When a Mate Wants Out

When a Mate Wants Out

SALLY CONWAY

JIM CONWAY

ZondervanPublishingHouse
Grand Rapids, Michigan

A Division of HarperCollinsPublishers

When a Mate Wants Out
Copyright © 1992 by Sally and Jim Conway

Published by Zondervan Publishing House
Grand Rapids, Michigan 49530

Library of Congress Cataloging-in-Publication Data

Conway, Sally.
    When a mate wants out / by Sally Conway, Jim Conway.
        p.   cm.
    Includes bibliographical references.
    ISBN 0-310-57370-X (hard)
    1. Marriage—United States. 2. Communication in marriage—United
States. 3. Marriage—Religious aspects—Christianity.   I. Conway, Jim.
II. Title.
HQ734.C77   1992
646.7'8—dc20   92-8295
                                                                                    CIP

Edited by Julie Ackerman Link
Designed by Blue Water Ink
Cover design by the Puckett Group

Printed in the United States of America

92 93 94 95 / DH / 5 4 3 2 1

To

John and Jacque Coulombe   Dennis and Karen Dirks

Our support group friends
who have been our
stretcher-bearers
during
Jim's recovery from his dysfunctional family,
Sally's breast cancer,
and the writing of this book.

Contents

Part 5—To Pastors and Counselors

Introduction

• • •

SINCE 1958, the two of us have spent a great deal of our energy helping people rebuild their crumbling marriages. We did it first while pastoring three different churches. Then in 1981 we formed an organization (Christian Living Resources, Inc./Mid-Life Dimensions) to help couples put their marriages back together.

Through the years many couples close to breaking up came to "Pastor Jim" for help. Since our first books were published at the end of the seventies, we both have been in touch with hundreds of thousands of hurting couples across the nation and in other countries. Of these couples, many have been success stories. So we can say with assurance: *there's hope for your marriage!*

Not everyone succeeds in rebuilding their marriage, but many do. Even the ones whose marriages finally end in divorce tell us they are glad they worked at restoration as long as they did. Instead of having regrets for giving up too soon—as many divorced people later have—they feel satisfied that they tried long and hard to save their marriage. In the process, they grew and became more complete individuals who were better prepared to live as healthy singles.

Not only have we helped others work on their marriages, we have had to work on *our own marriage*. The two of us have had some rough, scary times. Much of what we share with you, we have learned through our own thirty-eight years of marriage. Yes, we've read a lot of books and guided others in putting their marriages back together, but we know firsthand which ideas work. And we're happy to pass them on to you.

Part 1

AT FIRST . . .

Chapter 1

Don't Panic

• • •

CHERYL WATCHED as Ron jammed some of his clothes into a bag and stuffed his deodorant, hair dryer, and shaver in with them. He wouldn't look at Cheryl. Her eyes saw his every move, but she couldn't get her mouth to say a word. She had run out of things to say. All her pleading had proven useless, and now an awkward stillness hung in the air. Although she was outwardly quiet, a million clamoring noises were pounding inside.[*]

He's leaving! she thought. *Going—I don't know where. He's taking the older car and leaving the better one for the kids and me. It looks as if he's planning to leave forever.*

Ron had been warning Cheryl for weeks that he was going to leave, but she never took his threats seriously. Even though they argued a lot and there was tension between them, she always believed they could work out their problems. But now he was actually leaving! She was devastated.

---

[*] In this story and throughout the book, we are using real people to illustrate real life. In most cases, however, we have changed names and disguised circumstances to protect the privacy of the people involved.

A Common Problem

Unlike many women, Cheryl actually saw her spouse drive away. Many unsuspecting wives come home to find their husbands have moved out without so much as a bitter good-bye. Other husbands, instead of leaving physically, vacate emotionally. They become overly involved with their work, the guys, or another woman in an effort to shed themselves of their marriage relationship.

Women do it, too. Larry finally woke up when Joan demanded, "Just get out! I need some space." Larry would have seen the signs along the way if he'd been paying attention, but he was so wrapped up in his career that he had taken Joan and their marriage for granted.

Joan had been happy to mother their three children and keep up with all their activities while they were growing up, but when they became teenagers they were seldom home. Larry didn't realize how alone Joan felt now that the kids no longer needed her as much.

When the new associate pastor asked Joan to be his part-time assistant, Larry thought the experience would be good for her. He was unaware, however, of how many evenings she worked because he himself worked late nearly every night.

Larry also was unaware that Joan's boss made her feel like a new woman. He always complimented her on the work she did and took time to talk to her; in fact, he really seemed to understand her inner feelings. He sensed her loneliness and lack of fulfillment, so he encouraged her to take some college courses and consider a career of her own. Joan liked having a cheerleader.

Before long, Joan and the associate pastor were enjoying each other more than was appropriate. Larry should have sensed that something was wrong when Joan turned colder and colder toward him—but he didn't.

Then Joan announced she was going back to school. This didn't set well with Larry, and he wouldn't hear of it. "You've got enough to do around here without trotting off to college," he argued.

That did it for Joan. With hands on her hips, she yelled, "You're smothering me! It's time for you to get out!"

So What Are You Going to Do Now?

Whether you are a Cheryl whose husband is leaving or a Larry whose wife wants you out of the house, you are in a crisis situation. And whether your spouse is having an affair, threatening to leave, or has already left, beware of how you respond. Actions that are most natural in this type of situation usually make matters worse instead of better.

In the first hours and days after learning that your mate is leaving, you will be in a state of shock, and people have been known to do very foolish things during this critical period.

You may be tempted to shout and stomp and make unreasonable demands. You might feel like crying for hours on end or going on a shopping spree or drinking binge. Maybe you're a quiet tooth-grinder who vows to get revenge. Or perhaps you're the kind of person who withdraws into a shell, fooling yourself into believing that you don't care.

When the Unbelievable Is True

We know about these reactions because we ourselves have faced devastating crises and have often been surprised at how we behaved under stress—sometimes good; sometimes bad.

From those we have counseled over the years, we've learned how shattered they felt when they first learned their mate wanted out. Some of these people have expressed themselves very poignantly, such as in this letter:

> Please help me! I'm devastated. My husband tells me he doesn't love me like a wife anymore. . . . He has moved out. My pastor, friends, and family all tell me that he's preparing me for divorce, but he says he just wants time to himself to figure out who he is.

Yet he has a friendship with a woman that I find questionable. He is attending public functions with her but denies that anything is going on. The whole thing is driving me nuts. . . .

I love him, but he says he doesn't love me. I'm so confused. I'm ready to throw in the towel, but I really do love him and miss him so much. We've had a far from perfect marriage—but where is my husband? Please, if there is anything you can do, please help me.

Tom's story carries a similar theme of hurt. He and Dorrie had been married fewer than five years when she announced that she wanted a divorce. She despised him and wanted him out of the house *right now!*

She expected to get custody of their little girl, Amy, and was planning to take a promotion out of state. This meant Tom would have little time with their daughter. As all of these facts hit Tom, he thought he would die! He loved Dorrie very much and couldn't believe that her earlier wild passion for him had turned to such a cold, calculating hatred. And he dearly loved Amy. He had been home with her certain days of every week, and the extra hours of parenting had caused his heart to be deeply entwined with her life. It was unbearable to think of seeing her only once or twice a year for a few days!

Tom moved in with a bachelor friend and lived for the times Dorrie would let him care for Amy. Dorrie usually arranged for a third party to deliver Amy so she wouldn't have to face Tom.

Each new phase of the divorce proceedings smashed Tom into yet smaller pieces. But whenever Dorrie spoke civilly to him over the phone, Tom felt as if a few of the fragments had been glued together again. *Maybe this means she is changing her mind and won't go through with the divorce,* he dared to hope. But then she would strike another blow to his already fragmented life.

The anguish and uncertainty was about to kill Tom. He walked around in a daze and became so emotionally upset he had to see a psychiatrist.

This situation doesn't yet have a happy ending, but it shows that men as well as women suffer severe trauma when their marriages are threatened. There are, however, some differences in the way men and women respond to the suffering.

In our years of counseling we have found that men usually reach out for help only once or twice. If the marriage doesn't come together, they quit trying. Most women, though, are willing to work longer to rebuild a broken marriage.

According to several researchers, it is also true that men are more apt to hide their emotions than women. One report says that men, when their marriages start to come undone, tend to withdraw and become silent and secretive. Women, on the other hand, are more inclined to become exceptionally active.[1]

Panic Causes More Panic

At the first threat of separation, some people rush right out and start divorce proceedings. Others talk to everyone they know about what is going on, spreading the information under the guise of a "prayer request." Others dump out all the garbage they have collected about their mate. When a third party is involved, a few have even gone out and bought a gun to take care of the person! Others have wished they had the nerve. None of these solve anything, of course.

The first thing to tell yourself is, *Don't panic*. The truth is, you need to calm yourself and take a good look at the situation. Be still, and don't do anything rash. You probably won't feel like saying "God loves me and has a wonderful plan for my life" while your marriage is crumbling, but be assured that he does have some principles to guide you through this difficult period.

We know you hurt—a lot! You may even wonder if you can live through the awful, gnawing pain. We understand your problem and want to help you. Over the years, we have learned some specific methods to help people restore broken or breaking marriages, and we have discovered that the actions taken at the very beginning of the crisis can make the difference in whether or not a marriage ever comes back together.

The people who usually have the most success in saving their marriages are those who keep their panic under control. Most are not naturally serene people, but they develop a surprising degree of composure and find strength they didn't know they had.

You Are Normal

Don't be discouraged if you're not a super being who is able to handle any mess. The truth is, you *won't* handle everything correctly. No one ever does. We each have our own ways of managing stress, but none of us can save a broken marriage solely with our own wits and winsomeness. It will take God's power working in you and in your mate who's scrambling in the opposite direction.

Since you can't, with your own power, restrain your panic indefinitely—in spite of your best resolves—you will need the inner strength and wisdom that only God can give you. So ask him to control your emotions and perceptions as well as your circumstances.

When a mate leaves, or threatens to do so, there are two things you must do immediately:

Make a conscious decision to *be calm*.

Ask God to *make you calm*.

Thousands who have been in this predicament have been amazed at the courage and strength they received from God. Many have said words to this effect: "If you had asked me a few years ago if I could ever go through such a thing, I would have said that I simply would collapse. Instead, when it actually happened, I was surprised that I had the moment-by-moment ability to endure."

Patty found this to be true. She wrote and told us the sad story of how her husband left, without warning, and went to live with another woman. Then she added:

I keep busy. I go to ballroom dancing with a large group

of people. I go to school three nights a week after work. I go to movies with my girlfriends. I do crafts at home when I have time.

My children are proud of me. Friends at church have said how much I've grown and how great I am doing. My counselor tells me that all through this she has been pleased with how well I am doing.

As I have told them, the only way I'm getting through this, with my sanity, is because God has been with me all the way. I know he really does come to me in direct proportion to my needs. . . .

Once you stop the panic and feel quieter inside, you will be more able to believe that your marriage has a chance. God's peace is in itself a great power-booster and will give you hope.

Chapter 2

Have Hope

• • •

H OPE DOES NOT DISAPPOINT.... *Hope does not disappoint.... Hope does not disappoint....*[1] This verse has been going around in our heads ever since we began work on this chapter.

HOPE is a foundation stone for success in restoring your marriage. This belief comes from our own experiences and from those of people we've walked alongside during the marital rebuilding process.

Hope keeps the fires burning and the wheels turning. Without hope, plans and aspirations crumble and collapse. You simply won't make it through the inevitable hardships of rebuilding your marriage if you have no *hope* that it can happen.

Hope in the Face of Impossible Odds

Shirley paced the braided rug on the hardwood floor of her country-decorated bedroom. She couldn't bring herself to fluff the bedding and spread her grandma's cozy old quilt over the top as she usually did.

Her husband had left and was living with a younger woman he met at work.

When Gene stormed out of the house after a loud quarrel one evening, Shirley was sure he would be back by bedtime. But he didn't come home, and Shirley didn't sleep a wink all night. He had never stayed away like that.

She phoned him at work the next morning, and he informed her that where he had spent the night was none of her business. Then, timidly, she asked if he had another woman in his life.

"Of course not," he said. "I'm just sick of you."

In a few days, however, Shirley learned from a friend who worked with Gene that the news was all over the office: Gene had moved in with a young divorced secretary. Shirley was devastated! Not only had Gene left her and their two teenage sons alone, but he had gone against all the Christian principles they had held from the very beginning of their relationship.

As she agonized over the situation—her loneliness, pain, and feeling of betrayal, the boys' anger and bewilderment, their financial need, and Gene's comment that he "just had to have a change before he got any older"—she couldn't figure out what had gone wrong. One thing she did know, though. She wanted Gene back. And Shirley believed that God could and would save their marriage!

In spite of her resolve, however, Shirley's emotions ran the gamut in the early days of their separation—shock, hurt, jealousy, anger, depression, then back to shock. Part of the time she was very confused about what to do. Other times she knew exactly what needed to happen and determined to do it. She had strong hopes that things would soon be back to normal.

As the days went by and her attempts to win Gene back proved futile, however, her confidence diminished and her confusion increased. When she appealed to his sense of moral rightness, he said that was a bunch of religious garbage forced on people to try to keep them in line. When she reminded him of their good times together, he growled, "There never were any good times." When she described specific incidents that had been happy for her, he claimed that in his memory the events were nothing but disaster.

When she realized that reasoning with Gene would do no good, she became very frightened. She knew then that their problems were over her head. She asked her pastor to recommend a Christian counselor, and he gave her the name of a professional known for helping people put their marriages back together. Shirley made an appointment. During the following weeks, the counselor suggested ways for Shirley to relate to Gene whenever she got to talk to him. The counselor also advised Shirley concerning changes she needed to make. At first Shirley balked at the insinuation that something was wrong with her. She wasn't the one who had run off. She hadn't been unfaithful.

Eventually, though, Shirley did begin to work on herself even as she practiced the counselor's suggestions for relating to Gene. She believed that her changes would repair their broken marriage.

Her boys and her best friends were all praying with her for God to work a miracle. We, too, were praying for the restoration of Shirley's marriage. We were not the ones directly counseling her, but we kept in regular contact and did our guiding from the sidelines.

Even though communication with Gene didn't go well, Shirley remained undaunted. She had remarkably strong hope that he would come home. In fact, hope was about the only thing that kept her going.

Shirley could never have guessed at the beginning of the ordeal that she would have to "keep up her hopes" for years. *Almost eight years*, to be exact.

During that time Gene continued living with the other woman. They even moved out of the continental United States, which made contact with him more difficult for Shirley. But still she hoped—and prayed—and worked on her personal growth.

When she had nearly reached the end of her rope, she met a woman who gave her some spiritual direction that eventually changed her life. This person told Shirley that God would hear her prayers for Gene only when she let God completely rid her of the garbage within herself. Shirley heard the part about her need for change with only half an ear, but still the conversation renewed her hope.

It took some more time for her to earnestly get to work on her own problems, but finally she came to an absolute dead-end and simply had to let God take complete control of her and start the personal cleansing she needed.

Then one day she contacted us with the joyful news: "Gene has returned!"

We wonder what would have happened if Shirley had given up hope. The circumstances certainly made her confidence appear ridiculous. Most of the people around her thought she was crazy. Many urged her to give up and get on with a new life without Gene. But she didn't listen, and today Shirley and Gene are building a new, stronger relationship.

When Hope Doesn't Work

Hope doesn't always materialize into reality, though. Some people have done everything Shirley did and still haven't seen their marriage restored. Why? The answers aren't easy, and probably no human knows for sure. And certainly no one should heap guilt on those who are unsuccessful.

Some people want very much to save their marriages but simply have no idea how to go about it. Others have let their own anger, hurt, and need for revenge get in the way. But most have tried their very best to do the right things.

We need to realize that God has given us all a free will. And some people stubbornly insist on using that will to walk away from their marriage—in spite of all the good things their spouse does in an attempt to win them back.

We also know that Satan is looking for strongholds. He wants to ruin lives by taking over any space unoccupied by God. And the statistics show he is finding many vacancies!

However, you don't need to let Satan move in on you; you have Christ's power available to help you and your mate keep him out. In fact, praying for your mate is more powerful than anything you can say or do.

God can give your mate a corrected perception of the situation and a desire to change. He can relieve the frustrations that are driving your mate mad, and he can provide an escape from the alluring temptations.[2]

However, it still boils down to the fact that your mate has a free will and may choose to make wrong decisions.

Back to Hope

Despite the gloomy possibilities, the chances of saving your marriage *are* in your favor. The very fact that you are reaching out for help by reading a book like this is a good sign.

Also, God wants your marriage saved. And he's a powerful ally! "When you pour yourself into restoring love to your marriage, you can be sure that *the force of His will is at work with you in the process*" (italics added), says Dr. Ed Wheat, whose books have helped save and enrich many marriages.[3]

It is right to hope. It is therapeutic to hope. You know how depressed you feel when a situation seems hopeless. When you're depressed, you don't have the energy to try. When you don't try, it's like being in a boat without paddles. You'll never get anywhere.

Hope Moves You Forward

We had counseled Karen by letter for over four years, and about a year ago she wrote to let us know that her marriage was once again on safe ground. In a more recent letter she told us that her husband had even asked her to help counsel another couple who is having marital troubles.

She continued, "Isn't it wonderful to know that there is hope in the Lord! That hope, which had never meant much to me before, became the most important thing in my life during the years John was wanting a divorce. What a beautiful work God is doing in us!"

Ted is another person who learned to hope when his wife insisted their marriage was over and convinced him to file for divorce. Their relationship had never been an easy one, but they had shuffled through their conflicts and managed to keep hanging in there with each other.

Ted never told Connie he loved her or appreciated all she did for their family of five children. He did love her, but he certainly saw no need to say it again and again!

When they disagreed about anything, Ted always assumed he was right and never considered Connie's opinion. He usually overpowered her by raising his voice and insisting on doing it his way.

For years Connie let Ted have his way whenever they disagreed, but finally she had her "fill of it." Knowing she could never talk over her frustrations with Ted, she silently started to do her own thing.

She lost weight, got some cute clothes, and went out to see if she could attract other men. She did. And she had affairs with some of them—not so much because she wanted sex but because they listened to her and made her feel important.

When Ted found out, the fur flew! But by then he had lost any chance of influencing Connie. "Our marriage is over!" she insisted. "Just go ahead and start divorce proceedings."

Ted, numb with shock, thought divorce was the only possible outcome, so, for the first time, he did as she asked.

Even after their divorce was finalized, however, Ted couldn't give up hope that they would some day get back together. He ate, slept, and worked with that goal in mind. He talked for hours on end to us, and we guided him through changes he needed to make and suggested things he could do to win Connie back.

Months went by, and Ted kept hoping Connie would see that she had more with him than in her new life. He prayed for her. We prayed for her. And we prayed for Ted to make the necessary changes.

At times Ted wondered if he should just give up and find someone else. Other people were telling him Connie was gone for good. But he just couldn't ignore his all-consuming hope—that one day she would come back.

And hope paid off!

Eventually Connie got sick of the other men and had no place to go. She couldn't afford to live by herself, so, without much fanfare, she quietly moved back with Ted. At first she claimed she was only coming back to keep their family of grown children and grandchildren complete. This is common. A returning mate often does not yet feel "in love" with the other person, but being together gives them a better opportunity to work toward true marital love.

After several months of counseling with us and with their pastor, Connie and Ted were married again. Ted has learned to be more thoughtful of Connie's needs and to respect her right to be heard. And Connie has learned to speak up and not bury her feelings. They now have a strong relationship—and their family is complete!

If you can keep alive the hope that your marriage can be saved, you are ready to start the restoration process. And the first step is to learn what brought you to this place of disaster.

Chapter 3

Understand Why This Happened

• • •

L ES DECIDED TO BUILD a storage shed in his backyard, but he didn't want the prefabricated kind; he wanted it to be his own creation. He had never built anything before—except the rickety tree fort he and his brother had nailed together as kids. But he just wanted a simple shed. How hard could it be to build?

After drawing some crude plans and buying some materials and tools, he set to work. He didn't talk with anyone about the project because he didn't want any interference.

Les got the sides to stand up by nailing them onto a frame of two-by-fours. He decided the shed didn't need windows, so he didn't have to measure window frames or cut holes in the walls. The shed did need a door, however. It took Les awhile, but he finally got one installed so it would work. He didn't want to bother learning how to pour concrete, so he decided to have a grass floor.

Building the shed turned out to be harder than Les anticipated, but eventually he got the thing up. It didn't look great, but it was standing. After painting the little building, Les proudly moved in his tools and other items.

One morning after a windy night, Les noticed that his shed was leaning a little bit. No problem. He just went out and pushed it back into line.

The little building got skewed by the wind several more times, but each time Les just pushed it back up straight.

Then one night a fiercer wind blew and a hard rain beat down. The storm lasted all the next day, and the rain washed much of the soil from under the shed. When Les came home from work he found his shed completely down! Everything inside had been soaked by the rain and dented by the collapsing walls and roof.

Don't Cheat Your Marriage

Too many marriages are put together like that little shed. And when the hard times come, they can't stand up. When troubles knock our relationship out of balance, too often we just "push it back up" without making genuine corrections. Then suddenly—or gradually—the whole structure falls apart.

One of the tasks in rebuilding a broken marriage is to determine what caused it to collapse in the first place. In the case of the storage shed, Les thought the wind and rain caused it to fall. The real problem, however, was that the shed was improperly put together in the first place.

External forces did play a part, but buildings can be built to withstand storms. Some expert advice during assembly could have averted the disaster. The materials he used were fine, but he needed additional procedures—such as building a foundation. Even after the shed began to lean, it could have been salvaged and made strong if Les had recognized the problem and asked someone to help him pour a concrete foundation and properly brace the corners.

When marriages begin to totter, many think, *Oh, dear! I've married the wrong person. If I had a different partner, my marriage would be better.*

But you don't need a different spouse; you need new procedures. You probably received little or no counseling at the beginning of your marriage, but there is no reason you can't get it now. You may have developed poor patterns of relating to each other, but you can change them.

Take time to understand why your marriage is falling apart. What is the reason your mate wants to leave? Or has already left? Why is your spouse having an affair? What went wrong since those first days or years when you were madly in love?

It Takes Two to Tangle

A common mistake is to assume that the failing marriage is all the fault of the mate who wants out.

- "He always had a big ego and had to be in control of everything. When I began to challenge that, he couldn't take it and decided he didn't want me around anymore."
- "All she can think about is her own selfish interests. She became obsessed with fulfilling herself and following her dreams. I was in her way."
- "He's always been restless. I should have known that sooner or later he would fall in love with someone else."
- "She's chasing an older man because she needs a father figure."
- "She wants more than any normal man can give a wife."
- "He has a horrible temper and must always have his way. He's finally found someone he can walk all over."
- "He's just like his father. . . ."
- "She's just like her mother. . . ."

The list could go on forever. It always looks like the departing spouse is to blame. The truth is, however, both partners are at fault. There is no completely innocent party. Even the unsuspecting spouse has contributed to the problems. Personalities, temperaments, desires, choices, habits, and all that makes us the people we are, may drive a mate up the wall.

As the years go by, people change. Mates change. And little habits that used to seem like no big deal become as big as Pike's Peak. And the person with the irritating habit may not even realize how annoying it is.

Some people are totally caught off-guard when their spouse announces, "I've had all I can take. I'm getting out." We know of many who thought they had a happy relationship with their mate; the people around them thought the couple had an ideal marriage; and the church even used them as the model couple. It came as a big surprise to one spouse to learn that the other was so unhappy that he or she had already found someone else.

Other partners know very well that they have been a part of the problem. Perhaps they've been too domineering, a nag, a smotherer. Maybe they've been too much of a Milquetoast, never having an opinion of their own, never speaking up for what they believe or want.

Perhaps you are temperamental, rude, or disinterested in what interests your spouse. Maybe you've been sick or grieving and have been unable to meet your spouse's needs. Perhaps you've been negligent in communicating with your mate.

The point is, intentionally or not, you have contributed to your marital problems. It isn't one-sided. Your mate isn't totally at fault—even though that may be hard for you to see right now.

Blindness

Many mates who discover that their spouse is having an affair or is intending to file for divorce learn that they have been blind for years. They haven't noticed that their partner is struggling or unhappy. They have gone through days, weeks, months, even years, totally unaware of the other person's problems.

True, your unhappy mate should let you know that something is wrong, but often he or she doesn't. Your mate feels you should notice without being told. Or maybe your mate feels you wouldn't understand anyway or thinks things are so hopeless that it would do no good to try to talk about them. Some people actually think they are helping their marriage run more smoothly by keeping quiet. Of course, in the long run, the pain is greater than if the problem had been aired and worked out.

Others have tried to tell their partners of their unhappiness, but their words have fallen on deaf ears. An unsympathetic spouse will for some reason fail to tune in or even belittle the problem.

Perhaps you're the one who has been blind or who hasn't been communicating. Maybe you're the one with the hearing problem. In any case, it's time to wake up, find out how your mate really feels, and get to work!

Carelessness

In a troubled marriage usually both partners have been lax about common courtesies. We treat total strangers with more respect than we do the one we promised to love, honor, and cherish. We take each other for granted and often don't realize how rude we are.

People who want to save their marriages must forget about the carelessness of their mates. Rather than expose all the faults of their spouse, they go to work on their own.

Reflect on things you have said or haven't said, or on ways you have reacted or not reacted. Get down to the real reasons for your shortsighted behavior toward your mate.

I* remember how ashamed I was when, after at least twenty years of marriage, I began to see how thoughtless I had been toward many aspects of Jim's character. I had always thought of Jim as being especially tough and hadn't realized how sensitive he was in many areas.

With embarrassment, I recalled times I had stomped all over him, not realizing how tender he was inside. I didn't do it carelessly

---

* In chapters 1 through 20, the use of the first person "I" refers to Sally. In chapter 21, "I" refers to Jim.

or deliberately, but the effects were the same. I had to ask his forgiveness and train myself to be more alert to his real feelings.

Don't be overly hard on yourself, but acknowledge your thoughtlessness and ask God to make you more aware of your mate's needs and feelings. When you get the opportunity, tell your mate you're sorry and that you'd like to become more sensitive to his or her needs. Even if your mate has left or is involved with someone else, saying this may be a turning point in your soured relationship.

Preoccupation

Frequently we contribute to our marriage problems by being absorbed in many interests other than marriage. It's true, life consists of more than marriage and very important "musts" beg to be first on the priority list. But too often we put our mate at the end of the line.

While visiting a friend in the hospital recently we met a very cordial doctor who was making his weekend rounds. He told us of his busyness and even admitted that one Christmas morning he had left home after a brief time with his family and spent all day until after midnight making rounds.

We liked the doctor very much. It was obvious that he delighted in his work and enjoyed giving us a mini-education about our friend's illness. After nearly forty-five minutes with us, he said, "Well, I better be moving on. I have twenty-three more patients to see."

We thought, *If he spends forty-five minutes with each patient, it's going to be long after midnight again when he gets home!*

We couldn't help but wonder how his wife and children felt about his dedication. We were glad that our friend had a caring doctor, but sad that the doctor's family seemed to be so low on the totem pole of priorities.

It isn't just careers that erode marriages; it can be the church, P.T.A., children, hobbies, aging parents, illness, or anything that demands attention.

Sometimes you have no control over things that push their way into your life. If your child becomes seriously ill, you must drop everything and attend to all the details of health care. But while doing so, assure your mate that he or she still has a place in your life and that the preoccupation is only temporary. Vow to once again make your relationship the top priority as soon as possible.

Stress

While evaluating what has gone wrong in your marriage, take a look at the stresses and/or losses you have experienced recently. Often a person whose mate is leaving or is involved in an affair can enumerate a number of difficult things that have happened lately.

Problems at work frequently cause stress that can lead to marital problems. If a person has been laid off, passed over for a promotion, has too much to do, or has a difficult coworker, his or her prestige and identity have been undermined.

A mate with problems at work may come home grumpy and take out his or her frustrations on the family. But there is a more subtle problem. Often the mate under stress feels unable to discuss the problems for fear that his or her spouse won't understand or will be incapable of handling the anxiety.

Affairs have started when a person under stress confides in a third party who gives a sympathetic ear. Often the third party also has needs and is just waiting to get sympathy or "love" in return. In any case, the troubled mate feels this third person meets his or her needs better than the spouse does.

The following list of stresses might trigger your thinking so you can better understand your mate and the reasons he or she wants to run.

- Financial troubles
- Serious problems with aging parents or children
- Moving to a new location
- The death of someone close
- Learning that your children have been sexually molested
- Health problems for you or anyone in the family

- A car accident
- Misunderstandings with friends or neighbors

Anything that causes loss or disruption is a potential hazard to your marriage. And, of course, the more of these you have, the more likely you are to have problems.

Even if you only now realize that outside stresses or your preoccupations and actions helped cause your mate to come to the place of breaking your marriage, *it's not too late.* You can't undo the mistakes you've made, but acknowledging your part in the problems is the first step toward healing.

A Word of Caution

Don't use perpetual evaluation as an excuse to delay rebuilding. When you go out to assess why your shed fell down, don't keep kicking around in the debris forever. You'll never get it rebuilt by continually stomping through the broken mess.

Chapter 4

Listen and Speak Selectively

• • •

"**Y**OU BETTER WATCH those two, Tony!" laughed Fred as he gave Tony a hearty slap on the back. "Did you see all the smiles and winks bouncing between Joanne and Herb? Just like the old high school days."

Before Tony's back stopped stinging, another guy came by. "Well, do you suppose you'll ever get Joanne to go home with you now?" he snickered.

Tony was trying to get his wife to break away from a crowd of her former classmates. He had barely been able to tolerate the evening, and these latest remarks made him want to get out as fast as possible. These weren't his classmates; this wasn't even his high school, but he had agreed to come with Joanne because she hadn't been back to her school since graduation twenty-five years earlier.

When Joanne finally was ready to leave, Herb also was leaving. He walked out with his arm around Joanne, and Tony began to seethe. By the time Tony and Joanne reached their motel room, Tony was sullen.

Joanne asked what was wrong.

"Nothin'," he muttered. When they got into bed, he turned his back to her without so much as a goodnight. If there had been another bed in the room, he would have used it.

But Tony didn't go to sleep. Most of the night he mulled over what he should do. Joanne and Herb had talked almost exclusively to each other at the reunion. Tony winced as he recalled how they kept looking into each other's eyes. *So, Joanne had found Herb again and they really hit it off. Just like in high school. Apparently everyone else saw what was going on too. How embarrassing!*

By morning Tony had decided not to fight the inevitable. Joanne obviously thought more of Herb than of him. *They probably have been secretly contacting each other all along,* he concluded. *How could she be so deceitful? And how could she violate our marriage so easily?*

Tony vowed to sleep on the couch when they got home. He would have to start divorce proceedings as soon as he could. He didn't really want to break his marriage; he loved Joanne—but what else could he do? She loved someone else.

Tony was confused, but he thought the Bible taught that a husband was supposed to divorce his wife if she became involved with another man.

Little Remarks Can Make Big Trouble

Tony called a lawyer when they got home, but before actually filing for divorce he called us. He told us he had confronted Joanne and that she had admitted feeling some of the old feelings for Herb. She claimed she didn't want a divorce, however.

We suggested to Tony that just because some feelings had been aroused didn't mean Joanne was being unfaithful or even that she wanted to be unfaithful.

Tony protested. "But everyone could see the interest they had for each other. And I'm sure they're talking about it all over town right now."

Over a period of weeks we guided Tony about how to relate to

Joanne. Fortunately, the couple was able to talk over their situation and make some wise decisions. They each wanted their marriage. Joanne promised not to contact Herb, and Tony agreed not to make accusations. They both vowed to make a greater effort to be open and honest with each other. They decided to begin spending more time together and doing more things to show their love for each other.

Through this near tragic experience, they each learned more about what the other person needed to feel secure and happy. Joanne wanted Tony to spend more time with her instead of working on old cars so many evenings. Tony needed to hear that he was important to Joanne. They were each surprised that the other wanted to be first in their mate's life.

Today their marriage is solid. But what would have happened if Tony had continued to concentrate on the incriminating remarks of Joanne's classmates? His doubts and insecurities could have stirred up real trouble in their marriage. Then the gossips would have had plenty to talk about. In fact, the stories probably would have made a divorce more likely.

Don't Believe Everything You Hear

When something goes wrong with your marriage, rumors may fly faster than the wind. Truth may get stretched and bent so badly that only God knows the real facts. Even you and your mate will have different perceptions of the situation.

You've probably lived long enough to know that every person viewing a particular event or circumstance will see it differently. It's like the old poem about the blind men and the elephant. The first blind man approached the elephant, felt its side, and said, "The elephant is nothing but a wall." The second blind man, feeling the animal's tusk, said "an elephant is very like a spear!" The next blind man, who happened to take hold of the elephant's squirming trunk, said, "the elephant is very like a snake!" The fourth blind man reached out and touched the elephant knees and said, "the elephant is very like a tree." When the fifth man touched the elephant, he felt its ear and said, "an elephant is very like a fan!" And the sixth blind man, after grasping the animal's swinging tail, said, "the elephant is very like a rope!"

The stories circulating about your marital situation could be as varied as the blind men's descriptions of the elephant. Each one sees partial truth, but no one sees the whole truth.

That's why it's very important to be extremely selective in what you listen to when people make remarks about your mate.

Even well-meaning friends or family members can be biased. They may have received wrong information or their version of "truth" may have gotten twisted as it came through their thinking and speaking processes. Not intentionally. It's just that humans are fallible in hearing and interpreting information.

But I Was So Sure

Whenever I think of how mistakes can be made from what we *think* we hear, I recall an incident when I was a young pastor's wife. I had quit college to teach a year before getting married, but now we were living in a small town near a church-related liberal arts college and it seemed like a wonderful opportunity to go back to school part-time and finish my undergraduate degree.

We knew our congregation didn't respect this college; in fact, the church believed it was dangerously liberal. Whenever the subject came up, people were very vocal about how many young people had fallen away from the Lord after attending there. They considered it a ruinous place.

Jim and I reasoned that part-time attendance would not harm me. I would not be living on campus; I was a maturing Christian who could not be shaken from my faith; and I was simply taking the classwork to finish my degree. Nevertheless, we didn't broadcast the fact that I had enrolled.

During dinner one evening, the telephone rang and a deacon announced to Jim that the deacon board wanted to come to the parsonage that evening to hold an emergency meeting.

When the deacons arrived, Jim took them to the living room while I washed dishes, played with our two daughters, and folded laundry. Later in the evening I had to walk near the living room to get the ironing board from an adjacent room. Although I was in the room only a few seconds, what I heard set my hair on end! The deacons were talking about me. They didn't want me to attend that college.

The rest of the evening I felt sick to my stomach. My emotions were so churned up I couldn't think clearly, and I'm sure I ironed wrinkles into all of Jim's shirts. I didn't want to disappoint the people of the church nor damage the church's reputation, but I longed to finish my college education. I could hardly wait for the meeting to end.

When the deacons finally left, I said to Jim, "Well, they don't want me going to that college, do they?"

"What are you talking about?" he asked.

After explaining that I hadn't planned to listen in, I described the part of the conversation I had overheard.

Jim stood for a moment in shocked silence. Then he explained that the men never mentioned my name in the meeting! The deacons had come to discuss what to do about an elderly woman who was being severely beaten by her husband. It was a second marriage for both; their first spouses had died. Even though this new husband seemed very pious in public, someone had learned that he was abusing his wife and the deacons believed it was dangerous for her to stay in the home. They were deciding how to get money to help her live elsewhere. I overheard them say, "We want her out of there."

You can imagine how foolish I felt. Where did I get the crazy idea that the deacons were talking about me? And that they wanted me to quit college? I was *sure* I had heard words to that effect.

That incident has been a good lesson to me: *Not everything I think I hear is what is being said.*

You may need to remember that principle when people come to you with stories about your mate. They may not deliberately slant the truth, but be cautious about believing it all. You need a giant strainer.

Instead of simply taking in all the information you hear, filter it through what you already know about your partner. Separate the lies from the truth.

On the Other Hand, Don't Be Stupid

Sometimes, though, it pays to at least consider what you are hearing about your mate. If someone hints that your spouse is seeing someone else, it would be wise to check out the facts. If you think there is any truth to the story, talk it over with your husband or wife.

Your mate may get very angry, and that's scary. But waiting for the truth to finally emerge can be even more scary—and more painful. If you handle the matter kindly and your mate is innocent, the initial anger or hurt will subside. Then you can begin to rebuild trust.

But if your mate is a good liar, he or she may give a very convincing explanation. You'll have to decide whether to believe your mate or your informant. In most cases, it is best to give your partner the benefit of the doubt until evidence to the contrary becomes overwhelming. You probably won't be fooled for long if your mate is trying to deceive you. Truth eventually will emerge.

The Other Side of the Coin

Besides using discretion about who and what you listen to regarding your mate, be exceedingly careful about what *you* say and *to whom* you say it. We've known people who have ruined their chances for winning back their mate by the overuse of their mouths.

When Todd told Lynne he didn't want to be married to her any more, she shared the news with her Bible study group the very next morning. Of course Lynne was upset that he wanted to leave and she needed the support and consolation of friends. But she said *too much too early* and to *too large* an audience.

When Todd moved into his own apartment a few days later, the whole church learned about it. Todd worked at the same place as a couple of other guys from church, and he sensed right away that they knew he had left Lynne.

The entire church talked about Todd and Lynne's problem. For weeks it was the main topic at every prayer meeting. Everywhere Todd went, he ran into people who knew about his marital trouble. And they all either preached at him or ignored him. He felt like a leper with his flesh falling off right in front of their eyes.

As time went on, Todd began to wish he could rebuild his relationship with Lynne, but whenever he tried to see her he felt as if a bunch of other people were in the room with them. He heard all their words of advice floating out of her mouth. She quoted everyone from the preacher to her mother's cleaning woman's aunt. She had been talking and listening nonstop to everyone she knew.

Lynne asked Todd to attend church with her again, but he couldn't bring himself to do it. He didn't have the strength to face all the "judges" at church.

Lynne made church attendance a test of Todd's intentions. When he couldn't muster the nerve to attend, she decided their marriage would never work. In the end, they divorced.

If Lynne had quietly chosen a wise friend or two with whom to confide her pain, she might have saved her marriage. She mistakenly chose to enlist everybody she knew to pray for Todd. She also wanted them to sympathize with her and to ally themselves with her against Todd. She got people's support—but lost her husband.

When choosing how to share your marital troubles, we suggest the following:

1. Tell only one or two people. And choose people you know will keep the matter absolutely confidential. If you are in a small care group that is very close, you may choose to tell the group. But be absolutely certain you can trust each one of them *not* to talk outside the group.

2. Choose wise people. Older people who have experienced the good and bad of life will be able to give you a broader perspective than your peers. Friends who are walking closely with God will probably give wiser help than friends who are not in touch with the Lord.

3. If possible, choose people who can pray effectively. More will be accomplished inside your wandering mate by the power of the Holy Spirit than by all the wonderful words and tricky techniques people can devise.

4. Choose people of the same sex. If you are part of a small care group of couples you've known for a time, you may want to share with all of them. But we warn you not to tell your troubles to one person of the opposite sex unless it is your pastor or a trained counselor. Mates who initially want to save their marriage have often fallen into an affair themselves because they were vulnerable to the attentions of a "comforter" of the opposite sex.

5. Don't wear out your supporters. Yes, you are hurting. And, yes, you need the help of others, but be considerate of them and their families. Before dropping in and staying for hours, ask if it's a convenient time. If a friend says, "I'm always here for you," find out exactly what that means so you don't take advantage of their generosity. Make them promise to tell you when they need time alone or time for other people or projects.

Keep Your Eyes on the Goal

You are in a precarious spot, and you need a few good friends to lean on. But be discriminating about whom you trust. And use discernment as to which stories you listen to and how much you talk about your troubles.

Your goal is to rebuild your marriage. Everything you say and everything you listen to other people say should be done with restoration in mind.

Chapter • 5

Vow to Work Hard

• • •

W HEN DENNIS GOT INVOLVED in an affair he insisted that
his wife file for a divorce, but Bev refused. "I'm committed to
you and our marriage," she explained. "Let's give our relationship a
chance."

Dennis scoffed at her, claiming that their relationship was over.
After a few months, he pressed Bev again for a divorce, threatening
to quit making the house payments if she didn't get a lawyer and start
the proceedings. Bev's friends and family told her she might as well
end the marriage and get on with her life. Even her pastor advised her
to go ahead with a divorce.

Bev tenaciously stuck to her commitment. Although the possibility of restoring her marriage looked extremely bleak, Bev kept
saying, "I have vowed to love Dennis in spite of everything. He is my
husband; I am his wife. We can work on our problems and put our
marriage back together."

It took almost three years, but Bev is one of the happy ones who
achieved what she set out to get. She is convinced that her vow to her
marriage was the one thing that carried her through the times when
it seemed absolutely foolish to go on.

Some marital situations, however, have such major problems

that persistence alone is not enough. If one mate is violent and abusive or using all the family finances to support addictive behavior, the other mate needs to take dramatic steps for protection. As we discuss in greater detail in chapter 15, there may need to be a period of separation while both mates are in consistent, competent counseling. After both mates, especially the abusive one, make significant changes, they can begin to work on rebuilding their marriage.

Commitment

If you have decided your marriage is worth saving, it is time to take the next step, which perhaps is the most crucial of all—an all-out, true-grit *pledge* to keep your marriage. This commitment will be the foundation for everything you do and for everything you are likely to endure in the following weeks.

Initially, you are simply getting your emotional balance after learning that your marriage is in serious trouble. But now you need to buckle your seat belt for the long road ahead.

You won't like to hear this, but it will probably take months— maybe years—to put your marriage back together again. That's why it's imperative that you decide now whether or not you want to be married to your mate. Otherwise, when the going gets rough, as it surely will, you might toss out the whole idea of rebuilding your marriage.

Use Your Resources

Bev's experience may sound like a fairy tale with a happy-ever-after ending, but that's not how it was. You need to know that she worked hard—*really hard*.

Even though Bev vowed to save her marriage, she knew she couldn't do it on her own. God didn't make her to be the Lone Ranger. The commitment did have to come from her alone, but she needed other assets to draw on for the day-in, day-out work of rebuilding her marriage.

She realized she probably wasn't going to get any cooperation from Dennis. He wanted to be rid her. She knew she might also have to work against the tide of others' opinions and advice. Refusing to listen to the antagonists, she found some allies.

Your Greatest Help

Bev wrote and called us many times asking for encouragement for another day, strength for another step. Besides giving her words of hope, we prayed with her and steered her to a serious and regular reading of the Bible. Sometimes our encouragement was as simple as reminding her that

> GOD is on your side. He is the one who planned marriages and families. He also intended that marriage be monogamous, despite the lifestyles of some of our Bible heroes. Therefore, whoever tears and destroys marriages is doing so against the will of God; whoever works at building and reunifying a marriage relationship is pleasing God.
>
> Not only does the Lord think it's a great idea that you want to save your marriage, he wants to give you the wisdom and the power to do the job. You don't have to depend on your puny human strength, which will run out very quickly.

We continued to remind her:

> When you don't know which way to turn or which words to speak, ask God the Holy Spirit to guide you.[1] When you think you can't take another step, ask for his energy to keep you going.[2] God, as a devoted parent, truly cares for you.[3] If you can remember his concern for you when you're feeling down, perhaps it will be the nudge you need to lift your chin again. The King of the universe loves you!

Hundreds of people like Bev have told us that if it hadn't been for the Lord's loving hand holding on to them during the rough time after their mate's departure, they wouldn't have made it.

After Dennis moved out he did cruel things to Bev to force her to file for divorce. He would call to say he wanted to meet her at their favorite restaurant and then not show up. Once Dennis promised to meet Bev and the kids at his parents' house for his father's birthday dinner. He never came.

He would promise to buy new tennis shoes for the boys, but never follow through on his word. He quit making the car payments, although he had said he would make them.

Eventually Bev realized that Dennis was doing these things to test her commitment to take him back. So the more he hurt her, the more she leaned on God to help her keep working on their marriage.

On one occasion Bev wrote, "God has become my very best friend. I find myself praying all the time as if I were talking to a companion right beside me. His words in Scripture are like finding treasures tucked away just for me. I've underlined my Bible so much that I've practically worn it out. Sometimes God's promises are all I have to support me. I would never ask for this kind of pain, but it has driven me to a closer relationship with the Lord, which I wouldn't trade for anything."

Books, Magazine Articles, and Tapes

Other resources are any book, article, or tape that presents concepts to strengthen your marriage. The subject doesn't even have to deal directly with marriage; it could be about some part of the marriage relationship, such as effective communication or successful conflict resolution.

The advantage of books and tapes is that you can read or listen at your convenience and interact with the ideas at your own pace. You also can read and listen as often as you want to parts that are particularly helpful.

For a list of authors and our reading suggestions, see the Recommended Reading section, which appears after the notes in this book.

Counselors and Pastors

A wise pastor or professional counselor can help give you stability during this time. Competent pastors and counselors will aid you in getting a clearer perception of yourself and your situation.

Don't expect easy answers, but do expect to receive guidance so that you can work toward a resolution of your marital problem. The counselor may help you get rid of emotional baggage from your past and help you in areas where you need to grow.

Plan to see your counselor for several sessions. You didn't get into this predicament overnight, and the process of healing will take time. But you will probably begin to experience little changes and some relief from your pain after the first few visits.

Chapter 9 contains more help in how to choose a counselor.

Support Groups

You may be fortunate enough to live in an area that has a support group for people whose mates are in affairs or seeking divorce. Unfortunately, these groups are still scarce. Most community organizations and churches lack either the necessary staff or the courage to admit that such a group is needed.

Some people have found groups such as Al-Anon or another form of recovery group to be helpful. Proceed cautiously in this area and check out the group that you think is appropriate. Don't commit yourself until you're sure it will provide the right influence.

We warn against joining a divorce recovery group. Our experience has been that these groups, naturally, do not focus on marriage restoration and may in fact cause you to quit trying with your mate. Divorce recovery groups are great for the divorced. But if you're not yet divorced and want to recover your marriage, find a group that will give suggestions and support for rebuilding your marriage relationship.

Friends and Family

Your friends and certain family members may be important

sources of strength during this time. Rely most heavily on the ones who are unbiased. You don't need people jumping to your side, pitting you against the "wretch" who wants to break your heart.

Prejudiced friends can fill your head with more negative ideas than you can combat. We see too many people wrongly influenced against their mate because of the words and attitudes of close friends and family members who are trying to console them.

You do need emotional support and comfort, but not at the expense of balance. Tell your friends and family at the very beginning that you want them to be fair and to remain impartial in their judgments.

We have already talked about the danger of revealing your marital problems with too wide a circle so that your mate has an impossible hurdle to cross when he or she wants to come back. Choose a few wise people to be your confidantes and draw on them for the emotional support you need.

If you are in a situation where you need help such as child care, transportation, or even finances, don't be afraid to accept it when people offer. Not only is it good for you, it is also good for them. They get to live out the biblical direction to "bear one another's burdens,"[4] and you get some relief from your problems. God doesn't intend for you to struggle alone; he plans for someone to come alongside to help.

Legal Assistance

Even though we suggest caution about getting the gears of legal action turning too quickly, we recognize that some situations call for an attorney's advice to protect you and your children, especially in financial matters or potential custody cases. Try to get an attorney with a reputation for helping marriages get back together, not one whose clients always end up with a divorce.

If you see a lawyer for legal protection, beware of burning bridges that you may later want your mate to cross. Get the counsel you need without setting into motion anything that will hinder the restoration process.

Take a New Grip—Again and Again

Day after day you will need massive amounts of *patience*. You can't have all you're going to need stored away in some big container; there isn't one big enough. So for each day and for each unpleasant incident, you must depend on God to provide a fresh supply. But you must not let "your rights" and "your lawful needs" clog the channel. While not allowing yourself to be used as a doormat, you do need to say to yourself, "For now I'll turn the other cheek and walk the extra mile."

If time drags on with no sign of progress, or perhaps even a setback—your mate moves in with the other person, cuts off contact with you, blows up at you, or pushes anew for a divorce—be patient. When others urge you to get rid of your unworthy spouse, be patient.

Paint a mental picture of you and your spouse together again and keep it in mind when everything looks bleak. That picture represents your goal—a new, growing relationship that will be a joy to both of you.

Do you want your marriage? Is it worth all the trouble and pain you may have to go through to salvage and rebuild it? If so, now is the time to vow to work toward restoration—even if it takes years and unbelievable amounts of unconditional love. As Bev did, you may need to work very hard and call on every available resource. But you also may get to see your marriage restored, as Bev did.

Chapter 6

Handle Your Mate's Affair Wisely

• • •

YOU'VE JUST CONFIRMED the awful fact that your mate is having an affair! It may be a complete shock, or perhaps you've been suspecting it for some time. In any case, *you are devastated!*

You may feel indignation, anger, or perhaps even guilt if you are wrestling with the troubling thought that the affair is your fault. You may be depressed or vowing to get even. You may throw yourself harder into your work or other projects, or you may be unable to get moving at all. You may feel sick to your stomach or cry easily.

Before this is resolved you probably will feel all these emotions.

You have been betrayed! Your sacred marriage has been trampled on like so much dirt. What do you do next?

Go Carefully

Take time to catch your breath. If you are in a state of near panic, reread chapter 1 before you do anything foolish. Now is the time to act *rationally*, not rashly. Don't force your mate out of the house and don't start divorce proceedings. If adultery has been committed, you have every legal and biblical right to divorce, but God doesn't say you *must* divorce.

In the first few days, spend time asking God for wisdom and peace. Quietly take stock of your situation. If possible, talk to your mate. Don't demand to know details, but do offer to work on solutions. You may feel so hurt that you can't see your fault in the problem, but these things "don't just happen. Every action has a cause."[1] You may not be the direct cause of your mate's infidelity, but you can help make a better marriage that your mate will want to come back to.

Whatever you do, don't make decisions you'll later wish you could reverse. Take time to consider the outcome of any action you might take. For instance, you could:

1. Shoot your mate or the third party—or both. **But** you'd end up in prison and still lose your marriage. Murder is not a good solution.

2. Get revenge. You could put sugar in their gas tanks or make anonymous, threatening phone calls. **But** revenge often backfires, and your anger will probably give you ulcers and drive them closer together.

3. Have an affair yourself. **But** then you'd be guilty of breaking your marriage vows, and your conscience will eat you alive. Also, your mate may accuse you of violating your marriage and sue for a divorce.

4. File for divorce. **But** if you go through with it, you would be left without your mate and with a depressing sense of failure.

5. Work on restoring your marriage.

We, of course, are pushing for number 5, and we'd like to help you through the process.

Understand Why

Your mate may say, "I didn't choose to have an affair; it just happened." But the truth is, your mate *did* have a choice and chose wrong. At some point your mate knew the involvement was headed in an improper direction and failed to stop it.

However, to simply condemn the affair as evil and not discover what went wrong won't solve anything. There are reasons why your mate was easy prey for the devil and if you don't work to correct the causes, your mate will probably continue the affair or begin another.

Christie went to her pastor for help when she found out her husband, Tim, was having an affair with a woman in the church. The pastor was a take-charge kind of man and demanded to know the other woman's name. When Christie mentioned it, the pastor immediately picked up his phone and telephoned the other woman's home.

A male voice answered, and the pastor recognized it as Tim's.

"Tim, what in God's name are you doing there?" roared the pastor. "I want you to get out of there this very minute and don't you ever go back! Do you hear?"

Tim promised to leave and he did. But the pastor never helped Tim and Christie with their marriage. No one explored with them the reasons for Tim's unfaithfulness. Tim and Christie closed the book on that chapter without working on the source of their problems. In a few months Tim was in another woman's bed.

In *The Myth of the Greener Grass*, J. Allan Petersen says, "The affair is a sign of a need for help, an attempt to compensate for deficiencies in the relationship due to situational stress, a warning that someone is suffering."[2]

The reasons for infidelity don't fall into distinct categories; they overlap a great deal. And one inadequacy or condition can cause a chain reaction.

Sexual Addiction

Many women think their husbands are sex addicts because sex seems to be on men's minds so much—or at least that's the myth. True sexual addiction is very complicated, however. The sex addict is never satisfied and is usually involved in many kinds of unhealthy and ugly sexual pleasures. He is constantly driven by his compulsion.

Besides a relationship with his own wife, the sex addict gets kicks from lots of other women—either literally or in his mind. He uses pornographic magazines, videos, or films. He visits places of ill-repute. Wherever he walks or drives, he is always looking, looking, looking.

In fact, he often drives for hours just to enjoy "the sights." Many men talk about women they see at the beach, in the park, or on TV, but the addict is obsessed with women day and night, week in and week out.

Some women are also sex addicts. Their compulsions are as distorted as those of men. Sex addicts need the right kind of help. Reading a Bible verse about lust to them won't cure them. They need a counselor who has successfully treated other addicts. And they also need a mate who will see a counselor and be willing to stand alongside them while they work on the addiction.

Scripture is very clear about the seriousness of sexual sin.[3] It leads to bondage, and addicts are slaves bound tightly with ropes they cannot cut or wiggle out of. Their own will is definitely involved, but it has been so warped that only professional help will get it straightened.

Childhood Damage

Marie's parents neglected her as soon as she was able to fend for herself. Each new baby born into the family got attention only until the child had learned basic survival skills. The children always had enough food, but they had to prepare it themselves. Their clothes were few, but sufficient. What caused the most damage, however, was that none of them got tender nurturing from either parent. Marie's mother, because of her own deprived childhood, knew very little about taking care of children and even less about loving and valuing them. And in those days fathers weren't expected to take much interest in their children; they spent most of the time away from home making a living.

Marie grew up thinking her family was normal. But as an adult she began to feel a void she couldn't explain. She married, thinking that would fill the emptiness, but still something was missing. She gave lip service to her husband, but she always kept her eyes open for someone better.

She finally met a man who listened to her and told her how wonderful she was. She tingled all over and thought she had found true love. When he arranged secret meetings and made clandestine phone calls, she eagerly participated.

But eventually the empty feeling returned. The affair only added gnawing guilt to her lonely void.

When her husband learned of her involvement he was terribly hurt. But whenever Marie tried to break it off with the other man, he too was hurt and always managed to pull her back to him.

Marie was so miserable she finally went for professional help. In counseling she learned how much she had missed in childhood and how it was affecting her as an adult. The counselor encouraged her to grieve over her childhood losses and helped her fill some of the gaps in a healthy way. Eventually Marie no longer needed her lover and stopped looking for "something else."

To help you understand your mate or yourself better, consider the following causes of childhood damage:

- ◆ Neglect
- ◆ Abandonment
- ◆ An alcoholic family
- ◆ Family "secrets"
- ◆ Physical abuse
- ◆ Sexual molestation or attack
- ◆ Emotional battering
- ◆ Extreme poverty

False Expectations

People today are fed a lot of fantasies and lies about love. We expect marriage to be like love scenes in the movies—constantly full of sizzle and excitement. We forget that movies follow a script carefully created to make the story go just right.

In the real world, where we live, a lot of ordinary, routine living takes place. That doesn't mean we shouldn't experience romance, but we can't expect moonlight and roses every moment we're together.

Unfortunately, many couples enter marriage expecting a fairy-tale relationship. When they find out their mate has body odor, contrary viewpoints, and a selfish streak, they believe they've made a mistake. So they renew their search for the ideal lover.

Cultural Domination

The United States Declaration of Independence guarantees every citizen the right to "life, liberty, and the pursuit of happiness," but people today take the pursuit of happiness to a dangerous extreme. Many believe they have a right to be happy no matter what it costs or whom it hurts. A subculture of Christians and others with high moral standards holds out for marital fidelity, but almost everything we see on television or in movies, books, magazines, and newspapers makes the opposite look more attractive.

Not only do we see a lot of immorality, we are led to believe that nothing is wrong with it. In fact, we're made to look crazy for believing that old stuff about God's design for purity and marital happiness.

Therefore, when a mate is struggling with inner values and external conduct, it's easy for him or her to succumb to cultural standards because they endorse our own selfish desires.

Misunderstandings and Miscommunications

Marital infidelity also can occur when couples constantly disagree or have not learned effective ways to talk to each other. This causes them to lose all trust and respect for each other until finally they see no value in keeping themselves solely for the other.

Sometimes a mate is under a lot of pressure from a difficult situation and feels that his or her spouse wouldn't understand. Quite innocently, the person shares the burden with someone of the opposite sex, and the problem becomes a common bond which may grow into an emotional or sexual affair.

The Specter of Aging

Many affairs happen because of a need to prove oneself young and attractive. Women, as well as men, use sex to demonstrate that the aging process is having no dismal effects on them. They believe that sexual prowess will ward off wrinkles and thinning hair—or at least prove they are unimportant.

Attempts to appear youthful often begin with wearing fashions of the young. And no wonder: catalogs don't show many flattering clothes for anyone over age twenty-five. Few forty- and fifty-year-olds exist in advertising. And if they do, they're modeling "plus" sizes or trying to squeeze into stuff for twenty-five-year-olds. That may be one reason people fight growing older.

People discontented with their age also prefer the company of younger people and youthful activities because people their age or older remind them of the inevitability of aging. It isn't bad to spend time with a younger group except when it's done to try to escape from the reality of aging. The clock can't be stopped even by the best denial gimmicks.

Sagging Esteem

Some people get involved in affairs to prove their value. The victim of low self-esteem thinks, *If I can make that person love me, I'll know I'm worth something—I've really got it, after all. Or, I'll let myself be enticed by this stunning creature who makes me feel young and attractive.*

If you suspect that low self-esteem may have something to do with your spouse's affair, take comfort in knowing that the boost in self-esteem from affairs doesn't last. And when it dies down you can help your mate escape the affair by making it your goal to build his or her self-esteem. Chapter 11 tells how to do it.

Living with the Daily Nightmare

You probably want to step in and put a halt to your mate's affair immediately! That's understandable, but if you go in like a bulldozer you'll ruin everything, even what's good, and be left with no materials with which to rebuild your relationship.

Perhaps someone has even hinted that you are condoning the sin if you don't take a stand against such evil behavior. Actually, you aren't ignoring wrong by taking the inconspicuous approach. You intend to see the violation end. But you want to accomplish it in a way that will most likely insure the realization of your goals, which, by the way, are:

- ♦ To help your mate get disentangled from the affair
- ♦ To correct what has gone wrong in your relationship
- ♦ To build a new, strong, happy relationship

You won't achieve these goals by force. Nor will you accomplish them by inactivity. Pretending that nothing has happened or giving in to feelings of helplessness are not effective responses either.

Pray Like Never Before

If you have not already poured out your heart to God about your situation, now is a good time to start. Many people tell us they never spent as much time praying, day and night, as they did while their mate was being unfaithful. As a result, they found God to be their best friend.

"But," you may protest, "if God cares about me, why did he let the affair happen in the first place?"

As we mentioned before, God allows us to make choices—otherwise, we would be mere puppets—and often we make poor choices. God grieves more over your mate's sin than you do. He provided a way to escape,[4] but your mate didn't take it.

So you and your best friend, God, can talk over your awful situation. Happily, the Lord can do more for you than any human friend. He can give you peace as well as wisdom to say the right words and strength to perform the right actions. He will take all the hurt you hand to him.[5] And the Holy Spirit will move and work in you and in your mate—and even in the third party.

Appropriate God's Promises

Reading Scripture is one of the best ways to calm your agitated heart and to understand more about God. Find a translation that is easy to understand. Underline the verses that speak to you so you can find them easily. Memorize key phrases or verses so you can have the ideas with you all the time. Maybe you want to jot them on a card to keep in your pocket or purse or on the refrigerator or your desk.

The epistles of the New Testament, starting with Romans and ending with Jude, contain many rich thoughts and challenges. If Romans and Hebrews are too heavy right now, read and re-read the others. The Psalms, Proverbs, Isaiah, and Jeremiah in the Old Testament also contain a treasure of help and reassurance. For example,

> For I know the plans I have for you, says the Lord. They are plans for good and not for evil, to give you a future and a hope (Jeremiah 29:11 TLB).

> When you go through deep waters and great trouble, I will be with you. When you go through rivers of difficulty, you will not drown! When you walk through the fire of oppression, you will not be burned up—the flames will not consume you. For I am the Lord your God, your Savior (Isaiah 43:2–3 TLB).

Be Perfect

Of course, you can't be perfect, but your mate expects you to be. While your mate is comparing you to the third person and considering which way to turn, you won't be allowed one misstep.

Dr. Ed Wheat, in *How to Save Your Marriage Alone*, says:

> This [the need to be "perfect"] may come as a shock to you, but if you want to save your marriage, you cannot be just a "good" husband or wife. You have to be perfect in your behavior toward your partner. You must *do* and *be* everything the Bible prescribes for your role in marriage, and you must be very sensitive to avoid anything that will set your partner off. The least slip in word or action will give your mate the excuse he or she is looking for to give up on the marriage. Since resentment and rationalization are two of the key issues in the thinking

of an unfaithful partner, even one remark spoken out of turn can fan the flames of old resentments and give weight to rationalizations that the partner is manufacturing to excuse his or her behavior.[6]

This wise counselor stresses what we all know: we can't be perfect in our own strength. Any good we do or say will have to be by God's sufficiency as promised in 2 Corinthians 12:9–10: "He [the Lord] has said to me, 'My grace is sufficient for you, for power is perfected in weakness.' Most gladly, therefore, I will rather boast about my weaknesses, that the power of Christ may dwell in me. . . . for when I am weak, then I am strong" (NASB).

In working to save your marriage, Dr. Wheat also advises that you must:

1. Consistently do everything you can to please your mate and meet his or her needs and desires (while not violating your moral values or personhood).

2. Show your mate the respect and honor commanded in Scripture whether your mate personally merits it or not.

3. Totally avoid criticism of your mate.[7]

Tough orders to fill. But lots of successfully restored couples can tell you the ideas work.

Write and Burn

There's something therapeutic about writing, and putting your grief on paper may help you live with the distress of your mate's unfaithfulness. Write down what you know or suspect, how that makes you feel, prayer requests about the situation, and anything else that helps you. Pour out your whole heart, and write until you feel some relief. Then burn it all. You don't want anyone else reading your very personal notes. So after each session, get rid of what you've written.

Allow Yourself a Cry

It's better to pour out your agony than to keep it bottled up.

Stifling your feelings could lead to a violent explosion that you can't control, and suppressing tears may lead to physical ailments such as headaches, ulcers, or skin disorders.

Although it's important to let out your feelings, you need to be careful where and how you do it. Cry all you need to, but not in front of your mate or your children for now.

Enlist a Friend or Counselor

Although you shouldn't air your marital troubles to everyone, neither should you drag your burden alone. God doesn't intend for you to stand by yourself during this difficult time. Find at least one wise person of the same sex in whom you can confide, or be in regular contact with a counselor.

Scripture says, "Two can accomplish more than twice as much as one, for the results can be much better. If one falls, the other pulls him up; but if a man falls when he is alone, he's in trouble" (Ecclesiastes 4:9–10 TLB).

God will be your best help, but you also need a friend "with skin on." Carefully choose someone who can come alongside and carry part of your load.

As you live one day at a time—leaning on the Lord, letting someone else help you, and growing and changing personally—you will begin to see hope for the termination of your mate's affair.

Part 2

MEET YOUR
MATE'S NEEDS

Chapter 7

Walk in Your Spouse's Shoes

• • •

LAURA FELT AS IF BOB were keeping her in a bottle, and she didn't like it. She wanted to do more than keep a pretty house and be on parade at social functions with Bob.

Bob and Laura's two kids were nearly grown and soon would be totally gone from home. Missy had been living at home while attending a city college but was planning to transfer to a small Christian liberal arts college five hours away. Brad was a senior in high school and had a scholarship to play football at the same college Missy would attend.

Laura had not worked outside the home since Missy and Brad were born. She enjoyed being a wife and mother, but she was beginning to wonder what she would do with her time when the kids no longer needed her.

Two years earlier Laura had decided to use her talent as a pianist to accompany several church musical groups. Bob grumbled about her being gone in the evenings, but he didn't do anything with her when she was home. When he wasn't out with clients, he sat in his chair watching TV. The kids were usually out with their friends, at their part-time jobs, or with the youth group.

Laura wanted to do something productive during the daytime, but didn't want a career in music. She thought about pursuing a degree in nursing so she could provide better care for the elderly in their local nursing home. Or maybe she could go into real estate. That would be a little more glamorous and she could set her own hours. Or perhaps she could open a small boutique, a dream she had had for some time.

She tried to talk over her thoughts with Bob, but he just scoffed. He didn't want her so busy that she couldn't keep up with the housework and his business life. They didn't need the extra money, he argued, and if she couldn't make up her mind what she wanted to do she must not be very convinced she should be working. If she really wanted to work, why couldn't she just decide what to do and get on with it?

The tension between them made Laura nervous and depressed. She felt Bob didn't really care about her enough to listen to her desires. *How can he be so selfish after all the years I've given to him and the kids?* she wondered.

As the time came for Missy and Brad to leave for college, Laura became more despondent. She wasn't eating or sleeping well and couldn't get herself moving during the day. Not only was she going to miss the kids terribly, she felt she was in a cage. Every time she tried to talk to Bob about her ideas they ended up in an argument. She could hardly believe it when the thought crossed her mind that perhaps she should quietly slip away when the kids left for college.

Feel What Your Spouse Feels

As bystanders we can clearly see what Bob needs to do to hold on to Laura. "Hey, wake up," we'd like to tell him. "It's time to listen to Laura's needs for a change. Encourage her to do something creative with her extra time. Help her wrestle with the choices. Realize how lonely she feels with both kids about to leave."

It's easy to see what someone else should do, but what about you?

Are you trying to see life through the eyes of your spouse? Can you feel what it's like to be where your spouse is now?

The same as Bob didn't understand Laura, Carol couldn't understand Greg. He was threatening to leave home, and it seemed totally unreasonable to her when he said he just couldn't stand the pressure of being there anymore. He complained that the minute he stepped in the door at night, Carol was after him to take care of something around the house or make some decision. The kids were a headache too. Their teenage daughter kept the telephone line busy most of the time, and their two younger sons were usually at the dining room table asking for help with homework or in the family room fighting over video games.

Greg lost his temper several times every evening, so he always went to bed feeling guilty about being a rotten father and husband.

Still, he reasoned, *Carol and the kids demand a lot of me every minute I'm around, and they don't even know what I'm going through at work.*

The truth was, his job was more of a hassle than all the problems with his family. He managed to control himself at work even though he had to do the job of two people because an obnoxious colleague spent so much time patronizing the boss. By the end of the day Greg was so frazzled he took out his frustrations on Carol and the kids.

Then Greg's disgusting colleague got the promotion Greg felt sure he would get. He came home more irritable than ever, but no one even asked what was bothering him. *All they need me for is the money I earn,* he grumbled. *At least they could give me a little peace and quiet when I get home at night. This yammering drives me crazy!*

He thought about getting an apartment where he could have some peace and quiet. When he suggested the idea to Carol, she came unglued!

"How could you even consider such a thing?" she cried.

Greg wanted to tell Carol about all the problems at work, but she was too upset to listen. After a few more miserable weeks he rented a small, dingy apartment close to work.

Carol was sure this meant he wanted a divorce, and she insisted they see a marriage counselor. Reluctantly, Greg agreed. During the counseling sessions Greg finally had the opportunity to tell Carol what life was like for him.

She was astonished! For the first time she began to understand Greg's need for peace at home. When she realized what pressures he was dealing with at work, she decided to make their life more serene.

Greg consented to come back.

Carol made a concentrated effort not to remind Greg of all he needed to do as soon as he got home each night. She enlisted the kids to help by keeping down the noise. Their daughter's friends were not to telephone after Greg got home.

As Carol came to understand Greg and acted accordingly, their home quieted down and so did Greg.

Understand Your Mate's Perspective

If you really want to save your marriage, you must learn what it's like to walk in your mate's shoes. After you've walked a mile in them you will have a better understanding of why he or she is struggling with being married to you.

Perhaps all you can think of are reasons why it is a privilege to be bound to you. But with a little reflection you might remember a few teeny, tiny instances when you could have said something in a kinder tone of voice or acted in a slightly more loving way. You might even grimace as you recall times your mate tried to tell you about a problem or an idea and you didn't listen.

And have you considered your mate's childhood and young adult experiences? If you had weathered the same storms perhaps you'd react to life in a similar way.

As you realize that life looks different from your spouse's perspective, you can try to change yours. It's true that you can't exactly understand your mate's thinking, but you can come closer than you are now.

You *are* two different people with two different sets of life experiences. Even if you've been married a number of years, you still have separate events happening to you each day, and you each react differently to those events.

How, then, can you possibly see life from your mate's perspective? You start by making the determination to *be more sensitive* to your spouse and to *develop your empathy skills*.

Sometimes we identify more closely with a character in a movie or on a daytime TV talk show than we do with the person we promised to love and cherish. But by aligning ourselves as much as possible with our mates we can make a stronger connection with them.

"But I don't see life at all the way my spouse does," you may protest. "In fact, I think my spouse is totally off base."

The question right now is not a matter of right or wrong, but of accepting the fact that this is how your mate feels about circumstances (*and* your marriage) right now.

Being empathetic and sensitive doesn't mean that we wallow in the pit with people. It means that we "feel deeply with them" (the meaning of empathy from the Greek word *pathos*). But we don't get mired down in faulty thinking and behaviors. You don't help alcoholics by getting drunk with them, but you do help by caring and seriously trying to meet their needs. And one of their needs may be to get professional help.

How to Develop Empathy

Some people don't have the foggiest idea how to exercise empathy, but it's not all that difficult. You can begin by increasing your alertness, which means you will listen more carefully and be more observant of your spouse's unspoken signals.

The next thing to do is to *use your imagination*. The ability to be empathetic is closely tied to having a good imagination. Pretend you're actually looking through your mate's eyeballs. Mentally get inside his or her head and see, feel, and understand life from that viewpoint. When you deliberately identify with your mate's feelings you will be able to suffer or rejoice with him or her.[1]

When Jim was going through his mid-life crisis, he was questioning the meaning of life, full of self-pity, and very, very irritable. He was frightened about getting old and even more upset that I was getting old. He was tired of all the demands his family and congregation were making on him. He kept feeling the urge to run away and just escape the whole mess.

At first, I couldn't understand why he should be feeling as he did. Life didn't seem futile to me. I didn't feel old. We were only half-way through life and we had a lot of exciting things left to do.

As the months of his agony continued, I sometimes wanted to shout, "Just snap out of it! Grow up! Think of someone besides yourself for a change!"

Fortunately, I didn't say those things. Instead, just before Jim slid into his deepest despair, I asked him what counsel he gave to women who came to him for help with their husbands in mid-life crisis. He mustered enough objectivity to share some of his suggestions with me.

In a nutshell, these are what he had found helpful to the women he counseled:

1. Commit yourself to a **long time** of working through the crisis—perhaps three to five years.

2. Be your husband's **best friend**. Understand what he's going through and attempt to meet his needs.

3. Listen when he feels like talking, but let him have space and **quiet** when he needs it.

4. Be a **girlfriend** to him, not a mother. In other words, be fun and sexy instead of naggy or bossy.

Even though I wasn't feeling what Jim was feeling, I decided to try to imagine what he was going through. His shoes were definitely different than mine! He was a successful pastor and counselor and had the looks and vigor of someone younger than his age. I had spent my adult years as a wife and mother, had received little public affirmation, and looked every bit as old as I was.

But I was determined to at least speculate what it was like to be Jim at this time and place in life. I tried to imagine what it would be like to hate getting older. What would it be like to think I was being exploited? What would be the confusion in my mind as I questioned the meaning of life and didn't come up with any happy answers?

I'm sure I never did completely understand his world, but I was able to empathize better than I had previously. In fact, during the process I got more in touch with my own feelings about aging and the purpose of life.

Be Willing to Learn

Another way to understand your mate's world is to *ask questions*. Ask about their views on life—their own lives in particular. Ask what makes them feel happy or fulfilled.

Even if your spouse has left, you can ask questions whenever you do have contact. Ask appropriately, of course. You're not a Gestapo agent trying to force an enemy to talk. You want the experience to be as pleasant as possible.

If your mate is not available for discussion, ask other people who know from similar experiences what your mate is feeling. Piece together as much information as you can to get a picture of your mate's inner struggles.

By showing genuine interest in your mate's world, you will likely detect some softening in his or her determination to get rid of you. In turn, you will learn more about what's really going on in your mate's mind and heart.

Chapter 8

Listen Attentively to Your Spouse

• • •

SHARON GREETED PETER from the kitchen when he came home from work, but he didn't stop to talk. Later, during dinner, their three teenagers chattered nonstop about school and church events and their friends. Sharon joined in frequently, but Peter remained silent. When a phone call took Julie away from the table, Sharon asked Peter how his day had gone.

"Lousy," he mumbled. It was the first word he'd spoken since coming in the door. He picked up a dinner roll and was silent again.

"My day was hard too," replied Sharon, and she launched into a story about an argumentative customer she'd had at the bank where she worked as a teller. She was still relating the details when Julie returned to the table. The conversation again turned to the kids' interests.

Peter excused himself from the table after he had finished eating. He made a short business call from the bedroom phone and then sat down in the family room and turned on the television. Sharon joined him later. Their only conversation was a discussion of which programs to watch.

As they undressed for bed that night, Sharon rehashed some of her feelings about her irritating customer. Peter, lost in his own thoughts, didn't respond.

After they settled into bed, Peter gave a big sigh and said, "I'm not sure what to do about the mess at work."

"Oh, don't worry," Sharon said cheerily, "you'll think of something. You're tired tonight. In the morning the world will look better." With that, she turned over and went to sleep, leaving Peter to spend the night tossing and turning alone.

Listening to Problems

Many of us go through life not knowing how to listen. We can hold a conversation, but usually we focus on *what we have to say* rather than on *what the other person is saying*. While the other person talks, we think about what to say next and can hardly wait for the opportunity to jump in.

Women complain to us that they can't get their husbands to communicate. When we probe a little into the relationship we often find that sometime in the past the husband did try to say something, but his wife didn't listen and he finally gave up trying. We also find that many husbands don't listen to their wives because they think women talk all the time but not about anything important.

Both these problems are real—but there are solutions.

Although exceptions do occur, men generally use words to take care of business and to solve problems. They tend to get right to the point and very often don't say anything until they have a problem all figured out.

Women, on the other hand, use talking as a form of companionship. They think out loud, letting others share their reasoning process.

The talkative mate could learn a lot about the other one by truly listening to the few words he or she does say and by watching for nonverbal signals. In turn, the quiet spouse could better understand the chatty one by reading between the lines, watching body language, and realizing that all the words are an attempt to connect emotionally.

Peter needed Sharon to tune in on his one word—*lousy*. He might have talked further about his problem if she hadn't jumped in to tell about her bad day. In bed that night Peter again was willing to discuss his dilemma, but again Sharon turned him off by her overly simplistic response.

Eventually Peter quit trying to share his problems at all. Sharon accused him of never communicating because to her communication meant lots of conversation. She didn't realize that the few words he did say were his way of communicating, so she failed to follow up when he tried to get his feelings out.

Unfortunately, Peter found someone who did listen—Penny from work. She genuinely cared about his troubles and told him all the great qualities she saw in him. He hadn't intentionally looked for an affair, but if the relationship continued Peter would likely turn to this woman for sexual satisfaction as well as for emotional satisfaction.

How Do You Really Listen?

True listening is hard work and takes discipline. I have known about active listening (or creative listening, as it is sometimes called) for nearly twenty years, but I still don't have the skill down pat. It is easier for me to talk than to listen. Yet when I do switch into the "listen" mode, I am always amazed by what I learn.

Not only do I find out about the person to whom I'm listening, but often that person finds a solution to a problem or, at least, finds emotional release. When I actively listen to Jim, he often thanks me for helping him see an issue more clearly even though I haven't given him any answers. Just being able to "talk it out" gives him a perspective he didn't have before.

Following are some things we've learned about true listening.

Listening Takes Time

Listening is best done when we stop other activities and limit other noises. This means putting on the brakes, and that isn't easy in our hurried world where we never have enough time to do all the important things that need to be done.

If we really want to know what makes our spouses tick, however, we have to take time to let them talk. We must make listening a high priority. In fact, if we mean business about bettering our relationship, we will make listening our *highest* priority. And listening must be done in non-rushed moments. We can't hurry the process.

Listening Requires Focused Attention

Many events in life do not require 100 percent concentration because our minds can receive more than one stimulus at a time. But if we want to be sure we are catching every bit of the message our mates are sending, we must focus totally on them.

An important aspect of focused attention is eye contact. If we glance around the room, we indicate that something is more important than the person speaking. If we turn away from that person, drum our fingers on the table, or tap one foot, we show that we are bored. To truly connect with people and let them know they are significant to us, we must give them clues with our eyes and the rest of our body.

Not only will we detect the full meaning of what our spouses are saying by focusing on them, we also will give them the assurance that they are important to us. They will sense our concern. Our attention tells them that we'd rather be with them than anywhere else. When they feel confident that they are cared for they will be more likely to disclose their feelings and thoughts.

Listening Means "Be Quiet"

When we want to learn what is really going on with our mates, we have to be quiet and let them do the talking. That's hard when we have so much wisdom to dispense, so many observations to make, and so many experiences to share. However, information is not what they need right now. They simply need a listening ear. A time may come when talk is appropriate, but we need to make sure we've done sufficient listening first.

The Art of "Drawing Out"

When we actively listen to our mates, we may sense they're having trouble saying what's on their minds. They can't find the proper words or aren't sure how much is safe to talk about. If they hesitate, we may think they've said all they're going to say. But that's probably not so. This is the time to practice "drawing out." Try rephrasing the last comment made by your spouse. By assuring your mate that you are listening you can often spur more talk.

Sharon was learning to draw Peter out. One evening she picked up on a single word Peter said: *Penny*, and she suddenly realized he had been mentioning that name frequently. Sharon decided to listen more closely to everything Peter said, no matter how little it was, and to pay closer attention to the clues he was sending her. A few days later Sharon had the opportunity to put her resolve into practice.

"Boy, I sure do dread going back to work tomorrow," Peter said as he climbed into bed on Sunday night.

Instead of assuring him that he would be able to handle whatever came along, Sharon determined to find out more about what was troubling him, so she rephrased his comment.

"You don't want to go to work?" she asked, being careful to make the comment in a neutral tone of voice and softly phrasing it as a question so it sounded neither patronizing nor judgmental.

"Yeah, I have some tough decisions to make," he added tentatively.

Sharon wisely chose not to question him directly. Instead of demanding to know "What kind of decisions?" she simply said, "Decisions?" leaving him free to say as much or as little as he wanted.

Sharon desperately wanted to say something to fill the silence that followed, but instead she kept her focus on him, quietly expecting him to say more. And finally he did.

As Sharon continued to actively listen and occasionally repeat

Peter's last words, he felt liberated enough to continue talking. When Peter concluded, they both felt satisfaction. For the first time in years Peter felt that Sharon cared about the problems he was wrestling with, and Sharon felt as if Peter had let her in on the details of his business life, which he had always told her had "nothing to do with family."

Don't Pass Sentence

A major hindrance to self-disclosure is the fear of judgment. Perhaps the issue with which your spouse is struggling is one you have previously condemned. Knowing this makes your spouse fear that you will be overly harsh.

If he or she is involved in a moral problem, you certainly will have a strong opinion. But at this stage, it is important to convince your spouse that you want to hear his or her viewpoint and that you will listen without condoning or condemning.

If this sounds wishy-washy, we assure you that we are not advocating that you turn your back on your value system. Not at all. We simply want you to recognize that your spouse has the right to be understood and cared for, no matter what he or she has done or is struggling with. Your spouse needs to know that you can listen nonjudgmentally, that you want to understand, and that you care. When the whole story comes out, perhaps you'll have a viewpoint that surprises both of you.

Or perhaps your mate, after verbalizing his or her thoughts or actions, will come to see the situation more clearly. People are more apt to make the right decision, and stick to it, if they make it of their own free will and not because someone is preaching at them or pointing accusing fingers.

Keep Confidentiality

Some spouses are afraid to communicate for fear of what their mate will do with the information. They may be afraid it will be used against them or told to other people.

Our mates' struggles—whether problems at work, fear of the

future, unattainable dreams and goals, feelings of rejection, or temptation—must be treated with the greatest of respect. When they entrust this information to us, it is not something others need to know, nor is it something to use as a weapon against our mates.

No Need for the Shell Answer Man

A mistake people often make is to think they must give solutions to their mates' problems.

- "If you'd just tell your boss. . . ."
- "You can find fulfillment by simply throwing yourself more into our home. . . ."
- "You need to read what the Bible says about that. Here's a verse. . . ."
- "You should do it like this. . . ."
- "Just keep away from that woman. . . ."
- "The next time you see your father, simply say. . . ."

As easy as it is for us—with all our knowledge—to clearly see what our mates should do or feel, our answers are not what will help most at this point. For now we are to be *listening*, not giving wise advice. Before we start talking, we should be very sure we've listened and listened and listened.

When we do finally speak, we must do so carefully. Here again, God's wisdom is crucial.

As Sharon listened while Peter revealed more of his problems at work, she learned that Penny, a woman he had hired a year earlier, was very unproductive and causing a great deal of strife. Peter's boss had told him that he must get rid of her.

However, Peter felt sorry for Penny. She was a single mother with three children and had had a very rough life. This job was one of the best things that had ever happened to her.

As Peter further disclosed his dilemma, he acknowledged that he had become infatuated with her. She often came into his office to talk about her personal problems. He enjoyed talking to her, and he felt good that he had been able to help her.

In fact, he had talked to her about a personal relationship with Jesus Christ and she seemed close to making a decision. If he fired her she might never become a Christian and she certainly would feel that the world, and probably even God, was against her. But if he didn't let her go, his own job was in jeopardy. As he talked, he realized for the first time that his marriage would also be threatened.

He was in a predicament.

Very wisely, Sharon just listened. When he told her of his emotional attachment to Penny, she trembled inside but said nothing. She could have raged, "Get rid of that woman immediately or I'm leaving. Then see where you'll be!" Or, she might have said, "You'd better listen to your boss. How could you possibly blow your whole career for someone who's a liability?"

Instead, by letting Peter talk it out, she allowed him to clarify his thinking and determine the direction he needed to go. He realized his feelings for Penny were based more on sympathy than anything else. He had enjoyed being a rescuer, but she needed to carry her own weight on the job and take responsibility for her personal life as well.

Penny really was a detriment to the company, and he needed to find someone who could make a contribution. This would not only put him in better standing with the boss, but would actually help the entire organization be more productive.

A few days later Peter released Penny—although it wasn't easy—and began searching for the right person. He was much more at peace with himself; he even liked his job better. And it was much more fun coming home to Sharon at night.

"But My Mate's Not Here!"

You may say, "This chapter is fine for those people whose mate is around to be heard, but mine is gone!" Or "How can I practice listening when he only telephones about business matters?" Or "What's there to listen to when all she does is sit in the car while she drops off the kids?"

Jody's counselor gave her a crash course in how to effectively listen to her husband, Phil. Phil had disappeared without much warning and with no indication of where he was going. Jody, of course, was worried sick.

Three nights after leaving, Phil called. "I just want to let you know I'm all right and to see if you are too," he said almost tenderly. When Jody asked where he was, he turned cold and said, "That's my business. And don't ask when I'm coming back!"

Jody's counselor helped her see from that conversation that Phil had actually given her more information than his words alone revealed. He wanted her to know that he was safe and that he cared about her well-being. But he still needed privacy and to feel in control of his own life.

With each subsequent call, Jody received more insight into Phil's inner feelings. She learned to let him talk as he felt up to it. She didn't nag or give advice. He opened up more and more to her and finally offered to come get her for a "date" so they could talk some more.

Phil and Jody's communication certainly wasn't as full as it would have been if he were home and their relationship was healthy. But Jody learned to appreciate all that Phil was saying and meaning whenever they did talk. She found she was getting to know him better than she ever had.

It *is* much harder to listen to your mate when he or she is out of the home. However, unless your mate has completely broken all contact, you can still use the little snatches of time you do get.

When your mate telephones, stops by the house, or meets you somewhere, use the opportunity to genuinely tune in. Yes, you have your hurts and your agenda, but put them on hold for now. Focus your attention on your mate as a true friend would. Let your spouse know you care by listening and practicing the art of "drawing out."

Your mate may put up a front of anger or coldness, but look beyond the facade and try to see the struggle going on inside. Your mate is full of questions and doubts, even though the exterior shows otherwise.

Only God knows your mate's inner workings for sure. But you're aware of enough to know that something's going on and you need to find out more. Don't get angry or let your feelings get hurt because of your mate's hostility or distant emotions. Focus on your mate's needs, not your own.

At this point, these actions and attitudes may seem achievable only by a Super Spouse. Since you're a mere human being, you won't always do and say—and *not* say—everything correctly. But it will help to have listening as a goal you're working toward.

Over time, you will be pleasantly rewarded if you
- take time to listen,
- focus attention on your mate,
- keep quiet so you can hear,
- draw out your mate,
- be nonjudgmental,
- keep confidentialities, and
- give support rather than solutions.

Chapter 9

Deal with
Emotional Clutter

♦ ♦ ♦

RECENTLY THE TWO OF US cleaned our garage. Somehow the odds and ends we store there always outgrow the space. Some of the stuff just needed to be straightened and rearranged, but most of it needed to be thrown out—cans of old paint, a broken coffee maker, empty boxes, and stacks of plastic plant pots. When we finished the task, we were exhausted, as usual.

You may be in need of some intense emotional housecleaning if your mate is threatening to leave or has already left. The attic, basement, closet, and garage of your mind may be crammed with clutter from the past.

If you're like we were, you may be overflowing with emotional debris. But we didn't see our mess for years. We both had accumulated emotional garbage during childhood and had added to it during our years together. We hadn't had much adult life apart from each other because we were married as soon as Jim graduated from college. But some couples collect a lot of psychological junk during their single adult years.

At first you may have to do the cleaning and digging by yourself. Your mate may want no part of it. But you still have to consider his or her trash, along with your own, because your mate's emotional garbage affects you too.

You may think the task is too big, too ugly, or too painful. Or you may be blind to the mess you are in. The truth is, the longer it goes untouched, the worse it becomes. We wish we had started ridding ourselves of extra emotional baggage years ago, before some of it grew into serious disorders.

Even if you have gone a long time without dealing with your accumulated clutter, it's not too late. It's better to now so you can enjoy the years you have left. A couple we know had a miserable marriage for over sixty-one years. The wife died recently—without either of them ever having tried to work on their problems.

When we realized we had to get to work on the trash piles in our lives, we vowed not to waste any more time. Once we made the decision, Jim kept saying, "This is the year I'm going to get healed!"

He set out to find a therapist in whom he could have confidence. For years he had fought against seeing a counselor, because, as a counselor himself, he couldn't imagine what anyone could tell him that he didn't already know. And whom could he trust? But eventually his childhood pain became so great that he knew he had to find help. After a while I began seeing the same counselor.

Small Care Groups

About the same time Jim began therapy, we each became part of small—very small—care groups. Jim meets with two other men, and I meet with two other women. We can count on these people to listen to us and to keep whatever we share within the group.

Our friends have walked with us through very hard times as we have struggled to get free from the long, ugly tentacles of Jim's childhood experiences, which had severely affected our marriage and even our childraising. Sometimes we have been very difficult folks to be around, but our friends have loved us anyway.

Our friends also share their problems with us, and together we have become a true support for each other. Besides meeting together, we pray regularly for each other, telephone each other several times a week, and have many fun times together. These people have been like lifelines to two drowning people. In the early days they rescued us; now they keep us from going under again.

Time to Work Together

The two of us also began to do more talking and working together to clean out our old emotional clutter. It took time; and it still takes time—often at what seems the wrong time—and sometimes it hurts. But it's certainly worth it.

We have become more honest with each other. It isn't that we lied to each other before; but we often withheld the whole truth or tinted it a little to protect the other one.

We entered the waters of truthfulness gingerly. We didn't dare just plunge in. Little by little, one of us would say something like,

"I'm uncomfortable with what you just said. . . ."

"I'm left with a feeling I don't like. . . ."

"I wonder if I understand what you mean. . . ."

Previously, we would have stuffed the uneasy feelings deep inside and never come to a mutual understanding. We thought we were being Christ-like by not prolonging a disagreement or making the other angry. Instead, we were following patterns we had learned in childhood; and a lot of the misunderstandings and resentments we buried eventually germinated into an ugly mess we couldn't control.

Clutter from Long Ago

Your attitudes about life and patterns of living started forming in childhood. Even if you think you've changed your attitudes and behaviors a good deal from that of your parents, your world is still colored by what did or didn't happen to you as a child.

If you felt loved, valued, and listened to, you have a different picture of the world—and even of God—than if you were neglected, physically or sexually abused, and made to feel unimportant. You may have forgiven those who did these things to you, but those deeds still are part of the accumulation of experiences that makes you who you are.

Often people don't realize that their childhood experiences are still entwined in how they function as adults. Some attitudes and responses can cause strife in marriage without giving a clue as to the source.

For years, whenever Jim came home after a day at the church, I would ask, "What happened today? What did you do?"

If he was in a good mood, he'd answer, "Oh, I can't really remember. The day was so full." When he was in a poorer frame of mind, he'd say, "I don't feel like giving a report." If he was in an even worse mood, he'd grumble, "Why do I have to tell you everything I do? Just let me run things without having to give an account to you."

Many years down the road, we woke up to the influence of Jim's troubled childhood on his adult life and realized why we ran into trouble when I asked about his day.

His mother always suspected that children who were out of her sight were up to no good. She would greet them at the door with "Well, what trouble have you been into now?" Or, "You're five minutes late getting home from school! What have you been doing?"

Jim grew up being mistrusted and falsely accused. So even though I just wanted to know how things were going for him and to show I cared about his world, he heard his mother's inquistions.

Together we worked on the problem. I was more careful in how I asked about his day, and he reminded himself that I was asking because I cared about him, not because I was checking up on him.

If either you or your mate came from a troubled—or dysfunctional—home, you may need a lot of healing. The helpful steps to recovery from a damaged homelife are covered in Jim's book, *Adult Children of Legal or Emotional Divorce*.[1]

Other Clutter

Besides childhood debris, one of you may have rubble left from your adult life before marrying your spouse. This could include:

- A previous marriage or love affair
- Sexual assault
- Multiple career changes
- Military service
- Drug or alcohol addiction or other harmful habits
- Running with the wrong friends
- Living too long with your parents after becoming an adult

These must be dealt with as part of solving your present marital problems. Again, you may need outside help from a discerning counselor who understands dysfunctional families.

If either you or your spouse has been married before, reading books about remarriage and the "blended family" may help you. Insights from others' experiences can give you some tips to work on. Christian bookstores and some church libraries are well-stocked with books on remarriage and how to make new families successful. One book we highly recommend is *When You're Mom No. 2* by Dr. Beth Brown.[2]

Helpful books on addiction and codependency are also available. Some are listed in the Recommended Reading section.

Whatever your problems from your previous adult life or your mate's earlier life, it is important to face them and do what is necessary to put them at rest. They have cluttered your present life long enough.

You can't undo past events—especially if there are living reminders, such as children. So instead of pretending certain things never happened, decide now to face them and find some solutions.

Everyday Clutter

Cleaning away the garbage that has accumulated in marriage may be more difficult than getting rid of clutter from the past because we are less likely to see the mess we have become accustomed to. And even if we do see it, we're likely to blame it on our mate.

You probably have been married long enough to know that *old hurts* sting every time you remember them, and you probably have quite a supply by now.

Connie and Ted, the couple we mentioned in chapter 2 who divorced and then remarried each other, had to work on the emotional destruction caused by Connie's unfaithfulness. For months after they remarried, Ted worried whenever Connie left the house. He was a nervous wreck every time he thought of Connie's past affairs.

Finally, he came to the place where he knew he had to put all that behind him. Connie assured him of her loyalty and asked again for his forgiveness. When he specifically uttered the words, "I forgive you," he found a release.

Certain words or events may always activate memories of a grievance or start a new argument with your mate, so it helps to recognize these *triggers* and be on guard. If you can identify them and see them coming, you can prepare yourself and avert the usual consequences.

Secrets are another cause of damage in marriage. This doesn't mean Christmas or birthday surprises; it means withholding information that should be general knowledge between you and your mate.

Art and Susan had been married for over twenty-five years, yet Susan never knew how much Art made at his job. For years he kept the bank account in his name and gave her an allowance. When she got a job outside the home and started a bank account of her own, Art expected her to pay most of the household expenses from her earnings.

Several times during their marriage Art bought a new car and proudly drove it up in front of the house, expecting Susan to be delighted. She hadn't even known he was thinking of changing cars, and he never let her be involved in deciding the make or color.

Recently Susan discovered they had heavy debts and were in danger of losing everything. Art had wanted to keep the details to himself, but he was managing so poorly that he had to divulge some of his secrets. And Susan had to take a crash course in finance management and jump in to salvage what she could. The whole experience caused a great deal of division between the two of them. In fact, Susan's emotions were so on edge that she asked Art to move out for a while.

It's time to get those hurts, trigger events, or secrets cleaned out and make room to live life to the fullest! Left unattended, emotional garbage will take it's toll—sooner or later—on our physical well-being. The result may be headaches, ulcers, chemical imbalance, heart problems, or other diseases. Emotional tension saps our immune system so that our bodies cannot effectively fight infections and other ailments.

If you're beginning to see the garbage for the first time and think that you can get along by just covering it up, you're only adding to the mess. You can go on stumbling over it for a time, but how much better it would be to have an uncluttered, healthy, fun marriage!

Getting Help

To get rid of the junk in your marriage, you probably will need the help of a competent counselor. Look for one with at least a master's degree in psychology or in marriage, family, and child counseling (MFCC) from an accredited school. Therapists with a doctorate in marriage and family counseling are even more qualified to help you.

Education, however, is not the only guide. You will want a therapist whose values do not conflict with your own. You may want a Christian counselor, but keep in mind that being a Christian doesn't guarantee ability.

Choose a counselor known for helping couples put their marriages back together. Some therapists emphasize individual growth and independence to such an extreme that they actually encourage divorce rather than restoration. Other counselors become discouraged when a marriage doesn't heal quickly and begin to recommend divorce.

If either you or your spouse is also working on recovering from an unhealthy childhood, find a therapist who understands dysfunctional families.

For our own counselor we are pleased to have found a well-educated, well-qualified Christian who grew up in a dysfunctional home. Most of his clients are working through problems from dysfunctional childhoods.

Don't be afraid to ask questions about the person you are considering as a counselor. You have a right to know about the person's education, particular specialty, and personality. When you telephone the therapist's office, tell the receptionist that you are gathering information to make a decision about choosing the best counselor for your needs. The process should include a telephone interview with the counselor.

You also need to ask about the cost of counseling. If you can't afford the fee, the counselor may offer you a reduced rate. If the cost still is too great, look for a church or community agency that offers free or low-cost counseling. Some health insurance plans cover counseling costs.

In considering the price of counseling, also consider the cost of *not* getting professional help. Remember, a divorce costs a lot of money too—and it leaves you with nothing but a broken marriage.

Don't be afraid to change counselors if after several sessions you don't click with the first one you chose. You need to feel at ease with your therapist or you won't make much progress.

At First It Hurts

We know it takes hard work to dig through the debris in your lives, but you'll be glad for the good changes it brings. "What do you mean—good changes?" you may ask. "Things are worse than before."

Ridding yourself of accumulated junk sometimes causes a great deal of agony in the beginning. It's similar to having an appendectomy. The surgery and recovering are painful, but later you are much healthier than you would be with the rotten appendix.

By anticipating the pain and bracing yourself for it, you will be able to handle it. And knowing that you will eventually see signs of health will help you through the hard times. Little rewards along the way will encourage you on your journey toward recovery.

We knew it was going to be a day of hard work when we started to clean the garage. We got tired and dirty, but we couldn't quit once we had everything pulled out into the driveway. So we kept at it, and when we had finished sorting and had things in place we felt very good. The garage was clean and organized. We could walk through it again. The result was certainly worth the work.

Instead of being left alone with an attic full of old trunks crammed with ugly remnants of your past life, you can be on your way to clutter-free living. And we hope your mate will be with you for the trip.

Chapter 10

Consider the Career Pressure

◆ ◆ ◆

KEN WAS A QUIET, gentle man who loved his family, but he was on the verge of leaving them. No one would have guessed it a few months earlier. He had always been a spiritual leader in his church, and many admired him. For over a year, however, he had been so exhausted that he could barely move one foot ahead of the other. But he felt he had to keep going to provide for his family.

He worked extra shifts to earn enough money so his children could have music lessons, attend special activities, and so the family could live in a big house in a nice part of town. The mortgage was a huge drain on Ken's paycheck, but it was a wonderful house—a house where he spent very little time.

Eventually Ken just snapped. He began disappearing from work. He'd get in his car and drive until he ran out of gas. Although devoted to his wife, he became attached to a woman at work. He couldn't understand what was happening to himself. He decided he'd better leave town before he destroyed his family. *If I just disappear*, he reasoned, *it will save my wife and kids a lot of unhappiness. If I stay around here, I'll end up disgracing everyone.*

Fortunately Ken's wife, Ruth, came to us for counseling before Ken left for good. Alerted to his problem, Jim began to drop in on Ken at work. As they became closer friends, Jim learned how tired Ken was from overworking and that he felt confused and unable to make good decisions. Ken's bewilderment had led to the involvement with the other woman, and he felt so ashamed that he thought the best way out of the mess was to get away completely.

Less but More

Ruth continued to come for counseling. She began to see how Ken's many hours of work had brought him to this point. As she and Ken started to talk more openly about the complications, she assured him that she would forgive him for his unfaithfulness even though it had hurt her terribly.

She encouraged him to return to a normal work schedule and agreed to move to a smaller house, get rid of one car, and cut back on some other expenses. The older kids, who had become aware of the potential family breakup, willingly gave up some of their activities and hobbies to have Dad at home. It was hard to share crowded bedrooms, but it was far better than living in big rooms with no father.

Would you be willing to lower your lifestyle to save your marriage? Would your family move into smaller living quarters or do without some other things if doing so would keep your mate from leaving?

Work Equals Significance

My father was a hard-working farmer for much of his life and in later years he became a cabinet-maker. He owned his own shop and put in six long days every week at his craft. As he aged, this work too became difficult and he had to slow down because his legs and arms were becoming weak.

I visited him just before he retired at age 82. One evening while he sat in his big recliner, I perched near him and took his big, gnarly hands in mine. "How are you feeling, Daddy?" I asked.

"Oh, I feel pretty good. It's just that I'm 'no account,'" he replied sadly. "I can't lift those sheets of plywood like I used to, so I'm not much good to anybody."

I could see I needed to let my daddy know right then that he was special to me and the world, even if he couldn't work much.

Our mates also need to know they are of much more value to us than their paycheck or career accomplishments. And we need to stick by them while the tide of outside praise is out to sea.

This does not mean that we should underestimate the importance of our mate's career. We will be of no comfort if we say "Don't let your work bother you—it's not that important anyway! It's just a job." Work is important and our mates want it to run right.

A large portion of a person's identity comes from work, whether it's managing a household or working outside the home. When people are introduced at social or business gatherings, their names are almost always attached to their job identification rather than to their character. We don't say, "This is John Brown, an honest and caring husband and father." Instead, we say, "Meet John Brown, head of marketing at Acme Corporation."

Since work takes up so many hours of each day, we can see why job satisfaction or dissatisfaction affects everything else about a person's life. And families often bear the brunt when things go badly at work. Our niceness batteries last only so many hours—usually while we're at work—and then watch out! Our mean side kicks into action and all disgusting individuals within the four walls are in danger. (And everyone, especially the mate, is disgusting.)

Work Can Mean Destruction

Unhappiness at work can have several effects besides marital strife, including physical problems such as heart disease, ulcers, rashes, digestive disorders, and breathing difficulties. Job stress also accentuates negative emotional tendencies, which create an ever-widening circle of complications.

People desperate to change career circumstances may say something foolish to a boss or coworker that they would not say while thinking clearly. Or distress may cause people to make a poor choice in choosing a new job, grabbing the first available position whether or not it fits.

Job troubles can be anything from too little pay or a poor working environment to disagreeable employers or incompetent employees; from unfair promotion practices to a mismatch in career. Jobs can be too demanding—or too demeaning.

Some work situations tear away self-esteem. And people's value of themselves is greatly smashed when they are dismissed from jobs or can't find a job. Retirement also can be hard on self-worth. Most of us think our value is in "doing," so when we aren't doing we feel worthless.

Some men don't understand their wife's desire for a meaningful career. In the last two decades, many women have abandoned their husbands and children to find "their place." A wise husband will help his wife find fulfillment so she won't want to break the marriage.

For some women, a paycheck is an official sign that someone considers them worthy of reward. An assistant of ours used to say, "Money isn't everything, but a paycheck is one way of knowing you've pleased somebody."

Not every threatened marriage has work and money pressures, but sometimes that's where the trouble starts. And often we don't recognize job difficulties as the source of the friction, assuming instead that the problems are caused by a difficult mate.

Show You Care

We have seen many distressed marriages changed to happy ones when one mate recognized the job pressure of the other and cooperated to lessen it. Complete corrections usually cannot be made quickly. But by showing an interest and working together to diminish work stress you can bring about some relief, which then gives hope that the marriage as well as the job situation eventually will get better.

One difficulty in helping mates with job tension is that sometimes they don't want help. They may even push you away. What then? Practice listening and empathizing. Look for little ways to show interest without forcing yourself on your mate. Make sure your spouse feels free to discuss job problems with you and never act too busy or disinterested. Yes, you may have work problems of your own, but a healthy marriage requires that you have regard for your mate's job as well. As you show genuine concern, your spouse may begin to accept your care.

Suggestions for Change

While some mates may need to be encouraged to slow down in their job commitments, others could use encouragement to "Go for It!" Certainly there are no pat answers about work since each couple's situation is different and varies from one season of life to the next. However, if your mate wants out of your marriage and part of the problem is work-related, the following suggestions may help.

First, if too much work is the problem consider *downsizing*. This means cutting back or scaling down your lifestyle. In our society, we sometimes confuse wants with needs. Perhaps you should reevaluate your "needs" to coincide with a saner work schedule.

Occasionally families downsize by having both mates cut back on their work hours. Others decide that one partner will stay home and manage the family. Children who don't have all the newest clothes or toys won't grow up remembering all their parents *didn't* provide. But if mom and dad split up, they'll not only remember it but suffer damage that will affect them the rest of their lives.[1]

To help the person under job pressure, the family can pitch in to do the household tasks. Junior and Susy can mow the lawn and keep the car clean. They both can learn to help with the cleaning, cooking, and laundry. Children also can be enlisted to help make the home a refuge. Parents need an environment of peace and restoration when they come home exhausted. Children need a refuge too, so everyone needs to work together to make home a pleasant place.

Another way to lessen job pressure is to *shift sideways*. Instead of being promoted to a position where the demands are even greater, a person can sometimes make a "lateral" move to a job with less stress but similar pay.

Some people need to make a *complete career change* to decrease their stress. Perhaps they accepted a job that turned out to be a poor fit, or maybe the job itself changed so the skills required no longer match the person's abilities. A complete career shift must be done with a great deal of thought because education, experience, health insurance, and retirement benefits are probably tied up in this particular job. But switching to a totally different line of work may be a lifesaver—and a marriage saver—for some people.

Before making such a drastic decision, however, give serious consideration to getting some professional career counseling. If that is not an option, we recommend Richard Bolles' excellent book *What Color Is Your Parachute?*[2] It helps people identify their abilities and offers guidance for finding employment that matches.

Be a sounding board for your mate; listen while he or she mulls over the situation and give assurance of your support in whatever decision is made.

Often there are no easy answers to job stress, but if your marriage is coming apart because of it you need to find help and activate some changes quickly. A healthy, happy marriage is worth all the effort you exert to reduce work stress.

Chapter 11

Build Your Mate's Self-Esteem

• • •

J IM WAS UNRAVELING, and I didn't know what to do about it.
Almost every part of my Christian life was something I had learned
from him. Besides being my husband, he was my spiritual role model.
He always had been the optimistic one in our relationship. But now
this spiritual leader of a large church and the person who had effectively counseled hundreds of people was irritable and depressed himself. He sat around watching TV or staring out the window, asking,
"What is the meaning of my life?"

He couldn't remember ever doing anything significant or with
the right motive. He questioned his worth in every area. All he could
see in himself were faults and weaknesses.

He was grumpy because he was getting older and told me everything in his life was up for reevaluation, including his commitment to
our marriage.

I was astounded! I was also scared. How could this be?

Underneath it all, though, I felt a challenge to join myself with
God to make a difference in Jim's life.

Realizing I had grown lax in letting him know how highly I valued him, I determined to help him see his strengths and contributions to life. Others admired him and often let him know it by speaking to him after church, sending notes of gratitude, or talking to him during the week. Some of his admirers were young, intelligent, pretty women in our church from the local university. Many of them had come to Christ or were flourishing in their Christian lives because of Jim's ministry. They often told him how much they appreciated him.

Instead of taking Jim for granted, I decided to look at him through the eyes of a twenty-two-year-old and let him know what I saw. From this new perspective I saw many more things to admire than I'd seen before. I told him about those qualities and reminded him of his past accomplishments. I often complimented him on his appearance and thanked him for what he did for our family.

At first he brushed aside my words and wouldn't believe me. He acted as if he didn't want to hear me. But later he told me that all my comments were accumulating inside him. Because I appreciated him and let him know it, he began to move toward accepting himself again and his self-esteem began to thrive once more.

Wasted Possibilities

When we talk about a good self-image or high self-esteem, some people mistake this for arrogance. We've been taught all our lives not to blow our own horns nor to be puffed up with pride. However, having a good sense of our intrinsic worth is not pride. In fact, valuing ourselves is wise stewardship of what God has given us.

Yes, some people seem to have an exaggerated opinion of themselves, but many of these folks actually feel horribly inadequate deep inside. Their proud exterior is merely a coverup for their insecure interior. Self-important people often fear being honest with themselves because they know they are frauds.

People with a low opinion of themselves, on the other hand, are cheating themselves and others. They feel like such lowly peons that they waste their good qualities and abilities by never fully using them.

Their lives are like shriveled seeds that never get planted and therefore never grow and bloom.

Adults with low self-esteem seldom recognize the problem, but their behavior reveals their doubts about themselves. They may be jealous or critical of others; they may be cross with their children and other people; they may talk too much; or to impress others they may spend money they don't have. But worst of all, they may never try anything new for fear of failure; therefore they never develop their skills, and the world misses out on what they might contribute.

Men and women with a healthy self-image are not braggarts; nor are they drudges. They have an accurate assessment of their strengths and weaknesses. They have confidence that they can succeed in most things yet know that if they fail they can learn from it. They know they don't have every ability or talent, but they develop and use the ones they do have.

People with a truly wholesome self-esteem realize that their value does not lie within themselves. They are who they are and possess what they possess because of God's grace.[1] They recognize where they are strong and wise, but they also acknowledge that their strength and wisdom are gifts from God.

The Making of Self-Esteem

Our self-image begins developing at birth—perhaps while we are still in the womb. Among other things, it is affected by whether or not we are

- Lovingly touched and caressed
- Given eye contact
- Talked to
- Kept safe and warm
- Fed

As we grow, we sense from all the important people around us whether we are valuable or a bother; whether we can do things well or always mess up; and whether our ideas are worth listening to or better kept to ourselves. In those early years, we gather information about ourselves from how others act toward us. What others think of us forms what we think of ourselves.

Experts used to believe that self-image was entirely developed and fixed by our early twenties. Now, however, we know that self-image is never completely static; it changes with life's seasons and circumstances.

Adults continue to need positive input from the important people in their lives. Subconsciously, we use our friends, family, and coworkers as mirrors to reflect our worth. If we see that we are respected, listened to, and cared for, it is easier to esteem ourselves.

The two of us have known a few dynamic people who were able to see their worth even though they got little or no approval from others. These are unusual folks; most people are not strong enough to have good self-esteem when they are emotionally battered or ignored by people close to them.

Now, About Your Mate

By now you can see how crucial you are to the health of your mate's self-image. In fact, of all the people in the world, you are the most important.

"Wait a minute!" you may say, "My husband is so wrapped up in his career that he doesn't need me. What's important to him is whether or not he's succeeding at work." Or, "My wife only cares about what her friends think of her. They go shopping together, have a weekly Bible study, and talk about everything. If her friends approve of what she wears, thinks, or does, she's happy. She ignores my opinions."

Yes, other people are important to your spouse's self-image, but what the partners feel about each other is a more powerful force. Many marriage partners, however, grow lazy in showing appreciation, and a marriage that is falling apart is pretty strong evidence that at least one mate is no longer building the self-esteem of the other.

This is where you have an important part. As your mate decides whether to leave permanently or to return, your view of your mate's value is crucial. Not only should you appreciate your mate, you should communicate your appreciation.

Perhaps for the moment your mate has found someone whose opinion counts more than yours. However, you have history on your side. Your years of life together, shared joys and sorrows, children, friends, and extended family will count in the long run, and so will your new campaign to build your mate's self-esteem.

What Is There to Praise?

Right now you may think your mate is totally unworthy of any esteem from you. You certainly don't respect your partner's leaving or being involved with someone else, so what good can you say?

Start by thinking of all your mate's abilities and skills. Write them down so you can refer to them again when things get bleak and you have a hard time remembering anything good about your mate. Then list your partner's positive deeds from the past. Finish by noting all your mate's qualities. Qualities are different from abilities and deeds in that they are an inherent part of a person's character. Even if we lose our abilities or can no longer perform certain deeds, we still have attributes that make us worthwhile.

People use their qualities and abilities either negatively or positively. Someone who is aggressive can be abrasive and domineering or a wise administrator. Someone with a sense of humor may use it to cut others down or lift them up. Sometimes our point of view colors whether we think someone's qualities are negative or positive. Forcing ourselves to look at the positive side of our mate's qualities will give us a new appreciation of them.

After you've completed your inventory, jot down some words of appreciation you intend to say to your mate the next time you are together. Vow to carry out your intentions, no matter what else may transpire.

A Builder, Not a Destroyer

Commit yourself to doing and saying everything you can to build your mate's self-image. Don't allow yourself even one "put down." Following are some ideas that have helped us:

Use Words Wisely

When you are tempted to retaliate with spiteful or angry words—don't. Instead, speak soft words of kindness and affirmation. Recall your mate's past goodnesses and use those as a foundation for complimenting him or her.

Thank your mate for any positive thing you think of, past or present. Your spouse may be surprised that you noticed. On the other hand, don't be put off if he or she doesn't react with joy. I was saying all kinds of positive stuff to Jim, but at the time he didn't let me know that he liked it and was secretly storing it away.

Keep *unconditional love* as your key phrase when you speak to or about your mate. Think of God's unreserved love for you when you were no friend of his. Ask him for his power to speak lovingly to your mate.

Try Touching

For too long we've been wary of touching someone because of sexual implications. There are inappropriate ways to touch, of course. But you and your mate have a right to touch each other. God ordains loving touch between a husband and wife, as we know from reading *The Song of Solomon.*

Many scientific studies have shown the value of human touching to give a sense of well-being. Patients in hospitals or convalescent centers thrive when someone touches them regularly and tenderly. Premature babies struggling for life are more apt to survive and do well if they are touched and caressed.

Experiments have shown that customers are more likely to purchase an item when a salesperson touches them appropriately—a momentary touch on the shoulder or back of the hand. Restaurant patrons give better tips to waiters or waitresses who briefly touch them.

The two of us have learned the joy of touching each other. Sometimes it's with sexual motives, but many times it's just to show love and to communicate with each other. Anyway, touching certainly feels good!

Right now, however, your mate may not want to be touched. Don't be adamant about touching an unwilling partner, but look for times when you can tactfully and briefly touch his or her shoulder, hand, or knee.

If your mate allows more touching, do it. The more positive contact you have, the more materials you will have to use in rebuilding your marriage.

Give Respect

Another way to improve your spouse's self-esteem is to show that you value his or her opinions, preferences, and daily decisions. Nothing tears at self-esteem more than to be treated as if one's ideas and interests are unimportant or disgusting.

If you realize you've been disrespectful in the past, you need to make a concentrated effort to look for areas in which to give approval. Showing respect to your spouse is the right thing to do all the time, but now it's absolutely essential.

Respect will boost his or her self-esteem as well as show your mate that you have good motives. As your partner's self-worth increases because of your efforts, his or her bitterness or indifference toward you will likely lessen.

Reveal Your Admiration

Let your mate know what you admire about him or her, not only by your words but by your actions. Look into your mate's eyes when you speak.

If you can't think of anything to admire, remember what first attracted you to your spouse. Let your memories trigger some feelings of admiration.

Do your admiring both privately and publicly. Don't carry on like a love-sick calf in front of others, but let people know you value your mate.

Be Romantic

Sometimes a lack of romance is part of what has driven a mate away. When a mate does not feel accepted physically, his or her self-esteem lowers. So if your partner gives you any clues that it is permissible to show affection, go ahead.

This, of course, brings up the subject of whether or not you should have sexual intercourse. We used to advise, "Certainly, you should. You are the married partner. That's one way of meeting your mate's needs and redeveloping a closeness."

Now, however, we have the AIDS scare. If your mate has been sexually unfaithful to you, having intercourse may be unsafe for your health. "Safe sex" by use of a condom is a misnomer because accidents can happen, so don't put your full trust in a condom.

You and your spouse will have to determine if the risk of AIDS is an issue. Be certain you can trust your mate's words, and don't let the passion of the moment carry you away. AIDS is fatal.

You can, however, find safe ways of expressing affection without the complete act of intercourse. Until you know through a blood test that your mate is free from the AIDS virus or other sexually transmitted diseases, use safe expressions of love such as hugging and caressing.

As you have opportunity, be romantic. Do little things to show that your mate is special to you. For some, a candlelight dinner or flowers is the appropriate expression; for others, it's just being close and attentive. Some mates are pleased with unexpected love notes. Others like flirtatious gestures. You are the one who knows best what would delight your mate.

Whatever you do, do it with the idea of building your mate's self-worth. As your partner feels more valuable to you and to the world, perhaps you will begin to see a healing in your marriage.

Marv was a miserable person. Life had always seemed unfair to him. He was short, and the other kids at school teased him. He wanted to go to college but didn't have the money, so he took a low-paying sales job. He wanted to marry Lana, but she wouldn't look at him. He settled for Dottie instead.

After four kids and ten years of marriage, he began having an affair with Rhonda in another city. He told Dottie he was in that city on business, but much of the time he was actually living with Rhonda.

Dottie found out about Rhonda and did some serious talking with Marv over the next few months. At times he wanted to keep his marriage and end the adulterous relationship with Rhonda. He would promise to break up with her, but he insisted he needed to tell her in person. He'd go to the other city to do so and then not come home for two or three weeks.

Marv's feelings of inadequacy increased every time he said he'd break off the affair and couldn't follow through on it. He felt pulled between the two women. He was disgusted with himself for not being able to make his own decisions and stick to them.

He worried about messing up his family by his coming and going, so he finally announced he was going to stay away. He moved all his things into Rhonda's apartment.

Dottie was crushed, but she was determined to save their marriage. As part of her rebuilding efforts, she saw that Marv needed a better self-image and wisely decided to do what she could to help build his view of himself.

Marv still came by the house regularly to take the kids to a fast food restaurant, the mall, or a movie, so Dottie grabbed those moments to affirm him. She realized she hadn't done much of that in the last few years. Whenever she spoke of him to the kids, she praised and complimented him. She knew they would pass on the essence of her remarks to him.

She sent light-hearted cards and short letters to him at the office to keep him up on family news, making sure she always said something to show she valued his opinions and personhood. At first, he didn't let her know if he even received the letters or read them, but one time when he came for the kids, he mumbled, "I was glad to get your letter this week."

Marv began to step inside the door when he picked up or dropped off the kids. He acted as if he'd like to stay awhile, so one time Dottie invited him to sit down. As they chatted about insignificant matters, she used eye contact to communicate her positive feelings about him. As he stood to go, she gave him a slight pat on the shoulder. He didn't pull away.

After he left the house that evening, Dottie was on cloud nine. They had made progress! But then Marv didn't come around for nearly two weeks. Her spirits sank as she realized he must have felt they were getting too close again. But she mailed him a couple of cards and greeted him warmly when he finally telephoned.

Dottie kept up her crusade of building Marv's self-esteem whenever she had the opportunity. Over the next year, he began to stand straighter and look her in the eye when they talked. He walked with a more self-confident air. He again spent time visiting with her when he came to the house and began to return her little love pats on the knee or shoulder.

Then Marv told her that he had moved away from Rhonda and was living in his own apartment. He had also applied for a better job and got it. A short time later he told Dottie that he felt good when he talked to her and wondered if they could spend an evening together. Dottie complimented Marv on his new job; by then she found it easy to affirm him.

After three more months they decided to try again to make their marriage work. They went to a church-sponsored seminar that helped them better express their true feelings to each other. They decided they needed to see a marriage counselor to help them with long-standing problems.

After several more months Dottie and Marv were cautiously announcing, "Our marriage is on the road to healing!"

Marv credits Dottie for believing in him when he saw no good in himself. "She just kept hanging on, letting me know I was worth hanging onto," he says.

Chapter 12

Maintain "Externals"

• • •

BERNIE LOOKED OUT from his dingy apartment window over the irregular line of dilapidated rooftops. Utility lines sagged from one pole to the next, cluttering most of his view. Even the nondescript birds perched on the wires looked dismal. The dented, overflowing trash cans in the alley below didn't add any beauty to the scene either.

There was only one bright spot—the big, red K on a K-Mart sign. If Bernie stood close to the window and craned his neck to the right, he could see the gaudy sign over the rooftops. If he looked to the left, all he saw were the grimy bricks of another taller building.

This certainly isn't like home, Bernie thought as he envisioned the modest, but well-kept suburban home he and Linda had bought so proudly eleven years ago.

If he were looking out their bedroom window, he would be seeing their sparkling, green lawn with the kids' swing set and sandbox to the right and the picnic table under the pine tree to the left. The yard sloped down toward a line of trees at the back which nearly blocked the neighbor's houses from view. The side fences could use a new coat of stain, but they weren't bad yet. Linda's iris along the left fence would be blooming soon. The backyard had been a happy place, but the memory of it now pricked Bernie like a thorn. What a mess their marriage had become. He thought about what had gone wrong.

It all started when he took on a special project at work. It had meant more income, but it cost him hours away from his family. Before long he hardly had time to turn around at home before he had to go back to the office. Linda showed that she could manage the family without him, but she was becoming like a stranger to him. And he didn't like missing out on everything Mark and Timmy were doing.

Then he became involved with Dawn, a typist at work. When she rolled her big brown eyes at him, Bernie tingled all over. He began taking her to lunch and eventually he asked her to stay after hours to help him. He enjoyed being around this pretty young woman. The night he took her home to her apartment after dinner had been his downfall. They ended up in bed.

Dawn begged him to stay overnight, but suddenly he was sick of her and he sheepishly went home to Linda.

Bernie felt so ashamed that he woke Linda and confessed everything. He told her how sorry he was, but Linda was enraged. She didn't yell because she didn't want to waken the boys, but she was seething. He had deceived her into believing he was working late by himself, and she let him know how hurt and betrayed she felt. The rest of the night, she gritted her teeth and muttered, "How could you do this to me? How could you destroy our family?"

When morning came, Linda demanded that Bernie get out.

"Where do I go?" he asked.

"I don't care!" she retorted. "Rent a motel room or whatever, just get out of my sight!"

Bernie tried to talk to Linda during the next couple days, but she hung up on him whenever he called. One afternoon he went to the house when he knew the boys would be at school. She let him in, and he apologized again.

Linda smiled weakly and said, "I'd like for things to work out for us again. But, I don't know . . . we have a big problem."

Bernie declared that he was no longer seeing Dawn; in fact, he was going out of his way to avoid her at work.

Linda wasn't sure she could believe him, and she sent him away without forgiving him and without resolving anything. But she did make it clear that she didn't want Bernie back home yet. She felt a deep resentment toward him and thought he needed to pay for his failure.

Bernie decided to rent an apartment rather than live in a motel. He couldn't afford much because the family's monthly expenses ate up most of his paycheck. So here he was on a Saturday morning in a dumpy, run-down, cramped apartment. Linda had told the boys that Daddy was sick and had gone away to get better, so he couldn't even go to see them. He had work to do, but he didn't feel like doing it in these surroundings.

He was still stinging over Linda's announcement that he was to get a separate checking account. She was closing out their joint account and getting one with only her name on it because she didn't want his name on the checks with hers. The news made him afraid that she was also closing out their marriage.

When he stopped by the house another time, he noticed she wasn't wearing her wedding ring. He hoped she had it off because she was housecleaning.

Bernie was so discouraged over his isolation from his family that he just stayed around his apartment, letting his loneliness gnaw away at him. Then he made up his mind that he had to get out and be with people. But where? He couldn't go to any church meetings because Linda had him blackballed there.

He began spending more time at coffee breaks with the other employees. Previously, he would take a cup of coffee and drink it at his desk while he worked. Now he longed to chat.

He noticed an attractive woman about his age and began having conversations with her. He found out Ellie was divorced. She was also intelligent and fun to be around. He enjoyed taking her to dinner—even though he would rather have been home with Linda and the boys.

Then the big shock came. A coworker showed Bernie a Christmas card he had received from Linda. It contained a snapshot of the boys with their dog, but the card was signed only "Linda, Mark, and Timmy." Linda really was cutting him out of her life!

He called her and asked the meaning of the Christmas card. "Does this mean you want a divorce?" he demanded. "If you do, say so."

"Of course I don't want a divorce. Some day I'll be ready for you to come home." But inside she was still punishing Bernie.

Bernie was truly confused. If she wanted him, why was she sending so many signals that he was no longer part of her life?

Time went by and Bernie continued seeing Ellie—just for companionship. He called Linda often, but she was always cool to him.

Then one day Linda called him for the first time. She said that she was ready for him to come home and that he could return anytime.

Bernie was bewildered again. For nearly ten months she had shut him out, telling everyone they were separated because of his affair. Now she was waving him back in and he wasn't sure *he* was ready. He had grown fond of Ellie, and going home would mean breaking ties with her.

How could he ever take up a normal life at home? By now his boys thought he had abandoned them because he hadn't been allowed to see them. His neighbors and church friends all knew he had been gone and why. All the people on their Christmas card list assumed the marriage was over. He wasn't sure Linda had forgiven him, and he was afraid she'd hold his failure over his head like a club. Perhaps too many hurdles blocked the way between him and home.

Don't Burn Your Bridges

Many spouses, like Linda, change routines while their mate is away. This causes the partner to feel all the more estranged.

No harm is done by keeping up appearances while your mate is deciding whether or not to return. You aren't being a phony; you're simply making it easier for your mate to come home.

Leave your mate's belongings in place. Don't do as one man did: he gave all his wife's clothing to Good Will after she had been gone only a month. She hadn't taken everything with her because she felt she might return. But he was angry, and getting rid of her clothes was his way of retaliating.

Keep wearing your wedding ring. Don't change the locks on the doors. Keep your mate's name on the checking account unless you have some reason to think he or she will abscond with the funds. Don't tell a lot of people that your mate is gone. Make it as simple as possible for your mate to come back.

Include Your Mate

Keep your mate in the family as much as you can. Invite him or her to traditional family gatherings. Doing so may create an awkward situation for you, but that is better than the chilly isolation your mate might feel from being excluded. Banishment only pushes your mate toward intimacy with someone else.

Keep your spouse posted as to what the children are doing and try to involve your mate in their activities. Say nothing to your children to turn them against your mate, even though you may feel justified in doing so.

If your children question what is happening, give them a simple, honest answer in line with their ability to understand. For example, "Daddy and I are having some trouble right now, but we hope it will get better soon."

If they are angry because of the separation, help them work through their anger without tearing down your mate's dignity. Assure your children that your spouse will always be their parent. Discourage your children from taking sides.

If your mate feels he or she hasn't been ripped out of the family picture, it will make coming home easier. And that's what you're working toward.

Don't Muddy the Water

Rachel had been writing to us for help for about six months. Her husband had left and was living with another woman. Rachel and Bud talked often and sometimes even "dated." She had strong hopes that he would come back home although he hadn't done so yet.

Then we got a letter from Rachel saying:

> I think I'm going to start dating. I still believe that Bud is going to return before the end of the year, but I am so dreadfully lonely while I wait. Wherever I go, I'm like a fish out of water—I'm not divorced, but neither do I seem married.
>
> I don't drink, but lately I've been going to a bar with my girlfriends after work and just sipping a soft drink while we talk. Then sometimes we go eat and see a movie. Lately we've been meeting up with the same three guys at the bar, and they join us for the evening. One of them has taken an interest in me and has asked me out.
>
> Do you think it would be all right to accept? It wouldn't be anything more than a friendship, and it would give me something to do while I wait for Bud to get ready to come home.

Our advice to Rachel was, "Don't do it."

We understand how lonesome a person is while the mate is gone, especially knowing that he or she is with someone else. But if your goal is to make it easy for your spouse to return, you don't want a fourth party scrambled into the mixture—for several reasons.

First of all, you may have trouble keeping your emotions in check. Before you know it, you could become too enmeshed with the other person to make an easy break if your mate decides to come back.

A worse danger is that your mate will learn of your social life and will see it as verification that your marriage isn't working. Since your spouse is probably looking for excuses to justify his or her own unfaithfulness, you would be adding fuel to the fire.

We suggest you meet your needs for companionship by cultivating a few good friends of your own sex. If you are with mixed groups, be in an environment that doesn't lead to pairing up.

This is a tough time, but God is on your side. As you do everything possible to maintain the shape of your marriage, your mate will more likely see that he or she still has a place in it. And you will be glad you did all you could to "maintain the externals."

Chapter 13

Confront Sparingly and Practice Patience

◆ ◆ ◆

A PETITE, DARK-HAIRED woman was waiting for us at the back of the room after we finished speaking at a mid-life crisis seminar. She was attractively dressed and gave us a warm smile. When she introduced herself, we recognized her name from letters she had written to us. Jan looked almost too young to be at a mid-life meeting, but she clearly knew her mission:

"I just had to come see you when I learned you were going to be in my area. Your letters and materials have been a big help to me since my husband left, and I really thank you for them. But now I think it's time I take some action."

"What kind of action?" one of us asked.

"It's been three-and-a-half months since Roger walked out. I've tried all the things you've suggested, but he hasn't changed. You said to try to meet his needs, but how can I? His only need seems to be the other woman," she said firmly.

"Three-and-a-half months seems long now, but . . ." Jim started to say.

Jan interrupted, "That's long enough for him to change his mind, and he hasn't. We're getting together to talk this weekend, and I'm going to confront him. I've been nice long enough, and that isn't working. I think giving him some ultimatums will help."

Jan wanted us to endorse her actions against Roger. Instead we tried to calm her down and discourage her from pressuring him into making an immediate decision. We explained that many people work for months and years to restore their marriage. The ones who win are very glad they were patient. The ones who lose are still glad they didn't hurry into a divorce. They at least have the satisfaction of knowing they didn't give up too quickly.

"Why should I have to go through all that?" Jan asked. "I'll go a little easy on him when I talk to him, but he has to make up his mind one way or the other."

Two months later we heard from Jan. "I should have listened to you," she wrote. "I demanded that Roger either choose me or the other woman. He chose her. He hasn't contacted me since. Now what do I do? I really love him and don't want to lose him."

Ultimatums Get the Wrong Results

When people are pushed against a wall to make a hasty decision, they often choose the opposite of what the mate hopes. Had they been given time to think things through, to let God do his work, and for natural processes to take their course, the decision might have been in favor of the spouse.

Sometimes the best way for confused mates to come to their senses is for them to be on the other side of the fence long enough to learn for themselves that it isn't greener over there, after all. If others tell them that it isn't, they don't believe it; and if someone *demands* that they get back on the right side of the fence, they balk like stubborn donkeys.

Ultimatums cause mates to build barriers to protect themselves from the ultimatum-giver. Undecided mates already feel vulnerable, and when someone starts lobbing boulders at them, they erect a higher wall.

Some uncertain mates don't even stay around to build walls; they just run. And giving an ultimatum to a person on the run is like digging spurs into the side of a horse; it'll make him go faster, but it won't make him change directions.

Patience Is a Virtue

Days and weeks do drag on while you're waiting for your mate to want to be with you again. Each new incident rips at your heart and tries your patience even more. "I just learned he's taking her to Hawaii." "She's let a guy move in with her now." Patience is probably one of the hardest principles to carry out.

We live in a "hurry" society. We get immediate resolutions to problems in TV stories. Commercials promise instant relief from colds, stomach distress, and weight gain. Men and women even compete with each other over whose hair product takes less time to get the gray out.

We microwave our meals and gobble them down in less than ten minutes. We dash and zoom and don't have time to listen to anyone who utters a single "uh-h-h" when speaking.

But some things can't be rushed; they just take time. Restoring a marriage is one of those things that won't happen overnight. When people tell you that your mate is never coming back and that you might as well get on with your life, tell yourself that you can wait. God sometimes works miracles in a flash, but more often he chooses the "process" method—and with good reason. Changes that unfold in stages usually are more permanent than those made hastily.

Patience Requires All Your Resources

Each morning—and many times through the day—you'll have to murmur, "Patience. Patience. God, please give me patience." Perhaps you should even memorize James 1:2–4:

> Is your life full of difficulties and temptations? Then be happy, for when the way is rough, your patience has a chance to grow. So let it grow, and don't try to squirm

out of your problems. For when your patience is finally in full bloom, then you will be ready for anything, strong in character, full and complete (TLB).

Besides reading Scripture and praying for patience, keeping yourself busy will help the time go faster. Plan activities with friends or family. Take a class. Learn a new skill. Visit the elderly. It's usually better to do things with other people than to be alone. Doing something *for* someone else will also help reduce the intensity of your problem.

Enlist your friends who know about your situation to pray for you. We've seen amazing turn-arounds in marriages that seemed beyond rescuing. But someone was praying and the impossible happened.

Tina called our home one evening. She was crying and pleading desperately, "Please, please, pray for me and Jack. You know he has been threatening to leave. Well, at this very moment he's with another woman asking her to leave with him. Betty, Jack's secretary, just called to tell me. She happened to step into Jack's office and overheard part of their conversation."

Jack and Tina had been struggling for several months, and now it really looked as if their marriage might not make it.

We prayed with Tina on the phone, and then we prayed some more as soon as she hung up. We begged God to keep Jack from making a mistake. We asked him to do an extraordinary work in both Jack and Tina. We poured out our hearts for several minutes and then we committed Jack and Tina into God's hands. Several of their other friends were praying for them that night as well. So a whole band of folks was imploring God for his intervention during those hours.

The next morning we learned that Jack had not left with the other woman. He had gone home and talked briefly to Tina about his confused feelings before going to sleep. Their troubles were far from resolved, but the crisis had reached a climax. From then on, Tina and Jack cautiously worked to strengthen their marriage. Today they are still together with a much better marriage.

Patience Allows Time for Growth

If you have been taking giant strides in personal growth during your separation, your spouse needs a chance to catch up. If there's too big a gap between the two of you, your marriage could still break. Be patient and give your mate time to blossom.

When you find yourself fretting that this terrifying season is never going to end and you feel like demanding a decision, remember that forcing something to bloom before its time will kill it.

Our four-year-old granddaughter was with us one evening when we were given some long-stem roses. The flowers hadn't opened yet and were only beautiful red buds. We carried them around for a few hours, so they were looking rather droopy when we got to the house. Jim ran water in the bathtub and laid the roses in the water to soak up moisture before putting them in a vase.

After a few minutes I found our granddaughter standing beside the tub with one of the flowers in her hand. She was peeling back the layers of the bud.

"Oh, no, Honey," I said, "you're hurting the flower."

"But I want to see the whole flower," she explained.

Needless to say, that rose never blossomed because it was forced open before its time.

Instead of trying to force God's process of making your marriage blossom again, you can be patient because you have hope—hope in God's plan for you and your mate. You can also be patient because you want to meet your spouse's needs—and one of the needs is not to be pushed.

Keeping Silent about Sin?

Is all this patience simply an endorsement of sin? Are we just making it easier for people to keep committing adultery or to defect from their families?

Some people would argue that we are. They say we should attack the issue straight on. "Tell people to repent or you'll wash your hands of them!" they would advise.

We need to look at the example of Jesus. He, too, "hit the issue straight on." But his blunt and harsh words were directed to the hypocritical religious folks—the phonies putting on a spirituality show. Jesus, on the other hand, was very kind to adulteresses, tax cheaters, alcohol abusers, and people whose tempers got them into trouble. He got to the root of their problem, but he preserved their dignity while he did it. And he brought about permanent change.

Certain people believe we must confront sin with indignation and anger. We have found, however, that hostility will never bring a person to repentance. Even if you manage not to be antagonistic, if you are the slightest bit condescending or give any impression that you feel superior you will alienate the one you're trying to win.

A woman once told us that God had given her the gift of confrontation. As we watched her relate to people, however, we weren't so sure the gift was from God. It seemed more likely that she had an ax to grind and was grinding it on whomever got in her way.

We need to be very careful in challenging people about their sins. Too often the confronting is done more to satisfy the confronter's feelings of self-righteousness and need for power than out of genuine love for the other person.

Useful Confrontation

There will come a time when it is appropriate to speak to your spouse about your side of the situation, but only *after* you have carefully attempted to meet your mate's needs. Confrontation should come after much prayer for wisdom to say the right things and for love to say them kindly.

Be very sure God is telling you it's the right time. Sometimes we convince ourselves God is giving us a message when instead it's our own human nature urging us on. We confuse the Holy Spirit's direction with our human emotions. Timing is very crucial so that your good purposes will not be aborted.

As with any communication, your confrontation should be done quietly and courteously. Make sure your face has a pleasant expression when you use eye contact. Don't put your mate down or try to make him or her feel guilty. State your point simply. Then give your mate time to respond and ask questions.

Your mate needs to know that you want to restore your marriage. Tell your spouse you're sorry for your part in the deterioration and that you want to work on solutions. You want to understand what he or she needs and you'll try to meet as many of those needs as possible.

Don't be surprised if your spouse says it's too late or that he or she no longer has feelings for you. Words like that are often used to test the earnesty of your intentions. Your mate is probably still confused about what he or she wants; so, for now, the response may be cool or even angry. Remember to keep having hope beyond the wall your mate is holding up right now.

Putting It All Together

You are being asked to do some of the hardest things of your life. The natural response is to get angry, give up hope, or whine. But you need supernatural responses and actions if you're going to rebuild your collapsed marriage.

You need strength, patience, and love beyond your own supply as you work to meet your spouse's needs—needs that may take keen detective work to discover now that your mate wants out.

Remember, God stands ready to give you all the supernatural love and persistence you need. Each day, take a fresh grip on God's grace for you.

Chapter ◆ *14*

Flex, Change, and Grow

◆ ◆ ◆

CAROLYN CAME HOME from her job at the school cafeteria to find a note from her husband:

> I've gone away for a few days. I don't know when or if
> I'll be back. Don't try to find me. Here are some signed
> checks so you can pay the most pressing bills. Tell Rick
> I'm sorry to miss his wrestling tournament.
>
> Take care,
> Wes

Carolyn ran to the garage. Wes's pickup was gone. Then she went to the bedroom closet. Most of his clothes were still there, but he had taken enough to last several days.

Where could he have gone? What could he be doing? Why did he leave without saying goodbye?

She knew he had been nervous and agitated the last few months, and they had quarreled more often than usual. When she tried to show affection he had gruffly pushed her away, saying he wasn't in the mood.

She thought he'd be better once he sold the cattle. He got tense every year when he was watching market prices and trying to decide on the best time to sell his herd. But when Wes sold the cattle this year he made very little profit, so he remained discouraged and irritable. He complained about everything Carolyn did or didn't do. She couldn't seem to do anything right, and she was beginning to not care.

Wes did relate positively to their seventeen-year-old son, Rick, however. Wes was proud of Rick's wrestling abilities and went to all his meets, both home and away. Carolyn detested the smelly gymnasiums and the competitive atmosphere of the parents. She told Wes, "You like that stuff because you haven't really grown up yet." So Carolyn didn't go to the meets, and Wes drove alone while Rick rode with his team.

Now Carolyn wished Wes were around to invite her to the wrestling tournament! This time she'd say yes. She would put up with the miserable surroundings just to be with him.

Her heart was wrenching. She didn't think she could stand this agony of not knowing where Wes was and what was going through his mind. She missed him terribly. She began to think of all the things they had enjoyed together.

Carolyn winced as she realized how little she had done to try to build a good marriage. But she'd been so busy, how could she do more? She worked almost fulltime at the school and still did all the housework. She went to church at least twice a week, and she liked to attend the monthly women's agricultural extension meetings. Besides, she rationalized, Wes didn't do all that much for their marriage either.

Rick came home from the wrestling tournament a little bruised, but more discouraged than hurt. He had only taken third place in his weight class although he'd been expected to get first.

I just couldn't concentrate," he explained. Then he went off to bed without saying much more.

The next morning Rick added a few details to his story about the wrestling match. "I saw Dad last night," he said. "He came to the tournament after all." Rick hesitated and looked uncomfortable before he continued. "I think he had that woman, Trudy, with him. She didn't come with Dad to see me afterward, but I saw her sitting with him during all the events. And she was hanging around the back while Dad talked to me."

Rick banged the table with his fist, let out an expletive he didn't usually let his mother hear, and stormed out of the house, slamming the door behind him. He drove away in his old truck and didn't come back all day.

Carolyn was left alone, shivering and crying. Her hand shook so much that she had to set down her coffee cup. Then her crying turned to wailing. She made so much noise that the dogs outside began to howl. But what did it matter? She was utterly alone.

She didn't go to church that day. How could she face everyone without Wes and Rick? She didn't want to have to explain their absence. Besides, she would just sob all through the service anyway.

Carolyn had heard about us from a friend at church, so the next morning she called our office. Our assistant carefully listened to her and then suggested that our book *Your Husband's Mid-Life Crisis* might be of help.[1] She prayed with her over the telephone, promised to send her some other materials, and invited her to write.

We corresponded with Carolyn for several months, and reading her letters was like watching a cocoon turn into a butterfly. Carolyn went from being a dull, rather self-absorbed woman to a much more sparkling, appealing person. In a matter of days she had made a list of things she needed to do to win her husband back. Instead of moping around the house in the evenings, she attended an oil painting class at the community college. This was something she had always wanted to do but was afraid to try.

Carolyn even decided to attend Rick's last tournament of the season. She asked him to explain some of the rules and techniques so she would know more about what was going on. She put on her most attractive blouse and pants and got out her leather jacket to wear instead of her hooded carcoat.

Wes and Trudy were sitting together on a bleacher when she arrived at the tournament, but Trudy left a few minutes later and didn't come back. Carolyn felt miserable sitting alone, but she had made up her mind to enjoy watching Rick. Finally she got involved in the match, and her excitement and enthusiasm poured out.

After the tournament, Wes walked over. "Hello, Carolyn," he said. "You seemed to enjoy the match." He hesitated a bit and then said, "I was wondering if I could come to the house some night this week. If you want to, we can go eat somewhere." They agreed on a night and each went their separate ways. Carolyn wondered if Trudy was waiting for Wes somewhere.

She decided to put that question out of her mind and concentrate on planning the evening with Wes. She would fix his favorite meal. He'd like that better than eating out. She'd wear the sweater he liked. She wished her jeans fit better, but they'd have to do for now. She vowed to start losing weight so her clothes would look better.

The evening Wes came to dinner turned out better than Carolyn had dared to hope—even though she had prayed for a miracle. Rick ate with them, and it seemed like old times—before the quarreling had begun. They didn't get into any deep, meaningful conversation, but neither did they argue.

Carolyn could tell Wes was watching her every move. He carefully measured each word he spoke, and so did she. She wanted to let him see that she was growing, but she didn't want to tell him outright.

Before Wes left, he said, "Well, you probably wonder when I'm coming home."

Carolyn answered gently. "I think you probably have things you're working out. You'll be home when you're ready. We'll be very glad to have you whenever that is."

Wes seemed relieved by her answer.

"Are you planning to go to the national livestock show in Denver next month?" she asked.

When he said yes, she asked if she could go with him.

He blinked his eyes a moment and then said, "Livestock show? You hate those things."

"I used to, but I'm learning to enjoy things like that. I'd really like to go. I even have a new western shirt I'd like to wear," she said.

"Well, O.K. Sure you can go. I've never liked going by myself," Wes said, surprise still in his voice.

By the time they went to Denver, Carolyn had lost six pounds. Already her pants fit better. She felt peppier and a little like a teenager as she got into the pickup with Wes. They chatted about several family matters on the way. Carolyn even got up nerve to tell him she was taking the oil painting class.

He laughed just like she thought he would. "Oil painting? Isn't that a little classy for a rancher's wife?" he joked.

So, he still thinks of me as his wife, she thought. *That's good!*

At Carol's suggestion, they stayed in separate motel rooms in Denver. She didn't want Wes to feel as if she were smothering him.

When they got home, Wes came to the house more often. They had some good talks about changes they both needed to make if their marriage was going to work. After a few weeks, Wes told Carolyn that Trudy was no longer a part of his life. He still wasn't ready to come home, however, and Carolyn didn't push.

One week she invited him to a special dinner for his birthday. She groaned when she recalled that last year she had been too busy and tired to do anything for his birthday.

After they ate, Carolyn gave Wes a gift. He tore off the wrapping paper to find an oil painting of a Hereford cow under a tree in their pasture. The old windmill was part of the background.

"Wow! This is really good," Wes exclaimed. After studying the painting a minute, he said, "The best place I know for this is over my desk in the den." He immediately went to put it up.

Before leaving, he took Carolyn's hands in his. "I'd really like to move back home, if you'd have me," he said.

"I'd be glad to have you back if you're ready," she said carefully.

They talked a little more and decided he would move home on

Saturday. He gave her a peck on the cheek and walked to his pickup whistling.

Know Yourself

Right now your mate wants out or wants someone else. What you want is for your mate to want you. So part of what's still to be done is some personal work on yourself.

We've never met a married person who didn't need to keep adapting and growing. That's what makes a healthy marriage. Since yours is rather sick right now and you want to bring it back to health, you'll need to take a look at yourself.

If you're ready to admit that some changes in yourself might help your mate see your marriage more positively, hurray for you! Even if your marriage doesn't improve, you'll like the new you.

Before you undertake your self-improvement program, spend some time prayerfully taking an inventory of who you are and what changes you need to make. Jot down what kind of person you are—your personality characteristics, abilities, qualifications, and experience. Make another list of things you like to do or wish you could do.

Keep your lists where you can add to them during the days to come. When you are satisfied that your lists are complete, take your notes and mark the items that are pleasing to your spouse. Then list the things you know your spouse would like you to modify. After considering both lists, decide which areas to start developing and which ones to start changing. Choose those that will make the most difference to your spouse but won't violate your values and personal integrity.

Review Wes and Carolyn

Carolyn found out that she could learn to like wrestling matches and livestock shows without violating her convictions. She also knew that Wes would like her to be thinner—and she'd like to be also. So she went to work on losing weight. She changed some of her wardrobe so she no longer looked old enough to be Wes's mother.

Carolyn also very wisely started growing in a new dimension by taking the painting class. She found personal fulfillment from this and it made her a more interesting woman.

What convinced Wes that Carolyn intended to change was the attention she started giving him. He knew it took extra work for her to cook special meals for him, and he appreciated her effort to become involved in his interests. The painting of the cow was the first time she had ever *made* a gift for him.

He enjoyed having her focus on him. He felt special to her, and it made him want to do something special for her in return. When she spoke gently to Wes it helped him speak more kindly. He liked not fighting. He didn't feel like such a louse or that he was being treated like a little boy.

As he felt better about Carolyn, he also felt better about himself. Carolyn's growth started Wes on a journey of growth, and then he was ready to come home. And he was able to say, "I'm sorry for the pain I caused you by not being open with you and by being with Trudy."

Where There's Life There's Hope

Often we get into a rut in the way we relate to our mates. We forget that our relationship is a living entity, and living things need to grow to stay alive. Some couples fall asleep after the wedding ceremony and ignore the cultivating, fertilizing, and watering necessary for a thriving marriage.

We now live in California where—much to our delight—plants grow and bloom all year. However, California is very dry. It doesn't rain for months, so we must be sure to water our plants frequently. Because they have no dormant period, they also need fertilizer. And, of course, the weeds and pests have to be controlled.

We have a variety of plants and bushes on all sides of our house. One plant we've been enjoying the past several years is a robust geranium in a large pot that we can see from our kitchen and dining room windows. It is more than three feet in diameter and has bright pink blossoms all year long.

Sadly, it's not so healthy now. When Jim was away for a week of college lectures, I was sick and forgot to water the outdoor plants. By the time I remembered, the poor geranium was turning brown.

It kept getting browner until only about one-sixth of the plant was alive. Recently Jim cut away all the dead parts, leaving only a small green plant in the pot. It doesn't even have blossoms. He fertilized it and is watering it faithfully.

Even though only a little bit of the plant is left, it *is alive*. With proper care, it will again grow and bloom. We expect to see a much prettier plant in that pot in a few months.

As you tend your marriage and nurse it back to health, remember to consistently feed, water, and till it. And don't forget to prune the parts that irritate your mate or are dull and boring. You may have only a little sprig of life left now, but *it is life* and can grow into something beautiful again.

Part 3

MEET YOUR NEEDS

Chapter ◆ 15

Know Your Boundaries

• • •

TED TWISTED HIS wedding ring around and around on his finger. *Should I leave it on or take it off?* he wondered. The rock and roll music blaring over the speakers in the smoky cafe made it hard to think. He picked up his coffee cup, then set it down again on the greasy table top. He continued to turn his ring on his finger.

Melody had made it clear that she was ready to take off her wedding ring if he didn't make good on a few promises and pay more attention to her.

He hadn't bothered to eat breakfast with her that Saturday morning because she was still sleeping and he wanted to get an early start on his day. Before leaving the house, he'd helped Justin find new laces for his basketball shoes. But, no matter what else he was doing, his mind was constantly nagging him to do something to make things better with Melody.

As Ted started to chew his soggy toast, he looked at his watch. Time for him to leave. While he stood at the cash register paying his bill, he worried that he might be making Scott wait. He had told his friend he'd help him take down the dying tree in his backyard that morning.

While Ted and Scott were getting set up to cut the tree, Scott's wife called Ted to the phone. Ted's twelve-year old daughter, Jessica, was crying because he had forgotten to drive her to gymnastics lessons. Melody had already left to go to her part-time job.

"I'll be right there, Sugar," he said.

Ted was embarrassed to tell Scott he had to leave for awhile, but he promised to return as soon as he could.

After he dropped off Jessica at the Y, he saw a little old lady with her grocery carrier piled high. The rickety old cart looked as if it had hauled groceries one too many times; one wheel wouldn't move at all. The frail woman tugged at the cart to make it go and suddenly her tall pile of groceries toppled over.

Ted stopped to help her gather up the groceries. He put them in his car and drove the woman to her apartment. By the time he got her and the groceries inside, it was getting late.

He zoomed back to Scott's house only to find that Scott already had the tree down. He had called on a neighbor to help him. Ted pitched in to make up for lost time.

As he sawed the trunk into short pieces to be split for firewood, he realized he was half an hour late to pick up Jessica. He mumbled his apologies to Scott again and tore off to get her. She was standing near the curb with one hand holding her gym bag and the other on her hips. She scowled as she got into the car and pouted all the way home.

They reached the house as Justin was finishing off leftover pizza. It was an hour after lunch time, so Jessica and Ted each made a sandwich and ate in silence. While they were eating, Justin came into the kitchen carrying a new basketball hoop.

"O.K., Dad, I'm ready for you to help me mount my hoop on the garage," he announced.

Ted looked at the kitchen clock and pressed his temples with his fingers. "Wow, I almost forgot. This is the afternoon Grandma and

Grandpa are expecting you. I told them I'd bring you over about 1:30. It's been so long since they've seen you," explained Ted.

"Oh, Dad, how could you? How could you?" both kids moaned.

Ted decided he'd rather deal with grumbling children than disappointed parents, so with an ugly tension between them, Ted got the kids in the car and headed for his parents' home.

Near the end of the afternoon, Ted drove home with his two kids mad at him for staying too long and his parents annoyed because he didn't stay long enough. He entered the back door to find Melody ready to explode.

"Why isn't the bathroom light installed? It doesn't look like you picked up the drycleaning either. And the garage is as messy as ever. You didn't do one of the things you promised," she stormed.

When Ted tried to explain how he had spent the day, she gritted her teeth and said, "That's it! Everybody comes before me. I don't mean as much to you as a friend with a dead tree. We're finished. It's time for you to get out. Now!"

Out of Bounds

Before Ted got packed, Melody cooled down and asked him not to leave. "But we're going to a marriage counselor!" she declared.

After a couple of counseling appointments, the therapist asked to see Ted for a session alone. During that session the counselor showed Ted that he had a boundary problem. He was trying to please everyone—and wound up pleasing no one.

Ted needed to define himself, to establish priorities for his life and set limitations. He was so busy accommodating others that he was getting trampled and his marriage was being destroyed. He needed to put others in second place and devote time and creativity to make Melody feel special.

Protect What God Has Made

Many of us think we are being Christlike when we let people intrude on us. Even though Jesus poured himself out for people's needs, he rested and he didn't heal everyone. As God he could have; but he was also man, and he stayed within his human limits by touching or speaking healing words to only one or a few at a time.

While we should serve others, we can't help anyone if we exhaust ourselves. It is appropriate to have boundaries. It is not being selfish to recognize and protect the center that is self. Self is a gift God has given us.

A part of God's design for us is inner wholeness, and that includes knowing our value to God and protecting ourselves. We should not allow others to walk all over us. Protecting ourselves is not self-centered; it's good stewardship of God's gift.

We need to clearly know our boundaries in various areas of our lives—emotional, physical, financial, etc. Many of us can remember times we've been taken advantage of in these areas.

Demands on our time are probably the most common exploitations. These impositions can drain us both emotionally and physically. Other boundary violations are inappropriate touching, molestation, or sexual abuse.

Trampled Fences

The first time Bonnie met her boyfriend's father, she felt uncomfortable. He hugged her too closely and held her too long. He made comments about her physical appearance that sounded like a come on.

Oh, well, maybe I'm too much of a prude, she told herself.

Bonnie married her boyfriend, Eric, but was continually alarmed by her father-in-law's inappropriate touching and remarks. Thankfully, he lived halfway across the continent, so they didn't see each other often. Whenever he arrived for a visit, Bonnie would turn her face when he greeted her so his kisses would land on her cheek rather than her lips. But he still pressed his body too close to hers.

Bonnie avoided her father-in-law as much as she could whenever he visited. But he had sneaky ways of walking past her and moving his hands down her sides along her breasts and over her hips and quickly leaving the room before she could protest.

Eric dismissed his father's improper behavior. "That's just the way he is," he'd say. Since her husband downplayed the man's actions, Bonnie decided not to make a scene over the situation and just let each incident slide.

After thirty years, though, Bonnie became aware that her father-in-law's liberties were *totally wrong*. He had no right to touch her the way he did, and she became angry that Eric hadn't protected her all these years. She felt dirty and used.

When her father-in-law visited the next time and again violated her with inappropriate touching, Bonnie felt she had to speak to Eric about it and ask him to help her put a stop to it.

Bonnie knew she risked upsetting Eric and causing trouble in their marriage if she complained about his father, but she decided that she must do it for her own health and recovery. Surprisingly, Eric did not get angry. He admitted that his father was out of bounds, but still he did not act on her behalf.

Bonnie and Eric started seeing a counselor for help in their marriage, and then Eric saw how very wrong his father was. He realized that all his life he had justified his father's offensive sexual behavior as permissible because he was his father.

When the full impact of all that Bonnie had endured hit Eric, he was filled with remorse that he had allowed his father's improper conduct. He tried several times to confront his father about the matter, but his father denied any wrongdoing. Finally, for Bonnie's safety, Eric and Bonnie agreed that she would have no further contact with her father-in-law.

It is right to protect our boundaries, but sometimes we don't realize when our borders are being violated. Nor do we know what to do when we are aware of it. As we become more confident of our value as God's creation, we can more easily recognize boundary abuses. We also will be more self-assured so that we can calmly put a stop to the violations.

Scripture says:

Don't give holy things to dogs, and don't throw your pearls before pigs. Pigs will only trample on them, and dogs will turn to attack you (Matthew 7:6 NCV).

The Dilemma

A further question, though, is how can you balance self-protection with meeting your mate's needs? You want to do all the right things to heal your marriage, but how do you do that and not violate yourself?

Much of what we are suggesting to help your mate come back to the marriage does call for sacrifice on your part. But some of the suggestions are simply common courtesies that should have been a part of your relationship anyway—empathy, listening, encouragement, and patience, to name a few.

Balancing your marriage-rebuilding activities along with protecting your boundaries begins with *your own commitment* to save your marriage. You are the one deciding to go the second—or the ninety-second—mile to help your mate. No one else is making you do it.

It is your decision to turn your cheek, and you're doing it with the long-range goal of reclaiming your marriage. You are making the choices to sacrifice; the choices are not being forced upon you. You know who you are and what you want. What you want is a restored, mutually satisfying marriage.

Handling Abuses

While you're working to rebuild a healthy, happy marriage, how much mistreatment should you take from your mate?

If your mate is verbally abusive to you, be calmly assertive as you tell him or her that that kind of talk is neither helpful nor appropriate. If you have to, remove yourself from the verbal onslaught.

You do not need to be a doormat, but it is important to remember that being *assertive* is different from being *aggressive*. Assertiveness is expressing your opinions and observations in a non-violent manner and with confidence that your thoughts and feelings are worth considering. Being aggressive means you are offensive and warlike. You are argumentative and insensitive to the other person's feelings.

If, however, your spouse is being physically abusive, get away at once. We do not advocate unlimited patience while your face is getting smashed. Your goal of restoring your marriage isn't going to be met while you're being pounded black and blue. Protect yourself and get out of there.

Kathy frequently got so angry and frustrated that she yelled and pummeled her husband, Rob. She would become so distraught that she didn't realize what she was doing.

After one beating, Rob calmly said, "Kathy, I love you very much and I'll never divorce you. But I cannot live with you like this. You must get some help."

Kathy found a counselor and during the first session she became aware that she had been sexually molested as a child. Even though she had enjoyed many happy years of growing up and had done well throughout high school and college, this ugly, forgotten boundary violation was slowly poisoning her.

Marriage brought the damage from childhood attacks to the surface. Sexual intimacies began to be nightmares. Even in routine, daily matters, Kathy would become enraged if she thought Rob was taking even a slight advantage of her or getting too much power.

Through counseling, Kathy began the healing process. Rob also went to a therapist for a time, and today their marriage is back on a healthy track. Rob's quiet, but insistent demand that Kathy get professional help was much more effective than if he had retaliated or silently walked out.

You are a valuable person with God-given rights. You deserve respect.[1] You also want to reclaim an important relationship—your marriage. Therefore, use all your energies and abilities to bring about this recovery.

In so doing, you are not denigrating nor defaming yourself. You are engaging in a noble enterprise that adds dignity to you and to your mate.

Chapter 16

Esteem Yourself Too

✦ ✦ ✦

O PAL PULLED UP A CHAIR at the conference center dining room table and said, "I'm glad we can have a few minutes together. I have so much to tell you two since I last saw you."

We had met Opal a few years earlier when she looked more like a scared rabbit than a grown woman. She was being physically and verbally beaten by her husband who constantly cut her down for being dumb and worthless. She had a heart of gold, but her husband was trying to pound it out of her. For twenty years he yelled and swore at her, saying she could do nothing right.

Then suddenly he left her and three teenage children, filed for divorce, and was totally gone. This "worthless" woman now had full responsibility for providing for her family. Her income had been a nice supplement to her husband's salary but it was not nearly sufficient to pay all the bills.

Her kids said, "Mom, we'll make it," and they found after-school jobs to help meet expenses. They loved and respected their mother and encouraged her to get more education so she could find a better job.

But I could never study, she told herself. *I'm too stupid to learn anything new.*

Suddenly she realized those words were only menacing echoes from her former husband. Putting his lies out of her mind, she decided to try a few courses in nursing at a community college. She did very well, and with each succeeding semester felt increasingly confident about herself and her abilities. She went on to become a registered nurse.

Because of her caring heart and natural leadership abilities, she soon was made a supervisor in a home for the elderly. She thoroughly loved the work and the people. She even loved herself. Opal glowed as she rehearsed for us what delight she now had in life. She had learned she not only could do some things right, but she was *very* competent and needed.

Your Self-Worth

Right now you may feel like a rotten piece of rubbish, but that is not the truth. You are special, even if your mate doesn't think so. If you remind yourself of your good qualities and strengths you can esteem yourself whether or not anyone else does.

Your self-image has been influenced from birth by the responses you've received from the important people around you, just as we discussed in chapter 11 regarding your mate. If the majority of your life experiences have been happy and successful, your view of yourself is probably positive.

If you have been abused, ridiculed, or ignored, your self-esteem is likely to be poor. Or perhaps something has happened in later life to change your physical appearance or abilities, and, as a result, your self-image has been lowered. Life's tragedies—such as deaths, illnesses, and disappointments—can be so heavy and so numerous that your view of yourself suffers serious damage. Certainly, your mate's negative response to you right now is battering your self-worth.

Although people and events have been important in developing who you are, you can build your own self-esteem. You are not totally dependent on others for your value.

Learn Who You Are

The best place to find out your worth is from Scripture. God values you and wants you to value yourself.

First of all, you're worthwhile because God made you in his image, as recorded in Genesis 1:26. In addition, you are an asset to God. We are assured of this in such passages as Ephesians chapters 1 and 2. The Living Bible edition of the New Testament makes God's purpose and love for us very clear. Ephesians 1:11 and 18 are especially good, telling us that because of what Christ has done for us we are "gifts to God" and "God has been made rich" by us.

You're also needed for God's plan for the world and for the people in it, as expressed in Ephesians 4:16:

> Under his direction the whole body is fitted together perfectly, and *each part in its own special way helps the other parts*, so that the whole body is healthy and growing and full of love (TLB, emphasis ours).

Psalm 139:1–18 is a classic section of Scripture, assuring you of your worth. God knows everything about you and still loves you. He is always with you. He "precedes" and "follows" you and places his hand of blessing on you. Further along the passage tells you that God made "all the delicate, inner parts" of your body and "knit them together in [your] mother's womb." He was there while you were "being formed in utter seclusion." The Creator of the entire universe is thinking about you constantly. That ought to tell you that you're precious!

Evaluate Yourself

As you did when taking inventory of your mate, now make some lists about yourself. We suggest that you make a list for each of the following:

♦ Your abilities, skills, education, and experience (list at least twelve items).

- Your qualities and personality characteristics (list at least twelve items).
- All the things you like to do, whether or not you presently are doing them (list at least fifty items).

These three lists should help you make a fourth:

- All the things you would like to accomplish in your lifetime.

As you study these lists, you will get to know more about yourself. Are you a people person? A detail person? An administrator? A support person? An outdoor lover? An artist? A traveler or a homebody? Does solving problems intrigue you or frazzle you?

There are no right or wrong answers. The combination of abilities and preferences that makes up *you* is what's right. Whatever kind of person you are, you can be glad for what God has made!

Don't Run Yourself Down

Self-criticism is a serious disease. When you think poorly of yourself and make insulting remarks about yourself, you are really criticizing God. Do you ever make any of these remarks about yourself?

- "I can't do anything right."
- "I made the same dumb mistake again."
- "I look awful. (I'm too tall, short, fat, thin, bald, poorly dressed. . . .)"
- "I just can't do it—I'll fail again."
- "I can never be as talented as he or she is."
- "I'm not needed."
- "My illness or disability makes me undesirable."

These ideas are counter-productive! The more you feed yourself these thoughts, the more they become part of you.

Start telling yourself the opposite of the above:

- "I can do many things right."
- "I made the same mistake, but this time I'm going to learn from it."

- "I may be too tall (short, fat, thin, bald, or poorly dressed . . .), but inside I'm becoming more beautiful every day."
- "I will try to do it. Please guide me."
- "I may not have his or her talents, but I do have talents that are suited for me."
- "I'm an important part of God's design; someone needs me in some way."
- "My illness or disability may slow me a little, but I'm still necessary in God's blueprint for the world."

Vow to stop knocking yourself. Never, never say negative things about yourself. When the temptation comes, turn it into a positive remark or say nothing.

That commitment goes for the things you say to yourself as well. Put negative thoughts about yourself out of your mind. As you speak positive, godly thoughts about yourself and to yourself, you will begin to live up to them.

Respect Your Physical Body

"Take good care of yourself; you belong to me," are lines from an old popular song. If you understand that you are valuable, you will realize that you deserve good physical treatment.

Your ability to meet your mate's needs will be enhanced as you meet your own needs. You will do a better job of restoring your marriage if you are in good physical shape.

Get Sufficient Sleep

Being rested is important during this time of stress. Some people are too nervous and tense to get a good night's sleep, or they aren't in bed enough hours for sufficient sleep.

This is not the time to skimp on rest. Your perception of your mate and your situation will be hindered if you are tired. Matters may seem worse or bigger than life simply because you're worn out. You may snap at your mate when you don't intend to because your guard is down due to fatigue. Researchers tell us that three days of sleep deprivation can cause bizarre psychotic symptoms.

Consult a doctor if you are not getting enough sleep. It could make all the difference in rebuilding your marriage.

Weighty Problems

Proper weight is important to your physical well-being during this stressful time. If you are too much underweight, you may have a health problem that is not yet discernible to you. Also, if you're too thin, you may not have enough "reserve" for your immune system to fight disease.

Most of us, however, have more trouble with being overweight, which we all know is dangerous. Extra weight contributes to heart disease, makes us less peppy, and may be repulsive to our mate.

Whether your problem is being too thin or too fat, it is important to take care of your weight. You may be under too much stress to add a rigorous weight control plan to your life at this time, but you can start to improve your eating habits.

You Are What You Eat

It is crucial that you get adequate nourishment during this stressful time with your mate. A well-balanced daily diet consists of protein (meat, beans, legumes); dairy products (milk, cheese, yogurt); grains (bread, cereal, pasta); and fruits and vegetables.

For good health, choose more poultry and fish than beef and pork. Avoid rich gravies and sauces. Cut out as much fat as possible. Fat not only adds weight, it also clogs arteries. Lower your sugar and caffeine intake. You can substitute fruits or vegetable and fruit juices for sweets or soft drinks.

It's best to eat at least three small meals a day rather than to skip meals. You need all the vim and vigor you can get while you're under the tension of your threatened marriage. Good eating habits will help you have the emotional and physical strength to cope with a mate who wants out.

Move Those Muscles

Another way to increase your physical heartiness is through exercise. Exercise not only burns calories, it promotes the release of endorphins, which circulate in the blood and relieve tension.

Choose a regular exercise plan that fits your schedule and interests. You may like the stimulation and equipment of a health club, or perhaps you'd rather have exercise equipment in the privacy of your home. You may be a swimmer, biker, or jogger. Pick an exercise that is convenient and enjoyable and you'll be more likely to stick with it. Think of exercise as part of your daily routine, as you do bathing, dressing, and eating. You don't go without those!

We have found walking to be our best exercise. We don't need special equipment except for comfortable walking shoes. We don't have to do it at any specified time. We don't need to drive to another location. We don't have to take a shower afterwards. While losing a little weight, we get to enjoy the birds and flowers, plus we get away from the day's pressures.

We walk at least six times a week. Fortunately, we now live in a climate that accommodates our habit. When we lived where winter and wet weather were a problem, we used an inexpensive exercise bike during bad weather.

The generally accepted rule in exercising is to get your heart rate up to 120 for twenty minutes at least three times a week. Exercise should be done only with your doctor's approval, however, so check with a professional about how strenuously you should work out.

Keeping yourself physically fit will help you to value yourself and better cope with your marital stress.

Enjoy Your Appearance

"Man looks at the outward appearance, but the LORD looks at the heart" (1 Samuel 16:7) is a frequently quoted Scripture verse. Often we emphasize the second part of the verse—that God sees our hearts—and forget the first part.

Since our exterior is what others see, we generally feel better about ourselves if we're pleased with our appearance. Without putting undue importance on clothes, hair, and other externals, keep in mind that you're doing yourself a favor to look as good as you can. You are worth it.

Your mate likely will appreciate it too. In fact, people we know have started to reconsider their desire to break their marriage when they've seen their spouse lose weight, dress better, and get a new hairstyle. Appearance isn't all that makes or breaks a relationship, but it may have more influence than we imagine.

At a college reunion we noticed that the divorced women looked more attractive than the married ones. They were thinner, had hairstyles that were more becoming, and wore up-to-date clothes. Before their marriages broke, the divorced women had looked as mediocre as the others. Apparently they learned after their divorces the importance of a good appearance. Married people would do well to find the key to looking good while still married.

You may not have money to spend on new clothes, so do the best with what you have. Study TV and magazine ads to see what the people of your sex and age are wearing. Then improvise with inexpensive accessories or new combinations from your existing wardrobe. It's better to have a few clothes in style that you wear frequently than to wear a lot of out-of-date clothes that signal you must not know the difference.

Personal hygiene is also important. Clean hair, teeth, nails, and body will make you feel good, and everyone around you will enjoy you more.

You will like yourself better if you do the most with what you have, whether it's your clothes, face, nails, or hair. In many ways you're in competition with whatever force is pulling your mate away from you, so take some steps to be in the running.

Nourish Yourself Emotionally

Sometimes when we're under stress, we try to run on an emotionally empty tank. We're so consumed by our problem that we neglect to refuel our spirits.

Everyone needs to do some little thing that restores them every day, but the type of activity will vary for each person. For you it may be reading, running, taking a bubble bath, playing the piano, spending time on a hobby, working in the yard, or being with a friend. Choose whatever nourishes you and do it regularly. Much of the day depletes your emotional energy, so be sure to do something every day that refuels your spirit.

Part of emotional nourishment is accepting new challenges. Don't get in over your head, but try something different: develop a new sport or hobby, volunteer in a hospital, cultivate a new friend, or even take a different job.

Take time for reflection and meditation. If you're buzzing with activity to the point that you never have any thinking time, you're doing yourself a disservice.

Some of the most important growth the two of us have experienced has come from reading or listening to what others have learned about living successfully. You too can grow through the use of self-help books or tapes.

Nourish yourself emotionally by being with positive friends rather than negative ones. Instead of being dragged down by people who drain your emotions, spend time with the kind who fill you with joy and hope.

Find as many ways as possible to appreciate yourself. Be good to yourself. You aren't being selfish—you're filling your emotional tank so you have something to give to others. You especially need a full tank so you can give to your mate and restore your marriage. Caring for yourself is important to you, your mate, and your family.

Chapter 17

Put Yourself
in God's Hand

◆ ◆ ◆

T HE SAND BLEW IN the front door, across the living room
floor, and joined the dust balls around the unmade bed in the
barren three-room apartment where Ted was staying. Sand settled
between the pages of a book he had dropped on the floor after
reading in bed one night. That didn't matter; it was just another
example of the bleakness of Ted's life. A dismal feeling of power-
lessness nearly overwhelmed him. He felt desperately lonely and
utterly rejected. He was deeply aware of his failure, yet he could do
nothing to change the situation. Ted wasn't used to having his back
against the wall with no way to turn. He definitely didn't like
feeling so helpless.

He was an independent man. He didn't normally need help, but
he knew he needed it now or he might go crazy. While searching for
some relief from his torment, he remembered the Bible. He used to
read it a lot. In the last few years, though, he hadn't even opened the
cover. He had made a commitment to Christ as a teenager, but he had
almost forgotten about that. He and Connie hadn't been to church in

years; they had been faithful in attending until they got busy with their growing family.

Ted and Connie, you may remember from chapter 2, are the couple who divorced and then remarried each other.

Ted went to the house when he knew Connie would be gone and rummaged around until he found the small black Bible he had as a kid. He took it back to his apartment. He found the Psalms and began to read like a starving man at a banquet table. Wow! What great promises were in those verses!

He finished the Psalms in a few evenings and began reading the Gospels. He liked the teachings that assured him of Christ's love for him. He could tell that Christ was a powerful man but also had immense love and tolerance for people.

For the first time in years, he began to hold a prayer conversation with God that was more than "Bless me, my wife, and my kids. Amen." The further he read in Scripture, the closer he felt to God and the more he had to say in prayer.

As he went about his work each day, he talked to God silently. He sensed that he wasn't alone after all. He had a friend with him everywhere he went. Some of his desolation began to lift.

Even though Connie hadn't changed her mind about the divorce, some of the sting was gone because God shared the hurt.

As the months went by Connie began to show interest in getting back together, and Ted prayed all the more fervently. Eventually they worked out their differences and married each other again.

Ted then said to us, "I wouldn't want to have to go through that mess again, but it certainly did bring me back to the Lord. I might have cracked up if I hadn't been able to talk over my troubles with God."

Finding Your Security

"Friendship with God is reserved for those who reverence him. With them alone he shares the secrets of his promises" (Psalm 25:14 TLB).

Throughout Scripture we are guaranteed God's friendship, love, and protection as we turn to him. When we put ourselves in his hand—knowing we have no power[1] nor goodness[2] of our own—he will abundantly supply our needs. Christ, by his death and resurrection, paid for our very lives.[3] In him we have everything we could ever need.

John 10 compares believers to sheep who follow a trusted shepherd. Verse 27 says, "My sheep hear My voice, and I know them, and they follow Me" (NASB). Then we are given this wonderful promise of security with the shepherd and his Father:

> I give eternal life to them, and they shall never perish; and no one shall snatch them out of My hand.
>
> My Father, who has given them to Me, is greater than all; and no one is able to snatch them out of the Father's hand.
>
> I and the Father are one (John 10:28–30 NASB).

We can all place ourselves in this harbor of safety by a simple act of our will. We do this by confessing our unworthiness and accepting his worthiness in exchange.

In His Hand You Are Loved

Many people know John 3:16: "God so loved the world that he gave his only begotten son. . . ."[4] But many of us long to feel God's love more personalized. We want to know that God's compassion is for us as individuals rather than for one gigantic mass of people. The mass includes us, of course, but we are especially encouraged when we see that God knows us as separate persons.

As you search for this intimate love, begin with the plea in Psalm 17:7, "Show me your strong love in wonderful ways, O Savior of all those seeking your help" (TLB). Then watch for all the ways God reveals his love to you. Keep a list of God's kindnesses each day. "See for yourself the way his mercies shower down on all who trust in him" (Psalm 34:8 TLB).

Instead of concentrating on the times you feel ignored or misunderstood, look for the times when you are respected and appreciated. Count the times that things work well for you rather than only the times they don't.

Read the Psalms and underline the verses that speak of God's love and protection. You won't get very far before you'll be amazed at God's many assurances of his faithfulness.

As you read the New Testament, note how much God does for us because of his love for us. We are dearer to him than our own children are to us.[5]

You may or may not have had a tender earthly father, but you probably feel affectionate and protective toward your own children or grandchildren. Think of the person you love the most and realize that God's love far exceeds any earthly love you can feel. And nothing can ever separate us from his love. No person or force in heaven or hell or on earth is strong enough to tear us out of God's hand.[6] His love is forever!

In His Hand You Are Safe

Whether or not you ordinarily are a strong person, you probably feel very vulnerable now. Remember the symbols of safety the Bible uses. God promises we are safe in his hand.[7] He is like a shield to us[8] or a towering rock of safety.[9] We are safe under his wings, like baby chicks sheltered by a mother hen from storms and dangers.[10]

These are only a few of the figures of speech the Bible uses to show God's protection. Not only are we dearly loved, we are also dearly kept. Psalm 46:1–5 promises us that

> God is our refuge and strength, a tested help in times of trouble. And so we need not fear even if the world blows up, and the mountains crumble into the sea. Let the oceans roar and foam; let the mountains tremble!
>
> There is a river of joy flowing through the City of our God—the sacred home of the God above all gods. God himself is living in that City; therefore it stands

unmoved despite the turmoil everywhere. He will not delay his help (TLB).

God is on your side.[11] If God is for you, who can be against you?[12] Circumstances and people around you may be blasting you, but you are safe with the one who knows the best plan for you and has the power to carry it out.[13]

Lettie was shaking badly as she closed the garage door and went into the house. She was tempted to just let herself fall apart—to quit fighting for her marriage. Instead she took a deep breath and murmured a prayer for help as she put the teakettle on to heat.

She had just been out to the logging area to see her husband, Paul. For several weeks they had been having bitter arguments and long periods of cold silence, and for the past several nights he hadn't come home. She had heard he was sleeping at the trailer home of Violet, a woman who frequently took in "troubled" men. Lettie thought perhaps this afternoon she could talk to Paul at work.

She drove deep into the woods before she spotted Paul's truck. She was maneuvering her car to the side of the narrow road to park when she noticed an old pickup pulled off under the trees. As she got out of her car, she called loudly for her husband.

The door of the pickup opened and Paul got out, an embarrassed expression covering his face. Then Lettie saw Violet through the pickup window. Suddenly Lettie was so overcome that all she could do was scream, "Oh, Paul! Paul! Paul!"

Without another word she ran to her car and started back down the narrow road out of the woods. Above the noise of her sobbing, she heard the sound of a truck behind her on the bumpy trail. She looked in her rearview mirror and saw Violet coming in her old pickup.

Lettie could see Violet gripping the steering wheel with both hands, and the determined, angry look on the woman's scowling face scared her. Then Lettie felt the pickup ram the back of her car. It let up a bit and then rammed again even harder.

Lettie couldn't believe it! She was going as fast as she could over the narrow, rutty road. The wall of trees on each side prevented her from turning off to avoid the attacking pickup. Again and again she was rammed from the rear.

When they finally reached the main highway, Violet pulled out around her, violently honking her horn, and roared on down the highway. Lettie was trembling all over. She stopped the car to regain her composure before driving home.

When at last she reached their modest little house on the edge of town, she quickly pulled into the garage and began to sob. As her anguish poured out she felt God's strong arms around her. For some weeks now she had been learning to rely on God for her strength.

As she made herself a cup of tea, the telephone rang. When she picked it up, the person on the other end hung up without a word. In a few minutes, the phone rang again. Lettie let it ring twice before she picked it up. Again someone hung up.

The telephone rang throughout the evening. Sometimes she let it ring without answering it, but then she'd wonder if it were Paul trying to reach her. So the next time she would pick it up, only to be left in silence again.

Lettie was sure it was Violet trying to intimidate her. At first she cried out into the lonely house, "Oh, God, I'm not safe anywhere from that woman!" But then Lettie decided that instead of allowing this matter to rattle her she would turn it over to God. Throughout the evening she repeated to herself part of a Psalm: "You are my hiding place; you will protect me from trouble and surround me with songs of deliverance" (Psalm 32:7).

With that promise running through her mind, she was able to go to bed and sleep in peace. For many months Lettie had to draw on God's special protection and care.

Eventually Paul did come home. But he wouldn't get counseling to work on their problems, so their relationship was still stormy. Lettie knew she would need to stay in God's tender hand.

In His Hand You Are Enabled

We aren't kept in God's hand only to be treasured and preserved. We are also empowered to get moving. God has plans for us to carry out rather than stay cuddled in dormancy. Once we've had our batteries recharged, we can get back to the business of marriage restoration, knowing we can be recharged as many times a day as necessary.

Philippians 2:13 says, "God is working in you to help you want to do what pleases him. Then he gives you the power to do it" (NCV).

We don't have to live by our own fortitude. In fact, if all we have is our own resources, we will soon fail. Our courage and energy will quickly wear thin. But we are promised that we can "do everything through [Christ] who gives [us] strength" (Philippians 4:13).

God's mighty hand enables us to act. In addition, he loves us with a love deeper than any other known love, and he keeps us safe. He doesn't fail. In his hand we are truly protected.

Part 4

TOGETHER AGAIN AT LAST. . . .

Chapter 18

Rebuild Carefully

• • •

A N EXCITING TIME is here! You and your mate have decided to try again to make your marriage work. You no doubt have some questions and maybe some misgivings. You wonder if you'll be successful this time.

We hope you're not thinking, *Now that my mate has given up the third person, we can get on with life and be happy again.* Or, *Once we are under the same roof again, everything will be great! Just like the old days.*

Perhaps your mate doesn't want the "old days." Something in the old marriage caused your mate to want to leave, so you need to build a *new marriage*. You'll use the same two people, but both will have to change so you don't fall back into the same old habits that got you into trouble.

Careful consideration about many issues needs to go into your decision to get back together. If you reunite without confronting the problems that caused the collapse of your marriage in the first place, your relationship may fall apart again, making it less likely to ever be restored.

Include the Architect

You will want the best architect available to help you rebuild your marriage. Therefore, as you put your marriage together again, ask God to reveal exactly what needs to be done.

> If the Lord doesn't build the house, the builders are working for nothing (Psalm 127:1 NCV).

Each couple will have a different set of directions, but the following efforts should go into every marriage restoration project:

Build a Solid Foundation

Your marriage will crumble into ruins within a short time unless you take time to build a strong base. Remember the parable of the wise man who built on solid rock and the foolish man who built on sand.[1] The house on sand collapsed when the storms came, but the house on the rock stood firmly. The following things need to be done to rebuild your marriage on a sturdy foundation:

Deal with Past Problems

Clearing the obstacles that nearly ruined your marriage is perhaps the most difficult part of your rebuilding process. It could be compared to bulldozing the property where you plan to put your foundation.

The tricky part is that earlier bad habits and experiences are like landmines planted in your marriage. You and your mate may still be very tender or defensive about past problems. When you start to discuss them, your whole rebuilding process could blow up in your face. Somehow you and your mate have to defuse those explosives without destroying yourselves in the process.

Don't simply bury your grievances and try to get on with life. That's what you did in the past, and that's why you have landmines now. If you refuse to acknowledge and resolve the old hurts and complaints, you will spread another layer of dirt over the landmines and only delay the inevitable blowup.

Time is necessary to work through the past problems. You can't deal with everything in one marathon talk session. You will need to have many discussions over a period of time.

You may need a marriage counselor. Choose one who is skilled in restoring marriages. A wise counselor can give you insights you don't have. The therapist will probably give you assignments that will help you rid the old wreckage from your lives and get ready to continue building.

Forgive and Move On

Once you have uncovered all the landmines, you can begin to defuse them. And that is done through forgiveness. Forgive as much in little steps as you are able. Sometimes it is impossible to forgive all violations against us in one grand gesture.

Honest forgiveness quite frequently comes in stages.[2] The first stage is to acknowledge that you have been wronged. Granting forgiveness presupposes that an offense has been committed or there would be no reason for forgiveness.

Don't just say, "That's O.K. It was really nothing." It *was* something, and if you acknowledge it you can forgive it. If you deny any wrong occurred when it actually did, you cannot forgive it.

Another part of forgiveness is to grieve the losses that the offenses caused. Don't try to take a shortcut by omitting this stage. That would be like putting a bandaid over a wound that first needs to be opened and drained. Admit that damage has happened and pour your heart out to God about your losses.

You will eventually reach the place where you can grant a sincere "grace forgiveness." "Forgiveness is always unmerited. In the last analysis, no one can ever earn forgiveness. It must be granted as a free gift by the person who has been offended."[3]

What if your mate doesn't regret the wrongdoing? Do you still forgive? Yes, after you've worked through the stages of forgiveness. Many times true apologies from your mate will come later, and often they don't come stated as clearly or in as much detail as you would like. Your mate may feel that he or she is showing repentance simply by coming back to you. To demand an apology stated explicitly in your language may be unrealistic at this point.

Forgiveness is needed on both sides. You know your mate has offended you and needs forgiveness, but you also have offended your mate and need forgiveness. To help clear away the rubble in your relationship, start by asking for your mate's forgiveness. This may elicit apologies from your spouse, but that is not the reason for asking—you're asking because you need it.

Forgiveness is like a giant eraser. Once the old marks are wiped away, you and your mate will be able to start writing a new script on the clean surface.

State Your Expectations

Think through what you want in your new relationship. Both you and your mate should decide what will be important for happiness together. Be very specific. Don't just say, "I'd like harmony." Name what actions and attitudes you need to make you satisfied. For example:

- ◆ "I need some wind-down time when I get home from work."
- ◆ "I need more help with the housework. Perhaps we could alternate getting groceries and doing laundry."
- ◆ "I need my own closet and drawer space."
- ◆ "I need to be spoken to in a kinder and calmer tone of voice when something is bothering you."
- ◆ "I need to have my opinions respected and my viewpoints considered."
- ◆ "I need affection other than when you want sex."

The more clearly you each state your expectations, the fewer unpleasant surprises you'll have later on. Naming expectations also provides a ground rule when certain situations arise.

For instance, you may be ready to tromp all over your mate because you're upset about something. Then you remember your spouse requested that you speak in a gentle manner. This helps you change your attitude and tone of voice and may divert bad feelings.

Or, knowing your mate wants some quiet time after arriving home from work, you won't be surprised if he or she goes off to a room to be alone for a while.

As you each become aware of what will make the other happier in the marriage, you'll know what to do and not do. Instead of just stabbing in the dark, hoping to do the right things, you'll have a better idea of what actions and attitudes are needed.

By the way, go through this process about once a month for the first several months or until this is a natural part of your life with each other.

Use First-Quality Materials

A few years ago we surveyed 186 couples to find out what they thought were the most important ingredients for a lasting marriage. We sent an extensive questionnaire to couples in mid-life or beyond who had been married at least fifteen years. When we compiled the results, the following ten characteristics headed the list:[4]

1. Commitment to marriage (not only committed to stay married, but committed to enrich the marriage).

2. Good communication (able to dialog with each other).

3. Vital spiritual life (at least one and sometimes both partners were spiritually alive).

4. Effective conflict resolution (able to mutually work out differences).

5. Positive impact from other people (maintaining constructive friendships).

6. Sexual intimacy (mutually satisfying sexual relationship).

7. Fun, leisure, and humor (time was allocated for recreation and a sense of humor).

8. Realistic expectations (accepting and enjoying each other).

9. Serving each other (doing things to please each other on a basis of mutuality).

10. Personal growth (growing as an individual to bring a freshness to the marriage).

These traits would be good building materials as you reconstruct your marriage. A quality building is not made from shoddy materials and workmanship; neither is a good marriage.

In that sense, marriage is also like baking. For example, to make a torte you need the best ingredients. You can't say, "I don't have enough flour so I'll just use cornstarch and I don't have any fresh fruit so I'll use some canned fruit cocktail." You have to use what the recipe calls for. You also have to use the right procedures. You can't just gather all the ingredients and mix them together at one time. Unless you have the correct ingredients, in the correct amounts, and put them together in the correct steps, you won't have a torte. You may have something edible—if you're starving—but it won't be a delicate pastry.

In one sense, gourmet cooking is a better metaphor than construction work for marriage. Building a house is a one-time effort. If you make a mistake, you live with the consequences. But in baking you can learn from each experience. If your first torte doesn't turn out exactly right you can figure out what you did wrong and improve on it the next time you try.

The same is true of all the ingredients in marriage. If your first attempt at meeting your spouse's needs is a disaster, you can figure out what went wrong and improve on it the next time. The ingredients that go into a marriage won't be perfect all the time. You can aim for perfection, but in this lifetime you and your mate will never reach it. So give yourselves credit for the progress you are making in choosing the best ingredients and adding them in the right order and keep working *toward* perfection.

Correct Problems Right Away

You already know what happens when you let problems slide. They don't go away. They get worse and cause complications. In rebuilding your marriage, work on problems as soon as they arise. Don't simply patch something without correcting the basic problem. Everybody knows that it makes no sense to repair the ceiling plaster without first repairing the leak in the roof that caused the damage.

At one of the churches we pastored, the men of the congregation were constructing the new sanctuary themselves. A few retired men worked nearly every day, other men worked on their days off, and many others came in the evenings. George, an elderly man who had been a housebuilder in earlier days, came as often as his strength allowed.

George was proud of his work and didn't realize that he no longer was able to do a precise job. The other builders were very particular about their work and wanted each detail on their church done as perfectly as possible. The man who was the unofficial foreman always tried to give George jobs where accuracy wasn't a factor.

One day, however, the foreman was not present and George was. George spent several hours rough-framing two doorways. After he left, the foreman arrived and couldn't believe his eyes! Both doorways were so crooked that minor adjustments could not correct the problem. A decision had to be made. Should they leave the work as it was and try to compensate for the errors, or should they risk hurting George's feelings and redo both doorways? They decided to redo all the work. Far into the night, men took apart and redid what George had done.

Fortunately, George wasn't able to come back for several days. By the time he did, the building had progressed far enough that he never knew his rough framing had been redone. If it had been left as it was, the two doors at the front of the sanctuary would be out of line to this day.

Add Decorator Touches

You can build a plain concrete block house with a door and some windows, or you can add some enhancement. The plain house will shelter you, but the house with some added features will bring more enjoyment.

After you get your marriage on solid footing, think of ways you can enrich your relationship. Add a few touches of interest. Plan little pleasures and surprises for your mate. They may be as simple as an unexpected note or an inexpensive treat.

Put romance back into your relationship. Go carefully, however. Your mate may not be able to rush into playful intimacy with you right away. Intimacy needs to grow slowly, as when you first met.

First use eye contact. Then begin gentle touches. When both of you are ready, hugging, kissing, and caressing may be added. Finally, you both may want sexual intercourse. Don't be discouraged if it takes some weeks to get to the last stage. Love can be shown in many other ways.

For a long time our culture has believed that women wanted romance and affection while men only wanted sexual intercourse. Many of today's males want to be let out of that stereotype. They have learned to be more sensitive and aware of feelings.

Also, a psychological change takes place in men during their mid-years, and they actually become more feeling oriented than in their younger years.[5] They like to be caressed and hugged and given a light kiss. Touching doesn't necessarily have to lead to intercourse for them to feel loved and cared for.

Both men and women enjoy intercourse as well as romantic tenderness. But both also take pleasure in simply being close.

Don't be disheartened if you or your mate don't have intense love feelings for each other when you first come back together. You've been battered and bruised, and you may need some healing time before feelings return.

As you learn that you can trust each other, your emotions will become more loving. If you carry out loving actions—even when you don't feel loving—feelings will eventually come along.

As your marriage becomes more steady, look for new ways to grow. Take on small challenges and keep adding to your rebuilt structure. You may decide to build more than a plain little marriage—perhaps you can have a magnificent mansion!

Chapter 19

Encourage Hurts to Heal

◆ ◆ ◆

DIANE KEPT PUTTING her hand to her heart as she went about dusting her house. She felt as if someone was twisting a knife inside the pulsing muscles of her heart.

The pain started when she found out that her husband had been involved in an affair. It was over now, Charlie said, and he seemed truly sorry it had ever happened. But it wasn't over for Diane.

Every time she looked at Charlie, ugly thoughts raced into her mind and sent stabbing pain straight to her heart again. *How could he desecrate their relationship?* she wondered. *And why? She had been a good wife. What excuse could he possibly have?*

She became bitter even though she didn't want to. She looked at him through narrowed eyes with her mouth set in a firm, straight line. When he tried to touch her, she pulled away. She turned her back to him in bed. Sometimes she wondered if she even loved him any more, and then she'd realize that she truly did. But he had hurt her so much!

She started thinking wicked, revengeful thoughts about the

other woman and even wished she could put a curse on her. This wasn't the Diane she knew; she didn't like the hatred growing inside her, but she didn't know how to stop it.

The pain! It was becoming unbearable. She had to get some relief. She looked for verses in the Bible that would give her comfort, but her heartache took up so much room that she had no place to put anything else.

Finally the agony overwhelmed her. She had to have help. She found a counselor who helped her acknowledge her wounds and showed her what to do to help them heal. As she learned more about herself, she also understood Charlie better. She realized that he did love her and actually needed her to show more love to him.

Diane finally came to the place where she could start to forgive Charlie for the affair. Each time an ugly memory came to her mind, she would deliberately say, "I love him and I forgive him." Gradually her heart pain disappeared. It took a long time to be completely cured, but each day she made steady progress.

Honesty Pays

Even if you and your mate are together again, your lives probably are not completely whole and healthy. You have bruises and wounds that need to heal.

A first step toward healing is to admit you have been hurt and to identify the injuries. Some mates will be willing to talk a great deal; others will find it too painful and too out of character to discuss the offenses in detail.

When you talk about your hurts, don't attack your mate. Calmly state how you've been injured. As you speak, talk about *your* feelings and observations instead of assaulting your mate with "you did this or that" and "you are this or that."

Say "I feel . . ." in place of "You make me feel. . . ." Or say "I feel insecure when. . . ," not "You caused. . . ."

When you level with your mate, don't level him or her. Your

mate is not a hideous monster that needs to be flattened. Your honesty sessions will be much more rewarding if done in kindness and love.

Honesty is a two-way street. If you state your grievances, allow your mate the same opportunity. Be ready to admit your part in the failure of your relationship. It may be hard for you to hear, but listen to what your mate thinks went wrong.

Forgiveness Is Freeing

In *Forgive & Forget: Healing the Hurts We Don't Deserve*, Lewis Smedes reminds us that forgiving is usually done slowly and a little at a time.[1] Often forgiving is also done in confusion:

> Forgiving is wisdom's high art; most of us who work at it, however, are muddlers and bunglers. We usually move toward forgiving in the cross-currents of our confusion.[2]

As you get to the place where you want to forgive your mate, don't be hard on yourself if it doesn't happen easily. Just remember that forgiveness *is* eventually possible as you honestly work through the violations against you.

Perhaps it will help you to forgive if you realize you can do it because Christ has forgiven *your* wrongs. A key verse about forgiveness is "Be kind and loving to each other. Forgive each other just as God forgave you in Christ" (Eph. 4:32 NCV).

In *Healing for Damaged Emotions* Dr. David Seamands tells us to "get out of the setting right and getting even business, and into the forgiving and the loving business."[3]

Forgiving does not mean that you somehow erase history. What has happened is a fact. But as you heal, you will eventually reach the place where memories no longer feel like knives in your heart.

When you forgive, you must also give up your resentments. If you nurse the wrongs your mate did to you, they only grow larger and stronger. If you keep bringing up the affair or other events that disrupted your marriage you are conveying to your mate that you have not genuinely forgiven.

Getting rid of malice will give you a light heart. Carrying a grudge will only keep you earthbound when instead you could be flying free as an eagle.

Memories Can Be Healed

The problem with memories is that they aren't just vague thoughts. They trigger your emotions so it feels as if the event is happening again at that very moment. Each time you relive an unhappy experience, you are wounded anew.

How do you get your memories to quit gnawing at your heart and mind?

Those gruesome memories will eventually fade if you and your mate are sincerely working on the healing process. In *The Myth of the Greener Grass* J. Allan Petersen says, "Certainly where trust has been broken there may be questions for a period of time, occasional twinges of doubt, or echoes, but these will pass if there is a mutual effort to improve the marital relationship."[4]

God can make the pain of your bad memories subside. As you pray about your hurts, imagine that God is beside you and that together you are looking at the hurtful event as if it were just now happening. Visualize yourself asking for his help. Then pray for him to touch your mind and soul in the days to come.

Time is on your side in the healing of memories. If you deliberately confront your hurts, forgive them, and ask for God's healing, the memories will come less often and the hurt will lessen.

Imagine that your mind is a tape player. When an old hurt or a new suspicion starts to play its ugly song, just insert a different "tape"—the tape that assures you of God's love and your improving marital situation. If your mate is giving you positive signals about the progress of your relationship, concentrate on these signs rather than on the old painful memories.

Change Old Patterns of Living

Rick and Stacy sat side-by-side in a coffee shop booth enjoying a quick lunch together. Their arms were touching as they studied the menus. After placing their orders they chatted about how their morning had gone. The waitress interrupted occasionally to serve them, but their attention was on each other.

As they finished lunch, Stacy said, "I'm so glad we're taking time out of the day to see each other. It seems so long to go without seeing you from morning until night."

"I like it too. It makes me feel much closer to you," Rick added.

Outside the coffee shop, they each went to their cars to return to their respective jobs. "See ya tonight at home," Rick said as he kissed Stacy on the cheek.

Rick and Stacy's relationship hasn't always been so cozy. Two years ago they were both concentrating so much on their jobs, household responsibilities, and social obligations that they didn't make much time for each other.

Stacy began to feel that Rick thought of her only as someone to do the household tasks, provide sex, and help him look good socially. She was getting no nourishment from their marriage, and her emptiness became her weak spot.

When one of Stacy's coworkers took an interest in her, Stacy fell into an insidious trap. Steve made her feel pretty and important. They started going to lunch together just to talk. Then they began to take short rides after work.

One late afternoon they stopped at a secluded spot in a large park. Steve made bold sexual advances toward Stacy, and she got scared. She insisted that he stop immediately and take her to her car.

Stacy drove home as the sun set in front of her. Brilliant orange streaks beamed into the clouds on all sides around her. The brightness outside was a stark contrast to the dismal darkness inside her soul. She realized that her relationship with Steve was absolutely wrong and that she was in almost over her head. She knew she had to get out now.

She was starting dinner when Rick arrived home. She got the meal in the oven and then, with a trembling voice, said, "Rick, we need to talk." He sat with her in the family room as she tearfully told him what had been going on with Steve.

Rick was shaken and hurt. He walked around in circles and ran his fingers through his hair. Then he went for a walk by himself.

He did a lot of mental wrestling as he walked. Eventually he began to see that their situation wasn't hopeless. Stacy had come home instead of leaving him. She'd told him about the entanglement with Steve instead of hiding it any longer. She had been involved with Steve emotionally, but not sexually. She was extremely sorry and wanted to strengthen their marriage.

When he returned to the house he assured Stacy that he forgave her and wanted to do his part to get their marriage back on sure footing again. They decided they needed to do more things together and to do specific things every day to let the other know that he or she was loved.

They each had jobs that allowed them to take long lunch hours, so they agreed that at least twice a week they would meet for lunch. Sometimes they brought sack lunches and ate in a park.

They decided to help each other with the house and yard work on the weekends so they could be together. By working together they got the jobs done more quickly and found free time to go on inexpensive "adventures" nearly every week.

Rick and Stacy had to practice their new lifestyle for several weeks before it became a habit, but now they can't bear the thought of living the old way. "And to think we almost lost each other because of bad patterns we had set up," they say solemnly.

Create Healing Habits

Heal your old hurts by breaking harmful habits and creating healthy ones. Substitute activities that strengthen your marriage for ones that cause it to deteriorate. Practice new, kind ways of speaking to each other. Show a little love every day. Have some fun experiences—they don't have to be costly to provide enjoyment.

As you produce a new design for your relationship you will not only enrich your marriage, you will also replace ugly memories with new, happier ones.

When an old hurt starts throbbing again, go back to the Great Physician and let him apply his healing ointment. Remind yourself that these old memories have been cared for and that you don't have to let them hurt you.

Chapter 20

Invest for a Lifetime

✦ ✦ ✦

MARRIAGE RESTORATION ISN'T a once-for-all-time project. You can never say you're finished. No marriage is ever
complete, not even one that has never been threatened as yours has.
There is always more work and more growing to be done.

Wayne learned this the hard way. Although his wife, Jenny, was
a professing Christian, she always seemed to be meeting new men and
falling in love. Often the infatuation turned into a sexual relationship.
When Wayne accused Jenny of being nothing but a common slut, she
shook her finger at him and said, "I have nothing to keep myself pure
for. You're no husband to me. You're gone most of the time, and when
you are home, you're in your workshop. You don't go to bed when I
do, and you're always gone before I wake up."

Pastor Bob helped them reach an uneasy truce when they went
to him for help. They agreed to keep living together after Jenny
promised not to get involved with any other men and Wayne promised
to pay more attention to her.

Wayne was relieved when Jenny once again seemed to be trying
to be a homemaker and his wife. She kept her attentions off other men
and concentrated on being attractive to Wayne. It wasn't long,
though, before Wayne began to slip on his part of the bargain. His

company assigned him to a special project that required long hours and when he got home, he didn't want to go straight to sleep—he wanted to putter in his workshop.

Jenny frequently went to the site where Wayne was working to maintain a connection with him. She'd take him a cold drink and just chat for a few minutes. Wayne barely acknowledged her presence. He quickly gulped down whatever she brought and then plunged back into his work.

Some of the other men, though, took time to notice Jenny. They kidded her about bringing them something to drink too. So she started making iced tea in a large thermos and giving some to all the men. They would take a few minutes to talk with her while Wayne kept at his work. One particular man, Rusty, spent lots of time talking to Jenny, and she thoroughly enjoyed his attention.

Late one night Wayne tromped into the house and found a note propped against a pop bottle on the table:

> Rusty and I have left town. He won't be at work anymore. He really loves me, and we want to be together. Don't bother trying to bring me back this time.
>
> Your formerly lonely wife,
> Jenny.

Even though it was after midnight, Wayne frantically called Pastor Bob. He told him his story and they agreed to meet in the morning. As they talked the next day, Wayne began to see that he had been extremely careless in taking care of his marriage. Unfortunately, Jenny never did come back to Wayne, and they are divorced.

Increase Your Assets

Coming together again is not all there is to a successful relationship. You must not forget that you're in a rebuilding process that requires alertness and enthusiasm every day. You'll need a lifetime commitment.

Don't let that overwhelm you. You only have to live one day at a time, and you don't have to meet these demands in your own strength. God will empower you for the job. He will help you "take a new grip with your tired hands [and] stand firm on your shaky legs" (Hebrews 12:12 TLB).

Perhaps you are starting out with only one asset—your willingness to try. But from a feeble start you can, with God's help, build something strong and beautiful.

Storing Up Treasures

Rebuilding your marriage is similar to investing in a savings account or money market fund. You don't have to make one large deposit all at once; you can add to it as you go.

In rebuilding a sound marriage, you can make deposits into your account many times a day. Each time you do something favorable to or for your mate, you are adding to your investment.

The difference between investing in a bank account and investing in your marriage is that your marriage is a living organism. You and your spouse can interact with each other as you respond, react, and cooperate. Money has no feeling; your mate does. Money is temporary; your mate is eternal.

What Can You Deposit?

What each couple invests in their marriage-rebuilding account will vary according to the unique character of the two people in the relationship. There are, however, some investments everyone can make:

Improved Attitudes

Are you an optimistic person? Is your glass half empty or half full? Are you interested in others or consumed with your own concerns? Are you suspicious of others' motives and actions or do you grant the benefit of a doubt? Can you tolerate a difference in opinions or preferences? Do you value another's privacy? Are you cheerful and encouraging or crabby and complaining? Do you affirm or criticize others (your mate, in particular)? Do you boss and nag until people want to shake free from your dominance?

As you can see, a great number of attitudes affect our lives and relationships. Since you want to restore your marriage, you'll want to develop good attitudes in everything you do. Your mate will be watching you. He or she will be much more desirous to work on the marriage with you if you're a pleasant, upbeat person.

You won't regret investing in healthy attitudes. As your investment grows, your mate will enjoy you more, other people will enjoy you more, and you'll even like yourself better. You really do get a good return on your investment when you develop positive attitudes.

Beneficial Words

Some of us talk too much; others don't say enough. What some of us say is worthwhile; what others say is nearly useless or very damaging. The right use of words can help a marriage grow strong; the wrong use of words can destroy it.

James in the New Testament reminds us:

> We all stumble in many ways. If anyone does not stumble in what he says, he is a perfect man, able to bridle the whole body as well.
>
> Now if we put the bits into the horses' mouths so that they may obey us, we direct their entire body as well.
>
> Behold, the ships also, though they are so great and are driven by strong winds, are still directed by a very small rudder. . . .
>
> So also the tongue is a small part of the body, and yet it [is capable] of great things (James 3:2–5 NASB).

Words reveal attitudes, so use words to bless and encourage. Even if you are directing an employee or instructing your child, and especially when you're speaking to your mate, kind words get positive results.

Remember to *use* words. If you are the strong, silent type you may forget that your mate isn't a mind reader. Talk to your mate so that she or he isn't left watching a silent movie with no subtitles. Communication is one way to feel close to each other.

For those of you for whom talking is easy, don't forget to shut off the flow once in awhile. Give your husband or wife a chance to use words too.

Acts of Kindness

You are known by what you do. Good intentions only go a little way. If you don't carry them out, you are soon known as a pretender or a procrastinator.

Your behavior for investing in your marriage covers everything from common courtesies in daily life to specific, creative deeds to show your love.

I have recently undergone breast cancer surgery and intensive chemotherapy, which debilitated me for over a year. I could hardly care for myself, let alone keep up household duties or go about my counseling and writing ministry.

Jim let me know immediately that his major priority was my recovery. He waited on me when I couldn't care for myself. He took on the cooking, cleaning, laundry, grocery shopping, and managing the household. He did my share of the office and speaking ministry. He went with me for innumerable doctors' visits and tests.

He was my cheerleader, encouraging me that together we would make it through this ordeal. He said he didn't mind my lopsided chest or my balding head. He helped me go for short walks outdoors by letting me hang on to him. He listened to my moaning and groaning when I was too sick to be a nice person.

One of the most outstanding things Jim did for me was to dress a large, ugly wound where my breast had been. He did this for over nine months! I had complications, and a gaping hole developed in my chest following surgery. Every day Jim tenderly cleaned and wrapped that repulsive opening.

When I would thank him for all he was doing for me, he would say, "I'm glad to do it. I'm here to serve you."

What if, at the beginning of the cancer experience, he had said he would help me and then had ignored me most of the time?

His kind words would have been like a helium-filled balloon that escapes a child's grasp and floats upward out of reach toward endless space. Jim's loving actions conveyed more meaning than any words could have.

What can you do every day that shows your love for your mate and makes your marriage enjoyable? You're a busy person, but if you want a restored marriage you can't afford to neglect doing things for and with your spouse.

Deposits Now Pay Dividends Later

Remember the parable of the master who was going on a journey and distributed money among his servants? One man hid his money and did nothing with it until the master returned. The other two men invested their money and had a multiplied amount to give to their master when he came back.

The two servants who increased their money were praised. The servant who buried his money had it taken from him and was thrown out of his master's presence.[1]

Your opportunity to rebuild your marriage is like the money given to the servants. Don't bury your opportunity; use it. Make investments every day that will pay dividends of a stronger marriage. If you put more in, you'll get more out.

What you get from your investment in your marriage, however, is more than mere dollars and cents. A happy marriage benefits you, your mate, your children, your extended family, and everyone else in your world. Their lives will be healthier because yours is. An enjoyable feature of a savings account or money market fund is that you begin to get interest on your money as soon as it's deposited. The same is true when you invest in your marriage restoration project.

Not only will you enjoy the benefits now, but you'll also have profits later. "Increase" is a key word of investment. It's like a reward for faithfully storing up good things. Increase and dividends are what you'll get from rebuilding your marriage.

Since our marriage in 1954, each anniversary impresses us with the rewards of having lived so many years together. We used to grimace at Robert Browning's sentiment, "Grow old along with me, the best is yet to be." We wondered, *What's so great about growing old together?*

Our real question was *What's so great about growing old?* Since we can't escape growing older, we're finding it's a great adventure to do it together.

There's something comforting about coming home to someone who has known you since you were a well-intentioned, but immature pup. You have a long history together. You know what the other's parents were like. You shared joy when your kids were born and sorrow when those kids broke your heart.

You saw your mate make mistakes and learn from them. You know what it has taken for your spouse to get this far in life. You knew each other when you had more hair and a bouncier spring in your step. Just a phrase or a certain look triggers a whole panorama of connections between the two of you. You have your little private jokes.

Life may be hard, but you have someone who has been over the same bumps and is willing to keep on going with you.

We sincerely hope that you and your mate have the opportunity to enjoy an ongoing marriage. We want you to discover that "the best is yet to be."

May God bless and empower you.

Part 5

TO PASTORS
AND
COUNSELORS

Chapter 21

Work for Restoration, Not Divorce

◆ ◆ ◆

A FEW YEARS AGO I was getting ready to speak in one of the largest Baptist churches in Southern California. The man who was to introduce me was a divorce lawyer. He leaned over to me and said, "What you're going to be talking about this morning is very important for our people. Looking around the congregation, I see more than fifty of my clients who are in the process of divorce."

Since the Second World War, Americans have watched the divorce rate rise until its peak in the early eighties at slightly over 50 percent. In other words, if a hundred people in an average town got married in a given year, fifty people in the same town would get divorced.

In the early fifties Christians were quite smug about the spiraling divorce rate, thinking it happened only to "those people" on the outside. Some Christian writers even said that truly committed Christians would never get a divorce. They believed the slogan, "The family that prays together stays together." However, by the late seventies the divorce rate for Christians began catching up to that of the general population.

In the sixties and early seventies, pastors I surveyed thought that the divorce problem was outside of the church. Their simple response was, "I don't have anything to do with people who are divorced or remarried."

The fantasy of a Christian subculture without divorce or remarriage is no longer possible. Divorce has penetrated even the smallest towns and remotest parts of our country so that no pastor can put his head in the sand and say, "I don't have to be involved in this problem."

Marital stress even among churchgoers is not a figment of imagination. It's real life. It's tough life. It affects everything that happens in the individual family as well as in the church, community, extended family, and in generation after generation as people carry with them the baggage from a difficult family life.

So the question is, how do we deal with this reality? How can we counsel, put programs into action, and work together as a team of caring specialists to heal sick marriages and steer those at the point of divorce onto a course toward marital harmony?

The rest of this chapter suggests a perspective for counselors, pastors, small group leaders, elders, deacons—in short, anyone who is trying to rebuild marriages, reduce the divorce rate, or soothe the giant pain divorce is causing all across our country.

Counsel Toward Restoration, Not Divorce

Most couples in failing marriages will try several do-it-yourself approaches to help their marriage before they seek professional counseling. By the time they reach out for help, the situation has usually deteriorated so much that they probably are talking about divorce and one of them may have moved into separate quarters.

Many of these marriages appear to have little or no potential for reconciliation or stabilization. Because of a couple's longstanding problems, their disillusionment with attempted solutions, and their sheer fatigue, counselors frequently are tempted to concur with the bleak assessment of the marriage and encourage the couple to get divorced, accept God's forgiveness, and press on with life.

One of the most difficult battles we face in our office at Mid-Life Dimensions is that of encouraging people to keep working toward reconciliation and stabilization while Christian counselors and pastors are encouraging these people to divorce.

Many of these marriages could be saved if counselors or pastors understood developmental issues and were willing to consider additional approaches to counseling, which we'll be looking at in the rest of this chapter.

Our office is currently achieving about a 50 percent reconciliation rate for marriages that have been written off by most people. We consider a marriage reconciled when the couple report they are together again and are both resolving problems in their marriage.

When counseling a troubled couple, keep in mind the following ideas:

Divorce Is Not the Best Answer

Although the Bible permits divorce under certain conditions, it never suggests it as the best solution. People who divorce frequently believe they have solved the problem. They are, however, likely to marry another person very similar to the former mate and relate to that person in many of the same destructive ways as in the previous marriage. In addition, he or she may carry a haunting sense of guilt and hear the probing question, "Could I have made my first marriage work if only I had done something differently?"

It is important for the counselor to ask, "Am I pushing these people toward divorce because I am frustrated at the length of the healing process or the depth of the problems?"

Everyone's Not Getting a Divorce

Marital fidelity is being barraged by the idea that "everyone's doing it"—everyone is playing around and everyone is breaking up. Even many Christians feel justified in leaving their marriage or having an affair if their mate doesn't make them happy. One man told us, "My wife hasn't met my basic needs for the last five years. So, of course, I got involved with another woman. After all, what does my wife expect? . . . It's really her fault I had the affair, you know."

Some cynics are claiming, as they look at the high divorce rate, that expecting one marriage to last a life-time is a bankrupt idea. It's interesting to note, however, that marriage is more popular than ever. Even though the divorce rate is hovering around the 50 percent mark, a greater percentage of our population is married today than ever before.[1]

From our study of couples whose marriages have survived, and from the many couples we counsel, we have learned that successful couples are willing to say, "We don't care what everyone else is doing, we're going to make this marriage work."[2] These couples made this pronouncement in spite of the fact that divorce for married persons forty to sixty years of age rose more than 50 percent between 1968 and 1978.[3]

To survive, every marriage must develop the strength to swim against the tide.

An Affair or Separation Can Be an Opportunity for Growth and Reconciliation

Affairs often start because of a vacuum in one's personality or in the marital relationship. If the vacuum can be filled in legitimate ways, the need and urgency for the affair disappears. Counseling is more productive when it deals with the causes of the vacuum than when it commiserates about the evil of the affair.

A separation can provide the distance that facilitates heal-ing, but a separation does not require that one of the partners move out of the city, state, or even out of the house. Even "slight" separations can be extremely helpful if a couple is at the point of desperation.

A separate bedroom within the house can be identified as a retreat for one of the mates. And short-term separations can be accomplished through fishing trips, church retreats, and visits with old friends (of the same sex, of course).

The counselor should help slow down the process toward divorce. If separation must take place, encourage small, incremental steps. The fewer bridges burned, the easier it is to be reconciled.

Help the Counselee to Focus on the Mate

Counseling should work not only on the counselee's general well-being, but also on enabling the person to meet the needs of his or her mate. We believe that marriages are primarily held together because people meet each other's needs. Therefore, helping the counselee to understand the mate's needs and to actively meet those needs will provide a later basis for reconciliation.

Counsel from a Developmental Perspective

The study of adult development is a rather new phenomenon. Before the late 1920s, it was generally assumed that adults could not learn or change after their early twenties. In 1928,[4] Edward Thorndike shocked the educational world with his studies of adults in their thirties. He discovered that they *were* capable of continued learning.

Charlotte Buhler[5] was one of the early researchers studying the process of adult development (1939). Erik Erikson (1950),[6] Robert Havighurst (1953),[7] Bernice Neugarten (1964),[8] and a host of others in the late sixties through the nineties, have expanded the research and study of adult development and learning from an educational, spiritual/moral, and psychological point of view.

As a result, researchers have divided the adult era into many sub-periods. Adulthood, which had been considered a very stable period, is now seen as a time of growth with several important times of change.

A large group of researchers and writers, such as Alan B. Knox,[9]

Daniel J. Levinson,[10] Roger Gould,[11] Marjorie Lowenthal,[12] and many others, have helped to delineate these adult stages more precisely. It is now commonly accepted that the adult lifespan consists of a young adult era, a mid-life era, and an aging era. Each of these broad stages is then divided even more finely.

All through the adult stages of life a process of reassessment takes place as people realize they are moving into a new era. At each stage they ask, "Who am I?" "What should I do with my life?" and "How should I relate to others and to God?" These questions are asked by teens becoming young adults, young adults coming to mid-life, and mid-life adults turning older.

In addition to the normal developmental process of moving from one era to another, people also experience physical aging, work pressures, increased community and social responsibilities, an awareness of the shortness of life, and a decreasing amount of personal intimacy, particularly within marriage.

All of these developmental changes, cultural pressures, and internal questions may cause problems in marriage. Each partner may be so consumed with his or her own developmental concerns that no energy is left to maintain the marriage.

Counsel with an Insight into Changing Needs

In addition to the internal factors that may cause marriages to erode, there are also external forces at work.

For centuries marriage was necessary for physical survival; then it became a primary unit of economic survival. Some sociologists believe that in primitive cultures the word *love* may not have been associated with marriage because couples united for other reasons.[13]

In our culture people don't usually marry for economic or political advantages or to have children to work the land. Most people marry for love, companionship, and a secure relationship in a lonely and uncertain world.

Today's marriage partners have to be concerned not only about physical survival, financial stability, and family harmony, they also have to be good listeners, sensitive, caring, understanding, and terrific sexual partners with great-looking bodies! A contemporary marriage partner has to meet many of a mate's needs for friendship that in past days were met by the extended family or by church and community friends.

This century has seen a dramatic lengthening of American life expectancy. As recently as 1900, the average length of life was only about forty-nine years. In the eighties, however, average life expectancy rose to over seventy years.[14]

In past generations, unhappily married fifty-year-olds figured they didn't have many more years to put up with each other. Today's dissatisfied fifty-year-olds know they may have twenty to forty more years of potential marital misery.

Counsel with an Individual's History in Mind

All of us bring problems into marriage because we bring ourselves. We are a combination of strengths and weaknesses, positive experiences and crushing blows. We are people who have a light, transparent side as well as a dark, secretive side. We carry our total selves into the marriage relationship. Any unresolved problem, inadequacy, or family dysfunction from our past may be the seed of marital breakup.

I discovered in my fifties that I never fully trusted that Sally would not abandon me once she found out how inadequate I really was. My parents were emotionally divorced from the very first day of their marriage, and I thought that emotional distancing in a marriage was normal. As a result, I never fully committed myself to Sally. I felt deep down inside that sooner or later she would leave me, so I didn't invest everything in our marriage because that way I wouldn't get hurt too much when she abandoned me.[15]

Sometimes marriage dissatisfaction can be traced directly to dysfunctional baggage carried from childhood or teen years.

Frequently we hear a story like that of Ken, an insecure man married to a strong woman. In the early years Ken was glad that Carol helped him with many of his decisions, but in his late thirties he began to throw off all mentors. He resented having his wife continually "mothering" him.

In counseling it became apparent that their problems went back to their development in homes with dominant mothers. Ken had not realized that he married Carol partly because he admired her leadership abilities. She had learned from her mother to take control. He had learned from his father to be passive. It seemed like a perfect match.

As Ken grew older, however, he wanted to take more responsibility for personal decisions. Ken and Carol had to work on a new style of leadership to keep their marriage from disintegrating.[16]

Counsel with an Awareness of Predictable Divorce Ages

Courtship and the early married years include the new and novel—getting to know each other, exploring sex together, launching a new career, bringing children into the world, and rearing them. Then the focus moves to buying a home and getting the "extras"—a second car, a boat, a video cassette recorder, special trips—those things that mean "we have arrived."

Tragically, a subtle shift takes place that may go unnoticed until the middle years. The couple increasingly focuses on everyday activities and the accumulation of things rather than on each other. Couples justify this outward focus because "we're buying a house," "raising children," "starting a business," "buying the luxuries of life."

Suddenly a chilling realization descends. Though once deeply in love with each other, the couple has become boring people with no common interests except their children, investments, and properties. They have fallen into routines that are necessary but hum-drum and lifeless.

Another blow to marriage may be the awareness that it is turning out just like that of their parents'. They had promised each other that theirs would be different. Instead, they realize they married someone just like their father-in-law or mother-in-law, which isn't what either of them had in mind!

The apparent dissatisfaction with marriage is not a new phenomenon. A Detroit study done in the early 1960s showed that only 6 percent of the wives were satisfied with their marriages after twenty-two years.[17]

Also in the sixties, psychologist and columnist Dr. Joyce Brothers stated, "Marriage is a 'quiet hell' for about half of American couples, . . . four of twelve marriages will end in divorce, while another six become loveless 'utilitarian' relationships to protect children, property, shared concerns, and other goals."[18]

In a study of 2,000 married couples, Richard Strauss reported in 1973 that 60 percent of men would not marry the same partner if they had it to do over.[19] Some research is indeed pessimistic about the future of our western society in general and marriage specifically, but in spite of these gloomy views, there has been a definite turn from the seventies "me-ism" to concern for the group and marriage and family. That's good news!

The First Year

The most dangerous year for a potential divorce is the first. There are many reasons for the high first-year failure rate, but most boil down to inadequate preparation. Couples are carefully rehearsed on where to stand for the marriage ceremony, but few get the counseling necessary to help them deal with their own personal family history and prepare them for the realities of their own marriage.

During my many years as a pastor, I said to the congregation, to singles' groups, and to junior-high and high-school students that it was important to get premarital counseling. Ideally, I wanted to see the couple in the early stages of a relationship—while it was simply a serious friendship. Coming to see me didn't mean they were announcing a date to get married. But early visits gave me an opportunity to help each of them accelerate their emotional maturity so that, whomever they married, they would be better prepared.

In each church I pastored, I encouraged those in leadership to pass a resolution that no one on the pastoral staff could perform marriages for couples who would not commit themselves to six to eight hours of premarital counseling over a three-month period. Plus, the couples had to read several books, take appropriate tests, and follow through on any recommended referrals.

The result was that a number of couples did not get married right away—some never did. Some spent more time growing; others discovered they were not right for each other.

It is time for counselors, pastors, parents, wedding coordinators, and church officials to band together to insist on serious, in-depth premarital counseling so that we can head off the tragically high divorce rate of the first year.

The Late Twenties and Early Thirties

By this age many couples have been married about seven years. It isn't that seven years of marriage is automatically a bad time, but a divorce is more likely during a developmental reassessment time, one of which occurs at the end of the twenties or in the early thirties.

During the late teens and early twenties, individuals usually choose what they want to do with their lives. During that time people often decide to get married and start their family and career. All looks well until they get to the late twenties and begin to ask themselves, "Am I really on target? Am I accomplishing the goals I thought I would accomplish? Is my marriage really as satisfying and fulfilling as I hoped?"

If the answer to any of these questions is no, the partner may look at his or her mate and think that someone new would improve the situation.

Couples struggling with the question of whether or not to stay together usually do so alone. The rest of the community sees them as "well established" and out of danger. Everything seems to be O.K. Unfortunately, this can be a very dangerous period for marriages and is a crucial time for the community, church, counselors, and other leaders to plan marriage enrichment seminars or special classes to help couples work through this questioning period.

The Mid-Life Era

The time of highest risk for married couples is at mid-life. The potential for depression, anger, frustration, and rebellion is great. If one or both of the partners are experiencing mid-life crisis, their lives will be affected not only physically, but also socially, culturally, spiritually, and occupationally. Mid-life is a time when people reach the peak of the mountain and look back to see where they have come from and look forward to what lies ahead. How people evaluate accomplishments, hopes, and dreams will determine whether life ahead will be an exhilarating challenge or simply a demoralizing expanse that must be drearily traversed.

Mid-life, which is roughly ages thirty-five to fifty-five, was previously thought to be a settled time but now is seen as a potentially tumultuous era for marriage. It is during this period that people reassess their personal values and goals related to marriage, career, friendships, and social commitments, as well as God.

Mid-life has several sub-stages. The mid-thirties male, who quite often is an aggressive, single-focused individual trying to make his mark in the world, is very different from the early forties male who is wondering what life is all about and which values and lifestyles he should change. The man in his fifties is different from both groups. He has mellowed and is more willing to invest himself in the lives of younger people.

Mid-life men quite often experience a shock of realism about their careers. For the first time they may come to understand they're not going to go as far as they had dreamed. Frequently mid-life husbands who are angry about their career or other facets of life will project that anger onto their marriage. They may blame their wife for the limitations and frustrations they are experiencing.

A mid-life wife may feel that her husband is keeping her in a mother-only role. If their children are in high school or moving out of the nest, her mothering job is coming to an end. This loss may affect her self-identity and self-worth and may breed resentment toward her husband if he wants her to function only as a mother.

She may be tired of putting up with an absentee husband consumed by his career goals, and her own sense of cultural displacement may be setting in as she realizes that society no longer considers her "young and beautiful." The feeling of loss she experiences in many areas causes her to reassess her values.

Many couples of various ages feel trapped into pretending they like each other, themselves, and what they do. They live out a farce, acting as if all is well in their marriage and in their individual lives.

Changing Life Questions

Since the adult years have several reassessment times, the marital relationship will likely need to be readjusted to fit the changes at each transition.

The questions asked in the early twenties are future-oriented: "Who am I? What shall I do with my life? With whom shall I relate?" Most people marry during this early twenties adjustment period.

The questions asked in the late twenties and early thirties are progression-oriented: "How am I doing with the choices I have made? Am I progressing fast enough? What are the areas that need to be corrected in order to accomplish my life goals?"

At mid-life, the questions are now-oriented: "Who am I now? Who am I becoming? What will my values be? Am I satisfied with my career? Who will my friends be? Am I contented in my marriage? How does God fit into my life? How is my life making a difference in the world?"[20]

The perspective is, "Life is running out too fast. I need to make corrections *NOW!* I only have twenty to thirty more good years left."

At each developmental reassessment stage, marriage will take on a slightly different form because of the personal growth of each mate.

Counsel with Long-Term Patience

Keep the Counselee Focused

One of the major problems in the long-term counseling of an unstable marriage is that frequently the people lose perspective and give up hope. Each new event produces trauma—something bad happens at work, a letter is discovered, a teenager or aged parent causes trouble, or an angry fight occurs.

Frequently, the counselee exaggerates the situation and concludes that all of his or her work is for nothing. The counselor needs to help the counselee remember that the goal is a reconstructed, stronger marriage. The counselor should rehearse how to accomplish the goal and encourage the person to keep focused in positive directions that will achieve the goal.

Marriage Doesn't Mean Happiness

An unhappy person before marriage is likely to be an unhappy person after marriage. Marriage may provide a temporary change in happiness because of the novelty of the situation, but eventually each mate will settle back into the level of happiness experienced as a single adult.

Married life, after all, is not exclusively made up of picnics, dinners out, roses, and little surprise gifts. It is ordinary living, with not enough money, too much work, and too much stress in an uptight world. It is good mixed with bad. If a couple believes marriage is going to be just like courtship, they will be continually frustrated. They will blame themselves or each other for what appears to be a failed marriage. But it's not a failed marriage—it's just life.

Unfortunately, some people keep jumping from one marriage partner to another, ignoring the stark reality that marriage can only be as satisfying as the sum of its participants. Putting two unhappy people together ultimately means there is *double* the *un*happiness.

No Hope of Improving the Other One

Before marriage each one subconsciously said, "Well, he (or she) isn't exactly what I want, but I'll be able to make all the necessary improvements." And there will be *some* improvements. People do modify and adapt, but usually only in areas that are inconsequential.

When we were first married, Sally wanted me to be neater—to throw my dirty laundry in the laundry basket, etc.—and I wanted her to tolerate a little more messiness.

Another early difference was that after a hard Sunday morning of preaching and teaching, I wanted to leave the Sunday dishes and take a nap, turn off the world, hold each other, fall asleep together, or make love. But Sally would say, "I can't relax when I know there's a pile of dirty dishes in the kitchen."

These sound like some of the more easily solved problems of married life, don't they? We *have* adapted to each other. Both of us have made compromises. (We eventually got a dishwasher, so now we can go to bed. This arrangement is a lot more fun!) But after more than thirty-eight years of being married to each other, those conflicting traits continue to come up. Sally is basically tidy. I am basically messy. Recently I asked, "How do you handle my messiness?"

She said, "I learned early to just throw your socks in the laundry basket, close the closet door, and forget them."

After a few years of marriage, people either accept the fact that their mate is different or the very differences will eat holes in the relationship. Differences that once were "cute," can become maddening irritations that drive people apart.

Avoidance Becomes a Pattern

Poor marriages seem to be marked by avoidance. Both partners use ingenious devices to keep from communicating with the other about who they really are and the needs they have. Favorite avoidance tricks are: time away at the job, raising children, church or community activities, being a "couch potato" in front of the TV, or working extra hours or jobs to pay off a mortgage, buy a second car, a boat, or a cottage at the lake.

Eda LeShan tells of a woman who discovered that her husband was having an affair. "He was finally forced into admitting some of the negative feeling he had had about their relationship all along: the times he felt he was being manipulated; the times he became utterly weary of her histrionics; the times he had felt imprisoned by her dependency and proprietary attitude. [The wife] said, 'He kept telling me that he hadn't wanted to hurt my feelings—so instead he took the chance of destroying our marriage.'"[21]

Counsel in Partnership with a Support Network

In typical marriage counseling the counselor and one person meet periodically and concentrate on the problems or issues that are presented in the session by the counselee. We suggest that the counselor be more *proactive* by encouraging:

1. Standard counseling sessions.

2. Specific homework (books to read, tapes to listen to, Scripture assignments, new actions to practice).

3. Involvement in a support group.

4. Help with legal and financial concerns from competent laypeople within the church or community.

People who have a broad-based support network are more likely to continue working on their marriage than those who have a counselor-only support base. Also, a great deal of power and psychological change are accomplished by encouraging personal spiritual development in the individual and enlisting a prayer support group for the situation.

Think of the person with a marriage crisis in the same way you think of the alcoholic who needs frequent support and cannot wait for a counseling appointment. The counselee needs support from peers who have struggled through and survived problem marriages.

The counselor should continue to play an important role but should not try to be the primary support. The counselor is strategic in overseeing a synergistic process that includes counseling sessions, homework, group interaction, and outside legal and financial coaching.

Counsel with God Present

When I start a counseling session, my first question to the counselee generally is, "Well, what can I do for you?" While the person is telling his or her story and moving deeper toward the real problems, part of me is listening and part of me is praying, "Dear God, help me! Give me the insights I need. Give this person the courage to change. Work in the circumstances of his or her life. Help him or her to find the needed support group. Bring about growth and change so that the marriage can be saved."

When I was working on a graduate degree in counseling, I thought I was learning all of the answers, procedures, and techniques I would need to help people get better. My last course was a seminar where I was the only student. I had two professors—one psychologist and one psychiatrist. The sessions consisted of listening to excerpts from recorded counseling sessions I had held with people in my church and community. Then we would discuss the individual's problems and the procedures that ought to be taken.

On one occasion, I presented a tape from my first session with a particular woman. After listening to it I asked my two professors, "Well, what direction should I take with this woman?" They both looked at me blankly, and said, "We don't know."

I had imagined that these men were the fountains of all knowledge about the human psyche and that I would be able to absorb all of their insights and put them to work immediately. I was shocked by how little absolute knowledge they had.

On my way home I came to a deep spiritual awareness that

ultimately only God knew the heart and circumstance of any of my counselees. Unless I enlisted him in the healing process, I would never see the full healing that I wanted for people.

I'm glad for all the training I've had and you've had. The more, the better. But remember to carry out all of your counseling with a deep sense that God understands your people better than you do. And he wants to see them fully healed and restored.

I've also found that God can work inside people day after day, twenty-four hours a day, even when they are not in a counseling session or doing prescribed homework. I urge you to let God be the vital power that he wants to be in your people's lives.

Marriage restoration is a big job—but a "do-able one!" Many of the marriages that are breaking apart could be saved with proper *prevention* and *intervention!*

The Bible says, "He who finds a wife finds what is good" (Proverbs 18:22). We add, "Whoever restores a marriage is replacing generations of pain with health and happiness."

Keep on helping the people who have found a good thing— marriage—and help them keep it good.

Jim and Sally Conway
Fullerton, CA
1992

Notes

Chapter 1—Don't Panic

1. *The Orange County Register*, Santa Ana, CA, October 7, 1991.

Chapter 2—Have Hope

1. Romans 5:5.

2. 1 Corinthians 10:13; James 1:12–16; Jude 24–25. We can claim the *resurrection triumph of Jesus* to win over Satan's plots to destroy our marriage. Christ has defeated the devil for us, and we can appropriate that victory for our own (1 Corinthians 15:57–58; Romans 8:1). We can pray for God to give us wisdom in everything we say, every action we take, and every thought we have (James 1:5; John 16:13; Romans 8:26–28). We can ask for his peace and protection (Psalm 4:8; John 14:26–27; 1 Corinthians 15:58; 2 Corinthians 1:3–5). He will give us the courage to make the needed changes in ourselves.

3. Ed Wheat, M.D., *How to Save Your Marriage Alone*, (Grand Rapids, MI: Zondervan, 1983), 13.

Chapter 5—Vow to Work Hard

1. James 1:5; John 16:13.

2. Philippians 4:13,19.

3. Psalm 103:3–18; 1 Peter 5:7–11.

4. Galatians 6:1–3.

Chapter 6—Handle Your Mate's Affair Wisely

1. J. Allan Petersen, *The Myth of the Greener Grass*, (Wheaton, IL: Tyndale, 1983; rev. 1991), 29.

2. Petersen, 27.

3. Proverbs 2:16; 22:14; Mark 7:21–23; Romans 1:26–29; 1 Corinthians 6:9–10; Ephesians 5:5; Colossians 3:5–6; 1 Thessalonians 4:3–4; 1 Timothy 1:10–11; Hebrews 13:4.

4. 1 Corinthians 10:13.

5. 1 Peter 5:7.

6. Dr. Ed Wheat, *How to Save Your Marriage Alone*, (Wheaton, IL: Tyndale, 1983), 29–30.

7. Wheat, 31–32.

Chapter 7—Walk in Your Spouse's Shoes

1. Adapted from Jim Conway, *Making Real Friends in a Phony World*, (Grand Rapids, MI: Zondervan, 1991), 131.

Chapter 9—Deal with Emotional Clutter

1. Jim Conway, *Adult Children of Legal or Emotional Divorce*, (Downers Grove, IL: InterVarsity, 1990).

2. Beth E. Brown, *When You're Mom No. 2*, (Ann Arbor, MI: Servant, 1991).

Chapter 10—Consider the Career Pressure

1. From the research of Jim and Sally Conway as published in *Adult Children of Legal or Emotional Divorce* by Jim Conway, (Downers Grove, IL: InterVarsity, 1990).

2. Richard Bolles, *What Color Is Your Parachute?*, (San Francisco: Ten Speed Press, 1970, revised annually).

Chapter 11—Build Your Mate's Self-Esteem

1. 1 Corinthians 15:10.

Chapter 14—Flex, Change, and Grow

1. Sally Conway, *Your Husband's Mid-Life Crisis*, (Elgin, IL: David C. Cook, 1980, rev. 1987).

Chapter 15—Know Your Boundaries

1. Ronald Potter-Efron and Patricia Potter-Efron, *I Deserve Respect*, (Center City, MN: Hazeldon Educational Materials, 1989). This helpful booklet is available from Hazeldon, P.O. Box 176, Center City, MN 55012-0176. Telephone: 1-800-328-9000.

Chapter 17—Put Yourself in God's Hand

1. Psalm 40:1–4; Romans 7:14–25.

2. Romans 3:10–12; Isaiah 53:6; Romans 3:23.

3. Romans 5:8; 1 Corinthians 15:3–4; Ephesians 1:7.

4. John 3:16.

5. For example, see Matthew 7:9–11 and Psalm 103:13.

6. Romans 8:31–39.

7. John 10:27–30.

8. Psalm 5:12.

9. Psalm 61:3–4.

10. Psalm 61:4; Matthew 23:37.

11. Psalm 118:7.

12. Romans 8:31.

13. Psalm 138:8.

Chapter 18—Rebuild Carefully

1. Matthew 7:24–27.

2. From the chapter, "Forgiving the Past" by Jim Conway, *Adult Children of Legal or Emotional Divorce*, (Downers Grove, IL: InterVarsity, 1990), 205–220.

3. *Adult Children of Legal or Emotional Divorce*, 216.

4. Jim and Sally Conway, *Traits of a Lasting Marriage*, (Downers Grove, IL: InterVarsity, 1991).

5. For example, see H. Grunebaum, "Middle Age and Marriage: Affiliative Men and Assertive Women," *American Journal of Family*, Fall 1979, Vol. 7, No. 3, 46–50.

Chapter 19—Encourage Hurts to Heal

1. Lewis Smedes, *Forgive & Forget: Healing the Hurts We Don't Deserve*, (San Francisco: Harper & Row, 1984; New York: Pocket Books, div. of Simon and Schuster, 1986), pp. 125–157.

2. *Forgive & Forget*, 138.

3. David Seamands, *Healing for Damaged Emotions*, (Wheaton, IL: Victor, 1981), 128.

4. J. Allan Petersen, *The Myth of the Greener Grass*, (Wheaton, IL: Tyndale, 1983; rev. 1991), 139.

Chapter 20—Invest for a Lifetime

1. Matthew 25:14–30.

Chapter 21—Work for Restoration, Not Divorce

1. U.S. National Center for Health Statistics, *Monthly Vital Statistics Report*, Vol. 31, No. 12 (March 14, 1983).

2. Jim and Sally Conway, *Traits of a Lasting Marriage* (Downers Grove, IL: InterVarsity, 1991).

3. Hugh Carter and Paul C. Glick, *Marriage and Divorce: A Social and Economic Study*, rev. ed. (Cambridge, MA.: Harvard University, 1976).

Arthur J. Norton, "Family Life Cycle: 1980," *Journal of Marriage and the Family*, Vol. 45, No. 2 (May 1983), 267–275.

4. Edward Thorndike, *Adult Learning* (New York: Macmillan, 1928).

5. Charlotte B. Buhler (Malchowski), Edeltrud Baar, Lotte Danzinger-Schenk, Gertrud Falk, and others, *The Child and His Family*, Henry Beaument, trans., (New York: Harper, 1939).

6. Erik Erikson, *Childhood and Society* (New York: Norton, 1950).

7. Robert Havighurst and Ruth Albrecht, *Older People* (New York: McKay, 1953).

8. Bernice Neugarten, ed., *Personality in Middle and Late Life* (New York: Atherton, 1964).

9. Alan B. Knox, *Adult Development and Learning* (San Francisco: Jossey-Bass, 1977).

10. Daniel J. Levinson, *Seasons of a Man's Life* (New York: Alfred A. Knopf, 1978).

11. Roger Gould, *Transformations* (New York: Simon and Schuster, 1978).

12. Marjorie Lowenthal, Majda Thurner, and David Chiriboga, *Four Stages of Life* (San Franscisco: Jossey-Bass, 1975), 49–50.

13. William J. Lederer and Don D. Jackson, M.D., *The Mirages of Marriage* (New York: Norton, 1968), 27.

14. Floyd and Harriett Thatcher, *Long-Term Marriage* (Waco, TX: Word, 1980), 21.

15. Jim Conway, *Adult Children of Legal or Emotional Divorce* (Downers Grove, IL: InterVarsity, 1990).

16. Some of this material is taken from *Traits of a Lasting Marriage* by Jim and Sally Conway (Downers Grove, IL: InterVarsity, 1991).

17. James A. Peterson, *Married Love in the Middle Years* (New York: Association Press, 1968), 20.

18. Thatcher, 20.

19. Richard L. Strauss, *Marriage is for Love* (Wheaton, IL: Tyndale House Publishers, Inc., 1973), 9–10.

20. Jim Conway, *Men in Mid-Life Crisis* (Elgin, IL: David C. Cook, 1978).
Sally Conway, *Your Husband's Mid-Life Crisis* (Elgin, IL: David C. Cook,

1980, rev. 1987).

Jim & Sally Conway, *Women in Mid-Life Crisis* (Wheaton, IL: Tyndale, 1983).

Jim & Sally Conway, *Your Marriage Can Survive Mid-Life Crisis* (Nashville, TN: Nelson, 1987).

21. Eda J. LeShan, *The Wonderful Crisis of Middle Age* (New York: David McKay, 1973), 161.

Recommended Reading

Stephen Arterburn and David Stoop, *When Someone You Love Is Someone You Hate*, Word, 1988.

David Augsburger, *Caring Enough to Forgive/Not Forgive*, Regal, 1981.

Richard Bolles, *What Color Is Your Parachute?* Ten Speed, 1970, revised annually.

Beth E. Brown, *When You're Mom No. 2*, Servant, 1991.

Rich Buhler, *New Choices, New Boundaries*, Nelson, 1991.

Andre Bustanoby, *When Your Mate Is Not a Christian*, Zondervan, 1989.

Gary Chapman, *Hope for the Separated*, Moody, 1982.

Gary Collins, *You Can Make a Difference*, Zondervan, 1992.

Jim Conway, *Making Real Friends in a Phony World*, Zondervan, 1991.

Jim Conway, *Adult Children of Legal or Emotional Divorce*, InterVarsity, 1990.

Jim Conway, *Men in Mid-Life Crisis*, David C. Cook, 1978.

Sally Conway, *Your Husband's Mid-Life Crisis*, David C. Cook, 1980, rev. 1987.

Sally Conway, *Menopause: Help and Hope for This Passage*, Zondervan, 1990.

Jim and Sally Conway, *Women in Mid-Life Crisis*, Tyndale, 1983.

Jim and Sally Conway, *Maximize Your Mid-Life*, Tyndale, 1987.

Jim and Sally Conway, *Your Marriage Can Survive Mid-Life Crisis*, Nelson, 1987.

Jim and Sally Conway, *Traits of a Lasting Marriage*, InterVarsity, 1991.

Becki Conway Sanders, and Jim and Sally Conway, *Trusting God in a Family Crisis*, InterVarsity, 1992.

James Dobson, *What Wives Wish Their Husbands Knew About Women*, Tyndale, 1975.

Don and Jan Frank, *When Victims Marry Victims*, Here's Life, 1990.

Archibald Hart, *Healing Life's Hidden Addictions*, Servant, 1990.

Earl Henslin, *The Way Out of the Wilderness*, Nelson, 1991.

Gordon MacDonald, *Rebuilding Your Broken World*, Nelson, 1988.

Gavin and Patti MacLeod, *Back on Course*, Revell, 1987.

Josh McDowell, *Building Your Self-Image*, Tyndale, 1984.

J. Allan Petersen, *The Myth of the Greener Grass*, Tyndale, 1983; rev. 1991.

Dennis and Barbara Rainey, *Building Your Mate's Self-Esteem*, Here's Life, 1986.

Larry Richards, *When It Hurts Too Much to Wait*, Word, 1985.

David Seamands, *Healing for Damaged Emotions*, Victor, 1981.

David Seamands, *Healing of Memories*, Victor, 1985.

Jan Silvious, *Please Don't Say You Need Me*, Zondervan, 1989.

Gary Smalley and John Trent, *The Blessing*, Word, 1986.

Lewis Smedes, *Forgive & Forget: Healing the Hurts We Don't Deserve*, Harper and Row, 1984; Pocket Books, 1986.

Charles Swindoll, *Strike the Original Match*, Multnomah, 1980.

Jim Talley, *Reconcilable Differences*, Nelson, 1991.

Floyd and Harriett Thatcher, *Long-Term Marriage*, Word, 1980.

Ed Wheat, M.D., *How to Save Your Marriage Alone*, Zondervan, 1983.

Ed Wheat, M.D., *Intended for Pleasure*, Revell, 1977.

Ed and Gaye Wheat, *Love Life for Every Married Couple*, Zondervan, 1980.

Sandra Wilson, *Release from Shame*, InterVarsity, 1990.

H. Norman Wright, *Communication: Key to Your Marriage*, Regal, 1979.

Sally Christon Conway, M.S., and Jim Conway, Ph.D.

Jim and Sally are cofounders of **Mid-Life Dimensions/Christian Living Resources, Inc.,** a California-based organization that offers help to people struggling to save or rebuild their marriages.

Jim and Sally speak together at colleges, seminaries, churches, and retreat centers. They also make television appearances and can be heard on many radio programs. Besides their own books, which are listed in the Recommended Reading section, they have contributed to many other books and magazines. They previously were speakers on their own national daily radio program, **Mid-Life Dimensions**, broadcast on more than two hundred stations.

Jim served as a pastor for almost thirty years, while Sally served as pastor's wife. Sally also has been an elementary school remedial reading specialist. For five years Jim directed the Doctor of Ministry program at Talbot School of Theology, Biola University, and was associate professor of practical theology. Sally taught part-time at Talbot for five years.

Sally holds a Bachelor of Science degree in elementary education and a Master of Science degree in human development. Jim holds two master's degrees—one in psychology and one in theology—and two doctorates—a D.Min. in ministry and a Ph.D. in adult development and learning.

Jim and Sally have three daughters, three sons-in-law, three grandsons, and three granddaughters.

To contact Jim and Sally, write to them in care of Zondervan Publishing House, 5300 Patterson, S.E., Grand Rapids, MI 49530.

Around Atlanta

W I T H

Children

A GUIDE FOR FAMILY ACTIVITIES
Third Edition

Denise Black ◆ Janet Schwartz

Illustrations by Tonya Beach

LONGSTREET PRESS
Atlanta, Georgia

*To David and Nathan, my eager explorers, and to Bruce
for always supporting me in whatever I do. — D.B.*

*To Allison, Daniel and Ira, "the best family in the
whole wide world." — J.H.S.*

*And many thanks to Jill Dubin
for her enthusiasm, guidance and creative spirit.*

Published by
Longstreet Press, INC.
A subsidiary of Cox Newspapers,
A division of Cox Enterprises, Inc.
2140 Newmarket Parkway
Suite 118
Marietta, Georgia 30067

Printed in the United States of America

Third Edition, 2nd printing 1994

Library of Congress Catalog Card Number: 93-81141

ISBN 1-56352-133-4

This book was printed by Gilliland Printing, Incorporated, Arkansas City, KS

Cover illustration and design by Tonya Beach
Book design and typesetting by Laura McDonald

Table of Contents

We can hardly believe this is the third edition of *Around Atlanta with Children*. We are pleased and grateful that parents, grandparents, teachers and tourists have found this guidebook to be so valuable. In fact, the first two editions were so favorably received, we felt a desire and a responsibility to explore Atlanta once again to provide us all with an update on our ever-changing, diverse city. Indeed, we have unearthed many new and interesting places to go, clubs to join, trails to traverse and colorful festivals to attend. Some of our favorite discoveries are:

- Festival of Cultures—Atlanta's premier international festival
- IMAX Theatre at the Fernbank Museum of Natural History
- Cagle's Milk House—offering tours of the dairy
- Urban Nirvana Gallery—a unique combination of art and live animals
- Circus Arts Studio
- Kids Comedy Theatre
- Performing Arts Series for families
- Atlanta Chess Club
- Farmers Markets galore
- Dunwoody Nature Center
- Tennessee Aquarium in Chattanooga

While painstakingly updating all of the entries in the first two editions of *Around Atlanta with Children* and adding new ones, we found ourselves looking at many of the activities in a different light. Lo and behold, our children have gotten older, spanning kindergarten through upper elementary, so we have tried to be more conscious of broadening our listings and comments to include the views of the more worldly child.

So take this book in one hand, your child's hand in the other, and walk, drive, run and laugh all around our wonderful city. We wish you a *bon voyage, buona fortuna, safiri salama, buena suerte* and "a jolly good time."

Places
To Go

The listings in this chapter are arranged alphabetically to make it easier for you to locate all of the major attractions, museums, recreational facilities and historical sites in the metropolitan Atlanta area. If you cannot find an attraction that you expected to find, be sure to look in the next chapter, "Tidbits: More Good Things to Do," which contains information about the smaller or more unusual places to visit in this city.

We have placed symbols at the top of each listing to designate the general categories that best characterize the attraction. These symbols will help you recognize the essence of each "Place to Go" at a glance.

🍁   **Nature**

⚛   **Science**

◉   **Unique Attractions**

🏛   **History & Government**

★   **Performing Arts**

✎   **Fine Arts**

AMERICAN ADVENTURES

250 N. Cobb Pkwy. • (Next to White Water Park)
Marietta, Georgia 30062 • 424-9283

American Adventures is an exciting indoor/outdoor amusement park whose conceptual theme appeals to families with babies to pre-teens. The unique complex is bright, cheerful, clean and large, yet very manageable. Rain or shine, there is plenty to keep a family happily occupied for hours.

The outside portion of the park has lots of amusement rides, many of which have been added since the facility opened in 1990. For the younger crowd, the new Chuck Wagon, Tree Top Swings and Crazy Bus rides complement the Rio Grande Railroad train, Timberline Truckers (convoy trucks with steering wheels and horns that really beep), the Circus Spin animal ride, and the Barnstormers' airplanes where children can shoot a noisy gun and steer the plane up and down as it goes around.

Older kids who are racing enthusiasts can drive the Formula K cars. (If children are not quite tall enough to go it alone, parents can chauffeur the kids around the track!) Children who meet the height requirement can drive the Bumper Cars solo, and those smaller may co-pilot with parents. Our three and six-year-olds smiled and laughed through both of these great rides even though they were only passengers. The braver crowd can try the Balloon Ride, which goes higher and faster than the other rides; the Ridgeline Roller Coaster, a small-scale introduction to a fast and jerky roller coaster ride; American Revolution's spinning tea cups; and Galleon, a pirate ship that swings to and fro in a very high arc. Finally, there is the Hidden Harbor miniature golf course, complete with fun and scary sound effects.

An old-fashioned carousel ride and several interactive stations top the list of indoor attractions. Best of all for young children is Professor Plinker's Laboratory. Allow yourselves plenty of time to enjoy this play area because your children will not want to leave. Kids and parents take off their shoes and jump into Playport, a large area about two or three feet deep filled with plastic balls, with connecting slides and climbing rope areas. Children can also play with lots of Roller Racers and other fun equipment. The new Imagination Station appeals to pre-schoolers with its funny mirrors, craft corner, Bubbleworks, face painting, shadow maker, Storybook Theater and more. The main area of the rather typical Penny Arcade is geared toward school-age children, but a new addition offers a few games for preschoolers—easy basketball, little skee ball and Whack the Crocodile.

- Please note that signs are posted that inform parents that outdoor rides will not be halted midstream just because a child might be terrified. Watch the rides with your young child and discuss them ahead of time to try to gauge if your child is ready for the experience. Be careful. From personal experience I can say that it can be quite upsetting for a parent to see their child frightened and be helpless to do anything about it.

- Seasonal special events for Halloween, Christmas and Easter are a real hit, as are the two birthday party plans ($8.49 and $9.49 per child).

- There is a large, reasonably priced restaurant in the park and a new gift shop. Water fountains are also provided.

- The women's restroom has a changing table.

   * Handicapped access is available.

Hours: The park is open year-round from morning to evening. The hours change seasonally, so please call ahead.

Admission: There is a rather complex pricing policy with several options and daily specials. Tickets may be purchased separately for individual activities, but a better deal for most families is the All Day Fun Pass for $13.00 per child and $4.99 per adult. You might seriously consider the new Annual Pass for $39.99, which permits one child and one parent unlimited

use of the park for one year. (Exception: only one
Great Race ride per visit.) The pass pays for itself in
just two visits. Parking is $2.00 per vehicle.

Directions: Take I-75 to Exit #113, and follow the signs to
N. Cobb Pkwy. and the park, about 8 miles north
of downtown Atlanta.

ATLANTA BOTANICAL GARDEN

1345 Piedmont Rd. (between 14th St. and Monroe Dr.)
P.O. Box 77246 • Atlanta, Georgia 30357
24-hour recorded message: 876-5858
Offices: 876-5859 • Plant Hotline: 888-GROW
Plantmobile: 881-LEAF

The Atlanta Botanical Garden is a great place to go for a hike in the
woods, to smell spring flowers, to stroll through beautiful gardens,
or experience a tropical environment and commune with some rare
and exotic plants.

The map you get upon entering the garden is helpful in planning your
tour route and locating such essential services as drinking fountains
and restrooms. Once you orient yourself, you will realize that your
family can make a complete overview of the garden area before anyone gets tired. On subsequent visits you may want to focus in on just
a few areas, spending more time at each. When your family is in a
hiking mood, visit Storza Woods for 15 acres of walking trails
through one of five remaining hardwood forests in Atlanta. And for
an easier walk, visit the Upper Woodlands paved trail—it's great for
strollers. Or just wander around the display gardens and explore the
rose, herb, summer bulb and rock gardens, and the small but tran-
quil Japanese Garden.

The Dorothy Chapman Fuqua Conservatory deserves a special mention. The conservatory is a $5.5–million haven for thousands of tropical, desert, Mediterranean and endangered plants from around the world. You will see plants with leaves as big as small children, stunning desert flowers, Cavendish banana trees, a cocoa tree, and a vining orchid (*Vanilla planifolia*) from which we get the vanilla bean. On one of our visits we saw the amazing Ant Plants, an ecosystem wherein plant and ants feed off of and nourish each other.

Look for the special display showcasing the Olympic olive tree which was presented to the citizens of Atlanta from the citizens of Olympia, Greece in 1992. The tree is being nurtured at the garden and will remain there until the centennial celebration of the modern day Olympics begins in Atlanta in 1996. Visit the garden. You won't be disappointed!

- A good time to visit the garden is during the twice-a-year Plant Sales, the Fall Gardening Festival, Country Christmas, the Spring and Fall Moon Strolls, or the many flower shows and special events held throughout the year.

- The garden offers a selection of classes for children age 6–12 covering many diverse topics relating to nature and science. Another special program provides Brownie Scouts with an opportunity to earn three different badges at the garden. During the summer months, there are six week-long sessions of Environmental Summer Day Camp where children age 5–11 have an opportunity to explore nature and their environment.

- The Sheffield Botanical Library has begun expanding its children's collection, and the garden's library now has about 160 titles that cover a broad spectrum of topics for children. The non-circulating library is open to the public during regular hours.

- Self-guided tours are being developed for school children visiting the garden, complete with child-oriented activities and information. A Plantmobile outreach program is also available for schools and community groups.

- Picnicking is not permitted, but an informal cafe-style lunch is served Tuesday–Sunday from 11:30 a.m.–2:00 p.m., April through October on the Lanier Terrace overlooking the Rose Garden. Or combine a picnic in nearby Piedmont Park with your visit to the garden.

- There is an attractive gift shop jam-packed with cards, knick-knacks, garden supplies and lots of books for the serious and casual gardener and for children. A small greenhouse to the rear of the shop is stocked with healthy, interesting plants, many of which were grown in the garden's greenhouses.

- Strollers are not permitted in the conservatory.

- Restrooms and water fountains are available. Handicapped access is available for most of the garden. Call for more information.

Hours: *Garden:* Open Tuesday–Sunday from 9:00 a.m.–6:00 p.m. Longer hours during daylight savings time. Closed on Mondays and major holidays. *Conservatory:* Open Tuesday–Sunday from 10:00 a.m.–6:00 p.m. Longer hours during daylight savings time. Closed on Mondays and major holidays.

Admission: Cost is $5.00/adults; $4.00/seniors; $3.00/children age 6–12; and children under 6 are free. Free on Thursday after 1:00 p.m. A yearly Family Membership is $50.00 and includes many privileges, plus free admission.

Directions: Enter on Piedmont Rd. at The Prado, one block
south of Monroe Dr. and one block north of
14th St. By bus, take the #36 N. Decatur bus from
MARTA's Art Center Station directly to the garden.
On Sunday, take the #31 Lindbergh bus from
MARTA's Five Points or Lindbergh Station directly
to the garden.

ATLANTA CELEBRITY WALK

P. O. Box 54262, Atlanta, Georgia 30308 • 662-4348

The Celebrity Walk, Atlanta's version of the Hollywood Walk of Fame, contains the names of fourteen famous Georgians in a marble walkway beginning in front of the Chamber of Commerce Building on International Boulevard at Marietta Street. As more inductees are added, the walkway will stretch six blocks, going east along International Boulevard to Peachtree Street and Piedmont Avenue, connecting CNN and the Georgia World Congress Center with the Georgia Dome and Peachtree Center. The first fourteen inductees were Margaret Mitchell, author of *Gone With the Wind*; baseball great Hank Aaron; former President Jimmy Carter; civil rights leader Dr. Martin Luther King, Jr.; musician and singer Ray Charles; developer and architect John Portman; former Mayor Andrew Young; anesthesia developer Crawford W. Long; Girl Scouts founder Juliette Gordon Lowe; Coca-Cola founder and philanthropist Robert Woodruff; singer Lena Horne; newspaper editor Henry Grady; Delta Air Lines founder C.E. Woolman; and entrepreneur Ted Turner. Each marble slab bears a bronze nameplate and a bronze phoenix, the symbol of Atlanta, lying on a marble field sandblasted with the shape of the State of Georgia. About 46 more Georgians are up for nomination, including entertainers James Brown, Little Richard, Kim Basinger, Burt Reynolds and Gladys Knight. The public is encouraged to send in their nominations to the address on the preceding page. Long-term plans may also include an Atlanta Celebrity Walk Museum!

ATLANTA HERITAGE ROW

55 Upper Alabama St.
Atlanta, Georgia 30303 • 584-7879

On the Upper Alabama Street level of Underground Atlanta lies Atlanta Heritage Row, a small but unique museum showcasing important events and people in Atlanta's history. Dr. Martin Luther King, Jr., Harts-field Airport and the Civil War are all recognized in an interactive exhibit hall. Displays have been designed so visitors do not merely walk passively by, but instead, find themselves right in the middle of a display, able to touch, hear or experience the presentation. At the end of the exhibit area, visitors may enter an auditorium that features a brief film chronicling the history of Atlanta. We recommend a trip to this museum for children above pre-school age.

- Special events are occasionally sponsored by the museum.

- Visit the Olympic Experience, also on the Upper Alabama Street level, where you can learn more about the Olympic games and browse among a huge selection of ACOG merchandise.

Hours: Open Tuesday–Saturday from 10:00 a.m.–5:00 p.m., and Sunday from 12 noon–5:00 p.m. Closed Mondays.

Admission: Cost is $3.00/adults; $2.50/seniors and teenagers ages 13–18; $2.00/children age 4–12; and children under 4 are free.

Directions: Atlanta Heritage Row is located in Underground
Atlanta at the Upper Level between Peachtree St.
and Central Ave. at Alabama St. It is two blocks
west of the Georgia State Capitol Building. Exit at
the MARTA Five Points Station.

ATLANTA HISTORY CENTER – BUCKHEAD

Museum of Atlanta History
McElreath Hall • Tullie Smith House
Swan House • Gardens • Swan Coach House Restaurant
3101 Andrews Dr., N.W.
Atlanta, Georgia 30305 • 814-4000

The impressive Atlanta History Center, operated by the Atlanta
Historical Society and founded in 1926, is the largest history museum in Georgia and includes McElreath Hall, Tullie Smith House, Swan
House, extensive gardens, Swan Coach House Restaurant and a recent
addition, the Museum of Atlanta History. One admission ticket
includes all exhibits, museums, house tours and gardens.

MUSEUM OF ATLANTA HISTORY. The modern 83,000-square-
foot museum honors Atlanta's heritage by creatively tackling the challenging task of representing Atlanta's cultural diversity through the
permanent centerpiece exhibit "Metropolitan Frontiers: Atlanta
1835–2000." Temporary exhibits also intelligently portray Atlanta's
heritage. Also to be housed in the museum are some 25,000 items
from the Beverly M. DuBose, Jr. Civil War Collection, considered one
of the finest in the country, containing items from both sides of the
war; the Dickey Collection of 800 Civil War armaments; 32,000 decorative arts items, including the Shutze Collection of furniture, silver, ceramics and paintings presently housed in the Swan House; more
than 2,500 costumes and accessories dating from the antebellum peri-

od to the present; and 100 quilts and 500 textile items, including an extensive collection of lace and shawls from the 1860s. The new facility includes two classrooms, the Kennedy Theater, a museum shop and cafe, with discovery rooms for hands-on activities in the works.

McELREATH HALL. McElreath Hall contains a library and archives of local and state history, which includes one of the city's largest photograph collections; the Cherokee Garden Library, which is a gardening and horticultural research collection of current and rare material; an auditorium; and meeting rooms where lectures and special events are held year-round. Some materials from the Atlanta History Museum's permanent collection are exhibited here.

THE TULLIE SMITH FARM. The 1840s Tullie Smith Farm is typical of a pre-Civil War working farm with a plain style plantation house, kitchen, barn, well house, storage house, smokehouse, corn crib, log cabin and blacksmith shop. Tours sometimes include demonstrations of folk skills, such as basketry, open-hearth cooking, whittling and smithing. The small cabin and out-buildings provide the setting for the annual fall Folklife Festival, the spring Storytelling Festival, and Sheep to Shawl Day, the best times by far for you to bring your younger children to see this attraction.

THE SWAN HOUSE. The Swan House is a classically-styled mansion built in 1928 by an Atlanta family whose fortunes were made in railroads, cotton, banking and real estate. Tours of this opulent home presently include a look at the Philip Trammell Shutze decorative arts collection. (We're talking fragile pieces, so we suggest you don't bring young children here!) Behind the Swan House is a Victorian playhouse filled with toys authentic to the era, which may be of interest to your child.

GARDENS. There are over 32 acres of beautifully landscaped gardens and woodlands, including The Mary Howard Gilbert Quarry Garden, Frank A. Smith Rhododendron Garden, Swan and Tullie Smith gardens and the one-half mile "Swan Woods Trail," which is labeled for a self-guided study. The grounds and trails are pretty and educational, and are recommended for children, especially if they need a nice break after touring the rest of the center.

SWAN COACH HOUSE RESTAURANT. The restaurant (261-0636) is located in the former garage and servants' quarters for the Swan House. Lunch is served Monday–Saturday from 11:30 a.m.–2:30 p.m. A gift shop (261-0224) and art gallery (261-2636), open Monday–Saturday from 10:00 a.m.–4:00 p.m., are also housed here.

• There are occasional one-day classes and lots of weekend workshops and special events offered at the museum. Additionally, the center hosts festivals and special events, such as "An Old Fashioned Christmas" and "The Civil War Revisited: Atlanta Encampment," a living history extravaganza.

• There is a large and attractive gift shop housed in the Museum of Atlanta History, with traditional crafts, educational toys, books, jewelry, Civil War items and *Gone With the Wind* memorabilia.

• Restrooms and water fountains are available. Handicapped access to certain attractions is available, but call ahead for parking directions.

Hours: Open Monday–Saturday from 9:00 a.m.–5:30 p.m., and Sunday from 12 noon–5:30 pm. Reduced hours on Memorial Day, July 4th and Labor Day. Closed on Thanksgiving, Christmas Eve, Christmas Day and New Year's Day.

Admission: Cost is $6.00/adults; $4.50/students and seniors; $3.00/for youths 6–17; and children 5 and under are free. The center is free on Thursdays after 1:00

p.m. Group rates are available. A yearly Family
Membership is $50.00 and includes free admission.

Directions: Take the W. Paces Ferry exit on I-75 to Northside Dr.
and go east on W. Paces Ferry Rd. toward Buckhead
for just over 2 miles. Turn right on Andrews Dr.
(not W. Andrews). The AHC is the first driveway
on the left.

By MARTA, exit at Lenox station. Transfer to bus
#23 to Peachtree St. and W. Paces Ferry Rd. Walk 3
blocks west to Andrews Dr. Turn left and the AHC
is the first driveway on the left.

ATLANTA HISTORY CENTER – DOWNTOWN

140 Peachtree St.
Atlanta, Georgia 30303 • 814-4150

If you wish to explore Atlanta's history on any level, the Atlanta
History Center's small downtown annex is a logical and helpful place
to begin. The friendly staff can tell you the how, what, when and
where for exploring Atlanta's history with your family. The center presents numerous videos on Atlanta's history, including a
great 18-minute overview, free of charge. Numerous brochures are
available which provide up-to-date and enticing details on special
walking tours (guided and unguided) and major attractions found
in Atlanta. You may also browse through their research library and
view changing exhibits highlighting architecture, folk art, politics
and other topics about Atlanta.

•   Occasionally, the center presents free lectures and special
events, some of which might be of interest to older children,

such as programs featuring cartoonists, storytellers and craftspeople.

• The center's gift shop is small but unusual, stocked with books, toys, crafts and other memorabilia.

• Handicapped access is available to the first floor only.

Hours: Open Monday–Saturday from 10:00 a.m.–6:00 p.m. Call about holiday closing dates.

Admission: Free.

Directions: The Atlanta History Center is located downtown in the restored 1911 Hillyer Building. It is across the street from the MARTA Peachtree Center Station (take the Ellis St. exit from the station) and is convenient to the High Museum at Georgia-Pacific Center and the Atlanta-Fulton County Public Library.

ATLANTA MUSEUM

537 Peachtree St., N.E. • Atlanta, Georgia 30308 • 872-8233

Housed in the historical Rufus M. Rose House (the family residence of the founders of Four Roses Liquor) and listed on the National Register of Historic Homes, this curiosity of a museum (or historical flea market?) is a hodge-podge of over 2,500 items packed into eight small rooms on the upper level. Among its more notable possessions are an original model of Eli Whitney's cotton gin, furniture, books and photographs from Margaret Mitchell's house, a cache of Confederate weapons, Indian artifacts, a Japanese "Zero" airplane, Hitler's cigar box and other Nazi memorabilia, a stone from King Tut's tomb, Emperor Haile Selassie's throne and Queen Victoria's shawl. Just a sample . . . there's much more!

We recommend that you think twice about taking small children to visit the museum. (What would you do with their curious hands and wriggly bodies?). If you bring older children here, be prepared to answer a lot of questions; the collection is neither organized nor well-labeled.

* Handicapped access and restroom facilities are not available.

Hours: Open Monday–Friday from 10:00 a.m.–5:00 p.m.
             Open on weekends for groups of 20 or more, but
             by appointment only. We suggest you call ahead to
             make sure the museum is open.

Admission: Admission is $3.00/adults and $2.00/children.

Directions: The museum is about two blocks south of North
             Ave. on Peachtree St. across from Crawford Long
             Hospital and its medical museum.

BIG SHANTY MUSEUM

2829 Cherokee St. • Kennesaw, Georgia 30144 • 427-2117

Big Shanty Museum is a must for Civil War history buffs and children of all ages, but especially for children who are already train fanatics.

Big Shanty, the original name of the city of Kennesaw, was the start of the "Great Locomotive Chase" which took place during the

Civil War. (Yes, Disney made a movie about it!) You can touch history here, as it is only 100 yards from the spot where the locomotive "The General" was stolen by Northern troops on April 12, 1862, during the famous Andrews Railroad Raid debacle. The Northerners' plans were foiled when pursuers boarded the locomotive "Texas" (now enshrined at the Cyclorama), caught up with the raiders and recaptured The General for the Confederacy. The General continued to operate for the South throughout the War.

The museum, a converted cotton gin, houses The General's restored engine and tender. And is it ever an impressive sight! After you have had a chance to walk around the General, proceed upstairs to watch a narrated slide presentation about the raid. It will be easier for you to understand the importance of the museum and get answers to the many questions you will be asked by your children, once you view the program. Afterwards, when you go back downstairs and look at The General again, you will see the train in a different light. Next, look at the far wall for several historical photographs of The General as it looked way back then. Look at the Civil War relics in the room that help make the past more concrete and understandable to children as well as adults. There are quilts, clothing worn by ordinary people and soldiers, examples of food eaten by soldiers, stone bullets, a fife, bugle, both Confederate and State of Georgia money, news articles, personal notes and a miniature replica of Kennesaw and The General as they were over a century ago.

- On your way out, walk through the gift shop, but be forewarned—the toy engines, trains and other small items are very appealing to small hands.

- To make a day of it, we suggest you visit Kennesaw Mountain Battlefield Park for a picnic and hike, and then stop in at Big Shanty. Or visit during the Kennesaw Big Shanty Festival held in both April and October.

- Parking is free across the street by the old depot.

- For more information about "The Great Locomotive Chase" and to see the restored "Texas," we suggest you visit The Atlanta Cyclorama.

- Restrooms and water fountains are available. Handicapped access is available for the downstairs portion of the museum.

Hours: Open Monday–Saturday from 10:00 a.m.–5:00 p.m., and Sunday from 12 noon–5:30 p.m. Closed on Easter, Thanksgiving, Christmas and New Year's Day.

Admission: Cost is $3.00/adults; $1.50/children age 7–15; and children under 7 are free. Maximum cost per family is $10.00.

Directions: Go north on I-75 to Exit #117 (Chastain Rd.), and make a left on Cherokee St. Follow the signs to Big Shanty (about 2 miles). The museum is about 25 miles north of downtown Atlanta.

CALLANWOLDE FINE ARTS CENTER

980 Briarcliff Rd. • Atlanta, Georgia 30306 • 872-5338

Callanwolde is a Tudor-styled mansion built in 1920, as the home of Charles Howard Candler, eldest son of Coca-Cola founder, Asa G. Candler. The 27,000-square-foot mansion, which is now listed on the National Register of Historic Places, is surrounded by 12 acres of lawns, formal gardens and a small conservatory. But, most importantly, Callanwolde is a most unique art center.

Callanwolde presents a year-round program of concerts, performances, lectures, recitals, poetry readings, and productions for children by guest artists and Callanwolde's affiliate groups—the Poetry Committee, The Young Singers of Callanwolde, the Apprentice Dance Company and the Community Concert Band. The mansion is a marvelous location for musical performances since the sound system, which features a magnificent 3,752–pipe Aeolian organ, the largest of its kind in playable condition, was especially designed for and built into the mansion and extends to every major room in the house. Callanwolde is often the location for special events throughout the year, such as Christmas at Callanwolde every December. (See our chapter on "Festivals and Special Events" for more information about this event.)

Also, housed on the second floor of the historic mansion is The Callanwolde Gallery, presenting exhibits by local artists year-round, and the Art Shop, a gift store filled with collectibles created by artists and crafts people.

We strongly suggest that you and your children visit Callanwolde only in conjunction with a festival, performance or class. The grounds, conservancy and gardens, although quite pretty, are also formal and not the best place for a picnic or day's outing with high-spirited children.

- Callanwolde has a large selection of classes and workshops for preschoolers through adults, including offerings in dance, drama, painting, photography, pottery, writing and textiles. The Summer Arts Camp, "Kaleidoscope," for preschoolers and older children, includes visual arts, puppetry, writing, movement and dramatics.

- Callanwolde is available for private parties and events. Call 872-5338 for information.

- Restrooms and water fountains are available. Handicapped access is available, but call ahead for special directions.

Hours: Callanwolde and the art gallery are open
                  Monday–Saturday from 10:00 a.m.–3:00 p.m.;
                  the Art Shop is open Tuesday–Saturday from
                  10:00 a.m.–3:00 p.m.; and the Conservatory is
                  open Monday–Friday from 10:00 a.m.–2:00 p.m.
                  Closed on all legal holidays.

Admission: Admission to the grounds and art gallery is free. A
                  special tour of the mansion is available by appoint-
                  ment for groups of 15 or more at a cost of $1.50
                  for adults and 50¢ for children.

Directions: Callanwolde is located in the Druid Hills/Emory
                  section of Atlanta on Briarcliff Rd. in between
                  Ponce de Leon Ave. and N. Decatur Rd. Take I-85
                  to the N. Druid Hills Rd. exit and head east. Turn
                  right on Briarcliff Rd. and head south. Callanwolde
                  will be on the right side of the road, in between
                  N. Decatur Rd. and Ponce de Leon Ave.

CARTER PRESIDENTIAL CENTER
MUSEUM OF THE JIMMY CARTER LIBRARY

One Copenhill Ave. • *Atlanta, Georgia 30307* • *331-3942*

Housed in the Carter Presidential Center complex, the Museum of the
Jimmy Carter Library memorializes the life, career and presidency of
Jimmy Carter. It also offers a glimpse of the office of the American presidency and addresses modern day issues such as war and peace,
hunger and poverty, human rights, the environment and the economy.

The permanent exhibits in the museum are quite interesting and highly recommended for older children. We were also pleasantly surprised

to discover how much fun our preschoolers had here; there was much to see and do, and enough space and hands-on activities to keep everyone happy. Exhibits include a replica of the Oval Office as it appeared during Jimmy Carter's term; an interactive video display allowing us an opportunity to participate in one of Jimmy Carter's famous "town-meetings;" a special video presentation of children's thoughts on the presidency called "If I Were President;" a glimpse into the voluminous stacks in the Jimmy Carter Library; personal aspects of the presidency, such as a collection of elegant gifts from foreign leaders; and an exhibit recognizing Rosalyn Carter's important role as "Partner of the President." The museum also has changing exhibits which explore various historical aspects of the presidency and eras in America's history.

After visiting the museum, our family had a grown-up lunch at Copenhill Cafe, the center's restaurant, followed by a stroll through the lovely landscaped Japanese gardens which overlook downtown Atlanta.

- Members of the public are not allowed access to the library or the remainder of the Carter Presidential Center unless they have a legitimate research purpose.

- Restrooms, water fountains and handicapped access are available.

Hours: The museum is open Monday–Saturday from 9:00 a.m.–4:45 p.m., and on Sunday from 12 noon–4:45 p.m. Tours are available by special appointment. The museum is closed on Thanksgiving, Christmas and New Year's Day. The restaurant is open daily from 11:00 a.m.–4:00 p.m.

Admission: Cost is $4.00/adults; $3.00/seniors; and children under 16 are free.

Directions: *Going south*: Take I-75/85 south to Exit #100 (North Ave.) and turn left. Continue to N. Highland Ave. and turn right. Continue one block to Cleburne Ave. and turn right into the Carter Center parking lot. *Going north*: Take I-75/85 north to Exit #96A (Boulevard/Glen Iris) and turn left at dead-end. Turn right at Highland Ave. and continue ¹/₂ mile to Cleburne Ave. and turn left into the Carter Center parking lot. Parking is free.

CENTER FOR PUPPETRY ARTS

1404 Spring St., NW • Atlanta, Georgia 30309 • 873-3391

The Center for Puppetry Arts is the most comprehensive puppetry center in the entire nation, attracting masters of puppetry from all over the world! The puppeteers are serious professional students of world puppetry and its history. Their extensive knowledge of various culture's puppets, traditions and stories is demonstrated in productions of classic tales that have always appealed to American children, such as *Pinocchio, Rumpelstiltskin, Tom Thumb* and *The Velveteen Rabbit*. For the next few years, the center's Summer Festivals will feature performances by critically acclaimed international puppeteers. The productions are always unique, interesting, and fun, fun, fun! Rod puppets, full body puppets, hand puppets or marionettes might be used by black clothed puppeteers on stage in a theatre where every seat is a good seat. After each production, which lasts about an hour, the puppeteers remove their head coverings and explain to the audience just how they hold and manipulate the puppets. They then act out a couple of minutes of the performance in this manner, so children can get a "behind the scenes" glimpse of the voice, rhythm and fundamentals of puppet movement.

Before or after the performance, you should visit the center's International Museum, which features one of the largest exhibits of puppets in North America. There is a fascinating permanent collection of over 150 hand, string, rod and shadow puppets, including tiny pre-Columbian clay puppets, ritualistic African figures, puppets from Asia, the Soviet Union, South America, North America and Europe, and even Muppets by the late Jim Henson. One room in the museum is reserved for special exhibits, which might include a memorial exhibit dedicated to a great puppeteer, or an in-depth study and celebration of a contemporary puppetry artist. In PUPPETWORKS, the hands-on display area, children may operate rod, hand, string and shadow puppets on various stages.

- "Create a Puppet Workshop" and other innovative classes are offered year-round for children age 4 and up. Workshops are held on weekdays and Saturdays and last a little over an hour. Participants have an opportunity to create a unique puppet and learn how to bring it to life. "Puppet Camp" and "Create a Big Production Camp" are offered during the summer months. Call for information, costs and reservations.

- The Family Series consists of several puppet shows offered during the regular season. The Summer Festival consists of six different shows by famous international puppet companies (performed in English). See our chapter on "Performing Arts for Children" for more information about these series.

- You can have a puppet-making Birthday Party in a special room for children age 4–12 years. Combine the party with a puppet show which will be sure to delight everyone. Call for details.

- The annual "Travel Fund Benefit" in the spring features games, face painting, puppet shows, puppet making and refreshments.

- There is a small, but interesting gift shop.

- There are restroom facilities and water fountains. Handicapped access is available.

Hours: *Museum*: Open Monday–Saturday from 9:00 a.m.–4:00 p.m., and evenings on performance nights. *Ticket Office*: Monday–Friday from 9:00 a.m.–5:00 p.m., and Saturday from 9:00 a.m.–4:00 p.m. Closed on major holidays and Sundays.

Admission: Museum cost is $3.00/adult and $2.00/child, but complimentary for those attending a show. Shows are $5.50 per person. Reservations are required. The Family Series of three shows costs $9.23. A Summer Festival pass for six shows costs $18.00. There are several levels of annual membership, the minimum contribution being $25.00. Benefits include a 10% discount on tickets, classes, work-shops and gift shop purchases, as well as preferential seating for Family Series performances.

Directions: The center is located in midtown Atlanta. *Going south*: Take I-85/75 south to Exit #29. Take a right on Spring St. and the center will be a block and a half on the right. *Going north:* Take I-85/75 north to the 10th St. exit and turn right. Go to W. Peachtree St. and turn left. At 18th St. turn left and the center will be a block and a half on the left. Parking is free behind the center.

CHATTAHOOCHEE NATURE CENTER

9135 Willeo Rd. • Roswell, Georgia 30075 • 992-2055

Located on the river, the Chattahoochee Nature Center is a community nature preserve that is manageable and enjoyable for families with young children and, at the same time, holds the rapt attention of older children. Walking from your car to the nature center building, you will first notice the native garden clearly marked with plant identification labels. How many do your children recognize?

Once inside the building, you can view changing exhibits of live animals (sometimes snakes, opossums or turtles) and visit the nature store which stocks an intriguing collection of nature books, bird feeders, bird seed, rocks, T-shirts and many other items, including small bags of duck and fish food.

Then go out the back door to the duck pond where you can feed the ducks, fish and turtles inhabiting the especially serene and scenic pond near the river; and visit the bald eagles, a small mammal habitat and a hawk and owl aviary. Marked trails through the surrounding woodlands and a boardwalk through the marshes across the road are easy to traverse.

- After-school naturalist classes are scheduled during the school year for kids age 4–11. "Summer Nature Camp" for children age 6–10 offers sessions covering different topics about nature.

- Enjoy guided evening canoe rides during the summer down the Chattahoochee River (children must be at least 8 years of age), weekend guided walks, and moonlight prowls around the forest.

- No picnicking is permitted on the grounds of the center, but Chattahoochee River Park, which has picnic facilities and a playground, is only ½ mile away on Azalea Drive.

- There are bins in the parking lot area for recycling newspapers, glass (sorted by color) and aluminum cans.

- There are restrooms and water fountains. Handicapped access is available.

Hours: Open Monday–Saturday from 9:00 a.m.–5:00 p.m., and Sunday from 12 noon–5:00 p.m. Closed on legal holidays.

Admission: Cost is $2.00/adults and $1.00/children and senior citizens. A yearly Family Membership is $35.00 and includes free admission, discounts on classes and purchases in the nature shop, a free subscription to the monthly newsletter, and access to special member events.

Directions: The center is located outside I-285 in Roswell. Go north on Georgia 400 and get off at the Northridge exit. Go west to Roswell Rd. Turn right on Roswell Rd. and then left on Azalea Dr. (just after crossing over the Chattahoochee River). Take Azalea Dr. to Willeo Rd. passing by Chattahoochee River Park. Take a left on Willeo Rd. and travel 1/4 mile to the nature center, which will be on your right.

CHATTAHOOCHEE RIVER
NATIONAL RECREATION AREA

Park Headquarters & Information • 1978 Island Ford Pkwy.
Dunwoody, Georgia 30350 • 399-8070 or 952-4419

The Chattahoochee River is a national treasure and, luckily for us, it is right in our backyard. The Chattahoochee National Recreation Area is a series of beautiful park lands along a 48-mile stretch of the river. Even if you have already been to certain portions of the park, we strongly urge you to visit Park Headquarters and pick up a fistful of their informative brochures (especially maps of hiking trails so you don't get lost) to find out more about the recreation area.

SCENIC TRAILS: Some brochures describe the flora and fauna that inhabit the area, while others contain individual maps that detail scenic trails along the river and information on trail difficulty, parking, picnicking, telephones, restrooms, launch areas, handicapped access and horseback riding. We can attest that the trails are well marked and for the most part, appropriate for families with young children, babies in backpacks and dogs on leashes. All the ingredients you need for many wonderful and varied Sunday afternoons are along the river!

- **Sope Creek/Historic Mill Trail** system is located off Johnson Ferry and Paper Mill Rds. Take a pleasant woodlands stroll along the Sibley Pond Loop, but take care to watch your children on the unrailed platform that protrudes into the lake. Or hike along the East Bank Trail, taking care while crossing over Sope Creek, to view historic ruins of the Marietta Paper Mill. Built in 1854 by slave labor, the factory manufactured newsprint, stationery, and paper for Confederate money until it was destroyed by the Union troops during the Civil War. Later rebuilt, the mill supplied many types of paper, including wrapping paper and paper for the *Atlanta Journal* until 1902. There is a small parking lot at the start of the trail system on Paper Mill Road.

- **Vickery Creek Trail** system includes an easy hike from Allenbrook, 227 S. Atlanta St., Roswell, to the creek via the Ivy Woolen Mill ruins.

- **Island Ford Trail** begins at Park Headquarters and is a short, easy walk down to the Chattahoochee River. The walk alongside the river is ideal for small kids, grandparents, and dogs on leashes, with optional forks in the path for a more moderate hike. The trails are well marked with signs indicating trail configurations and degrees of difficulty. Our kids are always eager to head off to Island Ford.

FISHING: Other brochures provide information about fishing on the Chattahoochee, a designated trout stream. You should be aware that a valid Georgia fishing license with a trout stamp is required for those 16 years of age and older. Also, live bait, such as minnows, may not be used. For more information about fishing, see our chapter on "Sports and Recreation," or call Park Information.

CANOEING & RAFTING: Brochures are also available about boating, rafting, canoeing and kayaking on the river, including advice on river and land safety. Children of all ages may boat with families on the river, but a U.S. Coast Guard approved life preserver is required for each person aboard any water craft, including inner tubes! If you need to rent a raft or other water craft, see our chapter on "Sports and Recreation" for listings, or contact the Chattahoochee Outdoor Center (the park concessioner) at 395-6851. If you would like information on river conditions at Buford Dam call 945-1466, and at Morgan Falls Dam call 329-1455.

SPECIAL PROGRAMS: The park offers free ranger guided winter walks, which we recommend for families with older children, as these leisurely walks last anywhere from 2–3 hours. You can discover the many scenic trails along the Chattahoochee and learn about Native Americans, early settlers, plant life and wildlife. In addition to winter walks, there are nature and cultural programs held throughout the year at all branch units of the park.

CLAYTON COUNTY HISTORICAL TOURS

Clayton County Convention & Visitors Bureau
8712 Tara Blvd. • Jonesboro, Georgia 30236 • 478-4800

Clayton County is rich with antebellum plantation homes and historic mansions, cemeteries, churches and courthouses. The Convention & Visitors Bureau has compiled a brochure called "Visitors Guide Clayton County," which includes a Historic Jonesboro Driving Tour listing that includes approximately thirty-two of the county's historic sites and attractions. Also listed in the brochure are other Clayton County attractions, including two excellent stops for children: the Atlanta State Farmers Market, discussed in our section on Farmers Markets; and the Reynolds' Nature Preserve, a woodland and wildlife refuge, described in our section on "Ecology & Nature, Science, History & Politics."

Most notable among the historical Jonesboro plantations on the tour are Ashley Oaks Mansion and Stately Oaks Plantation Community. Ashley Oaks was constructed between 1879–1880, and is an example of a planter's town home. The refurbished home is open for tours Tuesday–Friday from 11:00 a.m.–3:00 p.m. (Group tours and other events are available by appointment.) Stately Oaks Plantation Community is the headquarters for Historical Jonesboro and the site of Clayton County's annual Fall Festival, moonlight storytelling sessions, as well as other special events throughout the year. Besides housing the 1839 Greek Revival-style mansion, the plantation community also includes the original kitchen outbuilding, an authentic period country store, Bethel Schoolhouse (c. 1898), and a formal colonial garden. Stately Oaks is open for tours Thursdays and Fridays from 11:00 a.m.–3:00 p.m. and the second and fourth Sunday of each month from 2:00 p.m.–4:00 p.m. (Group tours and other events are available by appointment.)

Further south, in Lovejoy, lies the historic antebellum Crawford-Talmadge Plantation, now called Lovejoy Plantation, said to be the inspiration for Margaret Mitchell's fictional Wilkes family home, Twelve Oaks, in *Gone With the Wind*. The privately-owned home is open by appointment only for groups of thirty or more.

This do-it-yourself tour of a portion of Georgia's Historic Heartland should be both interesting and educational for older children, and if done in moderation (with a stop at the Reynolds Nature Preserve and/or the Atlanta State Farmers Market), may even be enjoyable for younger children.

CNN STUDIO TOUR

CNN Center • 100 Techwood Ave., S.W.
Atlanta, Georgia 30303 • 827-2400

Take your older children on a tour of the international headquarters of CNN and Headline News, the two 24-hour all news networks, for a behind-the-scenes glimpse of TV news in the making. The exciting 45-minute walking tour also includes information about TBS, TNT and a weather demonstration.

The excitement begins when you enter the CNN tour waiting area. The room is covered with bright photographs of the CNN newscasters that you may soon be seeing. Overhead, television monitors air the current programs being broadcast on the many television channels owned by Turner Broadcasting System (TBS).

As your tour begins, you leave the waiting area and travel up the world's largest free-span escalator (eight stories!), from which you have a spectacular view of the CNN Center atrium. At the top of the escalator your tour guide will give a brief introduction, after which you have an opportunity to wander around a very polished photography exhibit highlighting TBS's holdings and accomplishments. Then the tour of the studios begins . . . .

Your tour guide will lead you around the offices of CNN until you reach the large glass windows overlooking the news floor. You get an excellent behind-the-scenes look at the entire process of producing the news program, seeing state-of-the-art technology and learning how it is used in all aspects of news production. You will watch writers, editors and producers working to produce the news broadcast, and through a clever use of mirrors, you will actually be able to see the news anchors reporting the news live. We watched as "hot" information came into the newsroom by wire from one of the station's correspondents in Eastern Europe, then traveled through the hands of writers, editors and the graphics department. A few minutes later, we heard it being reported live by the news anchors!

After leaving the CNN newsroom, you proceed to the glass windows looking out over Headline News, a smaller, scaled-down version of the CNN Studio. Once again we were able to view the live broadcast and learn more about how Headline News operates. We were impressed, and felt we now had an insider's view on how a television news program ends up in our living room.

• Arrive at least one-half hour early to buy your tickets because they are sold on a first come, first served basis. Allow even more time if there are a lot of conventions in town. After you purchase your tickets, wander around the CNN Center Mall and look through glass windows to see and hear the live broadcasts of two different radio stations.

• Shop at The Turner Store which is stocked with T-shirts, gift items, memorabilia and mementos from the classic films owned by TBS. Store hours are Monday–Friday from 9:30 a.m.–6:00 p.m., and Saturday and Sunday from 9:30 a.m.–5:30 p.m. Call 827-2100 for more information. Turner The Store is located at Lenox Square and carries the same merchandise, but also features Atlanta Braves gifts and the opportunity to be photographed in a mock CNN newsroom. Call 262-2700 for information.

• This tour is not recommended for children under 6 years of age. There are too many stairs and the information imparted by the tour guide will be well over their heads.

• You can combine this tour with a visit to the Federal Reserve Monetary Museum which is just two blocks away.

• There are restroom facilities and eateries in the building.

Hours: Open daily. Tours are on the half hour, starting at
              9:00 a.m., with the last tour beginning at 5:00 p.m.
              The tour lasts approximately 45 minutes. Closed
              major holidays.

Admission: The cost is $6.00/adults; $4.00/seniors; $3.50/chil-
              dren 5-12; and children under 5 are free. Groups of
              30 or more and handicapped tours require advance
              reservations. Tickets are on sale only at the tour
              booth and must be purchased in person on a first
              come first, served basis. Tickets may be purchased
              any time during the day, but only for a specific time
              that same day.

Directions: The CNN Center is located in the heart of downtown
              Atlanta and houses the Omni Hotel and Omni
              Sports Arena. The less expensive parking lots are
              located west of the Omni on Marietta St.

CYCLORAMA

800 Cherokee Ave., S.E.
Atlanta, Georgia 30315 • 624-1071 or 658-7625

Next to Zoo Atlanta lies the Atlanta Cyclorama, which brings to life
the hot summer day when Confederate troops led by General John
B. Hood made a desperate attempt to save Atlanta from Major General William T. Sherman's Union forces. This is an attraction like no
other in Atlanta.

When you enter the museum you are greeted by the famous steam
locomotive "Texas" which chased and caught "The General" south
of Chattanooga in the "Great Locomotive Chase." You can wander

around the downstairs portion of the museum and look at an assortment of Civil War artifacts while you wait for the production to start. The presentation begins with an impressively produced 12-minute slide show narrated by James Earl Jones, which chronicles the campaigns leading to the famous July 22, 1864 Battle of Atlanta.

Next, you enter the Cyclorama itself, where a revolving seating platform slowly turns you around the massive Civil War panoramic painting and the 30-foot wide, three dimensional diorama below it. (The painting is 42-feet high and 358 feet around—about the size of a football field!) Simultaneously, a multi-media production—complete with lights, sound effects and narration—highlights the stories memorialized in the amazing painting. During a second revolution around the painting, a guide talks about the history of the painting itself and provides some amusing trivia, such as how Clark Gable's face came to appear in the diorama.

For more in-depth exhibits about the Battle of Atlanta, be sure to see the upstairs portion of the museum. Here, photographs of the original and reconstructed parts of the painting are displayed side by side, as well as numerous Civil War artifacts, photographs, and exhibits honoring all soldiers of the War.

A visit to the Cyclorama is a must for older children. Although the sign on the museum door indicates that the attraction is not suitable for children under 3 years of age, we took a 2-year-old who made it through the 30-minute production with flying colors (albeit with some squirming and whispers).

- There is an excellent Civil War history bookstore in the museum.

- You might want to make a day of it by visiting Cyclorama, having a picnic in Grant Park and then going on safari to Zoo Atlanta.

- For more information about "The Great Locomotive Chase" and to see "The General," we suggest you visit Big Shanty Museum in Kennesaw.

- Restrooms, water fountains and handicapped access are available.

Hours: Open daily from 9:20 a.m.–4:30 p.m., October through May; and 9:20 a.m.–5:30 p.m., June through September. Tours are given every half hour. Closed on New Year's Day, Martin Luther King, Jr. Day, Thanksgiving Day and Christmas Day.

Admission: Admission is $5.00/adults; $4.00/seniors; $3.00/children age 6–12; and free for children under 6. For group rates call 658-7625.

Directions: Take I-20 to the Boulevard exit (one exit east of I-85/75). Follow signs to Grant Park, Zoo Atlanta and the Cyclorama.

DEKALB HISTORICAL TOURS

DeKalb Historical Society Museum
DeKalb Historic Complex • DeKalb Historical Tours
DeKalb Historical Society • Old Courthouse on the Square
Decatur, Georgia 30030 • 373-1088 or 373-3076

THE DEKALB HISTORICAL SOCIETY MUSEUM. The DeKalb Historical Society Museum is now housed on the first floor of the Old Courthouse on Decatur Square, and with the promise of new funds, will soon be expanding in size and increasing its exhibits. The three–room museum presently features two permanent exhibits:

"DeKalb: The First Hundred Years," containing artifacts, photographs, maps and memorabilia dating from turn-of-the-century Atlanta up through World War I; and "Johnny Reb and Billy Yank: The Life of the Common Soldier," honoring the common soldier of the Civil War and World War I and displaying his uniforms, guns and weaponry. Our six and seven–year–olds were fascinated by this second exhibit, especially the photograph of Johnny Clem from Newark, Ohio, the most famous drummer boy in the Civil War. Johnny went to war as a drummer boy with the Union army at the mere age of ten! The smashing of his drum at the battle of Shiloh by a stray bullet earned him the nickname "Johnny Shiloh," along with a big promotion in rank. Adjacent to Johnny Clem's photograph was the actual uniform of a Confederate drummer boy—the uniform was even smaller than the shirts and pants being worn by our boys that day! Our children could not believe that a 10-year-old boy that small had been allowed to fight in a real war. They stood silently staring at the photograph and uniform for a long, long time.

The DeKalb Historical Society is in the process of raising funds to expand the Old Courthouse into a multi-purpose community center. The Old Courtroom has already been attractively renovated and turned into a community room with catering facilities. The library and archives are being quadrupled in size, and a gift shop and snack bar are being planned, along with a special exhibit hall, which will house local arts and crafts shows, traveling cultural exhibits and musical performances. DeKalb's first Visitors Center has recently moved into the facility. Stop by the Old Courthouse with your children to see this small museum when you are in the Decatur area. Or make a day of it and visit the museum in conjunction with one of the historical tours highlighted below or a visit to the main branch of the DeKalb County library system on Sycamore Street.

- Restrooms, water fountains and handicapped access are available.

Hours: Open Monday–Friday from 9:00 a.m.–4:00 p.m.

Closed on all legal holidays.

Admission: Free. Donations are appreciated. A yearly Family Membership in the DeKalb Historical Society costs $25.00.

Directions: The Old Courthouse is located on the Square in downtown Decatur at the intersection of Clairmont Rd. and E. Ponce de Leon Ave., next to the Decatur MARTA Station.

DEKALB HISTORIC COMPLEX. A little further west from the Old Courthouse, on W. Trinity Place, lies the Historic Complex of the DeKalb Historical Society, a collection of early DeKalb historical dwellings that have, for the most part, been restored by the society. The center of the complex is the **Benjamin Swanton house,** home of an early entrepreneur who came south during gold-rush days. This furnished antebellum house is believed to be Decatur's oldest townhouse. Also at the complex are two log cabins—the **Biffle Cabin,** a restored log cabin built by a Revolutionary War veteran, which now serves as a kitchen for the Swanton House, and the **Thomas-Barber Cabin,** a rustic log cabin built by early pioneers. The latest edition to the complex is the **Mary Gay House,** the antebellum home of Mary Gay, whose *Life in Dixie During the War* tells the dramatic story of Decatur's Civil War days. Directly behind the complex lies Adair Park, complete with a play structure, swings and lots of space to run.

• During the summer months, the DeKalb Historical Society presents Wednesday morning story hours and pioneer activity programs for children age 5 years and older, which include demonstrations of pioneer activities such as open-hearth cooking and woodworking. See our chapter on "Festivals and Special Events" for more information about this program.

Hours: Open on weekdays by appointment only. Call the DeKalb Historical Society well in advance to schedule a tour.

Admission: The cost is $2.00 per person. A yearly Family Membership in the DeKalb Historical Society costs $25.00 and entitles you to free admission to the complex.

Directions: The complex is located on W. Trinity Place about four blocks west of the Old Courthouse Square and one block west of the Decatur Police Station.

DEKALB HISTORICAL TOURS. Two different tour brochures are available for those who enjoy being tourists in their own city and are eager to explore the historical sites of DeKalb County and downtown Decatur. Call the DeKalb Convention & Visitors Bureau (378-2525) to get a copy of the brochure "DeKalb Driving Tour" which presents five different tours of the historic homes, cemeteries, roads, churches, log cabins, museums and art centers found throughout DeKalb County. And for those who have energetic children and are up for a bit of walking, try the Decatur Historic Preservation Commission's (371-8386) brochure "Tour and Discover Historic Decatur." Although this brochure is meant to be used as a driving tour (it does include quite a few neighborhoods beyond the downtown area), there is no reason why you can't modify it to create a customized, self-guided walking tour of the downtown Decatur area for you and your family.

FEDERAL RESERVE MONETARY MUSEUM

Federal Reserve Bank Building
104 Marietta St., N.W. • Atlanta, Georgia 30303 • 521-8747

If you know a child who needs a lesson on the value of money, then the Federal Reserve Monetary Museum is certainly the place to visit! And even if lessons aren't needed, this museum will give your family an opportunity to see $100,000 bills, solid gold bars and many other rare and unusual currencies.

The museum is located in the imposing Sixth District Federal Reserve Bank Building on Marietta Street. Your family will sign in with the armed guard at the front desk and get directions to the museum. You will also be warned that the glass exhibit cases in the museum are hooked up to a sensitive alarm system, so that even a mere touch will set off the alarm. (Obviously, this is not the place to bring small children!)

The museum is housed in a small room that looks like a board room in one of the downtown banks. The exhibits showcase the history of currency through the ages, and include a 27-pound, genuine gold bar, trading beads, arrowheads, $100,000 bills, gemstones, salt and many other interesting and often beautiful examples of early exchange units. There is also a bowl filled with small packets of shredded dollar bills that you may take home with you. The excellent exhibits in this museum will certainly convince your family that money is serious stuff!

- Brochures which may be of interest to older children and adults are available in the lobby of the building, and include information about the Federal Reserve System, how to identify counterfeit money, and regional economic updates.

- Combine a visit to the museum with a tour of the CNN Studio, which is two blocks west on Marietta Street. Or stop by the *Atlanta Journal and Constitution*, which is one block east, for a quick look at their lobby exhibit. (See our section called "Ecology & Nature, Science, History & Politics" for more information.)

- Handicapped access is available.

Hours: Open Monday–Friday from 9:00 a.m.–4:00 p.m. Closed on Federal holidays.

Admission: Free.

Directions: The museum is located in the heart of downtown
Atlanta, two blocks east of the CNN Center.
Inexpensive parking is located west of CNN Center
on Marietta St.

FERNBANK MUSEUM
OF NATURAL HISTORY

767 Clifton Rd., N.E. • Atlanta, Georgia 30307 • 370-0960.

Fernbank Museum of Natural History, lying amid the beautiful
Fernbank Forest, is in the process of evolving into a grand showcase
of the natural and physical sciences. The 160,000-square-feet of floor
space uses hands-on exhibits, interactive displays and the most
modern communications and learning techniques available to help
us explore and understand our universe.

When entering the museum, be sure to quickly note the museum's
limestone-tiled floors sent to the museum from a quarry in Solnhofen,
Germany. These tiles are embedded with hundreds of 150-million-
year-old fossils, including ammonites (small, snail-like creatures),
belemnites (small cigar-shaped ancestors of the squid) and sponges.
My children were so intrigued with discovering each fossil in the floor-
ing, they inadvertently bumped into a lot of good-natured people
throughout the museum!

After you purchase your tickets, proceed upstairs to check out the
two small discovery rooms for kids. Fantasy Forest is for preschoolers and offers creative hands-on activities for young children. Kids
can use bee puppets to pollinate colorful flowers, wear special pinch-
er claws to feed worms to young chirping birds, or play hide-and-

go-seek in a special camouflage forest by donning an apron that matches the forest walls. Georgia Adventure, for children 6–10 years of age, is next door, and features Jekyll Island Pier, with a water play area; Oconee Camp, where children can use magnifying lenses and other tools to study wildlife specimens; and Turkey Mountain, where children can use spotting scopes to observe Georgia wildlife.

After finishing with the discovery rooms, we suggest you stop by Spectrum of the Senses, also on the upper level of the museum. Sony Corporation has donated about sixty-five different, high-quality, hands-on, interactive exhibits which explore the scientific concepts of light and sound. Although this large room has a few exhibits geared to preschoolers, the exhibit is more appropriate for elementary-age children and older. (Big people really have fun here as well.)

After finishing the Sony exhibit, go down one level to view the museum's permanent exhibit, "A Walk Through Time in Georgia." This innovative exhibit uses the State of Georgia as a springboard to understand the major stages of development of life on earth. While walking through fifteen galleries, your family will explore all of Georgia, from the mountains to the seacoast, and in a brief period of time, travel from the beginning of time to today, and into the future. Children especially enjoy the great Dinosaur Hall featuring seven life-size dinosaurs, and the Okefenokee Swamp exhibit, which recreates the sights and sounds you would find during a 24-hour visit to the mysterious swamp.

The lower level of the museum is where traveling and special exhibits are displayed, as well as "The World of Shells," a small but stunning display of shells from around the world. Part of the exhibit features a 1,000-gallon aquarium containing a living coral reef filled with brightly colored tropical fish.

If finances allow, we recommend that you indulge your family and view one of the two films playing at the special IMAX theatre housed in the museum. The IMAX films are projected on a three-story high screen and are enhanced by a six-channel, multi-speaker sound system. The spectacular IMAX system is designed to "drop you right in the middle of the on-screen action." Whether your family ends up munching on roots with mountain gorillas in the rainforest or riding rapids in the Grand Canyon, we can assure you that the IMAX experience will be unforgettable. (Some films can make young children feel slightly dizzy.)

- The atrium of the museum overlooks the Fernbank Forest and offers children space to run off their energy. You can also go outside on the terrace overlooking the forest and greet the Stegosaurus that was on exhibit at Fernbank Science Center. This beautiful atrium is also available for weddings and special functions.

- The museum houses the **Harris Naturalist Center** where amateur biologists, geologists, archeologists and families can use scientific tools and methods under professional guidance to identify and date objects found in the field. Call for information about the dates and times of open-houses at the center.

- An attractive dining room serves light meals and snacks. You can sit inside the dining room (watch out for the glass tables) or outside on the balcony overlooking the Fernbank Forest. The food is reasonably priced.

- The museum store is located adjacent to the main lobby, so you can shop there without having to pay an admission price. The gift shop carries T-shirts, books, science kits, dinosaur models, rocks and fossils, and other small souvenirs appropriate for children.

- Special workshops, programs and puppet shows for school-age children are in the process of being developed. Also, a summer camp program for elementary-age children is also in the works. Contact the Education Department for more information.

- Restrooms and water fountains are available. Handicapped access to the museum is available. However, special arrangements need to be made to enter the IMAX theatre.

Hours: The museum is open Tuesday–Saturday from 9:00 a.m.–6:00 p.m., and Sunday from 12:00 noon–6:00 p.m. There are extended hours during the summer season. IMAX films are screened on the hour, Tuesday–Saturday from 10:00 a.m.–5:00 p.m., and Sunday from 12:00 noon–5:00 p.m.

Admission: Admission is $5.50/adults; $4.50/children, senior citizens and students; and children under 2 are free. Special exhibits may cost an additional fee. IMAX theatre admission is $5.50/adults and $4.50/ children, senior citizens and students. If you just want to view an IMAX movie, tickets can be purchased without museum admission. Combination museum and IMAX admission tickets can also be purchased at a cost of $9.50/adults and $7.50/children, senior citizens and children. Family membership costs $70.00 and includes free admission to the museum, free admission to the Fernbank Science Center's planetarium shows and other benefits.

Directions: The museum is located south of Emory University in Decatur off Ponce de Leon Ave. *Going east* on Ponce de Leon, turn left on Clifton Rd. (a few miles past Briarcliff Rd.) and the museum will be immediately on your right. *Going west* on Ponce de Leon

turn left on Clifton Rd. (a few miles past Clairmont
Rd.) and the museum will be immediately on your
right. Parking is free, but space is limited. Valet
parking is available on weekends, during summer
months and at special events. Or take MARTA to
the North Ave. station. Get off and transfer to the
#2 bus, which will let you off at the intersection of
Clifton Rd. and Ponce de Leon Ave.

FERNBANK SCIENCE CENTER

DeKalb County School System • 156 Heaton Park Dr., N.E.
Atlanta, Georgia 30307 • 378-4311

FERNBANK EXHIBITION HALL. Fernbank Science Center's
Exhibition Hall displays various exhibits on the natural environment
and animal habitats of the southeast from prehistoric times to the
present. Highlights of the permanent exhibits include a reproduction
of the plants and animals of the Okefenokee Swamp, dinosaurs, meteorological exhibits, dioramas of insects, interactive computer display
terminals, an authentic *Apollo* space capsule, and a rock and precious
stone collection. Special exhibits change regularly. Most of the
exhibits in the hall are appropriate for preschoolers, others are
more interesting to older kids.

• Science and nature enrichment programs, workshops,
  lectures, film series, and open-houses for children and families are offered throughout the year, as well as an exciting
  roster of summer programs and workshops in astronomy,
  birding, science, gardening, forestry and meteorology. (These
  should not be missed.) Most of the programs are free or of
  nominal cost.

• A good time to visit is during the fall Science Book Fair.

- The small gift shop stocks T-shirts, dinosaurs, posters, books and other small items relating to science and nature. The shop, however, has irregular hours.

- Restrooms, water fountains and handicapped access are available.

Hours: Open on Mondays from 8:30 a.m.–5:00 p.m.; Tuesday–Friday from 8:30 a.m.–10:00 p.m.; Saturdays from 10:00 a.m.–5:00 p.m.; and Sundays from 1:00 p.m.–5:00 p.m. Fernbank has extended holiday closings, so call ahead before visiting.

Admission: Free. Sign up to be on the mailing list of events. Membership at the Fernbank Museum of Natural History entitles you to certain privileges at Fernbank Science Center.

Directions: Fernbank is located south of Emory University in Decatur off Ponce de Leon Ave. *Going east* on Ponce de Leon, turn left on Artwood Rd. (a few miles past Briarcliff Rd.) and follow the signs to Heaton Rd. Then turn right into the parking area. *Going west* on Ponce de Leon, turn right on Artwood Rd. (about 1 mile past Clairmont Rd.), and follow the signs to Heaton Rd. Turn right into the parking area. Parking is free.

LIBRARY AND LABORATORIES. Housed within Fernbank Science Center is one of the leading science reference libraries open to the public in the southeast. There is also a Media Distribution Center with slide sets, instructional media kits and traveling exhibits for use by schools, libraries and other non-profit organizations; a Meteorological Laboratory; an Electron Microscopy Laboratory; and a Human Development Classroom, all of which periodically conduct open-houses for individuals and families.

Hours: The library is open to the public Mondays from
             9:00 a.m.–5:00 p.m.; Tuesday–Thursday from
             8:30 a.m.–9:00 p.m.; Fridays from 8:30 a.m.–5:00
             p.m.; and Saturdays from 10:00 a.m.–5:00 p.m.
             Closed on Sundays.

Admission: Free.

Directions: See above.

FERNBANK FOREST. Outside the science center lies the 65-acre
Fernbank Forest where families may enjoy a serene walk along 2 miles
of paved trails, ponds, look-out points and instructional shelters. The
trails are perfect for younger children who, by following a simple map,
can wander through at their own pace and enjoy the area's original,
undisturbed vegetation. Of special interest is the "Easy Effort Trail"
for those with physical impairments. Tape narrations and Braille recorders
are available for the visually impaired.

* The paved trails make it easy to take babies and toddlers
  along in strollers.

* No running, jogging, picnicking or recreational activities are
  allowed in the forest. No pets are allowed. Children under
  12 must be accompanied by an adult.

Hours: Fernbank Forest is open to the general public
             Sunday–Friday from 2:00 p.m.–5:00 p.m. and
             Saturday from 10:00 a.m.–5:00 p.m. The forest is
             open to school groups by special appointment
             daily from 8:30 a.m.–5:00 p.m. Fernbank has
             extended holiday closings, so please call ahead
             before visiting.

Admission: Free.

Directions: See above.

THE PLANETARIUM. Fernbank's Planetarium is the largest in the southeast, boasting a 70-foot diameter projection dome, a Zeiss Mark V projector and seating for 500! Celestial theatre-in-the-round shows are presented year-round for families (children must be 5 years or older for regular planetarium shows) and special productions for children of all ages are screened year-round. Children under 12 must be accompanied by an adult.

Hours: Show times vary and Fernbank has extended holiday closings, so please call ahead before visiting.

Admission: The cost is $2.00/adults; $1.00/students; and senior citizens are free. Summer children shows are just 50¢ per person. Members of the Fernbank Museum of Natural History receive free admission to all planetariums shows.

Directions: See above.

THE OBSERVATORY. Fernbank's Observatory houses the largest telescope in the world dedicated primarily to public education. The 36-inch reflecting telescope is open to the public to view celestial objects, and older children will thrill at an opportunity to use such a powerful telescope.

Hours: Open Thursdays and Fridays on clear evenings, during the "dark hours" of 8:00 p.m.–10:30 p.m. On cloudy evenings, the observatory is open 8:00 p.m.–9:30 p.m. for tours only. Fernbank has extended holiday closings, so please call ahead before visiting.

Admission: Free.

Directions: See above.

FERNBANK GREENHOUSES. The Fernbank Greenhouses, located off Briarcliff Road inside the DeKalb Addiction Center, are small, but filled with many varieties of labeled plants, cacti, small trees and herbs. At the end of the visit, children are invited to take a small plant home, complete with instructions about its care. A short but sweet visit!

Hours: Open only on Sundays from 1:00 p.m.–5:00 p.m. Closed on all holidays.

Admission: Free.

Directions: The greenhouses are located inside the DeKalb Addiction Center at 1260 Briarcliff Rd. Take I-85 to the N. Druid Hills Rd. exit and head east. Turn right on Briarcliff Rd. and the DeKalb Addiction Center will be on your right just past N. Decatur Rd. and before you reach Ponce de Leon Ave.

FOX THEATRE DISTRICT TOUR

660 Peachtree St. • Atlanta, Georgia 30365 • 876-2040

During your guided tour of the Fox Theatre, conducted by the Atlanta Preservation Center (APC), you will hear all about how this absolutely unique 1920's Moorish/Egyptian/Art Deco fantasy movie palace was "saved" by the efforts of Atlantans, and how it came to be designated as a National Landmark. The tour is excellent for older school-age children who will enjoy seeing the stars on the ceiling, hearing about the amazing organ and thrill at the opportunity to go backstage.

•   The 1 ½ hour tour may include a neighborhood walk to

the Ponce de Leon Apartments, the Carlton Bachelor Apartments and the newly restored Georgia Terrace Hotel, weather permitting.

* Musical productions, ballets and movies are shown at the Fox Theatre throughout the year, and will delight children of all ages. Keep your eyes open for these performances, as this is an excellent way for children who are too young for a formal tour to be able to see and enjoy this imaginative building.

* After you finish your tour you can visit **The Road to Tara Museum**, 659 Peachtree Street, Atlanta (897-1939), across the street in the basement of the Georgia Terrace Hotel. *Gone With the Wind* buffs will appreciate the plethora of memorabilia related to both the film and the novel on display in this museum. Appropriately, the Georgia Terrace is where the cast of the movie stayed during the film's gala premiere. Trivia fanatics will love seeing autographed first editions, original costume sketches, a GWTW doll collection, posters, costume fragments, movie props, photographs, newspaper articles and more. You can also view a short film on the making of the movie. Open: Monday–Saturday from 10:00 a.m.–6:00 p.m., and Sunday from 1:00 p.m.–6:00 p.m. Admission is $5.00/adults, $4.25/seniors, $3.50/students, and children under 11 are free.

Hours: Tours are available year-round and begin at the Kiosk in the Fox Theatre Arcade. Tours are held on Mondays and Thursdays at 10:00 a.m., and on Saturdays at 10:00 a.m. and 11:30 a.m. No reservations are necessary.

Admission: Each regularly scheduled tour is $5.00/adults; $4.00/senior citizens; and $3.00/students. Free for

APC members. Group tours are by appointment only.

Directions: The Fox Theatre is accessible by the North Ave. MARTA Station, #N-3. It is located at the inter-section of Peachtree St. and North Ave.

THE GEORGIA GOVERNOR'S MANSION

391 W. Paces Ferry Rd., N.E.
Atlanta, Georgia 30305 • 261-1776

A few mornings each week, the public rooms of Georgia's executive residence are open to the public. The 24,000-square-foot mansion, built in the Greek Revival style, stands amidst 18 acres of informal and formal gardens. Volunteer guides stand at roped entrances to each of the formal rooms on the first floor level (you are not allowed to actually enter the rooms), and explain the historical significance of the 19th century furniture, art, carpets, crystal, silver and other ele-gant period furnishings found in each of the rooms. An impressive 19th century gilt-wood chandelier, a Benjamin Franklin French porcelain vase, bronze busts of George Washington and Benjamin Franklin made in 1778, and a cherry-paneled library will be of particular interest to children. Most of the furniture is American, and the home has one of the best collections of Federal Period furniture in the United States. The tour is short, pleasant and appropriate for older school-aged children.

• Many school groups visit the mansion during the holiday season to see the Christmas decorations, so be prepared for crowds during this time.

• The annual celebration of the lighting of the State Christmas

Tree is held in December; it is the best time to visit with younger children. See our chapter on "Festivals and Special Events" for more information about this event.

- Restrooms and handicapped access are available.

Hours: Tours are given on Tuesdays, Wednesdays and Thursdays between the hours of 10:00 a.m. and 11:30 a.m. Closed on all legal holidays.

Admission: Free. Reservations are needed for groups of more than 20.

Directions: Take the W. Paces Ferry exit from I-75 and go east on W. Paces Ferry Rd. toward Buckhead for about 2 miles. The Georgia Governor's Mansion will be on your left. The guard at the gate will direct you to the parking area.

GEORGIA STATE CAPITOL BUILDING & GEORGIA STATE MUSEUM OF SCIENCE AND INDUSTRY

Capitol Square, N.W. • Atlanta, Georgia 30334 • 656-2844

GEORGIA STATE CAPITOL BUILDING. The first thing everyone notices about Atlanta's skyline when driving up I-85/75 is the brilliant dome of our state's Capitol Building, the largest gold dome in the United States. The gold leaf covering the dome was mined near Dahlonega, the site of America's first gold rush, and brought to Atlanta by wagon train in 1958, and later in 1978 when the dome was regilded.

As you approach the Capitol, your children might get anxious to go inside, but see if you can take a few minutes to tour the Capitol grounds. There are many impressive statues, a replica of the Liberty Bell, a monument to the Spanish War Veterans and a sculpture on the northeast side symbolizing black Georgians' struggle for political power.

Upon entering the building through the main entrance, you will pass right by the Governor's office (this is really where he works!), and into the beautiful marble interior of this massive building. The 237-foot-high central rotunda is filled with marble busts and portraits of past governors and other famous Georgians. The north and south wings of the building are adorned with the flags of the fifty states as well as all of the different flags that have flown over the state of Georgia. Also, the north wing has a portrait of Dr. Martin Luther King, Jr., civil rights leader and Nobel Peace Prize recipient.

The many legislative chambers are located on the third and fourth floors of the Capitol, and the entrance to the galleries of the Senate and House are on the fourth floor. If your children are old enough, and the legislature is in session (January through March), be sure to go in for a few minutes. Prepare your children in advance not to expect to understand very much, as it is really difficult to figure out what is going on the floor of the legislature (even for us parents!).

GEORGIA STATE MUSEUM OF SCIENCE AND INDUSTRY. The Museum of Science and Industry is located primarily along the halls and corridors of the fourth floor of the Capitol, and consists of extensive exhibits and dioramas about the state's wildlife, including deer, fowl, native fish, birds and a large whale. Also showcased are hundreds of rocks and minerals from every county in Georgia, including an exhibit of rocks which glow under fluorescent lights. A Native American heritage exhibit includes artifacts and dioramas depicting four cultural periods dating back over 2,500 years. On the first floor of the Capitol, children can view tattered and torn flags of Georgia regiments from various wars and four cases of model airplanes depicting the history of aviation.

- Do not miss Indian Heritage Week held each November. See a teepee, a Native American dressed in native clothing, and listen to three 15-minute presentations on Native American culture in Georgia. This is very popular with school groups.

- Restrooms and water fountains are available. Tours for the hearing and sight impaired are available, and there is handicapped access.

Hours: Open Monday–Friday from 8:30 a.m.–5:00 p.m.; Saturday from 10:00 a.m.–4:00 p.m.; and Sunday from 12:00 noon–4:00 p.m. Tours are conducted at 10:00 a.m., 11:00 a.m., 1:00 p.m. and 2:00 p.m. weekdays. Group tours are available by appointment.

Admission: Free.

Directions: The State Capitol is located in downtown Atlanta across the street from Underground Atlanta and The World of Coca-Cola.

GWINNETT HISTORICAL TOURS

GWINNETT COUNTY MUSEUM, 455 Perry St., Lawrenceville (822-5178). The one-room Gwinnett County Museum (formerly the Lawrenceville Female Seminary) is packed with early educational material, furniture, books, clothing, dolls, antique school desks, historical documents, veteran's memorabilia and other similar items collected from all over Gwinnett County. Museum guides supplement the exhibits with stories and information that will help bring to life the history and heritage of the county. The museum is somewhat unusual and probably best enjoyed by your older children. Stop by during your historic tour of Gwinnett County.

- There is no handicapped access. The museum is on the second floor of the historical building.

- Restrooms are available.

Hours: Open Monday–Friday from 10:00 a.m.–3:00 p.m. Group tours need to schedule an appointment.

Admission: Free.

Directions: Take I-85 north to GA 316 to the Lawrenceville exit. Turn right off the exit ramp and head to the Square. At the Old Courthouse turn right on Perry St., which leads to the museum.

PLANTATION HOUSES OF GWINNETT COUNTY, P.O. Box 261, Lawrenceville, Georgia 30246 (822-5174). For a do-it-yourself driving tour of historical antebellum plantation homes in Gwinnett County, write to the Gwinnett Historical Society for a copy of their brochure *Plantation Houses of Gwinnett County— Self-Guided Driving Tour.* The brochure is full of information about the history of Gwinnett County. (Example: Did you know that Gwinnett County is named after Button Gwinnett, one of Georgia's three signers of the Declaration of Independence, even though he never actually set foot inside the county?) It also provides directions and information about seventeen historical homes and plantations in Gwinnett County.

Most of the homes on the tour are privately owned and not open to the public, so please respect the privacy of the property owners and stay in your vehicle. The following homes are available for tours by appointment only: the Wynne-Russell House (1826), now owned by the Lilburn Women's Club (call 921-2210); the Bowman-Pirkle

House (1818), operated by Gwinnett Parks and Recreation (call 822-8840); and the Elisha Winn House (1812), which was the county's first courthouse (call 822-5174). Or visit the Elisha Winn House the first weekend in October during the traditional Elisha Winn Fair. See our chapter on "Festivals and Special Events" for more information about this event.

This do-it-yourself tour lets you proceed at your own pace and gives you an opportunity to take a historical drive into the past.

VINES BOTANICAL GARDENS, 3500 Oak Grove Rd., Loganville (466-7532). The 90-acre park, donated to Gwinnett County Parks and Recreation by Myrna and Charles "Boe" Adams, features over twenty-five-acres of developed gardens, a three-acre lake which is home to a family of swans, an 18,000-square-foot elegant manor home, fountains, statues galore, and flowers, flowers and more flowers. A visit to this lovely, serene attraction is a must for any family visiting the Gwinnett County area.

The unfurnished mansion usually is open to the public one Sunday a month (Super Sunday) and during the Christmas holiday season when local florists and decorators decorate the home in holiday finery. Also, during the garden's Christmas celebration, the grounds and mansion are decorated in hundreds of strings of lights, a large Christmas tree appears on the deck behind the home, and Santa Claus makes special appearances for the children. On Super Sundays, the garden sometimes sponsors special activities for children, such as storytelling and gardening workshops. Call for information about Super Sunday dates.

- Most paths are easily accessible to strollers (excluding those around the home). A special garden tour map is available for the physically challenged.

- The mansion and grounds may be rented for weddings and other special events.

• There is a small picnic area, a water fountain and soft drink vending machine at the main entrance, but no food or drink are allowed beyond the picnic area. Presently there are only portable restroom facilities for garden visitors.

Hours: Open Thursday–Saturday from 10:00 a.m.– 5:00 p.m., and Sunday from 1:00 p.m.–5:00 p.m. Open additional hours during peak blooming seasons and the Christmas holiday season.

Admission: Cost is $3.00/adults; $1.00/children age 5–12; and children under 5 are free.

Directions: Take I-85 north to Highway 316, exit at Route 120 and turn right. Continue until you reach GA 20 and turn right. Continue on GA 20 through Grayson and then make a right onto Oak Grove Rd. The gardens are about 1 mile on the left.

THE HERNDON HOME

587 University Place, N.W. • (Near the Atlanta University complex) Atlanta, Georgia 30314 • 581-9813

Alonzo Franklin Herndon was Atlanta's wealthiest black person and one of America's foremost businessmen and philanthropists. A former slave from Social Circle, Georgia, Alonzo Herndon came to Atlanta in the late 1800s, and in 1905 founded Atlanta Life Insurance Company. After his death in 1927, his son Norris Bumstead Herndon carried on the family's tradition of business prominence, leading Atlanta Life to prosperity and making it the largest black-owned insurance company in the United States. The Herndon family's tradition of community service and philanthropy to black schools, churches and social agencies is now continued by the Herndon Foundation, which owns and operates Atlanta Life and the Herndon Home.

The Herndon Home is a Beaux Arts Classical mansion designed by Alonzo Herndon and his first wife Adrienne McNeil, a drama teacher at Atlanta University. The mansion was built by skilled African-American crafts people, and throughout the years has stood as a symbol of black achievement. Norris Herndon's collection of antique furniture, Roman and Venetian glass, silver, Oriental rugs and other decorative artwork completed the impressive home. A tour of the mansion begins with a short videotape about the Herndon family, followed by a comprehensive tour of the home.

Although we feel that a trip to the historical home by older children is a must, we recommend that you not take preschoolers. The mansion is full of valuables, the videotape and tour would be hard for a young child to follow, and your attention (and the rest of the tour group's) would probably be directed to amusing your child throughout the visit rather than to the enjoyment of the home.

• The annual Christmas Open House and Kwanzaa celebrations in December are good times to visit the house.

• Restrooms and water fountains are available. Handicapped access is available only for the first floor of the home.

Hours: Open Tuesday–Saturday from 10:00 a.m.– 4:00 p.m. Closed on all legal holidays. Reservations are required for groups.

Admission: Free.

Directions: Take I-85/75 to the MLK Jr. Dr. exit and travel west until you reach Vine St. Turn right at Vine St., and right again at University Place. The home is located near Clark Atlanta University.

HIGH MUSEUM OF ART

Robert Woodruff Arts Center
1280 Peachtree St., N.E., Atlanta, Georgia 30309 • 733-4200
Recorded Information: 733-HIGH

The High Museum of Art is a modern, light-filled architectural masterpiece that houses Atlanta's permanent art treasures and special exhibits from the museum's collection and other institutions. The museum offers children an opportunity to discover art in a spacious and attractive facility.

Prior to your visit, you may wish to call ahead to the Education Department (898-1116) and request a mailed hand-out explaining some fun ways parents can prepare older children for their upcoming visit to the High. "Viewing Guides" describing most of the permanent and special collections at the museums are also available. A lot of the works on display will probably be better appreciated by both you and your older children, if you take advantage of reviewing these resources prior to your visit. Our older children really appreciate the museum's extensive collection of Sub-Saharan African art and a lot of the contemporary art usually on display on the upper level (when there are not special collections). But be forewarned, the upper levels of the museum can be inappropriate for lively preschoolers—museum guards are quite strict about sticky fingers touching the works of art and little feet running down the enticing ramps spiraling around the museum.

The entire lower level of the museum is reserved for the Junior Gallery. Changing installations introduce children to the creative processes involved in making and looking at art and exploring line, motion, light, space, illusion, point of view, color and material. All of the children's exhibits invite kids to participate in "hands-on" activities that allow them the opportunity to touch, draw and create on their own. Unfortunately, the Junior Gallery will be closed until late 1994 or even early 1995 while a new exhibit is installed. The museum does plan to set aside a small area in the lower level for a small selection of hands-on art activities for children in the interim.

- The High Museum offers "Weekend Workshops for Families," that combine guided gallery visits with a studio art experience in drawing and painting, printmaking, mobile construction, sculpture, textiles or mixed media. Parents and children (age 5–12 years) attend the program together. Arrangements can be made to accommodate youth groups. Also offered are workshops tied into special exhibits and/or seasonal holidays. A summer camp program which focus on a variety of art media, including sculpture, printmaking, textiles, drawing and painting is also offered.

- Storytelling hours, puppet shows, children's films and family festivals are scheduled year-round, including the Children's Festival (held annually in the fall), and a Holiday Party for Children (held in December). Look in our chapter on "Festivals and Special Events" for more details.

- There is an excellent book and gift shop at the museum. It is stocked with unusual books, toys and art project kits for children, as well as handcrafted jewelry, hard-to-find art, posters and stationery. For those who don't want to travel to Midtown, check out the High Museum of Art Shop at Perimeter Mall, 4400 Ashford-Dunwoody Rd., Atlanta (913-9454) which carries an even larger selection of merchandise. *Open:* Monday–Saturday from 10:00 a.m.–9:30 p.m. and Sunday from 12:00 noon–6:00 p.m. Tickets can be

purchased at the Perimeter Mall shop for the Alliance
Theatre and Atlanta Symphony.

• Most afternoons, a small handcart in the atrium sells coffee,
tea, lemonade and assorted muffins and pastries. Tables and
chairs are also available for those who need to rest their feet.

• Restrooms, water fountains and handicapped access are
available.

Hours: Open Tuesday–Saturday from 10:00 a.m.–
5:00 p.m., and Sunday from 12:00 noon–5:00 p.m.
On Fridays the museum is open to 9:00 p.m.
Closed on Mondays and all legal holidays. The
children's exhibit on the lower level has different
hours. Call for more information.

Admission: Except during special exhibits (when admission
costs may be increased), the cost is $5.00/adults;
$3.00/students and seniors; $1.00/children age
6–17; and children under 6 are free. The museum is
free on Thursdays from 1:00 p.m.–5:00 p.m. A
yearly Family Membership is available at a cost of
$50.00 and includes free admission, discounts on
classes and summer programs, discounts in the gift
shop, and many other privileges.

Directions: The High Museum is located on Peachtree St.
between 15th and 16th Streets, and next to the
Woodruff Arts Center. Parking is available behind
the building for a small fee. The MARTA Arts
Center Station is directly behind the building.

HIGH MUSEUM OF ART FOLK ART
AND PHOTOGRAPHY GALLERIES

30 Dobbs Ave. N.E. • Atlanta, Georgia 30303 • 577-6940
Recorded Information: 733-HIGH

This small, attractive "extension" to the High Museum of Art, located in the heart of downtown Atlanta, inside the Georgia-Pacific Center, has just reopened its doors with a new name, new entrance and, most importantly, a new focus. The facility now has the space to display properly the museum's extensive fine photography collection (comprising nearly one-third of the museum's permanent collection) and to showcase special high-quality collections of folk art. This new focus is good news for our children because both photography and folk art are "kid friendly" art forms. Familiar images, intricate details and bright colors make it easy for children to understand and enjoy these mediums. For example, one of the exhibits on display in 1994 called "Asafo! Fante Flags From Africa 1850-1957," was very kid-friendly. "Asafo!" featured 201 spectacular flags patch-worked, appliquéed and embroidered by the Fante people of Ghana. Children of all ages could enjoy these colorful banners depicting African folk tales and vivid details about the everyday life of these people. Keep an eye on the *Atlanta Journal and Constitution's* Saturday "Leisure Guide" for information on current exhibits, or call the museum to get more details, if you need help in deciding whether an exhibit is appropriate for your child.

• Most of the special exhibits are accompanied by related workshops, classes, storytelling sessions or performances, most of which are free. Local folk artists, such as Howard Finster and Lonnie Holley, as well as professional photographers, have also offered workshops at the museum.

• The museum is in the process of developing a series of

guided tours and special programs for students of all ages. Teachers should call the Education Department (898-1116) for more information.

- Restrooms, water fountains and handicapped access are available.

- You might combine a visit to the museum with a stop at the main branch of the Atlanta-Fulton County Public Library located across the street, or the Information Center of the Atlanta History Center.

Hours:　Open Monday–Saturday from 10:00 a.m.– 5:00 p.m. Closed on legal holidays.

Admission:　Free.

Directions:　*Going south* on I-75/85, get off at the Butler St. exit and turn right on Dobbs Ave. *Going north* on I-75/85, get off at the Edgewood/Dobbs Ave. exit and turn left on Dobbs Ave. Pay parking is available at nearby lots. The museum is near the MARTA Peachtree Center Station. (Use the Ellis St. exit from the station.)

KENNESAW MOUNTAIN NATIONAL BATTLEFIELD PARK

Old Highway 41 and Stilesboro Rd.
P.O. Box 1167 • Marietta, Georgia 30061 • 427-4686

Kennesaw Mountain National Battlefield Park is an enjoyable place to go for a family picnic, to hike and to learn more about the Civil War. To start off your visit, first go by the Visitors Center and pick up some brochures about the park. You might choose to view a 10-minute slide presentation, which provides introductory information about the 1864 campaign and the Battle of Kennesaw and explains that the park was established to commemorate this major Civil War battle.

The park has two different picnic areas complete with tables, trash cans and barbecue facilities. The area near the Visitors Center has a small creek running by that provides another fun place for children to explore.

Families and youth groups really enjoy hiking on the marked trails that begin at the Visitors Center. Round-trip distances are two miles, five miles, ten miles and sixteen miles. (Make sure your group communicates about which path each other is taking, or some may have a long, unexpected wait at the bottom!) When our kids were little, we took the two-mile hike to the top of Kennesaw Mountain and it was a nice, wide trail of moderate steepness. There is an overlook at the summit of the mountain that provides a panoramic view of the battlefield. Our children loved running back down the trail! Take note—there is no water, food or shelter along the trails.

- During the summer months, living history demonstrations and programs are often presented at the park. The Kennesaw/Big Shanty Festival is held in April and October. See our chapter on "Festivals & Special Events" for more information.

- Parking is in short supply at the Visitors Center. Bicycles are not permitted, and dogs must be on a leash.

- There are restrooms and water fountains at the Visitors Center.

Hours: The Visitors Center is open daily from 8:30 a.m.–5:00 p.m.; the main gate is open from 8:00 a.m.–

7:30 p.m.; and the gate to the mountain road is open from 8:00 a.m.–7:00 p.m. The gates close earlier in the winter months.

Admission: Free.

Directions: The park is located 3 miles north of Marietta. Take I-75 to Exit #116 (Barrett Pkwy.). Turn left on Barrett Pkwy. which dead-ends at Cobb Pkwy. (US 41). Turn right on Cobb Pkwy. and go to the first light. Turn left at the light and continue about 2 ½ miles until you reach the park.

MARTIN LUTHER KING, JR. HISTORIC SITE

The Martin Luther King, Jr. National Historic Site is undergoing a comprehensive and impressive remaking, thanks to a $10.9-million appropriation by the U.S. Congress, which has been long overdue. The King Site receives well over three million visitors each year, making it one of our nation's most frequented attractions. Expectations for the new King Site are appropriately high: to provide a more complete interpretation of the civil rights leader's life in a beautifully landscaped setting; and to educate, enlighten and capture the heart of every visitor. Among the many changes in the works is the creation of a 7,500-square-foot Visitors Center which will house a museum containing artifacts from Dr. King's life and times, including his Nobel Peace Prize and other memorabilia contributed by his wife and collectors from around the country. The completion date for the work on the King Site is January 1996, during King Week, and in time for the 1996 Summer Olympics.

CENTER FOR NONVIOLENT SOCIAL CHANGE, 449 Auburn Ave., N.E., Atlanta, Georgia 30312 (524-1956). The center, founded by Coretta Scott King, is the only official national and international monument dedicated to the life of Martin Luther King, Jr. Its goal is to preserve and advance Dr. King's mission by applying his principles of nonviolence to all areas of human activity. The center sponsors numerous conferences, training programs, internships, workshops, community services and cultural events, and actively promotes nonviolent solutions to family, local governmental, national and international problems. It also houses a library and archives containing the world's largest collection of primary source material on the Civil Rights Movement and Martin Luther King, Jr.

An exhibition hall at the center displays photographs and memorabilia depicting Dr. King's personal and public life. A new exhibit is in the works which will focus on King's legacy and Coretta Scott King's current work.

In the courtyard of the center, in a simple reflecting pool, lies the marble crypt of Dr. King engraved with the words from his famous speech, "Free at last, free at last, thank God Almighty, I'm free at last!" His grave, the nearby eternal flame, and Ebenezer Baptist Church stand as moving reminders of the life and mission of Dr. King. A visit to this monument is important for people of all ages.

- The center sponsors King Week in January, a Nonviolent Film Festival, original theatrical productions, and KingFest (a summer-long series of musical and cultural performances). See our chapter on "Festivals and Special Events" for more information.

- There is a snack area in the center, and a gift shop with books, posters, postcards and other items.

- Restrooms, water fountains and handicapped access is available.

Hours: Open daily from 9:00 a.m.–5:30 p.m.

Admission: Free.

Directions: Located ½ mile east of Peachtree St. on Auburn Ave. Parking is available to the north of Auburn Ave., behind the King Community Center.

EBENEZER BAPTIST CHURCH, 407 Auburn Ave., N.E., Atlanta, Georgia 30312 (688-7263). Just a block down from the Center for Nonviolent Social Change lies the church where Dr. King, his father and his grandfather preached. Walk in and see the historical sanctuary. You are also welcome to attend Sunday services at 7:45 a.m. and 10:45 a.m., although this may not be the best activity for preschoolers and children who are not accustomed to religious services. (The King Site renovations include a new sanctuary with tours conducted by the Park Service.)

- Tours are offered Monday–Saturday from 9:30 a.m.– 4:30 p.m., and Sunday after services.

- There are restrooms and water fountains. Handicapped access to certain areas of the church is available, but call ahead for directions.

Hours: The church is open to the public Monday–Saturday from 9:30 a.m.–12:00 noon, and from 1:30 p.m.– 4:30 p.m.

Admission: Free, but donations are always welcome.

Directions: The church is a block west of the Center for Nonviolent Social Change.

MARTIN LUTHER KING, JR. BIRTHPLACE, 501 Auburn Ave., N.E., Atlanta, Georgia 30312 (331-3919). About one block east of the Center for Nonviolent Social Change lies the simple Victorian birth home of Martin Luther King, Jr. The 1895 home has recently been restored, and tours are scheduled every fifteen minutes. Walk down the street and see this historic home, even if just from the outside. Some of the funds from the Congressional appropriation for the King Site will permit the Park Service to continue renovating the entire block, restoring it to the way it was during King's childhood.

* There are no restrooms or water fountains. Handicapped access is not presently available.

Hours: Open every day except Christmas from 9:00 a.m.– 5:00 p.m. Tours begin at 9:30 a.m.

Admission: Free.

Directions: The home is about one block east of the Center for Nonviolent Social Change. It is distinguished by an American flag out front.

MARIETTA HISTORICAL TOURS

Marietta Welcome Center
Marietta National Cemetery
No 4. Depot St. • Marietta, Georgia 30060 • 429-1115

MARIETTA WELCOME CENTER & HISTORICAL TOURS. The Marietta Welcome Center occupies part of the original Marietta Railroad depot and offers historic films, slide presentations, walking tours, historic exhibits and information about the community and county.

When visiting the center, be sure to pick up the brochure called "Historic Marietta Walking • Driving Tour" which features a sampling of historic parks, churches, homes, businesses, hotels and cemeteries in downtown Marietta. The brochure provides a brief historic narrative about each of the fifty stops on the tour and a general synopsis of the history of Marietta. You can rent a portable cassette player and tour guide tape at the Welcome Center for $4.00 to supplement the brochure. Almost all of the homes and businesses on the tour are privately owned and not open to the public, although some can be seen during the Christmas holiday tour of homes.

*   The historic **Root House**, one of the stops on the tour, was the home of William Root, one of the founders of Marietta. The restored home should be open to the public in early 1994 and displays period furnishings and a small exhibit about the Root family. Another stop on the tour, **Kennesaw House Hotel**, is slated to be renovated as a Civil War museum in the not so near future.

*   Pick up a brochure about the new "Cannonball Trail," a 17-mile, 2-hour tour of Civil War sites.

*   Restrooms and water fountains are available. Handicapped access is available to the Welcome Center.

Hours: The Welcome Center is open Monday–Friday from 9:00 a.m.–5:00 p.m.; Saturday from 11:00 a.m.– 4:00 p.m.; and Sunday from 1:00 p.m.–4:00 p.m. Closed on all legal holidays. Guided tours are offered Thursdays at 10:30 a.m. and 2:00 p.m., April through November.

Admission: Guided tours cost $8.00/adults and $4.00/children.

Directions: Take I-75 north to Exit #113 (N. Marietta Pkwy.). Turn left onto N. Marietta Pkwy. and go 2.3 miles to Mill St. Turn left at Mill St. and the center will be immediately on your right.

MARIETTA NATIONAL CEMETERY. One of the stops on the tour is Marietta National Cemetery. Henry Cole, a Marietta citizen who remained loyal to the Union throughout the Civil War, originally offered land for a cemetery to be used as a burial ground for both Union and Confederate soldiers. He hoped that by honoring those who had fallen together, the living might learn to live together in peace. Unfortunately, this peace offering was rejected by both the North and the South, so Henry Cole donated the land to be used as a national cemetery (and a Confederate Cemetery was later built nearby). Approximately 10,000 Union soldiers (almost 3,000 of which are unknown) from 23 states are buried in the 24–acre Marietta National Cemetery, along with veterans of the Cherokee Indian War of 1836, Revolutionary War, Spanish American War and five subsequent wars— over 17,000 gravesites in all! The Veterans Administration maintains the cemetery and has an excellent collection of historical literature at the cemetery office.

Hours: The cemetery is open 24 hours a day, seven days a week. The office is open weekdays from 8:00 a.m.– 4:30 p.m. Call 428-5631 for more information.

Admission: Free.

Directions: Located at the corner of Washington Ave. and Roswell St. in downtown Marietta.

MEDICAL MUSEUM – CRAWFORD LONG HOSPITAL

550 Peachtree St., N.E. • Atlanta, Georgia 30365 • 686-4411

The lobby of Crawford Long Hospital of Emory University houses a small one-room museum of medical memorabilia and hospital artifacts. The hospital is named after Crawford Williamson Long, the first doctor in the United States to use anesthesia (ether) in surgery.

The museum's collection has furniture from Dr. Long's office and some of his original papers.

Also displayed are early medical and surgical equipment, Confederate memorabilia and an exposé leading us to believe that George Washington's death may have been caused by medical malpractice! It's a small, interesting exhibit—but for older children only. Take a quick peak if you happen to be in the neighborhood.

- The Atlanta Museum is across the street from the hospital.

- To learn more about Dr. Long, you may wish to venture to Jefferson, Georgia (about 65 miles northeast of Atlanta off I-85) for a visit to the Crawford Long Museum located at the historical site of Dr. Long's office. Call 706/367-5307 for more information.

- Restrooms and water fountains are available in the hospital. Handicapped access is available.

Hours: The museum is open Mondays, Tuesdays and Wednesdays from 10:00 a.m.–2:00 p.m.

Admission: Free.

Directions: Crawford Long Hospital is about 2 blocks south of North Ave. and Peachtree St. in midtown Atlanta, across from the Atlanta Museum.

MICHAEL C. CARLOS MUSEUM

Emory University Campus • 571 S. Kilgo St.
Atlanta, Georgia 30322 • 727-4282

Emory University's ancient art and archaeology museum is housed in a beautifully renovated marble building listed on the National

Register of Historic Places. The interior of the building, designed by internationally renowned architect Michael Graves, is contemporary, blending beautifully with the art and archaeological treasures found within. An impressive expansion has recently been completed which has tripled the museum's existing space, and added Caffé Antico and lots of instructional space.

The museum's permanent exhibits on the first floor focus on artifacts, sculpture, pottery, coins and everyday objects from Egypt and the classical cultures. We suggest you walk through the Egyptian exhibit first—thrilling your children with mummies, coffins and treasures from the museum's Egyptian collection. Make sure you spot the vibrant painting of the Goddess of the West on the underside of one of the coffins. This "new" addition to the museum was actually resting in obscurity at Emory for over 70 years. It was accidentally discovered in the museum's storage room on the bottom of a fragile wooden coffin that was being moved to make room for a new exhibit.

Point out to your children the "Floor Stencils" traced on the floor of each exhibit room. Whether it be the diagram of a mortuary temple from which a coffin was excavated or a map of the layout of an ancient city, your children will have an opportunity to use their map-reading skills (and imagination) to visualize the ancient site where an artifact on display was found. Our children were especially fascinated by the floor stencil of the River Nile, meandering through three exhibit rooms and leading our family past objects of everyday life used by ancient civilizations that lived along the Nile, from Lake Victoria in Uganda, up through the Nubian desert and Egypt, and ending at the Mediterranean Sea. A re-creation of an excavation site in Jericho filled with the remains of 25 skeletons, and a photographic display of Giza and the Lahav Research Project complete the lower floor's exhibit on ancient Egypt and the Near East. Also featured on the first floor are artifacts, sculpture and objects of everyday life from Greek, Indian, African, Oceanic and Asian cultures.

In addition to the permanent collection, special exhibits on loan from other institutions are displayed regularly on the second floor of the museum. Recent exhibits have included treasures from ancient Mexico, exhibits of North African ancient art on loan from the Louvre, and Egyptian Art from the British Museum.

You may be surprised to discover that children, even preschoolers, find this museum impressive and enjoyable. Its spaciousness allows children to move freely, the floor stencils entice children to move from room to room, and the exhibits, with some explanations from parents, are appropriate for children.

• Families who join the museum can also join the Children's Culture Club, which not only puts children on the museum's mailing list, but entitles them to invitations to special holiday parties, membership in a Birthday Club and invitations to special children's previews of new museum exhibits.

• The museum offers films, storytelling, holiday parties and a wide selection of Saturday morning workshops and programs for children in archaeology and the visual and performing arts. Overnight programs are also being considered for the near future. During the summer months, the museum offers "Dig It," where children age 5–18 years explore archaeology techniques, and older children actually get to work at local excavation sites. A new weeklong summer program, "Ancient Culture Camp: Sport in the Ancient World," exposes older children to the sports and games played by ancient cultures. Call to receive *Columns!*, the museum's art newspaper for kids, which contains notices about all upcoming events.

• The museum's annual B.C. Fest held in the fall is a must for children of all ages. See our chapter on "Festivals and Special Events" for more information.

• Parking on weekdays is difficult, so plan on a long hike to the museum if you want to park for free. Nearby parking at the Boisfeuillet Jones Center surface lot on campus is available for a nominal fee.

- There is a small, but excellent, gift shop stocking books on art, archaeology and architecture. The children's section has an impressive selection of books, games, activity kits and small gifts on the same subjects.

- Caffé Antico on the upper level serves breakfast, lunch, tea and dessert and is open to the public during regular museum hours. The restaurant's menu, however, may be a little too ritzy (and a little too expensive) for younger children. (Please note: the restaurant does not accept checks or credit cards.)

- Restrooms, water fountains, elevators and handicapped access are available.

Hours: Open Monday–Thursday and Saturday from 10:00 a.m.–5:00 p.m.; Friday from 10:00 a.m.–9:00 p.m.; and Sunday from 12:00 noon–5:00 p.m. Closed on major holidays.

Admission: Admission is free, although a donation of $3.00 is appreciated. Group tours are available for $10.00 with advance reservations. Call 727-0519. A yearly Family Pass costs $50.00. Members' children can join the Children's Culture Club for a cost of $10.00/child. Call 727-2251 for more information.

Directions: The museum is located in the heart of the Emory campus on the Quadrangle. Take I-85 to Clairmont Rd. and head south. Turn right on N. Decatur Rd. and continue to just before Emory Village. Turn right on Oxford Rd., which leads into the campus. Circle to the right on Mixell Dr. and bear left on Kilgo Cir. The museum is clearly marked on the right.

OAKLAND CEMETERY

248 Oakland Ave., S.E. • Atlanta, Georgia 30312 • 688-2107

Established in 1850, historic Oakland Cemetery was the only municipal burying ground in Atlanta, so nearly everyone, rich or poor, was buried here until 1884. Now listed in the "National Register of Historic Places," the 88-acre Victorian cemetery is filled with a large collection of Gothic and Classic Revival mausolea, ornate statutory and the graves and monuments of many famous Atlantans, including: golfer Bobby Jones; Atlanta's first mayor, Moses Formwalt; author Margaret Mitchell; and Morris Brown College founder, Bishop Wesley Gaines.

A visit to Historic Oakland Cemetery is not for everyone and is certainly not for every child. Full of important historical information, the cemetery is an open-air museum and presents an opportunity for your children to learn about the history of Atlanta. Yet any child's trip to a cemetery is sure to raise questions about death and mortality, so be sure you are ready to discuss the questions and concerns that your children have.

• The annual "Sunday in the Park" usually takes place in October and includes guided tours, a Teddy Bears' Tea, music and dance entertainment, storytelling, carriage rides, a Victorian boutique and other history-oriented events.

• A note about security: Although there is a security guard present, it is recommended that you take one of the guided tours offered on Saturdays at 11:00 a.m. and Sundays at 2:00 p.m., May through October, or schedule your visit during active hours.

Hours: Open daily from 8:00 a.m.–6:00 p.m. The cemetery office is open Monday–Friday from 9:00 a.m.–5:00 p.m., but is closed for lunch. Group tours for 10 or more people are available by appointment.

Admission: Free. A walking tour brochure is available at the cemetery office for $1.25.

Directions: Take I-85/75 to the Martin Luther King, Jr. Dr. exit and go east until the street dead-ends at the cemetery.

ROSWELL HISTORICAL TOURS

BULLOCH HALL, 180 Bulloch Ave., Roswell, Georgia 30075 (992-1731). This grand Greek Revival structure, built in 1840, was the antebellum home of Mittie Bulloch, President Theodore Roosevelt's mother and Eleanor Roosevelt's grandmother. A tour of this building will fascinate everyone in your family, as the tour guides are knowledgeable about architecture and history, and enjoy answering everyone's questions.

During your walk around the home, you will see period and museum rooms, an old-time kitchen with a "beehive" oven that astonishes children, gallery space, a reference library and antebellum gardens. Permanent exhibits include photos and documents from the James Stephens Bulloch and Theodore Roosevelt families, a collection of artifacts left in Roswell by the federal troops encamped in the area during July 1864, and a Roswell Textile Mills exhibition.

- Bulloch Hall also serves as a cultural center in Roswell. Special events are scheduled year-round, including lectures, readings, fine arts and crafts shows, storytelling, musical concerts, historical exhibitions, literary perspectives, theatrical performances, special festivals and living-history demonstrations. See our chapters "Festivals and Special Events" and "Performances for Children" for more information about those events which are appropriate for children.

- Workshops and classes are offered for children year-round in folk crafts and history. "Camp Bulloch" is a one-of-a-kind summer camp offering children in grades 1–5 an opportunity to experience first hand the way of life and recreation of children of the 1800s. Camp activities include arts and crafts, stories, songs and games, Native American lore, hikes and architectural explorations.

- There are restrooms, water fountains and a small gift shop. Handicapped access is available.

Hours: Tours are scheduled Monday–Friday from 10:00 a.m.–2:00 p.m. Special group tours for children in the third grade and up are available beginning at 3:00 p.m. One adult per ten children is required, and the cost per person is $1.00.

Admission: Admission is $3.00/adults; $2.00/senior citizens; $1.00/children age 6–16; and children under 6 are free. A yearly Family Membership costs $30.00 and entitles you to free admission, special invitations to events, a quarterly newsletter and discounts on heritage craft and art classes.

Directions: Take I-285 to the Roswell Rd. exit. Head north on Roswell Rd. and across the Chattahoochee River

until you reach the Town Square in Roswell. Turn
left at GA 120, then right on Mimosa, and then left
on Bulloch Ave. There are signs directing you to
Bulloch Hall.

ROSWELL HISTORICAL SOCIETY TOUR. Roswell Historical Society, Inc., 935 Alpharetta St., Roswell, Georgia 30075 (992-1665); and The Roswell Visitors Center, 617 Atlanta St., Roswell, Georgia 30075 (640-3253). Roswell is a beautiful city, and a walk around the historic downtown area can be quite pleasant, even for younger children. The headquarters of the Roswell Historical Society is located on the grounds of the Archibald Smith Plantation, but official and self-guided tours should begin at The Roswell Visitors Center where you may pick up a copy of the brochure entitled "Historic Roswell" (or write ahead to the Roswell Historical Society) for a do-it-yourself walking tour of the city. The tour takes you past historic homes, squares, churches, businesses, cemeteries and of course, the cotton and woolen mills of the Roswell Manufacturing Company.

One of your stops along the way will be Bulloch Hall, which is open to the public. The rest of the homes are private, some of them still occupied by descendants of Roswell's founding families, and are only open at certain times and by appointment.

- Roswell is the site of many special events during the year, including the Fall Arts and Crafts Festival and Christmas open-houses. See our chapter on "Festivals and Special Events" for more information on these and other festivals in Roswell.

- The **Archibald Smith Plantation** home with original family furnishings and outbuildings is open to the public Tuesday–Friday for tours at 11:00 a.m. and 2:00 p.m. On Saturdays, tours are conducted on the hour from 11:00 a.m.

to 2:00 p.m. Admission is $5.00/adult; $3.00/children age
6–16; and children under 6 are free.

• Stop by **Roswell Mill Square,** 85 Mill St., Roswell (552-
8716) where you can enjoy a meal in a restaurant overlooking the creek or shop around in the arts and craft stores. Or
you may wish to stop by the **Arts Pavilion,** which has moved
down the road, to see real artisans at work. (See our section
on "Small Art Museums, Galleries & Art Centers" for more
information.)

• Park your car at Founder's Cemetery (where Roswell King
and Teddy Roosevelt's grandfather Bulloch are buried),
which is about twenty-five feet beyond the trail entrance to
Vickery Creek Park – Roswell Mill Ruins Trail, and begin a
very interesting walk on a wide, well-designed trail of steps
and flat creek walks. Along the way are interpretive markers
explaining the unique history of the cotton mill and the
ruins that you can literally touch. All along the walk you
hear the suspenseful roar of the waterfall that powered the
mill, and at the base of the trail you are rewarded for your
patience by being able to walk right up to the top of the
falls. The water is polluted as the signs warn, so do not
expect to take a dip in the creek.

Hours: The Roswell Historical Society office is open
Monday–Friday from 10:00 a.m.–4:00 p.m. The
society conducts guided walking tours leaving from
the Roswell Visitors Center on Wednesday and Saturday mornings, weather permitting.

Admission: Guided tours are $3.00/person.

Directions: Take I-285 to the Roswell Rd. exit. Head north on
Roswell Rd. and across the Chattahoochee River to

Roswell Square. Keep right at the fork in the road, and the society will be on the right, just past the new city hall building.

ROSWELL FIRE MUSEUM, 1002 Alpharetta St., Roswell, Georgia 30075 (641-3730). This quaint antique museum houses early fire fighting equipment, including a fire rattle (used to wake up residents during a fire), a leather fire helmet, old tools, fire wagons once pulled by horses, a uniform and more. Children are welcome to ring a 19th century fire bell and sit in a 1940s red pumper truck! Take your camera. School and other groups are welcome by the very friendly firefighters.

Hours: The museum is pretty much open all the time, because the firefighters are usually there.

Admission: Free.

Directions: Take I-285 to the Roswell Rd. exit. Head north on Roswell Rd. and across the Chattahoochee River to Roswell Square. Keep right at the fork in the road which becomes Alpharetta St.

SCITREK

The Science and Technology Museum of Atlanta
395 Piedmont Ave. • Plaza Level
Atlanta, Georgia 30308 • 522-5500

SciTrek, Atlanta's hands-on museum, is recognized as one of the country's top ten physical science museums. Children are invited to explore, create and problem-solve in this exciting laboratory of physical sciences, technology and mechanics. The main portion of the museum is divided into three different areas: Mechanics and Simple Machines, Light and Perception, and Electricity and Magnetism. A new permanent exhibit has been erected here: the Eiffel Tower, a 44-foot tall replica constructed with 18,762 Erector set pieces, making this the world's largest Erector set model. Each area provides visitors with an opportunity to learn and experiment with state-of-the-art exhibits. There is also a special exhibit hall where fascinating, top-quality visiting shows are housed, providing visitors with something new at each visit. Throughout the day, the museum offers free "Mr. Wizard"–like demonstrations of principles of physics and chemistry. This section of the museum is guaranteed to capture the rapt attention of anyone over the age of five.

The spectacular, redesigned Kidspace is a separate area for children under the age of seven, where scientific principles and experiments are learned through play. In the "I Can Do" area, children explore music, drama, art and more by focusing on their senses. The "I Can Explore" gallery explores the principles of motion and light through various interactive displays. By far the most popular area is the water play section, complete with water hoses, dam construction, bubble-making and a selection of water toys to insure that your children will not leave the area dry!

- Workshops, family programs and walking tours are offered in conjunction with special exhibits at the museum, including "Science Around the Clock," an overnight program for families and groups. Also, the whole family can enjoy a Summer Film Festival which screens full-length feature films, animated shorts and science fiction.

- A Summer Day Camp Program is offered. SciTrek is also available for birthday parties.

- The museum gift shop is excellent, filled with unusual puzzles, books, toys, kites and more, but the merchandise is not cheap. (Museum members do get a discount.)

- There is a small food concession area with tables and chairs.

- Restrooms, water fountains and handicapped access is available.

Hours: Open Tuesday–Saturday from 10:00 a.m.–5:00 p.m., and Sunday from 12:00 noon–5:00 p.m. with extended hours during the summer. Monday mornings are available for school groups. Closed on Easter, Thanksgiving, Christmas and New Year's holidays.

Admission: Admission is $7.50/adults; $5.00/children age 3–17; and children under 3 are free. (Admission is $3.75 for all ages Tuesday–Friday from 2:00 p.m.–5:00 p.m., September through May.) Discounts are offered for groups of 12 or more with reservations. A yearly Family Membership costs $45.00 and includes free admission and lots of other privileges.

Directions: SciTrek is in the Atlanta Civic Center on Piedmont Rd. *Going south* on I-85/75 get off at the Courtland St. exit. Turn left on Harris St.; then turn left onto Piedmont Rd. At the first light, turn right onto Ralph McGill Blvd. At the first light turn into the parking lot. *Going north* on I-85/75 get off at Pine St. (Exit #98), and at the second light turn right onto Courtland St. Go to the second light and turn left onto Ralph McGill. Turn left into the parking lot. Parking fees are $4.00 for cars and $9.00–$12.00 for buses and recreational vehicles.

SIX FLAGS OVER GEORGIA

7561 Six Flags Rd., S.W. (at I-20 West)
Mableton, Georgia 30059 • 948-9290

Six Flags is a tremendously popular 331-acre amusement park that has over 100 thrilling rides, attractions and shows. The park is named for the six flags that have flown over Georgia. (Quick! What are they? Spain, France, England, Georgia, the Confederacy and the United States.) It is clean, well managed and full of cheerful young attendants. Warning: parents have as much fun as kids here, so be prepared to spend the day and perhaps part of the evening.

For young children, there is a mini-zoo, a train ride, the Dahlonega Mine Train roller coaster, Yosemite Sam's Playfort (featuring rope climbs, slides and ball baths) and Looney Tunes and Bugs Bunny Land, which have lots of great rides and play areas.

For brave children and adults, there are, of course, the thrilling, heart-pounding roller coaster rides: the fifty-seven-mile-per-hour Great American Scream Machine, the triple-loop Mind Bender, the Georgia Cyclone (a replica of the legendary Coney Island Cyclone) and the newest thriller, Ninja, which turns riders upside down five times! You can also enjoy the many water rides which greatly appealed to our seven and ten-year-old boys: Ragin' Rivers, a raft ride down four slides; Splashwater Falls (yes, kids are bound and determined to get wet); and the Log Flume, which our kids equated with the Olympics toboggan slide. "The Great Gasp," a parachute that drops 210 feet in a matter of seconds, the Looping Starship, and the many other exciting rides at the park make this a fun place for the entire family to visit.

And don't forget the shows, musical concerts, magic, fireworks and the daily stunts of the U.S. High Diving Team which entertain children of all ages.

- Six Flags reopens for "Fright Nights" during certain weekends in October, so that Atlantans can celebrate the Halloween holiday. Rides are sometimes operating.

- Restaurants and souvenir shops are numerous.

- Discount tickets can be found all over Atlanta. Look for them at Krogers, in newspapers and at other metro Atlanta locations.

Hours: Six Flags is open at 10:00 a.m. daily from Memorial Day to late August. Closing hours vary but are usually around 10:00 p.m. From about mid-March to Memorial Day, and late August through October, the park is open on most weekends. Call for the current schedule.

Admission: Call for current prices. A 1993 one-day pass to the park costs $26.00/adults; $18.00/children age 3–9; $14.00/seniors over the age of 55 years; and is free for kids 2 years and under. A season's pass costs $68.20 a person or $178.45 for a family of four. Parking is $4.00.

Directions: Six Flags is located 12 miles west of downtown Atlanta directly off I-20. You can see the park from the expressway and there are signs to direct you there.

SOUTHEASTERN RAILWAY MUSEUM

3966 Buford Hwy. • Duluth, Georgia 30316 • 476-2013

If your children like trains, you simply must explore this one-of-a-kind outdoor museum for retired railroad cars. Some of the cars at this 12-acre train yard have been restored by the Atlanta Chapter of the National Railroad Historical Society and are in top condition, while others are in various stages of decay. All are interesting. Kids can climb on some of the cars, including a working, shiny black steam engine, freight cars, a Pullman dining car and a few good-old red cabooses. (Haven't you always wanted to go inside a real caboose?) Watch your children carefully while they explore, since a few of the cars are not safe to climb on due to their severe state of disrepair. Be sure to peak into the busy "Corner Shop" to view engine and rail cars being restored.

On the third Saturday of each month, children can take an irresistible 10-minute ride on miniature trains, lovingly and painstakingly built by the North Georgia Live Steamers. Riders sit in gondolas built to scale which are pulled by powerful steam engines along 5,000 feet of railroad track with a little tunnel and bridge. You can also climb aboard a restored diesel locomotive, "Old 97," for a trip around the grounds. Call ahead to make sure that both the small and full-size trains are operating on the day you plan to visit. Longer excursions to Toccoa and Chattanooga are offered. (What a fun way to get to the impressive Tennessee Aquarium.) Call the museum for the weekend steam-up schedule.

A few of the restored railroad cars have been converted to museum use. The museum's library is housed in a U.S. Post Office railroad car and is a repository of over 7,000 items of railroad memorabilia. Among the more interesting documents for children to view are a train register with the real Casey Jones's signature, old signal lanterns, rail spikes and telegraph equipment. Snacks, beverages and souvenirs are for sale in the Central of Georgia Baggage Car No. 405.

•   The museum volunteers urge everyone to use safety precautions. Avoid walking on the rails and keep a safe distance from moving equipment.

- There are many interesting free brochures about the history of the Southern Railway System and on safety. There are also activity sheets just for kids.

- The terrain is gravel, so this is not a good place for strollers and wheelchairs.

- Dogs are welcome if on a leash.

- Birthday parties are a big hit here. Call 271-2442 for information.

Hours: Open on Saturdays from 9:00 a.m.–5:00 p.m., except on days set aside for the longer Southern Steam Excursions and holidays.

Admission: Admission is $4.00/adults, and $2.00/children under 12 and seniors over 60. Call 736-1431 for more information on the longer excursions to Toccoa and Chattanooga.

Directions: Take I-85 north to the Pleasant Hill Rd. exit. Turn left and go to Buford Highway. Take a left on Buford Highway and continue for about 1/4 mile. The museum will be on the left, immediately after a railroad spur.

STONE MOUNTAIN PARK

P.O. Box 778 • Stone Mountain, Georgia 30086
498-5600 or 498-5690

Georgia's Stone Mountain Park will be a host of the 1996 Summer Olympic Games, and deservedly so. It's 3,200 acres are filled with natural scenic beauty and numerous attractions and recreation facilities which provide year-round enjoyment for the whole family. Some of the facilities will undergo improvement in time for the Olympics, such as the relocation of the Ice Chalet and the renovation and expansion of a recently acquired large tennis facility. But the focal point of this attraction will always remain the mountain itself: the world's largest exposed granite outcropping, the north side of which displays Confederate Memorial Carving, a monument honoring Confederate President Jefferson Davis, and Generals Robert E. Lee and "Stonewall" Jackson.

Families of all ages hike to the summit of the mountain year-round for a breathtaking, panoramic view of Atlanta and its surroundings. (Our three-year-old makes it all the way, no problem, and then wants to climb it again the next weekend.) Every summer evening at 9:30 p.m., families picnic and enjoy the one-of-a-kind, 50-minute Laser show on the carving, complete with popular music, dancing laser beams and fireworks.

ATTRACTIONS. The larger of the park's attractions include the Antebellum Plantation, a re-creation of a typical southern plantation of the 1800s; the Antique Auto and Music Museum, a collection of vintage cars and musical instruments, including an authentic Tucker automobile; the Skylift, whose Swiss cable cars lift you to the mountain's peak where you may purchase souvenirs in the gift shop and enjoy a unique bird's-eye view of Atlanta; the Scenic Railroad Ride around the base of the mountain; the Paddlewheel Riverboat on the 363-acre Stone Mountain Lake; The Grist Mill; Indian Island, where we enjoy picnicking; and a family favorite, the Wildlife Trails and Traders' Camp Petting Farm, which has over 20 acres of natural woodland filled with cougar, elk, bison and other animals that were once indigenous to Georgia.

RECREATIONAL ACTIVITIES. The Ice Chalet Complex has full skating facilities and instruction, though a move outside the park, but still in the city of Stone Mountain, is scheduled for the summer of 1994. Boating, fishing, tennis, golf, hiking, running paths, camping, bicycle rentals, batting cages and miniature golf are also available. The Waterworks Beach Complex includes two white-sand beaches, a tube water slide, a playground, game room, bathhouse and snack bar. The park's "Master Plan" calls for many of these facilities to undergo improvements, some in time for the Olympics, such as the 28-acre tennis facility the park has recently inherited. And wait, there's more . . . Stone Mountain Park has a large play structure for children: a wonderful maze of slides, tunnels and climbing challenges. Adjacent to the structure is a toddler's play structure and lots of picnic tables, outhouses and a drinking fountain.

• There are restaurants, snack bars and picnic areas galore.

• Special events year-round bring families to the park, including the Antebellum Jubilee, Springfest, Fantastic Fourth, Yellow Daisy Festival, and Scottish Festival and Highland Games. See our chapter on "Festivals and Special Events" for a complete description of annual events.

• For information on fishing, boating and the sports facilities at the park, see our chapter on "Sports and Recreation."

Hours: The park is open daily year-round from 6:00 a.m.–12:00 midnight. Attractions and recreational facilities have varied hours, but most attractions open at 10:00 a.m. and close at 9:00 p.m. during the summer, and at 5:30 p.m. the rest of the year. Call the park for more detailed information. The Lasershow starts at 9:30 p.m. every evening from early May through Labor Day, and weekends through October.

Admission: The vehicle parking fee is $5.00 per family, per visit, or you may purchase a calendar-year permit for $20.00. Special rates are available for buses. Admission to most of the attractions cost extra, as do the recreational facilities. Call the park for more detailed information.

Directions: Take I-285 to US 78 (locally known as the Stone Mountain Freeway) going east. The park exit is clearly marked. When you enter the park you will be given a map and information brochure.

SWEET AUBURN DISTRICT

A stroll down Auburn Avenue yields families an essential historical and cultural perspective on Atlanta's African-American community. From Martin Luther King, Jr.'s Birthplace at one end, to the newly constructed Auburn Avenue Research Library on African-American Culture and History at the other, visitors will see buildings with rich histories, including churches, the Masonic Building, and the Royal Peacock Night Club, where artists such as Nat King Cole and Cab Calloway performed. (The MLK, Jr. Historic Site has its own separate entry in this chapter as does the nearby Oakland Cemetery.)

AFRICAN–AMERICAN PANORAMIC EXPERIENCE (THE APEX MUSEUM), Collections of Life & Heritage, Inc., John Wesley Dobbs Building, 135 Auburn Ave., N.E., Atlanta, Georgia 30303 (521-APEX). The APEX is a permanent collection of exhibits that depicts the cultural heritage of African-Americans and recognizes their contributions and achievements in helping to build America. Displays include a re-creation of the Yates & Milton

Drug Store; the Paul Jones Collection of African Art, representing aspects of African culture through media such as masks and sculpture; a trolley with a video production called "Sweet Auburn, Street of Pride"; and special exhibits chronicling African-American achievements in history and science. (Find out where the question, "Is it the real McCoy?" came from!) The museum also has exhibits which honor Atlanta's black community.

A visit to the APEX is recommended for all school-age children and their families. Currently the museum is small, but a major expansion is in the fund-raising stage. The museum hopes to add up to 90,000 square feet by the time of the 1996 Olympics to provide Atlantans and visitors with a more comprehensive and accurate picture of Atlanta and its people.

• Tours are available for groups at a reduced rate and by reservation. We strongly recommend the tour; the guides are excellent.

• The **Sweet Auburn Welcome Center** is located here, which provides information on black attractions and cultural events, business and other black institutions, and up-to-date information on black political, social and church organizations. The center also carries all of Atlanta's black-owned newspapers.

• Restrooms, water fountains and handicapped access are available.

Hours: Open Tuesday–Saturday from 10:00 a.m.–
              5:00 p.m., and on Wednesday from 10:00 a.m.–
              6:00 p.m.

Admission: Cost is $2.00/adults; $1.00/senior citizens and
              students; and children under 5 are free. A yearly

Family Membership is available for $50.00 that includes free admission and the museum's newsletter.

Directions: The APEX is located on Auburn Ave. about 3 blocks east of Peachtree St. in downtown Atlanta.

ATLANTA LIFE INSURANCE COMPANY, Herndon Plaza, 100 Auburn Ave., Atlanta, Georgia 30303 (659-2100). Atlanta Life Insurance Company, the largest black-owned insurance company in the United States, was founded in 1905 by Alonzo Herndon. The atrium of the modern high-rise houses a permanent exhibit on the Herndon family and the history of Atlanta Life Insurance, as well as a magnificent corporate collection of African-American art that is featured during an annual art exhibit. A quick stop into the building is worth your while before or after a trip to the APEX.

• Handicapped access and restrooms are available.

Hours: The artwork may be viewed on weekdays from 9:00 a.m.–3:30 p.m.

Admission: Free.

Directions: The Atlanta Life Insurance building is across the street from the APEX Museum.

THE TELEPHONE MUSEUM

Southern Bell Center, Plaza Level
675 W. Peachtree St., N.E. • Atlanta, Georgia 30375 529-3637

The Telephone Museum is a rare find and highly recommended for people of all ages. This small museum traces the history of the telephone from its earliest inception to the creation of telestar and fiber-optic technology. Your self-guided tour begins with an exhibit about Alexander Graham Bell and the significant events leading up to his invention of the telephone. (What were the first, now famous, words spoken over a telephone?) Next, children will marvel at the collection of telephone sets dating from the beginning of World War II and an old-fashioned switchboard which some of us have only seen on television shows. (If you happen to look over-head, don't be surprised by the life-size figure of a lineman, hard at work on the top of a telephone pole.)

There is a mini-theatre with a 15-minute movie about the history of the telephone. Exiting the theatre and continuing around the museum hall, you will enter the modern age of fiber optics and digital technology. The fun hands-on displays helped all of us understand the complexities of communication a little better.

- You can park behind the museum and go to lunch at the Varsity one block west of the Southern Building for a very unusual experience in fast-food eating. Or you may eat at one of the several eateries on the Lower Level of the Southern Bell Center.

- Restrooms and water fountains are available in the Southern Bell Center. Handicapped access is available, but please call ahead for directions.

Hours: Open Monday–Friday from 11:00 a.m.–1:00 p.m. Closed on all legal holidays.

Admission: Free.

Directions: The Southern Bell Center is located on W. Peachtree St. at the intersection of North Ave., behind the Fox Theatre.

UNDERGROUND ATLANTA

Between Peachtree Street and Central Avenue at Alabama Street
Atlanta, Georgia 30303 • 523-2311

The former business center of historical Atlanta is again alive with activity. Retail stores, restaurants, night clubs, street vendors and street performers populate the below-the-street levels. Above the ground, fountains, pedestrian promenades, Atlanta Heritage Row, park benches and a soaring 10-story light tower complete this miniature city. The new Underground, spanning across six city blocks, has become a major retail and entertainment center in Atlanta, with a historical twist.

Underground offers something for everybody—beautiful retail stores for the spenders in the family; over 70 different push carts selling unique and exclusive merchandise; and clowns, mimes, magicians, street performers and balloons for those younger family members who expect more out of life than just shopping.

• On the Upper Alabama Street level of Underground Atlanta, visit Atlanta Heritage Row, a small but unique museum described in the beginning of this chapter.

• Also on the Upper Alabama Street level lies **Olympic Experience** (658-1996), an information center and audiovisual exhibit celebrating a century of Olympic games and providing information about the upcoming 1996 Olympic Games in Atlanta. A merchandise mart has a huge selection of ACOG merchandise and Olympic collectibles. Open Monday–Saturday from 10:00 a.m.–6:30 p.m., and Sunday from 12:00 noon–6:00 p.m.

• There are several excellent restaurants, as well as a huge food court specializing in fast food from around the world. Restaurant and club hours vary.

* A good time to visit Underground is during one of its many year-round special events. Quite a few are geared to families and children. See our chapter on "Festivals and Special Events" for more information.

* If your family is energetic, combine your visit to Underground with a trip to the World of Coca-Cola, which is adjacent to Underground. Or visit the State Capitol which is just two blocks away.

* Restrooms and water fountains are available. Handicapped access is available, but call ahead for directions.

Hours: Open Monday–Saturday from 10:00 a.m.–9:30 p.m., and on Sunday from 12:00 noon–6:00 p.m. Closed on Christmas Day.

Admission: None.

Directions: Underground is located between Peachtree St. and Central Ave. at Alabama St. It is 2 blocks west of the Georgia State Capitol Building. Exit at the MARTA Five Points Station.

WHITE WATER PARK

250 N. Cobb Pkwy., Marietta, Georgia 30062 • 424-9283

White Water is the largest and most visited water park in the southeast. Yes, it is crowded—you can expect long waits for some attractions, but they are well worth it. Just ask any kid who has been there! Also of importance, White Water Park has a reputation of being a well-managed facility with good supervision. The forty acres of water adventures thoughtfully include areas designated for pre-school and elementary age kids only. Older kids can get a break from little brother or sister and enjoy exciting water play in The Atlantic Ocean (a water pool), White Water Rapids, the Gulf Coast Screamer, Bermuda Triangle slide (our nine-year-old's favorite), Bahama Bob-Slide, Black River Falls and more.

For the youngest children, there is Little Squirts' Island (you must be less than 48 inches tall) with more than twenty-five activities, including water and tube slides, water guns, and the Dragon's Tail (our six-year-old's favorite). The new Captain Kid's Cove (kids under age twelve only, please) boasts over 100 water adventures, including spiral slides, fountains, and swings. These two areas combine to make this the largest water playground for children under age 12 in the entire country. For those who want to cool off in the summer heat, this attraction can't be beat!

- The park is adjacent to the American Adventures amusement park complex that offers outdoor rides, miniature golf, play areas and a penny arcade.

- "Dive-in" movies are featured on Wednesdays and Fridays in July.

- Only appropriate swim attire is allowed. There are locker and shower facilities.

- There are restaurants/snack bars and gift shops. Picnicking is permitted in the parking lot area, but there are no picnic tables. Food, alcoholic beverages and glass containers may not be brought into the park.

Hours: Open weekends in May, and then daily from

Memorial Day through Labor Day. The park opens at 10:00 a.m. and closes around 9:00 p.m., with occasional late night openings.

Admission: Daily admission for adults is $16.99 plus tax; children under 4 feet tall pay $9.99 plus tax; and children under 3 years and seniors are free. A daily combo ticket with American Adventures for adults is $16.99 plus tax, and for children costs $11.99 plus tax. A season pass for a family of 2 is $79.99 plus tax, for a family of 3 is $99.99 plus tax, and each additional member is $29.99 plus tax. Group discounts are available. Parking is $2.00.

Directions: Take I-75 north to Exit #113, and follow the signs to N. Cobb Pkwy. and the park. It is about 8 miles north of downtown Atlanta.

THE WORLD OF COCA-COLA

*55 Martin Luther King, Jr. Dr. • Next to Underground Atlanta
Atlanta, Georgia 30303• 676-5151*

Coca-Cola has erected a stunning 45,000-square-foot pavilion that, despite the blatant self-promotion, offers a fascinating multi-media tour of the century-plus history of the world's favorite soft drink. Merchandise, memorabilia, interactive displays, radio and television commercials, and state-of-the-art technical displays glorify Coca-Cola's influence in over 160 countries.

To enter the pavilion, you walk under an 11–ton red and white neon sign that Coca-Cola believes will become one of Atlanta's most famous landmarks. Your tour is self-guided, though there are cheerful hosts who speak a variety of languages to answer your questions. The one to two hour tour will take you past rare and invaluable artifacts from the archives of the company, such as the original prototype for the first Coca-Cola bottle, trays, magazine ads, photographs and Dr. Pemberton's original book describing the Coca-Cola formula—a formula that, until recently, was top secret!

The pavilion also has a modernistic soda fountain that shoots a 20-foot stream of soft drink into your cup, supplies unlimited samples of soft drinks from around the world, and houses an 18-foot high Coke bottle, a simulated bottling demonstration (which one of our preschoolers thought was real), and a store stocking the world's largest selection of Coca-Cola brand merchandise. You may shop at the TradeMart for free if you choose not to take the tour.

No matter how you feel about the taste of Coke versus its rivals, or whether or not you want your children drinking soft drinks, Coke is certainly part of our pop culture; and this attraction celebrates that in a tasteful, fun presentation.

- There is a passenger drop-off in front of the attraction and nearby parking decks.

- Restrooms, water fountains, and lots of free soft drinks are available. Handicapped access is available. Certain video presentations are close-captioned for the hearing impaired.

- Another way to enjoy Coca-Cola products is to visit one of the old-fashioned soda fountains that can be found in older neighborhoods throughout Atlanta. Our family's favorite is **Fleeman's Pharmacy** (876-1566), located at the intersection of St. Charles and N. Highland Avenues in Virginia Highlands. This pharmacy, established in 1914, houses a large soda fountain area where bona fide soda jerks serve inexpensive ice-cream treats, such as floats, malteds, shakes, banana splits and ice-cream sodas—just like the "old days" when we were children. The pharmacy is also filled with Coca-Cola and pharmaceutical memorabilia dating back to the early 1900s. You can't miss the building—just look for the huge "Refresh Yourself" trademark sign painted on the side of the building.

Hours: The ticket booth is open Monday–Saturday from 10:00 a.m.–8:30 p.m., and Sunday from 12:00 noon–5:00 p.m. Visitors may remain in the attraction one hour after the ticket booth closes. Closed Easter, Thanksgiving Day, Christmas Eve, Christmas Day and New Year's Day. Reservations can be made Monday–Saturday from 9:00 a.m.–5:00 p.m. by telephone, by charging to your credit card. There is a $2.00 additional fee per transaction.

Admission: The cost is $3.50/adults; $3.00/seniors; $2.50/children age 6–12; and children under 6 are free. Admission includes complimentary soft drinks. Discounts are available for groups of 25 or more.

Directions: The attraction is located next to Underground Atlanta and near the Georgia State Capitol Building. It is 2 blocks from the MARTA Five Points Station.

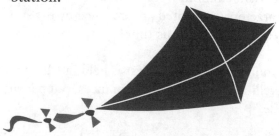

THE WREN'S NEST

1050 Ralph David Abernathy Blvd., S.W.
Atlanta, Georgia 30310 • 753-7735 or 753-7736

The Wren's Nest is a living tribute to Joel Chandler Harris (1848-1908), author of the Uncle Remus tales (Br'er Rabbit and Br'er Fox). Most importantly, it is Atlanta's main stage for the art of storytelling.

This National Historic Landmark houses the original Harris family memorabilia, books, photographs and furnishings. During your guided tour of the home, you will see a slide presentation about Mr. Harris and learn how his writing was heavily influenced by listening to his friend, Uncle Bob Capers, a black slave who told him irresistible folk tales and animal stories. Later, another slave, George Terrell, enchanted the young Joel with more African folklore. Harris' stories, which are written in the authentic middle Georgia dialect, tried to recapture these tales which had been changed and refined through the many tellings. For a period of time in the 1960s, his writings were deemed racist, but are now appreciated as a valuable contribution to African-American history and culture.

The art of storytelling that so deeply moved Mr. Harris is perpetuated at the Wren's Nest to the delight of children and adults alike. Members of the Southern Order of Storytellers perform every Saturday at 2:00 p.m. and involve the audience in each presentation. During our visit, children were invited on stage to play the parts of various characters (prompted and coached by the storyteller). All of the children had a marvelous time!

- The annual Wren's Nest Fest is held in May and includes storytelling, theatrical performances, puppet shows and a parade.

- The Christmas Festival and Open House at the Wren's Nest

takes place on the Sunday in December closest to Joel Chandler Harris' birthday. You can see the house decorated in Victorian Christmas finery, hear storytelling, school choral groups and enjoy refreshments.

- Located in the West End, Atlanta's oldest neighborhood, the Wren's Nest is featured on an Atlanta Preservation Center Walking Tour (876-2040).

- There are picnic grounds, a gift shop, restrooms, and water fountains, but no handicapped access.

Hours: Open Tuesday–Saturday from 10:00 a.m.–5:00 p.m., and Sunday from 2:00 p.m.–5:00 p.m., with the last tour conducted at 4:00 p.m. Closed on major holidays and Mondays.

Admission: Cost is $4.00/adults; $2.00/seniors and teens; $2.00/children age 4–12 years; and children under 4 are free. Group rates are available.

Directions: From I-85/75, take I-20 west to the Ashby St. exit. Turn left on Ashby St., then a right on Gordon St. There are signs to assist you in locating the attraction.

YELLOW RIVER GAME RANCH

4525 Hwy. 78 • Lilburn, Georgia 30247 • 972-6643

Along the banks of the Yellow River, sprawled over 24 wooded acres, are families of trusting deer waiting to be caressed and fed crackers from your children's hands. There are also many chubby rabbits who live in Bunny Burrows, waiting to be nuzzled and given some fresh carrots and lettuce.

Wildlife trails lead you past all sorts of animal exhibits, including the largest herd of buffalo on public display in the state of Georgia, cougars walking overhead on their special Cougar Catwalk, bears, birds-of-prey, foxes, owls, skunks, pheasants, porcupines and bobcats, to name a few. The large farm area houses cows, ponies, goats, sheep, donkeys, chickens, pigs, ducks and geese, all of whom make a lot of noise and show how pleased they are to see you and more food! We recommend that you bring your own snacks for the animals. Carrots, greens and crackers are favorites. If you forget, snacks can be bought at vending machines along the trail. There are always new baby animals on the trail, making the game ranch a little different, no matter how often you visit.

The game ranch is also the home of Georgia's Official Groundhog Weather Prognosticator, General Beauregard Lee, who yearly, on February 2nd—Groundhog Day—manages to get more attention than his northern (and often wrong) counterpart.

The trails are natural, the animals abundant, and the woods rustic. It is not hard to figure out why Yellow River Game Ranch is a favorite with families.

- There is a souvenir shop (try to get through it without stopping), concession stand, playground area, picnic areas, restroom facilities and old-fashioned mechanical horse-and-wagon rides.

- Strollers and red wagons are provided for little ones, free of charge. The paths, however, are rustic, making handicapped and stroller access a bit difficult.

- In May, the ranch hosts Sheep Shearing Saturday, described in our chapter "Festivals and Special Events." During the fall, special Wilderness Hayrides are offered.

- A special log cabin is available for birthday parties year-round. The Game Ranch's "Traveling Ark" is available for birthday parties and other special events. A more formal lecture and "show and tell" can also be booked for schools, libraries and community groups.

Hours: Open daily from 9:30 a.m.–6:00 p.m. During summer months, the ranch is open until 9:00 p.m.

Admission: Cost is $4.50/adults; $3.50/children age 3 –11; and children under 3 are free. Discount rates apply for groups of 15 or more.

Directions: Take I-285 to US 78 and go east toward Stone Mountain. Stay on Highway 78 past the Stone Mountain Park exit for 4 traffic lights. Yellow River will be on your left.

ZOO ATLANTA

800 Cherokee Ave., S.E. • Atlanta, Georgia 30315 • 624-5678

You never know which animal will be the "star" of your next visit to Zoo Atlanta. The zoo is undergoing a multi-million dollar redevelopment program, and every visit brings more new animals and exhibits in natural environment habitats. Everything is being done right here, and the zoo is a real delight to visit.

The newest exhibits at Zoo Atlanta are the Ford African Rain Forest, featuring Willie B. and the Yerkes gorilla families, housed in a re-creation of a West African tropical rain forest; Masai Mara, a re-creation of the savannas of Kenya and Tanzania, starring giraffes, ostriches, gazelles, lions, zebras, impalas, East African birds and black rhinos; the orangutans of Ketambe, an Indonesian rain-forest habitat filled with families of high-climbing orangutans; the Elephant Show, with Starlett, Victoria and Zambezi showing-off their special tricks; the Wildlife Show, featuring endangered species, birds of prey and other small animals; the Children's Railroad Train circling the Children's Zoo area; Flamingo Plaza, where you can be sure to see baby Pink Chilean flamingos; the Sumatran Tiger exhibit, displaying two rare cats; and the Small African Primate Center. And don't forget the Reptile House, one of the largest reptile collections in the U. S., now housing the zoo's latest acquisition—two rare Komodo dragons from Indonesia!

Exhibits for the future include a new Sea Lion Cove, which will feature underwater viewing of sea lions and regularly scheduled sea lion shows; the Okefenokee Swamp/Georgia Coast, displaying wolves, bears, alligators, otters and eagles; International Farms, which will be a petting farm of domestic animals from around the world; and South American Tropics, a jungle addition to the Reptile House, showcasing anteaters, tamarins, sloths and other animals from the Amazon.

Thank you Zoo Atlanta for a job well done. Year-after-year, this attraction has been voted #1 in our household.

• Times for the Elephant Show, Wildlife Show and feeding of the sea lions and gorillas vary. Call ahead, as you won't want to miss these events.

• Take your energetic younger kids to the Egleston's Ark, a smart playground where the play structures not only come in all shapes and sizes but are designed with safety in mind.

• Zoo Atlanta sponsors all sorts of special events throughout the year for children. See our chapter "Festivals and Special

Events" for information about the annual events at the zoo. Look for announcements about the many other special events held throughout the year.

- A large variety of educational programs for children and adults are sponsored throughout the year, including guided group tours, teacher workshops and summer camp programs. A sampling of programs: "Project Discovery Field Trips," a 30-minute program for elementary-age school groups; "Zoomobile Outreach Program," which brings small animals to preschools through high schools; and "Zoo Walkers," an hour-long program for preschoolers exploring reptiles and amphibians living at the zoo with hands-on encounters!

- "Night Crawlers," an overnight camp-in (which our cub scouters loved), includes a behind-the-scenes tour of the zoo, a night hike and lots of educational talks and hands-on experiences with animals and artifacts. The zoo's "Summer Safari Day Camp" offers behind-the-scene visits, hands-on encounters with small animals, art projects, games and lots of other animal-related activities.

- Concession stands, snack bars, restroom facilities and water fountains are plentiful. Handicapped access is available.

- Stroller rentals cost $2.00/day with a refundable $3.00 deposit.

- The zoo has an attractive gift shop that stocks T-shirts, stuffed animals, toys, puzzles, cards and beautiful jewelry, pottery and woodcarvings from Africa.

Hours: The ticket booth is open daily from 10:00 a.m.–4:30 p.m. During the summer, the zoo stays open on weekends until 5:30 p.m. Visitors may remain on the grounds for one hour after the ticket booth closes. Closed on New Year's Day, Martin Luther King, Jr. Day, Thanksgiving Day and Christmas Day.

Admission: The cost is $8.00/ adults; $6.00/children age 3–11; and children under 2 are free. Seniors pay $7.00 on weekdays. A yearly Family Membership costs $49.00 and entitles you to free admission and many other benefits. Discount rates for groups are available. The Zoo Train costs $1.00 per person.

Direction: Take I-20 to the Boulevard exit (Exit #26), one exit east of I-85/75. Follow signs to Grant Park, Zoo Atlanta and the Cyclorama. Parking is free.

Tidbits

MORE GOOD THINGS TO DO

This chapter includes smaller, sometimes more unusual places to go with children than described in the previous chapter. This does not mean that outings to these locations will be any less important or enjoyable for your family. Quite the contrary. Because of the uniqueness of some of these places and events, you may discover some real treasures. And, best of all, most of the activities in this chapter are free or of nominal cost! We recommend that you look through this chapter, experiment and visit some of the unusual places that we describe.

ECOLOGY & NATURE, SCIENCE, HISTORY & POLITICS

Many places to go with children involving ecology, nature, science, history and politics are described in our chapter "Places To Go." What is different about this section is that it contains tidbits of information on places to take children that few people know about, or that sometimes slip parents' minds, or that, without this information, you may not have deemed worth a visit at all. Some places and activities are for children of any age, such as Earth Day events, nature stores and nature preserves. Other places are for the more sophisticated or older child, such as Southface Energy Institute, observatories and space camps. Peruse these listings, for we are certain there are many places here your family will want to visit!

━━ ECOLOGY & NATURE ━━

AL BURRUSS NATURE PARK & WILDWOOD PARK

S. Cobb Dr. & Barclay Cir.
Marietta, Georgia • 528-0621

Located in Marietta one mile east of I-75 Exit #10, near Life College, these adjacent parks contain over 70 acres of woods, streams, trails and picnic areas, as well as a playground and challenge course. A special feature of Wildwood Park is a picnic shelter and trail that are accessible to the handicapped. *Hours:* Daily from dawn to dusk.

BUFORD TROUT HATCHERY

Trout Place Rd. • Buford, Georgia 30518
404/889-1150

This well-stocked fish hatchery is open for families to visit, and between the hours of 8:00 a.m. and 4:00 p.m., 365 days a year, someone should be there to answer your questions. Buford has a brood stock but also receives 3-inch fingerlings from federal hatcheries to raise to adults. The fish are released into the Chattahoochee when they are about 10-inches long. Approximately 190,000 trout are released each season. The hatchery is located on Highway 20 between Cumming and Buford. Coming from Buford, cross over the river, go about 1.3 miles to Pruitt Road and take a right, then take the next turn onto Trout Place Road. Free.

COCHRAN MILL PARK

6875 Cochran Mill Rd.
Palmetto, Georgia • 463-6304

Fulton County operates this 800-acre park that affords families a variety of hiking possibilities—from easy 3-mile walks to moderate and steep 4-mile hikes. Pick up a map to guide you on your trek and enjoy the natural beauty of the area. *Hours:* Daily from dawn to dusk.

DAVIDSON-ARABIA MOUNTAIN
NATURE PRESERVE

3850 Klondike Rd.
Lithonia, Georgia • 371-2631

Arabia Mountain is a large granite outcropping similar to Stone Mountain and Panola Mountain. Unlike those parks, however, Arabia Mountain is still undeveloped, and the county hopes to maintain its pristine quality as much as possible while providing limited access to visitors. There are plans to build a caretaker's house, new parking lots, picnic sites, hiking trails and fishing areas. The natural vegetation of mosses and wildflowers, which are on the endangered flora list, will be preserved, as will the natural ecosystems. The educational possibilities for families, school groups and other organizations will be explored and developed in the near future by the DeKalb County Department of Recreation, Parks and Cultural Affairs. Visit this special wilderness. *Hours:* Daily from dawn to dusk.

DUNWOODY NATURE CENTER

5343 Roberts Dr.
Dunwoody, Georgia • 394-3322

Imagine your family having a lovely picnic amidst a butterfly and bee garden, a shade garden or a sun garden, with nearby trails that wind through the woods near a creek and playground. If this scene appeals to you, be sure to visit the Dunwoody Nature Center, owned by DeKalb County but independently operated, where you can enjoy the beauty of the outdoors or explore indoor exhibits about plants and animals. A large selection of nature classes are offered for children of all ages. *Hours:* Open for classes and programs by appointment.

EARTH DAY

Earth Day has become a very important time of year in Atlanta as well as elsewhere in the country. Participating in Earth Day events, whether attending festivals or planting a seed in your yard, is a yearly lesson for children in the possibilities of people working together to better the human condition. It is an opportunity to discuss ecological issues of pollution (air, water, sound and visual), to discuss conservation and recycling, to get involved in politics by writing to government representatives and companies, and to study about endangered species, hazardous products and toxic wastes, pesticides, alternative forms of energy, the destruction of rain forests, and acid rain. The subjects, educational discussions and projects your family can get involved in are endless. Earth Day events are advertised well in advance. Look in the *Atlanta Journal and Constitution's* Saturday *Leisure Guide, Creative Loafing* and newsletters from your library. Also look for announcements about special events at the Atlanta Botanical Garden, Chattahoochee Nature Center, Fernbank Science Center, SciTrek, Zoo Atlanta and participating bookstores.

GEORGIA DEPARTMENT OF NATURAL RESOURCES

205 Butler St., S.E. • Suite 1352
Atlanta, Georgia 30334 • 656-3530

The Georgia Department of Natural Resources sponsors numerous special events, workshops and programs at all of the Georgia State Parks and Historic Sites. Programs include hiking and backpacking activities, nongame and wildlife classes, music and dance, folk skills and living history demonstrations, fishing, wildflower programs, canoe excursions, Native American activities and holiday programs. Send away for the department's brochure entitled "Georgia State Parks and Historic Sites—Special Events," which provides a comprehensive list of the year's scheduled activities and information on purchasing an annual "Georgia ParkPass."

GEOSPHERE CENTER

Chattahoochee River National Recreation Area, Barnwell Unit
Alpharetta, Georgia • 642-8386/518-1134

The National Parks Service offers a unique training program in environmental education for teachers and youth group leaders. It is believed that through active participation in outdoor activities and role playing exercises, enthusiastic and knowledgeable adults will spark students to become active in preserving and enhancing our environment. A secondary focus of GeoSphere is to host overnight camps and outdoor activities for groups of school-age children.

MONASTERY OF THE HOLY SPIRIT

Highway 212
Conyers, Georgia 30207 • 483-8705

If serenity is what you seek, take your family on a sojourn to this monastery set in beautiful natural surroundings. You may visit unannounced or you may call ahead to arrange a free group tour (760-0959), which includes a slide presentation and time to browse in the bookstore and gift shop. A special treat is the bread that is baked on the premises every Thursday and sold at the gift shop all week long until sold out. The monks suggest you bring a sack lunch (minus the bread, of course) and spend an afternoon visiting the monastery and picnicking by the lake.

NATURE STORES

• **The Nature Company,** Lenox Square, 3393 Peachtree Rd.,

Atlanta (231-9252); Perimeter Mall, 4400 Ashford-Dunwoody Rd., Atlanta (551-0266); and Underground Atlanta, 114 Lower Alabama St., Atlanta (525-3131).

• **The Discovery Store,** Phipps Plaza, 3500 Peachtree Rd., Atlanta (841-0081).

Children as well as adults are fascinated by the stunning museumlike displays and science toys (some of which may be touched) all over these stores, from ceiling to floor. There are rock and mineral specimens, magnifying glasses, puzzles, posters, T-shirts, jewelry, mobiles, games, fetishes, bug collecting and other nature kits, birdfeeders and more. Nature stores are fun and interesting places to go, especially on a rainy day when your family needs a special indoor activity. Also, keep these stores in mind when you need to buy a special birthday gift. The stores also offer year-round workshops and storytelling for children. *Hours:* The Nature Company: Monday–Saturday from 10:00 a.m.–9:00 p.m., and Sunday from 12:30 p.m.–5:30 p.m. Discovery Store: Monday–Saturday from 10:00 a.m.–9:00 p.m., and Sundays from 12:00 noon-5:30 p.m.

• **Birdfeeders, Etc.,** 5500 Chamblee-Dunwoody Rd., Dunwoody (393-2570). The nature gift store has an unusual selection of birdfeeders, birdbaths, plain and decorative birdhouses, pictures, decorated chairs, seed and a very large selection of bird books. *Hours:* Monday–Saturday from 10:00 a.m.–6:00 p.m.

NURSERIES

Even without spending a cent, nurseries can be visited and enjoyed for their displays of outdoor seasonal plants and interesting houseplant varieties. Visit at least once each season (not just springtime!) to get a sense of what grows in this part of the world in our kind of climate. For less than $1.00 per child, seeds may be purchased to plant indoors or out for an individual science lesson. Toddlers can plant a seed in a glass between a wet paper towel and the inside of the glass, and watch the roots and stem grow. Older children can choose a particular plant they like best and go to the library to learn more about it. Develop a project by keeping a journal, identifying parts of the plant or describing the many uses of the plant. Planning a serious flower or vegetable garden, or growing specialty plants such as Bonsai, takes many visits to nurseries and libraries to do a good job. Or just go for a spontaneous visit when your family needs something to do together. Note: There is a railroad garden (yes, real model trains) at **Hastings Nature and Garden Center**, 2350 Cheshire Bridge Rd., Atlanta (321-6981), and a koi fish tank that are particularly exciting for young kids. There is something for everyone at a nursery.

OUTDOOR ACTIVITY CENTER AT BUSH MOUNTAIN

1442 Richland Rd., S.W.
Atlanta, Georgia 30310 • 752-5385

Located only three miles from downtown Atlanta, the Outdoor Activity Center is aptly named "Atlanta's Forest in the City," because it offers three miles of hiking trails running through a twenty-six–acre Piedmont forest. The center offers guided nature walks, a discovery learning room, a traveling nature show, workshops, adventure teaching gardens, puppet shows, scout programs, Christmas in the Woods, Arbor Day educational programs, birthday parties, birdseed sales, a nature shop, a picnic and playground area, a treehouse classroom and Naturescapes, an outdoor environmental learn-and-play sculpture designed to teach children about different habitats in the forest community. A new Nature Science Center has allowed for an exciting expansion of programs offered to families. *Hours:* Monday–Saturday from 9:00 a.m.–4:00 p.m. or by appointment. The park is free, but there are small fees for tours, traveling nature shows and discovery craft projects.

PANOLA MOUNTAIN STATE CONSERVATION PARK

2600 Highway 155, S.W.
Stockbridge, Georgia 30281 • 389-7801

Located 18 miles southeast of Atlanta off I-20, this 100-acre granite monadnock is a beautiful conservation park sheltering rare plants and animals. Within the park are a picnic area, playground, nature center with interpretive exhibits, and six miles of well-marked hiking trails the whole family can enjoy. Bicycling is not permitted. Saturdays and Sundays throughout the summer there are films, slide shows, and/or storytelling sessions related to nature. Special early bird and moonlight walks are scheduled year-round as are nature programs, workshops and demonstrations on such diverse topics as wildflowers, birds of prey, bats and mushrooms. The hikes are free, as are most of the other programs. The park occasionally runs a summer "Environmental Discovery Program" for children. *Park hours:* Daily from 7:00 a.m.–dark. *Interpretive Center hours:* Monday–Friday from 10:00 a.m.–6:00 p.m.; Saturday from 10:00 a.m.–4:00 p.m.; and Sunday from 1:00 p.m.–5:00 p.m. Closed Mondays except on major holidays. Free.

PROVIDENCE PARK

13440 Providence Rd.
Alpharetta, Georgia 30201 • 740-2419

The salient features of this forty-two-acre park include family camping facilities, an accessible shoreline around a 28-acre lake (shore fishing permitted), picnic tables, and unique class offerings. Adventurous families may sign up for classes in backpacking, rock climbing and even rappelling. For us ordinary folk, there are simple hiking trails with maps available to chart your course. *Park hours:* Monday–Thursday from 9:00 a.m.–6:00 p.m., and Friday–Saturday from 9:00 a.m.–5:00 p.m. Free.

RECYCLING

Surely there is no longer anyone left who needs to be convinced that recycling is a good thing, even a necessity. Everyone knows recycling conserves natural resources, landfill space and energy, generates revenues and enhances the quality of the environment. But it can be a bit of a bother to do. Fortunately, county governments are increasing their curbside recycling, local schools have paper drives, many popular locales (such as Your DeKalb Farmers Market) have bins, and companies such as Mindis Recycling have recycling centers around town. Children really enjoy participating in recycling. My son loves taking his red wagon to the neighbors to collect their newspapers. Every little bit helps, and we feel better when we do it. Above all, we are teaching our children to care, and to care is to take an active role. The Sierra Club Atlanta Group has a comprehensive publication, *Recycling Directory for the Extended Atlanta Metropolitan Area*, that lists recycling places by area, notes what kinds of materials they accept and when. The book is available at most area bookstores and costs $2.00.

• **The Common Pond**, "An Environmental Awarehouse," 1402 N. Highland Ave., Atlanta (876-6368). This Morningside-area shop is reputed to be the only Atlanta retail store to deal exclusively in environmentally friendly products. Recycled merchandise, non-toxic and non-polluting products and packaging are some of the qualities the owners take into account when stocking their shelves. The items for sale range from household products to clothing to pet supplies—even fun and interesting games, books and toys for children, as well as baby gifts. This store, as you might have already imagined, provides food for thoughtful discussions well after your shopping is done. *Hours:* Tuesday–Thursday from 10:30 a.m.–9:00 p.m.; Friday–Saturday from 10:30 a.m.–10:00 p.m.; and Sunday from 12:00 noon–7:00 p.m.

W.H. REYNOLDS MEMORIAL NATURE PRESERVE

5665 Reynolds Rd.
Morrow, Georgia 30260 • 961-9257

This 120-acre preserve, run by the Clayton County Department of Parks & Recreation, is a fine place to go for a short hike in the forest among ponds and streams. Four miles of trails begin and end at the nature center, ensuring that no one can get lost! The center also houses an interpretive nature exhibit and is the site of many interesting nature classes for children and families throughout the year. Call early to reserve a space as the classes are quite popular. There are also two large picnic areas. *Preserve hours:* Daily from 8:30 a.m.–dark. *Nature Center hours:* Monday–Friday from 8:30 a.m.–5:30 p.m.; Saturday from 11:00 a.m.–3:00 p.m.; and Sunday from 1:00 p.m.–5:00 p.m. On the weekends, the nature center and bathrooms are sometimes closed, so be sure to call ahead. Free.

SOUTHFACE ENERGY INSTITUTE

158 Moreland Ave., N.E.
Atlanta, Georgia 30307
Mailing address:
P.O. Box 5506, Atlanta, Georgia 30307 • 525-7657

This institute is a non-profit public interest group that has promoted renewable energy resources through education and research of alternative technologies for over a decade. Your family can take a very interesting self-guided tour through their Southface Alternative Energy Center and see such innovations as toilets that dramatically reduce water usage, special insulated window coverings ("window quilts"), ellipsoidal reflector lamps and occupancy sensors that automatically turn on or off a light when someone enters or leaves a room. There is always someone available to answer your questions. The library and numerous free energy publications are of interest to adults and to upper elementary kids who might be doing a special project in this field. *Hours:* Monday–Friday from 9:30 a.m.–5:00 p.m. Free.

SWEETWATER CREEK STATE CONSERVATION PARK

Lithia Springs, Georgia • 732-5871
Mailing address:
P.O. Box 816, Lithia Springs, Georgia 30057

Located in Douglas County, about twenty-five minutes from downtown Atlanta, Sweetwater Creek is a beautiful, lush forest with lakes, streams and a reservoir. You can spend the better part of a day hiking on a five-mile nature trail, picnicking in one of many picnic shelters, boating, fishing or playing in one of the playgrounds. Not only is this vast area (1,995 acres) conserved for its natural resources, but it is also a site of historical significance: there are ruins of the New Manchester Manufacturing Company, a textile factory burned by Sherman's troops during the Civil War, and the remains of more than 60 workers' homes. Programs on nature, history and boating safety are offered throughout the year, as well as special events such as Summer Jr. Ranger camp and the annual New Manchester Days Celebration in July. Most activities are free, but a rental fee is required for boats. *Park hours:* Daily from 7:00 a.m.–10:00 p.m. *Office/Bait Shop hours:* Monday–Friday from 8:00 a.m.–5:00 p.m. Free.

CATOR WOOLFORD MEMORIAL GARDEN

1815 S. Ponce de Leon Ave.
Atlanta, Georgia 30307 • 377-3836

Located on the grounds of REACH, Inc., this beautiful garden is open to the public until dark each day. Through a cooperative effort between REACH, Inc. and Fernbank Science Center, high school students enrolled in a vocational horticulture program (Occupational Education Center/Central campus) take meticulous care of the garden, the stream and the paths, including all of the flowering bulbs and plants. If your family would like to take a quiet stroll through a beautiful garden, try this one. Free.

SCIENCE

BRADLEY OBSERVATORY & PLANETARIUM

Agnes Scott College
E. Hancock St. and S. Candler St.
Decatur, Georgia 30030 • 371-6294

Bradley Observatory is open to the public on the first Friday of every month during the academic year (except January) at 8:00 p.m. There is a brief lecture and a planetarium show, after which anyone may gaze through the telescopes. The program is geared for children eight years and older and adults. Be sure to call ahead as the schedule is subject to change. Free.

COMPUTER SCIENCE & ACADEMIC ACHIEVEMENT

Some of the Atlanta colleges and universities offer programs for children in computer sciences and advanced academic skills:

• **DeKalb College Continuing Education Department**, 3251 Panthersville Rd., Decatur (244-5050). DeKalb College offers summer classes introducing children to computer sciences.

• **Emory University Tennis & Computer Sports Camp**, Woodruff Physical Education Center, Atlanta (727-6547 or 727-6545).

Emory's summer program offers children age 8–17 an opportunity to learn and improve their computer and tennis skills. Session instruction is designed for each child's individual needs, and courses include Introduction to the Computer, Caring for the Computer, Computer Programming and Enhancement of Verbal Skills, and Math Skills Utilizing Simulation Games.

• **Georgia Institute of Technology**, Academic Affairs, 225 North Ave., Atlanta (894-8994). Georgia State offers "Summerscape," an excellent summer science and computer enrichment program for rising 7th and 8th graders.

• **Georgia State University Saturday School for Scholars and Leaders**, Department of Early Childhood Education, 917 Urban Life Center, University Plaza, Atlanta (651-2840 or 651-2581). Saturday School for Scholars and Leaders is an extensive program of extracurricular topics for gifted children offered year-round. On five consecutive Saturdays, "gifted" children (having an IQ of 120 or above, or results in school indicating a 90th percentile or higher ranking on a standardized achievement test) attending K–12th grade are eligible to attend. Courses encompass a wide range of subjects—computer, science, math, architecture, physiology, humanities, creative writing, journalism, art, music, dramatics, movement, ballet and foreign languages. There is also a preschool program.

• **Kennesaw College**, Division of Continuing Education, Professional Development and Extension, Marietta (423-6765). Year-round, Kennesaw College offers workshops promoting study skills and classes in computer proficiency. During the summer, the college offers a dazzling array of summer camp programs in computer, rockets, Chisanbop, music, foreign languages and cultures, calligraphy, business, visual arts, nature, sports, science, mythical monsters and super heroes.

GEORGIA STATE OBSERVATORY

Hard Labor Creek State Park
Rutledge, Georgia • *404/651-3579*

Georgia State University opened this observatory in Hard Labor Creek Park, which is about an hour east of Atlanta (Exit #49 off I-20). The observatory is open to the public in the evenings about once a month. Please call the observatory to find out the date of the next open house.

SPACE & ASTRONOMY CAMPS

• **CASS/Center for Astronomy & Space Science,** Roswell (641-1729). This non-profit educational organization offers an outreach astronomy program to local schools and a summer astronomy camp. The hands-on experience with science equipment and materials offered by CASS are unparalleled in Atlanta, including special computer systems tracking global warming, a portable Starlab, and a real meteorite. One-week classes for children age 7–12 are offered, and class sizes are kept small. Call for information on this exciting, fledgling program.

• **Challengers Club Space Camp,** Dr. Ronald E. McNair Foundation, P.O. Box 54392, Atlanta, Georgia 30308 (527-7452). Children age 10–14 years can sign on as one of the space camp crew for Challengers Club Space Camp, which is a five-day summer program offering children hands-on exposure to space and science education. The program may include a field trip to the U.S. Space & Rocket Center in Huntsville, aerospace experiments at Six Flags, space demonstrations at SciTrek, meetings with NASA scientists, rocket building workshops or an overview of careers in space.

• **U.S. Space & Rocket Center/U.S. Space Camp,** P.O. Box 1680, Huntsville, Alabama 35807 (205/837-3400) (For reservations:

800/63SPACE). Although not local, we could not resist including this listing! Year-round, children from all over the world can attend a one-week program at U.S. Space Camp to learn how they can become involved in science and space technology. Hands-on experiences in rocket propulsion, spacesuits, simulated space walks, astronaut training activities and Space Shuttle mission simulations are all a part of the program. In Alabama, overnight camp is offered for children in grades 4–6; in Florida, camp is offered for children in grades 4–7. Older children in grades 7–12 can attend U.S. Space Academy and the Aviation Challenge, which offer more advanced programs. There is also an Adult Space Academy and a special Teacher Program. Special parent/child sessions are available on certain holiday weekends for children age 6–12. Call for details and costs. Our family spent a day at the U.S. Space & Rocket Center, staying overnight in nearby Guntersville, and we all thought it was great to see real rockets, space vehicles and explore the hands-on indoor/outdoor museum.

▬▬ HISTORY & POLITICS ▬▬

In addition to the larger institutions we discussed elsewhere in this book relating to history and politics, there are more esoteric places to visit which might interest your family.

ATLANTA JOURNAL AND CONSTITUTION

72 Marietta St.
Atlanta, Georgia 30303 • *526-5286*

The lobby of the *Atlanta Journal and Constitution* has a small showcase of historic newspaper front pages; a special display featuring Ralph McGill, Margaret Mitchell and other individuals who have worked on the newspaper; and a large linotype machine. The exhibits are small and a bit out-dated, but a quick stop by the newspaper lobby, if you are already in the neighborhood, will be worth your while. (The newspaper is next door to the Federal Reserve

Bank's Monetary Museum and down the street from the CNN Center.) *Hours:* Monday–Friday from 8:00 a.m.–5:00 p.m. Free.

ATLANTA PRESERVATION CENTER TOURS

84 Peachtree St., N.W.
The Flatiron Building, Suite 401
Atlanta, Georgia 30303 • Hotline: 876-2040

The Atlanta Preservation Center is a non-profit association dedicated to promoting historic preservation in Atlanta through advocacy and education. Members provide assistance to people interested in preserving historical buildings and neighborhoods. The center has a newsletter, a speaker's bureau, and conducts walking tours of Atlanta as a means of increasing public awareness of, and appreciation for, the city's architectural heritage. Most of the tours offered by the center are probably too long and detailed for young children to enjoy. However, the year-round guided tour of the Fox Theatre, an exotic Moorish and Egyptian revival movie palace, can be enjoyed by older children. For information on and a description of the Fox Theatre tour, see "Fox Theatre" in our chapter "Places To Go." Other tours offered by the Preservation Center are Ansley Park, Historic Downtown, Inman Park, Sweet Auburn/MLK District, Underground Atlanta (which includes the Capitol, government buildings and churches), West End (including the Wren's Nest and Hammonds House), and Walking Miss Daisy's Druid Hills Tour. These tours are only offered during the months of April through November. The cost of the tours is $5.00 for adults, $4.00 for seniors and $3.00 for children. To make reservations for groups of ten or more, or for membership information, call 876-2041. The center also offers a unique "Heritage Education" program for elementary school children.

COBB COUNTY YOUTH MUSEUM

649 Cheatham Hill Dr., S.W.
Marietta, Georgia 30064 • 427-2563

The Cobb County Youth Museum is unlike traditional museums where children are instructed to "look, but don't touch." Here, children actually get to participate in the museum's exhibits by dressing in costume, using period props and interacting with the museum's staff in skits, puppet shows, parades and narrations centering on the exhibit's theme. For example, a recent program was called "The Drama of Science," which used skits, costumes and narration to highlight the accomplishments of George Washington Carver, Marie Curie and Thomas Edison. The museum is primarily for groups of school children from the second grade and up, but it is open to the public on a limited basis. *Hours:* Tours are open to the public from 2:00 p.m.–4:00 p.m. on the first Sunday of March, April, May, October and November, at a cost of $1.00. Please phone ahead. School tours are offered Monday–Friday at 9:30 a.m. and 11:30 p.m. during the school year at a cost of $4.00 per person. Teachers must schedule a visit in advance. (The museum is located in the Cheatham Hill section of Kennesaw Mountain National Battlefield Park.)

FORT PEACHTREE

2630 Ridgewood Rd., N.W.
Chattahoochee Water Treatment Plant Facility
Atlanta, Georgia 30318 • 355-8229

Fort Peachtree, located at the rear of the property of the Chattahoochee Water Treatment Plant, is a replica of the original fort built by the British on the shores of the Chattahoochee River as the first non-Indian establishment in Georgia. The original "Fort Peach Tree" served as a stronghold against the Creek Indians, and was also a strategically located trading post and ferry landing on the river. All that remains now is this replica of the original fort. (There are no exhibits, artifacts or documents other than two signs explaining the historical significance of the site.) Down the road from the fort is a pretty picnic area near the shores of the Chattahoochee. Although it would be difficult to expect a child to be able to imagine the original Fort Peachtree or the historical significance of the site, it is an unusual site for a picnic or fishing expedition. (There are no restroom facilities. Finding the fort is quite difficult, so be sure to call ahead for directions.) *Hours:* Monday–Friday from 8:00 a.m.–4:00 p.m. Free.

GEORGIA DEPARTMENT OF ARCHIVES & HISTORY

330 Capitol Ave., S.E.
Atlanta, Georgia 30334 • 656-2350

This striking building, a seventeen-story, windowless "ice cube" of marble, houses official records, state documents, census data, photographs, prints and maps dating from 1733. There is not much here for the casual sightseer, but some of the displays on the main floor might be of interest to older age children, such as the maps on permanent display and occasional special exhibits on genealogy. Tours are by appointment, and a special pass is required to use the archives. *Hours:* Monday–Friday from 8:00 a.m.–4:15 p.m., and Saturday from 9:30 a.m.–3:15 p.m. Free.

HAPEVILLE DEPOT MUSEUM

620 S. Central Ave.
Hapeville, Georgia 30354 • 669-2175

Housed in Hapeville's renovated train depot (originally built in 1890), the Hapeville Depot Museum is small and jam-packed with memorabilia from the 1900s. Exhibits highlight the role of airplanes, cars and trains in Hapeville's history. (Hartsfield International

Airport is nearby, the Ford Assembly Plant in Hapeville opened in 1947, and the museum is in the old train depot.) A whole room of the museum is devoted to a model railroad. Installed by the Hapeville Central Model Railroad Club, it has about 400 feet of track with tiny trains running through a village and mountains. *Hours:* Monday–Saturday from 11:00 a.m.–3:00 p.m., and Sunday from 1:00 p.m.–4:00 p.m. Free.

RHODES HALL

Georgia Trust for Historic Preservation
1516 Peachtree St., N.W.
Atlanta, Georgia 30309 • 881-9980

Rhodes Hall is a Victorian structure built in the Romanesque Revival style. Constructed in 1903 as a home for the Amos Giles Rhodes family, the design was inspired by Rhineland castles. It is currently owned by the State of Georgia and is the headquarters for the Georgia Trust for Historic Preservation. In the spring of 1990, restoration began with the installation of the original carved mahogany staircase and stained glass windows. Nine Tiffany glass panels depict the "Rise and Fall of the Confederacy." *Hours:* Monday–Friday from 11:00 a.m.–4:00 p.m. Admission is free. Guided tours cost $2/adult and 50¢/child.

THE SANDY SPRINGS HISTORIC SITE

6075 Sandy Springs Cir.
Sandy Springs, Georgia 30328 • 851-9111

A visit to the Sandy Springs Historic Site includes a very informative guided tour of the Williams-Payne House, a restored 19th-century farmhouse furnished in period antiques. (Learn where the expression "Sleep tight" came from!) You will also see an authentic 1860s, fully restored milk house; a 19th-century "privy"; and the natural springs for which Sandy Springs is named. This historic site is the location for the annual fall Sandy Springs Festival that features folk craft demonstrations, music, vintage car shows and other living history activities. A summer program for children includes storytelling and traditional crafts, such as candle-dipping and soap-making. *Hours:* Daily from 10:00 a.m.–4:00 p.m. The site is reserved for school tours on Thursday mornings. Call ahead to make sure other tours have not been scheduled. *Admission:* $2.00/adult, and $1.00/children and senior citizens.

ZACHOR HOLOCAUST CENTER

Jewish Community Center – Lower Level
1745 Peachtree St., N.E.
Atlanta, Georgia 30309 • 873-1661

The center houses a permanent exhibit of Holocaust history, photography and survivor's memorabilia. The center will be moving near the new Jewish Heritage Center, 1753 Peachtree Street, scheduled to open in late 1994 or early 1995. *Hours:* There are regularly scheduled hours, including some on Sundays, but because the museum is staffed by volunteers, coverage is not always certain. We suggest you phone ahead to make an appointment. Free.

FARMERS MARKETS & PICK YOUR OWN

FARMERS MARKETS

Food shopping is a weekly chore that cannot be avoided. We can try to add a little spice to the routines by frequenting different grocery stores in our neighborhood or venturing to various ethnic groceries; but even so, children (and parents, too), may still get bored.

Luckily, Atlanta offers a variety of alternatives to ordinary supermarket shopping that children and families will find fun, and in many instances, educational.

THE ATLANTA STATE FARMERS MARKET

16 Forest Pkwy.
Forest Park, Georgia 30050 • 366-6910

The Atlanta State Farmers Market is located about 15 minutes south of downtown Atlanta in Forest Park (off I-75 just south of I-275). It is the second largest wholesale market for fruits and vegetables in the United States. The huge complex is filled with produce, plants (pansies, begonias and ferns are favorites), shrubbery and local specialties such as honey, relishes, pickled vegetables and peanuts. During the summer and fall, the complex is filled with eye-catching displays of seasonal produce. From October through December, the market sells pumpkins of all sizes and plenty of interesting gourds, Christmas trees and other holiday greenery. (We go twice a year every year and thoroughly enjoy our special visit!) The market also houses an egg processing plant, a hamper house stocked with crates and baskets, and a cannery. *Hours:* The complex is open every day of the week, and the majority of the farmers' booths are set up and open for business from 8:00 a.m.–5:00 p.m. On site is a Davis Brother's Cafeteria which serves up southern-style meals using produce purchased from the market. Stop by for a country style breakfast or a meal of fresh vegetables, fruits, meats and southern desserts—a fitting end to your shopping. The cafeteria is open daily from 6:00 a.m.–8:30 p.m. Call 366-7414 for more information.

HARRY'S FARMERS MARKET

Three locations: 1180 Upper Hembree Rd., Alpharetta (664-6300); 2025 Satellite Point, Duluth (416-6900); and 70 Powers Ferry Rd.,

Marietta (578-4400). Now that Harry's Farmers Markets are open, the northern suburbs have fantastic farmers markets of their own. Harry's stocks a large selection of farm fresh produce, meats, fish, cheese, spices, dairy products, coffees, dried fruits and nuts, cookbooks, cut-flowers and plants. Unlike the DeKalb and International farmers markets, the stores do not have as large a selection of ethnic and gourmet foods. But nowhere in Atlanta will you find a better bakery—the selection and variety of the market's freshly baked goods (breads and desserts) have a wide-spread reputation. And the quality and variety of prepared fresh foods (like sushi, lasagna, quiche, pasta sauce, pizza, complete meals and unusual salads) cannot be beat. I stock our freezer with desserts and prepared main dishes for those hectic days when there just isn't time to cook, or I am suddenly informed by my son that it is my turn to bring dessert to a school function. Another Harry's Farmers Market is being planned near the Atlanta State Farmers Market. Also visit Harry's in a Hurry, 1875 Peachtree St., Atlanta (352-7800) and at other locations opening throughout metro Atlanta for take-out delicacies. *Hours:* Monday–Thursday from 9:00 a.m.–8:00 p.m.; Friday from 9:00 a.m.–9:00 p.m.; Saturday from 9:00 a.m.–8:00 p.m.; and Sunday from 10:00 a.m.–7:00 p.m.

INTERNATIONAL FARMERS MARKET

5193 Peachtree Industrial Blvd.
Chamblee, Georgia 30341 • 455-1777

The 90,000-square-foot facility is filled with produce, meats, fish, cheeses, coffees, spices, and baked goods, with a heavy emphasis on international food products. Not only will the array of interesting foods appeal to children, but so will the fish swimming around in huge tanks. You may choose one of the fish for dinner, and then watch while the fish is killed, gutted and filleted to your specifications. *Hours:* Monday–Friday from 10:00 a.m.–9:00 p.m., and Saturday and Sunday from 9:00 a.m.–9:00 p.m.

SWEET AUBURN CURB MARKET/
THE ATLANTA MUNICIPAL MARKET

209 Edgewood Ave.
Atlanta, Georgia 30303 • 659-1665

First opened in 1923, and currently open during an expensive renovation process, the Atlanta Municipal Market is located near the Martin Luther King, Jr. Historical District and Grady Hospital. The market is filled with vendors selling massive quantities of meats, fresh fruits and vegetables, as well as a selection of cheese and grocery items. Increasingly, the stalls and snack bar area are becoming more international in tone as Asian-Americans and African-Americans operate businesses side-by-side, resulting in an unusual mix of Asian and southern cuisines. For your first visit, we recommend that you not expect to do much food shopping— this market's rustic style may not appeal to everyone. Just plan on looking around at the displays and getting used to the unique atmosphere. Even if you decide not to buy any food at the market, we guarantee that your family will nevertheless long remember the visit. **Hours:** Monday–Thursday from 8:00 a.m.–5:45 p.m., and Friday and Saturday from 8:00 a.m.–6:45 p.m.

YOUR DEKALB FARMERS MARKET

3000 E. Ponce de Leon Ave.
Decatur, Georgia 30030 • 377-6400

Your DeKalb Farmers Market is a small city unto itself filled with fresh meats, fish, produce, cheeses, flowers, spices, dairy products, baked goods, deli items, coffees . . . and if that wasn't enough . . . ethnic foods, nuts, dried fruit, wine, beer and gourmet groceries. Each department is filled with eye-opening selections of unusual and varied products—all reasonably priced. Free samples of seasonal fruit, baked goods, sparkling juices and chunks of cheese are sometimes available for sampling, but if you still feel hungry, you can visit the cafeteria which features fresh baked goods, hot meals, salads and piping hot coffee. If you just want a special treat, go to the snack bar to purchase a yummy dessert you can eat while shopping, or buy the kids a fresh fruit smoothie (they can choose the fruits) or a frozen yogurt. No matter how sophisticated your tastes, you can be sure that you will find something in the market that you have never eaten before. Be brave— experiment, and eat well! Bring sweaters—the market is chilly. *Hours:* Monday–Friday from 10:00 a.m.–9:00 p.m., and Saturday and Sunday from 9:00 a.m.–9:00 p.m.

NORTH FULTON COOPERATIVE MARKETS

730-7000

Purchase fresh produce at tailgate markets operated through the North Fulton Cooperative Extension Service on Tuesdays, Thursdays and Saturdays from 7:00 a.m.–12:00 noon during the summer months. Locations are the Roswell Mall parking lot, Mount Vernon Presbyterian Church in Sandy Springs, and Wills Park Recreation Center in Alpharetta.

▬ PICK YOUR OWN FOOD ▬

Wouldn't it be wonderful if we all had the time and space to have our own gardens in the backyard filled with our favorite seasonal produce? And while we're dreaming, let's throw in a few fruit trees, berry patches and an herb garden. Our children could run outside and in a few minutes be back with everything we'd need for the evening dinner. Well, we may not be able to fulfill our fantasies, but we are lucky to have farmers who allow us, for a few hours (and a few bucks), to pretend their farms are our own and welcome us to pick vegetables, fruits and berries. A word of caution: please wear sunscreen and a hat.

Equally as much fun as the gathering of food is deciding as a family what foods to cook and letting the children participate in the preparation. Not only will children of all ages develop a deeper understanding and appreciation of farming and where food really comes from, but the lesson of *The Little Red Hen* will be most clearly understood!

• **Georgia Certified Farm Markets,** Georgia Farm Bureau Federation, Commodities/Marketing Department, P.O. Box 7068, Macon, Georgia 31298 (912/474-8411). For those who may want to take a ride in the country, venturing out beyond the metro Atlanta area to pick your own food, you can write to the Georgia Farm Bureau Federation at the address above for a copy of their brochure called "Georgia Certified Farm Markets." The brochure lists over 50 retail farm markets in Georgia certified by the bureau, and for each farm provides directions, telephone numbers, months of operation and, most importantly, a description of the seasonal produce available at the farm. The descriptions are mouth-watering peaches, plums, berries, apples, watermelons, butter beans, collards, Vidalia onions, pecans, honey, relish, peanuts, jams, jellies, pumpkins, syrup, corn, gourds, fried pies, firewood, cured hams and bacons, muscadine grapes, ciders, dairy products, sausages, Christmas trees, candies, hanging baskets, country crafts, quilts and soaps. Take your pick!

• **Lake Laura Gardens,** Burnt Hickory Rd., Marietta (427-1774). Lake Laura Gardens is a small garden complete with dog, cats and hammock, that is perfect for preschoolers and younger children. Families may wander about and pick seasonal vegetables, flowers, fruits, herbs and berries. And for the patient child, there is also a small trout pond stocked with large fish. Open every day. Call for availability of produce and fishing information.

• *Farmers and Consumers Market Bulletin.* The *Bulletin* is a weekly publication of the Georgia Department of Agriculture. Some of the summer and fall issues list the names, addresses, telephone numbers and information about farms that allow you to pick your own produce. The main branch of your library system should have a copy of the *Bulletin*, or you can call the Department of Agriculture (656-3722), which will be glad to send you a free copy. Below is information on some of the farms often listed in the May, July and August issues of the bulletin which are within an hour and a half drive of the metro Atlanta area.

Remember always to call ahead to find out:

- **What crops are in season**
- **The availability of the produce**
- **Picking days and times**
- **If you will need to provide your own containers**
- **Cost**
- **Detailed directions**
- **Bathroom facilities**

BARTOW COUNTY

- **Glen Cove Nursery,** 755 Indian Mounds Rd. (1/4 mile north of Etowah Indian Mounds Historic Site), Cartersville (706/386-0207 or 706/386-3656). This farm is a great one to visit in conjunction with a trip to the Etowah Indian Mounds and Museum. The farm's specialty is raspberries and blackberries.

CHEROKEE COUNTY

- **Aaron & Pat McLain,** 18040 Union Hill Rd., Alpharetta (475-6836). Blueberries are available for picking in the months of July and August. Bring your own containers.

- **Berry Patch Farms,** 786 Arnold Mill Rd., Woodstock (936-0637 or 926-0561). The owners of this Georgia Certified Farm say they do not use any chemical spray on their berry plants, so you may eat as you go without concern. They are really very nice to children and encourage them to both pick and eat. Besides seasonal berries, they also have apples, pumpkins and Christmas trees. Picnicking is available nearby. Containers provided.

• **Cagle's Milk House,** Rt. 12, Box 362, Stringer Rd., Canton (706/345-5591). Dairy products are produced and processed at this Georgia Certified Farm. Buy whole milk, two percent milk, whole chocolate milk and buttermilk. Farm tours are available of the milk processing facility for groups of 25 or more. Call for an appointment. Open year-round.

• **Dan Merrefield,** Route 13, Canton (706/479-9608). This farm grows white half-runner beans, butter peas, tomatoes and other vegetables.

COBB COUNTY

• **Salacoa Valley Farm,** 3050 Ellis Rd., Kennesaw (422-9318). This farm specializes in blackberries.

COWETA COUNTY

• **Don L. Stambaugh,** 757 Fisher Rd., Sharpsburg (2 miles from Peachtree City) (706/251-7161). The farm has blueberries, blackberries, tomatoes, cucumbers and squash.

FAYETTE COUNTY

• **Adams Farms,** 1486 Hwy. 54W, Fayetteville (706/461-9395). Pick corn, tomatoes, greens, peas, beans, spinach, carrots, onions and other vegetables in season at this Georgia Certified Farm. Tours are available.

• **David Richardson,** 701 Goza Rd., Fayetteville (706/461-7814). Thornless blackberries and purple hull peas are available for picking.

• **Harp's Farm Market,** 1692 Hwy. 92S, 4 miles south of Fayetteville (706/461-1821). Pick muscadine grapes, berries, pumpkins, Christmas trees, cotton, books, shrubs and more at this Georgia Certified Farm. Take a hayride around the farm and picnic nearby. There is a roadside country store with jams, jellies, flowers and more for sale. Containers provided.

FORSYTH COUNTY

• **Bill Callaway,** Route 1, Cumming (706/887-4443). Produce at this farm is "Certified Organic." Sweet corn, beans, peas, cucumbers, squash, tomatoes, blueberries and raspberries are available. Call for an appointment a day or two ahead of time.

FULTON COUNTY

• **Whimsy Haven Farm,** 552 Hwy. 279 (Old National Hwy.), Fairburn (706/461-6742). Berries, vegetables, herbs, flowers, shittake mushrooms and worms are available here. Picnic in the shade. Portable toilets and Spanish-speaking staff are some of the amenities at this Georgia Certified Farm.

• **William Brown,** 1055 Jones Rd., Roswell (993-6866). Seasonal blueberries may be picked here.

GWINNETT COUNTY

• **Green Acres Farm,** Bill Isaacs, 2839 Lenora Rd., Snellville (979-1336 or 972-6865). Besides blackberries, boysenberries, tayberries and strawberries, this farm has barns, horses, water wells and tractors to delight young children. Bring your own containers.

• **J. L. Duncan,** 2503 Cammie Wages Rd., Dacula (962-4990). Pick blackberries, blueberries, corn, grapes, peaches, apples and plums out in the country.

• **Pine Ridge Berry Farm,** John Craddock, 311 Scenic Hwy., Lawrenceville (963-0937). Pick blackberries when in season.

HENRY COUNTY

• **Bond's Peach Orchard,** 1315 Fairview Rd., Ellenwood (706/474-4160). Pick peaches by appointment July and August.

• **Gordon's Berry Patch,** Gordon Olmstead, 490 Dorsey Rd. (Exit #70 off I-75), Hampton (706/946-3525). Blueberries and blackberries are available during summer months, but please call ahead before coming.

• **Gardner Farms,** P.O. Box 177, Locust Grove (706/957-2113). Peaches, blueberries, blackberries and local produce are available for picking at this Georgia Certified Farm.

• **H.C. Seabolt,** 2323 Legion Mill Rd., Locust Grove (706/957-3196). Pick blackberries June through July. Containers are furnished.

NEWTON COUNTY

• **Margaret Dimsdale,** 4300 Salem Rd., Covington (706/786-4687). Blueberries are available for picking from July through mid-August. Bring your own containers.

OCONEE COUNTY

- **A.W. White, Jr.**, High Shoals Rd., Watkinsvillle (706/769-6237). Ten varieties of plums are available daily June–July.

- **B.A. Thomas Orchards**, 5850 Macon Hwy., Bishop (706/769-6472). Peaches, muscadines, plums, nectarines, scuppernongs and seasonal vegetables are available at this orchard from mid-May through mid-September.

- **Doug Felder**, 1010 Pete Dickens Rd., Bogart (706/725-9489). Blackberries are available daily in June and early July.

- **James Miller**, 1371 Union Church Rd., Watkinsville (706/769-6359). Eight to nine varieties of blueberries are available daily June through August. Bring your own containers.

SPALDING COUNTY

- **Buck Creek Farm**, 175 Chappell Mill Rd., Orchard Hill (706/228-2682). Blueberries, blackberries and raspberries are available for picking, and fresh tomatoes may be purchased. Picnic tables and restrooms are on the premises.

- **Futral Farms Peach Orchard**, 5061 Jackson Rd., Griffin (706/228-1811). Pick your own peaches daily from mid-June through mid-August. Ice water and portable toilets are available.

- **Bill Ison**, Highway 16 west, Brooks (10 miles west of Griffin, 6 miles east of Senoia) (706/599-6970). Pick blueberries, blackberries and muscadines when in season. Containers are furnished. Open June through November.

WALTON COUNTY

• **Hard Labor Creek Blueberry Farm**, Knox Chapel Rd., Social Circle (near Hard Labor Creek State Park) (706/464-2412). Blueberries are available during the summer months.

• **Nepenthe Farms**, 2259 Liberty Hill Church Rd., Monroe (706/267-7711). Blueberries are available daily during the summer months. Containers are provided.

■■■ CHRISTMAS TREES ■■■

Cut your own trees at the following tree farms: • **Bethany Tree Farms,** 606 Old Jackson Rd. McDonough (706/957-5608); • **Berry's Christmas Tree Farm**, 90 Mount Tabor Rd., Covington (706/786-1880); • **Farmer Red's**, 2296 Jacksonville Rd., Lithonia (482-6049); • **Harp's Farm Market**, 1692 Highway 92 South, Fayetteville (706/461-1821); • **King's**, Wilhelmina Dr., Austell (948-3051); • **Santa's**, Saw Mill–Smithtown Rd., Suwanee (945-1027); and • **Worthington Tree Farm**, 145 Twin Oaks Dr., Lovejoy (706/478-4355). Also, the *Atlanta Journal and Constitution* usually provides a rather comprehensive list of tree farms in their special "Holiday Shopping Guide" section that runs near the end of November or early December.

■■■ PUMPKINS ■■■

These farms grow lots and lots of pumpkins, although you cannot necessarily pick your own: • **Burt's Pumpkin Farm**, Hwy. 52, Dawsonville (near Amicalola State Park) (706/265-3701). School and other youth groups are welcome to have fun on a hayride. A special treat is the popcorn grown and processed at the farm. • **Harp's Farm Market**, 1692 Highway 92 South, Fayetteville (706/461-1821). Groups are welcome to enjoy a hayride around the farm, visit a small petting zoo and picnic on the grounds.

STORYTELLING, LIBRARIES & BOOKSTORES

▬ STORYTELLING ▬

Storytelling is an art form that is almost extinct in our era of television and videos. We may diligently read stories to our children, but the art of storytelling is something quite different. Fortunately this marvelous means of communication that combines story, drama, personal presence and sometimes audience participation, can be enjoyed by children and parents alike in Atlanta.

• A group of professionals—the **Southern Order of Storytellers** (**SOS**)—performs regularly throughout Atlanta at bookstores, such as Borders Book Shop, Oxford Book Stores, Hobbit Hall and the Children's Book & Gift Market. The SOS also presents the **Olde Christmas Storytelling Festival** every January at DeKalb College Central Campus, the **Atlanta Storytelling Festival** every spring at the Atlanta History Center, and performs weekly at **The Wren's Nest**. (See our chapter "Places To Go" for more information about this attraction.) Some members of the SOS perform at **Art Centers** and are also available to perform at birthday parties, in classrooms and other group situations. Call the SOS at 633-3277, or The Wren's Nest (753-7735) for a list of professional storytellers and their phone numbers.

• A few of Atlanta's professional storytellers, necessarily being multi-talented, are teachers of creative dramatics. The **Alliance Theatre School** offers storytelling classes throughout the year for children age 8–16 years. Call 898-1131 for information. Professional and amateur storytellers perform regularly at public library storyhours. These programs are free and open to the public. Call or drop by your local library for storytime schedules.

• Hear a story told by a member of the Southern Order of Storytellers on **Tele-Tale (270-8238)**, a 24-hour telephone storytelling service offered by the DeKalb County Library System. A different story is featured every day.

• Listed below are more locations to alert you to the fact that storytelling happens all over Atlanta all year long!
  • **Atlanta History Center** (814-4000)
  • **Bulloch Hall** (992-1731)
  • **Chattahoochee Nature Center** (922-2055)
  • **DeKalb Historical Society's Log Cabin Story Hour** (373-1088)
  • **High Museum of Art** (892-3600)
  • **Michael C. Carlos Museum** (727-4282)
  • **National Black Arts Festival** (biennial) (730-7315)
  • **Antebellum Plantation at Stone Mountain Park** (498-5600)
  • **Stately Oaks Plantation Community**, Jonesboro (473-0197)

━━━ LIBRARIES ━━━

Groundbreaking ceremonies are being held for new libraries in the metropolitan Atlanta area every year, and many older libraries have been or are currently being renovated. Newer libraries have attractive reading areas for younger children and are expanding their reference collections for older students.

• Besides offering a comfortable place for children to enjoy the pleasure of books, Atlanta-area libraries offer diverse programs and services for children ranging from sleepy **storytimes** in the evenings to after-school **film** specials, craft and even skateboarding **workshops**! Occasional workshops are offered for adults on enhancing parenting skills. The materials available to children go beyond the tremendous children's book and reference sections to foreign language books and periodicals, magazines, records, films, videos and cassettes. Every summer libraries have **reading clubs** and contests for school-age kids.

• Keep an eye out for the opening of the **Auburn Avenue Research Library for African-American History & Culture**, which is a research facility dedicated solely to African-American studies. The impressive collections for the library have been gathered from all over the nation and include private papers, rare books, an extensive photography collection and other sophisticated and rare research materials. The branch also has a huge auditorium with a full schedule of lectures, workshops and children's films. There will be storytelling hours for elementary-age children.

• Mark your calendar for the **Friends of the Library Annual Book Sale** held at the main branch of the Atlanta-Fulton Public Library System every June.

• You might also be interested to know that libraries provide services to homeless shelters, voter registration and hospital kits, and have a wide-range of ESOL audio-visual materials. Go to your local library today, pick up its brochures, ask questions and find out what's going on.

• Not all branch libraries provide all the services of the county's system. Contact your main branch to locate special items such as foreign language materials or videos and the branch nearest you:

Atlanta-Fulton Public Library
System Central Headquarters
1 Margaret Mitchell Sq., N.W.
Atlanta, Georgia 30303
730-1700

Cobb County Public Library
Headquarters
266 Roswell St.
Marietta, Georgia 30060
528-2320

Clayton County
Library System
865 Battle Creek Rd.
Jonesboro, Georgia 30236
473-3850

DeKalb County Public
System Main Library
215 Sycamore St.
Decatur, Georgia 30030
370-3070

Gwinnett County Public
Library System
1001 Hwy. 29 South
Lawrenceville, Georgia 30245
822-4522

BOOKSTORES

There are many bookstores throughout Atlanta that have tremendous children's book sections or cater solely to children. Some have programs for children, such as storytelling hours or science and nature workshops; others have toys for sale and/or play structures and lofts for children to enjoy while reading. We cannot list all of the fine bookstores in the Atlanta area; however, the following are some of the more popular choices and examples of what you might find.

• **Borders Book Shop,** 3655 Roswell Rd., N.E. (near Piedmont Rd.), Atlanta (237-0707). This serene and spacious bookstore has the ambiance of a library. You really get the feeling that books are very special and important—things to be revered. I like to think that the calm I feel when walking into Borders is also felt by children. The large, well-displayed children's section is easy to negotiate with a stroller. (This cannot be said of all bookstores.) A variety of events are planned throughout the year especially for kids, such as storytelling, group songs and nature programs. *Hours:* Monday–Saturday from 9:00 a.m.–9:00 p.m., and Sunday from 11:00 a.m.–6:00 p.m. (Borders will be moving to Peachtree Road, across from Phipps Plaza, in early 1995.)

• **Children's Book & Gift Market,** 375 Pharr Rd., N.E., Atlanta (261-3442). This bookstore is jam-packed with children's books, and the staff is as knowledgeable about children and children's books as you could ever hope for. And besides stocking a wonderful selection of books, the owners have developed a diverse program of events throughout the year, including the award-winning "Summer of Saturdays" program that offers professional storytelling, puppet shows, magic shows, science and nature activities, musicians, multi-cultural events, creative party ideas and much, much more. There are book signings, story hours, a book club (after 12 purchases you get a book free), as well as educational toys and games. *Hours:* Monday–Saturday from 9:00 a.m.–6:00 p.m., and Sunday from 1:00 p.m.–5:00 p.m.

• **Hobbit Hall,** 120 Bulloch Ave., Roswell (587-0907). As your children enter Hobbit Hall, you will want to carefully watch their faces as they take in their surroundings. You will marvel at their delight as they discover an entire house full of books on every subject imaginable. And interspersed throughout the books is a selection of educational games, puzzles, music, stuffed animals and other enrichment material interesting to children of all ages. All merchandise is attractively arranged, and the owners are friendly and knowledgeable. Each Saturday the store hosts a free event, such as breakfast with the Berenstein Bears, storytelling sessions with children's authors, theatrical performances, or music hours led by professional musicians. On Wednesdays, Hobbit Hall hosts a storytime hour for preschoolers at 10:00 a.m. The browsing deck, playhouse, puppet theatre and garden make this an ideal location for one of the birthday programs offered by the store. Teachers please note—the store offers a whole range of outreach programs for schools, such as storytelling in classrooms, assistance in selecting books for libraries, whole-language workshops, book fairs and school discounts. *Hours:* Monday–Saturday from 10:00 a.m.–6:00 p.m. Extended hours during the holiday season.

• **Oxford Book Store at Peachtree Battle,** 2345 Peachtree Rd., N.E., Atlanta (364-2700). This huge bookstore is literally packed with an incredible number of children's (as well as adult's) books. But don't let the cramped aisles daunt you. It really is quite fun to be in the midst of so many books, and the store has a very knowledgeable person in the children's section ready and willing to help you find what you are looking for. A climbing structure provides a cozy place to read and helps keep your children occupied, but my youngsters find the books and the maze of aisles interesting enough. Summer storytelling, book signings and other special activities are designed just for children. Visit Cup and Chaucer upstairs for a special dessert with your children. *Hours:* Sunday–Thursday from 9:00 a.m.–12:00 midnight, and Friday and Saturday from 9:00 a.m.–1:00 a.m. (Yes, 1:00 a.m.). Open 365 days/year. On the other side of the shopping center is **Oxford Too**, 2395 Peachtree Rd., Atlanta (262-3411), which carries publisher remainders, discounted and used books, a large children's section and comics, games and collector items. This store also offers year-round special activities for children. *Hours:* Sunday–Thursday from 9:00 a.m.–10:00 p.m., and Friday and Saturday from 9:00 a.m.–12:00 midnight. Open 365 days/year.

• **Oxford Book Store at Buckhead,** 360 Pharr Rd., N.E., Atlanta (262-3333). This bookstore is one of the largest in Atlanta. Yet, as big and comprehensive as it is, the atmosphere is warm and friendly. The children's section has a special play/reading cave built under a staircase. A new addition, off the children's section, is filled with a large selection of comic books, baseball cards, Star Trek paraphernalia and the like. Upstairs is the pleasant Oxford Espresso Cafe with a menu that includes sandwiches, desserts and ice cream. The Arts Connection, also upstairs, is an intimate gallery that often displays works by students and offers workshops for children year-round. The bookstore services and hours are the same as at Peachtree Battle. **Oxford at West Paces Ferry,** 1200 W. Paces Ferry Rd., Atlanta. (364-2488) has a children's book section with a climbing structure, but the bookstore is not as large and comprehensive as its sisters. *Hours:* Sunday–Thursday from 9:00 a.m.–10:00 p.m., and Friday and Saturday from 9:00 a.m.–12:00 midnight. Open 365 days/year.

• And be sure to visit these other book and toy stores that have many unique and hard to find children's books. Or check the *Yellow*

Pages under **Book Stores** and **Toy Stores** for telephone numbers and addresses for these and other stores in your area:

- **ABC Parent/Teacher Learning Center** (multiple locations)
- **African American Book Shop** (multiple locations)
- **Barnes & Noble** (multiple locations)
- **B. Dalton Bookseller** (multiple locations)
- **BookStar** (multiple locations)
- **Brentanos**
- **Chapter 11** (multiple locations)
- **The Children's Hour Toys**
- **Coles, The Book People** (multiple locations)
- **Doubleday Book Shop**
- **Family Bookstores** (multiple locations)
- **Final Touch Gallery and Books**
- **First World Book Store** (multiple locations)
- **Hakim's Book Store** (African-American children's books)
- **Hammett's Learning Center**
- **International Bookstore** (Spanish language children's books)
- **J & R Educational Supplies**
- **Just Imagine**
- **Kiddie City**
- **Media Play** (multiple locations)
- **My Storyhouse** (multiple locations)
- **The School Box** (multiple locations)
- **Scribner's**
- **Shakespeare & Co. Bookstore**
- **Shrine of the Black Madonna Bookstore & Cultural Arts Center**
- **Tall Tales Bookshop**
- **Teacher's Toolbox**
- **The Toy School**
- **The Toy Store** (multiple locations)
- **Waldenbooks** (multiple locations)

• For fellow catalogue shoppers, **World of Reading, Ltd.** (233-4042) offers books, cassettes and language learning materials in over 6 different languages.

• **AND DON'T FORGET:** Members of Atlanta's international and ethnic communities have opened bookstores throughout the city stocking all sorts of books, magazines, newspapers, comics and other reading material for children in their native languages. For a comprehensive list of these bookstores, check *Ethnic Atlanta, The Complete Guide to Atlanta's Ethnic Communities*, available in local bookstores.

TOURS OF THE WORKING WORLD

Below is a list of tours available around town (and a bit beyond). Although a few of these tours do allow individual families to join up with other groups, you will still have to call ahead and make reservations. You might consider a tour for your child's next birthday party for an unusual celebration. All of the listed tours are free unless otherwise noted.

• **Atlanta Baking Company,** 165 Bailey St., S.W., Atlanta (653-9700). Take a guided tour through the production plant of this large bakery to observe the bread-making process. Watch the dough being mixed, and the loaves being baked, sliced and wrapped. Proceed to the shipping department where you can watch the bread being loaded onto trucks. The tour lasts about 1/2 hour. Please call ahead to schedule a tour.

• **Atlanta Police Department,** 165 Decatur St. Atlanta (658-6795). Tours for children age 8 and older include the fingerprinting, identification and communication departments of the police station, as well as a trip to the courthouse. Tours are available Monday–Friday from 8:00 a.m.–4:00 p.m. for groups of no more than 15 children. There are no tours during the summer months. Write well in advance for reservations: Community Services, 2001 Martin Luther King, Jr. Dr. N.W., Atlanta 30310. Also, contact your local police department to see whether or not tours are available.

• **Atlanta-Fulton County Public Library,** 1 Margaret Mitchell Sq., N.W., Atlanta (730-1700). The Children's Department conducts tours of the downtown branch of the Atlanta-Fulton County Library for children in the 4th–7th grades. Groups must include at least 10 children. The tour consists of a floor to floor walk through the library with explanations geared to the age group, along with a stop at the Margaret Mitchell exhibit. Call in advance for reservations.

• **The Brumby Chair Co.,** 37 W. Park Sq., Marietta (425-1875). The Brumby family began constructing the now-famous Brumby Jumbo Rocker in 1875. Although the rocker has not been in continuous production since that date, it is once again being built by the Brumby family. Visit the store and see the hand assembling and staining processes, learn the history of the rocker and peruse the current inventory. Open Monday–Saturday from 10:00 a.m.–5:00 p.m. Call for information.

• **Cagle's Milk House,** Rt. 12, Box 362, Stringer Rd., Canton (706/345-5591). Dairy products are produced and processed at this Georgia Certified Farm. You may buy whole milk, two-percent milk, whole chocolate milk and buttermilk. Farm tours are available of the milk processing facility for groups of 25 or more. Call for an appointment.

• **Channel 2 – WSB Television,** 1601 W. Peachtree St., N.E., Atlanta (897-7369). Tours of the television station are offered Tuesdays and Thursdays at 9:30 a.m. and 10:30 a.m. for children age eight years and older. Groups can be as large as forty children, and individual families are also welcome. Call in advance to schedule your tour.

• **Channel 5 – WAGA Television,** 1551 Briarcliff Rd., N.E., Atlanta (875-5551). Tours are offered Mondays, Tuesdays and Wednesdays at 10:00 a.m. for children in the second grade and older. This is a very popular field trip for school children, so we suggest individual families make an appointment to tour the station on a school holiday. Call at least two weeks in advance for reservations.

• **Channel 46 – WGNX,** 1810 Briarcliff Rd., N.E., Atlanta (325-4646). This news-oriented tour is offered to groups of children age eight years and older Sunday–Thursday. The one-hour tours are booked months in advance, so plan ahead!

• **Chattahoochee Water Treatment Plant,** 2532 Bolton Rd., N.W., Atlanta (355-7310). Children age five years and older can see how water is collected and treated to make it safe to drink. Tours are given Monday–Thursday from 9:00 a.m.–2:00 p.m. for any size group. Call in advance for an appointment.

• **The Coca-Cola Bottling Company,** 1091 Industrial Park Dr., Marietta (424-9080). Group tours of the Coca-Cola Bottling Plant are given on Wednesdays at 10:00 a.m. for groups no larger than thirty-five children. This popular tour is usually booked six months in advance, so plan ahead.

• **Delta Air Lines,** Hartsfield International Airport, South Terminal Information Counter, Atlanta (765-2554). Delta Air Lines conducts tours of the technical operations area for children age twelve years and older on Tuesdays, Wednesdays and Thursdays at 9:30 a.m. The minimum group size is ten, and the maximum group size is thirty-five. Groups are booked months in advance, so call well ahead of time.

• **Dunkin' Donuts.** Locations throughout Atlanta. Your local Dunkin'

Donut store encourages you to bring children to the store to watch the hand-baking of a large variety of donuts and muffins. Each store has a glass window for viewing the baking area. It's free to watch, but samples must be purchased.

• **Federal Bureau of Investigation,** 275 Peachtree St., N.E., Atlanta (521-3900). Group tours for children age 6–12 are available on Tuesdays and Thursdays at 10:00 a.m. The tour is tailored to the age of the children, but usually includes a talk about the history of the FBI, a visit to the gun vault and computer room, a film about drugs, and sometimes a demonstration explaining fingerprinting and surveillance. A maximum of twenty children is allowed per group. Call ahead to make reservations.

• **Fire Stations.** Your local fire station will be more than glad to schedule a tour of the station. Some will even let you host your child's birthday party at the station.

• **Georgia Department of Transportation,** 15 Kennedy Dr., Forest Park (363-7510). The Georgia Department of Transportation's tours are for children age ten and older. Tours provide a view of the equipment and show procedures utilized to test the materials used in highway construction. They are conducted Monday–Friday during normal working hours. Maximum group size is fifteen children.

• **Georgia Dome,** 1 Georgia Dome Dr., Atlanta (233-TOUR). The Georgia Dome is now a landmark in Atlanta, rising to 275 feet in the center and covering 8.6 acres. Tours, available for groups of twenty-five or more, may include the 71,500-seat stadium itself, the visiting team's locker and dressing rooms, the Astroturf storage area, the press box, executive suites and the sports lounge. Tours are offered frequently, but must be scheduled around Georgia Dome events, so please call well in advance. Admission: $4.00/adults; $2.50/seniors and children age 5–12 years; and children under 5 are free.

• **G. M. Assembly Plant,** Doraville Assembly Plant, Doraville (455-5255). Tours are offered on Tuesdays at noon for school groups over sixteen years of age. Maximum group size is forty. There are no age restrictions on families. Call for reservations.

• **Goree's Ice House,** 5425 Buford Hwy., Doraville (451-2765). This small older building houses an ice-block factory that also occasionally makes ice carvings for hotels on Saturdays. Families are welcome to come and watch ice being artistically carved. We suggest you call ahead before visiting.

• **Krispy Kreme Donut Company.** Locations throughout Atlanta. Visit one of the Krispy Kreme locations for a free look through the viewing windows. But remember, samples must be purchased.

• **Lithia Springs Water & Bottling Co., Inc.,** 2910 Bankhead Hwy., Lithia Springs (944-3880). Children can tour the historic company that bottles the medicinal water rich in lithium (thus, the name of Lithia Springs). This rare metal is found in only three other springs in the world. Visit the Family Doctor Museum, Medicinal Gardens and "Frog Rock." Tours are given Monday–Friday from 9:00 a.m.–4:00 p.m., and on Saturdays from 10:00 a.m.–12:00 noon. Families are welcome to join a group.

• **McDonough/Atkinson Power Plant,** 5551 S. Cobb Dr., Smyrna (792-5368). The tour of this coal-fired plant includes a slide presentation and a chance to see the motors, pumps and generators used in producing power. Children should be at least ten years old and groups must be no larger than thirty children. Schedule your tour well in advance.

• *Marietta Daily Journal*/Neighbor Newspapers, 580 Fairgrounds St., S.E., Marietta (428-9411). The tour begins with a brief discussion about the history of this newspaper and how news is made. Your guide then leads you past the busy newsroom, the typesetters, the composition room and then, the tour highlight, the press room in operation. At the end of the tour, each child receives a newspaper hot off the press! The tour lasts about 30–45 minutes and is appropriate for children age eight years and older.

• **United States Post Office,** Federal Annex, 77 Forsyth St., Atlanta (765-7400). Children in the 4th grade and younger can take tours of a local branch of the U.S. Post Office where they can see postal workers, mail trucks and the inner workings of the branch. Groups of 10 or more children, 5th grade and older, may tour the downtown Federal Annex Building where the machines and the process by which mail travels through the building can be seen. The tour takes about an hour and a half.

▬ Tours for Older Children ▬

• *Atlanta Journal and Constitution,* 6455 Best Friend Rd., N.W., Norcross (263-3971). Tours of the Gwinnett printing plant of the *Atlanta Journal and Constitution* are available for children age 13 and older.

• **Chateau Élan, Ltd. Vineyards,** 7000 Old Winder Hwy. (I-85, Exit #48), Braselton (800/233-WINE). A visit to this replica of a 16th-century chateau may include a tour of the winery, lessons on wine-making, a visit to the wine history museum, hiking on nature trails, picnicking, golfing, dining in an elegant restaurant, or participation in one of the many special events held throughout the year. (The winery is located about thirty miles northeast of Atlanta.)

• **Neely Nuclear Research Center,** 900 Atlantic Dr., N.W. (Georgia Tech Campus), Atlanta (894-3600). Tours of the research center are usually only given to children over sixteen years of age, although younger children are sometimes allowed to visit the facility. The tour includes a visit to the research labs and the viewing gallery where children can see the hot cell and reactor containment building. Tours are Monday–Friday during normal working hours for groups no larger than thirty children, and must be scheduled in advance.

TRANSPORTATION
CARS, BOATS, TRAINS & PLANES

Children are fascinated by anything that moves. Most of the conversation in our car revolves around the different vehicles we pass along the way. Be it cars, buses, mail trucks, trains, taxis, ambulances, fire engines, police cars, backhoes, cherry pickers, boats, airplanes, jets, or helicopters, they all get noticed, including the out-of-state license plates. Preschoolers love to imitate the noises the vehicles make; they want to know everything about the vehicle and can't wait for a chance to be behind the wheel. Older kids can't understand why we won't let them drive, as they indignantly argue, "But I can reach the pedals!" Any trip that brings your child within an arm's reach of transportation is sure to be a big hit.

▬ TRAINS & BUSES ▬

• Why not leave the car behind the next time you go to a game at Atlanta Fulton County Stadium? The **MARTA Train Station** is a few blocks away and you won't have to deal with parking (especially now that Olympic-related construction has eliminated so many spaces). If you're really at a loss for something to do, take a MARTA train ride to Hartsfield International Airport, Peachtree Center or Underground Atlanta, and treat your child to an ice cream cone once you arrive. The fare is inexpensive, and an otherwise boring day will turn into a little adventure. Or take your child for a short trip on a **MARTA bus** the next time you have to run a simple errand. Call 848-4711 for MARTA bus and rail schedules. Call 848-3457 for stadium shuttle information.

• The **Amtrak Train Station** is the only passenger train station in Atlanta. Although small, it is the only show in town for those embarking on an old-fashioned railroad journey to another state. If you plan ahead, you may be able to schedule a visit to the station during boarding or arrival time. The station is located at the intersection of Peachtree and Deering Roads, near Pershing Point. Or the next time you plan a vacation, consider traveling by train. Many of our friends have ridden Amtrak to Washington D.C., and even New York. Their kids loved spending the night on the train! Call 800/872-7245 for schedule information.

• Every few years **Fernbank Planetarium** (378-4311) presents a Christmas show called "The Christmas Express," where a little engine named Casey saves the day for the children in a small mountain village. Take young children—they will love it!

• Also, be sure to look in our other chapters for information on these great places: **Big Shanty Museum, Cyclorama, Hapeville Depot Museum, Southeastern Railway Museum, Stone Mountain Railroad, Zoo Atlanta** and other metro Atlanta attractions that feature trains.

• One of Atlanta's more unique attractions, **The New Georgia Railroad**, has recently stopped its Saturday and dinner excursions around Atlanta and to Stone Mountain Village due to financial difficulties. There is a chance that a private group might take over the railroad and make the train available for private charters.

• For the more serious train collectors, railroad memorabilia abounds at **Gandy Dancers Toy & Hobby Shop**, 5460 Peachtree Road in the Chamblee Antique District (471-7425). (A gandy dancer was a laborer on a railroad gang.) The very knowledgeable staff can even repair antique train cars. Other stores specializing in trains and railroad memorabilia are opening up all over town. Check the *Yellow Pages* under "Hobby and Model Shops" for listings.

• Each winter look for the **Model Train Show** at the Cobb County Civic Center in Marietta (426-1264 or 528-8450) featuring displays, demonstrations, dealers and advice for the novice and advanced model builders. Or attend **The Model Train, Railroadiana & Collectible Toy Show** (987-2773) held in the spring featuring more than 80 exhibitors with trains, models and toys for trade or sale. In August or September visit the annual **SE Railroadiana Collectors Show** (233-7991) at the Georgia International Convention and Trade Center in College Park where over 300 tables display model trains and collectibles for sale or trade. Stop by **The Great American Train Show** at the Georgia International Convention Center in College Park (708/834-0651 or 997-3566), featuring over 10,000 model trains, operating model railroads and railroad antiques. Also, Big Shanty and the city of Kennesaw (427-2117) sometimes host the **Magical World of Lionel Trains**, the world's largest portable train display.

■■■ AIRPLANES & HELICOPTERS ■■■

Big airports or small, Atlanta has plenty of opportunities for children to get close to jets and airplanes.

• **Hartsfield International Airport** has it all—MARTA trains, buses, taxis, motorized transportation carts, moving sidewalks, people movers, elevators, long escalators, baggage claim areas, security checks and, of course, big jets. Try to plan ahead and take the Delta Air Lines Tour of the airport. (See our section in this chapter, "Tours of the Working World.") Most of the time, Delta can make arrangements for your children to tour the inside of one of their jets. For a change of pace, stop by the International Arrivals escalator and watch the reunions of families and friends who have not, in some cases, seen each other for years. There are a hundred stories to imagine, and watching all of the hugging and kissing will surely bring tears to your eyes. Take MARTA to the airport and give your children a full day of "moving" experiences.

• For a visit to a smaller airport, try our favorite, **DeKalb Peachtree Airport** (PDK) located on Clairmont Road in Chamblee. The historical airport used to be part of Fort Gordon, established during World War I to house the Emory Division of the 82nd Regiment, later the 82nd Airborne Division. Now it is a busy commuter airport with airplanes and small jets taking off and landing continuously. The airport has built a large observation deck overlooking the runways, and next to the deck is a grassy area complete with picnic tables and family swings. Bring a picnic and enjoy this perfect lunch spot. PDK is open 24 hours a day. Call 936-5440 if you need more information. See our chapter on "Festivals and Special Events" for information about Good Neighbor Day at PDK held in the fall.

For an extra special Sunday brunch, dine at the **57th Fighter Group Restaurant,** located at 3829 Clairmont Road right at the edge of one of the runways of DeKalb Peachtree Airport. This restaurant is a bit on the pricey side, but it contains lots of memorabilia and artifacts that airplane lovers and military buffs will enjoy. Inside the restaurant are headphones which allow you to listen in on the Air Control Tower at the airport. Outside is an old fighter plane, several jeeps, and a convoy truck which add authenticity to the World War II fighter theme. Call 457-7757 for more information.

• **Stone Mountain Britt Memorial Airport,** located on Bermuda Road in Stone Mountain, is open to the public daily from 8:00 a.m.–dusk. The airport used to be home to the Georgia Historical Aviation Museum, which has since closed, but it still displays four World War II fighter planes in various states of repair, including a TBM Avenger (the same kind of plane flown by George Bush during World War II). In addition to the museum area, there is a small grassy area where children can view the activity on the runways. Call 469-7604 for more information.

• **Fulton County Airport – Charlie Brown Field,** located off Fulton Industrial Boulevard (close to Douglas County), is open to the public daily 24 hours a day. There are a few benches and a small grassy area where children can observe the airplanes and jets. Call 699-4200 for more information.

• **Gwinnett County Airport,** Briscoe Field, is located off of Highway 316 on Airport Road in Lawrenceville. The airport sometimes offers tours by appointment on weekdays. Call 995-5592 for more information.

• **McCollum Airport** is located on McCollum Parkway, off of Highway 41 in Marietta, and is open to the public by appointment only. In certain years they offer tours of the airport that include a visit to the hangars and a chance to go inside a small aircraft. Call 528-1615 to schedule an appointment.

• **South Expressway Airport,** located on Tara Boulevard in Jonesboro, has a small, fenced-in grassy area with a few benches for viewing the runway activity. Open to the public daily from 8:00 a.m.–8:00 p.m. Call 471-0534.

• Occasionally, **Lockheed/Dobbins Air Force Base** hosts an openhouse in May or June as part of the Armed Forces Festival & Open House. Look in our chapter on "Festivals and Special Events" for more information.

• Up in Calhoun is **Mercer Air Museum** (706/629-7371), a "roadside collection of aircraft" you can see from I-75. Also be sure to check our chapter "Day Trips" for information on the **Air Acres Museum** in Cartersville.

• **AND FOR BIG SPENDERS** (and brave at heart), try **Historic Air Tours** (457-5217) where you can soar over the skies of Atlanta and experience a unique perspective of Atlanta's old south antebellum homes, plantations, Civil War battlefields and downtown landmarks. Your family can chose between 20-minute tours of the city of Atlanta that can cost as low as $35/person, or 55-minute tours that feature either landmarks, the Civil War or the Battle of Atlanta tours costing as much as $85/person. Custom tours are also available upon request. Planes seat three, operate daily, and take off and land at DeKalb Peachtree Airport. Reservations are required. (Children must be old enough to use seat belts or be in an approved car seat.) Or try a **Helixpres Atlanta by Air Tour** (451-7386) where for 20–60 minutes, depending upon which tour you select, you can whirl around the skies of Atlanta, Stone Mountain, or above the estates of the "Rich and Famous" along the Chattahoochee River for a cost of $65–$160. The helicopter seats two and rides are not recommended for children younger than 6 years. Tours begin and end at DeKalb Peachtree Airport. Reservations are recommended.

HORSE-DRAWN CARRIAGE RIDES ━━ & TROLLEY RIDES ━━

• Now this is really touristy! Take a 20-minute Horse and Buggy Tour of the historic Downtown area from Five Points to Underground Atlanta. The cost is about $12.50 a person and rides are given from 6:00 p.m. to midnight. Look in the *Yellow Pages* under "Carriages–Hire" and call ahead for reservations. Or just hire one on the spot.

• Or tour Atlanta with **Trolley Tours of Atlanta** (378-1146) in a turn-of-the-century trolley beginning at Atlanta Heritage Row and continuing through the older neighborhoods of Druid Hills and Inman Park, as well as Peachtree Street and the Sweet Auburn area. Tours run Wednesday–Saturday at 10:00 a.m. for a cost of $27/person. Shorter trolley tours can also be arranged.

▬ CARS ▬

• For those of you who have automobile enthusiasts in your family, keep your calendar free for the **Atlanta International Auto Show** held at the Georgia World Congress Center in March of each year and the spectacular **World of Wheels,** also held at the Georgia World Congress Center in the winter (223-4000). These mega-shows feature domestic and foreign cars, as well as vintage classics and cars that have made it to the movies. Also check the *Atlanta Journal and Constitution's* Saturday *Leisure Guide* for information about smaller automobile collector shows, motorcycle shows, and auctions scheduled throughout the year. Information about championship race car driving and motorcycle racing at **Road Atlanta** and elsewhere, can be found in our chapter "Sports and Recreation," and information about the **Antique Auto and Music Museum** at Stone Mountain Park can be found in our chapter "Places to Go."

▬ BOATS ▬

• The **Paddlewheel River Boat Ride** at **Stone Mountain Park** is the only attraction in Atlanta which offers children a hands-on experience with larger boats. However, you can rent canoes and other watercraft for fun family boating and fishing on the Chattahoochee River, Lake Allatoona, Lake Lanier, at Callaway Gardens and elsewhere. See our chapters "Sports and Recreation" and "Day Trips" for more information.

• There is also the annual **Atlanta Boat Show** held at the World Congress Center in March of every year (233-4000), and what a show it is! This is the largest inland Marine Show in the United States, featuring over 350 exhibitors and over 500 boats. Smaller shows, such as the **Boat Expo** and the **Great Southern Boat Show,** sometimes come to Atlanta. Check local newspapers for announcements.

━━ . . . AND MORE ━━

• Don't miss the Atlanta Fire Department's annual **Metro Atlanta Fire Apparatus Show and Muster** held each summer, featuring, among many other things, displays of antique and modern fire-fighting vehicles. For more information about this event, check our "Festivals and Special Events" chapter. And don't forget the obvious, but sometimes overlooked visit to your local:

- • Fire Station
- • Post Office
- • Police Station
- • Neighborhood Construction Site

PLAYCENTERS

━━ INDOOR PLAYCENTERS ━━

It's raining or freezing cold outside and your active kids need somewhere to go. Or you have a child who is reluctant to engage in sports, and you would like to encourage him/her to be more physically active. What might you do? Try one of Atlanta's new indoor playgrounds, a concept that is sweeping the country, and for a good reason—kids absolutely love it. In over 11,000-square-feet of play space, children ages twelve and under slide down plastic tubes, crawl through a maze of tunnels, jump in ball pits, climb in overhead tunnels, bounce on air-filled bubbles, roll, leap, skip and run. Everyone can join in comfortably and safely. In fact, safety, security and sanitary equipment are of utmost importance to the owners of these facilities. A security system is in place, and parents are encouraged to participate with their children (though this does not really seem possible in the older kid area). Trained staff, non-slip floors, padded or rounded edges on equipment, knee pads, and a stocking feet only requirement make these playcenters about as safe as they can be, given the number of children who are energetically playing. A special area for infants and toddlers has equipment appropriate for their size and physical development to ensure good exercise, success in their explorations, and safety from exuberant older kids. Thoughtfully, the owners have included a separate room for parents to relax in, yet the play area is still visible. Now and then there are special activities such as face painting, arts and crafts, and group activities like the "Bunny Hop" and "Hokey Pokey." Not only will your children have fun (My 10-year-old said, "If I had a credit card, I could live here!"), but they should also have a good night's sleep afterwards.

On the down side, these places can get quite crowded and loud, especially with the background music adding to the children's gleeful noises, but only parents seem to mind this—the kids sure don't. There are also birthday party rooms, family-oriented snack areas serving the usual kid's fare, small arcade rooms and restrooms. Several more of these indoor playscapes are planned for the Atlanta area.

• **Discovery Zone,** 1630 Pleasant Hill Rd. (Pleasant Hill Plaza), Duluth (923-8889) and 4400 Roswell Rd., Marietta (565-5699). Admission is $4.99/child the first two hours; $1.49 each additional hour; and parents are free. Adult supervision required. Open Sundays 11:00 a.m.–8:00 p.m.; Mondays 12:00 noon–8:00 p.m.; and Tuesday–Saturday from 9:00 a.m.–9:00 p.m.

• **Leaps & Bounds,** 5370 Highway 78, Suite 1100 (Stone Mountain Square), Stone Mountain (413-5880). Admission is $5.95/child, and parents are free. Adult supervision required. Open Monday–Thursday from 9:00 a.m.–9:00 p.m.; Friday–Saturday from 9:00 a.m.–10:00 p.m.; and Sunday from 9:00 a.m.–8:00 p.m.

• **Play Daze,** 1570 Holcomb Bridge Rd. (Holcomb Woods Village), Roswell (642-7529). Admission is $5.45/child, and parents are free. Group rates are available. Permits parents to drop-off their children. Open Sunday–Monday 11:00 a.m.–8:00 p.m., and Tuesday–Saturday from 9:00 a.m.–9:00 p.m.

═══ Outdoor Playcenters ═══

These outdoor play arenas offer a group of activities that kids can't find in the larger theme parks that are featured in our chapter "Places To Go." Most outdoor fun parks offer miniature golf, bumper boats, batting cages, go-carts, arcade games and snack bars.

• **Malibu Grand Prix,** 5400 Brook Hollow Pkwy. (west of I-85 between Indian Trails and Jimmy Carter Blvd.), Norcross (416-7630) and (George Busbee exit off I-75), Marietta (514-8081). Malibu has a simple miniature golf course, batting cages, bumper boats, an elaborate arcade room, a restaurant, a figure-eight go-cart course for kids and the only scaled Formula 1 racing facility in the mid-south. They have Virage, Gran Virage and Sprint cars. Cars can reach speeds of 70 miles per hour on the half-mile track. Birthday party packages are available.

• **Mountasia Fantasy Golf & Games/ Mountasia Fantasy World,** 8510 Holcomb Bridge Rd., Alpharetta (993-7711); 175 Ernest Barrett Pkwy., Marietta (422-3440); 1099 Johnson Ferry Rd., N.E., Marietta (977-1200); and 1100 Highway 120 N.W., Lawrenceville (339-0250/339-1002). Mountasia has miniature golf, batting cages, bumper boats, arcade games, and kid-sized Indy car race tracks. Birthday party packages are available. The Lawrenceville location is the largest of the facilities.

• **Dixieland Fun Park,** 1205 Highway 85N (4 mi. south of Riverdale Rd.), Fayetteville (460-7135). Indoor and outdoor miniature golf, arcade games, bumper boats, batting cages and three go-cart tracks entertain families. Birthday party facilities are available. But what is really unique about this entertainment park is that it features a real bungee jump tower. The jump is 75 feet, participants wear a full body harness and there is an airbag. Jumpers must be at least 16 years old, and 16–17-year-olds must be accompanied by a parent. The first jump costs $20.00. For bungee information call 719-9339.

PETS & ANIMALS

If your household already has a family pet, then you know how much pleasure an animal can bring to a child. As further proof, visit Zoo Atlanta, Yellow River Game Ranch and the Wildlife Trails at Stone Mountain Park which are filled with excited children eager to get close to the animals. The petting areas of these attractions are, by far, the favorite part of each visit. Children can touch the furry bodies and figure out ways to get wet tongues to lick their hands. Read on to find out about other places in Atlanta where children can discover more animals who also deserve enthusiastic attention.

ANIMAL SHELTERS & ■ HUMANE SOCIETIES ■

The best animal petting can be found at the animal shelters and humane societies in Atlanta. Playful kittens, puppies, cats and dogs (and in some instances, rabbits, hamsters and mice) are glad to see friendly faces. They seem to know instinctively just what to do to successfully audition for a new home. Your children will have plenty of hands-on opportunities with these animals. (A word of caution—make sure your children understand ahead of time whether or not you are going home with a new pet. We didn't deal with this issue very well during our first visit, and our children got very upset when they watched other families leave with pets. They could not understand why we were leaving empty handed!)

• **Buying a Pet.** If you are in the market to buy a pet, the animal shelter or humane society is the right place to be. The animals are healthy (most come wormed with their first shots, and a coupon good for a discount on spaying or neutering). And, most importantly, these pets are in need of a good home.

• **Tours and Programs.** Animal shelters and humane societies offer an excellent opportunity for your children to learn more about animals. Almost all of the metro Atlanta animal shelters and societies listed below offer guided tours of the facilities for elementary age children. These tours often include films and discussions relating to the care of animals. The Atlanta Humane Society has an excellent series of educational touring programs on a variety of topics that can be presented at your child's school free of charge. Humane societies also sponsor special animal adoption events at local shopping malls, as well as amateur pet shows and fundraising art contests.

Call the numbers below for more information about visiting hours, tours and pet adoption. Also, look in *Creative Loafing* for the names and addresses of other non-profit animal shelters.

Atlanta Humane Society
981 Howell Mill Rd., N.W.
Atlanta, Georgia 30318
875-5331

Cobb County Humane Society
1060 County Farm Rd., S.E.
Marietta, Georgia 30060
428-5678

DeKalb Humane Society
5287 Covington Hwy.
Decatur, Georgia 30035
593-1155

DeKalb Animal Control Shelter
845 Camp Rd.
Decatur, Georgia 30032
294-2930

Clayton County Animal
Control Shelter
7810 N. McDonough St.
Jonesboro, Georgia 30236
477-3509

Gwinnett Humane Society
Hwy. 316 and Hi Hope Rd.
Lawrenceville, Georgia 30243
662-9566

▬ PET STORES ▬

Metro Atlanta has an excellent selection of pet stores featuring a large variety of species on display—iguanas, snakes, tame and talking birds, spiders, hamsters, guinea pigs, mice, tropical fish and even monkeys— sort of "mini-zoos" in their own right. There are also those stores that specialize in exotic birds and tropical fish (some of their displays rivaling aquarium attractions in other cities). Look in the *Yellow Pages* for pet shop listings near your home. Some of our favorite stores are: • **The Aviarium** at Market Square (634-5930) – fish and birds; • **Piccadilly Pets** at Ansley Mall (892-2473), at Buckhead Crossing (261-6902), and at College Park (768-3816) – fish, birds, reptiles, small animals; • **JunglePets** on Lawrenceville Highway in Gwinnett County (923-0752) – birds, reptiles, fish and small animals; • **Tropiquarium** on Piedmont Rd. in Atlanta (875-6121) – fish galore!; and • **For Birds Only** in Buckhead (851-1800) – fish and birds. Most pet store owners do not want you touching the animals unless you are serious about buying a pet; but, if you are interested in some inexpensive animal-watching, then a visit to a pet store is a sure-fire way to please children.

▬ PET SHOWS ▬

Year-round, Atlantans are showing off their pets, whether it's at a nationally recognized **Purebreed Championship Show** sponsored by the Greater Atlanta Cat Club, the Atlanta Kennel Club, or one of the many other championship purebreed clubs; or an amusing amateur pet show or pet parade sponsored by your local humane society or parks and recreation department. Wills Park Equestrian Center in Alpharetta is the location for two national dog shows held in the spring and fall of each year. Championship shows are not inexpensive. They are serious competitions with little opportunity for a child to get close to or actually touch the animals. But, if your child is really interested in animals, then the shows are a fascinating way to see them. (The shows may not be a good idea for preschoolers. Mine were not welcome at a cat show; they had too much energy for the already nervous pets.) Amateur shows, on the other hand, such as the frisbee catching dogs at the **Stone Mountain Frisbee Championships,** are great events for children to watch. Check with your local humane societies and parks and recreation departments for a schedule of upcoming events.

And don't forget the annual **Fish Show and Auction** sponsored by the Aquarium Society of Georgia, the annual **Pet Parade – A Walk For Animals** sponsored by the Atlanta Humane Society, the **Exotic Bird Mart** held yearly at the Farmer's Market Exhibit Hall, or the big **Pedigree Atlanta Pet Show** (892-2002) featuring cats, dogs, ferrets, monkeys, reptiles, birds, fish and more at the Georgia World Congress Center. Check *Creative Loafing* to keep up with the many shows scheduled year-round.

■ ANIMAL FARMS ■

• **Cobb County Petting Farm,** 1060 County Farm Dr., Marietta (499-4136). You will need an appointment to visit this farm that features sheep, goats, a pig and a pond filled with ducks eagerly awaiting your tidbits. Families and groups are welcome to arrange a visit Monday–Saturday, but call well in advance.

• **Dauset Trails,** Indian Springs (404/386-0159). The wildlife refuge is located forty-five miles southeast of Atlanta, but it is well worth the trek—just ask the more than 30,000 people who visit the center every year. Snakes, alligators, buffalo, deer, a bear, a bald eagle and other animals have found a home here. Though the refuge is privately owned, the state Department of Natural Resources and the U.S. Fish and Wildlife Service bring injured animals here to be treated and released if they can be fully rehabilitated. The center offers educational programs, such as its popular ecology class that includes a three-hour trail hike lead by a naturalist. Visitors must call ahead for tour reservations or to participate in special programs.

• **Noah's Ark Rehabilitation Center,** 1425 Locust Grove Dr., Locust Grove (957-0888). Children are encouraged to touch the 500 animals that frolic in the yard of this 122-acre rehabilitation center for wild and exotic creatures. If your children seem to be a bit wild, they too are welcome to romp! Open Tuesday–Saturday from 12:00 noon–5:00 p.m. Donations are welcome. You might consider stopping nearby at Gardner Farms (957-2113) to pick seasonal berries.

• **The Red Barn,** 800 Old Rucker Rd. (near Harry's Farmers Market), Alpharetta (442-1617). Feed and pet animals, collect eggs from the hens, and ride ponies at this working farm! Pre-arranged group visits only please, as this farm is a family home. There is a per child fee for groups, with the exception of the two-hour birthday party program which has a set fee. Days and hours are flexible.

• **Urban Nirvana,** 15 Waddell St., N.E., Atlanta (688-3329). Located in historic Inman Park, the name Urban Nirvana may give you a hint of the setting for this unique art gallery which showcases the pottery of Christine Sibley and other visual artists. Visitors are surrounded by a lush garden of flowers, shrubs and arbors and, believe it or not, rabbits, turkeys, peacocks, goats and sheep to pet. Our young children thought this was a "super neat" place.

SMALL ART MUSEUMS, GALLERIES & ART CENTERS

Visiting a gallery can be a special activity, even a regular event for a family on a rainy or cold day. Artists tell us that children exposed to art at a young age and on a regular basis, will develop a fine appreciation of art that will enrich them throughout their lives.

Atlanta has a large number of small art museums and galleries scattered around the city. The *Atlanta Journal and Constitution's* Saturday *Leisure Guide* is the best source for discovering what is being exhibited and where. You should then call the various museums and galleries to figure out if the current exhibits would be enjoyable for your child. During the National Black Arts Festival (held in July and August biennially), numerous galleries have special showings of outstanding art work by black artists. The July issues of *the Atlanta Tribune, Creative Loafing* and *Atlanta Magazine* are good sources for locating these galleries as well as other festival events.

Below are descriptions of some small art museums and galleries that are worth noting, either because their exhibits can always be appreciated by children, or because the museum or gallery has tried in the past to offer at least one exhibit each year for children. Unless we have indicated otherwise, admission to these galleries and museums is free.

There are also numerous community art centers spread throughout the Atlanta area. In addition to offering a broad range of exciting activities for children throughout the year, many have galleries which frequently exhibit art work done by children or art work that a child would enjoy. We have included all of the community art centers, even those without galleries, so you will have an idea of where to look for interesting visual art classes for your children.

You will find a wide range of choices here, from fun explorations for preschoolers to classes for serious young students.

ABERNATHY ARTS AND CRAFTS CENTER

254 Johnson Ferry Rd.
Sandy Springs, Georgia 30328 • 303-6172

The arts center, which is a program of the Fulton County Arts Council, offers a full range of classes in the visual arts and occasional workshops. Afternoon and early evening youth classes in drawing and painting, portraiture, pottery and sculpture are available year-round, as well as a summer program, "Art in the Park," held at Chattahoochee River Park. Future plans include extending the camp program to include a wide range of visual, performing arts and recreational activities. Abernathy's small gallery periodically exhibits the art work of its students, so children and adults attending the classes have a forum to display their creations. *Gallery hours:* Monday–Friday from 9:00 a.m.–5:00 p.m., and when classes are in session.

THE ART PLACE—MOUNTAIN VIEW

3330 Sandy Plains Rd.
Marietta, Georgia 30066 • 509-2700

The Art Place–Mountain View is a facility of Cobb County Parks, Recreation & Cultural Affairs offering classes for preschoolers and children in drawing and painting, clay, weaving, sculpture, ceramic, mobile making, print making, cartooning, multi-media exploration and collage/assemblage. Some classes are also offered in the performing arts. Summer camp programs are offered in both the visual and performing arts. The Art Place's gallery often has exhibits appropriate for children, including shows of students' art work displayed at the end of each class session. *Gallery hours:* Monday–Friday from 10:00 a.m.–5:00 p.m.

ARTSBUSTERS/CREATE

627-2707

CREATE sponsors "Artsbusters," a visual and performing arts summer camp and school-holiday program (winter break, spring break and teacher workdays based on the City of Atlanta school calendar) for children 2–12 years of age, which includes activities in both the visual and performing arts. The program receives rave reviews from participants. Classes are held in different locations in the Midtown area. Call for more information.

ART STATION, INC.

The Trolley Barn
5384 Manor Dr.
Stone Mountain, Georgia 30086 • 469-1105

ART Station, one of the four not-for-profit art centers in DeKalb County, houses two art galleries, a theatre, dance studio and six classrooms. The center presently offers a wide variety of year-round classes for children in the visual, literary and performing arts, and its Summer Arts Camp program offers activities in drawing, painting, sculpting in clay, creative dramatics, dance and music. A special student artists gallery features works which were created by students taking ART Station visual arts classes or participating in the summer camp program. The other galleries feature year-round exhibitions of work by local, national and international artists. *Gallery hours:* Monday–Friday from 9:00 a.m.–5:00 p.m., and Saturday from 11:00 a.m.–3:00 p.m.

THE ARTS EXCHANGE

750 Kalb St., S.E.
Atlanta, Georgia 30312 • 624-4211

The Arts Exchange is a multi-cultural, multi-disciplinary arts resource center located near Zoo Atlanta. The center houses the Gallery at the Arts Exchange, which features exhibits reflecting the multi-cultural orientation of the center. A wide variety of afterschool and Saturday class offerings for children include creative dramatics, voice, piano, dance, martial arts and tai-chi chuan. A special all day Summer Arts Academy offering an enrichment program in both the visual and performing arts runs for ten weeks, and the cost is more than reasonable. For the next few years, the center will host a series of festivals and performing arts events in conjunction with the Cultural Olympiad, which will reflect the diversity in ethnic background of Atlanta's many communities. *Gallery hours:* Monday–Saturday from 10:00 a.m.–5:00 p.m.

THE ATLANTA COLLEGE OF ART

1280 Peachtree St., N.E.
Atlanta, Georgia 30309 • 898-1164

The gallery displays faculty and student art and hosts traveling exhibitions of work by regional and international artists. Some exhibits address issues that may be more appropriate for older children (AIDS, human rights, etc.). The college offers a range of classes for children in drawing, painting, cartooning and photography, including a popular preschool program and a Saturday "Creative-Kids" arts class for school-age children. *Gallery hours:* Monday–Saturday from 10:00 a.m.–5:00 p.m., and Sunday from 2:00 p.m.–6:00 p.m.

ATLANTA INTERNATIONAL MUSEUM OF ART & DESIGN

285 Peachtree Center Ave. – Marquis Two Tower
Atlanta, Georgia 30303 • 688-2467

The Atlanta International Museum is located in downtown Atlanta in the Marriott-Marquis Two Tower. This one-room museum exhibits work from around the world showcasing the arts and designs of the world's many cultures, past and present, such as recent exhibits of Turkistan art, Japanese tapestries and an American craft exhibit. When visiting the downtown area, be sure to take a quick look inside; the museum is quite enjoyable for the entire family. *Hours:* Tuesday–Friday from 11:00 a.m.–5:00 p.m.

CHASTAIN ARTS CENTER/ CITY GALLERY AT CHASTAIN

135 W. Wieuca Rd., N.W.
Atlanta, Georgia 30342 • 252-2927 or 257-1804

Chastain Arts Center offers year-round classes in the visual arts, including instruction in drawing and painting, weaving, clay and sculpture. A summer art camp program, "Artventures," offers children an opportunity to explore different media. The center has a small art gallery which occasionally displays works that might be of interest to children. The same building also houses the City Gallery at Chastain featuring exhibitions of contemporary fine art and craft work by local, regional, national and international artists. *Gallery hours:* Tuesday–Saturday from 1:00 p.m.–5:00 p.m.

GILBERT HOUSE

2238 Perkerson Rd., S.W.
Atlanta, Georgia 30315 • 766-9049

This community art center, listed on the National Register of Historic Homes, is the location for a wide-range of classes, workshops, exhibitions, festivals and activities for children emphasizing
the visual arts. On certain Saturdays, usually during Kwanzaa and
Black History Month, the Gilbert House is the location for storytelling
sessions and holiday workshops. The house may also be rented
out for special functions. A gallery located at the center often features works of interest to families. *Gallery hours:* Monday–Friday
from 10:00 a.m.–6:00 p.m. Open on Saturdays for special occasions.

GWINNETT FINE ARTS CENTER/ GWINNETT COUNCIL FOR THE ARTS

6400 Sugar Loaf Pkwy., Building 300
Duluth, Georgia 30136 • 623-6002 or 623-5577

The Gwinnett Council for the Arts' new 14,000-square-foot facility houses three galleries, three painting studios, a ceramics studio and
kiln room and a gift shop. Permanent and changing exhibits are often
appropriate for children. A large selection of courses are offered year-
round in drawing, painting, cartooning, pottery, mixed media and
drama. Private art lessons are also available. *Gallery hours:* Tuesday–Friday from 10:00 a.m.–5:00 p.m., and Saturday from 1:00
p.m.–4:00 p.m. The Gwinnett Council for the Arts also sponsors a
satellite gallery, Norcross Studio & Gallery, located at 116 Carlyle
St. in Norcross (840-9844) that exhibits work by local artists.
Gallery hours: Tuesday–Saturday from 10:00 a.m.–5:00 p.m.

HAMMONDS HOUSE GALLERIES
& RESOURCE CENTER

503 Peeples St., S.W.
Atlanta, Georgia 30310 • 752-8730

The Hammonds House is a gallery and resource center of African-American art housed in a restored 1857 Victorian home, formerly the home of Otis T. Hammonds, a physician and arts patron. The Fulton County Council for the Arts has acquired the home along with Dr. Hammonds' vast art collection, and the Hammonds House now serves as a cultural facility and resource center in historic West End. Although the educational programs, forums, lectures and workshops offered by the gallery are generally geared to adults, the permanent collection is delightful and can certainly be appreciated by children. Special traveling exhibits, which change about six times a year, are usually quite appropriate for children. There is a small but well-stocked African-American gift shop in the gallery. The gallery is spacious and the staff friendly. Stop by the next time your family visits the Wren's Nest. *Gallery hours:* Tuesday–Friday from 10:00 a.m.–6:00 p.m., and Saturday and Sunday from 1:00 p.m.–5:00 p.m. *Admission:* $1.00 for adults and senior citizens and children under 12 are free.

KENNESAW STATE COLLEGE ART GALLERIES

3455 Frey Rd.
Sturgis Library Gallery & Fine Arts Gallery
Kennesaw, Georgia 30061 • 423-6239 or 499-3223

Kennesaw State College has two galleries that display works of art primarily of interest to adults; however, some exhibits are more fun and feature work children can enjoy. Studio art classes are usually offered for children age seven years and older throughout the year. During the summer months, the college offers a dazzling array of summer camp programs, including classes in the visual arts. Call 423-

6765 for information about classes. *Library Gallery hours:* Monday–Friday from 10:00 a.m.–4:00 p.m., and Saturday from 1:00 p.m.–5:00 p.m. *Fine Arts Gallery hours:* Monday–Friday from 10:00 a.m.–4:00 p.m.

MABLE HOUSE/SOUTH COBB ARTS ALLIANCE

5239 Floyd Rd., S.W.
Mableton, Georgia 30059 • 739-0189

The historical antebellum home which was taken over by federal troops during the Civil War is now the site of an art gallery with changing monthly exhibits and art classes for children and adults year-round. The South Cobb Arts Alliance also hosts festivals and special events at the Mable House, including appearances by visual, literary and performing artists from Cobb County and the summer Candlelit Concert Series. *Hours:* Tuesday–Saturday from 10:00 a.m.–5:00 p.m., and Sunday for special events.

MARIETTA/COBB MUSEUM OF ART

30 Atlanta St.
Marietta, Georgia 30060 • 424-8142

The museum's mission is to serve as an educational facility for both children and adults alike, presenting a well-rounded offering of special exhibits, workshops, classes and lectures appropriate for the entire family. Younger children can enjoy Kid's Place, an interactive learning gallery featuring lots of hands-on experience with the arts. Families with older children can utilize the "Family Guides," which are prepared in conjunction with the permanent and special collections. Teachers can schedule special student tours of the museum or take advantage of "in service" training programs. Afternoon and weekend classes for children include instruction in pottery, painting and drawing, photography and creative expression. A summer art camp offers comprehensive activities in drama, drawing, print-making, painting, clay and papier-mâché. *Hours:* Tuesday–Saturday from 11:00 a.m.–5:00 p.m. *Admission:* Price varies with the special exhibits, but is usually $4.00/adults, $3.00/senior citizens, $2.00/students age 6–21, and $1.00/children age 4–5.

JOHNNY MERCER EXHIBITION

Georgia State University, 8th Floor of the Pullen Library South
103 Decatur St., Atlanta, Georgia 30303 • 651-2477

Georgia State's library has a small exhibit entitled "I Remember You," honoring Georgia native Johnny Mercer, writer of the hit songs "That Old Black Magic," "Moon River" and "Days of Wine and Roses." Posters, photographs, and Oscar and Grammy awards are available for viewing while a tape recording of continuous Mercer hit songs plays on. *Gallery hours:* Monday–Friday from 8:30 a.m.–5:00 p.m.

NEXUS CONTEMPORARY ART CENTER

535 Means St.
Atlanta, Georgia 30308 • 688-1970

Keep your eye out for announcements about the Nexus Kids Club, an art club for children age 4–12 years, meeting one Saturday a month and offering children an opportunity to experience fine arts and crafts. Activities in painting, sculpture, collage, photography and printing are offered. Recently, Nexus joined forces with the Academy Theatre to present Kids Klub on Imagination Street, a creative arts and drama program featuring "issue-oriented programming."

PINCKNEYVILLE ARTS CENTER

4300 Holcomb Bridge Rd.
Norcross, Georgia 30092 • 417-2215

Located between Spaulding Drive and the Chattahoochee River, the Pinckneyville Arts Center is a facility of the Gwinnett County Parks and Recreation Department offering a dazzling selection of classes and workshops for children in drawing and painting, sculpture, ceramics, art explorations, music, movement, jewelry and cooking. One-day workshops are also featured during holiday seasons. The center has no gallery, but it does hold open houses during the year showcasing the children's art work. Summer Art Camps are offered for preschoolers and school-age children and include a variety of classes in the visual and performing arts. A family performance series on most Friday evenings runs throughout the year.

RAY'S INDIAN ORIGINALS

90 Avondale Rd.
Avondale Estates, Georgia 30002 • 292-4999

Ray's Indian Originals is part gallery, store and souvenir shop. Featured are permanent and touring museum-quality exhibits of Native American pottery, clothing, baskets, fetishes, jewelry, totems and artifacts; but there are also general and souvenir quality items as well. Prices in the gallery may seem high, but for those interested in Native American history and culture, a visit would be worth your while. The gallery occasionally sponsors special storytelling sessions and other unusual events relating to Native American culture and traditions. *Gallery hours:* Monday–Saturday from 10:00 a.m.–6:00 p.m. or by appointment. (We recommend you still call ahead to make sure they are open.)

SOAPSTONE CENTER FOR THE ARTS

One South DeKalb Center
2853 Candler Rd., Suite 8
P.O. Box 370219
Decatur, Georgia 30037 • 241-2453

Funded largely through the DeKalb Council for the Arts, this burgeoning center for folk, ethnic and fine arts has year-round children's workshops and classes in drawing and painting, cartooning, textiles, crafts, dance, acting, character development, foreign languages, musical instruments and voice. The Soapstone Gallery often exhibits works by local, regional, national and international artists appropriate for children of all ages. *Gallery hours:* Monday–Friday from 10:00 a.m.–6:30 p.m., and Saturday from 9:00 a.m.–5:00 p.m.

SOUTH FULTON ARTS CENTER

4645 Butner Rd.
College Park, Georgia 30349 • 306-3087

This arts center is a program of the Fulton County Arts Council, offering inexpensive afternoon and Saturday classes for children year-round. During the summer it also offers Arts Camp, a comprehensive summer camp for children age 6–13, featuring many kinds of hands on experiences in the visual and performing arts. The eight-week program includes visiting artists, field trips, activities in all of the visual arts, along with music, drama, dance, swimming and free play.

SPRUILL EDUCATION CENTER/
SPRUILL CENTER FOR THE ARTS

North DeKalb Cultural Center
5339 Chamblee-Dunwoody Rd.
Atlanta, Georgia 30338 • 394-3447

Year-round classes for children are offered at the Spruill Education Center (formerly the North Arts Center) in visual arts, ceramics, literary arts, drama, music and cartooning. Summer camp programs include a wide-range of instruction in the visual and performing arts, including a special drama camp program. The Education Center's Hallway and Library Galleries exhibit a diverse selection of works by local, national and international artists that are specifically geared to or are appropriate for children. Also featured are special exhibits showcasing works created by students participating in classes or summer camp programs at the center. The recently opened Spruill Center for the Arts, housed in the historic Spruill family home at 4681 Ashford-Dunwoody Rd., Atlanta (394-3447), also features works of art by local artists appropriate for older children. Guided tours of the historic Spruill home and its gallery are offered for student groups. *Gallery hours:* Monday–Friday from 10:00 a.m.–5:00 p.m., and Saturday from 10:00 a.m.–1:00 p.m.

TULA ARTS COMPLEX

75 Bennett St.
Atlanta, Georgia 30309

The TULA Arts Complex, located at the end of Bennett Street (off Peachtree Road, behind Mick's and Brookwood Shopping Center), is an attractive and airy complex featuring over 45 galleries, artists' studios and arts-related businesses. All forms of media are represented, including paint, sculpture, photography, art glass, pottery, native art, graphics and holography. The public is welcome to watch the artists in their studios. Each of the galleries has its own hours of operation, although most are open Tuesday–Saturday from 11:00 a.m.–5:00 p.m. Bennett Street itself houses numerous galleries, antique shops and furniture stores, so if time and energy permit, plan on walking up the street to continue your adventure in art appreciation. One of the stops on your walking tour should include **Folk-Art Imports Gallery**, 25 Bennett St., Suite A-1, Atlanta (352-2656) where you will discover a delightful selection of folk art from around the world. The gallery is open daily from 12:00 noon–5:00 p.m.

CATHERINE WADDELL ART GALLERY

Trevor Arnett Building
Clark Atlanta University
223 James P. Brawley Dr.
Atlanta, Georgia 30314 • 880-8671

This magnificent collection of work by African-American artists was begun in the 1940s when Atlanta University started sponsoring one of the only black arts competitions in the country. Works of art shown during the annual competitions were acquired by the university over the next three decades. The competitions ended in the 1970s, but the collection has still grown thanks to the generosity of various donors who have helped the university acquire important pieces by Henry Ossawa Tanner, William H. Johnson and Romare Bearden. Plans are underway to move the gallery upstairs and quintuple the exhibition space. *Gallery hours:* Monday–Friday from 12:00 noon–4:00 p.m. Group tours for elementary age children are available by appointment.

■ OTHER GALLERIES WORTH VISITING ■

You will be pleasantly surprised to discover that all around Atlanta are many venues, including commercial galleries, theatre lobbies, bookstores and government buildings, that exhibit works of art by local, regional, national and international artists. You can view all of this wonderful art work for free. A sampling:

• **Arts Connection,** Oxford Books–Upstairs, 360 Pharr Rd., N.E., Atlanta (237-0005). This lively art gallery will charm children of all ages. A special exhibition of children's art work is featured every winter. *Gallery hours:* Monday–Saturday from 10:00 a.m.–10:00 p.m., and Sunday from 1:00 p.m.–10:00 p.m.

• **The Arts Pavilion,** 1158 Canton St., Roswell (552-8716). This artists' co-op (about 15 artists) sells a wide-range of fine arts and crafts that might be quite enjoyable to children. The public is welcome to watch the artists work in their studios. *Gallery hours:* Tuesday–Saturday from 10:00 a.m.–6:00 p.m.

• **Centro Cultural de Mexico,** 3220 Peachtree Rd., N.E., Atlanta (264-1240). This gallery features exhibits and art work relating to the history and culture of Mexico. *Gallery hours:* Monday–Friday from 10:00 a.m.–6:00 p.m.

• **City Gallery East,** 675 Ponce de Leon Ave., N.E., Atlanta (817-6815). The new City Hall annex (formerly Sears, Roebuck & Co.) houses a large art gallery which is committed to showing works by Atlanta artists. *Gallery hours:* Monday–Saturday from 8:30 a.m.–5:30 p.m.

• **Cricket Gallery,** 3108 Roswell Rd., Atlanta (814-0600). This gallery exhibits "cels," which are original drawings from classic cartoons and animated features. The gallery is a distributor for 20th Century Fox, Hanna-Barbera, Warner Bros. and Disney. *Gallery hours:* Tuesday–Saturday from 10:00 a.m.–6:00 p.m., and Friday from 12:00 noon–8:00 p.m.

• **Le Primitif Galleries,** 631 Miami Cir., Suite 25, Atlanta (240-0226). The exhibits by Haitian artists are colorful and interesting to children. *Gallery hours:* Monday–Saturday from 11:00 a.m.–5:00 p.m.

• **Oglethorpe University Museum,** 4484 Peachtree Rd., Atlanta (364-8555). The university's new museum features works of art from around the world. *Hours:* Tuesday–Sunday from 1:00 p.m.–4:00 p.m.

• **Unitarian Universalist Congregation of Atlanta,** 1911 Cliff Valley Way, Atlanta (634-5134). Changing exhibits of work by local artists, including children's creations, are featured at this church. *Gallery hours:* Monday–Friday from 9:00 a.m.–5:00 p.m., and Sunday from 9:00 a.m.–1:00 p.m.

• **Urban Nirvana Gallery & Gardens,** 15 Waddell St., N.E., Atlanta (688-3329). This unique one-of-a-kind gallery, pottery shop (Christine Sibley pottery), petting farm and garden is a favorite in my family. *Gallery hours:* Monday–Friday from 9:00 a.m.–5:00 p.m.; Saturday from 10:00 a.m.–5:00 p.m.; and Sunday from 1:00 p.m.–4:00 p.m.

SHOPPING & HOBBIES

Atlantans love to shop. Whether we're talking malls, strip shopping centers, super discount stores or small boutiques, there is little doubt that the retail industry in this city has grown tremendously through the years. But shopping is not for every kid. In fact, my two-year-old was known to scream, "No, not again!" every time I tried to convince him to take a quick peek inside a clothing store. But, that's only when it was a clothing store. Toy stores, hardware stores, sporting goods stores, and even drug stores were quite a different story. During cold or rainy weather, a shopping excursion often took the place of a trip to the neighborhood park. These days our older children can spend hours in stores such as The Sports Authority and

Sports Town where they bounce balls, try out bicycles and exercise machines, swing tennis rackets, try on catcher's masks, and insist they need every sports accoutrement in the store.

Families may wish to explore some of Atlanta's ethnic and international groceries, retail stores and strip shopping centers. Whether it be an adventure to Chinatown Square in Chamblee, the Buford Highway Flea Market also in Chamblee, Asian Square in Doraville, Woodcliff Shopping Center at Briarcliff and N. Druid Hills Roads or another international emporium elsewhere in Atlanta, parents and children will have an opportunity to learn more about the foods, clothing, arts and crafts and cultures of our fellow Atlantans. Most importantly, your children will be able to see that Atlanta has truly become an international city inhabited by warm and friendly people from all over the world. For a comprehensive listing of international and ethnic shopping centers, retail establishments, restaurants and more, check *Ethnic Atlanta, The Complete Guide to Atlanta's Ethnic Communities*, available in local bookstores.

■■ SHOPPING CENTERS ■■

Shopping centers abound in Atlanta. Spacious, modern and attractive, these malls have it all—glass bubble elevators, long escalators, food courts, arcades, elaborate fountains, running space and, of course, shopping. The malls have recently become a common locale for year-round special events, such as **art festivals, book fairs, fashion shows, concerts, collector & hobby shows** and **community awareness events.** During holidays, almost all of the malls arrange visits by **Santa Claus** or the **Easter Bunny** and provide **Safe Trick-or-Treat Halloween** events. During summer months, a lot of the malls sponsor special events for younger children to encourage families to visit the air conditioned malls.

• Our favorite mall for preschoolers is **Market Square Mall** located on Lawrenceville Highway in Decatur. The small "regional" mall has a small selection of stores that children enjoy, such as **The Aviarium** (a well-stocked fish and bird store); **Kay-Bee Toy & Hobby Shop,** a small store with a well-rounded selection of toys; **Everything's $1,** where everything in the store costs a mere dollar; **Woolworth's; Cole's The Book People;** and **Challenger's Arcade,** a game room with a special area for younger children. But the best thing about the mall is that it is filled with preschoolers. Whether you are at the clock tower, the cookie stand or the food court fountain, there is always a good chance that you can find a temporary play partner for your sociable child!

• **Phipps Plaza,** Atlanta's ritziest shopping mall, located in the heart of Buckhead on Peachtree Road, has undergone a major renovation and expansion. Although you may want to hold on tight to your wallets as you speed your older children past the beautiful designer boutiques and up-scale department stores, you will be able to breathe a sigh of relief once you reach some of the more unusual and less-pricey stores. Our children's favorite store for browsing is super-cool **Nike Town,** a one-of-a-kind sports store cum shrine featuring Nike-brand sports shoes and clothing for the whole family. Scattered throughout the store are photographic action images of Michael Jordan, Deion Sanders and other sports super stars who endorse Nike products, along with encased displays of their worn Nike shoes and clothing. Also visit **The Discovery Store,** displaying all sorts of nature and science merchandise, including educational toys, microscopes, musical instruments, puzzles, posters, jewelry, collecting kits, puppets, books and more; and the **Museum Company,** showcasing reproductions and replicas of treasures displayed in museums around the world plus top-quality educational toys, art supplies and books. And when you're through shopping your family can take a break at the food court, recently voted "Best Food Court in Atlanta" by *Atlanta Magazine.*

• And don't forget neighborhood strip shopping centers which can also offer an usual mix of stores. For example, visit **Ansley Mall Shopping Center** located on Monroe Drive and Piedmont Road in Midtown that houses **Piccadilly Pet Shop** (selling fish, exotic birds, kittens, snakes, iguanas, lizards, and more), **The Toy Store** (stocking imaginative, hard to find toys and crafts from around the world), **Chapter 11 Books** (offering an attractive and well-stocked children's section and discount prices), **Baskin-Robbins, Woolworth's** and **The Royal Bagel,** recently voted Atlanta's best Jewish-style bakery.

▬ TOY STORES ▬

The trouble with visiting toy stores with preschoolers is that there is no way you are going to walk out empty-handed unless you have a heart of stone. So if your budget allows for the purchase of another toy, puzzle, art supply or book, then a trip to a toy store can become a purposeful and fun-filled excursion. The larger toy store chains, such as Toys R Us, have not officially set aside play areas in the store where children can experiment and play (hint, hint!). Nevertheless, our children have managed to make themselves at home, and test ride the bicycles, play cars and spring horses. And almost all of the other toy stores in Atlanta have some products set out for temptation—Brio train sets, race car tracks, Lego tables and erector sets are favorites. Even if your child doesn't get everything he or she wants at the end of your visit, the trip still should be quite enjoyable.

• An award-winning toy store in north Atlanta is **The Toy School,** 5517 Chamblee-Dunwoody Rd. (Dunwoody Village), Dunwoody (399-5350). The Toy School's philosophy is "Every Child Deserves Some Success Today." Immediately upon entering the store you will have no doubt that your child will be successful in finding hundreds of top-quality toys, games, puzzles, art supplies, tapes, Brio sets and stuffed animals that she will absolutely want to take home with her. Or perhaps she will be successful in convincing you to read to her one of the 10,000-plus children's book titles found in the store's roomy "library" area, or if she is older, in convincing you to buy quite a few of the carefully selected titles. Your child will also be excited to come on one of the days when a special workshop, concert, or storytelling session is in progress or when a renowned literary figure—such as Lyle the Crocodile, Spot the Dog or Curious George!—is visiting the store. The Toy Store also offers an award-winning summer camp program for preschoolers and houses two different party rooms where birthday celebrations can be customized to meet your child's wishes. Recently the store has developed a special area of the store just for older children. Besides a large selection of books for highschoolers, the Toy School also carries games, science kits, puzzles and more for your older children. *Hours:* Monday–Friday from 9:00 a.m.–6:00 p.m., and Saturday from 9:00 a.m.–4:00 p.m. (Extended hours during the holiday season.)

Some other popular stores with interesting selections of toys are:

- **ABC Parent/Teacher Learning Center** (multiple locations)
- **Children's Book & Gift Mart**
- **The Children's Hour Toys**
- **The Disney Store** (multiple locations)
- **FAO Schwarz**
- **Hobbit Hall**
- **Just Imagine**
- **Kay-Bee Toy & Hobby Shop** (multiple locations)
- **Kiddie City**
- **Kids Central**
- **My Storyhouse** (multiple locations)
- **Puzzled at Phipps Plaza**
- **Sanrio Surprises & G. Whiskers**
- **The School Box** (multiple locations)
- **The Toy Store** (multiple locations)
- **Warner Brothers Stores** (multiple locations)
- **Zany Brainy**

■■ HOBBIES ■■

A hobby is something that can occupy and amuse a child for long periods of time. Children are natural collectors. (I am reminded of that every time I go into my daughter's room and look at her shelves and closet!) Whether your child chooses collecting (rocks, baseball cards, coins, dolls, stamps, etc.), model building, arts and crafts, reading, photography, comic books, computers or any other hobby, you can be sure that these interests will become part of the entire family's life. The excitement is contagious, and trips to **hobby stores, bookstores, specialty stores** (photography, stamps, baseball cards, dolls, etc.), **trade shows** and **collector fairs** will become part of the regular routine for the family.

When your child gets older, he or she may want to join one of the many collector clubs thriving in Atlanta, a place where your child is sure to meet others with similar interests. For example, our family belongs to **The Georgia Mineral Society** (242-0556), a non-profit association which has over 400 members in the Atlanta area alone. A special "Junior Section," open to children of any age, meets the second Monday of each month at Fernbank Science Center at 7:15 p.m. Each meeting features a presentation by one of the society's knowledgeable "rockhounds" on such subjects as gold-panning, gem identification, fossils or volcanoes, including hands-on experiences and a question and answer period. The meeting is followed by free refreshments for the kids and drawings for door-prizes (rocks, minerals and gems, of course). This enthusiastic society also leads four field trips each year just for the Junior Section, offering kids an opportunity to collect fossils and rock specimens in the North Georgia mountains. During the **Gem & Mineral Shows** held in May and November at the Cobb County Civic Center, a professional display area showcases some of the specimens found on these outings with each child's name clearly marked. The show also features more than fifty different exhibitors from around the country displaying amazing collections of rocks, minerals, fossils, jewelry, gemstones, carvings and more.

Or perhaps your child is interested in chess? The **Atlanta Chess Center,** 3135 E. Ponce de Leon Ave., Scottsdale (377-4400) is a chess club for children in grades K–12 (as well as for adults). Members meet once a month for tournament play. Beginners are welcome, although even the youngest are encouraged to write down their games. Winners are awarded with impressive trophies.

You can help your children find a hobby by exploring the various possibilities with them. Visit one of the many toy and hobby stores found throughout the city specializing in baseball cards, sports items, comic books, model cars, toys, rocks and minerals, dolls or just about anything else that is collected. Look in the *Yellow Pages* under **Hobby & Model Shops, Baseball Cards, Collectibles, Coin Dealers** and **Stamps for Collectors** for current listings. Walk around the stores and see what appeals to your child. Look for announcements about unusual hobby and collector shows. Almost every weekend, you can be sure to find some kind of collector's fair, whether it features antique automobiles, dolls, toys, flowers, baseball cards, comic books, railroad models, gems and minerals, radio control vehicles, coins, stamps or some other collector's item. Check the *Atlanta Journal and Constitution's* Saturday *Leisure Guide* and *Creative Loafing* for listings. Perhaps you will be rewarded by sparking an interest in your children that will bring them enjoyment for the rest of their lives!

■ HARDWARE STORES ■

We know that going to a hardware store is one of the many chores frequently appearing on your "To Do" list. But we cannot think of a better place to bring children of all ages. Whether it's a mega-hardware store like **Home Depot,** a helpful **Ace Hardware** or a small neighborhood shop, children are fascinated by the machinery, tools and gadgets on display. Sitting on a riding lawn mower, ringing door bells, hiding in bathroom display cabinets and picking favorite colors of paint are common activities on our trips. Older children can help parents make decisions on purchasing items for a home-improvement project or enjoy finding all the materials necessary for a school project. And since we discovered this pastime, most of the repairs needed at our home actually get done!

HOTEL HOPPING

We all know that Atlanta's number one industry is tourism, and our city has the hotels to prove it. There are the ritzy downtown tourist hotels—the Hyatt Regency, Westin Peachtree Plaza, Ritz-Carlton, Atlanta Marriott Marquis, Atlanta Hilton Towers and Omni Hotel—with glass bubble elevators, revolving roof-top restaurants, elegant shopping malls, elaborate water fountain displays, exotic gardens and sun-filled space. There are also the magnificent hotels springing up in Buckhead and around the city's perimeter. The growth is phenomenal!

• **Hotel Hop!** Visit the hotels and tour the architectural marvels. Spend some time in the bustling lobbies which are filled with tourists from around the world, business people and convention-eers. The people-watching is fascinating. So if it's a rainy day or you and your children just need to get out of the house for a while, stop in, ride some elevators, eat lunch, sit in a lobby and enjoy the people show at a nearby hotel!

• **Sunday Brunch.** For those with children old enough to appreciate and enjoy elegant dining or as a special birthday surprise, try one of the gourmet Sunday brunches offered by Atlanta hotels. These are usually listed in the *Atlanta Journal and Constitution's* Saturday *Leisure Guide.* Or take your older children to afternoon tea at the opulent

Hotel Nikko (365-8100) in Buckhead which is served in the hotel's lobby overlooking a stunning Japanese water garden. Afterwards, wander around the hotel which houses over 125 pieces of Japanese art spanning three and one-half centuries.

• **Swimming.** Recently, Atlanta hotels have begun realizing that hotels should not be for tourists only. For example, the **Atlanta Marriott Northwest** (952-7900) at Windy Hill Road, will allow a family to use the hotel's indoor pool facilities for a small fee . . . a great idea for mid-winter doldrums. They also allow birthday parties at the pool, with the hotel providing food, ice cream cake, decorations, towels and lifeguard. Call around to other hotels in your area to see if they will allow you to use their facilities.

• **Overnight Stays.** If you're desperate to take a family vacation but budgetary or time constraints don't allow a long trip, visit your own city by staying overnight at one of Atlanta's fancy hotels or suites. You will be amazed to discover that it costs less than $100/night for a family of four to enjoy overnight weekend accommodations, including breakfast, access to health clubs and pools, cable television and free newspapers!

On the Horizon

There are a few museums and attractions "On the Horizon" struggling to get enough money to become a reality. We hope their sponsors find enough financial support to make these new facilities available to the children of Atlanta.

• **The Children's Museum of Atlanta** (875-KIDS). The Friends of the Children's Museum aspire to construct a 80,000-square-foot museum on property at the corner of 11th Street and Peachtree Walk.

The program is still being developed, but will certainly include hands-on activities and other exhibits designed for educational, aesthetic, entertainment and social purposes. Possible exhibits include a mock courtroom with children playing the roles of lawyers, judge and jury, and a "bank" run and operated by children. The ideas are exciting and creative, and fundraising continues.

• **Gone With the Wind Country Theme Park.** A theme park based on the motion picture *Gone With the Wind* is scheduled to open in 1995 in Villa Rica. The park will feature recreations of various sets from the movie *Gone With the Wind*, including Scarlett O'Hara's Tara, Ashley Wilkes' Twelve Oaks Plantation, Rhett Butler's mansion, the Charleston jail where Rhett Butler was imprisoned, and old downtown Atlanta. Other activities under consideration include a riverboat ride, craft-making activities, shops and a chance for visitors to take screen tests to be in the movie. The site will also eventually include space for recreational vehicles, horseback riding, a golf course, a $35-million hotel and a condominium complex. Contact the Douglas County Development Office (942-5022) for more information.

• **Margaret Mitchell House** (870-2360). Many tour buses drive by the boarded-up and vacant Crescent Apartments on 10th Street and Crescent Avenue in midtown Atlanta to view the site where Margaret Mitchell lived with her husband while writing most of *Gone With the Wind*. Although the apartment building is presently in a horrible state of repair, plans have been developed to completely renovate the structure to house a museum and library honoring Margaret Mitchell and women authors. Fund-raising is in process, and a completion date by the 1996 summer Olympics is hoped for.

• **The Professional Photographers of America, Inc.,** 57 Forsyth St., Suite 1600, Atlanta (522-8600). The technical school has recently relocated its headquarters and photography school to downtown Atlanta and hopes to establish the Professional Photographers of

America Museum of Photographic History and research library by the end of 1994.

• **Sportspark 2000** (840-7655). A twenty-acre, sports-centered, family theme park is being planned for Gwinnett County that will include trails, racing courses and stunt props for in-line skating, training and tournament sites for roller and street hockey, facilities for teaching and practicing bouldering and rappelling, and beach volleyball and badminton events. Another section of the park will feature a concert area designed to seat 5,000 people. Crazy Eight Skate Co., the developer of SportsPark 2000, also hopes that the park will offer health and fitness programs and serve as the venue for festivals, exhibitions, corporate team-building events and other such activities.

• **Undersea World.** The proposed $50 million mega-aquarium will boast three one-million-gallon tanks of sea life, a series of smaller tanks, an educational theatre, a tidal pool, a laboratory, gift shop and snack bar. The attraction will make use of a technological breakthrough in plastics that permits not only gigantic tanks, but also an exciting acrylic tunnel to provide walk-through visitors with the sensation of being surrounded by an underwater environment. Undersea World will most likely be located near Underground Atlanta and be oper ated by Zoo Atlanta. A feasibility study is underway.

• **AND IN THE FAR, FAR FUTURE . . .** • Rumors keep brewing about a possible theme park in Cartersville at the same location where **Anheuser-Busch Inc.** has already built a $300 million brewery. Anheuser-Busch, who is the owner of Busch Gardens in Florida, has not confirmed the rumor but has acknowledged that a welcome center is being built at the brewery. • Preliminary plans have been drawn up for an $180 million, 80-acre **Country and Western Theme Park** in Canton, Georgia. This family-oriented park is expected to include a large theatre, a television and recording studio, hotels, shopping center and many other attractions. • Those interested in seeing a **Georgia Sports Hall of Fame** (875-8509) in the Georgia Dome should contact this number to offer support. • A group of dedicated southerners has a dream of building a museum which would showcase southern culture and stress the diversity of the south. This non-profit association, **The Institute of Southern Cultures** (681-7549), is first planning to open a gallery where they can exhibit southern art, but their long-term dream is to establish a full-fledged museum. • The recently deceased Ruth Carter Vanneman, known as "The First Lady of Vinings," has directed in her will that the historic **Pace House** be preserved and opened to the public as a museum. This home in Vinings was built from slave cabins by Mrs. Vanneman's great-grandfather, Solomon K. Pace, in 1864, a descendant of Hardy Pace, who ran a river ferry and for whom Paces Ferry Road is named. Contact the Vinings Homeowners Association for more information.

Performing Arts

FOR CHILDREN

People of all ages are thrilled by the illusory world created through the various performing arts media. Young children in particular seem to become transfixed by stage performances which often blur the distinctions between fantasy and reality. Their imaginations are titillated, their emotional intensity ebbs and flows, the realm of the possible expands, and ultimately their knowledge of themselves and the world around them grows. Your child can experience the excitement and wonder of the performing arts by attending classes and by watching other children as well as adults perform in a variety of settings. Peruse the number of opportunities listed below, and then you may think as we did: "There are so many performances we'd like to go to with our kids, how can we possibly find the time?"

The *Atlanta Journal and Constitution's* Saturday *Leisure Guide* has a special section called "Fun Stuff" which lists the week's upcoming performances and special events for children. This comprehensive list is the best resource around. Or you can try calling the city of Atlanta's **ARTS HOTLINE—853-3ART**—which has a 24-hour/7-day listing of festivals, performances, classes and special events. Also, the two parenting newspapers, *Atlanta Parent* and *Our Kids*, have detailed calendars describing upcoming events for kids. And if you're interested in finding out about performing arts series, the *Atlanta Journal and Constitution* publishes an annual guide to the arts in late August/early September that lists the season's schedule for most of the performing arts organizations in Atlanta. A few of the children's series are also listed.

We suggest you phone the organizations listed below that interest you and your children and get on their mailing lists to receive periodic up-to-date information. It is the best way to plan ahead. And keep in mind that ACOG's Cultural Olympiad is planning a full schedule of diverse international cultural events in the next few years leading up to the Olympics. All of these programs will feature special programming for children.

SERIES FOR CHILDREN

• **Abracadabra Children's Theatre** at Onstage Atlanta, 420 Court-land St., N.E., Atlanta (897-1802). Onstage presents five shows for children each year in its Abracadabra Children's Theatre series. Per-formances are on Saturdays at 10:30 a.m. and 2:00 p.m. and run for five to eight consecutive weeks. Each series includes a story from *Winnie the Pooh*, an adaptation of a classic children's tale such as *The Frog Prince* or *Rumpelstiltskin*, and the annual holiday per-formance of *The Littlest Angel*.

• **Academy Theatre** (525-4111). The Academy Theatre, in con-junction with the Georgia Tech Theatre for the Arts, presents three different performances for children each year "that are guaranteed to educate as they entertain." The Academy also has an "Artist-in-Schools" tour that brings "issue-oriented" performances to schools and to the Atlanta History Center, so children who can't come to the theatre have an opportunity to experience these performances. In col-laboration with Nexus Contemporary Art Center, the Academy presents Kids Klub on Imagination Street, a creative arts and drama program also featuring "issue-oriented" programming. A four-week acting program for children age 9–12 and teenagers age 13–16 is offered during the summer months at the Georgia Tech Theatre for the Arts. Call for more information about these programs.

• **Alliance Children's Theatre**, 1280 Peachtree Rd., N.W., Atlanta (892-2414 or 898-1132). The Alliance Theatre presents two full-scale productions each year in their Family Performance Series. The professional actors, the extravagant costumes and the elaborate sets have delighted Atlanta families for over twenty years. The plays are either original plays commissioned by the Alliance or are selections from the best adaptations of classic children's literature such as *The Snow Queen* and *The Velveteen Rabbit*. Call for program information.

The Alliance offers after-school and Saturday classes year-round in creative dramatics, music play, storytelling, television and film. A selection of camp programs are offered during the summer months.

• **Atlanta Symphony Orchestra**, Woodruff Arts Center, 1293 Peachtree St. N.E., Suite 300, Atlanta (898-1189 or 892-2414).

> *Family Concert Series.* The Family Concert Series on Sunday afternoons features a unique combination of the ASO, visual arts, dance and mime in programs lasting one hour each, perfect for children. This three-concert series is very popular and has sold out in past years. Season tickets are made available to the general public in early May. Special family Holiday Concerts are also scheduled during Halloween and the December holidays.

> *Symphony Street Concerts.* About half of the ASO, a narrator and dancers perform forty-minute programs for preschoolers through second grade in various locations throughout the Atlanta area. The symphony believes that younger children can better enjoy music in a more relaxed atmosphere, because they are really too young to sit in Symphony Hall for a full-scale performance. Call the Education Department (898-9572) for this year's locations of concerts.

> *Young People's Concerts.* Special weekday performances are held in Symphony Hall for elementary and middle school students. Call the Education Department (898-9572) for this year's performance dates.

> *Atlanta Symphony Youth Orchestra.* The Youth Orchestra is composed of musicians age fourteen through twelfth grade, selected by audition, and performs three Sunday concerts each year in Symphony Hall.

• **Center for Puppetry Arts,** 1404 Spring St., Atlanta (874-0398 or 873-3391). The Center for Puppetry Arts is the most comprehensive puppetry center in the U.S. featuring master puppeteers from all over the world. There are two performance series that will appeal to every child. The Family Series consists of three productions of classical children's tales, such as *Winnie the Pooh, Hansel and Gretel* or *Peter Pan.* Individual or season tickets may be purchased, and reservations are required. The International Summer Festival for families presents six different tales from around the world, some performed by international puppeteers. (All performances are in English.) These stories, as well as the Family Series productions, are performed in different puppetry styles. You can purchase a Summer Festival season pass for the incredibly low price of $18.00 per person. See our chapter "Places To Go" for a comprehensive description of the center.

• **Kids Comedy Theatre** at The Punchline Comedy Club, 290 Hilderbrand Dr., Atlanta (256-KIDS). Throughout the year, the comedy club presents a full calendar of "fractured fairy tales" appropriate for children age 3–10. These classical tales with a comical twist have included *The Ugly Duckling, How the Camel Got His Hump, The Boy Who Cried Wolf,* and *Beauty and the Beast.* Shows change monthly and performances are held Monday–Saturday at 10:00 a.m. and 12:00 noon; and Sunday at 12:30 p.m. and 3:00 p.m. During the summer months, shows change more frequently. Cartoons, funny-face videos and frozen snacks are included in the admission price. Soft drinks and a few snacks are available for purchase, or you may bring your own food. School groups and birthday parties are welcome. Call for information about group discounts.

• **Pinckneyville Arts Center,** 4300 Holcomb Bridge Rd., Norcross (417-2215). Throughout the fall, winter and spring seasons, the Pinckneyville Arts Center presents Friday Night Specials two or three times a month featuring the Vik Chik Puppets, storytelling by members of the SOS, and theatrical performances. During the summer months there is a Saturday evening outdoor storytelling series.

Call for a schedule of upcoming events. The center also offers a large selection of classes for children in the visual and performing arts, a summer art camp for children age 4–14, and special programming during Halloween and the December holidays.

• **Stage Door Players,** North DeKalb Cultural Center, 5339 Chamblee-Dunwoody Rd., Atlanta (396-1726). The Stage Door Players have recently started a children's series consisting of three quality productions of children's classics presented on Saturdays (and occasional Sundays), for five consecutive weeks. Recent performances in the series were *The Red Rose* (an adaptation of Beauty and the Beast), *Robin Hood*, and *Just So Stories*. Performances are held at the North DeKalb Cultural Center and sometimes feature children. The Stage Door Players also offer acting classes for children during the school year, and each class session ends with a special theatrical performance starring the students.

PERFORMANCES FOR CHILDREN

■ DANCE ■

• **African Cultural Dance Company** (991-9468). This vibrant dance group performs traditional West African dances and can be enjoyed at Atlanta's international festivals and during special events at Zoo Atlanta. During the summer months, the dance company offers classes for children at The Arts Exchange.

• **The Atlanta Ballet,** 477 Peachtree Rd., N.E., Atlanta (892-3303). The Atlanta Ballet performs five ballets for families each year at the Atlanta Civic Center, including the traditional holiday performance of Tchaikovsky's *The Nutcracker*.

• **Atlanta Dance Unlimited** (993-2623). This dance company presents two programs each year at the Roswell Municipal Auditorium and performs at festivals and special events such as The Festival of Trees and the Jazz on Tap Festival. Some of the productions feature older children from the junior and apprentice dance companies.

• **Ballethnic Dance Company** (762-1416). Ballethnic is considered Atlanta's premier African-American ballet company. Performances combine classical and ethnic dance and appeal to children as well as adults. Special programs, such as their *Urban Nutcracker*, offer young children and teenagers an opportunity to perform along-side professionals. Performances are usually at the Georgia Tech Theatre for the Arts. Other programs such as the Buddy Project (in conjunction with the Atlanta Project) and the Danseur Development Project target urban children, offering them an opportunity to train and dance with the company. Ballethnic also offers summer classes for children.

• **Carl Ratcliff Dance Theatre** (266-0010). This dance company is considered the first professional modern dance company in the southeast and has received national recognition for its artistic excellence. Special programming for children in elementary through middle school can be booked by calling 589-0644.

• **The Georgia Ballet**, 999 Whitlock Ave., S.W., Marietta (425-0258). The Georgia Ballet presents three performances each year at the Cobb Civic Center, including *The Nutcracker*. Occasionally, the ballet will even present a musical such as *You're A Good Man, Charlie Brown*. All performances are appropriate for children.

• **Gwinnett Ballet Theatre**, 2296 Henry Clower Blvd., Snellville (921-7277). The semi-professional dance company presents *The Nutcracker*, along with another classic production in the spring, such as *Cinderella*. Performances are at the Gwinnett Civic and Cultural Center in Duluth.

• **International Ballet Rotaru,** 2 Ravinia Dr., Suite 330, Atlanta (395-5322). This superb ballet company led by Pavel Rotaru has returned, performing colorful and exciting ballets at the Fox Theatre, including the seasonal favorite, *The Nutcracker.* In addition to evening performances, matinees are scheduled for each program, making it easier for parents to bring children. Ballet Rotaru also presents special performances for public schools at different locations throughout metro Atlanta. Dance classes for children are offered at Rotaru Performing Arts Academy in Norcross. Call 662-0993 for more information.

• **Jamaican Dance Theater** (243-6914). Under the direction of Paulette Cousins, this dance company's performances are reflective of the African heritage in Jamaica. Some of the dances are performed by "The Rosebuds," children members of the dance troupe. Saturday classes for children in Caribbean dance, movement and history are offered year-round.

• **Lee Harper & Dancers,** 721 Miami Cir., Atlanta (261-7416). This dance company's performances combine a variety of styles and often feature children dancers. Special touring programming for elementary-age children can be booked by calling 589-0644.

• **Ruth Mitchell Dance Theatre,** 3509 Northside Pkwy., Atlanta (237-8829). The professional dance company blends jazz, ballet and contemporary movement in its productions which, in recent years, have included *Cinderella* and *The Nutcracker.* Some performances feature children from the junior and apprentice dance companies. Special touring programs for school-age children can be booked by calling 589-0644.

▬ MUSIC & OPERA ▬

• **African-American Philharmonic Orchestra & Chorale** (Music South Corporation Orchestra & Chorale) (346-3417). Atlanta's first professional all-black orchestra performs works by black composers in pop, gospel, jazz and classical fields. The programs are appropriate for families, and groups such as the Boy Scouts often attend productions. In recent years, the orchestra was able to work with the Fulton County School System to develop a special program to bring to the schools. If the orchestra receives more funding, it will continue to develop programs specifically tailored to young audiences.

• **Atlanta Chamber Players,** 1447 Peachtree St., Atlanta (651-1228). The Atlanta Chamber Players performs its regular concert series at the Georgia State University Concert Hall, and the group can sometimes be enjoyed at various art galleries and Sunday brunches at select restaurants in Atlanta. It also presents touring programs for children consisting of skits about musical instruments and "light" classical fare. What a great way to introduce your child to chamber music! These productions can be booked by school groups by calling 589-0644.

• **The Atlanta Opera,** 1800 Peachtree St., Atlanta (355-3311). The Atlanta Opera has a special Studio Program that brings a taste of opera to children in K–12th grades. The opera performs 200 one-act operas a year in the public schools and at community centers. The productions are carefully tailored to the age group, yet professional quality is maintained as "the best singers in town" are hired to perform in English. To enhance the scene, the singers are dressed in ornate period costumes and perform on carefully designed stage sets.

• **Cobb Symphony Orchestra,** P.O. Box 452, Marietta 30061 (424-5541). The Cobb Symphony Orchestra's regular subscription series consists of five concerts performed at Stillwell Theater at Kennesaw State College, which includes a special children's concert in December. A special Summer Pops Series can also be enjoyed for free at the Galleria Amphitheatre and other locations in Cobb County.

• **DeKalb Symphony Orchestra,** DeKalb College, 555 N. Indian Creek Dr., Clarkston (299-4270). The orchestra's regular series of about seven performances throughout the year are held mainly at DeKalb College Central Campus. Every January the orchestra sponsors a special Children's Concert at the college's gymnasium featuring WSB TV's Monica Kaufman as host and narrator, along with dance, magic, clowns and other special entertainment.

• **Pandean Players,** 30 Trammell St., Marietta (427-8196). The Pandean Players is a small professional chamber music group performing on reed and wind instruments. The group has a wonderful selection of touring programs for children in grades K–6th, such as "Kids Pops," "Movie Madness," and "Zoo Music," created in cooperation with Zoo Atlanta. All of the programs are exciting and educational. Recently, the group received funding for a series of ten free concerts designed to entertain the entire family with well-known music, including Broadway show tunes, Joplin rags, marches, movie themes, jazz, light classics and more. Call for a complete schedule of these performances.

• **Southeastern Savoyards Light Opera Company** (396-0620). For over ten years, the Savoyards have been performing light operas, mostly Gilbert and Sullivan, of course, to rave reviews. These operas are full-scale, lavish productions supported by a 14-piece orchestra, which is really exciting for families with elementary-age children and older. Since much of the enjoyment of these operas is Gilbert's clever lyrics, the Savoyards thoughtfully provide the audiences with librettos in advance of the performances. Be sure to request one and sing at home ahead of time with your children! In addition to their regularly scheduled program, "Gilbert and Sullivan Samplers" are offered to schools, churches, and other community and business groups at nominal cost. Occasional diversions from the usual Gilbert and Sullivan repertory have included productions such as *The Student Prince*.

▬ THEATRE & PUPPETRY ▬

• **Atlanta Shakespeare Company**, Atlanta Shakespeare Tavern, 499 Peachtree St., Atlanta (874-5299). The works of Shakespeare and other period writers are presented in an informal tavern atmosphere Thursday through Saturday evenings and Sundays at 5:30 p.m. Special matinee performances for groups of students can also be arranged. The company estimates that its performances have been enjoyed by over 8,000 students since the opening of the tavern.

• **Clayton State College Music Theatre Ensemble**, 5900 N. Lee St., Morrow (961-3510). The college's performance company presents at least one play each year for families, such as *Charlotte's Web* and *You're A Good Man Charlie Brown*. Performances are at the world-renowned Spivey Hall.

• **The DeKalb Children's Theatre**, DeKalb College Central Campus, 555 N. Indian Creek Dr., Clarkston (299-4146). January through May, this children's theatre offers a touring program for elementary-age children consisting of an adaptation of a classic such as *Cinderella*. One performance is also presented at DeKalb College's Fine Arts Building.

• **DeKalb Music Theatre**, DeKalb College, 555 N. Indian Creek Dr., Clarkston (299-4270). The theatre company presents at least two musical family performances each year, such as *The King and I* and *Cabaret*. Performances are at DeKalb College Central Campus.

• **Down Right Theatre**, 3087 N. Peachtree Rd., Duluth (476-7926). Most of the productions presented by this new theatre company are appropriate for families with older children. The **Down Right Fun for Kids Theatre** (664-1058) sometimes performs original works for preschoolers through elementary age children at this location. Each production combines comedy, music, magic and audience participation.

• **Jomandi Productions** (876-6346). Jomandi Productions' performances combine drama, dance and music to dramatize the African-American experience. Many of the performances are quite appropriate for children.

• **Kennesaw State College Classic TheaterWorks,** The Stillwell Theater, P.O. Box 444, Marietta 30061 (423-6151). The Theater-Works series often consists of family-oriented performances such as *The Mikado, The Adventures of Huckleberry Finn* and *Romeo and Juliet.* Additionally, the college is the location for the **Story Theatre of Kennesaw State College** (423-6298), which presents professional storytelling programs for audiences age 10 and older, featuring folktales and music.

• **The Neighborhood Playhouse,** 430 W. Trinity Place, Decatur (373-5311). The Neighborhood Playhouse is a family-oriented community theatre. Recently expanded, the company intends to use its new Discovery Arena for more children's programming, including a few productions featuring neighborhood children. Other performing groups, such as Theatre Gael, Piccadilly Puppets and Tell-Tale Theatre, also use the theatre for limited engagements. Call for a schedule of upcoming events.

• **Open City Theatre/CREATE.** CREATE has a repertoire of over twenty different productions available for audiences K through high school. The programs use the arts to entertain, educate and excite the creative spirit of the children. Performances are participatory and allow children to interact with the actors. Workshops for smaller groups are also available. CREATE sponsors "Artsbusters," an excellent visual and performing arts summer camp and school holiday program for children age 2–12 years, which includes activities in the visual and performing arts. The theatre company can be booked by school groups by calling 589-0644.

• **Piccadilly Puppets.** Piccadilly is an internationally acclaimed touring company that performs original works for children at various theatres, festivals, schools and special events in the Atlanta area. The puppet theatre has quite a large repertoire, so it's possible to see five different shows in the span of just a few weeks. The puppet theatre can be booked by school groups by calling 589-0644.

• **The Playmakers at Oglethorpe University,** 4484 Peachtree Rd., N.E., Atlanta (261-1441). The Playmakers usually include at least one special children's performance each year in its performing arts series, such as *Snow White and the Seven Dwarfs* and *The Thirteen Clocks.* During the summer, the college is the location for a special dance and drama camp co-hosted by the Atlanta Workshop Players (998-8111) and for "Camp Shakespeare," a two-hour program for children age 5–12 co-hosted with the Georgia Shakespeare Festival (264-0020).

• **Roswell Village Theater & The Village Center Playhouse,** 617 Holcomb Bridge Rd., Roswell (998-3256). These two theatres are the location for fourteen different productions each year, almost all appropriate for families. Recent shows have included *Harvey, Arsenic and Old Lace,* and an annual holiday performance of *A Christmas Carol.* During the summer, the theatre companies often present Storybook Theater, a special children's theatre performing such classics as *The Red Shoes* and *A Little Princess.*

• **Southside Theatre Guild,** 200 W. Campbellton St., Fairburn (969-0956). This theatre company puts on one production each summer for children such as *The Velveteen Rabbit* or *Charlotte's Web.*

• **TellTale Theatre,** 30 Trammell St., Marietta (427-8206). Professional actors and actresses put on high energy, imaginative and educational performances for children. Although the company has no theatre of its own, it will perform at schools, recreation centers and other locations throughout metro Atlanta. Call for dates of upcoming performances. In June and July the theatre runs a summer drama camp for children age 7–17, where professional actors invite children to explore the world of acting. The theatre also has a special program called "Pull, Push, Click," developed in conjunction with Egleston Children's Hospital, promoting the use of seat belts.

• **Theatre League of Atlanta** (800/477-7974 for season tickets; 873-4000 for group discounts). This series features high-energy Broadway shows in the Fox Theatre, complete with spectacular sets and lavish costumes. *My Fair Lady, Tommy, Hello Dolly* and *The Wizard of Oz* were recent productions.

• **Theatre of the Stars** (252-8960). Theatre of the Stars brings performances to Atlanta which are appropriate for families, such as *Annie, Cats,* and *Phantom of the Opera.* Performances are at the Fox Theatre.

• **Theatre Gael,** 776 N. Highland Ave., N.E., Atlanta (876-1138). Theatre Gael's Worldsong Children's Theatre offers special children's programming which can be enjoyed at various locations in Atlanta, including the Neighborhood Playhouse and 14th Street Playhouse. These productions can also be booked by school groups by calling 589-0644. Also, Theatre Gael's regular productions, usually performed at the 14th Street Playhouse and Agnes Scott College, are often appropriate for families.

• **Theatrical Outfit,** 1012 Peachtree St., N.E., Atlanta (872-0665). Many of the Theatrical Outfit's performances are appropriate for children, such as their annual production of *Appalachian Christmas.* Call for information about the suitability of upcoming performances.

• **Theatre in the Square,** 11 Whitlock Ave., Marietta Square, Marietta (422-8369). This community playhouse presents a full schedule of performances each year, most appropriate for family audiences. The theatre's "Square One" program offers at least one production each year specially geared to students, complete with study guides for teachers. This program may be expanded if funding can be secured. During the summer, the theatre sometimes co-sponsors a summer acting workshop for children with TellTale Theatre.

OTHER LOCATIONS FOR SPECIAL ▬▬ PERFORMANCES ▬▬

• **Agnes Scott Theatre,** Gaines Auditorium of Presser Hall, 141 E. College Ave., Decatur (371-6430). Agnes Scott hosts a special concert, theatrical program or dance performance for children each year during the holiday season. Past performances have included *The Littlest Christmas Tree, Bob Humbug the Christmas Gump* and a special holiday dance program. The college is sometimes the location for unique performances, such as the world-famous Bao Dao Acrobats of the Republic of China whose exciting and unique performance included acrobatics, magic and dance.

• **The Art Place–Mountain View,** 3330 Sandy Plains Rd., Marietta (509-2700). This Cobb art center is home to the Centerstage North Theatre which presents a full season of performances appropriate for families with older children. Special children's programming is also scheduled throughout the year, including shows by the Youth Players of Cobb, a repertory company of children age 10–18 which studies at the center.

• **ART Station, Inc.,** 5384 Manor Dr., Stone Mountain (469-1105). ART Station, one of DeKalb County's non-profit art centers, usually has a few events each year specifically geared to kids, such as theatrical performances by the ART Station's Youth Company, storytelling sessions and musical concerts. In past years, the center offered a Children's Series and is hoping that it will be able to reinstate the series in the near future. Quite a few of the performances in the ART Station's regular Performing Arts Series, especially the folk music concerts co-sponsored by Atlanta Area Friends of Folk Music, are appropriate for school-age children.

• **Atlanta Civic Center**, 395 Piedmont Ave., N.E., Atlanta (523-6277). The Atlanta Civic Center, home to the Atlanta Ballet, is also the site of a large variety of concerts, productions and events for adults and children throughout the year. An advance schedule is not available, so check for announcements or call for a recording about current and upcoming events.

• **Atlanta Jewish Community Center**, 1745 Peachtree Rd., Atlanta (875-7881). The AJCC presents a few plays and events each year appropriate for children. Check for performance schedules in the AJCC's newsletters and the *Atlanta Jewish Times*. The AJCC regularly offers classes in acting and improvisation for children age 10–12, as well as a summer camp program, "Midtown Experience in the Arts," taught by professional artists, actors and directors. Call for more information.

• **Callanwolde Fine Arts Center**, 980 Briarcliff Rd., N.E., Atlanta (872-5338). Callanwolde presents a few children's theatrical and puppetry performances each year. Regular theatrical, musical and dance performances may also be appropriate and enjoyable to older children. Callanwolde supports the Young Singers of Callanwolde, described in the next section, and hosts various festivals and special events throughout the year. The art center offers a large selection of classes and workshops for preschoolers through adults, including offerings in dance, drama, improvisation, movement and the visual arts. "Kaleidoscope," a summer arts camp for children age 6–12, always features activities in the performing arts.

• **Clayton County Performing Arts Center**, 2530 Mt. Zion Pkwy., Jonesboro (473-2875). Clayton County Board of Education's new, large and impressive facility is the location for many productions and special events featuring Clayton County school groups. Touring dance companies, musicians, singers and theatrical companies also perform at the facility. Call for a schedule of upcoming events.

• **The Fox Theatre**, 660 Peachtree St., Atlanta (881-2100). Throughout the year, the Fox is a popular site for a wide variety of events for adults and children. The Fox Family Film Festival features evening movies, cartoons and sing-alongs during the summer months. An advance schedule for the Fox is not available, so look weekly in your local newspaper or call the above number for information about current and upcoming events.

• **Georgia Tech Theatre for the Arts**, 350 Ferst Dr., N.W., Atlanta (894-9600). Georgia Tech's new theatre is the location for a full schedule of high-quality performances, including ballet, music, dance, opera, acrobatics, mime and theatre. Almost all of the productions are appropriate for families.

• **Omni Coliseum**, 100 Techwood Dr., Atlanta (681-2100). The Omni is the location for numerous special events for children and families, including Ringling Brothers and Barnum and Bailey Circus, performing in late January and/or early February; Sesame Street Live, arriving in mid-September; and Disney's World on Ice, performing in November. An advance schedule is not available, so look for announcements about current and upcoming events in your local newspapers.

• **Seven Stages Performing Arts Center**, 1105 Euclid Ave., N.E., Atlanta (523-7647). Seven Stages' performances represent Atlanta's ethnic diversity through dance, music and the performing arts. Almost all are appropriate for families. From time to time, certain performances at the theatre are created especially for children.

• **Soapstone Center for the Arts,** One South DeKalb Center, 2853 Candler Rd., Decatur (241-2453). Many special events, concerts, puppet shows and recitals are held at Soapstone each year, most featuring the performing arts. Soapstone's resident dance company, Harry Bryce African American Dance Theatre, also presents unusual programs throughout the year. The art center offers an enticing year-round schedule of classes and workshops in dance, music, voice, instruments, acting, language, arts and crafts, and martial arts. Soapstone will also bring performances, classes, exhibits, art workshops and many other cultural programs to your school, recreation center, or youth and religious group. Call for more information.

FOR MORE INFORMATION ABOUT TOURING COMPANIES that are eager to perform at your child's school, recreation centers, birthday parties or other special group events, call **Alternate ROOTS** (577-1079), **Atlanta Theatre Coalition** (873-1185) or **Young Audiences of Atlanta** (589-0644). These service organizations have lists of theatre companies, puppeteers, storytellers, musicians and dancers who have programs appropriate for school-age children.

AND PLEASE DON'T FORGET the many other excellent performing groups established by members of Atlanta's international and ethnic communities. Whether it be Chinese dance, Greek bouzouki music, Israeli folk dance, Scottish bag pipe music, multi-cultural storytelling or the like, you can find it in Atlanta. For a comprehensive listing of international and ethnic performance groups, check *Ethnic Atlanta, The Complete Guide to Atlanta's Ethnic Communities*, available in local bookstores.

■■■ PERFORMING CHILDREN ■■■

• **The Atlanta Boy Choir,** 1215 S. Ponce de Leon Ave., Atlanta (378-0064). Only boys, age 5–13, are permitted to sing in this choir which performs classical concert repertoire at various locations throughout Atlanta, including churches, festivals and parades. The choir also performs with the Atlanta Symphony Orchestra as part of the symphony's regular series. The Atlanta Boy Choir makes an annual tour to Europe where it performs at many distinguished churches and institutions. Auditions are held yearly in late August.

• **Atlanta Children's Chorale** (728-0643 or 255-6869). This singing group is for children K–8th grade who love to sing in a fun and relaxed atmosphere. (No previous music experience is required.) The choir takes an eclectic approach to its musical repertoire, offering songs in foreign languages, ensemble singing, musical games, music training, vocal training, musical movement as well as secular and sacred music. The choir presently performs seasonal concerts and during special events throughout Atlanta. Rehearsals are in Sandy Springs or Roswell.

• **The Atlanta Music Club**, P.O. Box 15455, Atlanta 30333 (872-9670). The Atlanta Music Club is a non-profit association that supports young musical performers in Atlanta. One of its programs, the Young Performers of Atlanta, is a series of recital meetings held to provide young students with an opportunity to perform in professional settings. The club also supports the Atlanta Community Orchestra and provides scholarships for young performers.

• **Atlanta Workshop Players** (998-8111). The Atlanta Workshop Players is a non-profit professional children's theatre company comprised of adults and children age eight years and older, which offers a full schedule of musicals throughout the year, all involving comedy, singing, dance and audience participation. Recent productions have included *Rewind*, a musical adventure through history; and *A Play on Words*, a musical journey through the pages of literature. The Players also has a touring company that presents fully mounted productions with costumes and props at schools and recreation centers throughout the city, with optional workshops on either mime, improvisation, stage movement, diction, theatre games, auditioning techniques, dance or musical comedy. Additionally, the group offers acting classes for children at nine different locations in Atlanta and a summer camp drama program at Oglethorpe University.

• **Cobb Children's Theatre,** The Center in Powder Springs, 4181 Atlanta St., Powder Springs (941-1391). Child performers, seventh grade through high school, present two performances each year at The Center in Powder Springs, such as *The Trouble With Angels* and *The Hobbit.* Saturday acting classes are also offered for preschoolers through elementary-age children. Call for audition and performance information.

• **Cobb Civic Ballet,** Cobb Academy of the Performing Arts, Inc., 3301 New MacLand Rd., S.W., Powder Springs (943-7038). The Cobb Civic Ballet is comprised of children age 8–15 who perform in at least two different productions each year, including an original ballet during the holiday season. Other productions have included *The Wizard of Oz* and *Peter Pan.* Most performances are held at the Cobb Civic Center, although there are sometimes free performances at different schools in the Cobb County area and at festivals. Call for audition and performance information.

• **Cobb Youth Chorus of Georgia,** P.O. Box 316, Marietta 30061 (425-2271). The Cobb Youth Chorus provides voice training and performance experience for children age 7–14. Younger children are accepted without auditions, but selection for the older chorus is by audition only. The chorus performs at special concerts during the year, at many locations during the December holiday season and at area festivals. All productions integrate singing with dancing and costumes.

• **DeKalb Center for the Performing Arts at Avondale High School,** 1192 Clarendon Rd., Avondale Estates (289-ARTS). DeKalb County's Performing Arts Magnet School presents many special theatrical and dance performances throughout the year, all appropriate for children and families. It also presents a Children's Theatre on certain weekday mornings for very young audiences that is free for school groups. The public may attend on Saturdays for a small admission fee. The center also has a musical touring group and ongoing gospel performances.

• **Doraville Arts Musical Theatre,** Doraville Community Center, 3765 Park Ave., Doraville (451-0573). Throughout the year, children age 6 and up present musical revues and theatrical performances appropriate for children of all ages, including preschoolers. These productions include professional scenery, costumes and lighting. Musical theatre classes and workshops are offered year-round. Look for audition advertisements in local newspapers.

• **Festival Ballet Company,** 2286 Lake Harbin Rd., Morrow (366-3494). The performers of the Clayton Festival Ballet are students who are training at the Clayton Festival Ballet School, as well as a few others from outlying communities. The ballet has an active performance schedule, including its annual production of *The Nutcracker* at Clayton City Schools Performing Arts Center, and its appearances, representing Clayton County, at numerous festivals and special events throughout Atlanta. A few of the performances have included guest artists from the Atlanta and Joffrey Ballets and International Ballet Rotaru.

• **Freddy Hendricks Youth Ensemble** (366-4912). This theatrical performing group is comprised of children age 9–20 who perform works that have social and political relevance to today's youth. Led by Freddy Hendricks, who has years of experience in the dramatic arts, this performing group is currently in residence at Seven Stages Performing Arts Center. Their productions, such as their signature *Rhymes and Reason* and *Soweto, Soweto, A Township is Calling*, may be seen at Seven Stages and at festivals and special events throughout the Southeast.

• **Harmony: Atlanta's International Youth Chorus** (881-1456). Harmony is an in-residence program at Emory University's Department of Music, whose mission is to provide high-quality choral training and performance opportunities for youth who reflect the international, interracial and multicultural diversity of Atlanta. The music the choir sings emphasizes an international repertoire and ranges from classical literature to popular and regional folk music from a variety of ethnic origins. Children age 5–16 are invited to audition. Previous musical experience is not necessary. Scholarships are available.

• **Horizons Youth Theatre**, 1900 DeKalb Ave., Decatur (371-9609). Students from Horizon School write, produce, direct and perform four "issue-oriented," main-stage productions each year, most of which are appropriate for preschoolers through 12th graders. Performances are held at the Horizons School, Seven Stages Performing Arts Center and festivals throughout the city. This unusual program also presents smaller productions, seminars, workshops and a Summer Arts Laboratory. Children are admitted free to all performances.

• **Kids' Talk & Teen Talk** (395-1700). Atlanta area kids are offered an opportunity to gain experience in acting, producing, directing and camera operation by participating in the production of TV shows to be aired on local television stations. Productions include "Kids' Talk," for children age 8–12, and "Teen Talk," for children age 13 and older. One-day workshops are also offered on the basics of television production. These programs are operated by International Communications Project, a nonprofit media education corporation.

• **Young Singers of Callanwolde**, 980 Briarcliff Rd., N.E., Atlanta (377-6081). The Young Singers of Callanwolde is a choral group for boys and girls in the 3rd–9th grades. Children are instructed in voice and music, and have an opportunity to perform in special concerts throughout the year at Callanwolde, Emory University, with the Atlanta Symphony Orchestra, and at festivals and concerts throughout the United States and Europe.

• **Youth Players of Cobb,** The Art Place–Mountain View, 3330 Sandy Plains Rd., Marietta (509-2700). This repertory company produces live theatre shows for family audiences. Children age 10–18 learn acting, directing, choreography, dancing, singing and the technical aspects of theatre from professional directors and teachers. Most rehearsals and productions are at The Art Place–Mountain View in Marietta.

KEEP IN MIND . . . There are numerous opportunities for children to perform with school-based orchestras and bands throughout Atlanta and to attend concerts performed by these groups. One such orchestra is the **DeKalb Youth Pops Orchestra.** Comprised of students in DeKalb County schools who are in the seventh grade and older, its repertoire includes calypso, classical, country, jazz, gospel, reggae, spirituals and Top-40 hits. In the past the group has performed at the Civic Center, Six Flags Over Georgia, the Omni and many other civic and social functions locally and nationally.

AND PLEASE DON'T FORGET . . . Many of Atlanta's international and ethnic communities and religious associations have established folkloric dance and music troupes that perform at special events and festivals throughout the city. Almost all of these groups feature children. For a comprehensive list of these groups, check *Ethnic Atlanta, The Complete Guide to Atlanta's Ethnic Communities*, available in local bookstores.

ANNUAL PERFORMANCE FESTIVALS & CONCERTS FOR FAMILIES

▬ JANUARY–MARCH ▬

• **Coca-Cola International Series,** Fox Theatre, Atlanta (881-2012). This series features world-class performers—acrobats, orchestras, dancers and singers—from around the world. Performances are at the Fox Theatre.

• **DeKalb Symphony Orchestra,** DeKalb College Central Campus Gymnasium, Clarkston (299-4270). In January, the orchestra presents a Children's Concert at the college's gymnasium, featuring Monica Kaufman as narrator, along with dance, magic and other special entertainment.

• **Hispanic Festival of Music and the Arts** (938-8611). This event features a variety of Hispanic music played by the renowned Atlanta Virtuosi under the direction of Juan Ramirez.

• **Russian Arts Festival,** Atlanta Jewish Community Center, Atlanta (875-7881). This cultural arts festival allows families to sample the tastes and sounds of the cultures of the former Soviet Union. The festival features an evening performance of music and dance presented by Russian émigrés living in Atlanta.

▬ SPRING ▬

• **Atlanta College Dance Festival,** Agnes Scott College, Decatur (371-6360). Agnes Scott Studio Dance Theatre, Emory Dance Company, Spelman College Dance Company, Emory at Oxford and Georgia State Dance Company have all participated in this annual festival of dance held at Agnes Scott.

• **Atlanta Film & Video Festival,** Image Film Video Center at TULA and the High Museum of Art, Atlanta (352-4254). Some of the films screened during this quality week-long film festival are not appropriate for children, but certain of the animation films and other works are. Call for a schedule and decide for yourself.

• **Blue Sky Concerts,** Old Courthouse Square, Decatur (371-8386). Outdoor concerts are held each Wednesday in May at noon on the Courthouse Square lawn. Bring your lunch and blanket. Free.

• **Brown Bag Concert Series,** Glover Park, Marietta (528-0616). Live entertainment can be enjoyed mid-day each Thursday in May. Bring your lunch and blanket. Free.

• **Concerts on the Square,** Old Courthouse Square, Decatur (371-8386). Family-oriented outdoor concerts are held each Saturday evening in May on the Courthouse lawn. Bring your dinner and blanket. Free.

• **Glover Park Concert on the Square,** Glover Park, Marietta (528-0616). Evening outdoor concerts are held in the Square the last Friday of May through August. Bring your dinner and blanket. Free.

• **Jazz on Tap,** Atlanta (516-7229). This three-day event features over twenty-five different dance companies from throughout the Southeast performing jazz, tap and contemporary dance. A special Saturday matinee features three hours of performing children.

• **Peach Blossom Bluegrass Festival,** Southern Tech, Marietta (498-0097). This annual fund-raiser for WRFG (89.3 FM), a non-profit radio station, features continuous bluegrass performances.

• **Dahlonega Folk Festival,** Blackburn Park, Dahlonega (706/864-4127). Traditional, contemporary and international folk music, along with old-time square dancing and storytelling, highlight this weekend festival.

• **Spring Music Festival,** Hiawassee (706/896-4191). Country singers and fiddlers perform Friday night and all day Saturday at the Georgia Mountain Fairgrounds.

▬ SUMMER ▬

• **Atlanta International Jazz Festival,** Atlanta (817-6815). Held during the last weekend of May and the first weekends of June, July and August, the Atlanta Jazz Series offers concerts, workshops, dance performances, gallery exhibitions and film videos featuring local, national and international jazz artists. The outdoor concerts in Grant Park and brown bag concerts in Woodruff Park are free, although other music and dance events may have an admission fee.

• **Atlanta Symphony Orchestra Free Concerts in the Parks,** Atlanta (892-2414). Sunday evening concerts are held June through August at various locations throughout metro Atlanta, including Piedmont Park and Lakewood Amphitheatre. Free.

• **Atlanta Symphony Orchestra Summer Pops Series,** Atlanta (892-2414). Families can enjoy an eight-concert series on either Wednesday, Friday or Saturday evenings at Chastain Park Amphitheatre, all featuring superstar entertainers. Concerts begin at 8:30 p.m., rain or shine. "Stars & Stripes Forever," a special July 4th extravaganza, is a favorite spot for patriotic music and a spectacular fireworks finale.

• **Atlanta Symphony Orchestra Country Series,** Atlanta (892-2414). This series consists of six concerts featuring country music stars at Chastain Park Amphitheatre. Concerts begin at 8:30 p.m., rain or shine.

• **Candlelite Concert Series,** Mable House, Mableton (739-0189). Saturday evening performances on the grounds of the historic Mable

House are held twice a month May through July. Bring your dinner and blanket. Free.

• **Center for Puppetry Arts International Summer Festival**, Atlanta (873-3391). The Center for Puppetry Arts, in collaboration with ACOG Cultural Olympiad, presents an international puppetry festival consisting of six different family performances June through August. All shows are performed in English.

• **DeKalb International Choral Festival**, DeKalb Chamber of Commerce, Decatur (378-2525). The largest festival of its kind brings world-class choral groups from over fifteen different countries to perform at various venues throughout DeKalb County. The five-day festival ends with a choral finale at Stone Mountain Park and an international festival event complete with ethnic food, international vendors, and folkloric music and dancing.

• **Film Festivals at Commercial Theatres.** Almost all of the larger theatre companies (Capital Cinemas, Storey Theatres, General Cinema, etc.) feature free admission to the 10:00 a.m. and 10:30 a.m. features on certain weekday mornings during the summer. Check the parenting newspapers for announcements about this summer's schedule.

• **Fox Family Film Festival**, Atlanta (881-2000). Family movies, cartoons and sing-alongs are scheduled in the fabulous Fox Theatre throughout the summer. Evenings only.

• **The Summer Garden Concerts on the Great Lawn**, Atlanta Botanical Garden, Atlanta (249-6400). Enjoy a three-concert evening series amid the beautiful flowers of the garden. Picnicking is encouraged.

• **Georgia Shakespeare Festival**, Oglethorpe University, Atlanta (688-8008 or 688-8009). Oglethorpe University is the location for professional theatre, featuring three classic works by Shakespeare and other period playwrights performed in rotating repertory. Picnicking and pre-show entertainment offer families with children an excellent opportunity to sample Shakespearean works.

• **Glover Park Concert on the Square**, Glover Park, Marietta (528-0616). Evening outdoor concerts are held in the Square the last Friday of the month all summer long. Bring your dinner and blanket. Free.

• **High Museum of Art Children's Film Festival**, Atlanta (892-3600, ext. 433). When funding permits, the museum sometimes offers a children's film festival during the summer months. The films, screened on Saturday mornings, are usually free. Children must be accompanied by an adult.

• **Jubilee Summer Concert Series**, The Galleria Amphitheater, Atlanta (953-3722 or 988-9641). Evening concerts under the stars are held on eight Sundays during June through August. Bring your dinner and blanket. Free.

• **Lakewood Amphitheatre**, Lakewood Freeway, Atlanta (627-5700). A varied line-up of pop, rock, country and blues concerts are scheduled throughout the summer.

• **Montreux Atlanta International Music Festival**, Atlanta (817-6815). Opera, jazz, blues, zydeco, classical, folk, pop and improvisation performers from around the world participate in this annual event held in August and September at different locations throughout Atlanta. There are usually free brown bag concerts at Woodruff Park and a day-long free concert in Piedmont Park over the Labor Day weekend.

• **Roswell Concerts on the Square**, Roswell Square, Roswell (641-3760). The gazebo at Roswell Square is the location for evening outdoor concerts held the first Saturday of each month, May through October. Free.

• **The Roswell Mill,** Mill St., Roswell (249-6400). The outdoor theatre at historic Roswell Mill is the setting for numerous pop, rock, country and blues concerts throughout the summer.

• **Six Flags Over Georgia Summer Series,** Mableton (948-9290). Special children's concerts are featured at the park throughout the summer. Most are free with regular park admission, but some may have surcharges added.

• **Dahlonega Bluegrass Festival,** Dahlonega (706/864-3711). This June festival in the North Georgia mountains features four days of bluegrass music and plenty of good things to eat.

• **Appalachian Music Festival,** Unicoi State Park (706/878-2201, ext. 282). Enjoy this musical festival at Unicoi State Park in July, featuring concerts, instrumental displays, dancing and workshops on Irish, folk, blue-grass, gospel, and old-time mountain music.

• **The Reach of Song, Appalachian Drama,** Georgia Mountain Fairgrounds, Hiawassee (800/262-SONG). During June through early August, "The Official State Drama," re-creates the flavor of the homeland of Pulitzer Prize nominee Byron Herbert Reece.

■■■ SEPTEMBER ■■■

• **Blue Sky Concerts,** Old Courthouse Square, Decatur (371-8386). Outdoor concerts are held each Wednesday in September at noon on the Courthouse Square lawn. Bring your lunch and blanket. Free.

• **Coca-Cola International Series,** Fox Theatre, Atlanta (881-2012). This series features world-class performers—acrobats, orchestras, dancers and singers—from around the world. Performances are at the Fox Theatre.

• **Concerts on the Square,** Old Courthouse Square, Decatur (371-8386). Family-oriented outdoor concerts are held each Saturday evening in September on the Courthouse lawn. Bring your dinner and blanket. Free.

• **Fall Brown Bag Concert Series,** Glover Park, Marietta (528-0616). Live entertainment can be enjoyed mid-day each Thursday in September. Bring your lunch and blanket. Free.

• **Georgia Music Festival,** Georgia Department of Industry, Trade and Tourism (656-7526). The 10-day statewide show of appreciation for the musicians of Georgia features concerts, shows, performances and musical events throughout the state.

• **Montreux Atlanta International Music Festival,** Atlanta (817-6815). Opera, jazz, blues, zydeco, classical, folk, pop and improvisation performers from around the world participate in this annual event held in August and September at different locations throughout Atlanta. There are usually free brown bag concerts at Woodruff Park and a free, day-long concert in Piedmont Park over the Labor Day weekend.

• **Sesame Street Live,** Omni Coliseum, Atlanta (681-2100). Each September, the Sesame Street Muppets' Stage Show visits Atlanta and presents a musical show for children filled with familiar songs, dancing and audience participation.

• **North Georgia Folk Festival,** Sandy Creek Park, Athens (706/613-3620). Georgia's rich musical heritage is celebrated with blues, bluegrass and string-band musicians. Also showcased are pioneer skills and games, farm animals, and folk arts and crafts.

■■■ OCTOBER–NOVEMBER ■■■

• **The Atlanta Folks Festival,** Atlanta (396-5033). About fifteen multiethnic folk dance groups perform in native costume during this annual fall folk dance festival.

• **Cirque du Soleil.** Cirque du Soleil, the award-winning theatrical circus from Montreal, comes to Atlanta every other year to present a one-of-a-kind performance. The circus without animals features a ninety-member troupe of tumblers, contortionists, clowns, acrobats and musicians in a series of dramatic scenes set to original rock-jazz scores. Some performances are not recommended for children under five.

• **Coca-Cola International Series,** Fox Theatre, Atlanta (881-2012). This series features world-class performers—acrobats, orchestras, dancers and singers—from around the world. All performances are at the Fox Theatre.

• **Festival of Ethnic Dance,** Soapstone Center for the Arts, Decatur (241-2453). This festival has featured over ten different international dance groups from such diverse countries as Peru, Senegal, Laos, Jamaica and Greece. Future plans include expanding this event to include an even greater variety of international entertainment. The festival is not held every year.

• **Festival of Southern Performance,** c/o Alternate ROOTS (577-1079). Sponsored by Alternate ROOTS, an actor's service group, this festival schedules a variety of theatrical, dance, music, puppetry and storytelling performances over a one-week period, featuring artists from all over the Southeast. A whole day is reserved for children's performances. The festival is held every second or third year.

• **The Fall Celebration,** Hiawassee (706/895-4191). Bands, pickers, singers, cloggers and gospel singers entertain for nine days in

October at the Georgia Mountain Fairgrounds.

• **Walt Disney's World on Ice,** Omni Coliseum (681-2100). Walt Disney's incredible ice show featuring Disney characters comes to Atlanta each November and dazzles families with spectacular skating performances.

■■■ DECEMBER ■■■

• **Fernbank Planetarium Show,** Atlanta (378-4311). Each year, the planetarium presents a special holiday show such as "The Christmas Express" or "The Littlest Star." These favorite planetarium shows are screened at the Fernbank Science Center.

• **Holiday Performances.** December is the month for hundreds of performances celebrating the December holidays. Check the late November edition of the *Atlanta Journal and Constitution's* Saturday *Leisure Guide* for a comprehensive listing of holiday theatrical, dance, musical and storytelling performances scheduled throughout the metro area.

Sports

AND RECREATION

Unfortunately, in our highly advanced technological society, the value of physical exercise has almost been lost. In elementary schools, former full-time Physical Education instructors have too often been replaced with part-time instructors, and daily recess time has been considerably shortened. This requires parents to be more actively involved in their children's athletic development.

If your family does not have a "family sport," we urge you to skim through this chapter. We are sure you can find something enjoyable. Remember, in family sports skill levels need not be important, for even the youngest member can fit in a backpack on a family hike.

SPECTATOR SPORTS

PROFESSIONAL SPORTS

• **Atlanta Attack** (National Division, American Indoor Soccer Association). Home games are at the Omni Coliseum from November through March. For information call 431-6111. Attend on your birthday and have an autographed soccer ball and birthday cake delivered to your seat! Listen to home and away games on WCHK–105.7 FM.

• **Atlanta Braves** (National Baseball League). Home games are at the Atlanta-Fulton County Stadium from April through October. For single game tickets call 249-6400; for season tickets call 577-9100. Celebrate your child's birthday at the ballpark. Parties are for children age thirteen and younger. The Braves and Colonial Baking Company will supply everything—cake, invitations, ice cream, Coca-Cola and party favors! You must purchase a minimum of 10 tickets and make advance reservations. Call the Birthday Coordinator at 522-7630. You can buy Braves merchandise at the Braves Clubhouse Store at CNN Center, Atlanta (523-5854).

• **Atlanta Falcons** (National Football League). Home games are held at the Georgia Dome beginning in September. There are eight regularly scheduled home games, and pre-season games are held in August. For information, call 945-1111; for tickets call 223-8000. Falcon football practice is at the Falcon Complex in Suwanee.

• **Atlanta Hawks** (National Basketball Association). Home games are held at the Omni Coliseum from October through March. For general information and tickets call 827-DUNK.

• **Atlanta Knights** (National Hockey League). Home games are held at the Omni Coliseum from October through April. Call 525-8900 for ticket and schedule information. Home and away games are broadcast on SportsRadio 680, and most games are televised.

• **Atlanta Thunder.** Team tennis features top ranked players, and the Atlanta Thunder boasts Martina Navratilova. Home games are at the Peachtree World of Tennis, 6200 Peachtree Corners Cir., Norcross (449-6060). Season tickets may be purchased by calling 250-3428. For other information call 872-6422.

■■■ COLLEGIATE SPORTS ■■■

• **Georgia Tech Yellow Jackets Basketball.** (ACC Division I). Games are at the Georgia Tech Coliseum November through February. For information, call 894-5425.

• **Georgia Tech Yellow Jackets Football.** (ACC Division I). Games are at the Bobby Dodd Stadium September through December. For information, call 894-5420.

• **Georgia Tech—Other Sports.** Call 894-5445 for schedules and information.

• **University of Georgia Bulldogs Football.** (Southeastern Conference). Games are at Sanford Stadium in Athens from September through December. For information, call 706/542-1231.

• **University of Georgia Bulldogs Basketball.** (Southeastern Conference). Games are at UGA Coliseum in Athens from November through February. For information, call 706/542-1231.

• **University of Georgia—Other Sports.** Call 706/542-1231 for schedules and information.

• **Other College Sports.** There are many other colleges and universities in the greater metropolitan area whose sporting events are open to the public. Here are the phone numbers of just a few: Emory University (727-6547); Clayton State College (961-3400 and ask for the athletic director); Georgia State University (651-2772); Oglethorpe University (261-1441); and Atlanta University (880-8126).

▬ AUTO RACING ▬

• **Atlanta International Raceway,** 20 miles south of Atlanta in Hampton (946-4211). Events include Grand National stock car races—the Coca-Cola 500 in March, and the Atlanta Journal 500 in November. Regular events include NTPA tractor-pulls and Bobtail 200-truck races.

• **New Atlanta Dragway,** 1 hour northeast of Atlanta in Commerce, Exit #53 off I-85 at US 441 (706/335-2301). Races include Jet Funny Cars, Top Fuel Dragsters, The AC Delco Southern Nationals, the annual Ingles/96 Rock Nite of Fire, the SCAA Pro Racing Spectacular and the Coca-Cola Kudzu Nationals.

• **Road Atlanta,** 30 miles north of Atlanta in Braselton, Exit #49 off I-85 at Hwy. 53 (Road Atlanta Hotline: 706/967-6143. For a schedule of events call: 881-8233). This 1,000-acre world class facility is home to many road racing events, including the International Motor Sports Association GT series, the annual SCCA National Championship Valvoline Runoffs and the American Motorcycle Association. Parking is $5.00. Fees for races vary. Camping is permitted on Saturday nights only for no fee. Children age twelve years and under are free.

▬ BICYCLE RACING ▬

• **Dick Lane Velodrome**, 1889 Lexington Ave., Sumner Park, East Point (765-1085). Every Friday night, amateur and professional cyclists compete in a variety of races, including USCF track events on the southeast's only Velodrome. Races are $3 for adults ($5 for Grand Prix Races–General Admission), and free for children twelve years and under.

• **Road Atlanta**. 30 miles north of Atlanta in Braselton, Exit #49 off I-85 at Hwy. 53 (881-8233 or 872-4809). Road Atlanta hosts USCF races such as the Circuit Course, a 2.52-mile loop on the Road Atlanta road course. It also hosts the Southeast Cycling Festival, which has included the Coors Light NORBA National Point Series Circuit Race.

• **Outdoor Cycling Races**. Races to benefit various charities are held all year long. A source for finding out information about these events is the *Atlanta Journal and Constitution*. Sponsor a bicyclist for a worthy cause and have fun at the same time!

▬ CRICKET ▬

• **Atlanta Cricket Club** (971-6097, 381-0727 or 447-9248). Atlanta's Cricket Club began in 1989 and has already grown from just two teams to nine. British expatriates, Indians, Pakistanis, South Africans and West Indians compete every Sunday, May through October, at four fields in metro Atlanta. • **Cricket Champions of Atlanta Tropical Sports Club** (455-8482 or 428-9350). Call these clubs for information about dates and times of play.

▬▬ GEORGIA STATE GAMES COMMISSION ▬▬

• **Georgia State Games Commission** (853-0250). The commission holds state-wide competitions in over thirty events, ranging from archery to volleyball. The games are open to the public for a small fee, and many are held at Georgia Tech, as well as elsewhere in the Atlanta area. Children may enter certain events such as archery, track and field, and judo. Games Hotline: 877-7578.

▬▬ GOLF ▬▬

Golf is big in Atlanta, and there are many tournaments throughout the year. One of the most well-known is the Bell South Atlanta Classic held every May to benefit Egleston Children's Hospital. A recent event raised over a half million dollars!

▬▬ GYMNASTICS ▬▬

Several major gymnastics meets are held in Atlanta throughout the year, including the Peachtree Classic, an international gymnastics meet held in February.

▬▬ HORSE SHOWS & RODEOS ▬▬

Greater Atlanta is host to several riding events each year. Among the more popular are:

• **Atlanta Steeplechase**, Seven Branches Farm, Cumming (237-7436). Held in the spring to benefit the Atlanta Speech School. Tickets are available by mail order only on a first-come, first-served basis. Write: Atlanta Steeplechase, 3160 Northside Pkwy., Atlanta 30327. There is a parking fee.

• **DeKalb Sheriff's Posse Rodeo** (498-5600). The Posse hosts an annual two-day Wild West event each May at the Stone Mountain Coliseum that features bucking broncos, barrel riding, calf roping and more. They also host the State High School Rodeo in September.

• **The Hunter-Jumper Classic,** Wills Park Equestrian Center, 11915 Wills Rd., Alpharetta (740-2400). Sponsored by the Georgia Hunter Jumper Association, this two-week event held in July benefits charity.

• **Pro-Am Benefit Horse Show,** Henderson's Horse Show Arena, 4380 Stacks Rd., College Park (763-3002). The annual show, featuring riders from all over the country, helps raise money for Egleston Children's Hospital and Scottish Rite Children's Medical Center.

• **Wills Park Equestrian Center,** 11915 Wills Rd., Alpharetta (740-2400). This beautiful 46-acre facility is operated by Fulton County. Horse shows for all breeds are held throughout the year in both covered and open show rings. Of special interest to youngsters is the Little Britches All Youth Open Show held in June. There are picnic and camper areas. Farm tours are available on the weekends. Open daily. Admission is free or nominal.

▬ POLO ▬

• **The Polo Fields,** 6325 Saddlebridge Ct., Cumming, Exit #8 off GA 400 (688-POLO). The Polo Fields is the home of the **Atlanta Polo Club.** Every Sunday from the first Sunday in June through October from 2:00 p.m.–4:00 p.m., your family may enjoy watching polo in a picnic-like, fun atmosphere. You may tailgate it or purchase soft drinks and sandwiches from the concession stand. The stands are not covered, so bring a hat or sunglasses. Though it is rare for a match to be canceled, if you are in doubt, tune your radio to WPCH (94.9 FM) from 12:00 noon–1:00 p.m., and it will be announced if the fields have been closed for the safety of the riders and horses. The fee is $10.00 per carload.

▬ TENNIS ▬

Because Atlanta is an important tennis city, it is home to the **Atlanta Thunder** (mentioned above). The **AT&T Challenge,** which draws many of the top world-ranked players, is held every spring in Atlanta. And keep your eyes open for the location of the **Junior National Championships,** which has been held in Atlanta and may be again.

INDIVIDUAL, FAMILY & TEAM SPORTS

▬ ARCHERY ▬

Archery clubs for children under age eighteen are located in almost every metro Atlanta county. Kids as young as four years can enjoy archery! Many clubs offer lessons on Saturday and compete with other clubs in their area. For Junior Olympic Development Program certified instructors call: Fayette (460-0513); Morrow (361-8866); Gwinnett (962-3525 or 972-4022); and Lilburn (925-7866). Contact your local archery store listed in the *Yellow Pages* under "Archery Equipment & Supplies" and "Archery Ranges," for information on clubs in your area.

• **Buckskin Archery,** 2396 Cobb Pkwy., Kennesaw (425-2697). This well-stocked store carries top-of-the-line archery equipment and is the base of communication for several archery clubs. Call for store hours and club information.

▬ BADMINTON ▬

Not only is badminton great fun, but it also develops hand-eye coordination and speed. The equipment is not expensive and can be set up in your yard if you have the space. If not, the equipment can easily be transported to a park. Badminton can be played at almost any age level by adjusting the net, and injuries are almost non-existent because the playing surface is grass. The game can be easy-going, but for the more skilled, you will be surprised to discover how vigorous and competitive it can be.

━━ BALLOONING ━━

Hot air balloons are fascinatingly beautiful to the youngest child ... and the oldest adult. See our chapter on "Festivals and Special Events" for regularly scheduled balloon races. If you are interested in a ride, you can gather information at the festivals. Look under "Balloons – Manned" in the *Yellow Pages* or call the **Georgia Hot Air Balloon Association** at 288-1867.

━━ BASEBALL & T-BALL ━━

Contact your city or county Department of Parks and Recreation, your area religious organizations, YM/YWCAs, and other groups listed below in this chapter, to locate an association or youth group that has a team for your child to join. Some of these facilities also offer special summer camp programs.

━━ BASEBALL BATTING PRACTICE ━━

Baseball Batting Ranges, listed in the *Yellow Pages*, are located in Marietta, Duluth, Decatur and Scottdale. The **Stone Mountain Park Sports Complex** also has batting cages which are open daily March through December, and on weekends year-round. For 50¢ you get twelve practice balls.

━━ BASKETBALL ━━

Contact your city or county Department of Parks and Recreation, your area religious organizations, YM/YWCAs, and other groups listed below in this chapter, to locate an association or youth group that has a team for your child to join. Some of these facilities also offer special summer camp programs.

■■■ BICYCLING ■■■

Bicycling is not only great exercise in the beautiful out-of-doors, but an activity that a family can enjoy together. Some of the more beautiful and relaxing family bicycle rides are on designated trails in city and state parks. A few places are listed below to get you started. You can also contact the **Southern Bicycle League** at 594-8350 for information about the many programs, rides and tours available through the association, including in-school cycling safety programs for children. Also, keep in mind that more and more, children are participating in youth bicycle races. **The Children's Life Cycle** is an annual bicycle ride through the neighborhoods of North Atlanta to raise money for UNICEF. Call 636-5597 for more information. Another popular event is the annual **Tour D' Town** in Buckhead for all levels of bicyclists. This race, which benefits the American Cancer Society, includes a fun Celebrity Challenge at noon. Call 841-0700 for information. For the more adventurous, contact the **Southern Off Road Bicycle Association** at P.O. Box 1191, Decatur, Georgia 30031.

• **Piedmont Park**, Piedmont Ave. & 14th St., Atlanta (658-7406). Bicycling is permitted on paved trails. Bicycle rentals are available across the street at **Skate Escape**, 1086 Piedmont Ave., N.E., Atlanta (892-1292).

• **Stone Mountain Park** (469-9831). Bike rentals are available for children of any age on weekends from March through November, and on a daily basis from June through August. Single speeds are $2.50/hour, 10-speeds are $4.00/hour and tandems (for two) are $6.00/hour. Babysitters are also available.

• **Callaway Gardens.** Beautiful scenery and 7 ½ miles of level bike paths await you. Bike rentals are available for children and adults. See our chapter on "Day Trips" for more information.

BOWLING

Bowling is one of those rare participant sports that the whole family can play together with everyone playing at his/her own skill level. In other words, it can be just as challenging and enjoyable for parents as for kids, or great non-competitive fun when family members only play against themselves. There are numerous bowling lanes in the metro Atlanta area that have leagues for children. Did you know children can join as young as age three? (Bowling balls come as light as six pounds and inflatable bumpers prevent gutter balls.) Saturday mornings are a popular time for kid's league practices and games. Also, during the summer months, there are daily bowling league activities. Call or go to your nearby lanes listed under "Bowling" in the *Yellow Pages* for more information.

CAMPING

Georgia is made for camping with its natural beauty of forests, streams, lakes, waterfalls and mountains. For the novice camping family there is **Stone Mountain Park,** which has about 400 campsites by the lake. Not too far away to the north are **Allatoona Campground and Beach** (974-3182), **Lake Lanier Islands** (945-6701), and **Unicoi State Park** (706/878-2201). Be sure to call ahead for reservations. A fun way to get youngsters used to camping is to let them sleep in a sleeping bag in the living room or pitch a tent in the backyard. Seasoned campers should contact the Georgia Department of Natural Resources Division of Parks, Recreation & Historical Sites (656-3530) to obtain an informative brochure about campsites all over the state.

CAVING

The 400 or so caves in Georgia are not developed, so it is recommended that those interested in the sport of caving contact an organized group of cavers for information on locations, specific cave information, and whether or not the type of cave is within the range of your family's interest and experience. Contact the club described below for assistance. The not-so-brave may just wish to visit the **William Weinman Mineral Museum** in Cartersville (706/386-0576), which has a simulated cave, or head to **Cave Springs** (706/777-8439 or 748-9443), which has a natural limestone cave. Take a fun day trip to Chattanooga, Tennessee where even three-year-olds can hike down to the spectacular **Ruby Falls** at Lookout Mountain. (See our chapter on "Day Trips" for more information.)

• **Dogwood City Grotto,** 1865 Ridgewood Dr. NE, Atlanta, Georgia 30307. Children up to age 16 may join this club if the parent is a member. Dues are $10 and entitle members to receive *The Georgia Underground* magazine, access their library, and rent caving equipment.

CIRCUS ARTS

• **Circus Arts Studio,** 887 W. Marietta St., Atlanta (892-2727). In a non-competitive, playful environment, children and adults develop fitness, balance, grace, strength and self-confidence. Participants utilize the low trapeze, rings and Spanish Web, and learn juggling and acrobatics. Classes are ongoing 6–8 week sessions, and a summer camp is offered. Private workshops and performances are available, as are birthday parties for children ages three and older.

FENCING

• **The Atlanta Fencer's Club,** 40 7th St., N.E., Atlanta (892-0307). This club is a good place to begin for information on fencing instruction for young children. They have offered classes to children as young as five and six years of age, and private and group instruction is available depending upon the child's age. Older children have an opportunity to participate in fencing tournaments throughout the southeast.

• **Fayette Fencing Academy**, 330 N. Fayette Dr., Fayetteville (461-3809). The very professionally run fencing school offers classes at all levels for all ages, from beginners to nationally-ranked competitors. The serious fencing student would do well to seek information here.

▬ FISHING ▬

FISHING SAFETY:
   • Georgia State law requires all boaters to wear Coast
   Guard approved life jackets.
   • A fishing license is required for fresh-water fishing in
   Georgia for everyone over the age of 16 years. Call
   493-5770 for more information about licenses.
   • Fishing is permitted in all streams, lakes and ponds
   unless otherwise designated. Check with your local city or
   county Department of Parks and Recreation for informa-
   tion about fishing in your neighborhood parks.

For the child or novice angler, the first fishing trips should be kept simple. You may want to purchase a cheap (about $15.00) pre-packaged spincast rod and reel outfit which has everything you will need except bait. Pick up some crickets, a box of worms, and maybe a few dozen minnows to add interest. Bank fishing is a safe way to introduce very young children to fishing, but most children would be thrilled to have an opportunity to go out in a boat and would probably be satisfied even if no fish were caught. We suggest you bring food and beverages to ward off boredom as well as hunger, along with life vests, hats and sunscreen.

• **Lakes and Rivers. Stone Mountain Park** has a special fishing store that sells licenses, bait, snacks and rents boats on a large, stocked lake. Across the street from the store is an area for bank fishing with picnic tables. Fishing is seasonal from mid-March to the latter part of October. **Sweetwater Creek State Park** and the **Chattahoochee River** are spots for both bank fishing and boating. **Twin Brothers Lake** in Tucker (496-0002) is a stocked lake, and a fee is charged for fishing. Bait and bathrooms are available. Look under "Fishing Lake–Public" in the *Yellow Pages* for more fishing spots in the metro Atlanta area. And don't forget to venture to the many lakes surrounding Atlanta, such as **Lake Allatoona, Lake Hartwell** and **Lake Lanier.** Call 656-3524 for information on these and other lakes around Georgia.

• **Special Events.** "Kids' Fishing Day," sponsored by the Upper Chattahoochee Chapter of Trout Unlimited, is held in March of each year at the Chattahoochee River Park (on Azalea Drive between Willeo and Roswell Roads in Roswell). The event is free for kids under 16, but they must bring their own bait and tackle. The chapter releases trout in the river one half hour before the event begins. For more information, call 266-0577 or 447-9772. **Lake Oconee,** at the Old Salem Recreation Area, holds fishing tournaments for kids age 4–14 with trophies and prizes (706/485-8704). **Reynolds Nature Preserve,** on the south side of Atlanta, has a fishing tournament for children age 6–14 (961-9257).

• **Fisharama,** sponsored by the Georgia Wildlife Federation, is usually held at the Atlanta Exposition Center (929-3350). The show has over 400 exhibitors displaying the latest in fishing and boating equipment. Demonstrations and a casting contest for kids will keep the whole family happy.

■ FOOTBALL ■

Contact your city or county Department of Parks and Recreation, your area religious organizations, YM/YWCAs, and other groups (listed below in this chapter) to locate an association or youth group that has a team for your child to join. Some of these facilities and high schools offer special summer camp programs.

• **Atlanta Colt Youth Association** (551-8956), one of the largest youth football associations in the country, is an example of what is possible for kids interested in playing football in Atlanta. Kids age 5–7 play flag football. Girls and boys age 8–15 are assigned to teams based upon weight, age and football experience. The Colts have been in existence for over 25 years and have won nine national championships and produced 26 All-American scholar-athletes.

■ GOLF ■

• **Atlanta Junior Golf Association** (850-9040). Golf seems to be an increasingly popular sport among Atlanta's youth, and this association is a good source of information for the serious junior.

• **Junior Tournaments.** There are a number of junior tournaments each year, such as the DeKalb Junior Classic and Griffin Junior Golf Classic, as well as other competitive events for both boys and girls from about age seven on up. The "Participant's Calendar" in the Friday *Atlanta Journal and Constitution* Sports Section lists upcoming golfing events. You can also make inquiries at the more than thirty public courses or the many private courses in metro Atlanta.

• **Public Golf Courses.** Please note that there are several upscale public golf courses, such as Mystery Valley in Lithonia (469-6913), Stone Mountain Park (498-5715), The Metropolitan Club in east DeKalb (981-5325), River's Edge Plantation in Fayetteville (460-1098),

River Pines in Alpharetta (442-5960) and North Fulton Golf Course (255-0723).

• **Practice, Practice, Practice.** There are over fifteen "Golf Practice Ranges" listed in the *Yellow Pages,* some of which offer golfing lessons.

• **Miniature Golf.** There are more than twelve "Golf Courses— Miniature" listed in the *Yellow Pages.* Additionally, there is miniature golfing at **Red Top State Park.** At the **Stone Mountain Sports Complex,** you may play miniature golf daily from March through December, and weekends year-round on a very simple course. And good news! You can even golf in the rain at the indoor miniature golf course at **Pebble Beach** in Marietta (973-7828) or Dixieland Fun Park in Fayetteville (460-7135).

■ Gymnastics ■

Gymnastics is one of the best individual sports to help children build self-confidence, flexibility, agility and body control. They can work and develop skills at their own pace in a fun, active environment. For those who are ready and interested, an array of events in competitive gymnastics is available at the more notable private gyms in Atlanta. Also, Emory University's six-week **Summer Sports Fitness Camp** includes daily tumbling and gymnastics instruction. Classes are also offered at recreation centers, YM/YWCAs and other youth organizations. *Yellow Page* listings under "Gymnasiums" and "Gymnastic Instruction" are good resources. Some of these facilities are available for birthday parties, too!

■ Hiking & Nature Trails ■

We are fortunate to live in an ideal geographic area for outdoor activities. And what kid doesn't like to be outdoors every day? Hiking is a year-round activity—only heavy rain or snow will keep enthusiastic hiking families indoors. Some people need only walk around their neighborhood for a good hike, but for those who are looking for something more, there are good trails nearby. A supplemental resource for interesting walks is the book by Ren and Helen Davis called *Atlanta Walks*.

We provide in-depth descriptions of all the places listed below in our chapters "Places To Go" and "Tidbits—Ecology & Nature, Science, History & Politics." Look up the places that intrigue you in the "Index" at the back of this book for exact page numbers.

- **Al Burruss Nature Park and Wildwood Park**, Marietta
- **Atlanta Botanical Garden**, Atlanta
- **Atlanta History Center**, Atlanta
- **Chattahoochee Nature Center**, Roswell
- **Chattahoochee River National Recreational Area**, Atlanta and environs
- **Cochran Mill Park**, Atlanta
- **Davidson-Arabia Mountain Nature Preserve**, Lithonia
- **Dunwoody Nature Center**, Dunwoody
- **Fernbank Science Center—Nature Trails**, Atlanta
- **Kennesaw Mountain National Battlefield**, Marietta
- **Outdoor Activity Center at Bush Mountain**, Atlanta
- **Panola Mountain State Conservation Park**, Stockbridge
- **Providence Park**, Alpharetta
- **Red Top Mountain State Park**, Lake Allatoona
- **W.H. Reynolds Memorial Nature Preserve**, Morrow
- **Stone Mountain Park**, Stone Mountain
- **Sweetwater Creek State Park**, Lithia Springs

And don't forget the North Georgia Mountains! (See our chapter on "Day Trips" for more information.)

━━ (ICE) HOCKEY ━━

The Georgia Amateur Hockey Association has seasonal league play

at **Stone Mountain Ice Chalet** and **Parkaire Olympic Ice Arena.**
For children under age 10 there is an instructional program, and
House League Play for boys begins at age 10. For more information,
call the association at 249-4836.

■■ HORSEBACK RIDING ■■

Most stables in the Atlanta area do not rent horses for young children to ride; you should have better luck outside the metro area in
the North Georgia Mountains. English and Western lessons are
available at many of the stables listed in the *Yellow Pages* under "Riding Academies" and "Stables," as well as at private polo clubs in Atlanta.

• **Summer Riding Camps.** The **Huntcliff Stables** (993-8448), located on River Run Road in Dunwoody, has weekly sessions for children age six and up during the months of June, July and August. **Pounds
Stables** (394-8288) in Doraville has a horsemanship day camp for
children age five and up during the summer months. For fun with
horses on a real working farm, call **Jan Serafy's Riding Camp** (355-
5519) and contact **Fox Hollow Farm** (971-3437). **Little Creek Farm
School** (634-9209) in Decatur offers lessons for children throughout the year.

• **Clubs.** Your county Extension Service is a good source for finding
out about scheduled events. They often sponsor equestrian events and
will be happy to mail you information. You may also contact the following associations and clubs: **Georgia Pony Club** (893-3751),
Georgia Horse Foundation (261-0612), **Atlanta Equestrian Society**
(475-5551) and the **Quarter Horse Association** (483-2818).

• **Pony Rides** are a big hit at birthday parties and carnivals. There
are several pony rental groups that cater specifically to parties and
carnivals. Look for ads in *Atlanta Parent* and *Our Kids* newspapers,
as well as the *Yellow Pages* under "Carnivals" and "Party Planning
Service."

▬ ICE SKATING ▬

For the ice skating enthusiast or the neophyte, your best bet for skating is one of the two indoor facilities in Atlanta.

• **Parkaire Olympic Ice Arena,** 4859 Lower Roswell Rd., N.E., Marietta (973-0753). Ice skating is available year-round. Call for exact hours. The cost for adults is $5.00, plus $1.00 skate rental. For children under 12 the cost is $4.50, plus $1.00 for skate rental.

• **Stone Mountain Ice Chalet,** at the new facility in Gwinnett called Atlanta Iceplex (813-1010). Skating, lessons and other programs will continue to be year-round at the new facility in Stone Mountain.

KARATE & OTHER MARTIAL ARTS

• **Karate** (meaning "empty hand") is the development of the whole self, body and spirit. Discipline of the mind and emotions is as important as discipline of the body. Thus, karate and all martial arts develop, among other things, a child's self-confidence, his/her ability to focus and concentrate, and a respect for other people. Remember that good karate instructors emphasize the defensive nature of the activity, and they make this very clear to the students at all times. Karate involves defensive blocking, punching and kicking techniques.

• **Aikido** (meaning "way of harmony") is a unique martial art that teaches youngsters how to resolve conflict through tumbling, falling and rolling techniques. Through games and the study of movement, children learn to focus their energy, to maintain balance and composure in the face of conflict, to blend with an attack, and to redirect negative or aggressive energy. Aikido is both a serious and a fun approach to the study of balance. Call Dogwood Aikikai (364-0005) for more information.

• **Instruction.** For schools of martial arts in Atlanta, look in *Creative Loafing, Atlanta Parent* and *Our Kids* newspapers, as well as the *Yellow Pages* under "Karate and Other Martial Arts Instruction." Some recreation centers and art centers also offer martial arts classes. Be sure to observe a class before you enroll your child.

▬ RAFTING & CANOEING ▬

If you haven't already, you simply must **"Shoot the Hooch"**—it's an Atlanta tradition and great family fun! For first-timers or families with preschoolers, we suggest the approximately two–hour drift from Powers Island to Paces Mill. Along the way we paddled ashore to have a picnic and found places shallow enough to explore the river bottom. We took a hike up the mountain and made exciting discoveries along the river's edge. (Keep those sneakers on!) We were in awe as several people dove off a rock from a breathtaking height, but such diving is discouraged by the park. There is a bathroom halfway along this rafting route. To get you back from Paces Mill to your car, use the Outdoor Center's shuttle bus at a cost of $2.50 for adults and $1.25 for children.

If the river and all the in and out points are unfamiliar to you, don't worry. The folks at the Chattahoochee Outdoor Center (the official park concessionaire) are very willing to explain it all. A family of four might consider a six-man raft to have plenty of room for a cooler, camera, sunscreen, towels, etc.

Yes, children can learn to canoe safely and easily in calm water. Contact the **Georgia Canoeing Association** (421-9729) for general information about training, races and trips for canoeing and kayaking. There are guided evening rides down the Chattahoochee in the summer led by the **Chattahoochee Nature Center** (992-2055).

RIVER SAFETY:
    • Georgia State law requires that all people aboard a water-

craft (including inner tubes) wear Coast Guard approved life-jackets.

- The National Recreation Area recommends no swimming.
- Wear old sneakers to protect your feet from any sharp rocks, shells and broken glass.
- Do not dive or jump into the water, as it is difficult to see submerged objects and rocks. (But don't be surprised to see people diving from breathtaking heights on your rafting trip.)
- No glass is allowed on the Chattahoochee River.
- Take along a plastic bag for litter.
- Call 945-1466 or 329-1455 for up-to-the-minute river conditions, if you are planning to raft in a Class II or Class III section of the river.

• **Chattahoochee Outdoor Center** (395-6851). Rental and put-in sites are 311 Johnson Ferry Rd. and 285 Powers River (Powers Island). Take-out facilities are at Powers Island (I-285 at Northside Pkwy.) and Paces Mill (intersection of the river and Hwy. 41). Rental is seasonal: May (weekends only); June through mid-September (daily). Hours are Monday–Friday from 10:00 a.m.–8:00 p.m.; Saturday, Sunday and holiday hours from 9:00 a.m.–8:00 p.m. The cost for canoe rental is $30/day. Raft rental is $36/day for a 4-man, $54/day for a 6-man, and $74/day for an 8-man craft. Life jackets and paddles are provided for both canoe and raft rentals at no extra charge. Food, beverages and sundries are available at all sites, and reservations using a major credit card are suggested for the weekends. Shuttle service is available from all locations. To secure a rental, you will need a valid driver's license and make a refundable security deposit of $75–$100.

• **Chattahoochee Canoe & Raft Rental** at Chattahoochee River Park, 199 Azalea Dr. (between Roswell and Willeo Rds.), Roswell (998-7778). Rental is seasonal: April through September on Fridays, Saturdays and Sundays from 9:00 a.m.–7:00 p.m. There is no shuttle transportation until May 1. Canoe prices are $10 for two hours, $15 for four hours. Raft prices are $20/day for a 4-man, $25/day for a 6-man, $40/day for an 8-man craft.

• **Stone Mountain Park** (498-5683). Rent canoes, rowboats, pedal-boats and pontoon boats at the park. The cost for canoe rental is $4.50/hour; rowboats are $6/hour; pedalboats are $2.50/20 minutes; and pontoon boats range from $25/hour–$35/hour. The park also permits private boating (limited to 10 HP), but not after 11:00 a.m. on weekends and holidays between April 1 and September 20.

• Those of you who are experienced and adventurous might want to join the **Atlanta Whitewater Club** (299-3752). Be sure to check out our chapter on "Day Trips" for some other places to rent canoes, rafts or kayaks, including Lake Allatoona, Callaway Gardens and Lake Lanier Islands.

■ ROLLER & IN-LINE SKATING ■

Remember the helmets, knee pads and wrist guards—don't leave home without them!

There are about fifteen roller rinks, including the **Stone Mountain Park Roller Rink,** listed in the *Yellow Pages* under "Skating Rinks." Don't forget that roller skating birthday parties are great fun for school age kids, boys and girls alike. Call your nearest rink for individual and group prices, skate rentals and availability.

Speed skating may soon be in the Olympics. For speed skating fun visit **Skate-A-Long USA** roller rink in Lilburn (921-0800). "Roller Hockey" or "Street Hockey" is a new sport that is being organized at Piedmont Park's **Skate Escape** (892-1292) and elsewhere in Atlanta.

In-line skating has become quite the craze. Contact **High Country**

Outfitters (several locations in Atlanta) for demonstrations, skates, rentals, safety equipment, instruction and race information.

■ RUNNING ■

People of all ages run, and at all times of the day, in light rain, and up the steepest hills . . . in their neighborhoods and in parks. Many elementary schools have running clubs and annual "fun runs" for the whole family. Atlanta-area festivals have begun including races as one of the activities of the day, and many non-profit organizations are holding "fun runs" as fund-raising events.

• **Peachtree Jr.** The Atlanta Track Club has established a tradition in Atlanta with its annual 3K children's race for 7–12-year-olds. Held in June of each year at Piedmont Park, it's the children's version of *the* Peachtree Road Race. Almost 2,000 kids participate. Applications are in the *Atlanta Journal and Constitution* in early April. Keep your eyes open as enrollment is limited! For information, phone 231-9064.

■ SCUBA DIVING ■

According to the P.A.D.I. (Professional Association of Diving Instructors) regulations, the minimum age for kids to begin scuba diving is 12 years old. If you are interested in pursuing diving for your older child or anticipating instruction for your near-12-year-old, see the *Yellow Pages* under "Diving Instruction." Be sure to look for aquatic centers that have P.A.D.I. certified instructors. Scuba equipment is expensive, but can be rented. For more information, contact the **Atlanta Scuba and Swim Academy** (973-3120) or the **Atlanta Reef Dwellers** (477-5176), a group that dives almost everywhere, including the Chattahoochee River. Take heed—lessons are absolutely vital.

▬ SKATEBOARDS ▬

If your kids are skateboard enthusiasts, remember that helmets and padding should be worn at all times. To try an actual skateboard rink, visit **Surf's Up Street Waves** in Lithonia (482-7471) or **Skate Zone Skateboard Park** in Tucker (491-0656).

▬ SKIING ▬

The North Georgia Mountains provide fine snow skiing for families. Locally, the **Atlanta Ski Club** (255-4800), can help you with questions and other information. The Club offers ski instruction for school-age children beginning in October.

Water skiing requires no lessons—just hold on to the rope, bend your knees and let the boat pull you up! Lake Allatoona is used by the **Atlanta Water Ski Club** (425-7166), which hosts the annual Atlanta Open ski tournament. Lake Lanier is great for skiing and is an easy drive. Just remember to adhere to the boating laws in Georgia.

▬ SOCCER ▬

According to the Soccer Industry Council of America, only basketball is more popular among kids under the age of 12. Soccer has mushroomed in popularity all across our country in recent years, and is available at recreation centers and churches. Many youth groups also have teams. For those children who want serious information about the sport, call the **Georgia State Soccer Association** (452-0505). For information on private soccer clubs, see "Soccer Clubs" in the *Yellow Pages*. **Summer Soccer Camps** are held at colleges, such as Agnes Scott and Emory University, and are hosted by the Atlanta Attack (431-6111 or 577-9600) at numerous metro Atlanta locations.

▬ Special Olympics ▬

For information on the very active **Georgia Special Olympics** organization and events, contact their main office at 3772 Pleasantdale Rd., Doraville (414-9390). They will put you in touch with an area coordinator.

▬ Summer Sports Camps ▬

• **Comprehensive.** Summer sports camps are offered at many educational facilities throughout Atlanta, such as Agnes Scott College (371-6491), DeKalb College (244-5050), Emory University (727-6547), Georgia Tech (894-5400), Kennesaw State College (423-6400) and Oglethorpe University (261-1441).

• **Unique.** One-of-a-kind camps are offered by the Atlanta Attack (431-6111) in soccer, and the City of Atlanta's Outdoor Survival Camp (658-6381). Emory University (727-4280) offers the unusual "Ancient Culture Camp: Sport in the Ancient World" during which children age 8–12 learn a wide variety of sports from five ancient civilizations.

Also, see our section, "Recreation Centers & Youth Organizations" for names and phone numbers of many other facilities offering summer sports programs.

▬ Swimming & Aquatics ▬

• **Pools and Lessons.** Whether you wish to swim for pleasure or take swimming or lifesaving lessons, your local recreation center and YM/YWCAs have good programs for children of all ages and abilities. Some residential areas have community clubs with pools as do apartment complexes and condominiums. Be creative. If your club or residential pool does not offer lessons by certified instructors, try to organize such a service through the governing board. If enough of your neighbors are interested, the cost might be acceptable, and it would certainly be convenient. Swimming instruction is available at larger facilities such as **Dynamo Swim Club** in Chamblee (451-3272) and **SwimAtlanta,** located in Lilburn (381-7926), Roswell (992-7665) and Decatur (981-7946). See the *Yellow Pages* under "Swimming Instruction."

• **Teams.** Many community clubs have swim teams that all member children may join. The only requirement is that the child be able to make his or her way unassisted from one end of the pool to the other. Swim meets are organized with local clubs competing with one another, and the season usually ends with an awards dinner. Whether fun takes precedent over competition or vice versa depends upon the club, so find out if you are comfortable with the philosophy before you commit. **Dynamo Swim Club** in Chamblee (451-3272) has a U.S.S. Swim Team for ages seven and up.

• **Public Pools.** There are numerous outdoor, summer only public pools in cities and counties in and around Atlanta, and a few indoor year-round public pools in the city of Atlanta. Admission varies from free for youngsters to a nominal charge for adults depending upon the facility. Look in the *Blue Pages* under your county's or city's Parks and Recreation Department.

• **Beaches.** There are manmade white sand beaches at Stone Mountain Park (469-9831), Lake Lanier Islands (945-6701), Lake Allatoona (974-5182) and Sun Valley Beach in Powder Springs (943-5900). See our chapters "Places To Go" and "Day Trips" for more information. Be alert for beaches that are closed because of unacceptable levels of pollution.

━━ TENNIS ━━

Atlanta is a mecca for tennis enthusiasts. There are many public tennis centers and private courts available year-round for beginners as well as the most accomplished, top-ranked players. Tennis in metro Atlanta is impressively large and well-organized. Atlanta has a very active U.S.T.A. division and A.L.T.A., the local organization, which allow players to be on teams all year long. Many public and private courts offer lessons as well as team play for children.

There are many public courts managed by the city of Atlanta and sur-rounding counties. Call the numbers listed below for information on locations, children's lessons and teams. Some centers offer junior ten-nis camps, so be sure to inquire if you are interested.

- **Atlanta City Courts** – 658-7277
- **Clayton County Courts** – 477-3766
- **Cobb County Courts** – 424-0204
- **DeKalb County Courts** – 371-2548
- **Fulton County Courts** – 572-2526
- **Gwinnett County Courts** – 448-4464

Some recreation centers and YM/YWCAs have tennis facilities and offer lessons to children. **The Stone Mountain Sports Complex** (498-5728) has eight lighted courts available seasonally at a low per-hour fee. Ask about their free summer tennis lesson program. A huge new tennis complex is being built in Stone Mountain in time to be the venue for Olympic tennis in 1996.

- **Atlanta Lawn Tennis Association (ALTA)** (399-5788) is the world's largest local tennis association. Juniors (age 8 and up) as well as adults can join and be involved in competitive play. Call for the location of a team near your home.

- **Summer Tennis Camps** abound for juniors. *Net News*, a publi-cation of ALTA free to all members, contains ads for camps as well as other pertinent information for the serious tennis player. Check out the summer programs offered at Agnes Scott College, Emory Uni-versity and Georgia Tech.

RECREATION CENTERS & YOUTH ORGANIZATIONS

▬ RECREATION CENTERS ▬

Recreation Centers, both city and county run, provide an incredible variety of programs and facilities for children and youth in metro Atlanta. **Classes** are offered in swimming, karate, basketball, gymnastics, tennis, baton twirling, chess, ballet and tap, double dutch, drama, arts and crafts, horseshoes, guitar, cooking, scrabble and roller skating. Some facilities have **Preschool Classes** all year long and **After School Programs** during the school year. In the summer time, most recreational facilities have **Summer Day Camp** programs for elementary-age kids, which may include arts and crafts, swimming and field trips. A few offer extended care after regular camp hours. The day camp programs vary from location to location; some have a series of one week programs, others offer only one week-long program at a particular center, and yet others have developed a summer camp your child can attend all summer long. But inquire as early as March for these camps!

Non-profit **Youth Associations** provide competitive sports opportunities for children in football, baseball, softball, soccer and even cheerleading. Many counties in Georgia require that all coaches be trained and certified annually through the National Youth Sports Coaches Association (NYSCA), a non-profit certification program begun in 1981 to improve the quality and safety of out-of-school sports. Coaches learn first aid and safety, teaching techniques, the psychology of coaching, how to make practices interesting and fun, and sports ethics. Youth Associations are independently run, but use county and city playing fields.

For information on the sports your children wish to play, contact your local county and/or city recreation department. They will provide you with the name and phone number of the person you should contact.

- City of Atlanta (653-7111)
- City of Decatur (374-0494)
- City of Lawrenceville (963-3510)
- City of Marietta (528-0627)
- Clayton County (997-5945)
- Cobb County (427-7275 or 428-1300)
- DeKalb County (371-2631)
- Fulton County (730-6200)
- Gwinnett County (822-5151)
- Tucker Recreation Center (270-6226)

Handicapped persons should contact the following city or county offices: DeKalb (377-3616), Cobb (944-0868), Fulton (303-6181), Gwinnett (822-5150) and City of Atlanta (658-6381).

◼ YOUTH ORGANIZATIONS ◼

• **Boy Scouts of America** (577-4810). The scouts provide a broad range of activities in the arts, sciences, social skills and out-of-doors, while encouraging self-confidence, skill development and lots of fun! They perform various activities and earn badges upon completion of specific tasks. Boys can enter scouting as a Tiger Cub at age six, then move up through the ranks as they get older. Scouts normally meet once a week. Call for information on scouting in your area.

• **Boys Clubs of Metro Atlanta** (527-7100). Although the Boys Clubs are part of a nationwide organization called Boys and Girls Clubs of America, each club operates autonomously. The metro Atlanta clubs serve boys age 6–18. Programs and times may vary from club to club, but most are open from 2:30 p.m.–9:00 p.m. during the school year with transportation being provided from nearby schools for after school programs. There are summer programs for children, and the clubs are usually open a full day during school vacations. Activities may include arts and crafts, drama and poetry clubs, T-ball, ping pong, pool, a sign language club and a newspaper club.

• **Campfire Boys and Girls** (527-7125). Campfire offers programs for both boys and girls that include camping, community service and learning to take care of oneself. Campfire accepts children age five and up. The Atlanta Council of Camp Fire Boys & Girls, Inc. presents vacation camps during school holidays and teacher work days. Call for the location of a program near you. For information on Campfire's Summer Camp Toccoa, call 800/822-9541.

• **4-H And Youth.** This organization is not what it used to be! It has greatly expanded to include an urban/suburban focus emphasizing leadership skills and community service. Operating through the Extension Service of the University of Georgia, this organization serves children age 9–19. During the school year there are after school programs and occasional Saturday activities. Summer programs and summer camps might include field trips, talent shows, cooking, swimming, arts and crafts, woodworking and photography. Transportation is provided for some programs. Contact your nearest 4-H office for up-to-date information: **Clayton** (473-5450), **Cobb** (528-4076), **DeKalb** (371-2821), **Fulton** (730-7002) and **Gwinnett** (822-7700).

• **Girl Scouts of America** (527-7500). Girls may enter scouting at age five (Daisy's) and participate until they are 17 years old (Seniors). The primary goal of scouting is to help the girls develop self-esteem, appreciate nature, gain new friends, acquire social skills, and have experiences in the arts and sciences. Troops usually meet once a week, and girls earn badges by performing various activities. For information on Girl Scout Day and Overnight Camps, call the number above.

• **Girls Inc.** (881-8444). Formerly Girls Clubs of America, Girls Inc.

provides essentially the same services as Boys Clubs and are staffed by paid professionals. Each individual club operates autonomously, and may admit boys. There is a new focus on developing a science and math project called Operation Smart, but the main focus of the organization is still on bolstering girls' self-esteem. Call for the location of the club nearest you.

• **Indian Guides and Princesses.** This is a very unique and little known organization whose primary purpose was originally to afford fathers and their children (ages five and up) a very special, fun-filled time together on a regular basis. However, more and more "tribes" are involving moms too. They operate through local YMCAs, so you will need to call your local "Y" to find out if one is available. Since the programs vary in size and in program offerings, we will describe one of the more comprehensive ones as an example of what is possible. In Cobb County, there are currently 38 tribes consisting of eight pairs of parents and kids. Each tribe has its own special name. There are two meetings a month; the first is at alternating family homes and deals with any business that must be conducted, followed by activities such as crafts and singing. The second is an outing, such as to Stone Mountain Park, a bike rodeo, or a swimming and pizza party. Twice a year, in the fall and spring, all the tribes get together for a weekend campout! Call the **YMCA General Metropolitan Program Information** number 588-9622 for the location of your nearest YMCA.

• **The Salvation Army Boys and Girls Clubs.** The Salvation Army's programs are essentially the same as the offerings at other boys' and girls' clubs in Atlanta serving children in K–5th grade. Transportation is *not* provided from schools. For further information, visit 3500 Sherrydale Lane, Decatur, Georgia 30032 (284-9671).

• **YMCAs & YWCAs.** Family memberships are available at a low cost and usually include reduced fees for programs and a newsletter with updates on special events and programs. Additional fees are charged for a wide range of programs that *may* include:

- Summer Day Camps
- After-school child care (on site or at public schools)
- Sports lessons (basketball, swimming, soccer, tennis, etc.)
- Programs for preschoolers
- Babysitting while parent is participating in a class
- Indian Guides and Princesses (see above)

We are fortunate to have numerous "Ys" all over the Atlanta metropolitan area; there is sure to be one near you. For the exact location and telephone number of the YWCA or YMCA closest to you, call: YMCA-General Metropolitan Program Information (588-9622) or YWCA of Greater Atlanta (527-7575).

Festivals

& SPECIAL EVENTS

With a few exceptions, the festivals, parades and special events listed below are annual events. (We have included some first year events as it seems likely that they will receive enough community and financial support to become annual affairs.) Many of the newer listings describe festivals that have emerged in the last few years sponsored by Atlanta's many international and ethnic communities who are eager to share their heritage. These colorful events offer children an opportunity to explore the many diverse cultures and heritages of our fellow Atlantans by sampling delicious food, purchasing traditional arts and crafts, enjoying performances of folkloric music and dance, and mingling with families having different traditions and backgrounds. These events almost always feature children's areas complete with moonwalks, pony rides, games of skill, face-painting, hands-on art activities, and many more of the usual festival activities.

You may discover that the dates, locations and telephone numbers of the sponsors of these festivals vary from year to year, but we have tried to provide you with enough information to plan ahead and notice announcements about those events which are of interest to you. Please be sure to check the last section of our chapter "Performing Arts" for additional listings of annual festivals and concerts, which consist primarily of film, musical, theatrical, dance or puppetry performances.

■■■ JANUARY ■■■

• **Peach Bowl Parade & Game,** Atlanta (586-8500). Each year in late December or early January, Atlanta hosts the post-season college championship Peach Bowl in the new Georgia Dome. Prior to the game, downtown Atlanta is the site for the Peach Bowl Parade, featuring floats, bands and the usual parade excitement.

• **Olde Christmas Storytelling Festival,** DeKalb College Central Campus, Clarkston (971-7076). Besides two days of storytelling seminars and evening storytelling concerts for adults, this festival also presents special daytime storytelling sessions for children, featuring well-known local and national storytellers. Many other activities for children are offered.

• **Martin Luther King, Jr. Week,** MLK, Jr. Center for Nonviolent Social Change, Atlanta (524-1956). A week of events at the Martin Luther King, Jr. Center and other Atlanta locations are dedicated to the memory of Dr. King and his philosophy of nonviolence. The week's events include the Martin Luther King, Jr. National Parade in downtown Atlanta featuring, black stars and sports figures, and outstanding Georgia and out-of-state bands and specialty units. Monday, the official national holiday, features the National March of Celebration, where over half a million participants proceed down Peachtree Street to the King Center. Also, on the day of the official observance, an Ecumenical Service is held at Ebenezer Baptist Church.

• **Chinese New Year Celebration,** Chinese Community Center, Chamblee (451-4456). The public is invited to join the Chinese community in their celebration of the lunar New Year, which falls in January or February each year. Chinese food booths, traditional dances, martial art demonstrations, folk songs, music and children's activities are all offered during this celebration.

• **Ringling Brothers Barnum & Bailey Circus,** Omni Coliseum, Atlanta (249-6400). The "Greatest Show on Earth" comes to Atlanta every year, late January and/or early February, and dazzles children with the largest and most spectacular of circus shows.

▬ FEBRUARY ▬

• **Groundhog Day Juggler's Festival,** Virginia Highlands, Atlanta (451-4847). This weekend-long festival presents juggling of all kinds, other forms of object manipulation, magic, balancing, unicycle riding and special children's activities.

• **Atlanta Sports Carnival,** Georgia Dome, Atlanta (249-6400). Each January or February, the Georgia Dome is transformed into a giant carnival midway, complete with rides, games and prizes for children. Celebrities and famous sports figures sign autographs and delight children with demonstration games. Clowns, magicians, musicians, cheerleaders and team mascots perform.

• **Black History Month** features numerous month-long educational activities, TV specials, visual art exhibitions, films and performing arts events throughout the city honoring African-American accomplishments. Contact the APEX Museum's Welcome Center (521-2654) for more information, look in local newspapers or call the Atlanta-Fulton County or the DeKalb County Library Systems for a calendar of events.

• **Atlanta Flower Show,** Atlanta Apparel Mart/INFORUM, Atlanta (220-2223). The premier gardening event in the Southeast is sponsored by the Atlanta Botanical Garden and features trees and flowers, landscaped gardens, photography, educational exhibits, lectures, demonstrations, retail booths and a special children's corner.

• **Arbor Day.** The third Friday in February is Arbor Day, and numerous outdoor activities are sponsored by state, county and city park departments. Watch for announcements in local newspapers.

• **Mardi Gras Parade & Party,** Atlanta (392-1272). The parade, featuring illuminated floats, krewes, bands and party-goers, begins at Harris and Peachtree Streets and proceeds to Kenny's Alley in Underground Atlanta for an evening of celebration.

• **Fireside Arts & Crafts Show,** Unicoi State Park (706/878-2201, ext. 282). This high-quality arts and country crafts show is held the third weekend in February.

■■■ MARCH ■■■

• **St. Patrick's Day Parade,** Hibernian Benevolent Society of Atlanta (392-1272). This procession, one of the oldest in the country, proceeds down Peachtree Road to Underground Atlanta. The boisterous celebration continues later in the evening with live entertainment, games and audience participation events in Kenny's Alley at Underground Atlanta.

• **St. Patrick's Day Parade & Festival,** Buckhead/Bureau of Cultural Affairs, Atlanta (392-12725). The parade usually begins at Frankie Allen Park, proceeds down Pharr Road to Bolling Way, to E. Paces Ferry Road, and then back to the park. A family carnival, complete with rides, games, amusements and food at the corner of E. Paces Ferry Road and Bolling Way, is sometimes part of the festivities.

• **St. Patrick's Day Celebration,** Village of Stone Mountain (498-2097). Celebrate St. Patrick's Day with traditional Irish dances, Irish "specials" in the village restaurants and lots of other holiday excitement.

• **Musical Marathon Family Fest,** Woodruff Arts Center, Atlanta (898-1184). The Atlanta Symphony's annual extravaganza for kids, held in February or March, offers hands-on musical activities and an opportunity for families to enjoy special performances in each of the performing arts. Children can also delight in a musical petting zoo (hands-on playing with musical instruments), clowns, jugglers, face-painting, balloons and lots more festival activities.

• **Antebellum Jubilee,** Stone Mountain Park (498-5702). During late March and/or early April, the Antebellum Plantation is the scene for a special celebration that allows families to experience life as it was during the antebellum era. Living history demonstrations, musicians, storytelling, period dancers, old-time traveling shows, folk music and crafts, an authentic Civil War encampment, marches, drill and firing demonstrations, all bring the Civil War era to life.

• **Atlanta Fair** (740-1962). This traveling amusement park brings carnival rides, games, food, exhibits and shows to Atlanta each year, including the world's largest Ferris Wheel at seven stories high. The fair is usually set up across from Atlanta-Fulton County Stadium, but because of construction may move to a new location this year.

• **Kidsfest & Spirit of South DeKalb,** Soapstone Center for the Arts/ South DeKalb Mall, Decatur (241-2453). Soapstone Arts Center sponsors Kidsfest in conjunction with the Spirit of South DeKalb Festival. The children's portion features interactive performances, hands-on visual arts projects and lots of other fun children's activities. The festival is not held every year.

• **Kaleidoscope Fine Arts Festival,** Cobb Civic Center, Marietta (426-3404). This festival, held in late March or early April, highlights Cobb County students' visual and performing artistry. Performances include choral groups, bands, orchestras, cloggers, ballet dancers and more.

• **Tapestry Arts Festival,** Gwinnett Fine Arts Center, Duluth (623-6002). The Gwinnett Council for the Arts presents a festival of art and performances by student, amateur and professional artists.

• **Azalea Festival,** Callaway Gardens, Pine Mountain (800/282-8181). While the world's largest azalea gardens are in full bloom, families can enjoy storytellers, puppeteers, musicians, face painters, jugglers, magicians and other entertainers.

• **Athens International Festival,** Athens (706/546-1805). The Athens Chamber of Commerce and the University of Georgia sponsor four days of visual and performing arts from around the world. Included are international displays, a fashion and talent show, art lectures, garden exhibits, ethnic cuisine and performances of international music, dance and comedy. The festival is sometimes held in early April.

• **Macon Cherry Blossom Festival,** Macon (912/751-7429). With over 160,000 Yoshino cherry trees in full bloom, Macon—"The Cherry Blossom Capital of the World"—celebrates spring with an international celebration featuring arts and crafts, entertainment, tours, parades and lots of food. Japan and one or two other countries are featured each year, and festivities spotlight the culture, entertainment and cuisine of the selected countries.

EASTER

• **Easter Sunrise Service,** Stone Mountain Park (498-5600). The park opens at 4:00 a.m., so families can attend two non-denominational sunrise services—one at the top of Stone Mountain, the other on the bottom. Easter Egg Hunts sometimes follow later in the day.

• **Eggstravaganza,** Zoo Atlanta, Atlanta (624-5600). A giant Easter bunny, real rabbits and bunny games highlight Zoo Atlanta's special Easter celebration.

• **Easter Egg Hunts** can be enjoyed at many parks, recreational centers, nature preserves, museums, attractions and shopping centers all over the city. A sampling: Old Courthouse Square in Decatur, Atlanta Speech School, Laurel Park in Marietta, Smyrna Community Center, T.W. Briscoe Park in Snellville, Mable House in Mableton, The Art Place–Mountain View in Marietta, Roswell Mill in Roswell, Wills Park in Alpharetta, Autrey Mill Nature Preserve in Alpharetta, Hammond Park in Sandy Springs, Jonesboro Recreational Center and Riverdale Recreational Center. Families can also brunch with the Easter Bunny at hotels and local restaurants. Check *Our Kids*, *Atlanta Parent* and local newspapers for announcements.

• **Easter Egg Hunt & Carnival,** Lake Lanier Islands, Gainesville (932-

7200). A giant Easter Bunny presides over this Easter Egg hunt which is usually held at Presentation Point. DJ's, carnival games, prizes, horseback rides, hot air balloon rides and food may also be enjoyed.

• **Magical Eggstravaganza Parade & Egg Hunt,** Cleveland (706/865-5356). Billed as "one of the world's largest egg hunts," this event features 26,000 eggs, along with a parade, arts and craft show, games, contests and, of course, a visit by the Easter Bunny.

• **Easter Eggstravaganza,** Callaway Gardens, Pine Mountain (800/282-8181). During Easter weekend families can enjoy a fun egg hunt on Robin Lake beach on Saturday afternoon and a sunrise service at the ski pavilion on Sunday morning.

▬ APRIL ▬

• **Earth Day.** Earth Day is a month-long national celebration that brings the urgency of environmental problems to the public's attention. Exhibits, festivals, performances, lectures, tree-planting ceremonies and other similar activities are scheduled throughout the month by municipalities, nature centers, parks, galleries, book stores and other business establishments. Special children's events and activities are often sponsored by the Atlanta Botanical Garden, Chattahoochee Nature Center, Fernbank Science Center, Fernbank Museum of Natural History, SciTrek, Underground Atlanta and Zoo Atlanta.

• **Atlanta Dogwood Festival** (952-9151). The Dogwood Festival's special events take place throughout Atlanta in conjunction with Earth Day events. Weekend in the Park at Piedmont Park is the focal point of the festival, where arts and crafts, environmental exhibits, a children's parade, hands-on art activities, carnival games, kite-flying contests, a Sunday concert, and hot-air-balloon races can be enjoyed. At the Midtown Dogwood Festival, special children's performances, arts and crafts, an international market, ethnic music and lots of other great family activities can be enjoyed. House and garden tours are also held throughout the Atlanta area as part of the event.

• **Buckheadesque & Earth Parade**, Buckhead, Atlanta (525-6145). In conjunction with Earth Day celebrations, the Buckhead Chamber of Commerce sometimes presents a small festival featuring arts and crafts, exhibits saluting the cultural diversity of Atlanta, a children's parade, a road race, a tree-planting ceremony, games and lots of good food.

• **For Kid's Sake Day**, Zoo Atlanta, Atlanta (624-5630). This special children's event, held the last Saturday in April, is co-sponsored by WXIA 11-Alive Television and the Georgia Council on Child Abuse. Different activities are featured each year, but events usually include storytelling, safety programs, games and other fun activities.

• **Celebration of Children**, Apparel Mart, Atlanta (527-3500). The emphasis is on fun and information at this very unusual family festival sponsored by United Way. Over eighty exhibitors of the latest products on the market for children are featured along with seminars on parenting, vision and hearing screenings, storytelling performances, puppet shows, theatre and more.

• **Sheep to Shawl Day**, Atlanta History Center, Atlanta (814-4000). Children can watch the sheep at the Tullie Smith Farm have their winter coats sheared, and then see the fleece washed, sorted, handspun, dyed and hand-woven into a shawl. Other period activities and demonstrations are also featured at this very unique living-history festival.

• **Atlanta Hunt & Steeplechase**, Seven Branches Farm, Cumming (237-7436). Distinguished horses and riders meet at this beautiful farm in Cumming in March or April and race to benefit the Atlanta Speech School. Spectators bring gourmet tailgate picnics and entertainers perform continuously. Tickets must be purchased in advance.

• **TV Turn-Off Week.** For one week in April, families throughout the United States are encouraged to turn off their televisions and discover alternative family activities. At the end of the week, many neighborhoods and schools sponsor special festivals and celebrations rewarding those families who survived the week without turning on the tube.

• **Inman Park Spring Festival & Tour of Homes,** Inman Park, Atlanta (242-4895). Residents of historic Inman Park welcome you inside their homes. Outside, a neighborhood arts and crafts festival entertains families with an artist's market, continuous performances, a wacky parade, pony rides and many other children's activities.

• **Yaarab Temple Shrine Circus, Carnival & Flea Market,** Jim R. Miller Park, Marietta (875-0318). This 10-day circus and carnival, presented by the Shriners, features the George Coronas Circus, complete with lions, tigers, trapeze artists, acrobats and clowns. The midway has over thirty rides and games appropriate for younger children, including the world's largest portable Ferris Wheel and carousel. Proceeds benefit Shriner charities.

• **Kennesaw/Big Shanty Festival,** Kennesaw (427-2117). Reenactment of the Battle of Kennesaw, arts and crafts booths, local business booths, old-time village demonstrations, live entertainment and food highlight this annual festival. A special children's activity area features rides on a small train and other fun activities.

• **Jonquil Spring Festival Arts & Crafts Show,** Smyrna Community Center, Smyrna (434-3661). Smyrna's annual craft festival features a parade, carnival, antique car show, arts and crafts, races, festival food and continuous entertainment. An entire area is devoted to children's activities, including games, pony rides, a petting farm, kiddie train, moon walk, face-painting and clowns.

• **Georgia Renaissance Festival,** Royal Festival Grounds, Fairburn (964-8575). For six weekends (and Memorial Day) beginning late

April and ending early June, families can enjoy a 30-acre Renaissance Village reenacting the times, customs, crafts, characters and culinary habits of the Renaissance in authentic detail, complete with jugglers, magicians, fire-eaters, comedia troops and minstrels. Knightly games and activities, an authentic crafts village, and food and drink fit for a king and queen (or prince and princess) round off this very unusual festival.

• **International Cultural Festival,** Emory University Quadrangle, Atlanta (727-3300). Students from more than 50 countries participate in this friendly outdoor festival to share information about the cultures and heritage of their homelands. Folk dancing, travel information, a fashion show, martial arts demonstrations, traditional foods and displays of jewelry, crafts and clothing are all spotlighted at this fun festival.

• **Indian Heritage Day,** Stately Oaks Plantation, Jonesboro (473-0197). Jonesboro's spring festival features entertainment, face painting, arrow making, blowgun demonstrations, finger weaving, a green corn ceremony and other living history demonstrations. In the evening, there is a one-hour mock council meeting conducted by Native Americans. The activities take place in an authentic Creek Indian Village on the grounds of Stately Oaks Plantation.

• **Fiddlin' Fish Arts & Crafts Festival,** Lake Lanier Islands, Gainesville (932-7200). This annual festival features delicious dishes from area fish restaurants, an arts and crafts festival, fiddling, clogging, spring boat excursions, carnival games and lots more festival fun.

• **Appalachian SprinGreen Festival,** Blue Ridge (706/632-5680). SprinGreen celebrates the greening of the North Georgia mountains with traditional music and dance, regional crafts and lots of country cooking.

• **Return to Long Swamp Creek Pow Wow & Indian Festival,**

Tate House, Tate (800/342-7515). The three-day celebration of Native American culture and spiritual traditions includes traditional dancers, food, crafts and athletic events featuring members of the Cherokee, Chippewa and Sioux nations.

■ MAY ■

• **Stay and See Georgia Week**, Underground Atlanta, Atlanta (432-4986). The Georgia Chamber of Commerce hosts a travel show highlighting the different attractions and vacation spots around Georgia. Some booths have dioramas, others have people dressed in costume, and all have information packets and lots of brochures. Learn about Georgia's different cities and attractions and enjoy special street performers, special promotions and vacation give-aways.

• **Kingfest**, MLK, Jr. Center for Nonviolent Social Change, Auburn Avenue, Atlanta (524-1956). Starting in May, and continuing every other Saturday through mid-August, the center is the location for numerous afternoon and evening arts and performance festivals for families. Each weekend has a special theme, such as International Day, Gospel Day and Kid's Day, which features hands-on arts and crafts activities and music, dance, poetry, storytelling, theatre, comedy and juggling.

• **Atlanta Storytelling Festival**, Atlanta History Center, Atlanta (814-4000). This annual festival, presented by the Atlanta Historical Society and the Southern Order of Storytellers, features the best storytellers from the southeast as well as musicians, entertainers and special guest celebrities who, for two days, bedazzle families with tall tales, folk stories from around the world, songs, lying contests, jugglers, mimes, musicians and more.

• **Buckhead Arts Festival at Chastain**, Chastain Park, Atlanta (633-9609). Chastain Park is transformed into a huge outdoor gallery featuring over 200 artists, an auction, live entertainment, food and children's activities.

• **Springfest/Bar-B-Q Cookoff,** Stone Mountain Park (498-5702). This springtime celebration features cooks from all over the south dishing up samples as they compete in a "Bar-B-Q Cookoff," along with over 200 arts and crafts people, fireworks, clogging and other live entertainment. Springfest usually marks the debut of the summer Lasershow.

• **Taste of the South,** Stone Mountain Park (498-5702). Sample some of the many tastes of the South from one of the food tents dishing out delicacies from all over the Southeast. Other events, such as Carolina beach dances and Louisiana crawfish races, round off this tasty event.

• **Memorial Day Celebration,** Stone Mountain Park (498-5702). Memorial Day weekend marks the opening of the beach and water sports at Stone Mountain Park. As part of the holiday celebration, families can enjoy a special concert and Lasershow.

• **Atlanta Peach Carnival,** Woodruff Park, Atlanta (220-0158). This three-day annual folklife festival for children and adults celebrates the rich artistic and cultural heritage of the Caribbean. The highlight of the festival is a parade down Peachtree Street filled with bands, costumed dancers and celebrities. Woodruff Park is transformed into a Caribbean marketplace with dance, literary, visual and performing arts, retail vendors, folklife demonstrations and great food. A whole afternoon is set aside for a special Children's Carnival featuring a costume parade, food, games and lots of family activities.

• **Baby & Kid Expo,** Gwinnett Civic and Cultural Center, Duluth (509-7324). The Baby & Kid Expo showcases the latest merchandise, fashion information and services for parents, parents-to-be and children. Entertainment, health screenings, and lots of activities for children are also offered.

• **Willie B. Birthday Celebration,** Zoo Atlanta, Atlanta (624-5630). Zoo Atlanta celebrates Willie B.'s birthday with a special birthday cake filled with gorilla treats and lots of fun events for the entire family, including storytelling, face-painting and clowns.

• **Very Special Arts Festival**, Brook Run, Dunwoody (551-7000). This visual and performing arts festival provides a special chance for people with disabilities to have fun and show others they are capable of enjoying and producing art. Besides arts and crafts activities, there are performances and other fun family activities.

• **TechFest**, Southern Tech, Marietta (528-7222). Southern Tech holds an open house and educational family festival where young people are given an opportunity to see, feel and touch exhibits pertaining to science and technology. Besides participating in workshops and hands-on activities in different college laboratories, children can also enjoy roving entertainers, hot-air balloon rides and food.

• **Armed Forces Festival & Open House** (752-3392). Each year, the armed services (Army, Navy and Air Force) take turns hosting an open house and inviting the public to view flying demonstrations, military displays, hand combat demonstrations, parachute jumping and band concerts. Refreshments are also offered. Watch for announcements about this year's location.

• **Sheep Shearing Saturday**, Yellow River Game Ranch, Lilburn (972-6643). Yellow River Game Ranch's entire flock of sheep receive their once-a-year barbering during this event, each sheep rendering approximately five pounds of wool or the equivalent of two pairs of long underwear and one pair of men's socks. Visitors may try their hand at shearing, and a hand spinner demonstrates the various stages of making yarn.

• **Atlanta Celtic Festival**, Atlanta (394-4081). The annual celebration of Irish, Scottish, Welsh and Celtic heritage features Celtic food, beer, exhibits, wares, music, dance, bag pipe music, theatre, folklore and workshops. The festival has also featured an *Irish Feis*, a competitive music festival with Irish step dancing. The location for this unique festival varies from year to year.

• **Chamblee International Festival,** Chamblee (455-0471). This multi-cultural event is held in conjunction with the Chamblee Spring Antiques Festival. The international portion of the festival includes entertainment by folkloric music and dance groups, international food booths, numerous exhibits about Atlanta's ethnic and international communities, and a small children's area.

• **Greek Glendi Festival,** Cobb County Civic Center, Marietta (977-1350 or 971-6015). Authentic Greek bands, folk dancing, food, wine, pastries, artwork, costumes, religious gifts, jewelry, imported gifts, records, tapes, CDs, great T-shirts (Raise Hellas!) and entertainment for children highlight this annual Greek *Glendi* (festival) hosted by the Holy Transfiguration Greek Orthodox Church in Marietta.

• **Georgia Renaissance Festival,** Royal Festival Grounds, Fairburn (964-8575). *See* April festival listing.

• **Decatur Arts Festival,** Old Courthouse Square, Decatur (371-8386). Throughout Memorial Day weekend, downtown Decatur comes to life with a three-day arts festival celebrating the visual and performing arts. The entire family can enjoy a juried artists' market, neighborhood flea market, continuous live entertainment, food court, classic car show, book sale and evening Cajun Street Party. On Saturday, a whole day of children's activities is featured, including hands-on arts and crafts, pony rides, a moonwalk and special dance, music and storytelling performances.

• **DeKalb Sheriff's Posse Rodeo,** Stone Mountain Coliseum Park (498-5600). The two-day rodeo presents buckin' broncos, barrel riding, calf roping, cowboys, cowgirls and lots more "Wild West" fun.

• **Children's Art Festival,** Glover Park, Marietta (424-8142). Sponsored by the Marietta/Cobb Museum of Art, this children's arts festival offers hands-on arts and crafts activities, demonstrations, clowns, theatre and dance performances, jugglers, musicians, puppets, balloons, food and lots more fun activities.

• **Historic Marietta Arts & Crafts Festival**, Glover Park, Marietta (528-0616). This fun family festival in Marietta Square features arts and crafts displayed by artists from throughout the southeast, live entertainment and food.

• **Sweetwater Fever Fine Arts & Crafts Festival**, Mable House, Mableton (739-0189). Mableton's annual springtime festival, held the second weekend in May, includes a fine arts and crafts market, children's activities, performing arts and lots of good food.

• **Roswell Antebellum Spring Festival**, Roswell (640-3253). Historic Roswell is the setting for this springtime arts and crafts festival which always includes lots of hands-on children's activities and storytelling performances.

• **Georgia Folklore by Moonlight**, Stately Oaks Plantation, Jonesboro (473-0197). Storytellers dressed in 19th-century costumes present a special storytelling festival on the grounds of Stately Oaks Plantation. Fables, folklore, ghost stories and Civil War tales transfix the audience. Recommended for families with older children.

• **Snellville Days**, T. W. Briscoe Park, Snellville (985-3500). Arts and crafts, children's activities, country and western music, magic shows, food, and lots more fun are offered during this spring festival in Gwinnett.

• **Grayson Day Festival**, Grayson (963-8017). Families can enjoy arts and crafts, clogging and other entertainment, festival food, pony rides and children's activities at this annual festival held the third Saturday in May.

• **May Fest in the Mountains,** Helen (706/878-2181). Helen presents a festival during two weekends in May featuring Bavarian food, music and dance.

• **Dahlonega's Wildflower Festival of the Arts,** Dahlonega (706/864-3711). During the third weekend in May, Dahlonega Square is the location for a visual and performing arts festival that features programs and exhibits on wildflowers of the area, work by juried exhibitors, and a children's area with hands-on art activities.

• **Prater's Mill Country Fair,** Dalton (706/275-6455). This spring arts and crafts show re-creates the atmosphere of an old-fashioned country fair complete with entertainment of the 1800s period, country cooking, canoeing on Coahulla Creek, pony rides and many other children's activities. The operating grist mill at the site adds to the period atmosphere. Families can also enjoy a fall festival at the same location.

• **Reverend Howard Finster Art Festival,** Summerville (706/857-1048). This enjoyable festival is held in honor of the world-renowned folk artist and Summerville resident, Reverend Howard Finster, who exhibits his unique work alongside his family members and many other folk arts and crafts people. Families can also enjoy authentic country music and southern food.

• **Cherokee County Indian Festival & Powwow,** Hwy. 5 on the Etowah River, Boling Park, Canton (706/735-4930). This festival celebrates the culture and spiritual traditions of Native Americans with traditional dances, food, crafts, athletic events, a wildlife exhibit, a teepee competition and fire dancing. Members of several Indian nations are represented, including the Cherokee, Chippewa, Ute, Omaha, Lakota, Blackfoot, Creek and Sioux.

• **Cotton Pickin' Country Fair,** Gay (706/538-6814). This country fair is located on an old cotton-ginning complex that includes an

1890s vintage plantation home. Arts and crafts, antiques, continuous entertainment, children's activities and southern cooking are offered. Families can also enjoy a fall festival at this same location.

■■■ JUNE ■■■

• **A Taste of Atlanta,** Midtown, Atlanta (248-0066). The three-day celebration of "eating" features samples from more than fifty of Atlanta's leading restaurants, including many of Atlanta's ethnic haunts. Live entertainment, children's activities, clowns and street entertainers make this a very exciting event for families. Proceeds benefit the National Kidney Foundation.

• **Underground Atlanta's Anniversary Celebration,** Atlanta (523-2311). Underground Atlanta celebrates its anniversary with a big bash, including interactive exhibits, Georgia athletes and celebrities, lots of entertainment and evening fireworks.

• **Kingfest,** Martin Luther King Jr. Center for Nonviolent Social Change, Atlanta (524-1956). *See* May festival listing.

• **Summerfest,** Virginia Highlands, Atlanta (222-8244). The streets of trendy Virginia-Highland are the location for a popular juried arts and crafts show featuring exhibitors from all over the southeast. Families can also enjoy live entertainment, food and a large children's area with face-painting, clowns, magicians, pony rides, a petting zoo, moonwalk and lots of hands-on children's activities.

• **Beach Party,** Old Courthouse Square, Decatur (371-8386). Forty tons of sand transform the Old Courthouse Square into a beach area where the entire family can enjoy volleyball, wading pools, beach music, dancing, a dunking booth and lots of good beach-style food.

• **Log Cabin Story Hours,** DeKalb Historical Complex, Decatur (373-1088). Wednesday mornings, June through August, the DeKalb

Historical Society presents story hours and pioneer demonstrations for children at the restored log cabins located at the DeKalb Historical Complex at Adair Park. Reservations are required.

• **Arts and Crafts Festival**, Village of Stone Mountain (498-2097). More than 250 exhibitors from the southeast present their arts and crafts, antiques, and collectibles, while cloggers, storytellers, singers and musicians entertain the crowds.

• **Celebrate Israel**, Zaban Park Branch of the Atlanta Jewish Community Center, Dunwoody (396-3250). This annual celebration of Israel features an Israeli marketplace, hands-on arts and crafts activities for children, a Sesame Street theatre, a petting zoo, pony rides, singing, dancing, Maccabean games and ethnic food.

• **Young at Art**, Stately Oaks Plantation, Jonesboro (473-0197). This family festival features performances, art exhibits, children's arts and crafts, workshops, storytelling and magic shows.

• **Renaissance Festival**, Royal Festival Ground, Fairburn (964-8575). *See* April festival listing.

• **Indian Games Festival**, Etowah Indian Mounds Historic Site, Cartersville (706/387-3747). During this sporting festival, demonstrations of traditional games of southeastern Native Americans are played, such as chunkey, games of chance and stick ball.

• **Helen to the Atlantic Hot-Air Balloon Festival & Race**, Helen (706/878-2271). Over 75 hot-air balloons participate in this famous hot-air balloon race to the Atlantic. Meanwhile, back at the festival, families can enjoy tethered balloon rides, hay rides and live entertainment.

▬ JULY 4TH ▬

• **Peachtree Road Race,** Peachtree Road, Atlanta (231-9064). Atlanta's July 4th officially begins with the running of the Peachtree Road Race sponsored by the Atlanta Track Club. Over 45,000 Atlantans, alongside world-class runners, race down Peachtree Road to the finish line at Piedmont Park. Spectators line Peachtree Road and gather in the park to cheer on the runners and celebrate the start of the Independence Day holiday. The Peachtree Junior race for children is held in June. See our chapter on "Sports and Recreation" for more information.

• **WSB Salute 2 America Parade,** Atlanta (897-7452). The largest Independence Day parade in the United States begins early afternoon at the CNN Center, proceeds up Marietta Street and turns north up Peachtree Street. Each year elaborate floats, marching bands, clowns, unicycles and other specialty units participate in this Atlanta tradition.

• **July 4th Fireworks & Parades.** A sampling of locations for parades and/or evening fireworks displays: Old Courthouse Square in Decatur, Lenox Square Shopping Mall, Six Flags Over Georgia, South DeKalb Mall in Decatur, Underground Atlanta, Atlanta-Fulton County Stadium, Chastain Park Amphitheater, Wills Park Recreation Center, Peachtree City's Drake Field, Smyrna Community Center, Marketplace Shopping Center in Lilburn, New Courthouse in Lawrenceville, Adams Park in Kennesaw, Village of Stone Mountain, Glover Park in Marietta, and Lillian Webb Field in Norcross. Check your local newspapers for a current calendar of July 4th events.

• **Fantastic Fourth,** Stone Mountain Park (498-5702). Major concerts, patriotic music, clogging and beach activities entertain the daytime crowds while the Lasershow and spectacular fireworks atop the mountain entertain spectators at dusk.

• **Beach Concert & Fireworks Extravaganza,** Lake Lanier Islands (945-6701). An evening July 4th concert on the beach is followed by a spectacular fireworks display.

• **Float the Fourth Tube Parade & Fireworks,** Helen (706/878-2181). The July 4th celebration in the Georgia mountains includes an old-fashioned barbecue and an annual tube parade down the Chattahoochee River.

• **July 4th Family Day Celebration,** Dahlonega (706/864-3711). Fourth of July events include arts and crafts, music and dance, colonial demonstrations and lots more activities for the entire family.

▬ JULY ▬

• **The Civil War Encampment,** Atlanta History Center (261-1837 or 814-4000). Over 100 reenactors in authentic costumes stage a living history demonstration of Civil War camp life. Storytelling, lectures and hands-on displays are also featured.

• **Festival of Cultures,** Atlanta (392-1272). Over 80 different ethnic and international groups participate in this two-day mega-festival celebrating Atlanta's rich ethnic and cultural diversity. Families can enjoy an international marketplace, cultural exhibits, cooking demonstrations, food booths offering a variety of ethnic delicacies, and two entertainment areas providing continuous ethnic and folk dancing, music from around the world and multi-cultural storytelling. The large children's area offers cultural games, ethnic face painting, piñatas, moon walks, Sumo wrestling, a petting zoo, and lots of other hands-on activities and games.

• **National Black Arts Festival,** throughout Atlanta (730-7315). Held biennially late July and/or early August, this arts festival, the only one of its kind, celebrates the accomplishments of African-American artists in a big and exciting way, presenting over seventy-five concerts, plays, films, dance performances, storytelling sessions, book fairs, workshops, and art exhibits at over forty different locations in Atlanta. The festival is attended by over one million people! There are specially scheduled storytelling and puppetry performances during the 10 festival days, a large parade, an outdoor arts and crafts market, and many other activities that the whole family can enjoy.

• **Kingfest,** Martin Luther King Jr. Center for Nonviolent Social Change, Atlanta (524-1956). *See* May festival listing.

• **Log Cabin Story Hours,** DeKalb Historical Complex, Decatur (373-1088). *See* June festival listing.

• **Old Fashioned Jubilee,** Old Town Lilburn (921-2210). Old Town Lilburn celebrates its birthday with a festival that includes arts and crafts, street vendors, live entertainment and children's activities.

• **The Children's Art Festival,** Henderson's Indoor Arena, South Fulton County (438-4743). This festival offers lots of hands-on activities in the arts for children age 7–13, including puppet making, weaving, stenciling, mask making, pottery, printing, wood sculpture and fabric collage. There is also a small preschool area for children age 3–6. Live entertainment at the festival features music, dance, theatre and puppetry.

• **Metro Atlanta Fire Apparatus Show & Muster,** Atlanta Fire Department, Atlanta (955-2700). Twenty different teams compete in the Atlanta Fire Department's annual muster competition in fire service events. Families can also explore displays of antique and modern equipment, demonstrations, a flea market and more. Profits benefit the Georgia Firefighter's Burn Foundation.

• **New Manchester Days,** Sweetwater Creek State Park, Lithia Springs (944-1700). Travel back to the 1860s and a weekend experience memorializing the events surrounding the devastation of the 1800s village of New Manchester during the Battle of Atlanta.

━━ AUGUST ━━

• **National Black Arts Festival,** throughout Atlanta (730-7315). *See* July festival listing.

• **Festival of the Painted Rock Fine Art Festival,** Chattahoochee Nature Center, Roswell (992-2055). During the third weekend in August, the nature center sponsors a fine arts and crafts festival for families and also offers food, live entertainment and children's activities. This festival is sometimes held in the spring.

• **African Pride Cultural Celebration,** Underground Atlanta, Atlanta (523-2311). Underground Atlanta hosts African drummers, dancers and a fashion show, and a parade winds through Underground featuring costumed dancers and drummers.

• **Kingfest,** Martin Luther King Jr. Center for Nonviolent Social Change, Atlanta (524-1956). *See* May festival listing.

• **Koreatown Festival,** Flowers Park, Doraville. The Korean community welcomes the public to its annual festival showcasing Korean culture and heritage. Great Korean food, martial arts demonstrations, folk dancing, music, a Korean fashion show of traditional clothing and lots of children's activities are offered. As a special treat, festival goers can view a mock traditional Korean wedding ceremony.

• **Latin American Fiesta,** Chamblee Civic Center, Chamblee (451-3068). Representatives from many of Atlanta's different Latin American countries invite families to share their cultures. The festival features Latin foods, music and entertainment, folkloric dancing, a children's corner with many fun activities, a silent auction and more.

• **Cajun Festival,** Atlanta (955-1408). Enjoy a full day of live Cajun music and dance, storytelling, a fair with Cajun food, clowns, face-painting and other entertainment, as well as a Cajun dinner and dance in the evening.

• **Log Cabin Story Hours,** DeKalb Historical Complex, Decatur (373-1088). *See* June festival listing.

• **Arts Festival,** South DeKalb Mall, Decatur (241-2431). The best of African-America's heritage is featured during this nine-day event showcasing music, visual arts, books and live entertainment.

• **Tucker Days,** Main Street, Tucker (923-9381). Continuous live entertainment, an arts and crafts market, a family road race, and lots of children's activities highlight Tucker's annual family celebration.

• **Arts on the Courthouse Grounds,** Courthouse Square, Lawrenceville (623-5577). The Gwinnett Council for the Arts sponsors this annual event that features over 70 exhibitors of arts and crafts. Festival food and other entertainment abound.

• **Georgia Mountain Fair,** Hiawassee (706/896-4191). For 12 days, Lake Chatuge is the site of one of the largest of Georgia's state fairs, featuring farm, home and craft exhibits, music and dancing, parades, rides, shows and lots more "mountain fun" for the whole family.

• **Harvest Celebration,** Chateau Élan, Braselton (800/233-WINE). Families can view the annual harvesting of the grapes, learn about the wine-making process, enjoy country music and other entertainment, and purchase hand-made crafts.

• **Mountain Heritage Days,** Unicoi State Park (706/878-2201, ext. 282). This living-history festival features demonstrations of old-time skills such as spinning, weaving, woodworking, basketry and blacksmithing.

• **Nacoochee Valley Indian Cultural Festival,** Helen (706/878-2938). Three days of dancing, arts and crafts (25 booths), skill demonstrations and food (buffalo burgers, alligator and Indian fry bread) prepared by Native Americans from across the United States and Canada, afford visitors an insight into Native American culture.

■ SEPTEMBER ■

• **Labor Day Celebration,** Stone Mountain Park (498-5702). Celebrate the Labor Day holiday at Stone Mountain Park with continuous entertainment and other special events. The evening Lasershow is the last regular show of the season.

• **Arts Festival of Atlanta,** Piedmont Park, Atlanta (885-1125). Atlanta's most famous outdoor arts and crafts festival showcases arts and crafts in every possible media, some of the south's finest performing artists, unusual street performers, a sand castle-building contest among Atlanta's architectural firms, and a large selection of ethnic and southern food. A children's area offers exhibits of children's art, hands-on arts and crafts activities, performances for children—music, dance, puppetry, theatre and storytelling—face-painting, sand-art, balloons, mimes, jugglers, acrobats and more. This festival draws over two million visitors each year!

• **Yellow Daisy Festival,** Stone Mountain Park (498-5633). This celebration of the rare Confederate Yellow Daisy flower is rumored to be the south's largest arts and crafts show, featuring around 475 exhibitors. A flower show, live entertainment and lots of southern cooking are also offered.

• **Starlett Birthday Celebration,** Zoo Atlanta, Atlanta (624-5630). Zoo Atlanta celebrates Starlett's birthday with a special birthday cake filled with elephant treats, painting demonstrations by Starlett and lots of other fun events for the entire family, including storytelling, face-painting and clowns.

• **Wren's Nest & West End Festival,** West End Park, Atlanta (505-0075 & 753-7735). The West End puts on a neighborhood festival complete with a parade, walking tour, arts and craft show, marketplace of African jewelry and art, entertainment and a children's tent. Area schools feature a week-long arts program, and neighborhood restaurants offer food sampling. Nearby, the Wren's Nest, home of the famous children's book writer Joel Chandler Harris, has its own festival with storytelling, musical entertainment, jugglers, clowns, pony rides, and many other special children's activities. And at Howell Park (Ralph David Abernathy Boulevard and Peeples Street), a Children's Festival (371-9609) includes hands-on experiences for children age three years and older in jewelry, puppets, tie-dye, painted T-shirts, masks and more.

• **Good Neighbor Day,** DeKalb Peachtree Airport, Atlanta (936-5440). Antique airplanes, corporate and military jets, helicopters and ultralight aircraft are exhibited to the public, together with displays, exhibits and booths providing information about everything from whirly birds to emergency medical care. Aerial demonstrations, parachuting shows, and inexpensive airplane and helicopter rides over Atlanta are a very special treat for children. The festival is sometimes held in October.

• **Sweet Auburn Heritage Festival,** Auburn Avenue, Atlanta (525-0205). Street vendors, a children's carnival area, rides, historical tours, a cultural marketplace, an international art pavilion, southern food, and a variety of entertainment, including gospel, jazz, hip-hop, pop and reggae, all can be found during this three-day festival held on historic Auburn Avenue. Celebrities and over 500,000 people come together to join in this celebration of African-American heritage. Recently, the festival has begun saluting other groups in the Auburn Avenue neighborhood, such as the Ethiopian, Jamaican and Korean communities. The festival is sometimes held in the spring.

• **Grant Park Festival & Tour of Homes,** Grant Park (627-5033). This two-day event offers arts and crafts booths, live entertainment, food, pet parades, a moonwalk and lots of other children's activities.

• **Garden Hills Ice Cream Social,** Garden Hills Park, Atlanta (261-6124). The family event includes a parade, games, face painting, pony rides, crafts, consignment sale, hot dogs and hand-dipped ice cream.

• **Atlanta Greek Festival.** Greek Orthodox Cathedral of the Annunciation, Atlanta (633-5870). Over the years, the four-day festival has become a favorite for Atlantans who take advantage of this unique opportunity to experience Greek culture and tradition. Festivities include Greek entertainment, travel movies, lectures about Greece and Atlanta's Greek community, tours of the cathedral and a *bakaliko* (marketplace) selling a selection of Greek art, clothing, jewelry, handbags and imported items. Large quantities of Greek food, wine and pastries are served continuously throughout the festival.

• **Family Fun Day,** Zaban Park Branch of the Atlanta Jewish Community Center, Dunwoody (396-3250). A carnival, moonwalk, pony rides, matzah ball hunt, haunted house, games and prizes, and live entertainment highlight this children's festival at the beautiful Zaban Park facility.

• **Art in the Park,** Glover Park, Marietta (528-0616). Marietta's Labor Day festival, formerly known as Founder's Day, is a large fine arts show that exhibits arts and crafts, photography and a juried art show. Horse and buggy rides, walking tours and live entertainment can also be enjoyed.

• **Acworth Pioneer Days Arts & Crafts Festival,** Lake Acworth (974-4221). Lake Acworth is the backdrop for this annual Labor Day weekend festival showcasing arts and crafts, carnival rides, music and other live entertainment. The festival begins with a parade and closes with a spectacular fireworks display.

• **A Blue Ribbon Affair**, Jim R. Miller Park, Marietta (423-1330). This authentic country fair, which precedes the North Georgia State Fair, exhibits a mix of traditional arts and crafts and decorating trends. A special children's area is offered.

• **North Georgia State Fair**, Jim R. Miller Park, Marietta (423-1330 or 528-1170). The second largest county fair in the state features country crafts, amusement rides, games, agricultural exhibits, live entertainment and lots of country cooking.

• **Heritage Days Festival**, Bulloch Hall, Roswell (992-1731). The Roswell Historical Society presents an old-fashioned country fair with an 1860s theme. Civil War weaponry, encampments, antiques, storytelling, crafts, music, pony rides and lots of other children's activities are offered.

• **Roswell Arts Festival on the Square**, Roswell (992-0832). Families can enjoy arts and crafts, a children's activity area, the sounds of live entertainment and other festival activities.

• **Sandy Springs Festival**, Williams-Payne House, Sandy Springs (851-9111). Folk craft demonstrations, needlework, jewelry, music, cloggers, car shows, races, and tours of the historical Williams-Payne House highlight this outdoor festival at the Sandy Springs historical site.

• **Apple Chill Arts & Crafts Festival**, Wills Park, Alpharetta (740-2414). A variety of arts and crafts and performing arts can be enjoyed at this covered center, including a baseball card show and other children's activities.

• **Gwinnett County Fair**, Gwinnett County Fair Grounds, Lawrenceville (963-6522). This is a real state fair, complete with farm animals, home and craft exhibits, clogging and other live entertainment, amusement rides, games, barbecue and lots more.

• **Duluth Fall Festival & Parade,** Duluth (476-3434). The city of Duluth puts on a fall arts and crafts show that includes artist booths, a large parade, retail vendors, entertainment and more festivities.

• **Suwanee Day,** City Hall, Suwanee (932-2917). Suwanee hosts an annual arts and crafts festival the third weekend in September, complete with a parade, live entertainment, children's activities and evening fireworks.

• **Peachtree Crossings Country Fair,** Fairgrounds (Exit 12 off I-85), Peachtree City (434-3661). Artists and craftpersons, a pre-1840 frontier camp, folk crafters, muzzle-loaded rifle demonstrations, bluegrass and Army brass music, cloggers and pony rides highlight this Labor Day weekend country festival.

• **Powers' Crossroads Country Fair & Art Festival,** Newnan (706/253-2011). This nationally recognized southern arts festival on Labor Day weekend features over 300 arts and crafts exhibitors, bluegrass music, barbecue, clogging and other country fair activities. There is a very large children's area filled with hands-on activities, rides and other fun things to do.

• **Riverfest Arts & Crafts Festival,** Boling Park, Canton (706/479-9224). Families can enjoy over 100 artists and crafts people as well as demonstrations of blacksmithing, stained glass, pottery and quilting. A children's activity area featuring a coal-powered train and musical carousel, festival food and live entertainment are also offered.

• **Old Town Sharpsburg Fall Festival,** (6 miles west of Peachtree City), Sharpsburg (251-1234). This arts and crafts festival, housed in authentic rural buildings dating from the late 1800s and early 1900s, presents antiques, entertainment, children's activities and great food.

• **Oktoberfest,** Helen (706/878-2181). Every Thursday, Friday and Saturday in September, the mountain village of Helen celebrates the fall harvest with Bavarian food, music and dancing. Mid-September, a large parade kicks off the holiday celebration.

• **Cumming Falling Leaves Festival,** Cumming (706/889-8821). Arts and crafts exhibits, a live auction, Native American dances, dulcimer music, bluegrass, country and western music, and more activities highlight this annual fall festival in downtown Cumming.

• **Cherokee Homecoming Day,** New Echota Historic Site, Calhoun (706/629-8151). Each year, about 100 Cherokees demonstrate dancing, music and song, blow guns, cooking, crafts and games at their former national capital. Educational programs describe how the Cherokee lived in the 1800s.

■ OCTOBER ■

• **B.C. Fest!,** Michael C. Carlos Museum, Emory University, Atlanta (727-4282). This one-of-a-kind festival and educational experience introduces children to the life and culture of the ancient worlds. Emory University Quadrangle is transformed into ports-of-call of ancient civilizations, each having a selection of children's activities related to the theme of the festival. For example, when ancient Egypt was featured, children could enjoy mummy-wrapping demonstrations, hieroglyphic coloring walls, pyramid building, hands-on arts and crafts activities, music and belly dancing performances, gift stalls and wonderful Middle Eastern food.

• **Great Miller Lite Chili Cookoff,** Stone Mountain Park (498-5702). Cooking teams from all over the southeast compete in a chili-cooking championship. Plenty of samples are available for tasting while families enjoy continuous live entertainment.

• **Fall Gardening Festival,** Atlanta Botanical Garden, Atlanta (876-

5859). Gardening seminars, demonstrations of gardening products by retailers, celebrity gardeners, media personalities, vegetable growing contests, prize giveaways and lots of children's activities highlight this annual fall festival.

• **Folklife Festival,** Atlanta History Center (814-4089). Children can discover what life was life for an 1840s Piedmont Georgia family by watching demonstrations of traditional crafts, such as butter churning, quilting, open-hearth cooking, spinning and other daily-life crafts. Traditional songs and storytelling are also featured.

• **Fernbank's Children's Day,** Fernbank Museum of Natural History and Fernbank Science Center, Atlanta (378-0127). The two Fernbanks join together to present a special outdoor festival for children which could include road races, costume contests, pizza and other great festival food, special planetarium shows, bird walks and other fun activities for children.

• **Scottish Festival & Highland Games,** Stone Mountain Park (498-5702). Kilted clans compete in highland athletic events while pipe-and-drum bands, Scottish folk dancers, sheep herding contests, parades and pageantry entertain the crowds. Clan and Tartan information tents, Scottish shops and food abound. Over 100 different clans and societies participate in this unique event.

• **Festa Italiana,** Galleria Gardens, Atlanta (988-8085). This huge Italian-themed festival includes entertainment, a bocce ball tournament, cultural exhibits, Italian jewelry and marble, children's activities, games and rides, fireworks, delicious Italian food and more.

• **Hispanic Festival,** Immaculate Heart of Mary Catholic Church, Atlanta (888-7839). Festival Hispano celebrates the cultures of Central and South America and Spain with Latin and Spanish foods, salsa music, and arts and crafts. This very popular festival also features children's activities.

• **Ye Olde English Festival.** St. Bartholomew's Church, Atlanta (634-3336). Children love this re-creation of Merry Olde England, complete with costumed characters and jesters, period food and decorations, Renaissance, Baroque and folk music, jugglers, handicrafters, and other period activities. A large children's area is filled with games, rides and lots of fun. Members of the Society for Creative Anachronism, dressed in reproductions of Middle Age and Renaissance costumes and weaponry, hold demonstrations and mock tournaments.

• **Atlanta Jewish Festival,** Zaban Park Branch of the Atlanta Jewish Community Center, Dunwoody (875-7881). This community event features live music, storytelling, folk dancing, Judaic and Israeli gift items, ethnic delicacies and other fun activities for the whole family.

• **Ormewood Park Street Festival & Tour of Homes,** Ormewood Park, Atlanta (627-4313). The neighborhood street festival and tour of homes presents a flea market, arts and crafts exhibitors, pet parade, food court and live entertainment.

• **Decatur's Heritage Festival,** Old Courthouse, Decatur (371-8386). Children are offered an opportunity to learn about traditional country crafts by observing demonstrations in quilting, weaving, candle-making, soap-making, blacksmithing, bee-keeping, spinning and pottery. Storytelling, a petting zoo, puppet shows, pony rides, music, food and ghost stories round-off this very exciting festival.

• **Fall Festival of the Arts,** Paideia School, Atlanta (377-3491). This children's festival, held in late October or early November, features a large artist's market, tree-climbing, lots of hands-on art activities, a moonwalk, games, entertainment and great festival food.

• **Friends School of Atlanta's Fall Festival,** Decatur (373-8746). The annual fall festival and street fair for families features lots of hands-on arts and crafts activities for children, pony rides, a moon walk, a pumpkin sale, an Italian bistro featuring home-cooked food, a large flea market and lots more fun family activities.

• **Historic Marietta Arts & Crafts Festival,** Glover Park, Marietta (528-0616). This weekend arts and crafts festival presents many arts and crafts exhibitors, antique shops, historical walking tours, entertainment, food and special children's activities.

• **Sweetwater Valley Fall Festival,** Mable House, Mableton (739-0189). Look for an artist's market, Civil War encampment, children's activities, live entertainment and great food at this fall festival.

• **Vinings Fall Festival,** Vinings (438-8080). Antiques, arts and crafts, family entertainment, clowns, music, storytelling, and pony rides can all be found during this historic village's annual festival.

• **Jonquil Fall Festival,** Smyrna Community Center, Smyrna (434-3661). Arts and crafts, live entertainment, children's activities, a carnival, an antique car show, a Civil War reenactment and festival food highlight the Jonquil city's annual fall festival.

• **Harvest Fest,** Galleria Gardens, Atlanta (953-3750). This two-day celebration of American heritage and the pioneer spirit features an authentic Native American village; a reproduction of a pioneer village, including the raising of a log cabin; hands-on pioneer activities for children, harvest foods and country music. The festival benefits the Foundation for Medically Fragile Children.

• **Octoberfest in Roswell,** Canton Street, Roswell (642-2055). Arts and crafts, samplings of German cuisine, carriage rides, live entertainment and children's activities highlight this fall celebration.

• **Youth Day Parade & Festival,** Roswell (641-3760 or 640-3250). Roswell honors its youth with week-long activities culminating in a weekend parade and luncheon on Roswell Square.

• **Historic Jonesboro's Fall Festival & Battle Reenactment,** Stately Oaks Plantation, Jonesboro (473-0197). Jonesboro's fall festival includes a reenactment of the famous Battle of Jonesboro, a tour of the historic plantation, great food, demonstrations of traditional arts and crafts, music and other entertainment.

• **Festival of Nations,** Gwinnett Council for the Arts, Gwinnett (623-6002). October is international month in Gwinnett, and the Council for the Arts celebrates with a month-long festival featuring exhibitions and events of "world-wide interest." The event always includes artwork and performances by school children.

• **Elisha Winn Fair,** Elisha Winn House, Dacula (822-5174). During the first weekend in October, the Gwinnett Historical Society opens the doors of the Elisha Winn House and presents historical and Native American craft demonstrations, exhibits and living-history activities at the historical site.

• **Lilburn Daze,** Old Town Lilburn (921-2210). Lilburn hosts an arts and crafts fair complete with community and educational exhibits, live entertainment, festival food and lots of children's activities, such as pumpkin decorating contests, hands-on art activities, a moonwalk and balloons.

• **Oktoberfest,** Helen (706/878-2181). Throughout October (except on Sundays), Helen celebrates the fall harvest with Bavarian food, music and dancing.

• **Gold Rush Days,** Dahlonega (706/864-3711). During the third weekend in October, Dahlonega becomes an open-air stage for special performances and activities celebrating Dahlonega's gold mining history. Gold-panning, a large parade, games and other children's activities abound.

• **Prater's Mill Country Fair,** Dalton (706/275-6455). This quality arts and crafts show re-creates the atmosphere of an old-fashioned country fair complete with entertainment of the 1800s period, country cooking, canoeing on Coahulla Creek, pony rides and many children's activities. The operating grist mill at the site adds to the period atmosphere. Families can also enjoy a spring festival at the same location.

• **Georgia Apple Festival Arts & Crafts Fair,** Ellijay (706/635-7400). Besides a sampling of apples of all kinds, festival participants can enjoy arts and crafts, square dancing, clogging, singing, pony rides, a moonwalk and southern cooking.

• **Heritage Holidays,** Rome (706/291-3819). "Fall in the mountains" is the theme for Rome's annual festival that features concerts, boat rides, wagon train and trail rides, living history demonstrations, a parade, dancing, concerts and lots more activities.

• **Mule Camp Market** (formerly the Corn Tassel Festival), Gainesville (706/532-7714). Arts and crafts, puppet shows, bluegrass and Appalachian music shows, storytelling, quilt exhibits and plenty of country cooking highlight this traditional mountain festival.

• **Fall Festival,** Callaway Gardens, Pine Mountain (800/282-8181). Celebrate fall amid the splendor of Callaway Gardens and enjoy festival food, storytelling, entertainment and gardening demonstrations.

• **Cotton Pickin' Country Fair,** Gay (706/538-6814). This country fair is located on an old cotton-ginning complex that includes an 1890s vintage plantation home. Arts and crafts, antiques, continuous entertainment, children's activities and southern cooking are offered. Families can also enjoy a spring festival at this same location.

• **Georgia Marble Festival,** Jasper (706/692-5600). Guided tours of the Georgia Marble Company's quarries in Tate, a marble sculpture competition, historical tours and exhibits, arts and crafts, food, live entertainment, games and other children's activities highlight this North Georgia festival.

■ HALLOWEEN ■

• **Great Halloween Caper,** Zoo Atlanta (624-5630). A haunted house, costume contest and lots of real bats, spiders and snakes highlight Zoo Atlanta's annual Halloween celebration held the last Saturday in October.

• **A Tour of Southern Ghosts,** Stone Mountain Park (469-1105). The ART Station presents a Halloween storytelling festival at the Antebellum Plantation complex that includes lots of great storytelling, a candle lit walkway, fortune tellers and refreshments.

• **Little Five Points Halloween Festival,** Little Five Points and Bass Field, Atlanta (522-2926). Live entertainment, costume fashion shows, food and a moonwalk highlight this October festival.

• **Halloween Happenings,** Glover Park, Marietta (528-0616). Look for costume contests and other special Halloween activities on the Square during the Halloween holiday.

• **Halloween Carnival & Haunted Forest,** Laurel Park, Marietta (429-1115). Elementary-age children can visit the Land of Make-Believe, a Haunted Forest and participate in lots of games and fun.

• **Fright Nights,** Six Flags Over Georgia (739-3400). On October weekends, Six Flags reopens to celebrate the Halloween holiday. Enjoy some of the amusement park's rides, a special Haunted House and lots of other Halloween activities.

• **Harvest Moon Stroll,** Atlanta Botanical Garden (876-5859). This evening event features a costume parade for children, carved jack-o-lanterns, spooky sounds and other holiday decorations. Music and refreshments are also available.

• **Ghostly Gathering,** Williams-Payne House, Sandy Springs (851-9111). A covenant of ghostly storytellers gather at the historic home and tell spooky tales appropriate for children age six years and older. Costumes are welcome.

• **Safe Trick or Treat.** Cobb Center Mall, Cumberland Mall, Market Square Mall, Perimeter Mall, Greenbriar Mall, Southlake Mall, Northlake Mall, South DeKalb Mall, Town Center Mall, North Point Mall and Gwinnett Place Mall, all offer special Halloween activities for children and allow children to go from store to store gathering special AND SAFE Halloween treats. Check *Our Kids, Atlanta Parent* or local newspaper for listings of other safe trick or treat locations.

• **The Great Pumpkin Arts & Crafts Festival,** Lake Lanier Islands (932-7200). Jack-o-lantern contests, fall foliage boat excursions, arts and crafts, live entertainment, festival foods and pony rides are just some of the special activities offered for children at this fun festival.

■ NOVEMBER ■

• **The Children's Festival,** Woodruff Arts Center, Atlanta (333-0779 or 898-1184). This festival, co-sponsored by the Atlanta Symphony Orchestra, High Museum of Art, Alliance Theatre Company and Atlanta College of Art, is considered the premier children's visual and performing arts festival in Atlanta. Quality hands-on art activities for children, clowns, magicians, jugglers and other street performers, and continuous performances of dance, music, storytelling, theatre and puppetry (including a few performances featuring children), are always offered.

• **Veteran's Day Parade,** Atlanta (321-6111, ext. 6256). The second largest Veteran's Day Parade in the United States proceeds down Peachtree Street with military and veteran units, high school bands, clowns, floats and other specialty units.

• **Mideastern Festival,** St. Elias Antiochian Orthodox Church, Atlanta (633-5749). Delicious food and pastries, imported gift items, performances of traditional music, song and folk dance, cultural displays, tours of the sanctuary and children's activities highlight this annual event. The festival is sometimes held in October.

• **Indian Heritage Week,** Georgia State Capitol, Atlanta (656-2844). The State Capitol is the location for this special event celebrating Native American history and culture. Lectures, demonstrations and special exhibits geared to elementary-age children are featured, along with presentations by engaging Native Americans.

• **Holiday Festival,** The Art Place–Mountain View, Marietta (509-2700). This winter festival features an artist's market, gallery of trees, children's activities and a full schedule of theatrical, dance, musical and storytelling performances.

• **Holiday Open House,** Village of Stone Mountain (498-2097). The village dresses up for the holidays and opens its doors to the public. Holiday performances, refreshments and storytelling are offered during the event.

• **Holiday Celebration,** Stone Mountain Park (498-5702). To help celebrate the holiday season, Stone Mountain Park and Santa Claus present the south's largest "Tree of Lights." Also, horse-drawn carriage rides, ice skating shows, the spectacular Lasershow, holiday entertainment and a traditionally decorated antebellum plantation mark this holiday celebration. The festival is held throughout November and December.

• **Lighting of the Great Tree,** Underground Atlanta (523-2311). Thanksgiving evening, Atlantans gather in a new location—Underground Atlanta—to watch the night-time lighting of the huge Christmas tree. Atlanta school choirs sing Christmas carols as the official holiday season begins.

• **Fidelity Tree Lighting & Concert,** Fidelity Bank Building, Decatur (371-8386). The 60-foot tree atop the Fidelity Bank Building in downtown Decatur is lit the last Friday evening in November. Choirs and carolers sing, and the crowd celebrates the start of the Christmas season.

• **Lawrenceville Christmas on the Square,** Lawrenceville (822-8000). Thanksgiving evening, carolers sing in the Square in Lawrenceville as the crowd watches the lighting of the great Christmas tree, signifying the start of the holiday season.

• **Grayson Christmas Tree Lighting,** Grayson (963-8017). The city of Grayson officially starts the holidays in late November or early December with Christmas caroling, the lighting of the Christmas tree and a visit from Santa Claus.

• **Callaway Christmas & Fantasy in Lights,** Callaway Gardens, Pine Mountain (800/282-8181). Enjoy a five-mile drive through Callaway Gardens, passing by beautiful Christmas scenes composed of millions of tiny lights. A Christmas village, carolers, storytellers, craft people, entertainment and food are also featured during the holiday season. The spectacular drive-through light show is held late November through January 2nd.

• **Magical Nights of Lights,** Lake Lanier Islands (932-7200). Take your family on a two-mile drive around Lake Lanier, which is bedecked with thousands of tiny twinkling lights forming 60 different larger-than-life holiday displays. This light extravaganza is held late November through January 2nd.

• **Magical Alpine Christmas in Helen,** Helen (706/878-2181). Helen celebrates a Bavarian Christmas in the mountains late November through December.

• **Cabbage Patch Kids Appalachian Christmas Celebration at Babyland General,** Cleveland (706/865-2171). After the Great Christmas Tree is lit and Santa Claus makes a special appearance, Babyland General provides special entertainment for children of all ages. This holiday celebration is usually held Thanksgiving evening.

━━ DECEMBER ━━

• **Festival of Trees,** World Congress Center, Atlanta (325-NOEL). The Festival of Trees showcases hundreds of elaborate Christmas trees, wreaths, vignettes and gingerbread houses created by Atlanta's businesses and civic associations. Many of Atlanta's international and ethnic communities participate by decorating a booth depicting how the December holidays are celebrated in their native countries. Also featured are center-stage entertainment, rides on the famous pink pig monorail and a southern fair carousel. The large children's area has many hands-on art activities, a Lego play area, face-painting and other special activities for children. This benefit for the children's hospital is held late November and early December.

• **Art of the Season,** Atlanta Apparel Mart (250-2140). Scottish Rite Children's Medical Center presents a holiday event where children of all ages can participate in over 25 hands-on art, craft and holiday activities promoting children's self-esteem. Play areas and a visit by Santa Claus are also featured. This benefit for the children's hospital is held late November and early December.

• **Egleston Christmas Parade,** Atlanta (264-9348). The star of the parade, Santa Claus, leads celebrity guests, clowns, award-winning bands, holiday floats, giant helium balloons, and costumed storybook and cartoon characters up Peachtree Street as part of

Atlanta's celebrated Christmas parade.

• **Christmas at Callanwolde,** Callanwolde Fine Arts Center, Atlanta (872-5338). Callanwolde's seasonal fundraiser showcases the talents of Atlanta's interior and floral designers. Enjoy the rooms of the mansion which are decorated in Christmas splendor, a collectibles shop, a toy and gift boutique, the art shop and gallery, the courtyard cafe, the garden center and daily holiday performances. Recommended for older children.

• **Lighting of the State Christmas Tree at the Governor's Mansion,** Buckhead, Atlanta (261-1776). The public is invited to the Georgia Governor's Mansion for an evening lighting of the official Christmas Tree of Georgia. The ceremony includes caroling, tours of the first floor of the Governor's Mansion and refreshments served in the downstairs ballroom.

• **Chanukah Celebrations.** Members of the Jewish community celebrate the eight-day Festival of Lights privately in homes and in temples throughout the city. One of the more popular Chanukah celebrations open to the public is the Or VeShalom Bazaar (633-1737), featuring holiday gifts, books, children's games and hands-on activities, and wonderful holiday sweets.

• **Kwanzaa Celebrations.** The week-long African-American cultural holiday is celebrated privately in homes and publicly around Atlanta, including a parade in southwest Atlanta, theatrical performances, fashion shows, workshops, marketplaces, feasts, lectures, special library events, puppet shows, storytelling and many other special programs. Look in the *Atlanta Tribune* and local newspapers for a schedule of events or call the Metro Atlanta Kwanzaa Association (521-9014).

• **Holiday Party for Children,** High Museum of Art, Atlanta (892-3600). This day of family holiday entertainment usually includes a play, singing, holiday food, games, and hands-on arts and crafts activities.

• **Underground Atlanta,** Atlanta (523-2311). Underground Atlanta celebrates the Christmas season during December with street performers, carolers, a strolling Santa Claus and a talking Christmas tree. On New Year's Eve, the giant peach drops at midnight.

• **Country Christmas,** Atlanta Botanical Garden, Atlanta (876-5858). The Atlanta Botanical Garden hosts a traditional holiday celebration with carolers, chestnuts roasting on an open fire, horse-drawn carriage rides, holiday entertainment, arts and crafts, and lots of fun activities for children.

• **Christmas Festival & Open House at the Wren's Nest,** Atlanta (753-7735). The annual open-house is held on the Sunday in December closest to Joel Chandler Harris' birthday. The Nest is decorated in Victorian Christmas finery and hosts a very special children's Christmas storytelling festival with refreshments.

• **Old Fashioned Christmas,** Atlanta History Center, Atlanta (814-4000). Families can enjoy special Sunday afternoon performances and activities throughout December, including craft workshops and other holiday programs.

• **Christmas on the Square,** Glover Park, Marietta (528-0616). Marietta starts the Christmas holiday in early December (or occasionally, late November) with a celebration featuring community group carolers, storytellers, the lighting of the Christmas tree and a visit by Santa Claus.

• **Sugar Plum Festival,** Village of Stone Mountain (498-2097). Strolling carolers and seasonal entertainment in the village's gazebo highlight this Christmas season festival.

• **Merry Market,** Old Courthouse, Decatur (371-8386). The Old Courthouse in Decatur is transformed into a holiday market filled with handmade crafts, gifts and holiday decorations.

• **Christmas at Bulloch Hall & Christmas Candlelight Tour,** Roswell (992-1732). Bulloch Hall and other historical homes in Roswell are decorated with seasonal greenery and become the sites for special tours and holiday events throughout the month. The city of Roswell (640-3253) also has special holiday events with many activities for children.

• **Candlelight Tours of Stately Oaks,** Jonesboro (473-0197). Tour Stately Oaks Plantation in all of its holiday splendor.

• **Christmas in the Woods,** Laurel Park, Marietta (528-0616). Christmas caroling, storytelling, hayrides and a visit with Santa Claus are part of this children's holiday celebration.

• **Holiday Celebration,** Stone Mountain Park (498-5702). *See* November festival listing.

• **Grayson Christmas Tree Lighting,** Grayson (963-8017). See November festival listing.

• **Callaway Christmas & Fantasy in Lights,** Callaway Gardens, Pine Mountain (800/282-8181). *See* November festival listing.

• **Magical Nights of Lights,** Lake Lanier Islands (932-7200). *See* November festival listing.

• **Magical Alpine Christmas in Helen,** Helen (706/878-2181). Helen celebrates a Bavarian Christmas in the mountains throughout the month and presents an Altstadt Christmas Market each Friday through Sunday in December.

• **Dahlonega's Old Fashioned Christmas,** Dahlonega (706/864-3711). During the first weekend in December, Santa Claus and families visit Dahlonega to enjoy the holiday caroling, a winter parade and other holiday entertainment.

• **First Night New Year's Eve Celebration,** Midtown, Atlanta. Atlanta now has a spectacular event for families to enjoy while celebrating the start of the New Year. The midtown area, between 14th and 17th streets along Peachtree, is transformed into a giant block party featuring theatre, music, dance, storytelling, visual arts and lots of unusual hands-on activities for children. The non-alcoholic celebration also offers four large food tents and a fireworks display at midnight.

Day Trips

Sometimes you just need to get away from it all, but it's not time for the family vacation, or you're not up to a long drive and don't have time for an overnight stay anyway. A day trip that won't require more than a two–hour drive is the perfect solution! We have described many of our favorite day trip activities and organized them into eight areas, each one being chock full of things to do and see.

We have placed symbols at the top of each listing to designate the categories that describe each day trip.

🍁   **Nature**

⚛   **Science**

◉   **Unique Attractions**

🏛   **History & Government**

☆   **Performing Arts**

✑   **Fine Arts**

ATHENS

Fondly known to many Atlantans as the home of the University of Georgia Bulldogs, Athens also is home to the State Botanical Garden of Georgia, the Georgia State Museum of Art, Sandy Creek Park and Nature Center and Bear Hollow Wildlife Trail, all of which are appealing to youngsters . . . and even some die-hard Dogs fans. There is also a popular Cajun Mardi Gras Weekend and the North Georgia Folk Festival, to which many Atlantans flock each year.

If you are unfamiliar with Athens, you might want to stop by the Welcome Center located in the Church-Waddel-Brumby House, 280 E. Dougherty St. (706/353-1820). Built in 1820, it is the oldest residence in Athens and also serves as a house museum. It is open Monday–Saturday from 9:00 a.m.–5:00 p.m., and Sunday from 2:00 p.m.–5:00 p.m.

THE STATE BOTANICAL GARDEN OF GEORGIA

The State Botanical Garden of Georgia, 2450 S. Milledge Ave., Athens, two miles south of the University's main campus (706/542-1244). The garden is located on over 300 acres of land, much of which is in its natural state, with streams, woods, ravines and frontage on the Oconee River. It displays ordinary as well as rare and unusual plants, and is a natural habitat for numerous wildlife, with five miles of nature trails that are really fun to explore! In addition, the garden has special collections such as the Rose Garden, Herb Garden and Dahlia Garden to complement the azaleas, rhododendrons, dogwoods and other indigenous plants.

The strikingly modern and magnificent glass-enclosed Visitor Center/Conservatory Complex is the reception area for the garden, with a continuous slide show providing garden information and housing a gift shop, offices and the Garden Cafe. It is home to many tropical and semi-tropical plants, a stream and a wishing pool, and features the work of various regional artists. The Callaway Building nearby is a center for teaching and research and includes a reading room, library and art exhibits.

Conservatory & Visitor Center: Open Monday–Saturday from 9:00 a.m.–4:30 p.m., and Sunday from 11:30 a.m.–4:30 p.m. *Cafe:* Open for lunch Monday–Saturday from 8:00 a.m.–dusk, and Sunday from 12:00 noon–3:00 p.m. *Garden:* Open daily from 8:00 a.m.–dusk. *Callaway Building:* Open Monday–Friday from 8:00 a.m.–5:00 p.m., and by appointment. Free.

GEORGIA MUSEUM OF ART

Georgia Museum of Art, Jackson Street, North University Campus, Athens (706/542-3255). This is the official state of Georgia Art Museum and contains a permanent collection of over 5,000 works, including 19th and 20th century American paintings, as well as European and Oriental art. A visit here would only be of interest to the more sophisticated child. Open Monday–Saturday from 9:00 a.m.–5:00 p.m., and Sunday from 1:00 p.m.–5:00 p.m. Closed on major holidays. Free.

SANDY CREEK NATURE CENTER & PARK

Sandy Creek Nature Center and Park, Old Commerce Rd., Athens (706/354-2930). This nature center, a division of the Clarke County Department of Parks, is similar in concept to Fulton County's Chattahoochee Nature Center. The setting is 200–acres of woods, marshes and fields with nature trails weaving throughout. There are exhibits and numerous exciting educational programs offered throughout the year for people of all ages. There is also a gift shop. *Trail hours:* Daily from sun-up to sun-down. *Center hours:* Monday–Friday from 8:00 a.m.–5:00 p.m., and Saturday from 12:00 noon–5:00 p.m. The center is closed on weekends from Thanksgiving to March. Free.

About 1½–miles down the road from the center is the 700–acre **Sandy Creek Park**. There are many recreational facilities, including tennis courts, volleyball nets, picnicking and a primitive campground that is available for Friday and Saturday nights. There is a 260–acre lake for boating (though motors are restricted to trawling), and swimming is permitted at a designated beach. Open Thursday through Tuesday from 7:00 a.m.–7:00 p.m. (closed Wednesdays). Unlimited daily park use is $1.00/adults; 50¢/children age 7–12. Children age 6 and under and seniors over 65 are free.

BEAR HOLLOW WILDLIFE TRAIL

Bear Hollow Wildlife Trail, 293 Gran Ellen Dr., Athens (706/613-3580). Located in Memorial Park, this wildlife trail features animals native to Georgia, such as deer, skunk, owls and river otters. The trail is paved and comfortably accommodates strollers, takes about twenty minutes to traverse, and is open Tuesday–Sunday from 9:00 a.m.–5:00 p.m. Free.

Directions to Athens: Athens is about a one-hour drive from Atlanta on US 78.

CALLAWAY GARDENS & THE LITTLE WHITE HOUSE

CALLAWAY GARDENS

Callaway Gardens, Pine Mountain (800/282-8181). An easy 90-minute drive southwest of Atlanta lies the beautiful 12,000–acre world class resort of Callaway Gardens. But don't let the reputation of this facility daunt you; it is a place for everyone to enjoy, over and over again.

Callaway features **Robin Lake Beach,** a mile-long white sand beach for digging and building sand castles, swimming and watching water skiing spectaculars. You may ride on the riverboat Robin E. Lee and the miniature train Whistlin' Dixie. Miniature golf, ping-pong and the usual beach sports such as volleyball are available, and there are picnic areas and terrific playgrounds. Open daily from 8:00 a.m.–6:00 p.m. Memorial Day to Labor Day. The cost is $12.00/adults; $6.00/children age 6–11; and children under 6 are free.

Your family may **Bicycle** on over seven miles of paths that wind through beautiful woods, azalea gardens and along the lake. Bring your own bikes or rent them at Callaway. They actually rent small bikes for children! Rental prices are $3.00/hour or $9.00/half a day.

There are many **Walking Trails** through Callaway Gardens, but three of them are particularly suited to families. The Azalea Trail, which of course you would want to traverse in the spring, can take as little as 15 minutes or as long as 90, depending upon your pace. There is a Wildflower Trail, which might take 25 or more minutes, featuring ferns and wildflowers. The Rhododendron Trail is at its peak of beauty in late spring and would take a family about 30 minutes to enjoy. Remember, children do love nature walks, especially if you point out the varieties of plant life, discuss who lives in the animal holes, examine insects up close, and guess what makes the various sounds you hear.

Mr. Cason's Vegetable Garden is a 7¹/₂–acre demonstration garden that is featured on the television series "Victory Garden South." A wide variety of crops and flowers are grown, such as berries and grapes, in the Upper Terrace, and corn, beans, broccoli, lettuce and collards in the Middle Terrace. The Lower Terrace is the site of the Herb Garden, which has medicinal and fragrant herbs as well as culinary herbs. A recent addition is the water garden, which is home to many water plants and goldfish.

The **Pioneer Log Cabin** is an authentic 1800s log cabin which may be toured for a better understanding of daily life in early Georgia.

The **Cecil B. Day Butterfly Center**, the largest free-flight conservatory in North America, is home to about 50 species of tropical butterflies. This is truly a wondrous experience for young and old alike that should not be missed. But before you enter the free-flight area, try to convince your kids to visit the theatre and gallery that explain the life-cycle of butterflies and provide other information to help orient you. Now, full of anticipation, enter the breathtaking conservatory. You will find the butterflies to be stunningly beautiful and very cooperative; they gracefully rest on leaves while you stare at them. One even landed on a friend of mine and stayed on her shoulder throughout her visit! After you exit, you may want to visit the gift shop that sells lots of butterfly-related items.

Walk through the **John A. Sibley Horticultural Center** on a curving footpath where each bend brings a whole new landscape of flowering plants in view. The greenhouse garden is meticulously maintained and boasts a beautiful two-story waterfall surrounded by a flower display. There is also an outdoor garden of labeled plants and trees, and changing exhibitions, such as topiary gardens, that are a special delight.

- **Azalea Festival Weekends** in March and April, **Fall Festival Weekends** in October and **The Twelve Days of Christmas Festival** in December have storytelling, puppetry, magicians, music and other family-oriented activities and entertainment. See our chapter on "Festivals and Special Events" for more information.

- **Fantasy in Lights** is a Christmas drive-through light show with millions of lights glittering all over Callaway. Sixteen-foot-tall nutcrackers, a 24-foot wreath you drive through, huge toys, a nativity scene, colorful butterflies and an animated leaping frog are some of the bright sights you will see. Then visit the 22,000-square-foot Christmas Village filled with trees, elves, crafts people at work, gifts, snacks and, of course, Santa Claus. Fantasy in Lights is held late November through early January from 5:30 p.m.–11:00 p.m. Admission costs $15/vehicle Monday–Thursday, and $20/vehicle Friday–Sunday.

- **Family Adventure,** the summer recreation program, includes circus performances in the Beach Dome, water skiing, swimming, hiking, sailing, tennis, puppet shows and more.

• If you have ventured to Callaway via the Little White House, chances are you have some hungry children. We suggest you stop at the Country Kitchen and Store (intersection of GA 190 and GA 27) for delicious southern cooking you can eat on a verandah with a panoramic view of the valley. The Country Store has jarred jams, candy, souvenirs, arts and crafts, and more for sale.

Hours: Open daily from 7:00 a.m.–7:00 p.m. during the summer, and 9:00 a.m.–5:00 p.m. during the winter.

Admission: $7.00/adult; $1.00/children age 6–11; and children under 6 are free.

Directions: **From Atlanta:** Take I-85 south to I-185, exit on GA Hwy. 27 South. **From The Little White House:** Go right on Hwy. 85 West, right on GA 190 West and right on GA 27.

LITTLE WHITE HOUSE

The Little White House, Warm Springs (706/655-5870). Franklin Delano Roosevelt, four times President of the United States, used to visit the warm springs (88°F year-round) in this area because they were of therapeutic value to his polio-stricken body. Nestled in the beautiful Georgia woods near the natural spring waters, FDR built his "country home," which has been left exactly as it was on the day he died here, April 12, 1945.

The grounds of the Little White House have been more extensively landscaped since his death, and a museum, shop and picnic area have been added. Children enjoy the fountains and meandering up the terraced path that goes between rows of flags from every state of the union. Also lining the path are large stones in the shape of each state made from materials indigenous to that particular state. At the top of this path is the **museum** which houses various mementos worth seeing. Be sure to see the short 12-minute movie, a documentary about FDR, which most children will enjoy.

Another path leads to the guard house, servant's quarters and the garage. Inside the garage is the glass-enclosed **1938 Ford convertible** that FDR actually used to drive around the grounds. You can view how the automobile was modified with hand controls to accommodate FDR's paralyzed legs, and you may push a button to hear a voice describe some interesting details about FDR and his car.

Next is the **Little White House** itself, where there is tape recorded tour information and staff available to answer your questions. Children as well as baby boomers will enjoy the history lesson of seeing how few amenities even the rich had not too many years ago. The kitchen and its utensils can be viewed and compared to the modern kitchen of the 1990s, but you will soon be jolted out of your contemporary complacency. Entering the living room, 1945 does not seem so long ago as you stand just a few feet from the desk FDR was sitting at when he died. From that point on, the brief tour takes on a poignancy and immediacy we had not anticipated. You see Roosevelt's wheelchair, leg braces, his dog's chain, other personal effects, photographs and additional memorabilia.

- There is a small snack bar and gift shop at the entrance gate.

- The town of Warm Springs has over seventy stores and restaurants as well as the Warm Springs Hotel.

- The Warm Springs **U.S.D.I. Fish Hatchery** (706/655-3620) is located one mile south of the town on GA 27A. It has outdoor ponds and an indoor aquarium. It is open daily from 7:30 a.m.–4:00 p.m. Free.

Hours: Open daily from 9:00 a.m.–5:00 p.m.

Admission: $4.00/adults; $2.00/children age 6–18; and
              children under 6 are free.

Directions: Take I-85 south to GA 27A through Warm Springs.
              Turn left on Highway 85 W South.

PINE MOUNTAIN WILD ANIMAL PARK

Pine Mountain Wild Animal Park, 1300 Oak Grove Rd., Pine
Mountain (800/367-2751 or 706/663-8744). The 500-acre drive-
through park features nearly 300 species of animals, including
goats, sheep, camels, zebras, giraffes, elk, antelopes, llamas and buffalo. Even though signs warn drivers to keep the windows rolled up
and not to feed the animals, someone forgot to inform the animals.
They do not hesitate to approach the car, much to the delight of the
children inside, looking for a handout (or maybe they think we are
the curiosity in the cage?). The trip ideally should take up to three
hours, but this may depend on just how patient your children are.
A bus tour is also offered, but the kids may balk at this idea.

The second half of your visit will include a walking visit of Old Mac-
Donald's Farm, which has small animals such as peacocks, chickens,
pot-bellied pigs and monkeys. You will see snakes and alligators in
a "serpentorium" and enjoy the petting zoo.

*   A fast food restaurant and snack bar are open seasonally.
    There is a picnic area if you prefer to bring your own food.

*   There is a gift shop.

Hours: Daily from 10:00 a.m. to one hour before sunset.
              Open year-round except for Thanksgiving, Christ-

mas and New Year's Day.

Admission: $10.95/adults; $9.50/seniors; $7.50/children age
3–9; and children under 3 are free.

Directions: Take I-85 south to I-185 Exit #14. Turn left on US
27 and go about seven miles. Turn right onto Oak
Grove Rd.

CARTERSVILLE

The following terrific recreational, educational and historic sites may
be visited one at a time, or several may be combined into one
visit. Each place has much to offer, and the time you spend at any
one facility will depend upon the ages and interests of your family members. And since these attractions are less than an hour's drive
north of Atlanta, there is no need to hurry through any of them; you
know you can always return.

LAKE ALLATOONA &
RED TOP MOUNTAIN STATE PARK

Lake Allatoona (404/382-4700) and Red Top Mountain State Park
(975-4203), Cartersville. Your best bet is to access Lake Allatoona
at **Red Top Mountain State Park** (I-75, Exit #123), which is located on a peninsula along the lake. Here you may use the lake and park
facilities during the day for free. There is a Trading Post which
stocks refreshments, snacks and ice cream, has bathroom facilities
and many useful free brochures.

Among the many activities you may enjoy are: swimming at the beach
where you have use of a bathhouse from Memorial Day to Labor

Day, a small playground with four picnic tables and grills, a small miniature golf course, tennis courts and seven miles of nature trails. For families who bring their own boats or rent one here, there are boating ramps and docks with waterskiing and fishing permitted. If you are interested in camping, there are 286 tent and trailer sites, and if you want a quick getaway, stay in one of their eighteen, two-bedroom, fully-equipped rental cottages. Call 975-4200 for reservations. Another option is the Red Top Mountain Lodge that allows children to stay free, with dining at the Mountain Cove Restaurant which overlooks Lake Allatoona.

If you have time to spend the day and explore around **Lake Allatoona**, you will find 350 picnic sites, several shelters and thirteen pleasant sandy beaches. Stop in at the **Resource Manager's Office & Visitors Center** (I-75, Exit #125), which is open every day, and view video exhibits about the area's history and information about the dam itself. The fishing is good and hunting is permitted, so watch the kids. Also, the woods are wild and inhabited by bobcat, fox, wild turkey and black bear. All recreational use of Lake Allatoona is free, except camping. There are about 700 campsites (first come, first served) located in eleven campgrounds.

- An interesting historical site is near the dam—Cooper's Iron Works, a 143-year-old building where ammunition for the Civil War was manufactured.

- If you intend to fish and do not have a fishing license as required by Georgia State Law, there is a gas station at Exit #123 where you can purchase one.

- Dogs are permitted on leashes.

Hours: *Park:* Daily from 7:00 a.m.–10:00 p.m. *Park Office:* Monday–Friday from 8:00 a.m.–5:00 p.m. *Trading Post:* Daily from 8:30 a.m.–9:30 p.m.

AIR ACRES MUSEUM

Air Acres Museum, I-75 to Exit #124. Follow airplane signs through Cartersville (404/382-7030). "The Home of the Georgia Boys" houses many airplanes, from vintage World War II planes which are kept in mint condition, to a sleek glider and a modern ultralight. These planes are not only shiny clean and interesting museum pieces, but they are also operational. Kids can touch the airplanes, look in some of the cockpits, and on one bomber, see up inside the belly of the plane.

- The museum is in an old hangar alongside a runway of the airport.

- The museum will not take long to tour, and since it is about a fifty-minute drive from Atlanta, we suggest you combine a visit here with a trip to Etowah Mounds State Historic Site (see below), and/or berry picking at Glen Cove Nursery (706/386-0207), 1/4 mile before you get to the historic site.

Hours: Open Monday–Saturday from 9:00 a.m.–5:00 p.m.

Admission: Free, but donations are welcome.

ETOWAH INDIAN MOUNDS
STATE HISTORIC SITE

Etowah Mounds State Historic Site, 813 Indian Mounds Rd., S.W., Cartersville (404/387-3747). Take I-75 to Exit #124 and follow the brown "Etowah Mounds" signs. The **Etowah Archaeological Museum** is your introduction to the lives and culture of the Mississippian Indians who inhabited this beautiful, serene, fertile valley from about 1000–1500 A.D. Be sure to view the film which discusses the history and culture of the Etowah people and describes the significance of some of the artifacts on display in the museum. Among the artifacts excavated from the area are items that suggest the Indians decorated themselves with paint, copper and shell jewelry, tattoos and feathers. You will see pottery and marble statues as well as the burial site of a priest-chief excavated from a mound.

Exit the museum and begin the peaceful, almost mystical walk to the **Etowah Indian Mounds.** This is a self-guided tour, and the museum staff provides you with a very informative map and explanatory essay. You look down into a Borrow Pit, and have a difficult time comprehending how this enormous pit was dug by people carrying out hundreds of thousands of basketfulls of dirt in order to build the mounds. The task appears overwhelming. Your imagination comes alive picturing homes scattered around the clean swept central plaza and the bustling activity of people fishing, preparing food, and crafting pots and jewelry, and you can almost hear the laughter of children playing.

The steps of the mounds are not steep (there are just a lot of them, about 100 to the top of the tallest), so little legs can easily make it to the top. Two of the mounds were ceremonial and the third was a burial mound. From this mound scientists have gathered invaluable information about burial practices, diet, diseases, trading practices and class structure. It is from this third mound that the world famous marble figures displayed in the museum were excavated.

The conclusion of the tour takes you alongside the river where the Indians fished, and by trees that provided fruit and river cane that was the raw material for baskets, roofs, mats and arrow shafts. This **River Walk** has benches shaded by trees that are labeled with their names. When it was time to leave, my kids ran through the lush meadow—a timeless act, since meadows must have always beckoned children.

- There are several special programs offered here throughout the year, such as Indian Skills Day in the spring, Artifacts

Identification Day in April and November, plus astronomy programs. Call for information about the current offerings.

Hours: Open Tuesday–Saturday from 9:00 a.m.–5:00 p.m., and Sunday from 2:00 p.m.–5:30 p.m. Closed Mondays.

Admission: Museum admission is free. The Mound Tour costs $1.50/adults; 95¢/children age 6–18; and is free for children 5 years and under.

WILLIAM WEINMAN MINERAL MUSEUM

William Weinman Mineral Museum, Mineral Museum Dr., Cartersville (404/386-0576). Take I-75 to Exit #126. The museum is on the left next to Denny's restaurant. As you approach the museum, your children will probably spot the old rusty mining equipment, a truck and a train used to carry iron ore, and a rock garden to touch and talk about. Inside, the museum is divided into several rooms, each with a theme. In the Main Hall you may walk through a simulated limestone cave with stalactites and a fluorescent rock display, and see specimens from the state of Georgia, including fossils (which are always fascinating to kids). The Mayo Wing houses an international collection of specimens, petrified wood and an incredible array of geodes—some as high as three feet—that beg to be touched. The Paleontology Hall has numerous cases of fossils and Native American artifacts, some over 10,000 years old! You may want to time your visit to the Annual Rock Festival held the second Saturday in June. Festival admission is free and kids can bring their favorite rocks to be identified, pan for gold and gemstones, and watch special demonstrations.

• The Frank Mayo Junior Rockhound Club for children age 6–18 meets monthly at the museum.

- The gift shop is stocked with lots of rocks, books and jewelry.

- Restrooms and water fountains are available. The museum is accessible to the handicapped.

- There are educational and research facilities and specimen identification services for serious geologists.

Hours: Open Tuesday–Saturday from 10:00 a.m.–4:30 p.m., and Sunday from 2:00 p.m.–4:30 p.m.

Admission: $3.00/adults; $2.50/seniors; $2.00/children age 6–11; and children under 6 are free. Group tours are available.

CHATTANOOGA, TENNESSEE

A visit to Chattanooga is a must for every Atlanta family. Take a leisurely two-hour drive for a wonderful day trip to the Tennessee Aquarium and downtown Chattanooga—a trip we have enjoyed more than once. And even more fun was the time our two families spent the night in Chattanooga, with one family's kids thrilled by their night in a real railroad sleeper at the Chattanooga Choo Choo hotel. On that visit we saw other sights such as Ruby Falls, Incline Railway, Regional History Museum, the Tennessee Valley Authority (TVA) building and more. And with an expansion of the aquarium on the drawing boards, we know we will be back.

TENNESSEE AQUARIUM

Tennessee Aquarium, One Broad St., Chattanooga (800/262-0695). The stunning aquarium overlooks the beautiful Tennessee River, which is what this attraction is all about. Families meander through the well-designed aquarium much as a river fish might slowly swim downstream. The look of the aquarium is that of the river itself—with swamp areas, waterfalls, trees, and boulders—so it is as though you are walking along the river and then below the surface. Most of the marine life in the tanks is actually from the river, so a visit to the aquarium is a study of the Tennessee River. The freshwater aquarium is an impressive 13,000-square-foot building holding 500,000 gallons of water and marine life in over forty exhibits. The Nickajack Lake exhibit, at 140,000 gallons, is the largest freshwater tank in the world. Needless to say, this attraction is enormously popular, drawing up to 11,000 visitors on summer weekends. (We went on a weekday and it was not busy.) But don't let the crowds daunt you. The three major galleries are so enormous that even when occupancy is at maximum, everyone has a vast, unobstructed view inside. What is guaranteed to be crowded is the nice gift shop which sells books, jewelry, posters and souvenirs.

After you purchase your tickets for your admission time, possibly a few hours later in the day, take a moment to enjoy the panoramic view of this vital river. Your children will probably be wading (or maybe "accidentally" sitting down) in the simulated river-fountain area in the aquarium plaza. Someone sure had a great idea here. It certainly kept our children very happy on a hot summer day while we waited a bit to enter the aquarium. But if your wait is long, take the free shuttle bus which runs every five minutes down the street to **Warehouse Row** where you can shop and eat. Also, be sure to stop in at the **Chattanooga Visitors Center** located beside the aquarium to gather brochures and get up-to-date information on the attractions listed below and others you may find of interest.

Plans are already being developed to double the existing aquarium space. Tentative plans include a tropical rain forest inhabited by birds and monkeys, a simulated desert with snakes, lizards and desert vegetation, and an Alaskan Arctic environment inhabited by some creatures indigenous to the area.

Hours: Open daily from 10:00 a.m.–6:00 p.m. Extended hours on weekends May through Labor Day. Closed Thanksgiving and Christmas Day.

Admission: Cost is $8.75/adults; $4.75/children age 3–12; and children under 3 are free.

Directions: Take I-75 north to Chattanooga and follow the signs to the Aquarium.

OTHER CHATTANOOGA ATTRACTIONS

• **Chattanooga Choo Choo,** Holiday Inn, Terminal Station, 1400 Market St., Chattanooga (800/872-2529). In addition to the usual hotel rooms, there are forty-eight restored sleeper railroad cars where families may spend the night. For $105 plus tax, two adults and their children may sleep in a queen size bed and a day bed that holds two small children. This was, and still is, the home of the Chattanooga Choo Choo, famous to some of us only by song. The restored terminal and surrounding yard attracts visitors with four railroad themed restaurants, gift shops, a train shop, a formal garden, and the fantastic **Chattanooga Southern Model Railroad.** This is one of the largest exhibits open to the public, with over 3,000 feet of track, 150 switches, 120 locomotives, 100 freight cars, 80 passenger cars and more, chugging along a miniature recreation of Chattanooga and Cumberland County. This is a must for all train lovers. There is a nominal admission fee to see the model railroad.

• **Warehouse Row,** 1110 Market St., Chattanooga (615/267-1111). The designer factory outlet boasts among its many shops, J. Crew, Guess?, Bass, Ellen Tracy, Gitano and Napier. A food court is downstairs. Open Monday–Saturday from 10:00 a.m.–7:00 p.m., and Sundays from 12:00 noon–6:00 p.m.

• **Museums & Galleries: Hunter Museum of Art,** 10 Bluff View, Chattanooga (615/267-0968), is a beautiful modern mansion, overlooking the Tennessee River and Maclellan Island Wildlife Sanctuary, that houses art from pre-revolutionary times to the present. The permanent collection includes works by Mary Cassatt, Andrew Wyeth and John Singer Sargent. There is a museum gift shop. Open Tuesday–Saturday from 10:00 a.m.–4:30 p.m., and Sundays from 1:00 p.m.–4:30 p.m. Several galleries are within walking distance: **Rising Fawn Folk Art** (615/265-2760) and **River Gallery** (615/267-7353) offer fine crafts.

LOOKOUT MOUNTAIN

Lookout Mountain, Tennessee. Even though this is a very touristy place, with all the hype and inappropriate razzle-dazzle, there are some marvels of nature behind it all that are worth seeing, albeit only once. After all, where else can you go safely down into a *real cave?* **Lookout Mountain Caverns** has stalactites, stalagmites, crystals and **Ruby Falls** (615/821-2544), a natural 145–foot waterfall, 1,120 feet underground. If you are ready for more, ascend the mountain on the breathtakingly steep (72.7% grade) **Incline Railway** (615/821-4224), where you will find Lookout Mountain Tower and be able to view the spectacular Tennessee Valley. **Rock City Gardens** (615/820-2531) is at the top also, with rock gardens, beautiful vegetation and "Lover's Leap," where it is reputed one can see seven states on a clear day. Some of the rock formations are estimated to be 200 million years old. Among the 10 acres of gardens is **Fairyland Caverns & Mother Goose Village** (615/820-2531) for the little ones. When you need a break from the touristy stuff, visit the **Chattanooga Nature Center** (615/821-1160) located at the west side base of the mountain, which features wildlife exhibits, picnic areas, walking trails and a Wetland Walkway that is entirely handicapped accessible. Admission is charged for all of the above attractions.

DAHLONEGA

The cry of "We've found gold!" in Dahlonega in 1828 marked the start of the first major gold rush in North America. By 1833, Dahlonega was a bustling, vibrant town built to accommodate the numbers of pioneer gold-miners who came to strike it rich. Between 1838 and 1861, over $6 million in gold was coined by the U.S. Branch Mint in Dahlonega! The peaceful mining town in the foothills of Georgia's Blue Ridge Mountains is now a nice place to visit to view historic sites and scenic drives; to visit the beautiful and historic campus of North Georgia College; buy Appalachian crafts; and enjoy canoeing, fishing, hiking, horseback riding and many other outdoor activities.

Start your visit to Dahlonega with a walk around the historic town square area. The **Chamber of Commerce** (706/864-3711) is located right on the square and can provide you with handfuls of pamphlets and brochures, including ones describing self-guided walking tours of the town. You can also visit the many retail stores on the square which are filled with historical books and maps, Native American pottery and jewelry, antiques, quilts, crafts and other treasures.

• In the middle of the town square lies the Old Courthouse Building, now the site of the **Dahlonega Gold Museum State Historic Site** (706/864-2257). The exhibits, films and slides shown at the historic museum tell the story of the town's gold rush. You will learn about the mining techniques of the prospectors, see samples of the gold coins which were minted here and get a glimpse of the lifestyles of the town's mining families. Hours: Monday–Saturday from 9:00 a.m.–5:00 p.m., and Sunday from 10:00 a.m.–5:00 p.m. (open Sundays until 6:00 p.m. May through October). Closed Thanksgiving and Christmas Day. Admission: $1.50/adults;

75¢/children age 6–12; and children under 6 are free.

• After your tour, you can have a huge lunch at the **Smith House** (706/864-3566), Dahlonega's most famous dining facility. Meals are served family-style; you will be seated at a long table with other visitors, and huge platters of Southern-style meats, vegetables and biscuits will be brought to your table. As long as you can keep eating, more food will be served! (Closed on Mondays).

After your meal, there are more activities that await you. On the front lawn of the Smith House and at other locations throughout the town, children can, for a small fee, learn how to **pan gold** and other gemstones. Rocks, fossils and semi-precious gemstones are all available for purchase at local stops.

• Behind the Smith House is **Dahlonega's Fire Station**, which is staffed with friendly volunteers. Our children had a wonderful time with firefighter "Mike," who let them sit in the trucks and showed them the tanker truck and other kinds of fire-fighting equipment city children usually don't get to see.

• As you head out of town, you will pass lots and lots of signs leading you to camping facilities, horseback riding, stables, canoeing adventures, gold-panning attractions and scenic sites such as Amicalola Falls State Park and Unicoi State Park (discussed in "North Georgia Mountains" later on in this chapter). You might consider the underground tour of the **Consolidated Gold Mine** (706/864-8473) located ¹/₂ mile east of Dahlonega. Yes, you can see *real gold* on the walls of the mine. The tours run daily, include panning for gold, and there is a gift shop. Cost is $7.00/adults; $4.00/children 6–12; and children under 6 are free.

• A great time to visit is during one of Dahlonega's special festivals, such as Gold Rush Days in October, and Old-Fashioned Christmas in Dahlonega in December. These events are described in our chapter on "Festivals and Special Events."

Directions: Dahlonega is about 1½-hours north of Atlanta. Take GA 400 to Hwy. 60 and head north. You will dead-end into Dahlonega.

HELEN

Back in the late 1960s, a few of Helen's business owners got together to figure out what to do about the dying lumber mill town. A local artist, John Kollock, envisioned the entire village in Alpine design, and a few watercolor sketches later, the business community fell in love with the idea. Without much more fanfare, the village began its renovation and now, over twenty years later, the small village is a "Bit of Bavaria" in the North Georgia Mountains.

There are over 150 retail stores selling Alpine, Scandinavian and country gift items, such as music boxes, trolls, Viking hats, crystal, dinnerware, sweaters, quilts and so forth. And, not to worry, for those shoppers who prefer modern retail stores, there is also Alpine Village Outlets which has two small shopping malls filled with factory outlet stores, including the Van Heusen Factory Store, Corning/Revere Factory Store and Bass Shoes Outlet Store. Stores are open for the most part Monday–Saturday from 10:00 a.m.–9:00 p.m., and Sunday from 12:00 noon–6:00 p.m. (Earlier closing hours during winter months.)

Helen is the site of year-round festivals, parades and special events such as Fasching Karnival and Parade (German Mardi Gras), Mayfest in the Mountains, Helen to the Atlantic Hot Air Balloon Festival & Race, Float the Fourth Tube Parade and Fireworks, Oktoberfest and Magical Alpine Christmas in Helen. These special events are described in our chapter "Festivals and Special Events," or you may call the Chamber of Commerce for more information (706/878-2521). And for those who like water, contact Alpine Tubing (800/782-8823) or Garden Tubing (800/438-7742) for information about tubing down the Chattahoochee.

• **Alpine Amusement Park**, Main St., Helen (706/878-2306). Bumper boats, antique cars, go-carts and lots of other rides and games are available at this small amusement park. The park is open Fridays from 4:00 p.m.–11:00 p.m.; Saturdays from 10:30 a.m.–11:00 p.m.; and Sundays from 12:00 noon–9:00 p.m.

• **The Museum of the Hills**, Main St., Helen (706/878-3140). This is a self-guided tour through displays of the lifestyles of the hill country people in the south during turn-of-the-century America. There is also a Fantasy Kingdom containing castles and cottages, and characters from nursery rhymes and fairy tales. The museum is open daily from 10:00 a.m.–9:00 p.m. Admission is $4.00/adults; $3.00/children age 13 and older; $2.00/children age 5–12; and children under 5 are free.

• **Nora Mill Granary & Store**, Helen (706/878-2927). Located on GA 75 just a few miles south of Helen. This is a real working mill where you can see grain being ground on stones over 100 years old, powered by the Chattahoochee River. It is an awesome sight. Wholesome, natural grains, such as grits, cornmeal, whole wheat flour, rye and buckwheat flours, and even pancake mix, can be purchased at the store. If you are very lucky, they will have samples of their freshly made porridge with chunks of apple. The store is open daily from 9:00 a.m.–5:00 p.m.

• **Sautee-Nacoochee Indian Mound**. This Native American burial site on the National Register of Historic Places, is located at the junction of Georgia Highways 17 and 75. About 75 Native American skeletons have been unearthed here as well as numerous artifacts dating as far back as 10,000 B.C.

• **Storyland Petting Zoo & Castle of the Dolls,** Hwy. 75 (4 miles south of Helen) (706/865-2939). Storyland Petting Zoo has over 100 animals at the "zoo." Castle of the Dolls has miniature villages filled with over 150 Naber Kids, McGuffy Porcelain Dolls, Sweetheart Dolls and Raikes Bears. The attractions are open daily from 10:00 a.m.–6:00 p.m. The zoo is free. Castle of the Dolls costs $2.00/person, and children under two are free.

Directions to Helen: Helen is located about 1½-hours north of Atlanta off GA 75. See our section below called "North Georgia Mountains" for a description of attractions only about a mile or two north of Helen.

BABYLAND GENERAL HOSPITAL

Babyland General Hospital, 19 Underwood St., Cleveland (706/865-2171). Imagine a full-sized community hospital complete with a delivery room, nurseries, intensive-care units and play areas. Picture hundreds upon hundreds of Cabbage Patch Kids of all ages, sizes and color, standing in cribs, sitting on rocking chairs, playing in classrooms and going on various outings throughout the hospital complex. Next, visualize a large gift shop filled from top to bottom with Cabbage Patch Kids that are just waiting to be "adopted" by your children. And finally, listen for the announcement, "There's a Cabbage in labor!" and run to the delivery room to witness the delivery of a Cabbage Patch Kid (from a Mother Cabbage, of course). Are you interested? If so, visit Babyland General Hospital.

• For those of you who have children who do not like Cabbage Patch Kids, not to worry. Babyland also houses Moody Hollow General Store which is filled with Furskins Bears and other country craft gift items.

Hours: Open year-round Monday–Saturday from 9:00 a.m.–5:00 p.m., and Sunday from 1:00 p.m.–5:00 p.m. (Later closing hours during the summer months.)

Admission: Free. (It is difficult, however, to leave without buying something!)

Directions: Babyland is about one hour north of Atlanta off US 129.

GOURDCRAFT ORIGINALS

Gourdcraft Originals, Foot of Mt. Yonah on GA 255, Cleveland (706/865-4048). Gourdcraft Originals began as a lark in 1976, but is now a serious museum displaying unusual gourds from around the world as well as early American exhibits. Besides the museum area, there is a retail store where you can buy decorative gourds for use as containers, utensils, planters, toys, puzzles, mobiles and more. As they say at Gourdcraft, "Have a Gourd Day!"

Hours: Open Monday–Saturday from 10:00 a.m.–5:00 p.m., and Sunday from 1:00 p.m.–5:00 p.m. May through December. Open weekends and by appointment January through April.

Admission: Free.

Directions: The museum is about one hour north of Atlanta. Take GA 129 to GA 115 to GA 255.

LAKE LANIER ISLANDS

Lake Lanier Islands, 6950 Holiday Rd., Lake Lanier Islands (932-7200). About forty-five minutes from downtown Atlanta lies one of the city's most precious resources. Lake Lanier provides us with beauty to nourish our souls, drinking water to nourish our bodies, and a recreational beach and lake to rejuvenate our spirits.

There is something for everyone at "Atlanta's Classic Resort," from horseback riding and camping to boating, golfing, bicycle riding and, of course, the **Beach and Water Park**. At the white sandy beach you may avail yourselves of lounge chairs, locker facilities, life preservers, inner tubes and shade umbrellas. The Water Park has a wave pool and lots of splashing, twisting slides and tube rides as well as water attractions: a dark, tunnel-like slide aptly called the Typhoon, a waterslide called the Twister that has six 180-degree turns, the new TripleThreat, Intimidator, and a Kiddie Lagoon for young children that has slides, waterfalls, stationary water guns and more. Admission includes the use of sailboats, paddleboats and canoes.

The Water Park also has an 18-hole miniature golf course, a gift shop, a cafe that serves kids' favorite foods, a restaurant with barbecued chicken and hamburgers, and a refreshment stand for cold, unique drinks and ice cream.

Horseback Riding is available on miles of trails, and for young children there are pony rides. Rental rates are $12.00 for a one-hour trail ride and $5.00 for a 30-minute pony ride. **Bicycle Riding** is wonderful here. You may bring your own bikes or rent them at a cost of $2.50/hour or $10.00/day. Horse and bike rental facility operating hours are limited, so call 932-7233 in advance.

Boat Rentals are available for houseboats, group boats, pontoons, fishing, run-abouts and skimmer boats. Canoes, paddleboats and sailboats may also be rented. Call 932-7255 for detailed information, including rates and hours of operation.

Campground facilities include lakeside tent and RV sites complete with amenities such as water and electricity, a convenience store and laundry facilities. Call 932-7270 for rates and reservations.

If a high class vacation is what you are after, Lake Lanier can accommodate you at its new **hotel** (945-8787), or the **golf club**, or one of two elegant **resorts**. There are two–bedroom modern **cottages** also available.

• **Lanier Museum of Natural History**, 2601 Buford Dam Rd., Buford (932-4460) has exhibits that trace the history of the people and land of northern Georgia. There is an observation tower to view the lake, a log cabin built by Cherokee Indians, an 1818 homestead and a nature trail. Several summer programs are offered, such as "Wildlife Wednesdays." Call for program information. Open Tuesday–Friday from 12:00 noon–5:00 p.m., and Saturday from 10:00 a.m.–5:00 p.m. Admission: Free. Call for directions.

Hours: The Water Park is open Monday–Friday from 10:00 a.m.–6:00 p.m., and Saturday and Sunday from 10:00 a.m.–7:00 p.m. between Memorial Day and Labor Day. Open weekends only in May and September. Call for the hours of other amenities.

Admission: Entrance Fee: $4.00 for daily parking (annual pass $16.00). Beach and Water Park: $11.99/adults (season pass $45.95); $4.99/3-year-olds or those under 42" (season pass $18.95); and free for those age 2 and under and age 60 and over. A season pass for a family of four is $130. There is an additional fee for locker, tube and umbrella rentals.

Directions: Take I-85 north to I-985 and get off at Exit #1 or #2 and follow the signs to the lake. Or take GA 400 to GA 20 and follow the signs.

MACON

Millions of years ago, ocean waters reached the edge of what is today Macon, Georgia. As the ocean receded, it left behind enormous deposits of kaolin—white clay used today to give paint, china and stationery a stark white color. In these kaolin deposits, people have found sea shells and fossils from prehistoric times. The first inhabitants of this fertile area were Native Americans, who settled here almost 10,000 years ago. In more recent history, the kaolin industry, the Ocmulgee River and the railroad combined to make Macon an important and thriving antebellum town economically. Today, Macon is dwarfed by Atlanta, but the lives of Native Americans, white settlers, aristocrats, and African-Americans in these parts are chronicled in the many historical tours available, as well as through visits to the Ocmulgee National Monument and the Harriet Tubman Historical and Cultural Museum.

Stop by the County Convention and Visitors Bureau at I-16 and Coliseum Drive for a free slide show which will orient you to the area, maps and brochures. There is a Welcome Center at I-75 south (912/745-2668) and one at 200 Cherry Street, Terminal Station (912/743-3401) for brochures and information. Both are open Monday–Friday from 9:00 a.m.–5:30 p.m.

OCMULGEE NATIONAL MONUMENT & MUSEUM

Ocmulgee National Monument and Museum, 1207 Emery Hwy., Macon (912/752-8257). Mississippi Indians settled here as well as in other locations throughout Georgia and built enormous mounds for ceremonial and burial purposes. (We discuss the Etowah Indian Mounds in our section on Cartersville in this chapter.) The highest in this particular region is a ceremonial 45-foot-high plateau built around 1,000 A.D. which you may climb. There is a reconstructed ceremonial "earthlodge" and nature trails on the grounds.

In the **Visitors Center** you will see a short film called "People of the Macon Plateau," dioramas, artifacts, and exhibits that describe what is known about these people's culture and the Creek Indians who succeeded them and occupied this site until their forced expulsion in the 1830s. There is also a gift shop. Handicapped access is limited. The center is open daily from 9:00 a.m.–5:00 p.m. Closed on Christmas Day and New Year's Day. Admission is $1.00/person, and children age 12 and under are free.

HISTORICAL WALKING TOURS

Three different walking tours are available for the energetic family, and we suggest that you acquire detailed brochures at the Convention and Visitors Bureau to assist you in planning your walk. These brochures will also be helpful if you prefer to drive around Macon to get a sense of its history.

HARRIET TUBMAN HISTORICAL & CULTURAL MUSEUM

Harriet Tubman Historical and Cultural Museum, 340 Walnut St., Macon (912/743-8544). This museum displays the history, culture, art, and achievements of black Americans of African and Caribbean descent. There is a Resource Room and a shop that sells books, art and crafts, posters and more. The museum is open Monday–Friday from 10:00 a.m.–5:00 p.m., and Saturday from 2:00 p.m.–5:00 p.m. Admission is free, but donations are appreciated.

MUSEUM OF ARTS AND SCIENCES & MARK SMITH PLANETARIUM

Museum of Arts and Sciences/Mark Smith Planetarium, 4182 Forsyth Rd., Macon (912/477-3232). This museum houses fine arts exhibits, a gem and mineral collection, displays some artifacts unearthed in the area (including one 40-million-year-old whale skeleton), and sometimes offers hands-on experiences for children, such as a "Muddy Hands" exhibit which permitted children to watch a real potter at work and then work with clay themselves. **Live Animal Shows** are sometimes held indoors. Be sure to pick up your tickets (free with museum admission) when you arrive. There is a gift shop. Open Monday–Thursday and Saturday from 9:00 a.m.–5:00 p.m.; Friday from 9:00 a.m.–9:00 p.m.; and Sunday from 1:00 p.m.–5:00 p.m. Call for current prices. There are certain days and hours that the museum is free.

The **Planetarium** is the second largest in Georgia (second to Atlanta's Fernbank Planetarium). Shows are offered on Fridays at 7:30 p.m. and 9:00 p.m.; Saturdays at 2:00 p.m. and 3:00 p.m.; and Sundays at 3:00 p.m. The **Observatory** is open on Friday and Saturday evenings.

• Outside you will find a petting zoo and nature trails.

• The building has limited handicapped access. Call for specific access information.

FESTIVALS

You might try to arrange a trip to Macon to coincide with one of its fun festivals. The most spectacular is, of course, the 10-day annual **Cherry Blossom Festival** which boasts 130,000 pink and white blossomed Yoshino Cherry Trees. Macon calls itself the "Cherry Blossom Capital of the World," and indeed it has many more trees and flowers than Washington, D.C. This festival has an international theme and features a parade, street party with music, dancing and food, hot air balloons, sports, tours and exhibits, cooking contests, storytellers and, in all, over 150 events.

Directions: Take I-75 south from Atlanta directly to Macon.

NORTH GEORGIA MOUNTAINS

If you need an unhurried, relaxed day in your life, head to the North Georgia mountains! There are many places to go where you can picnic, hike, raft, bicycle, horseback ride, or enjoy the numerous waterfalls and scenic areas. Below are descriptions of some of our favorite places for a day trip that are not more than a 90-minute drive from Atlanta.

UNICOI STATE PARK

Unicoi State Park, two miles NE of downtown Helen via GA 356, Helen (706/878-2201). Just a few minutes north of Nora Mill Granary is Unicoi State Park, an area which is terrific for hiking, water play at the lake and beach, and camping (day or overnight). If you want to stay overnight but do not want to camp, Unicoi has a lodge and cottages. (Our family spent a night at the lodge and the kids thought it was great fun.) Both book up at the beginning of the season, so call well in advance. Unicoi also features special monthly programs, a Fireside Arts and Crafts Show in February and an Appalachian Music Festival in July. See our chapters "Festivals and Special Events" and "Performances" for more information about these events.

ANNA RUBY FALLS

From the northern boundary of Unicoi, drive on Anna Ruby Falls Road, park at the Visitors Center ($2.00) and take a short, scenic half-mile hike to the spectacular twin Anna Ruby Falls. These falls feed into Unicoi Lake, join the Chattahoochee River, flow across Florida and empty into the Gulf of Mexico. The path is smooth and wide enough for a stroller. Don't expect to be alone—this is a popular attraction, but definitely worth a visit. There are picnic sites in the Anna Ruby Falls Scenic Area with tables, grills and drinking water. Sanitation facilities are not available in the winter. Call 706/878-1448 for more information.

DUKE'S CREEK RECREATION AREA

Duke's Creek Recreation Area, near Helen on GA 348, 1.5 miles west of its junction with GA 356. This is a great place for a family to spend a Sunday afternoon. You can take a brief 15-minute walk down to Duke's Creek Falls, hike back up (about 30 minutes), then have a well-deserved picnic. This is a fairly popular place, so if you find there are too many other families for your liking, head off on one of the side trails to find a quieter spot.

RAVEN CLIFFS

Raven Cliffs, just north of Helen on Richard Russell Scenic Highway (GA 348) about 1.3 miles from the Duke's Creek Recreation Area sign. Park in the gravel parking lot and begin your trek to Raven Cliffs along a 2.5-mile trail that is the most diverse of any hike we have taken in Georgia. There are a series of waterfalls, streams, a beautiful forest, and, of course, magnificent cliffs. This hike is wonderful for families with young children, even if you can make it only part way. A word of caution: Stay on the main path and avoid the side paths that head directly to the water, as they are often very slippery.

AMICALOLA STATE FALLS PARK

Amicalola State Falls Park, on Hwy. 52 west of Dahlonega (706/265-2885) is pushing our 90-minute driving limit for family day trips. Amicalola is a Cherokee Indian word that means "tumbling waters." These 729-foot falls are the highest and most magnificent in the state. There are 3½ miles of hiking trails around the mountains and falls, three playgrounds, fishing and camping. If you do not wish to hike and picnic, you can drive your car to the falls and eat nearby at a new restaurant with a panoramic view of the area.

DILLARD HOUSE

Dillard House, Highway 441 in Dillard (800/541-0671 or 706/746-5348). If you live on the northern outskirts of metropolitan Atlanta, you should definitely take a 90-minute day trip to the Dillard House, where you can eat your fill of a delicious meal served in a family-style restaurant, visit their small petting zoo, and take the kids horseback riding. Even the youngest can ride, while you walk the horse around a grassy area. They also have more extensive facilities for daylong family horseback riding. The gift shop sells handicrafts, gift items, and their own jams, jellies, hams, peanut brittle and local honey. Dillard House also has overnight accommodations.

REVEREND HOWARD FINSTER'S
PARADISE GARDEN

Paradise Garden, Rena St., Summerville (706/857-2926). Reverend Finster is a folk artist of world renown whose work is increasingly popular. He did the cover artwork for David Byrne's Talking Heads album "Little Creatures," and his work has appeared in many galleries, including a show at the Georgia State Capitol. A special trip to Summerville is worth your time: wander around the unique, interesting and playful yard of sculptures made from everyday items put together in provocative ways. See 14-foot Coke bottles, Reverend Finster's casket-in-waiting, surreal images of famous deceased people and angels. We guarantee your conversation on the ride back to Atlanta will not be boring, as everyone, young and old, will have had their imaginations titillated. Open: Daily from 10:00 a.m.–6:00 p.m. You might want to time your visit to coincide with the annual Howard Finster Festival held in May in Dowdy Park, Summerville. Call 706/857-4033 for dates and times.

Resources

SPECIAL ASSISTANCE TELEPHONE NUMBERS

Ambulance, Fire & Police 911

Al-Anon & Alateen Family Groups 843-0311

Alcoholics Anonymous 525-3178

American Red Cross 881-9800

Auditory Education Center for
the Hearing Impaired .... 352-4145 or 351-4327

Battered Women's Shelter 873-1766
    Cobb County 427-3390
    DeKalb County 688-9436

The Center for the Visually Impaired 875-9011

Child Abuse Hotlines:
    Clayton County 996-4357
    Cobb County .... 528-5015 or 499-3911
    DeKalb County 370-5066
    Douglas County 489-3000
    Fulton County 756-4200
    Gwinnett County 995-2122

Child Care Solutions—Save the Children 885-1585

Easter Seal of North Georgia 633-9609

Egleston Children's Hospital 325-6000

Emergency Mental Health/Drug Abuse:
    Clayton County 996-4357
    Cobb County 422-0202

DeKalb County... 892-4646
Douglas County.. 422-0202
Fulton County 730-1600
Gwinnett County .... 963-8141 or 985-2494

Georgia Council for International Visitors
Language Bank... 873-6170

Georgia Council on Child Abuse
24–Hour Help Line 870-6555

March of Dimes 350-9800

Missing Children Hotline 800/843-5678

Pediatric Dentists—Northern District
Dental Society Referral Service 270-1635

Pediatrician Referrals—
Medical Association of Atlanta 881-1714

Poison Control Center.. 589-4400

Runaway Hotline 800/231-6946

Scottish Rite Children's Medical Center..................... 256-5252

Time/Temperature 455-7141

Toy Safety Hotline... 800/638-2772

Traveler's AID of Metropolitan Atlanta 527-7400

United Way First Call for Help Hotline 527-7370

Visiting Nurse Corporation of
Metropolitan Atlanta 454-0900

CONVENTION & VISITORS BUREAUS

Atlanta Convention & Visitors Bureau — Main Office
233 Peachtree St., N.E.
Atlanta, Georgia 30303
222-6688

Atlanta Convention & Visitors Bureau Information Centers:
Peachtree Center Mall (Weekdays)
233 Peachtree St.
Atlanta, Georgia 30303

Lenox Square Mall (Wednesday–Sunday)
3393 Peachtree Rd.
Atlanta, Georgia 30326

Underground Atlanta (Daily)
Pryor & Alabama Sts.
Atlanta, Georgia 30334
577-2148

Sweet Auburn Welcome Center
(Inside the APEX Museum)
145 Auburn Ave., NE
Atlanta, Georgia 30303
521-2739

Clayton County Local Welcome Center
8712 Tara Blvd.
Jonesboro, Georgia 30236
478-4800

Cobb County Convention & Visitors Bureau
1100 Circle 75 Pkwy.
P.O. Box 672827
Marietta, Georgia 30067-0048
933-7228

The DeKalb Convention & Visitors Bureau
750 Commerce Dr.
Suite 201
Decatur, Georgia 30030
378-2525

DeKalb Welcome Center
Old Courthouse on the Square
Decatur, Georgia 30030
378-7013

The Gwinnett Convention & Visitors Bureau
1230 Atkinson Rd.
P.O. Box 1245
Lawrenceville, Georgia 30246
963-5128

Marietta Welcome Center & Visitors Bureau
4 Depot St.
Marietta, Georgia 30060
429-1115

North Fulton County Chamber of Commerce
1025 Old Roswell Rd.
Suite 101
Roswell, Georgia 30076
993-8806

Georgia Department of Industry, Trade & Tourism
285 Peachtree Center Ave.
Atlanta, Georgia 30303
656-3590

Georgia Department of Natural Resources
Division of Parks, Recreation & Historical Sites
205 Butler St., S.E.
Atlanta, Georgia 30334
656-3530

PUBLICATIONS

• *The Atlanta Jewish Times* (352-2400). This weekly publication features articles about local, national and international events of interest to the Jewish community, along with calendars listing community events, performances and festivals. Available at bookstores and Jewish establishments throughout the city. Cost is 75¢/issue; subscription rate is $29/year.

• *The Atlanta Journal and Constitution*'s Saturday *Leisure Guide* (522-4141). The *Leisure Guide* provides a comprehensive summary of the upcoming week's events as well as feature articles on attractions, festivals and cultural events. The *Leisure Guide* is included in the Saturday paper. Newsstand price is 50¢/issue. Subscription rate is approximately $95.00/year for the Saturday and Sunday papers.

• *Atlanta Magazine* (872-3100). The monthly magazine's overview of upcoming major events usually includes some events of interest to families. Cost is $2.50/issue; subscription rate is $15.00/year.

• *Atlanta Parent* (325-1763). This monthly parenting newspaper is filled with articles, calendars and advertisements geared to families with children. The free publication is available at libraries, schools, stores and other locations.

• *The Atlanta Tribune* (587-0501). The newsmagazine features articles, business news, calendars and advertisements catering to African-American Atlantans. The semi-monthly publication is available at some libraries, bookstores, groceries and other locations. Cost is $1.00/issue; subscription rate is $20/year.

• *Atlanta Walks,* by Ren and Helen Davis and published by Peachtree Publishers, Inc. This pocket-size book describes about thirty different walks throughout the metro Atlanta area., some of which may be of interest to families with older children. $9.95.

• *Bed and Breakfast Directory* (651-9461). The Georgia Department of Industry, Trade and Tourism publishes a free annual guide to bed and breakfast inns in Georgia. Call the above number to obtain the directory.

• *Creative Loafing* (688-5623), *Topside Loaf* (642-9774) and *the Gwinnett Loaf* (923-7181) are good sources for finding information about festivals, performances and special events around town. *Creative Loafing* covers the metro Atlanta area, *Topside Loaf* specializes in places and events of interest to north Atlanta (Roswell, East Cobb, etc.), and *the Gwinnett Loaf* specializes in Gwinnett County. The free weekly publication is available at stores, newsstands, restaurants and other locations.

• *Ethnic Atlanta, The Complete Guide to Atlanta's Ethnic Communities* by Janet Schwartz and Denise Black and published by Longstreet Press, Inc. $14.95. This is the first-ever, comprehensive guidebook to all of Atlanta's ethnic communities, describing:

— restaurants
— festivals & special events
— markets, groceries & bakeries
— import stores & shopping centers
— schools & classes

— attractions
— entertainment
— community groups
— museums & galleries
— newspapers, books & videos

• *Georgia Byways* (664-6432). This quarterly magazine contains information about attractions and events throughout Georgia that are off the beaten path. The publication is available in bookstores throughout the city. Cost is $3.50/issue; subscription rate is $14.00/year.

• *North Georgia Journal* (642-5569). The quarterly magazine is filled with articles about the history, lifestyles, attractions, festivals and special events of various locales in North Georgia. The publication is available in bookstores throughout the city. Cost is $3.95/issue; subscription rate is $15.00/year.

• *Our Kids* (438-1400). This monthly parenting newspaper contains a detailed calendar listing festivals, performances and special events of interest to families with children. The free publication is available at libraries, schools, stores and other locations.

• *The Ultimate Atlanta Guidebook,* compiled by the staff of the *Atlanta Journal-Constitution* and published by Longstreet Press, Inc. This handy reference guide to Atlanta covers where to shop, eat, party and sleep and includes photographs and helpful maps. $7.95.

TOP 25 PLACES TO GO & THINGS TO DO

Airport Visits
Alliance Children's Theatre
American Adventures
Atlanta Botanical Garden
Atlanta History Center
Big Shanty Museum &
   Kennesaw Mountain
Bookstores & Libraries
Center for Puppetry Arts
Chattahoochee Nature Center
   & Chattahoochee River
   National Recreation Area
Farmers Markets & Pick Your
   Own
Fernbank Museum of Natural
   History & IMAX Theatre
Fernbank Science Center
   Planetarium Show

Festivals
Georgia State Capitol Building
   & Georgia State Museum of
   Science and Industry
High Museum of Art
Michael C. Carlos Museum
SciTrek
Six Flags Over Georgia
Southeastern Railway
   Museum
Stone Mountain Park
Sweet Auburn District &
   Martin Luther King, Jr.
   Historic Site
White Water Park
Wren's Nest
Yellow River Game Ranch
Zoo Atlanta

FREE ACTIVITIES FOR FAMILIES

Airport Visits
Animal Shelters & Humane
   Societies
Art Galleries
*Atlanta Botanical Garden
Atlanta Celebrity Walk
*Atlanta History Center

Atlanta International Museum
   of Art & Design
*Atlanta Journal and
   Constitution* Lobby Exhibit
Bookstores
Bradley Observatory &
   Planetarium

* During limited hours these attractions are free to the public.

Buford Fish Hatchery
Bush Mountain Outdoor
Activity Center
Chattahoochee River National
Recreational Area
Cobb County Petting Farm
Cobb County Youth Museum
** Day Trips
Decatur & DeKalb County
Historical Driving Tours
DeKalb Historical Society
Museum
Family Concerts
Farmers Markets
Federal Reserve Monetary
Museum
Fernbank Science Center
(except the Planetarium Show)
** Festivals
Fort Peachtree
Galleries
Georgia Department of
Archives and History
Georgia Governor's Mansion
Georgia Historical Aviation
Museum
Georgia State Capitol Building
& Georgia State Museum of
Science and Industry
Gwinnett County Museum
Gwinnett Plantation Historical
Driving Tour
Hapeville Depot Museum
Herndon Home
*High Museum
High Museum of Art Folk Art
& Photography Galleries
Hiking & Nature Trails
Hotel Hopping
Jonesboro & Clayton County
Historical Driving Tours

Kennesaw Mountain National
Battlefield Park
Martin Luther King, Jr.
Historic Site
Libraries
Marietta Historical Walking
Tours
Marietta National Cemetery
Medical Museum of Crawford
Long Hospital
Michael C. Carlos Museum
Johnny Mercer Exhibit
Monastery of the Holy Spirit
**Movie Theatres Special
Summer Festivals
**North Georgia Mountains—
Day Trips
Nurseries
Oakland Cemetery
Panola Mountain
Pet Stores
W.H. Reynolds Nature Preserve
Rhodes Hall
Roswell Historical Tours
Roswell Fire Museum
Shopping Malls—Browsing
Southeastern Railway Museum
Southface Energy Institute
Sweet Auburn Curb
Market/Atlanta Municipal
Market
Sweetwater Creek State Park
Telephone Museum
**Tours of the Working World
Toy Stores
TULA
Underground Atlanta
Urban Nirvana
Cator Woolford Memorial
Garden
Zachor Holocaust Center

** These attractions sometimes have nominal admission or parking fees.

BIRTHDAY PARTY PROGRAMS

Abracadabra Children's Theatre at Onstage Atlanta
American Adventures
Arcades
Atlanta Attack
Atlanta Braves/Colonial Baking Co.—Birthday Party Program
Birthday Party sections of *Atlanta Parent* and *Our Kids* newspapers
    provide names of clowns, magicians, musicians and other
    performers available to entertain at parties.
Bowling
Center for Puppetry Arts
Circus Arts Studio
Cobb County Petting Farm
Fernbank Science Center
Fire Departments
Gymnastic Centers
Ice Skating
Kids Comedy Theatre
Miniature Golf
Movie Theatres
Peachtree DeKalb Airport Observation Area
Playcenters—Indoors
Pony Rides
The Red Barn
Roller Skating
SciTrek
Southeastern Railway Museum
Southern Order of Storytellers
Stone Mountain Park—Play Structure & Wildlife Trails
Swimming—Atlanta Marriott Northwest, private pools & some
    YM/YWCAs
Tours of the Working World
Toy Stores—Party Rooms such as the Toy School
Yellow River Game Ranch
Wren's Nest
Zoo Atlanta Night Crawlers (overnight fun)

RAINY WEATHER IDEAS

African-American Panoramic
  Experience (APEX Museum)
American Adventures
Atlanta Journal & Constitution
  Lobby Exhibit
Animal Shelters & Humane
  Societies
Art Galleries
Atlanta History Center
Atlanta Museum
Big Shanty Museum
Bookstores
Bowling
Bulloch Hall
Carter Presidential Center—
  Museum of the Jimmy Carter
  Library
Center for Puppetry Arts
CNN Studio Tour
Cobb County Youth Museum
Cyclorama
Day Trips to Tennessee
  Aquarium & Other Indoor
  Attractions
DeKalb Historical Society
  Museum
Farmers Markets
Federal Reserve Monetary
  Museum
Fernbank Museum of Natural
  History & IMAX Theatre
Fernbank Science Center
Georgia Department of
  Archives and History
Georgia State Capitol Building
  & Georgia State Museum of
  Science and Industry
Gwinnett County Museum

Hammonds House Galleries &
  Resource Center
Hapeville Depot Museum
Hardware Stores
Hartsfield Airport
Herndon Home
High Museum of Art
High Museum of Folk Art &
  Photography Galleries
Hobby Shows & Collector Fairs
Hotel Hopping
Ice Skating
Libraries
Medical Museum—Crawford
  Long Hospital
Michael C. Carlos Museum
Miniature Golf—Indoors
Movies
Nature Stores
Performing Arts Events
Pet Stores & Pet Shows
Playcenters—Indoors
Road to Tara Museum
Roller Skating
Roswell Fire Museum
SciTrek
Shopping Malls
Sweet Auburn Curb Market/
  Atlanta Municipal Market
Swimming—Indoor
Telephone Museum
Tours of the Working World
Toy Stores
TULA
Underground Atlanta
World of Coca-Cola
Wren's Nest

SCHOOL & SCOUT GROUP ACTIVITIES

Note:
- Be aware that some places are booked well ahead of time
- Verify group age and size
- Ask for special group rates
- Ask if a tour guide is available

Airports & Air Museums
Animal Shelters, Animal
  Societies & Pet Stores
Art Museums & Galleries
Atlanta Botanical Garden
Atlanta History Center
Bowling
Bulloch Hall
Cagle's Milk Farm
Camping
Carter Presidential Center
CASS/Center for Astronomy &
  Space Sciences
Center for Puppetry Arts
Chattahoochee Nature Center
CNN Studio Tour
Cobb County Petting Farm
Cobb County Youth Museum
Cyclorama
Day Trips
Farmers Markets
Fernbank Museum of Natural
  History & IMAX Theatre
Fernbank Science Center &
  Planetarium Shows
Festivals
Georgia Dome
Georgia State Capitol &
  Georgia Museum of Science
  & Industry
GeoSphere
High Museum of Art
High Museum of Folk Art &

Photography Galleries
Hiking & Nature Trails
Martin Luther King, Jr. Historic
  Site & Sweet Auburn District
Michael C. Carlos Museum
Monastery of the Holy Spirit
Nurseries
Outdoor Activity Center at
  Bush Mountain
Panola Mountain
Performing Arts Events—e.g.,
  Kids Comedy Theatre, Atlanta
  Shakespeare Company
The Red Barn
Roswell Fire Museum
Sandy Springs Historic Site
SciTrek Museum—overnight
  fun
Skating
Southface Energy Institute
Stone Mountain—Wildlife Trail
  & Petting Farm, Hike to the
  Top, Train Ride, Riverboat
  Ride & Overnight Camping
Sweetwater Creek State
  Conservation Park
Tours of the Working World—
  Fire Stations, Police Stations
  & Television Studios
World of Coca-Cola
Wren's Nest
Yellow River Game Ranch
Zoo Atlanta—Overnight Fun

CLASSES & WORKSHOPS
SUMMER PROGRAMS & CAMPS

There are extensive classes, workshops and summer programs for children of all ages offered by profit and non-profit facilities throughout the metropolitan Atlanta area, including courses in the visual arts, performing arts, literary arts, foreign languages, sciences, nature, computers, cooking and other fields. Our list could not be all inclusive, so we limited it to the classes and programs offered by museums, art centers, nature centers, those schools and colleges which offer varied or unique classes, and a handful of other organizations of which you may not be aware.

■ CLASSES & WORKSHOPS ■

Computers & Academics
CASS/Center for Astronomy &
   Space Science
Georgia State University
Kennesaw State College

Folk Art & History
Atlanta History Center
Atlanta Preservation Center
   Tours
Bulloch Hall
Chattahoochee Nature Center
DeKalb Historic Complex
Georgia Department of Natural
   Resources
Georgia State University
Michael C. Carlos Museum
Sweetwater Creek State
   Conservation Park

Foreign Languages
The Arts Exchange
Georgia State University
Soapstone Center for the Arts

Literary Arts
The Arts Exchange
Georgia State University
Pinckneyville Arts Center

Music
A.R.T. Station
The Arts Exchange
Georgia Department of Natural
   Resources
Georgia State University
Pinckneyville Arts Center
Soapstone Center for the Arts
Spruill Education Center

Nature & Sciences
Atlanta Botanical Garden
Atlanta Humane Society
Chattahoochee Nature Center
Dunwoody Nature Center
Fernbank Museum of Natural
   History
Fernbank Science Center
Georgia Department of Natural

Resources
Georgia State University
GeoSphere
Nature Stores
Outdoor Activity Center at
Bush Mountain
Panola Mountain
W.H. Reynolds Nature Preserve
SciTrek
Spruill Education Center
Sweetwater Creek State
Conservation Park
U.S. Space Camp

Performing Arts
Alliance Theatre School
The Art Place—Mountain View
Artsbusters/CREATE
A.R.T. Station
The Arts Exchange
Atlanta Jewish Community
Center
Atlanta Workshop Players
Bulloch Hall
Callanwolde Arts Center
Center for Puppetry Arts
Circus Arts Studio
Cobb Children's Theatre
Doraville Arts Musical Theatre
Georgia State University
Gwinnett Fine Arts Center
Jamaican Dance Theater
Kid's Talk & Teen Talk
Michael C. Carlos Museum
Nexus Contemporary Art
Center/Academy Theatre's
Kids Klub on Imagination
Street

Pinckneyville Arts Center
Soapstone Center for the Arts
Spruill Education Center
Stage Door Players

Visual Arts
Abernathy Arts and Crafts
Center
The Arts Connection (Oxford
Book Store at Pharr Road)
The Art Place—Mountain View
A.R.T. Station
The Arts Exchange
The Atlanta College of Art
Atlanta History Center
Bulloch Hall
Callanwolde Arts Center
Chastain Arts Center
Georgia State University
Gilbert House
Gwinnett Fine Arts Center
High Museum of Art
Kennesaw State College
Mable House/South Cobb Arts
Alliance
Marietta/Cobb Museum of Art
Michael C. Carlos Museum
Nexus Contemporary Arts
Center
Pinckneyville Arts Center
Soapstone Center for the Arts
South Fulton Arts Center
Spruill Education Center

■■■ SUMMER PROGRAMS & CAMPS ■■■

Abernathy Arts and Crafts
  Center
Academy Theatre
Agnes Scott College
Alliance Theatre School
The Art Place—Mountain View
Artsbusters/CREATE
The Arts Exchange
A.R.T. Station
Atlanta Attack
Atlanta Botanical Garden
Atlanta College of Art
Atlanta Hawks
Atlanta Jewish Community
  Center
Atlanta Workshop Players
Bulloch Hall
Callanwolde Fine Arts Center
CASS/Center for Astronomy &
  Space Sciences
Center for Puppetry Arts
Challengers Club Space Camp
Chastain Arts Center
Chattahoochee Nature Center
Children's Book & Gift Market
Circus Arts Studio
Clark Atlanta University—
  African Summer Camp
DeKalb College
DeKalb Historical Society's Log
  Cabin Story Hours
The Discovery Store
Emory University Sports Camps
Emory University Tennis &
  Computer Camps
Fernbank Museum of Natural
  History
Fernbank Science Center
Georgia Department of Natural

Resources
Georgia Institute of Technology
Georgia State University
Gwinnett Fine Arts Center
High Museum of Art
Hobbit Hall
Kennesaw State College
Kennesaw Mountain National
  Battlefield Park
Mable House/South Cobb Arts
  Alliance
Marietta/Cobb Museum of Art
Michael C. Carlos Museum
The Nature Company
Oglethorpe University
Outdoor Activity Center at
  Bush Mountain
Outdoor Survival Camp
Panola Mountain
Pinckneyville Arts Center
Private Schools (Westminster,
  Paideia, Montessori Schools,
  Children's School, Friends
  School of Atlanta, Galloway,
  etc.)
Recreation Centers & Youth
  Organizations
SciTrek
Soapstone Center for the Arts
South Fulton Arts Center
Spelman College
Spruill Education Center
Stone Mountain Park
Sweetwater Creek State
  Conservation Park
TellTale Theatre Camp
The Toy School
Zoo Atlanta

Index

escapes!

• • •

true stories from the edge

Laura Scandiffio

true stories from the edge

escapes!

ANNICK PRESS

TORONTO + NEW YORK + VANCOUVER

Annick Press Ltd.

All rights reserved. No part of this work covered by the copyrights hereon may be reproduced or used in any form or by any means — graphic, electronic, or mechanical — without the prior written permission of the publisher.

We acknowledge the support of the Canada Council for the Arts, the Ontario Arts Council, the Government of Ontario through the Ontario Book Publishers Tax Credit program and the Ontario Book Initiative, and the Government of Canada through the Book Publishing Industry Development Program (BPIDP) for our publishing activities.

Edited by Pam Robertson
Copy edited by Pam Robertson
Cover art by Scott Cameron
Design by Irvin Cheung/iCheung Design

Cataloging in Publication Data

Scandiffio, Laura

    Escapes! / written by Laura Scandiffio ; illustrated by Stephen MacEachern.

(True stories from the edge)
Includes index.
ISBN 1-55037-823-6 (bound).—ISBN 1-55037-822-8 (pbk.)

    1. Escapes—Juvenile literature. I. MacEachern, Stephen II. Title. III. Series.

G525.S23 2003   j904   C2003-901897-0

The text was typeset in Bembo.

Distributed in Canada by	Distributed in the U.S.A. by	Published in the U.S.A. by
Firefly Books Ltd.	Firefly Books (U.S.) Inc.	Annick Press (U.S.) Ltd.
3680 Victoria Park Avenue	P.O. Box 1338	
Willowdale, ON	Ellicott Station	
M2H 3K1	Buffalo, NY 14205	

Printed and bound in Canada by Friesens, Altona, Manitoba

Visit us at **www.annickpress.com**

Contents

Introduction
Struggles for Freedom

A SLAVE, CHAINS ON HER ANKLES AND WRISTS, is tugged to the auction block. A man sent to prison for his beliefs watches his guard close the cell door and fears that he has seen daylight for the last time. A soldier, hands on his head, is marched at gunpoint through the grim gates of his enemy's prisoner of war camp.

All very different people, from different times and places, and all dreaming of the same thing —

Escape!

It's an impulse every human being feels when trapped. No one is willingly confined, and every captive dreams of freedom. A special few will act on this slim hope.

Men and women have used their wits and courage to escape from all sorts of threats: from slave owners, from dungeons, from enemy armies, from physical danger. They may be fleeing jailers or governments. Some have been shut in by four walls, while other prisons are the kind you can't touch, but which trap people alive — in slavery or oppression.

The greater the obstacles to be overcome, the more impossible escape seems, the more the stories fascinate us. Across the ages, different places have come to mind as the ultimate challenges for escapers. Each era has had its notorious prisons — from England's Tower of London, where people who posed a threat to the government awaited execution, to France's Bastille, where inmates could be locked away their whole lives without a trial. Slavery — whether in ancient Rome or in many of the American states during the 1800s — was a fate millions dreamed of fleeing. The prisoner of war camps of the Second World War (1939–45), with their barbed wire, armed guards, and spotlights, seemed inescapable to all but a determined few. And the "Cold War" that followed, between the Soviet Union and the Western powers, brought with it the infamous East German border wall, which kept all but the most desperate defectors behind its barrier of concrete, mines, and armed patrols with orders to shoot.

And yet despite the odds, a few found ways past these deadly traps, ways that show the amazing range of human creativity. They got out with clever disguises or ingenious hiding places; by patiently waiting or boldly dashing forward; by using whatever materials were at hand, crafting tools of escape from even the most innocent-looking objects.

★ ★ ★

"I looked at my hands to see if I was the same person now I was free. There was such a glory over everything, the sun came like gold through the trees, and over the fields, and I felt like I was in heaven."

Harriet Tubman, an American slave who escaped from her master in 1849, remembered her first thrilling taste of freedom. Her reaction is surprisingly similar to the feelings recalled by other escapers, whatever the place and time. Many speak of the same exhilarating moment when, though they could scarcely believe it, they were actually free.

Once Harriet Tubman made it north to freedom she wasn't content to stay there, however. Despite the dangers, she returned south again and again to help other slaves escape, more than three hundred in all. She became part of the network of antislavery helpers known as the Underground Railroad, people who hid runaway slaves on their journeys north out of the slave states, often all the way to Canada.

Still, escape from the slave states was no easy matter. Often thousands of miles had to be crossed, with professional slave catchers close on runaways' trails. But until the Emancipation Proclamation freed all slaves in 1863, many were desperate enough to try. One slave even had friends package him inside a wooden box, three feet by two feet, and mail him to the state of Pennsylvania, where slavery was illegal. He spent 27 hours inside, and no one paid much attention to the label: This Side Up, With Care. Amazingly, he survived, and Underground Railroad workers unpacked Henry "Box" Brown, as he became known, in Philadelphia.

Some people have managed to escape all on their own, without aid, but many others could not have been successful without the bravery of secret helpers on the outside. The Underground Railroad was the most famous of such networks in the 1800s. A hundred years later, the Second World War saw the birth of secret organizations dedicated to helping Allied soldiers escape or evade capture by the enemy.

★ ★ ★

"It is every officer's duty to escape..."

An Allied combat pilot of the Second World War faced huge risks every time he climbed into the cockpit. If shot down, he hoped to bail out and parachute to safety. But even if he survived the landing his troubles were only beginning. His mission had probably taken him far over enemy territory — maybe Germany or occupied France. Chances were he'd been spotted on the way down, and enemy soldiers were already rushing to take him prisoner.

Military intelligence in England realized how critical it was to get these pilots, as well as the soldiers stuck in prisoner of war (POW) camps, back into action. A new branch of the British Secret Intelligence Service — dubbed MI9 — was formed. Its job was to do everything possible to keep downed pilots out of enemy hands and to help prisoners of war to escape. Working round-the-clock, the people at MI9 came up with gadgets and schemes to stay ahead of the enemy. The "science" of escape was born.

One unconventional technical officer at MI9, named Christopher Clayton-Hutton, realized that many escape tricks had already been discovered — by the soldiers of the First World War. Clayton-Hutton recruited schoolboys to read memoirs from World War I for clues to what a soldier needed in order to escape. He was impressed by the boys' work. Many of the ingenious escape methods of the previous war had been forgotten.

Clayton-Hutton scanned the boys' list of escape aids, and came across "dyes, wire, needles, copying paper, saws, and a dozen other items, some of which I should never have dreamed of."

He set to work on an "escape kit" that every pilot could carry in the front trouser pocket of his uniform and that held essentials to keeping him at liberty: compass, matches, needle and thread, razor, and soap (looking grubby was a sure giveaway when you were on the run!). Food was provided in small, concentrated form: malted milk tablets or toffee.

MI9 also wracked its brains to help prisoners of war escape their German camps. Getting out was hard enough, but once outside a crucial item was needed if they hoped to stay free — a map. Escaping POWs hoped to cross the German border into Switzerland, a country that had remained neutral in the war. From there they could make contact with helpers and get home.

But without a map, they were more likely to be recaptured while wandering near the border, lost. And it couldn't be just any old map. It had to open without rustling (escapers often consulted maps while search parties were combing the area nearby), and it had to be readable even when wet, and no matter how many times it was folded and creased. MI9 hit upon the solution: reproduce maps on silk.

But how would they get them to the prisoners? All POWs received mail from home, so MI9 came up with ways to sneak the maps in through letters and packages from "relatives." Working with the music company HMV, they inserted thin maps inside records, which would be sent to prisoners by nonexistent aunts.

As the war continued, MI9's tricks got cleverer. POWs were sent blankets that, once washed, revealed a sewing pattern that could be cut and stitched to make a German-looking jacket — a perfect disguise. The razor company Gillette helped to make magnetized razor blades that worked as compasses. Wires that cut bars were smuggled in shoelaces, screwdrivers inside cricket bats.

The stories of the lucky Allied soldiers who escaped from Germany were kept secret for many years, and important details were changed in or left out of books published after the war. Many people feared that a new war with the Soviet Union was on the horizon, and it would be foolish to give away escape tricks and routes that might prove useful during the Cold War. After all, a known escape trick is a useless one.

It was the Cold War that gave rise to one of the most famous symbols of imprisonment, and of the dream of escape: Germany's

Berlin Wall. This concrete barrier, topped with barbed wire and dotted with watchtowers and arc lamps, was begun by the Communist government of East Germany in 1961 to halt the flow of thousands of citizens defecting to West Germany. Soon the entire country was split in two by the border wall. In East Berlin some people could look out their apartment windows and see into the homes of West Berliners living on the other side. And yet they were completely cut off from one another. As one border guard put it, even though the other side "was only six or seven meters away I would never go there. It would have been easier to go to the moon. The moon was closer."

Although many residents of East Germany accepted their government and living conditions, others found they could not. Freedom — the freedom to travel, to say and write what they believed without fear of punishment — beckoned. Until the wall was torn down in 1989, countless escapes were attempted at the wall, and many died trying to get across it to the West. They tried climbing over it, tunneling under it, driving past it hidden in the cars of West Germans. Once again, it seemed that the bigger the obstacle placed between a person and freedom, the more human creativity is inspired to meet the challenge.

★ ★ ★

Imagine for a moment that you have been taken prisoner. You and your fellow captives are marched in a long line toward barracks behind barbed wire. As you file along the winding path leading to the compound, the guards at the head of the line suddenly disappear around a corner. You twist your head around. The guards bringing up the rear are also momentarily out of sight as you round the bend. For this one instant, you won't be spotted if you dive out of line and roll under the bushes along the path. You have mere seconds to make up your mind. What do you do? Stay in line and face the misery — but safety — of captivity? Or seize the moment and make a break for it?

Anyone in your place will dream of escape, but only a few will act on the impulse. MI9 estimated that far fewer than one percent of Allied prisoners of war took the plunge and escaped in World War II. But who? What kind of person?

Psychologists have found that people who escape often share the same character traits. They're not necessarily the strongest or the boldest, but they are open-minded and flexible — people who can improvise on the spot and adapt quickly to changes. If one tactic fails, they try another. They are willing to take risks and learn from mistakes. Often they are good actors, able to blend in with locals and to hide their fear or their intentions. And they're not the type to freeze when placed in a difficult situation, as many people do. They can keep a clear head and not panic. Perhaps most importantly, they firmly believe that their future survival depends on themselves, and no one else.

Pierre Mairesse Lebrun, a French cavalry lieutenant imprisoned by the Germans in World War II, felt that in some ways the personal bravery needed for an escape was even greater than that needed for the battlefield: "I think it's easy to be brave in war, unless you are a complete coward. Escaping is a voluntary act of bravery, which is very difficult. Very difficult when you are risking your life."

Lebrun himself certainly had his share of courage. Using his friend's cupped hands as a stirrup, he vaulted over his prison camp's barbed wire fence in plain view of the guards. Under fire, Lebrun dashed for the outer wall, bobbing and weaving like a hunted rabbit. He waited until the guards stopped to reload their guns, then scrambled over the second wall. Even his enemies had to admire his nerve: "For sheer mad and calculated daring," wrote the camp's German security officer, "the successful escape of ... Pierre Mairesse Lebrun, will not, I think, ever be beaten."

Perhaps not, but it certainly faces some tough competition. What follows are ten stories of real people who refused to give up their dreams of escape, no matter how huge the struggle.

Some are stories of people born into slavery, but who dreamed of freedom. And of those whose freedom was taken away from them, but who fought to win it back. Sailors kidnapped by slave-traders and dragged across the Sahara. A man captured in his homeland by the army of ancient Rome and condemned to fight to the death as a gladiator. A family that took to the air to cross a wall that seemed to have sprung up overnight, dividing their country in half and holding them prisoners in their own land.

These are dramas from across time and around the globe. From medieval knights trapped with their lady in a castle under siege, to modern diplomats who slipped through the fingers of captors in an embassy hostage-taking that shocked the world. From political prisoners who found ingenious ways out of some of history's most feared prisons, to soldiers who hatched a bold plan to break out of Germany's "escape-proof" camp, and a fighter pilot who faced every airman's worst nightmare — being trapped alive in a crashing plane.

All true stories of human courage, but also stories of hope — because hope is what kept these remarkable people going in the face of the most overwhelming obstacles and dangers.

Paris, France, 1754

A GUARD PEERED THROUGH THE SMALL HOLE in the heavy wood door. With a sigh he watched the prisoner inside — writing again! This flood of letters, begging for his case to be reviewed, was a nuisance. The guard let the metal flap slam over the hole and walked away, shaking his head. Henri Latude could write until doomsday, he thought. It would come to nothing.

Inside the cold cell, the prisoner rubbed his ink-stained fingers to warm them. Blinking wearily, he angled his sheet of paper into the shaft of light streaming from a small chink in the stone wall. He had been locked up in the Bastille for five years without a trial, put away by a *lettre de cachet* — a piece of paper that let officials arrest someone in the King's name and keep him in prison for as long as they liked.

A foolish prank had landed him here. Like countless young men, Latude had left the countryside to seek a career in Paris. But that expensive city soon gobbled up his savings, and he could barely pay the rent on his tiny room. Favor at the royal court must be the key to success, Latude brooded. Why, people from backgrounds humbler than his had been raised to positions of honor by making the right impression there!

Latude came up with a scheme to gain favor with Madame de Pompadour, the close friend of King Louis XV. People said she was the real power behind the throne. They also said that she was terribly afraid of being poisoned or attacked by her enemies. Day and night she kept doctors and antidotes to poison at her side. She would never be the first to taste any dish.

That gave Latude an idea. What if he were to warn her of an attempt on her life and save her? She would be so grateful — surely she would promote him to some high office for his actions!

Latude bought four glass toys that would break with a bang when the ends were snapped. He sprinkled them with talcum powder and bundled them in a package. The outer wrapper was addressed to Madame de Pompadour. On the package inside he wrote, "Madame, I beg you to open this in secret." Smiling excitedly, Latude put his harmless toy bomb in the mail.

Then he rushed to court and begged to be allowed to see Madame. He had overheard a plot to send her a bomb!

The detective assigned to the strange case had his doubts about this loyal informer. He asked Latude to write down what had happened. Sure enough, the handwriting on Latude's statement matched the writing on the package.

No one laughed at Latude's prank. Perhaps he really had meant to hurt Madame, but was too foolish to do it properly. And surely he hadn't acted alone — this must be part of a larger plot. When Latude finally confessed to his little plan, no one believed him. The *lettre de cachet* did the rest.

Once the Bastille's heavy doors slammed behind him, Latude felt as if he had been buried alive. Since childhood he had heard stories of Paris's notorious prison, and they had filled him with dread. Its eight huge towers, linked by stone walls, cast a gloomy shadow over the Saint-Antoine district. No one seemed to know what went on behind those walls: any prisoner lucky enough to be released was sworn to silence about life inside. But the rumors were enough to terrify Latude's young imagination. It was where dangerous people — traitors, political enemies of the King — were locked away. And never heard from again.

And so he wrote letter after letter, asking for mercy, for justice. Most importantly, he begged those on the outside — Don't forget me! He wrote to the prison governor, to the chief of police, to ministers, to Madame de Pompadour herself. Letters were his lifeline to the outside world, and he clung to them.

At first prison officials mailed his letters. Then as time passed — and no one answered him — Latude's letters got stranger. He sent one minister an envelope full of cut-out letters of the alphabet, asking him to put them together himself in whatever words would move him to pity. Prison censors wondered, Is Latude going mad?

The governor of the prison ordered that Latude's ink and paper be taken from him. To the governor's horror, Latude kept writing — on a torn piece of his shirt, in his own blood.

★ ★ ★

Everything changed when Latude was given a roommate — Antoine Allègre, another troublemaker. The police hoped that putting the two men together would get them talking. Maybe they would let slip some new information about their crimes.

The result was surprising: Allègre and Latude started behaving themselves. The flood of letters stopped, as did Allègre's shouts and violent outbursts. Bastille officials sighed with relief.

What they never suspected was that Latude and Allègre had given up on letter-writing and screaming at the guards for a reason. They had a new idea now, and it filled all their thoughts. Escape.

A spark of hope Latude hadn't felt in years took hold of him. All the same, doubts preyed on his mind. Everyone knew that escape from the Bastille was impossible — wasn't it? Maybe I'm going mad after all, he thought.

He kept his fears to himself, as he and Allègre went over all the possible exits. Their room was on the fourth floor of one of the Bastille's eight towers. There was no getting out through the cell's heavy double door. It was locked with iron bars, and guards were right outside, day and night. They had one tiny window, but it was too small for a child to squeeze through, never mind a grown man.

And even if they could fit inside the window opening, four sets of iron grids barred their way through the six feet of stone wall. What's more, guards constantly checked the grids to make sure they were solid.

"The only way left is up," Latude said, half-joking.

Latude and Allègre raised their eyes to the chimney over their fireplace — in winter it barely kept the prisoners warm in the damp tower. Guards didn't search it often, since it was always filthy and smoke-filled.

Allègre stuck his head in the fireplace and peeked up the chimney. He quickly ducked back out and, brushing the soot off himself, shook his head. It was at least 30 feet to the top, and high up he could see layers of iron gratings, blocking the way.

"We could pry them out, one by one," Latude suggested.

"With what? We have no tools," Allègre answered. "And say we did, and could climb all the way up. We'd be at the top of the tower. How would we get down? It's at least an 80-foot drop — straight into a moat! Not to mention the huge wall on the other side of that."

Latude counted off the obstacles on his fingers. They would

need to make tools to remove the gratings. Plus ladders and ropes to climb up the chimney and down the tower wall, then to climb over the wall on the far side of the moat.

And guards were always listening in at the door, surprising them with searches. They'd have to build everything in total silence, then hide it in a flash. Latude and Allègre looked around the nearly empty room and at its meager furniture. All of it was regularly searched.

"Where would we hide everything?" Allègre asked.

They both fell silent. That was where their talk of escape always ended. They had no answer.

★ ★ ★

Latude and Allègre lay on their cots, staring at the ceiling. Latude listened to the prisoner above pace back and forth, the floor creaking with every step. "What a racket," he grumbled. "Why doesn't he just sit down?"

Allègre didn't answer at first. Then his eyes widened. He sat up. "But listen to the prisoner below."

Latude shook his head. "I can't hear a thing."

"Neither can I," answered Allègre. He paused. "But in my last cell, I could hear the man above me *and* the man below me."

"But there's someone down there," said Latude, sitting up. "I saw him myself on the way back from chapel."

So why couldn't they hear him?

"There's only one explanation!" Allègre whispered excitedly. "There's a space between the ceiling of the cell below and our own floor!" They both knew what that meant. A hiding place!

At 6:30 p.m. the guard brought their supper. The prisoners lowered the hinged table from the wall and ate in silence. As the food was taken away, Latude and Allègre exchanged glances. They knew no one would disturb them until morning. The guards were settled in their routine, and the two men were model prisoners now.

As soon as the door closed, Allègre and Latude began to wrench off the iron hinges that held the tabletop when it was down. They had their first tools! All they had to do was take their meals on their laps from now on and leave the table up.

With his hinge Allègre pried up one of the floor tiles, and the two men began to scratch at the mortar beneath. For six hours they scraped, barely noticing the aches in their arms and backs. Latude wiped his brow and glanced up — it would be dawn soon. The first guard of the day would arrive at five a.m.

Suddenly Allègre's tool pierced through the mortar. Latude joined Allègre as he scrabbled in the dust, clearing it aside. Allègre peeked through the hole, then motioned to Latude to do the same. Latude had to stop himself from shouting out loud. There *was* an empty space between the floor and the ceiling below — and it was at least three feet deep.

Allègre replaced the tile and carefully dotted mortar around it. No one would be able to tell it had been moved.

The two men collapsed onto their beds, exhausted. But Latude's head was spinning with happiness. He knew they were taking on a near-impossible task — and it would be painfully slow. But what did he have, other than time? From now on it was all he would think about by day, and toil at by night.

Each evening after the guard left they set to work. First they ripped the hems of their shirts and unraveled the threads, winding them into balls. Then they carefully braided the threads into a rope. As the rope grew longer, it began to eat up everything they could lay their hands on — shirts, underwear, stockings and breeches, napkins. As winter wore on, Latude and Allègre shivered half-dressed in their cell. They even unraveled the edges of their bed sheets, carefully stitching the hems back up and hoping the laundress wouldn't notice that their linen was getting smaller!

And before each dawn they hid it all under the floor, carefully laying the tile back in its place. The guards shrugged when the prisoners began napping during the day. It must help them pass the long hours, they thought.

Next they needed steps for their ladder. Each day they saved a bit of the wood the guards brought for the fire, and stashed it in their hiding place. At night they filed the logs into rungs — as quietly as they could.

Latude fitted the rungs one by one onto the rope, and laid out the 20-foot ladder for inspection. "Eighteen months' work," he said, stretching his back.

"Time for the chimney," said Allègre, nodding. Latude groaned — this would be the hard part!

"You first," Allègre smiled. "You're the nimble one."

Latude rolled up the ladder. Tucking it under one arm, he ducked through the fireplace and wedged himself inside the narrow chimney. He tossed the ladder up over one of the bars high above and climbed up to the first layer of gratings. Hanging in the gloom, he reached out to scrape at the cement around the grids, nearly losing his balance at first. His hands chafed on the rough stone and began to bleed.

An hour later he couldn't take it anymore, and scrambled down to give Allègre a turn.

Slowly, painfully, they pried out the chimney gratings one by one, and climbed a little higher. Each time Latude pried a bar loose, he gently placed it back in its hole on the way back down. You never knew when guards would inspect the chimney. But it was ready to be plucked out when the moment came.

And after hiding their tools each morning, Latude scanned the room for any sign of their work — the smallest chip of mortar could give them away.

★ ★ ★

Latude wound a strip of cloth around yet another rung. It had taken them six months to clear the chimney and braid a safety rope, and now he was halfway through the second ladder. This one would need at least 150 rungs to reach down the outside tower wall. Wrapping it in cloth was Allègre's idea — that way it wouldn't scrape noisily against the stone.

As he worked, Latude finally voiced the question that had been on his mind for months.

"What about the outer wall beyond the moat?" he blurted out. It was the most dangerous part of their exit route. Sentries patrolled the top all night long.

Allègre paused before ripping another strip of material. "There's only one way. We'll have to go through the wall — not over it." He handed the cloth to Latude. "We'll chip away the stones once we're in the moat."

Latude lowered his eyes, saying nothing. The doubts that had haunted him now made him turn cold. Could they do it? With a sentry walking over their heads? Maybe this was turning out to be madness after all.

★ ★ ★

Daylight was just piercing their small window as Latude slipped the last rung of the long ladder in place. He stared at it. He had thought it would go on forever! When he looked up at Allègre, he saw tears in his eyes. After seven years as a prisoner — eight for Allègre — Latude could scarcely believe this moment had come.

It was February 25, 1756, the day before Mardi Gras. The winter nights were long and dark, the river around the Bastille was high, and fog made it hard to see very far. There would never be a better time to escape. They would go that night.

The day seemed endless, but at last the guard came with their dinner and left. Latude hastily packed what clothes they had left in a watertight case. If they made it across the moat they would be soaked. And wet clothes would surely give them away in the city, if not freeze them to death first!

Allègre pulled the long rope ladder from its hiding place and began to piece it together, rung by rung. He counted as he went — 151 steps in all. They hauled everything over to the fireplace.

The prison bell tolled eight o'clock. Time to get going! As agreed, Latude began to climb up the chimney first, wedging his hands and feet against the sides, pulling out the iron gratings as he went. Let's hope it's for the last time, he thought. As he climbed, breathing hard, the chimney's walls seemed to press in on him. He grimaced as the rough stone rubbed the skin off his knees and elbows. Blood trickled from his elbows to his hands, making them slip.

Almost there, he told himself. Soot stung his eyes and made him choke.

At last he grasped the chimney top. Pulling himself up with his arms, he popped his head out into the air. The cold night wind blew on his face, and it felt delicious. He was outside! With a big push Latude hoisted himself out and sat astride the opening. He looked around at the foggy night — perfect! In the distance, a band played a march.

Latude lowered a cord back down the chimney, and the two

men worked fast to haul up their equipment — including two iron bars pulled from the chimney. At last Allègre sent up the short ladder, and Latude let it dangle down so the heftier Allègre could climb up.

Once Allègre had clambered to the top, the two men quickly scaled down the chimney's outer wall, landing on the platform between the towers. Latude glanced around through the fog — no sentries! He and Allègre pulled the long rope ladder down after them, and began to roll it up. All together, the pile of rope and wood was huge — nearly five feet high. Struggling under its weight, they carried it to the neighboring Trésor Tower, which they had agreed offered the best route down.

The two men tied the long ladder to a cannon and together they heaved the rest of it over the edge. Latude's stomach lurched as he watched it drop noiselessly down the side of the tower and disappear into the moat far below. He closed his eyes for a second to steady himself.

Allègre had already started rigging the safety rope to the cannon. It was 360 feet long, and Latude recalled how they had braided it inch by inch. Strong winds swept across the platform as Latude fastened the rope around his thigh, and he was glad they had been so careful. If the wind knocked him off the ladder, the safety rope would be his last hope.

With a nod to Allègre, Latude lowered his foot over the edge and onto the first rung of the ladder. He felt as if he were stepping into an abyss. Gripping the rope sides, he waited for his fear to pass, and then moved down rung by rung. Above him, Allègre fed the safety rope as he went. The wind whipped at his back in the darkness, and the ladder began to sway, brushing against the stones. Latude closed his eyes and held on. When it stopped rocking he took another step.

A sudden gust blew the ladder away from the wall and Latude felt himself swinging in midair like a kite, before falling against the stone again. He peered down into the blackness beneath him. It seemed to spin under his feet. Quickly he looked up again, and the dizziness left him. Step by step he kept going — down 80 feet of sheer wall.

When his foot touched the mire at the edge of the moat, Latude breathed a silent prayer of thanks. Allègre passed down the case and tools on a rope. Then, tying the safety rope to his own waist, he took his turn on the ladder. Latude pulled with all his might to secure the rope from below.

Once Allègre was at his side they peered across the moat. Latude could make out the silhouette of a sentry on top of the wall. As Allègre had predicted, they would have to do it the hard way — using the iron bars from the chimney to force a hole in the wall, which was four and a half feet thick.

Warily, they stepped down toward the water. Latude braced himself for the cold — but the shock was worse than he expected! They waded forward through the dirty, icy water, deeper and deeper. Soon they were up to their chests.

Once across, Latude got out their crude tools and began to pierce a hole between two stones. Suddenly a flash lit up his hands on the wall. He glanced up — the sentry was coming toward them along the wall top, swinging his lantern. Latude and Allègre sank down into the water to their chins, and listened to his footsteps pass over their heads. As soon as the steps died away, Latude stood up and kept scraping with all his strength.

The iron bar broke through the mortar, and Allègre was instantly at his side. They wedged in both iron bars and struggled to pry the stones loose, sinking down each time the sentry passed overhead.

Latude's hands and feet started to numb. They worked fiendishly, but their progress was slow. Too slow! Panic washed over Latude when he tried to guess how many hours had passed. Dawn was not far off, but he could not work any faster. A clumsy scrape of his bar or a splash of stone in the water would easily be heard by the patrol above.

As their hole grew, stones and debris rose in a pile above the water. Latude glanced up — the sentry was coming back. They sank down, splashing as they fell against the pile. The sentry's footsteps stopped.

Latude and Allègre froze. Had he heard them? Above, there were a few more footsteps as the sentry moved to the edge of the wall. Latude clenched his teeth to stop them from chattering. He wished he could sink underwater, but didn't dare — the splash would signal where they were.

He's right above us, thought Latude. Has he seen us? What is he doing?

A stream of water hit the top of his head. Latude nearly jumped out of his skin. Then it dawned on him — the sentry had stopped to relieve himself! Latude forgot to be disgusted. A few seconds later, he heard the sentry's steps again as he backed away from the edge and walked on.

After what seemed like an eternity, their hole reached the other side of the wall. As quickly as they dared, they pulled away the broken stone to make the opening big enough to fit through.

Allègre squeezed through first. Latude pushed the case after him. As he grabbed the stone sides to pull himself through, he glanced up. The sky was lighter now. How many hours had it taken them to break through the wall — six, seven, maybe more? Daylight was practically upon them.

Latude hurled himself through the opening. In his blind rush

he barely noticed the jagged stones that scraped his frozen skin. Every second counted now.

One more moat lay between them and the road. Latude tested the slope with his feet, and realized with horror that it was much steeper than the first one, and the water much deeper.

He and Allègre looked at each other. Neither of them could swim! But there was no going back. Side by side they plunged down the bank into the icy water. Latude soon lost his footing on the steep bank, and the water rushed over his head. He groped blindly forward. Suddenly he felt Allègre thrashing wildly near him, then gripping him in panic, pulling him down. Latude's mind raced frantically — he hadn't come this far only to drown!

With a kick he freed himself of Allègre. Then, with flailing arms, he grasped a root on the opposite bank. Reaching back into the water, he felt Allègre's hair and closed his fist around it, pulling him up. The two men gasped for air, clinging to the slope. Latude spotted a large object floating away — the case of clothes! He reached out and grasped it by the edge just before it moved out of reach.

They scrambled up the bank and collapsed onto the road above. Panting, Latude looked back at the stone walls looming behind them. *Behind,* he thought with sudden joy. They were outside! Free!

In the distance a church bell sounded five o'clock. Shivering, Latude fumbled to open the case. He could have wept with happiness — it was dry inside! Forcing their frozen limbs to move, he and Allègre tore off their wet clothes and pulled out the dry ones. With stiff fingers, the two men struggled with the clasps and buttons.

Then, in the pale light of morning, they set off down the rue Saint-Antoine, free men.

★ ★ ★

Latude stared into his empty coffee cup, now and then glancing up through the café window. Across the street, he could see the post office. A dozen times he'd made up his mind to get up and go in, but still he remained rooted to his seat. Would the police be waiting for him there?

He'd been on the run for nearly three and a half months. Allègre had escaped out of France first, disguised as a peasant.

He'd sent Latude a message telling him he was safe in Brussels, confident that the French police couldn't touch him in an Austrian domain. Latude had followed him there, but soon learned that Allègre had been arrested. So he *wasn't* safe, even outside France. He fled even further, to Holland this time.

Now he watched the people come and go from the Rotterdam post office, not far from the city's bustling seaport. In desperation, he had written to his mother in France, asking her to send him money under a false name. By now her letter would be waiting for him. He wondered if he had been foolish.

But if I had the money, he thought, I could go so far away they'd never find me. How big was the risk? Only a few seconds in a post office. He would do it.

His jaw set in a firm line, Latude stood up and strode across the street toward the office.

"A letter for Monsieur D'aubrespy?" he asked the clerk.

"Just a moment, sir."

Out of the corner of his eye, Latude saw a figure move. Then a hand clapped on his shoulder. Before he turned around, he knew it was all over.

★ ★ ★

Latude lay on a bed of straw in a dungeon deep beneath one of the Bastille's towers, shackles on his wrists and ankles. Moat water seeped in and soaked the floor. Rats roamed fearlessly, eyeing his rations of bread and water.

By the winter of 1781, Latude's letters were no longer sent to anyone.

With a few coins he'd managed to scrounge, Latude bribed a guard to take one last letter to a councilor at Parliament. But the guard carelessly dropped it outside in the snowy road, forgetting all about it.

A woman trudged through the snow on an early morning errand. She spotted something in the slush at her feet and stooped to pick it up.

It was a letter. Water had erased the address. Madame Legros turned it over — the seal was broken. She peeked inside for an address so she could deliver it.

Her eyes ran down the desperate plea for help on the page inside. She raised a shaking hand to her mouth as she read the long signature: "Masers de Latude, prisoner for 32 years at the Bastille, at Vincennes, and now at Bicêtre, on bread and water, in a cell 10 feet underground."

Forgetting her errand, Madame Legros raced back to the small shop she ran with her husband.

It was two years before Latude saw the woman who was working to free him. Madame Legros knocked on the doors of anyone she thought could help, pleading with their servants to let her in for a few moments.

Surprisingly, a few people did let this unknown woman inside, and listened to her story. Word spread of her cause, and she found more and more supporters — some of them powerful. When the queen herself was moved to pity, it was only a matter of time. On March 23, 1784, King Louis XVI issued a new *lettre de cachet,* this time freeing Latude forever. He was given no apology or reason for his long imprisonment without trial, only a small pension, which he used to live with his new friends, Madame and Monsieur Legros. He had been a prisoner for 35 years.

Five years later, the Bastille was stormed by an angry mob. The French Revolution had begun, and the downfall of France's monarchy and ruling class was close at hand. For revolutionaries, the Bastille was a symbol of power used badly. In 350 years it had held nearly 6,000 prisoners. Only seven ever escaped.

Days after the storming, revolutionaries began to tear down the massive prison, stone by stone, while crowds of people watched. One them was Latude.

"From here there is no escape..."

Germany, 1941

COLDITZ — THE NAME WAS ENOUGH to send a chill through the boldest prisoner of war. During the Second World War, the Germans turned this medieval castle into their greatest *sonderlager:* the highest-security, most heavily guarded camp for captured enemy soldiers. Hermann Goering, Hitler's second in command, had personally declared the camp absolutely escape-proof. Here the Germans sent the troublemakers from every other prisoner of war camp — especially those determined to escape. As the war raged on outside, Colditz was home to hundreds of Allied soldiers — Polish, British, Canadian, French, Belgian. And in 1941, they were joined by 68 Dutch.

"For you the war is over," the new prisoners were told by the German guards who herded them through the castle gates at gunpoint. As the young Dutch lieutenant Hans Larive looked around him, it wasn't hard to believe. During their march through the town below he had admired the fairy-tale castle high on a cliff. But that illusion disappeared with a closer look. Inside, the castle's high, gray stone walls blocked the sun. Glancing up from the damp courtyard, he spotted pale faces peering down through the barred windows all around him.

"Appell!" barked a German officer — time for roll call. The Dutch snapped to attention, forming neat ranks in the courtyard.

With sideways glances they watched the other prisoners drift in. One by one they came, or ambling in pairs. Some wore torn uniforms ragged from battle, some were half-dressed — one seemed to be in his pajamas! The Germans' frustration mounted as they tried to impose order, but every time they thought they'd finished counting they spotted an officer wandering out of his place or lined up with the wrong nation.

Larive was surprised by the chaos, but then slowly he understood the game the other prisoners were playing. Keep the guards frustrated and confused: it was a kind of psychological war. The French and British seemed to be the worst offenders of all. He watched as the British were lined up closest to the armed guards — obviously this was the "bad boys'" place during roll call. The Germans seemed to eye the Dutch with relief. They were so disciplined and quiet — at least there was one country they didn't have to worry about!

Or so they thought. From the moment Larive arrived he watched for a chance — any chance — to get out. He had to rejoin the fighting! But as the days passed he learned that this was no ordinary camp. Everything about Colditz was a cruel reminder that escape was out of the question. Constant roll calls made sure no one was missing. Prisoners and their quarters were searched day and night. There were as many guards as prisoners, and they kept the inmates in check with guns and bayonets, with searchlights to spot them, microphones to listen in on them, dogs to sniff them out.

And yet one thing kept Larive's hopes alive — the memory, still fresh in his mind, of a strange twist of events that had followed his capture. After escaping from another German camp, Larive had been caught near the border of neutral Switzerland. He was then taken for questioning by a Gestapo agent, a huge bull of a man who began by shouting threats. But when the agent had learned that Larive was Dutch, he relaxed. He had worked in Holland before the war and liked it there.

"The only clever thing you did was to get off the train at Singen — all the rest was stupid," he had told Larive.

"Why?"

"You must have known that Singen was the last station where anyone could get off the train without showing an identity card."

In fact, it had been a lucky guess. The "Bull" had then asked Larive why he hadn't just walked across the border.

"I didn't know how to get through the defense line," Larive admitted.

"Defense line!" he stormed. "Defense against whom? The Swiss? What a crazy idea. There are no defenses at all. You could have walked straight across."

To Larive's amazement, the Bull even got out a map and showed him where the Swiss border jutted into Germany, and the road he could have taken to walk across it. How could he talk so carelessly? Larive wondered. Then he realized: of course, the Germans believe they will soon win the war. Where I'm going there's no hope of escape, and I'd be a fool to get shot trying. Larive had nodded and listened — and memorized the map.

★ ★ ★

Larive settled into the prison's dreary routine, but he kept wondering if there wasn't more than met the eye at Colditz. He watched officers milling about the courtyard, lying on their bunks. So much time on their hands, he thought — surely enough time to plan escapes.

He had guessed right. Colditz was a maze of a castle, and Larive soon heard rumors of out-of-use passages and hidden rooms where prisoners worked on one scheme after another — from tunnels to disguises. The place is seething with escape plans, Larive realized, his pulse quickening at the idea. In fact there were so many in progress that the different "countries" began to cooperate so they wouldn't mess up one another's schemes by mistake.

Larive and the other Dutch wasted no time fitting in. They would need to choose a leader for their own escape "team." The obvious choice was the burly, quick-minded Captain Machiel van den Heuvel, whom the British quickly nicknamed "Vandy." It was an important job, but there was a catch. The escape officer was not allowed to escape himself — he would mastermind escapes for others, and always stay behind. Vandy accepted.

Larive and Vandy soon discovered that the Germans had made a mistake when they locked up all the troublemakers in one prison. Now every kind of escape artist — from lock pickers to explosives experts — was in one place. Some had gained valuable experience on their failed escape attempts. Larive was one of them.

Vandy was all ears as Larive told him in hushed tones the story of his capture and questioning by the Gestapo. Now the Dutch at Colditz knew a way across the border, but how could they get out of the castle? That was the puzzle Vandy set his mind to. The outer walls were monstrous and heavily guarded. But prisoners had one opportunity to be outside the walls — even if it was under an armed escort. The key had to be "the walk."

Exercise was impossible in the castle's cramped courtyard. And so the prisoners were regularly marched to a nearby park surrounded by a high fence. The guards knew this was the weakest point in their security and grumbled about the extra trouble it caused — the manpower needed to take the prisoners back and forth, plus all the roll calls before, during, and after to keep track of the men.

It was also a prime opportunity for the prisoners' favorite pastime — annoying the guards, or "goon-baiting." When called for the walk they would show up slowly one by one, then drop things and stroll back for them. Vandy knew the Germans were glad that at least the Dutch didn't stoop to these games. They were always orderly and easy to count. That could be useful too, Vandy mused.

As Vandy strolled around the park, he noted the armed sentries along the fence, the barbed wire, the guard dogs. He sighed and looked down. What he saw at his feet made him pause — a cement square set into the ground, covered with a wooden lid. It was shut with a heavy nut and a bolt, and dotted with small airholes. He quickly looked up and kept walking before the guards could see what had caught his attention. But his mind was racing.

On the next trip to the park, Vandy casually sat down on the wooden lid and pretended to watch the prisoners' rugby game. Never moving his eyes from the players, he reached into his pocket and pulled out the pebble he had tied to a long piece of string. Slowly he fed it through one of the small airholes. How far down would it go? He lowered it further and further. Two feet, three feet, four, five — *plop!* The pebble hit water. So it was an old well! He lowered it further, and it dropped another five feet or so before hitting the bottom of the well. Perfect! Vandy's expression didn't change, but he was so pleased it was hard not to smile.

In the days that followed, the German guards shrugged when they noticed the Bible study club Captain van den Heuvel had started leading during the exercise hour. What was the harm? Sitting quietly in a circle, always on the same spot, the men were easier to track. It also served Vandy's purposes nicely. With the well hidden from view, he set to work measuring the nut and bolt, making plans, barely hearing the voices that droned on around him.

* * *

Hans Larive walked aimlessly around the park, too anxious to join in the rugby, too restless to sit down. The waiting was driving him crazy. Nights ago, he had helped prepare two Dutch officers for their escape, drilling them on the route to the Swiss border. He knew the escape plan concerned the well in the park, but he was puzzled. The well was a dead end, so how did they get out? The scheme appeared to have worked, but Vandy had not let him in on the details, not yet. He kicked at the dirt. When would his turn come? On the grass, a shadow lengthened and moved toward him. Looking up, he saw the large form of his escape officer striding toward him, a smile on his broad, ruddy face. Before Vandy spoke the words—"Are you ready?"—Larive's answer was already on his lips, a confident "Yes."

On a hot August afternoon, Larive took his place in line to march to the park. Ahead of him he could see his friend Flanti Steinmetz, the other Dutchman who would make the break today. Almost every Dutch officer had a role to play. Vandy had gone over each man's part and had stressed the obstacles to be overcome. Somehow Larive and Steinmetz had to get into the well unseen by the guards. Then the guards and their dogs must be kept from closely searching the grounds, even though the Dutch would be two men short at the roll call that ended the exercise hour. And the Germans must stay confused for as long as possible to let the escapers get a head start.

Once at the park, every man took his place. Far from the well, several of the Dutch began a noisy game of rugby. The bored guards turned to watch. Larive and Steinmetz, meanwhile, joined a circle of officers who were lazily throwing a ball to one another across the well cover. At the same time, Lieutenant Gerrit Dames settled down against the fence between two guards and quietly read a book. Another officer strolled aimlessly along the barbed wire. The minutes passed.

Vandy gave the agreed-upon signal. This was it! The circle around the well started closing in. The rugby game got rougher and noisier than ever. The officer near the fence began to pull playfully at the wire like a naughty schoolboy. And Dames, still looking at his book, began to slowly cut a hole in the fence behind his back.

Finally, a guard lost his temper at the Dutchman playing with the wire, and his angry shouts caught the attention of the other guards. Screened from view, one of the officers around the well dropped to the ground. From his pocket he drew the homemade wrench Vandy had built over many nights, sized just right to loosen the nut and bolt on the well cover. Working fast, he removed the bolt and passed it to Larive, who stashed it in his pocket. The shouts of the guards continued in the distance as they led the troublesome officer away from the fence.

In a flash, the lid was lifted and Steinmetz slipped into the darkness below, followed by Larive. Above them, their helper closed the lid and put the finishing touch in place. It was Vandy's small stroke of genius. He smiled as he gently centered the new "bolt" — a carefully painted piece of glass that looked just like the real thing, but would smash easily when the lid was lifted from inside.

By now Dames had finished cutting his hole in the fence. He turned around and, with clumsy slowness, began to creep through. As expected, a guard's whistle pierced the air. Dames shouted toward the woods beyond the fence, "Run, run!" He felt the barrel of a rifle at his back and, slowly drawing his head out of the hole, raised his hands in the air. Seconds ticked by. Dames exhaled heavily — they weren't going to shoot.

A quick count of the prisoners was taken in the park. Two men missing! The German guards combed the park with their dogs, but found no one. They gave the well cover a quick glance, but it was clearly undisturbed with the bolt still in place. Their suspicions were confirmed: the two men must have escaped into the woods before the guards had spotted the third man, Dames. The Dutch were marched back to Colditz, while a widespread search of the woods began.

"Sonderappell!" Back in Colditz castle, the other prisoners weren't surprised by the shouts announcing a surprise roll call. A common nuisance. But as they streamed into the courtyard they noticed the atmosphere was tenser than usual. Guards were rushing back and forth, commanders talking in small groups. Then whispered rumors began to make their way through the ranks of prisoners. It's the Dutch... someone is missing! The British officers nearest the guards strained to overhear. No, make that two men. Wait a minute, I think it's more... four, five... *seven* missing? Impossible!

The Dutch group was marched in at gunpoint. All faces turned to look at them, but as usual their dignified expressions gave nothing away. The lines of prisoners made way as the Dutch were marched past their usual place in the courtyard. Then the guards ordered the British and French ranks to stand aside. A cheer went up through the prisoners as Vandy and his countrymen were led straight to the bad boys' place nearest the guards. Applause and whistles echoed through the courtyard, but the Dutchmen looked calmly ahead.

In fact, seven men weren't missing, but four were. Vandy had succeeded in tricking the guards. Two men had left through the well days ago, and the Poles had helped Vandy make up the numbers at roll call. Now, while Larive and Steinmetz hid in the well, three more men were hiding in the castle itself to help confuse the guards. Vandy knew the Germans' Operation Mousetrap would spring into action. Rail and police stations in the area would be alerted, and guards would scour towns and roads for miles around the camp, quickly spreading a net to catch the escapers. But they would be looking for seven men, not two. And those two weren't running to a station or town, not yet. They were hanging inside a well under the feet of the guards looking for them.

Vandy wasn't finished with the well, either. He wanted to get two more officers out fast, before the Germans found it, before they'd expect another attempt. He knew he couldn't use the fence trick twice, so the "third man" was out. Vandy stared straight ahead, barely hearing the German officers shouting around him. His mind was already forming a new scheme. His thoughts went back to the fake glass bolt he had painted. And to his friends in the Polish group, particularly one who was a sculptor. And to how appearances can be deceiving, especially when there's something you expect to see.

★ ★ ★

Larive's arms ached and his back was sore from crouching. For hours he had been hanging from the iron rungs on the side of the well, half of his body underwater.

At first he and Steinmetz had crouched on the rungs, but they realized that if the guards opened the lid they'd be seen immediately. Quietly, they had lowered themselves into the water, then draped a gray blanket they'd brought over their heads. If things went wrong and the guards opened the well, they'd see a gray mass — maybe they'd think it was the dirty water below and move on.

Hanging in the darkness, they listened to the guards' whistles and shouts above their heads and the sound of running feet. Then dogs barking in the distance. A murmur of voices nearby, growing fainter. And finally silence. Hours passed. The lid had closed over their heads at three o'clock, and it wouldn't be safe to come out until nine or ten, when darkness forced the Germans to call off their search for the night.

Time crawled by slowly. Larive's head was splitting and it was getting harder to think straight. He tried to take a deep breath, and his lungs heaved slowly with the effort. He watched Steinmetz's chest move up and down, as if he were panting.

"We are breathing like fish on land," Larive gasped. And then he realized why — not enough oxygen. They were slowly suffocating!

Steinmetz dragged himself up the rungs toward the lid. Slowly he pushed it open a crack and, careful not to break the glass bolt, propped it up with his pocketknife. He and Larive put their mouths to the opening and drank in the fresh air.

Outside, dusk was turning to darkness. They peered out the narrow opening. No lights, no sounds. It was time. They pushed up the lid, smashing the glass bolt as planned. Steinmetz hopped out and picked up the broken pieces, while Larive fished the real bolt out of his pocket and replaced it on the closed lid.

Quickly scrambling over the fence, they walked and crawled toward the nearest rail station, hoping to catch the first train at dawn. It was a gamble. Police would already be looking for anyone suspicious. They'd have to count on the civilian clothes they had faked and Steinmetz's perfect German to help them pass as tourists.

Luck stayed with them all the way to Singen — the last train stop before their walk to the Swiss border. As they set out along the dirt road that ran next to the tracks, Larive had an eerie sense of coming home. He had traveled the same road after his last escape — and had landed in front of the Gestapo. In his mind he went over the Gestapo agent's words: "Did you see where the road split from the tracks? An hour more of walking, a left turn through some fields, and the border would have been straight ahead of you."

The road veered from the tracks and led into the woods. Remember, Larive told himself, the Bull said there's no defense line. But he couldn't shake a feeling of dread as they entered the forest.

Then, rounding a corner, he saw something that turned his

blood cold: a German guard up ahead, moving toward them along the same side of the road. Larive and Steinmetz slowed down. What now? If they turned back, he'd suspect them for sure. Maybe he wasn't there to check papers.

"Let's cross the road," Larive whispered. "If he crosses, too, we'll know he means to check up on us."

Casually they strolled to the other side of the road.

"He is crossing!" Steinmetz exclaimed under his breath.

A few steps ahead Larive saw a narrow path heading off the road through the trees. But it led away from the border! No choice now. The guard was closing in and picking up his pace. "Turn right up the path — and run," Larive whispered. The two men bolted.

"Halt!" they heard the guard shout from behind. Larive forced his tired legs to move faster.

A shot was fired, and a bullet whistled past Larive's head. They dove off the path and kept running through the trees, the leaves and branches whipping their sides and faces. Larive waited for another shot but none came. He slowed a little to look back. No guard. He's gone back to raise the alarm, thought Larive. The two men slowed down and circled back, creeping from shrub to shrub to the edge of the woods. Crouching deep in a thicket, they watched the road.

Across a field they could see some commotion at a distant guardhouse. The sky grew darker and Larive felt a few drops of rain. Good, he thought. The harder the better. It will make us tough to spot tonight. Soldiers were now leaving the guardhouse and taking up posts along the road. The road they needed to cross to get to Switzerland! Suddenly, rifle shots made Larive jump. Then loud barking. The hunt had started.

"They're trying to scare us into running, so the dogs will hear us and pick up our trail," Larive whispered. He and Steinmetz sunk further into the thicket and covered themselves with their blanket. Their best chance was to stay quiet and perfectly still.

The barking grew louder and voices were getting clearer. More shots, closer this time. Larive's heart was pounding as he willed himself not to move, not to breathe too loudly. The guards' footsteps were very close now. This is crazy, thought Larive. Even if they don't see us they'll step on us! Then slowly the voices became dimmer, the barking moved further off. Soon only the rain falling on the leaves broke the silence.

Darkness came, and the two men crawled slowly out of the woods on their stomachs. Larive looked for some landmark to guide them, but everything looked the same in the pitch-black night. They found another dirt road, but was it the right one? They kept going. In the distance, Larive could make out the shapes of houses. That might be the Swiss village on the other side of the border. Or the town they had just left — were they going in circles? They passed signs but couldn't read them in the dark. Steinmetz climbed a signpost and struck a match before the words. In a flash, he dropped down. "German Customs!" he hissed.

Half running, half stumbling, they came upon a small group of houses. Were they Swiss or German? It was too dark to tell. Steinmetz leaned against a wall to catch his breath out of the rain. Larive joined him.

They discussed the situation in hoarse whispers. Maybe it was best to stay put and not get more lost. At dawn, they could get their bearings and make a final dash for the border. Larive leaned back. He'd never been so tired. Two and a half days on the run, without sleep and almost nothing to eat. His clothes were soaked and he felt cold and numb. Stay sharp, he told himself. This is when your mind dulls, and you do something stupid.

Suddenly the white beam of a flashlight stung his eyes, blinding him. He and Steinmetz froze, as if pinned to the wall by the light. Larive could hear the sound of boots squishing in the mud, coming closer. But he could see nothing beyond the glare of the light. Then a voice confirmed his worst fears — it spoke in German.

"Who are you? What are you doing here?"

Tears stung Larive's eyes. Not again! They couldn't be more than a few hundred yards from the border. Then anger replaced his exhaustion. No, he thought. I won't go back this time.

The beam of light moved to Steinmetz and back again. Behind it, Larive glimpsed a soldier with a rifle strapped across his back. It would take a few seconds for him to grab his weapon and aim.

Larive whispered to Steinmetz, "We must kick hard, both at the same time, then run. I'll say when." Steinmetz nodded grimly.

As the soldier came closer, they slowly lifted their right legs and pushed their hands against the wall behind them.

"Where did you come from? Are you prisoners of war?"

Larive took a deep breath. As he opened his mouth to say "Now!" the voice spoke again.

"You are in Switzerland. You'll have to come with me."

It took a moment for the meaning of the words to sink in. They were free.

★ ★ ★

In a corner of the Dutch quarters at Colditz, Vandy frowned as he inspected the two dummy heads from different angles. At last, he stepped back and gave a grunt of satisfaction. They were remarkable! His Polish friend had outdone himself. The amateur sculptor had modeled them out of plaster — obtained from a castle repairman who was always willing to take a bribe. The faces had then been painted by a Dutch lieutenant, who had snuck paints from a prisoners' art class.

Attached to frames, draped with long Dutch coats, and topped with officers' caps, the dummies — which the Dutch nicknamed "Max" and "Moritz" — were ready for action. Two more officers were about to escape through the well in the park. While they made their run for the border, Max and Moritz would stand in for them at roll calls, hiding their absence for as long as possible.

Vandy had noticed that the guards now took a shortcut when counting the Dutch prisoners. The orderly Dutch always stood in neat rows of five. The guards simply counted the rows, and so many rows times five gave them the right number. During the noise and confusion before roll call, while the British and French were stalling and goon-baiting, the Dutch walked out in a large group. They tucked Max and Moritz in the center, held by the officers on either side, who slid two extra pairs of boots under the dummies at the last minute.

It worked brilliantly — for a time. Months after the well escapes, a suspicious German guard took a closer look at the Dutch.

He raised his hand. "All from here to the right, move to the right. All from here to the left, move to the left," he ordered.

As the prisoners shifted position, one was left alone in the middle. The guard pointed at the prisoner with the blank expression and repeated his order. No response. The guard stormed toward him, and his anger turned to astonishment. Max had been found out. But Vandy didn't mind — by this time his two escapers had followed Larive and Steinmetz to freedom in Switzerland.

★ ★ ★

Escape attempts continued at Colditz, some ingenious, some out-rageous — through a trapdoor under the theater stage; hidden in garbage; disguised as German officers, workers, women. In a secret attic room, the British even built a glider to carry escapers over the castle's high walls to the valley below. The glider never had a chance to take flight, however. It was found by the amazed American GIs who liberated the castle in 1945.

Through Traitor's Gate

London, England, 1716

IT WAS NEARLY EVENING AS A LADY, wrapped in a cloak, her face almost hidden by her riding hood, stepped down from a horse-drawn coach onto the cobblestones. She looked up for a moment at the gray stone walls that rose before her, then lowered her gaze and strode ahead with a determined step. As she passed through the arched gateway, the sentry gave her a fleeting look of sympathy, but his face quickly hardened again into its usual cold stare. He was sorry for her troubles, but her husband was a traitor, after all.

The lady shivered as she made her way forward. Was it her imagination, or was it really colder, the air stiller, now that she had stepped inside the walls of the Tower of London? Ahead, across the small green, rose another stone wall. High above, she could see slits in the stone — tiny windows that lit the cells inside. Silently she counted the slits and found the one that cast its dim light on the room where her husband waited for her. And for the day of his execution.

It was out of family loyalty that William Maxwell, Lord Nithsdale, took up the doomed cause that had brought him here. In 1715 a plot was hatched to replace King George I with the exiled James Stuart. Many nobles, especially Scottish ones such as William, believed that James was the rightful heir to the throne.

And the time seemed ripe for swift action — the people were grumbling about the German-speaking King George, who knew little English and showed even less affection for his British subjects. William joined his friends and allies in a march south to England, rallying support along the way.

Their rebellion was over within the year. Surrounded and defeated at Preston by King George's forces, the rebel lords were led through London's streets on horseback, their hands tied behind their backs, past the jeers and shouts of the crowds. Soon afterward, the disappointed Stuart prince fled back to France, where he had been living in exile.

Three Scottish lords were found guilty of treason and sentenced to death — their heads to be cut off with an axe. Once sentenced, they were thrown into separate cells inside the Tower of London, the gloomy stone fortress that for centuries had held traitors and notorious criminals within its many dungeons. There the men were to stay until their executions.

★ ★ ★

In the frozen garden outside the family manor in Terregles, Scotland, Winifred leaned on her spade and surveyed her handiwork. Her palms were blistered from the shovel's handle, but she paid them no mind. It had been only a few hours since the news of her husband's death sentence had reached her at home in Scotland. She had choked back her tears. There was too much to do.

Quickly she had buried the deeds to the family lands in the garden. Her son would need them someday to claim his inheritance — without them all their property would be seized by the king. Snow would cover the hiding place soon enough.

Brushing the dirt from her hands, she next took a hard look

at the facts. William had pleaded guilty. The date for his execution was set — February 24, only days away. Things looked grim indeed.

But one hope remained. She'd race to London herself, and beg the King for mercy.

Winifred set out at once to hire a stagecoach, but none dared to travel in the heavy snowstorm that blocked all the roads. If she would just wait for the storm to pass, the drivers offered. But Winifred knew that every day was crucial. Very well, she decided, her jaw set stubbornly. I'll ride on my own.

Winifred and her trusted maid, Evans, mounted their horses and set off at a gallop for London — hundreds of miles away. Through the day and past nightfall they rode south, stopping to rest only when they were too exhausted to go on. The weather grew worse, and the horses shied from the sharp winds and deep snow ahead. With grim determination, Winifred dismounted and called to Evans to do the same. Together they walked through the waist-high snow, pulling their frightened horses forward by the reigns.

At last they staggered into London and found lodgings for the night. There, sympathetic friends tried to reason with Winifred. It was hopeless. She must accept it: William and the others would have to die as an example to all traitors. But Winifred shook her head.

The next day she asked for an audience with the king, but was turned away. Unwilling to give up, she dressed in black mourning clothes and went to St. James's Palace, planting herself in a corridor where she knew the king would pass. There she waited. And waited.

After what seemed like an eternity, a bustle of activity made her look up. There he was — the king! — striding in her direction, surrounded by attendants. Winifred wasted no time. Blocking his way, she knelt before him, and began to plead her cause. But he just brushed her aside and kept walking.

Winifred struggled up and followed him — in a moment he would be gone, taking her hopes with him. Squeezing through the attendants, she tried to push her written petition into his pocket, but it fell to the floor. Tears began to blind her, but this was no time to worry about dignity. Just before he moved out of reach, she lunged forward and grabbed his coattails. The angry king strode on, dragging her behind.

Gasps could be heard all around as horrified royal attendants rushed toward her. No one could touch the king! Soon firm hands were pulling her away. She stood up and shook them off, but it was too late. The king was gone. And with him goes any hope of a pardon, thought Winifred.

Which left only one other way.

★ ★ ★

As Winifred passed under the Tower archway, walking toward the stone Lieutenant's Lodgings where her husband was locked up, her eyes took in everything — the sentries along the green and at the entrance, the two flights of stairs, and at the top the grand Council Chamber full of warders, the Tower guards. Across the guardroom was the heavy door to William's cell.

Before it stood a warder armed with a halberd. With a nod, he opened the door for Winifred. She smiled sweetly and slipped a generous tip into his hand.

Inside, William rose swiftly from his seat and stepped forward, grasping Winifred's hands in his. After their heartfelt reunion, Winifred listened patiently as William paced the floor and spoke his mind. He was resigned to his fate and was ready to face execution with dignity, without flinching, so his family could be proud of him. He had even written his final words.

Winifred, however, had other ideas. She began unfolding her plan. William's room was high in a stone tower, its door well guarded, its only window a mere slit in the stone 40 feet above the ground. What's more, the cell door opened onto a crowded guardroom. There was no hope of sneaking out or jumping.

"But there is another way..." Winifred paused. She'd have to lead up carefully to the crucial part. "You could walk out in plain view of the guards, disguised — only for a few moments mind you — as a visitor... a lady visitor—"

William raised a hand to silence her.

He was a proud man. To face the axe was one thing. Walk up the scaffold with a steady step, looking bravely ahead — yes, he believed he could do it. He would do it for honor's sake. But to be caught sneaking out of the Tower in a dress!

"Can you imagine the laughter, the sneers? No," he said, folding his arms. "My family would never live down the shame. No."

"But that is if we fail, and we won't!" Winifred cried. She spoke passionately, quickly explaining the rest of her scheme.

William listened in silence. She'd thought of everything, there was no doubt. It was clever, he admitted. And it was one last chance for life.

When Winifred had used up all her arguments, she sat back, waiting breathlessly for his answer. William stood for a while with a hand on the stone wall, looking down. When he looked at her again his eyes were gleaming. He would do it.

★ ★ ★

Winifred poured the afternoon tea into porcelain cups, her movements calm and delicate. She waited a moment before raising her eyes. When she did, her maid and their landlady, Mrs. Mills, were both looking at her expectantly. Winifred took a breath, silently running through the phrases she had rehearsed in her head all morning. She prayed they would be persuasive enough.

Then in a flood of words she told the ladies everything. Her husband was not going to be pardoned. Tomorrow he would be executed. There was only one chance left — to help him escape, tonight. Everything was ready. But she needed their help. Would they do it?

Evans readily agreed. Winifred smiled and squeezed her hand. Then she turned to Mrs. Mills. Winifred knew she was loyal to the Stuart cause. But would that be enough?

Their landlady was dumbstruck, clearly astonished. Winifred bit her tongue as she waited for her answer. Had she been right to spring the idea at the last minute like this? She had hoped that the surprise and urgency would keep the women from considering the danger. At last Mrs. Mills nodded mutely.

They would need one more helper. Who else could they trust? Evans quickly sent for her friend Miss Hilton, and Winifred's dramatic pleas won her over as well.

Her accomplices in hand, Winifred moved fast. She ushered the three women outside and into a waiting coach, which she had arranged beforehand. Throughout the ride she kept chatting — that way no one would have a chance for second thoughts.

Her scheme sounded complicated, but it was based on a very simple idea: to confuse the guards with women coming and going from the prisoner's room.

"For days before an execution, all men visiting the Tower are stopped and challenged to identify themselves," she explained.

"But not the women! And what coldhearted guard would stop a grieving lady, crying as she said farewell to a prisoner for the last time?"

As the speeding coach lurched and bumped over the stone roads, Winifred reminded each lady of the part she would play. Mrs. Mills was a large, tall woman, and a few months pregnant. Lady Nithsdale had noticed that with her pregnant belly she was just about the same size and shape as her dear William! It was as "Mrs. Mills" that William would make his walk to freedom.

Miss Hilton, on the other hand, was tall and thin, and could easily wear two riding cloaks, one over the other, without looking suspiciously bulky. Winifred cast a critical eye over the lady and was satisfied that no one would guess she was smuggling in a disguise.

The sun was low in the sky as the coach pulled up alongside the Tower's arched entrance. Weaving through the stream of Tower workers still coming and going, the women headed for William's prison house.

"Prisoners are allowed only two visitors at a time," Winifred told them. Leaving Evans and Mrs. Mills at the foot of the stairs, she guided Miss Hilton up to William's cell.

The warder before William's door straightened and stepped forward as the two women approached. Winifred knew that for their plan to work, she would have to break the Tower rules — on the night before an execution, the prisoner's wife could visit only if she stayed with him until morning. That would ruin everything! She linked arms with Miss Hilton and strode forward, praying that the tip she had given the guard the day before had done the trick.

On cue, Miss Hilton began to sniffle and sigh, but Winifred, in a loud voice, told her not to fear. "At this very moment the king is considering my petition for a pardon. All will be well, Mrs. Catharine!" she said, adding the lady's first name for everyone to hear.

Turning to the warder, she added, "I am afraid I must leave after seeing my husband tonight. I have an audience with His Majesty."

The warder's face softened, and he nodded slightly as he opened the door. The other guards exchanged glances, then looked down. Her hopefulness was touching, but they knew there wasn't much chance of a pardon.

As soon as the door closed behind them, Miss Hilton slipped off her top riding cloak, and William tucked it out of sight. The two women waited anxiously for a few moments, and then walked out together.

In a worried voice, Winifred called for her maid. There was no answer. She called again, and the guards turned their heads toward Winifred. As they listened to her shouts they scarcely noticed the quiet Miss Hilton slipping past and down the stairs.

Winifred continued to cause a scene. "Pray send up my maid at once to help me dress — it is nearly time to present my last petition to the king!"

Below her, the stout Mrs. Mills was already huffing on her way up the stairs. Winifred took her by the arm and lead her past the guards toward the cell. As planned, Mrs. Mills pressed her handkerchief to her face and sobbed loudly the whole way. The guards looked away, embarrassed. Good, thought Winifred. The less closely they look, the better!

Lady Nithsdale smiled and patted her friend's arm, saying loudly, "I have high hopes, Mrs. Betty, that the king will pardon my husband this very night."

Inside William's room, Mrs. Mills took off her cloak and put on the one Miss Hilton had left. She handed her own cloak and handkerchief to William. Then she straightened up and prepared to walk out with her head held high.

"No crying this time," Winifred reminded her. "You must look like a different lady than the one who went in with her face in her handkerchief."

Winifred led her by the hand into the guardroom. Glancing around, she noticed that the room was fuller now. The guards' wives and daughters were sitting in small groups, whispering. After all, it wasn't every day that three executions were to take place at once!

A hush fell as the two ladies passed, their footsteps echoing under the high, timbered ceiling. Winifred turned to the disguised Mrs. Mills and addressed her as if she were Miss Hilton.

"My dear Mrs. Catharine," she said with growing alarm in her voice, "go in all haste and send me my waiting-maid, she certainly cannot reflect how late it is. I am to present my petition tonight, and if I let slip this opportunity I am undone, for tomorrow will be too late."

From the corner of her eye Winifred could see the looks of pity on the ladies' faces. "Hasten her as much as possible," she called after Mrs. Mills as she hurried down the stairs, "for I shall be on thorns till she comes."

Winifred turned and walked back toward William's cell, noting with satisfaction that the guards on either side looked away as she passed. Inside his room, William had already put on Mrs. Mills's riding cloak. Now it was time to complete the transformation!

Winifred fished out the tools she had hidden under the folds of her clothes. First she must do something about his heavy, dark eyebrows — Mrs. Mills's were a light sandy color. She brought out the paint she had prepared and began to disguise them. Next she fitted a light-haired wig over his head. With quick, sure strokes she powdered his face and painted his cheeks with rouge, to help hide his stubbly beard — he'd had no time to shave! Over it all she pulled the hood of his cloak, close around his face.

Finally, she stepped out of all of her petticoats except one and slipped them under William's cloak.

Winifred glanced up at the small window and noticed it was growing dark. This was the time she had planned for their exit — in the twilight that would hide their faces, but before the candles were lit.

They stood together before the closed door, blocking the rest of the room from view. Winifred turned to William and raised her eyebrows.

He nodded and pressed the handkerchief to his face. As Winifred pulled the door open, William began to make loud sobbing noises. Holding his hand, Winifred stepped out and guided William through the doorway.

The murmurs in the guardroom died down as they appeared.

"Evans has ruined me by her delay!" Winifred said for all to hear. "How could she do this to me?"

They started walking, past the guards and their wives. Only their footsteps and William's sobs broke the silence. The guardroom seemed endless, and Winifred felt the ladies' curious eyes boring into them. Was she walking too quickly, too suspiciously? She took deep breaths to slow her racing heartbeat.

"My dear Mrs. Betty," she said to William, her voice catching and sounding tearful, "for the love of God run quickly, and bring her with you. You know my lodging, and if you ever hurried in your life, do it now. I am almost distracted with this disappointment."

They were halfway there now. William kept his face buried

in the handkerchief, his head turned into Winifred's shoulder.

At the far end of the room servants were starting to light the candles. Winifred held her breath — a moment more and the room would be brilliantly lit. She picked up her pace.

Not so fast, she scolded herself. The heavy oak door was right before them now. Only a few steps more.

Suddenly a guard sprang forward, blocking their way. Winifred stopped in her tracks, and tightened her grip on William. She felt the blood drain from her face. They were trapped!

The guard bowed slightly and opened the door for them, his face full of sympathy. Winifred tried to hide her relief. She began to steer William through the door toward the long staircase flanked by sentinels. Not far now.

As William passed before her through the door she nearly gasped in horror. He was walking like a man! Dress or no dress, it was a miracle no one had noticed before now. She grasped him by the elbow and pushed him in front of her. They moved forward awkwardly, with Winifred's wide skirt hiding William's masculine walk from the sentries.

Past the guards, down the stairs, on and on Winifred begged anxiously — "Please hurry and send my maid." All the while, William cried loudly in his handkerchief, never daring to raise his eyes and counting on Winifred to steer him. The sentries stood aside to make way for them, the sympathy on their faces turning to exasperation.

All these women, all this weeping and calling after maids. Such a ruckus — there must have been three or four of them at least — or was it more? They felt sorry enough for the ladies, but this was getting tiresome. If only they would just leave!

At the bottom of the stairs stood Evans, and the sight of her loyal face steadied Winifred's nerves. She handed William over,

and Evans led him across the green toward the outer gate.

Outside the Tower walls, Mrs. Mills's husband was waiting for them. His wife had convinced him to help by having a safe house ready for the fugitive, but he had doubted very much that the women would succeed.

Now, there they were — Evans and Lord Nithsdale coming toward him through the archway! Mr. Mills was so astonished that he forgot what he was supposed to do. Surprise and joy crowded out every other thought, and he stood rooted to the ground, gaping. A few passersby slowed down and stared curiously at the group.

Glancing around, Evans saw the attention they were attracting. Time to take things firmly in hand, she thought.

Hailing a coach, the maid quickly pushed William inside and climbed in after him. She could sort things out with Mr. Mills later! Now they had to put as much distance between themselves and the Tower as they could.

★ ★ ★

Winifred walked slowly back up the steps and through the guard-room toward William's empty chamber. She had a final role to play out inside the Tower. She must buy time for William to get away — before the guards raised the alarm, before searchers flooded the streets and gave chase.

Again the warder politely let her into William's room. Winifred watched the door close behind her. She took a deep breath and began to talk to William as if he were still there. She paced up and down — as if they were walking together — to make it more convincing.

A sudden thought made her heart jump. They might wonder why they could hear her, but not him! She began to answer her own questions in his deep, quiet voice. All the while her mind was calculating — have they had enough time to clear the guards, cross the Tower green, and slip through the outer gate?

She kept up the illusion as long as she dared, then glanced outside at the dark night. It was time to make her exit as well.

Slowly she opened the door. Standing halfway out so that the guards could hear her words, but holding the door so close that they could not see inside the room, she bid farewell to her husband.

"Something unusual must have happened to keep Evans," she said. "She has always been faithful in even the smallest matters. But I can afford to wait no longer."

The guards kept their eyes discreetly lowered as she talked.

"I will go directly to the king now," Winifred said reassuringly. "My task completed, if I can still gain admittance to the Tower, I will see you tonight. But if I cannot, do not worry, my love. I will be here tomorrow morning as early as they will let me in. With good news, I trust," she added, smiling bravely.

Just before shutting the door, Winifred pulled through the string of the latch. Now it can only be opened from the inside, she thought with satisfaction, and there's no one there to do that! She gave the handle a sharp tug and slammed the heavy door firmly shut.

Turning to leave, she looked up and started in surprise. A servant was heading straight for her. He was carrying William's supper on a tray!

"My lord is praying now," she said quickly, stepping in the servant's way, "and does not wish to be disturbed. He has no need of supper or candles — he plans to fast until his pardon arrives." The servant nodded and turned away.

With a sigh of relief, the sentries watched Lady Nithsdale pass down the stairs and out into the night.

★ ★ ★

A few days later Lord Nithsdale escaped to Italy disguised as a servant on the Venetian ambassador's boat. Lady Nithsdale mounted her horse and rode back to Scotland, where she dug up the deeds for their lands. It was a risky journey for her. King George was furious about Lord Nithsdale's escape, and search parties combed the country for Winifred. The king swore that Lady Nithsdale "had given him more trouble than any woman in the whole of Europe!" But Winifred slipped through the searchers' fingers and joined her husband in Rome, where they lived near the court of the exiled Stuart family for the rest of their lives.

•

Fugitives in Iran

Tehran, Iran, 1979

THE CHANTING HAD DRONED IN THE DISTANCE since early that gray November morning. Crowds of student protesters were a daily sight outside the walls of the American embassy compound in Iran's capital. But now the voices were getting louder, sounding closer

Set back from the main entrance, the fourteen Americans in the consulate building felt far away from the noise. They ignored the angry shouts and kept working, processing applications from Iranians for visas to study or travel in the U.S. The protest was not their concern, and no doubt the police would soon break it up. But a panicked cry from an Iranian secretary destroyed their illusion of security.

"They're inside the walls!"

Staff rushed to the window. The students had broken the main gate and were streaming into the compound. The grounds were filling up with people — young men in khaki fatigues, women in head scarves or the full-length black *chador* that covered them from head to foot. Some carried pictures of their spiritual and political leader, the Ayatollah Khomeini, on poles. Others were armed with knives, lead pipes, or guns.

"Stay calm." From behind, the voice of Sergeant Lopez, a young marine, sounded reassuring. "It could just be a sit-in protest."

They had all known something like this was bound to happen. Since the Shah, Iran's former ruler, had fled his country, Iranian revolutionaries had shown more and more resentment toward his American allies. The return of the exiled Ayatollah Khomeini — an Islamic scholar who believed the country should be run by clerics — had focused people's anger into a full-fledged revolution.

Walking through the city, the American diplomats had sensed the growing fear and suspicion — especially toward them. What were these foreigners doing in Iran anyway, the revolutionaries demanded. Trying to run our country for us? When President Carter had allowed the Shah into the U.S. for treatment at a hospital, tensions had reached a boiling point.

The sound of footsteps on the roof made everyone tilt their heads up. Seconds later they heard a window shatter in the washroom. Lopez rushed there just in time to push back a student trying to climb in from the roof. The marine fired a tear-gas canister out the window. Retreating quickly, he then wired the washroom door shut with a coat hanger and herded the staff and Iranian visitors further back into the building.

"How can this be happening? They can't do this to an embassy! We're diplomats," sputtered the shocked employees. The Vienna Convention of 1961 was supposed to guarantee the protection of ambassadors and their staff in foreign countries. The embassy and its grounds belonged to the U.S., and could not be entered without permission.

"Can't you guys do something?" someone asked the marine. Lopez shrugged. The guards were there to defend the staff, not attack anyone. It was another rule of diplomacy: embassies must count on the host government to protect them. "I can't fire on citizens of this country," he explained, "unless someone's life is in immediate danger."

Robert Anders, the senior diplomat in the building, took charge. "We'll barricade the doors and hold out until the police or the army arrives to restore order," he announced.

The staff huddled closer together. The group of visiting Iranians spoke little English, but the anxious looks on their faces showed they understood the situation. They were about to be caught in the den of the enemy by the most extreme of the revolutionaries. How would the militants deal with them?

Outside, the roar of the mob, now three to five hundred strong, was frighteningly loud. Over his two-way radio, Lopez learned that the main embassy building, the chancery, had already been stormed by the revolutionaries. But so far no one else was trying to get into the consulate.

"They've forgotten about us," Anders thought aloud. "For now."

Suddenly the room went dark. "The lights! They've cut the electricity!" Panicked voices filled the darkened room. Lopez talked rapidly into his walkie-talkie, but received no answer. He tried again. Still nothing.

His face was in darkness, but the others could tell how he felt by the grim tone of his voice. "They must have captured the other marines. We're cut off."

Slowly the words sunk in. The handful of staff understood: they were on their own.

"We've got to get out now, before they find us!" someone wailed.

"Our best chance is the exit on the north side," Anders reasoned. On the side of the building facing away from the demonstrators in the compound, a sliding door opened directly onto the street.

Two by two, the Americans and Iranians filed down the stairs toward the north door. Close behind Anders were two young couples: Joe and Kathy Stafford, and Mark and Cora Lijek. Lopez followed at the rear, locking doors behind them, buying time for their escape. He stayed behind on the ground floor to smash visa plates, so no forgeries could be made by the invaders. He would leave last — if at all.

At the north door, Anders raised a hand to signal everyone to wait. Slowly he slid the door open a few inches and peered up and down Bist Metri Street.

To his surprise, he saw no one. No protesters, not even any passersby.

"Okay, move out in small groups. That will attract less attention."

The Iranian visa seekers slipped out first, followed by Iranians who worked at the embassy. Anders led the Staffords and the Lijeks out next. The rest followed behind.

All was quiet outside, but for the heavy rain. They dashed down the wet street, the sounds of protest faint in the background.

"Where to now?" Breathless, Joe Stafford voiced the question on everyone's minds. The nearby British embassy was the safest bet, they agreed. But to avoid the protesters they'd have to stick to the back streets — a confusing maze of alleys in the ancient city. They'd be lost in minutes.

Most of the Iranians in the group were already out of sight, but one woman had stayed behind "I can show you the way," she bravely offered. The Americans nodded, grateful. Picking up some newspapers to protect their heads from the rain, they began to weave their way though the alleys, turning their faces away whenever they passed anyone.

Coming out of a lane, they stopped across from the square that separated them from the British embassy. Their hearts sank: it was full of protesters.

The Americans slunk back into the alley. They thanked their Iranian guide, and she slipped away. One of the men urged them all to go to the house of the consul general. But Anders shook his head. It was too obvious a hiding place. And it would mean backtracking toward the American embassy, something no one wanted to do.

Unable to agree, the group split up. Five of them — Anders, the Staffords, and the Lijeks — began a long walk across the city to Anders's apartment. Creeping through the alleys, they arrived there by mid-afternoon, drenched and exhausted.

Anders quickly got on the phone, calling the homes of other embassy staff in the city — surely someone else had slipped out. But no one answered.

"Does that mean we're the only ones who got away?" Cora Lijek asked.

Growing frantic, Anders called every contact he could think of. Then, in the middle of a call, the telephone line clicked and went dead.

Anders slowly replaced the receiver. "Calls always get cut off in Tehran, it could mean nothing," he told the others. But they looked unconvinced.

Joe Stafford pulled out a radio, one that all the diplomats carried, and tried to contact the embassy. But on the crackling line they heard only shouting in Farsi, the Iranian language. The embassy was under the students' control.

Why hasn't the government sent in troops? Anders wondered. A sudden realization made him turn cold. Because they support the takeover, that's why. Or else they know they're powerless to do anything.

The five Americans looked at each other in silence. They were far from home in a hostile place, and a revolution had stripped away their last shreds of protection. Everyone was thinking the same thing: Where can we go?

★ ★ ★

Robert Anders was running out of ideas. The American fugitives had been on the run for days, moving from place to place. Revolutionary Guards were combing the city, picking up Americans on the streets and in offices. Anders and the others had spent a few days hiding with British diplomats, but their hosts grew uneasy, so they left. Servants had let them into the empty apartments of Americans trapped on the compound. But everywhere they had sensed they were being watched. At night they lay awake, jumping at every little sound. Sometimes they felt sure the servants were whispering about them.

Within hours of taking over the embassy — or the "Den of Spies" as the militants called it — the armed students released their demands to the media. They would hold the 60-odd trapped Americans hostage until the United States returned the exiled Shah to Iran to stand trial. If not, they would put the hostages on trial for spying.

To make matters worse, Iran's moderate prime minister, Mehdi Bazargan, had resigned. The country was now being run by the Revolutionary Council and the Islamic clergy it looked to for guidance — in particular, the Ayatollah Khomeini. There would be no help from such a government.

Anders knew the American government was in a tough position. Agreeing to the demands would not only mean handing over their ally for certain execution. It would be saying to the world, If you seize our embassies, we'll do what you want.

And where did that leave the five of them? Was it just a matter of time before they were dragged back to the compound to join the rest? That's what must have happened to Lopez and the others who'd split from their group. Anders was sure of that by now.

Desperate, Anders called an old friend — John Sheardown, Canada's chief immigration officer in Tehran.

"Why did you wait so long to call me?" Sheardown blurted out before Anders could finish his story.

The next day a car pulled into Sheardown's driveway, and inside the five fugitives sighed with relief. Finally a safe haven — for the moment, at least.

Sheardown quickly ushered them inside, where his wife Zena was waiting. Within seconds Canada's ambassador, Ken Taylor, arrived as well. When Sheardown had told Taylor about Anders's phone call, the ambassador had responded without hesitating: "Okay, where will we hide them?"

It was the kind of reaction Sheardown expected from his boss, who was energetic and unconventional, eager to cut through red tape to get to the heart of a matter. After a speedy coded message to the Ministry of External Affairs in Ottawa, Taylor got the official go-ahead to help the Americans.

As the fugitives gathered in Sheardown's living room, the Canadian ambassador went over the situation with them.

"We can't hide you at the embassy — downtown is too dangerous. So we'll be splitting you up. The Staffords will come to my house in the north of the city. The Lijeks and Bob Anders will stay here with the Sheardowns. No one will expect you to hide in our homes.

"How about extra security? Can any Canadian military be posted to the houses?" Sheardown asked.

Taylor shook his head. "No, that would only draw attention. It would give us away in a second. Life has to go on normally. No changes."

"But you must have Iranian staff at your homes — servants. Can we trust them?" Joe Stafford asked.

"We'll tell them you're Canadian tourists, friends of mine," Taylor said. "But you'll have to stay inside, especially during the day. You mustn't be spotted by the *komitehs,* the patrols who make the rounds of the neighborhood. Remember — stay out of sight."

After some hurried goodbyes, the Staffords left for the Taylor residence, and the Lijeks and Anders followed Zena Sheardown to their rooms. Cora carried all they'd brought with them in one small suitcase. They'd fled their last hiding place in such a panic, the clothes were still running in the washing machine.

★ ★ ★

Mark Lijek sat chin in hand, drumming his fingers on his cheek and staring at the Scrabble board. Now and then he glanced up at Cora, who sat across the coffee table, waiting for his move. Nearby, Anders was sunk in an armchair, reading a magazine. The silence in the house seemed to wrap around them.

I can't take much more of this, Mark thought. Reading, playing cards — it was all they could do to pass the long hours trapped inside the Sheardowns' house. For the first weeks they slept in, but still the days seemed endless. Mark and Cora were playing three hours of Scrabble a day! Cora had started running up and down the stairs to blow off steam. Anders had told them to pretend they were at a luxury resort, with a storm keeping them inside. But it hadn't helped. It's feeling so helpless and nervous, Mark thought, with nothing to take your mind off the fear — that's what's unbearable.

At Ken Taylor's house, the Staffords had the same cabin fever. Joe, who spoke some Farsi, listened all day to local radio, desperate for information on the hostages at the embassy and what — if anything — was being done to free them. What if the American government doesn't give in? he wondered. Will the militants start executing the hostages for spying?

Worst of all, he knew the Iranian staff at the Taylor home were getting suspicious. He'd overheard questions from the head servant and the cook — Why would tourists have so little luggage and never go out? They like to travel light, Taylor's wife, Pat, had answered. They're resting before they start sightseeing. But even to Joe the excuses sounded lame.

Then, a few weeks into their hiding, Taylor sprung some good news on them. Someone else had slipped through the students' fingers. Lee Schatz, an American attaché who leased space at the Swedish embassy, had been there when the takeover happened. He'd been hiding with the Swedes ever since.

The Swedish ambassador had called Taylor. Sounding apologetic, he asked if Canada could possibly hide Schatz — he wasn't likely to pass as a Swede, but he might have better luck posing as a Canadian. Taylor, with his mischievous sense of humor, had savored the moment. No problem, he'd told the shocked Swedish ambassador, we're already hiding five!

Schatz's arrival at the Sheardowns' gave everyone something new to talk about. As American Thanksgiving approached at the end of November, Taylor decided it was worth the risk to sneak Schatz and the Staffords over for a reunion dinner with the Lijeks and Anders. It would help keep everyone's spirits up. When the turkey was finished, someone joked, "Let's hope we're not all here for Christmas!"

There was silence around the table. That was a possibility no one wanted to talk about.

★ ★ ★

Ken Taylor went about his daily business, but it was getting harder with so much weighing on his mind. All through December he'd watched the Americans growing more restless and desperate. How much longer could he keep them a secret?

Some North American journalists had noticed that the original number of staff at the American embassy was greater than the number of hostages announced by the students. Where were the others? they asked. Government officials had asked them to keep it quiet, since lives were at stake, but sooner or later it was bound to leak out.

And rumors were spreading of a rescue operation. The U.S. military might storm the compound and whisk the hostages out by helicopter.

Then what would become of the six left behind? Taylor knew there'd be only one chance for an airlift — they couldn't fly back for the others. And the Iranian militants could argue that since the Canadians had been hiding them, the six must be spies, and as such had no diplomatic protection. They'd stay and stand trial, along with their Canadian accomplices!

Clearly, it was time for them all to get out.

Christmas came and went as Taylor weighed the options for escape. They could drive the Americans northwest to the city of Tabriz, then over the border to Turkey, where a helicopter could pick them up. Or take them west to the Persian Gulf and get them on a British tanker.

Both plans were risky, and they meant traveling through dangerous areas — some parts of the country had been plunged into even greater turmoil by the revolution than Tehran. Plus they would need safe houses along the way, and a Farsi-speaking guide they could trust.

No, Taylor realized, there was only one way. Confront the Iranians head-on. Take the Americans straight through Tehran's airport and onto a jet to Europe. It was the boldest option, but the swiftest, and the only one that stood a chance.

★ ★ ★

"Who is this?" A man's voice demanded over the telephone at the Taylor residence.

"Pat Taylor. And who is speaking, please?" Pat didn't recognize the voice, and an uneasy feeling told her to be careful what she said.

The man's reply turned her blood cold. "I'd like to speak to Joseph or Kathy Stafford. I know they're there."

Pat swallowed and answered steadily, "I don't know who you're talking about. There's no one here by that name." She glanced over at the Staffords, who had risen from their chairs and were standing nearby, watching wide-eyed.

The stranger began to argue with her, but Pat insisted he was mistaken. The man hung up suddenly.

Joe put an arm around his wife. This felt like the last straw in a series of scares that had tormented the Americans. Days before, a helicopter had mysteriously circled over the Sheardown home, terrifying Zena and the Americans hiding there.

Pat quickly phoned the ambassador, who rushed home. "Don't worry," Taylor reassured the frantic Staffords. "We're getting you out."

Taylor, together with officials in Ottawa and Washington, had worked out an escape plan. First of all, the fugitives would need new identities: Americans might not be let out of the country. But Canadians could still come and go.

Canadian Prime Minister Joe Clark had quickly issued six Canadian passports. For the next step, Ottawa turned to the Central Intelligence Agency in the U.S. They'd need the CIA's expert help to forge Iranian stamps on the passports, showing that the "Canadians" had entered Iran. And they'd need fake visas allowing them to enter and exit the country.

By mid-January the passports and visas arrived in a diplomatic pouch under the arm of a Canadian embassy courier. The CIA had also provided driver's licenses and credit cards to make the identities seem more real. As hoped, the pouch was not checked at the airport. Luckily some diplomatic privileges were still respected!

But when Taylor looked at the visas, he gasped. The dates were wrong! The CIA had followed the old calendar used by the Shah and not the Islamic calendar reintroduced by Khomeini. According to the visas, the Americans had arrived in Iran a month after they were leaving! Taylor said nothing to the hostages. His staff hastily doctored the date — and hoped it wouldn't show.

The last days before the escape ticked by in a nerve-wracking countdown. The plan was to leave during the national elections, when confusion throughout the city would help mask their departure.

On January 26, 1980, the night before the escape, Taylor sat down with the six Americans and the few remaining Canadian diplomats. Taylor knew the Canadian embassy's days in Iran were numbered, so staff had been leaving the country bit by bit, all the while keeping up the illusion that everything was business as usual.

Huddled in a circle, the Americans were handed their passports and began studying their new identities.

"You are a group of Canadian business people in the oil industry," Taylor explained to them as they eyed their new passports. "You came to Iran in early January, stayed with embassy staff, and are now returning home. Everyone ready? Let's start."

The Canadians began drilling the Americans on their new identities. Together they rehearsed every kind of question that might come up at the airport. Where was your visa issued? Where were you born? What was your business in Iran? The slightest hesitation before answering, a little confusion over details — any number of small blunders could give them away.

Next they studied a map of the airport terminal and its many checkpoints. Taylor showed them where they would run into police, guards, and immigration officials, and where their visas would be checked and double-checked. The toughest spot was about halfway through, at the third checkpoint — a barrier guarded by National Police and Revolutionary Guards.

Finally, Taylor circled the waiting area where they'd stand before boarding. "But don't relax once you're there!" he warned them. "You can't let your guard down until the plane is in the air. Even when you're sitting on the runway, Revolutionary Guards could board the plane for one last check of papers." The Americans nodded.

"Remember," Taylor added. "If one of you is arrested, the rest of you mustn't panic. Walk away — slowly — to the exit. Two cars will be waiting for you outside."

It was late and they all needed rest. Taylor stood up, wishing them luck. He wouldn't be with them the next day — if they all left together, it would raise suspicions.

He smiled on his way out, but silently he worried about the Americans. They'd done well in the mock interrogations. But they'd been cooped up for three months. They're healthy, Taylor thought, but dazed. Are they still sharp enough to react quickly to the unexpected? Because, as he knew, something unexpected was bound to come up.

★ ★ ★

At dawn the Americans piled into a car and prepared to face the many roadblocks on the way to the airport for their 7:35 a.m.

flight to Frankfurt, Germany. They arrived at the terminal without incident, but Anders was nervous. He had processed visas for so many Iranians at the consulate. What if someone recognized him?

One by one the travelers checked in their bags, then headed for the first of the security stations. At a distance, two Canadian diplomats strolled around the airport, watching their progress.

When the group reached the third checkpoint, the official stared at Schatz's passport, looked up at him, then back down. Suddenly he snatched it up and slipped out of sight into an office.

Don't panic, Schatz told himself. As moments passed and the man didn't return, Schatz raised his sleeve to mop the sweat on his brow. He sensed the others standing nervously behind him, but didn't dare make eye contact.

The official abruptly returned and held out the passport, his face expressionless. Schatz reached for it, tensing his hand to stop it shaking.

Mark and Cora's hearts were pounding as they strode toward the final checkpoint, where their visas would be examined. But no one was there. Mark and Cora hesitated. Should they just walk through? Mark eyed the departure gate, and was tempted to sprint toward it.

But Anders grabbed his arm to hold him back. If anyone spotted them, guards would be all around them in a second. Mark groaned as Anders went in search of help. I can't believe it: we're actually going out of our way to talk to guards, he thought.

But Anders had done the right thing. A nearby guard found the missing official, who apologized and waved them through.

The minutes ticked by slowly as they strolled around the waiting area. It's not over yet, Anders told himself.

A voice blared over the loudspeakers. Joe quickly translated the Farsi announcement — mechanical difficulties were delaying the Swissair flight. Panic spread through the group.

"What if it's just a ploy to stall us?"

"We're like sitting ducks here."

Twenty minutes went by. In low mutters, the Americans ran through Taylor's back-up plans. They could split up and catch other planes — each of them had a ticket for another flight, just in case. Or they could slip out of the airport and make a run for the safe house Taylor had rented as a last resort. It would buy them a couple of days, or at least a few hours.

"No, let's wait it out," Anders urged. "Bolting now would look suspicious."

An hour passed as they agonized. At last another announcement ended the torture: passengers were now boarding the Swissair flight. One by one, the fugitives filed past the Revolutionary Guards on either side of the gate and mounted the steps to the airplane.

Taking their seats, they stared anxiously at the door, watching for any sign of guards boarding at the last moment. The minutes passed and none came. The plane began to move along the runway, slowly picking up speed. As it lifted off the ground, the Americans felt themselves soaring. They were in the air! To the surprise of the other passengers, the six "Canadians" broke into tears and laughter. They were going home.

★ ★ ★

Once news of the escape broke, Americans said a big "thank you" to Canada. Towns and cities across the U.S. flew the Canadian flag, people pinned maple leaves on their lapels, and thousands of thank-you messages, as well as flowers and cakes, arrived at Canadian embassies.

But in Iran the crisis wasn't over yet. The embassy hostages still faced another year of captivity. A sympathetic guard showed a few of them a magazine story on the escape, and it gave them new hope. One hostage, worn out by months of confinement, blindfolds, and fear, later called the escape story "the most incredibly beautiful thing I've read in my whole life."

The U.S. military did attempt to rescue the hostages by helicopter, but the mission was a tragic failure, killing eight members of the rescue team. In the end it would take the sudden death of the Shah and a war with Iraq to spur Iran to negotiate a release for the hostages. The captive Americans came home on January 20, 1981, after 444 days as prisoners.

Falling from the Sky

England, 1941

IT WAS A PERFECT DAY FOR FLYING — a warm August morning with scattered clouds at 4,000 feet, and above them clear, blue sky. Into it rose three squadrons of Spitfire fighter planes, climbing steadily over the countryside, bound for the English Channel. The pilots' mission was to escort British bombers on their way to a German military target in occupied France.

In the air battles that had raged over the past year of the Second World War, England had pinned its hopes on the fast and nimble Spitfire. When the skies over England had darkened with squadrons of German bombers, the sight of a Spitfire sparked hope and defiance in those on the ground. Across the country, school kids had memorized its sleek outline, and would spot it at once, waving furiously as it soared overhead.

But on that August day, the weather was about the only thing going right. Wing Leader Douglas Bader had trouble with his radio from the start. Then, soon after takeoff, the needle on his airspeed indicator began to swing up and down, and suddenly dropped to zero. The mission needed precise timing — impossible if he couldn't tell how fast he was flying. Someone else would have to steer the group to its target. Bader handed over the job to one of his trusted pilots, "Cocky" Dundas.

Dundas wasn't alarmed. He trusted Bader's judgment and his

brisk, on-the-spot decisions. The pilots were a tight-knit group, with confidence in one another.

It hadn't always been that way.

★ ★ ★

Now it seemed like ages since the Royal Air Force pilots of 242 Squadron first heard they were getting a new commanding officer. Word quickly spread that he was a bit unusual — he had no legs. He'd lost them both in an accident. The pilots groaned.

"I don't suppose we'll be seeing much of him," they said, rolling their eyes. Just what they needed: a passenger, not a leader. A useless figurehead who would sit in an office.

They couldn't have been more wrong. In fact there was nowhere Bader would rather be than in the air, where his legs didn't matter. A pilot needed good hands and eyes, not feet. And ever since he joined the Royal Air Force at 18, he had lived to fly. Confident and energetic, he had been a bit of a show-off during his training — taking the plane through loops and rolls that were against the rules. But he was so friendly that people readily forgave him.

His RAF report said it all: "Plucky, capable, headstrong." His flying was rated as "above average," which satisfied Bader. The only higher rating was "exceptional," a mark so rare that it seemed mythical.

Bader learned a lot in his first two years, becoming confident in the air, maybe a little over-confident. His instructor had to lay down the law with him: no more stunts. He'd taken his instructor's words to heart, but his friends didn't let the matter go so easily. It wasn't long before he was asked to show his stuff in the air.

"No," said Bader firmly. The requests turned to needling. One sounded an awful lot like a dare, and that stung Bader. No one could say he was afraid. His mouth set in a grim line, he climbed angrily into a nearby biplane. While his friends watched, he took off and prepared for a strictly forbidden piece of aerobatics: a low roll close enough to the ground to silence any of his doubters.

He pushed the control column over and the plane began to roll to the right as he sped forward. Now the wings were vertical... halfway there.

And then the plane began to drop. Upside down, Bader struggled to complete the roll. Suddenly the left wing hit the grass, bringing the plane's nose down. The plane cartwheeled and plunged into the dirt, smashing the propeller, sending the engine flying. Bader blacked out.

Later, he'd heard the doctor say, "I'm afraid we've had to take off your right leg," but the words didn't mean anything — not yet. Through the haze of pain that followed he learned that the left leg had to go as well, because infection had set in. And once, while in a dreamlike state, he heard a nurse outside his hospital room hush a noisy orderly: "Shhh! Don't make so much noise. There's a boy dying in there."

A shock ripped through Bader. He opened his eyes. That's what *they* think! The challenge kept him going, through his recovery, through the pain of learning to walk on artificial legs. He'd been offered a cane, but stubbornly threw it away. "Never!" he snapped. "I'm going to start the way I mean to go on."

It was a long road back. "I *know* I'll still be able to fly," he'd said, but the RAF didn't agree. He settled down to a desk job. It was 1933.

Six years later, England was at war. Germany's massive, highly trained air force — the Luftwaffe — would soon be poised in occupied France. Thousands of bombers and fighter planes would stand ready to cross the Channel and begin their assault on England. Their plan was to smash England's air bases before the German army invaded on land. The Battle of Britain — the summer and fall of dogfights over England, and the devastating bombing of London — would soon begin.

The RAF's Fighter Command knew the odds were against them — their small force was outnumbered three to one. They had to build more planes fast, and they desperately needed pilots to fly them. The RAF agreed to give Bader another chance. He'd have to take a refresher course and pass a test.

As Bader reported to the airfield, he realized it had been over seven years since he'd flown an airplane. Aircraft had changed — a lot. He would be rusty, there was no doubt. For a moment, his confidence flagged. What if I fail? He put the thought out of his mind.

At the end of the course Bader had a chance to read his report. His eyes scanned the page. There was the heading he was looking for: "Ability as a pilot." Under it was scrawled, "Exceptional."

Legs or no legs, they'd have to take him back.

In the air once again, Bader was rapidly promoted — from flying officer to flight lieutenant to squadron leader in four months. And the skeptical pilots he was about to lead were in for a surprise.

The moment Bader arrived at the airfield as the new commander of 242 Squadron, he strode energetically toward one of the Hurricane fighter planes squatting on the runway. No cane, the pilots noticed. In fact, it was hard to tell that this dynamo, full of restless energy, had two metal legs. The only clue was the lurch in his stride as he threw his right leg forward, cracking it like a whip to bend the steel knee and straighten it out again. Bader pulled himself up on the wing and, swinging his leg over the side of the plane, settled into the cockpit.

For half an hour he put the Hurricane through its paces over the airfield, as the pilots stood watching from below. Three loops in a row, then straight ahead in a spin. Climbing up for a final loop, the Hurricane began to spin at the top, then came out of the spin and finished the loop. After a neat landing, Bader hauled himself out without help and marched briskly past the pilots, who stood openmouthed and speechless.

The squadron was a battle-weary group of Canadians, who'd been let down by commanders before. It wasn't long before Bader won them over. He had a temper and could be gruff. But he seemed fearless, and his confidence was contagious.

In the brief lull before the battle he knew was coming — after the fall of France but before Germany launched its assault on Britain — Bader took his squadron through grueling sessions in the air, testing their skills with loops and spins, all in tight formation. He knew the pilots must not be afraid to push themselves and their aircraft to the limit. They must be able to lock onto the tail of an enemy plane and never be shaken off, no matter how wildly it maneuvered to escape.

Never forget, Bader would tell them, he who gets in close shoots them down.

And when the calls started coming from the Operations Room — enemy aircraft sighted, all pilots "scramble!" — they were ready.

★ ★ ★

Now, a year after the Luftwaffe's first savage air strikes, the Spitfires kept climbing as they crossed the Channel. They flew in "finger four" formation, the planes in each group of four spread out like four fingers on an outstretched right hand. Leading his pack of four, Bader was easy to recognize by the large "DB" on the side of his camouflage-colored Spitfire. Bader had painted it there so his men could spot him. A cheeky pilot had jokingly asked if it stood for "Dogsbody," and the name had stuck. Now it was Bader's call sign.

The sun's glare pierced the cockpit glass. Bader's eyes were already burning under his goggles, his body sweating. But that was the least of his worries, he realized. He knew the sun hid their enemies, the Germans' silver-colored fighter planes — Messerschmitt 109s.

That much had not changed since World War I, when dog-fighters such as Billy Bishop had warned, "Beware the Hun in the sun." It was the enemy's favorite direction for attack, coming out of the sun, their prey blinded by the glare.

Now, high above the French coast, Bader rolled his head from side to side, scanning the sky for the dark outlines of enemy planes. Glancing down through the broken clouds he glimpsed bursts of fire from the Germans' anti-aircraft guns, then the patchwork of farmers' fields.

In his mind Bader quickly went over the setbacks so far. It was not one of his best days. First the radio, and then his airspeed indicator. Now one of the squadrons was missing. They were supposed to fly above Bader's group, covering them. They must have gone astray.

A voice crackled over the radio. "Dogsbody, 109s below, climbing up."

"Where are they? I can't see them." Bader's tone was crisp.

"Under your port wing."

There! Ahead, to the left, he could see a dozen Messerschmitt

109s. They were flying about 2,000 feet below the Spitfires, climbing slowly and turning toward them.

Perfect, he thought. A climbing aircraft is a sitting duck for an attack — it's moving slowly and is hard to maneuver. As Bader well knew, the pilot flying the highest controls the battle. The advantage was definitely theirs.

"Dogsbody attacking." Leading his group of four, Bader dove. Too fast! He had misjudged and was now hurtling toward one of the enemy planes much too steeply.

There was no time to fire. Bader swerved and dove under the 109, barely missing it. Plunging far below the battle, he finally leveled out at 24,000 feet and looked around. Nothing but blue sky. He was alone.

Bader cursed his bad judgment. He was too tense. He hadn't flown so rashly since the first time he'd seen an enemy plane. Now he knew better: it was useless to rush at the enemy like that. Always approach the target slowly. You'll never get him in a hurry. Maybe his exhaustion was showing — he'd been flying missions almost daily for five months.

But what now? He could continue toward the mission target and hope to link up with the others. Or he could follow the advice he gave his pilots when they found themselves alone — dive to ground level and go home. It was too dangerous to be on your own in a hostile sky.

Then a sight up ahead took him by surprise. Three pairs of Messerschmitt 109s flying with their tails to him. He knew where they were headed — for the British bombers.

Bader dropped below and patiently closed the distance between them. If they see me, he thought, I'll dive and return to base. No 109 can keep up with a Spitfire in a dive.

But they didn't see him. His own words to his pilots surfaced again in his mind — Don't try to fight alone. But he couldn't let them reach the target! He looked behind him — there was no one on his tail.

Ignoring his own advice, Bader closed in on the middle pair and fired. The rear 109 plunged down, streaming flames and white smoke. The other planes kept flying. Bader was surprised. Were they blind?

Bader couldn't resist the temptation to take one more shot. He quickly closed in on the plane still in the middle, steadying his Spitfire in the 109's rough slipstream. Then, lining it up in his sights, he opened fire.

His thumb was still pressed against the fire button when he suddenly glimpsed the two planes on his left turning their yellow noses toward him. In seconds he would be trapped.

Bader shot a glance at the pair of 109s on his right. They were still flying straight ahead, the sunlight shimmering on their silver bodies, the black crosses visible on their sides. He knew that with their guns fixed to fire ahead they were harmless to him, unless they turned. I'll pass over them, he thought, then dive and head home.

Bader banked sharply to the right. The next instant he felt a jolt behind the cockpit. Out of the corner of his eye he saw the tail of a 109 pass behind him.

Then he had the strangest feeling — as if something had grabbed the tail of his plane and pulled it out of his control. The nose of his Spitfire plunged downward. Bader quickly pulled back on the control column to right it. Nothing happened. The stick moved loosely backward in his hand. He looked behind him, and the sight sent his mind reeling.

There was nothing behind the cockpit. The body, the tail of his Spitfire — all gone. The 109 must have hit me, he thought. Sliced me in half with its propeller. But it all seemed so unreal.

Out of habit he glanced at the controls. The altimeter's needle was spinning fast — he had already fallen 4,000 feet. The broken airspeed indicator was still stuck at zero. Never mind that now. Bader was well aware he was hurtling toward the earth in a terrifying spiral.

He forced back a surge of panic. Then, as he plunged earthward, he was amazed at how clear, how detached his mind was. In the seconds that followed, one thought filled his head. He had to get out. Now.

He tore off his oxygen mask. Reaching above his head he pulled the rubber ball suspended there. The transparent hood over the cockpit tore off and flew away.

Bader was in the open now, and the noise was deafening. The wind roared around him as he spiraled downward in the open cockpit, strapped tightly in his harness.

I'm moving too fast... I'm in the wrong position. What if I can't push myself out with only my arms? Bader struggled to focus his mind as the wind howled and buffeted him.

Held fast by his harness, Bader found he could still move his hands. He fumbled with the harness pin and unfastened it.

Right away he felt as if he were being sucked out by a giant vacuum. The wind tore his helmet and goggles off his head. His body began to rise out of the cockpit. Almost out!

And then he stopped.

Something was holding him, he thought wildly, holding onto his right leg. He struggled uselessly. His right foot was caught — hooked under something. What?

The battered Spitfire continued its plunge, pulling Bader with it. As he writhed to free himself, a great pounding noise filled his

head. In his right hand he gripped the parachute release ring, and vaguely he remembered that he must hang on.

Time seemed to slow down. The noise and speed made any more thinking impossible as Bader twisted and pulled on his trapped leg.

Then, with a snap, the leather and steel belt that held his metal leg to his body burst under the strain. Bader had the strange feeling of falling upwards. He was free. The hammering noise stopped, and Bader closed his eyes. Then with a jolt his mind focused again.

The parachute release!

Bader pulled the ring. The parachute spread open above him, and now he was floating in the sunlight. Below he could see white clouds. I must be at about 4,000 feet, he thought. Just in time. A Messerschmitt 109 buzzed past, but left him alone.

Bader looked down at his flapping pant leg and saw that his right leg was gone. And suddenly it occurred to him: If my leg had been real I'd have gone down with the plane. For the first time he felt lucky to have detachable legs.

Once he was through the clouds he could see the farms of northern France below. Drifting gently, he watched a man in a cap carrying a yoke on his shoulders, and a woman with a scarf over her head. They were opening a gate between two fields when they looked up and spotted him. They froze and stared.

I must look pretty odd, Bader thought. Floating down with no leg.

A quiet feeling of peace, of freedom crept over him. He knew the calm was an illusion. Later would come the shock of landing, when the ground rushed up at him and he crashed down inside enemy territory.

But for now, after the chaos of the hour he'd survived, he gave himself over to this strange feeling of silently floating toward earth.

★ ★ ★

Douglas Bader was found by German soldiers who took him to a hospital to recover before continuing on to a prisoner of war camp. He soon learned that the Germans had heard of him, and were amazed that the RAF would let a legless man fly. They were so impressed by his determination that they even let him sit in the cockpit of a Messerschmitt 109! For a few seconds Bader toyed with the idea of taking off, but a German officer kept his pistol aimed squarely at him the whole time. Bader did convince his captors to retrieve his leg from the crash site and mend it, as well as radio England with a request for a new one. He secretly hoped that call would let everyone at home know he was still alive.

At the hospital, a sympathetic nurse smuggled a note to him from the French Resistance — the underground network of men and women working in secret against the Germans who occupied their country. The Resistance would hide Bader if he could find a way out. He escaped out of the hospital window with a rope made from knotted bed sheets, and followed his French contact through the dark to a farmhouse.

A German search party soon banged on the door. Bader slipped out to the barn and hid under the hay, lying still as the soldiers searched the barn. Then, to his horror, he glimpsed the steel of a bayonet piercing through the hay, moving closer with each stroke. When it struck his sleeve, Bader knew there was only one thing he could do. He jumped to his feet before the next stroke could hit home, his arms in the air.

Bader's new leg did arrive — dropped by parachute from an English bomber. But his German captors were so worried he would try another escape on the way to the camp that they took both his legs away for the trip! Bader spent the rest of the war as a prisoner in Germany. But he never stopped trying to escape.

When Douglas Bader returned home after the war, he was asked to lead 300 RAF planes in a special victory fly-past over London, to commemorate the country's triumph in the Battle of Britain. Londoners filled the streets to watch the sky darken once again — not with enemy bombers this time, but with their own beloved Spitfires and Hurricanes.

Under Siege

Oxford, England, 1142

THE DISTANT POUNDING STOPPED. The hail of stones on the castle's curtain wall had slowed and then ended suddenly. The king's great catapults and army of slingers had withdrawn — for the moment at least. Deep within the castle walls, knights and foot soldiers paused at the sudden silence. A sense of relief swept through the garrison. They knew it would not last long, and archers scrambled to prepare for the next assault.

Above them high in the keep, their lady, the Empress Matilda, pulled her robes closer around her and paced the floor to keep warm. The December wind seemed to pierce the stone walls, despite the heavy tapestries that blanketed them, and the fire in the great hearth could not be built up any further. Every piece of wood was precious now.

For nearly three months she and her followers had lived as prisoners within her own castle, surrounded by King Stephen's army, deafened by the battering of his siege engines. Looking around the crowded garrison quarters, she had seen the hunger in her men's gaunt faces, the growing panic in their eyes. And now the castle's great well was nearly dry. Where were her allies? They must come soon to break the blockade. If they didn't...

Matilda pushed the thought from her mind with a defiant toss of her head. Peering sideways through a narrow window, she could see Stephen's flags, the glint of his men's armor in the winter sun.

Anger flared inside her. Who was he to call himself King of England? She had the stronger claim — the only claim — to the throne. She was the daughter of the late King Henry. Stephen was only his nephew. Her father had made all the powerful men of the country swear an oath of loyalty to her, and promise to recognize her as their next queen.

King Henry had still hoped for a male heir — a grandson was his last chance. And so Matilda became a pawn in her father's search for a powerful alliance. At twelve she was married to a German emperor in his thirties. After his death she was betrothed to the thirteen-year-old son of the French Count of Anjou. When at last her father recalled her to England, she had lived away longer than she had ever been at home. As she listened to the barons' oaths, she realized her country had become a land of strangers to her.

And where were those loyal barons now? When her father died, Matilda had been away in France, expecting a child. The barons who had never liked the idea of a woman ruling England jumped upon the chance. At their urging, her young cousin Stephen seized the crown.

And now to be trapped like this! She bristled at the thought.

Then she smiled bitterly — they wouldn't have a woman, but look at the state of the country under Stephen! These were lawless, dangerous times. Barons declared their loyalty to the king, but it was mere words. They raided the countryside, seized lands, took what they liked, and then retreated into their castles.

Stephen may have acted boldly when he snatched the crown, Matilda mused, but he was too mild-mannered, too forgiving to keep the barons in line. When Stephen did not punish them, they smelled weakness.

It had been easy to lure many of the barons back to her side when she sailed to England to challenge Stephen. But she knew they would switch sides again when it suited them. They would be watching for any sign that she or Stephen was gaining the upper hand. No one wanted to be caught on the losing side — and their new leader would be certain to reward their loyalty generously.

Matilda's eyes shone with defiance as she watched the royal troops outside. Whatever happened, she told herself, she must never show weakness.

★ ★ ★

Beyond the castle's curtain wall, across the wide moat, the king's army was a hive of activity. For weeks, the noise of hammering had filled the air as carpenters built a siege tower to soar into the sky. From it Stephen's men would be able to spy on the garrison inside the castle.

Further back other men were repairing a shed on wheels. Under its cover, miners would crawl close to the walls and dig under the stone, hoping to weaken the wall and bring it crashing down. Here and there assaults were being planned, as teams with crossbows or slingshots prepared to storm the castle walls.

And in the midst of it all sat Stephen, on horseback, watching. His gaze now and then returned to one of the castle walls rising out of a huge mound of stone and earth, and the massive ten-sided stone tower that stretched high before him.

A weary sigh escaped his lips. The castles of England, once built to help the king impose his rule across the land, were now being used against him. The kings before him had laid down two rules — no baron could build a castle without the king's permission, and the castle's keys must be surrendered when asked for in the king's name.

Now Stephen's barons sneered at these rules. Ever since Matilda's ship had brought her back to England's shores, she had given the rebel barons a cause around which to rally. She egged on their treachery, urging them to fortify castles to stand against the royal army.

Stephen bitterly remembered the day when at last, like a man shaken from sleep, he had been roused to anger. But was he too late? By then nearly all of southwestern England had fallen into Matilda's hands, her knights controlling a strong belt of castles that stretched from the port of Bristol to her headquarters at Oxford.

After raising an army of loyal subjects in the north, Stephen had begun a grim march — laying siege to Matilda's castles along the way. Some garrisons he had terrified into surrender. Others he had found empty, the soldiers having fled when they heard he was coming. These Stephen burned. Castle by castle, the royal army closed in on Matilda's stronghold at Oxford, cutting her off from her helpers.

Near the end of September, as the feast of Michaelmas approached, Stephen's army had paused before the Thames River. At the head of his troops, Stephen gazed across the water at the city of Oxford. It was well protected by the deep river. To one side a timber palisade guarded the city; on the other rose its castle and soaring tower.

Stephen hadn't waited for long before the enemy showed itself. They came running out of the city gates, toward the Thames. Some shouted insults across the river, others shot arrows over the water. With the river lying between them and the invaders, Matilda's troops felt invincible.

Stephen had seethed with rage. He turned to his advisers. Was there no way across?

One showed him the shallowest point of the river, but warned that even it was very deep.

Stephen wasted no time. He boldly plunged in, leading his men into the deep water. The army waded across, then swam when the water rose over their heads. Their heavy chain mail dragged them down as they struggled to hold their flags above the water.

Streaming up the opposite bank, they charged. Matilda's men were quickly overwhelmed, and ran back through the city gates.

Stephen's troops followed in hot pursuit, pouring through the gates in a fierce column. Once inside, they spread through the streets, throwing firebrands among the houses, capturing as many of Matilda's followers as they could find. Their new prisoners were put in chains — they could be traded for a ransom later.

The rest of Matilda's force fled with their lady in a desperate retreat to the castle, where they shut themselves inside. And left Stephen with no choice but to do this the hard way.

★ ★ ★

Once the heavy doors closed behind her, Matilda had felt safe in her stronghold. Inside the high stone keep, she was confident she could withstand anything Stephen brought against her. She knew the three enemies of people under siege — hunger, thirst, and fire. Her castle had ample supplies and a deep well, and its towering stone walls would not burn.

Let him come, she thought. And her knights braced themselves for the assault.

They did not have to wait long. First a rain of stones slung against the walls, then showers of arrows from a host of crossbows. Stephen's methods were simple: surround the castle and bombard it nonstop.

Matilda's knights fought back. They rained down stones and quicklime on the attackers from the top of the castle, and aimed their bows through the arrow-loops that slit the stone walls. They kept a strict watch for any scouts or assault teams who might try to crawl up the mound at the castle's base. And they waited anxiously for the siege engines they knew the King could bring to batter the castle defenses. Monstrous catapults that hurled rocks into or over the walls. Battering rams to break down the doors.

While her men held the king's army at bay, Matilda plotted her next move. She could take her time. She knew sieges moved slowly — weeks, months could pass with both sides in a stand-off. There was plenty of time for reinforcements to arrive. Time for her half-brother, Earl Robert, or her husband to come to her aid. Months ago, Robert had sailed to France to convince Matilda's husband, Geoffrey of Anjou, to join her cause. But she had heard nothing since. Where were they?

Robert was always one to play for time, Matilda reasoned. He'd wait for the right moment. But deep down she knew that any help from her husband was doubtful. They were not close. Still, he might act for their son's sake, if not hers — to protect young Henry's birthright in England!

Just hold out, she told herself. Help is on the way.

★ ★ ★

Stephen knew that laying siege to Matilda and her knights would be a long, ugly struggle. Matilda was no fool and had surely stocked the castle well with food and supplies. But Stephen had already learned that as long as she was on the loose he would have no peace. It seemed he had spent most of his reign dashing from castle to castle, laying siege to rebel after rebel. No sooner was one rebel army defeated than another reared its head, defying him to attack. This time he would not budge.

Messengers arrived, breathless with news. Matilda's allies had joined their forces about 15 miles down the Thames at Wallingford. Then word came that Earl Robert had returned from France and attacked Stephen's garrison at Wareham. The royal troops inside the castle were "shaken and terrified by the Earl's siege engines," they said. The castellan had asked Robert for a truce so he could summon help from the king.

But Stephen refused to be lured away from the Oxford siege. "No hope of gain, no fear of loss will make me go away," he declared, "unless the castle is surrendered and the empress brought into my power."

Nothing would drag him from his goal — to capture Matilda and end the war.

★ ★ ★

Staring at the dying embers of her small fire, Matilda could no longer ignore the doubts that plagued her mind. The siege had entered its third grueling month. Winter deepened.

She and her knights were famished. Scarcely eating, they tried to make their meager supplies last as long as possible. When the well dried up, they drank wine. Now that was nearly gone.

Day by day, Matilda's fears had mounted. Now she was certain. No help was coming. And outside, an army of more than a thousand enemy knights surrounded the castle, battering it with stones. It was only a matter of time now before her garrison would be forced to surrender.

Unconditional surrender. It was an outcome Matilda had never dreamed of. Now she imagined the long line of defeated knights streaming from the castle, Stephen's trumpets sounding in victory. And she pictured the part that tradition held for her — to walk out barefoot and in tears, her hair loose around her shoulders, begging Stephen for her very life.

No, she thought, rising and crossing the room. She was too proud to play that role. She must escape, before the walls crumbled and the starved garrison fell to the King. But how?

Stephen had posted guards all around the castle walls, with orders to keep a strict watch day and night. No one must be allowed to sneak out. How could she get past his watchmen? And even if she could, the whole of Stephen's army lay around the castle, his soldiers blocking every route.

Matilda gazed at the frozen landscape outside. Icy winds swept over deep snow as far as the eye could see. And where would she go in that wasteland? Why, it was so cold this year the Thames was frozen solid!

She drew in sharp breath as a sudden idea came to her. Perhaps the harsh winter could be a friend as well as a foe. But she would need help. In her mind she cast over the knights in her service. She would need to choose carefully — she wanted men who were wary, sensible, and absolutely loyal. No hotheads! Yes, three knights came to mind. She would speak to them at once. Alone.

★ ★ ★

In the stillness of a pitch-dark night, just before Christmas, Stephen's sentries paced at the foot of the castle walls, blowing on their frozen hands, stamping their feet to keep warm. High above their heads, a rope snaked its way out of a tower window, down the steep wall toward the ground.

Unseen by the guards below, Matilda clung to the rope as it was lowered down the sheer wall. The wind lashed at her face and made her white garments flap. Suddenly her descent halted and for a nerve-wracking instant she just hung there, swaying. She squeezed her eyes shut and tightened her grip.

Then she felt herself drop again. Willing her eyes open, she forced herself to look down. Below, one of her trusted knights was waiting for her. In his white clothes, she could hardly make him out against the snow. Good, she thought, their camouflage was working.

The wind picked up, and sharp, wet snow stung her cheeks. But she didn't mind. She knew a snowstorm would make it hard to see your hand in front of your face. It could be the stroke of luck they needed!

Below, one of her accomplices held up his arms to guide her to the ground. When Matilda had first proposed this scheme, the knights had wondered if the hunger had gone to her head! Walking out through Stephen's troops, dressed in white so they would disappear against the snow? It was madness! But Matilda was determined. Her subjects were familiar with her fierce will. Once her mind was made up there was no changing it.

Above Matilda, the last of her escape party was inching his way down. As soon as he touched the ground, the four of them set out cautiously across the snow, toward the royal troops whose camps lay in every direction.

Silently they tiptoed forward, threading their way through the sleeping army. No one stirred. Moving slowly through the blowing snow, Matilda and her knights circled around the tents of sleeping soldiers and little pockets of watchmen.

Matilda fought the urge to run, to dash through the encampment and be off! But she did not dare quicken her careful pace. She could barely see a few steps ahead in the storm. It would be too easy to stumble on an enemy foot or leg in the darkness. One false step would be their undoing.

Then, out of the corner of her eye, Matilda spotted a sudden movement. She froze and signaled to her knights to stop in their tracks. A figure was moving toward them through the darkness. Matilda prayed they would be invisible through the swirling snow. As the figure drew closer, she could see it was a sentry. But could he see them?

The sentry peered through the darkness, his eyes scanning back and forth in their direction. Matilda stood frozen in place, not daring to speak or move. The sentry blinked as if to clear his eyes, then started walking straight toward her.

The knight at her side silently crouched down and began to creep in a circle around the approaching soldier. As the sentry came closer, his eyes widened — he had seen them! He opened his mouth to shout, but a firm hand clapped over it. While the knight held him from behind, Matilda and her two companions moved swiftly forward.

Making a silent plea with her eyes, Matilda slipped a fistful of coins into the sentry's palm, and placed her finger to her lips. He blinked and nodded slightly.

The white-clad group moved on, faster now. Matilda could feel the wind pick up, and she knew the icy expanse of the Thames lay ahead. They were almost at the riverbank. A moment later Matilda placed a wary foot on the ice, and then her whole weight. It's solid, she thought with relief. She and her knights spread out and crept forward cautiously, testing the ice with each step.

Behind them the silence of the night was suddenly broken by loud shouts and blaring trumpets. Curse him, Matilda thought, the sentry must have raised the alarm! She pressed ahead as quickly as she dared. The wind swept around her as she moved across the frozen water, and she felt keenly how exposed she was — out in the open for everyone to see!

Or perhaps not, Matilda reminded herself. Her only hope was that their white clothes were once again hiding them from their pursuers. Without a backward glance, she kept going, struggling to keep her footing on the ice.

With a surge of relief, Matilda stepped onto the opposite bank. The clamor of enemy soldiers sounded distant now. How remarkable, she thought suddenly. To think I have crossed with dry feet, without wetting any of my garments, the very waters into which the king and his troops plunged up to the neck!

But her odyssey was far from over. Six miles of frozen countryside lay between her and her nearest friends. The four escapers trudged close together for fear of getting lost in the blizzard — through snow and ice, down steep ditches and up treacherous hills. Exhausted and frozen, they stumbled toward Abingdon, where supporters of Matilda's cause gave them horses.

They did not dare rest at Abingdon for long. Mounting their horses, the group galloped to Matilda's stronghold at Wallingford, where her allies welcomed her with astonished joy.

When Earl Robert heard of Matilda's daring escape he rushed to join her. He had been at Cirencester, trying to rally an army of supporters to march to her aid at Oxford. Upon Robert's arrival Matilda sprang forward to greet him, but was stopped in her tracks by the odd smile that played on her brother's features. As he stepped to one side, she saw what he had been hiding behind his back — her nine-year old son, Henry, brought with him from France. No other sight could have so restored Matilda's hopes. As she wrapped her arms around him, the past months seemed to slip away, forgotten.

★ ★ ★

Once Matilda's getaway was assured, her garrison at Oxford surrendered to Stephen's army. Stephen stayed a while in Oxford, bringing that rebellious part of the country under his control at last. And the townspeople and peasants of the ravaged countryside — always the first to suffer hunger and loss during a siege — began to piece their lives back together.

The chroniclers of the Middle Ages marveled at Matilda's cunning. One wrote, "Certainly I have never heard of any woman having such marvelous escapes from so many enemies threatening her life, and from such exceeding perils." But for all her cleverness, Matilda was never able to take the throne back from Stephen. In time she was rewarded, though — when her son became King Henry II.

The Gladiator War

Capua, Italy, 73 B.C.

THE YOUNG THRACIAN LIFTED HIS SWORD to ward off the blow. Then another. Sweating now, he dodged around his larger, heavily armed opponent, looking for an opening to make a thrust with his own weapon. The combat was fierce, and the midday sun beat mercilessly upon the two men. Then, lunging desperately forward, the Thracian opened himself to attack. Quickly he swiveled behind his small shield, but it was too late — with a forceful blow his opponent's sword fell across his bare chest.

Panting, the young man stopped and looked down to where the weapon pressed against his skin, but drew no blood. In the heat of the contest, he'd almost forgotten — the sword was wooden.

But in the arena it will be real, he thought, as he let his own wooden blade and shield fall to his side. And I won't get off so easily then.

Standing nearby, his trainer shook his head and spit into the sand. It was his job to turn the slaves assigned to him into gladiators — men who fought each other with weapons in public spectacles. The young man's name was Spartacus, but to his trainers he was just another slave, like the rest of the outcasts who crowded the barracks of the *ludi,* or gladiatorial school.

To Spartacus, it seemed like a lifetime since he was captured by the Roman army in his homeland of Thrace, a land of nomadic shepherds. Bound in chains, he had been taken over sea and land to Rome, to be sold as a slave. Seeing that he was young and strong, his captors forced him to serve in the Roman army for a time, before selling him to be trained as a gladiator.

His story was a common one. As the Roman army conquered the lands around the Mediterranean Sea, more and more prisoners were shipped back to Italy to work as slaves for wealthy Romans. The Roman Republic's demand for new slaves seemed endless — they needed them to farm their huge tracts of land, to shepherd their flocks, to work in their dangerous mines, to entertain them.

And Roman taste in entertainment ran to the spectacular — and the violent. In a warrior state such as theirs, martial skill and courage were highly prized. The strongest and healthiest of the slaves might be bought by a *lanista,* a man who owned and trained gladiators — "men of the sword." In giant amphitheaters these trained fighters would engage in armed combat for the entertainment of crowds, and the honor of the powerful men who paid for the spectacle.

For even more variety and excitement, gladiators with different fighting styles and armor would be pitted against each other. A lightly armed *retiarius,* holding a trident and a net to entangle his opponent, might face off against a slower, armored *secutor,* whose helmet and large shield offered some protection from the *retiarius's* three-pronged spear.

The rituals of the arena may have been dramatic, but there was nothing staged about the fighting. Contests were often fought to the death. The defeated gladiator's only hope was to appeal to the crowd and the patron of the games for a *missio,* a decision to let him live. But this was granted only if he had fought bravely enough to capture the spectators' sympathy. And they were not easy to impress.

For while the Roman crowds adored the performances, at the same time they held the gladiators in contempt. These fighters were the dregs of society, only slightly better than *bestiarii,* the slaves trained to fight wild animals.

Of course the Romans knew enough to keep a close guard on these men they had trained for combat but doomed to slavery. In the barracks that circled the *ludi's* sandy training yard, the fighters were locked in cells at night, their weapons secured in an armory well away from them.

Still, the Romans weren't unduly alarmed. Everyone knew Rome's army was all-powerful. And these slaves — riffraff from Gaul, Germany, Thrace, Syria. They couldn't be much of a threat.

No one seemed to realize just how desperate Spartacus and men like him were. What could he hope for at the end of his harsh training? After the discipline and punishments of the school barracks, with its stocks and chains? A banquet the night before the gladiatorial games. A few hours before the cheering crowds. What then? Some of his fellow slaves clung to the hope of winning their freedom — they'd heard stories of a few talented fighters who'd been set free. Or maybe they'd survive long enough to become trainers themselves.

But Spartacus knew the chances of that were slim at best. Most gladiators could hope to fight two, maybe three times in the arena before being killed. It wouldn't be long now before he was riding in a cart, on the way to his first combat. His first and perhaps his last. Yet what choice did he have?

Master and slave. It was the way things were, and always would be.

Wouldn't they?

In the days and months ahead, Spartacus would shatter this idea, and others the Romans held dear, forever.

★ ★ ★

Word quickly spread through the cramped barracks: There's going to be a breakout. Will you come? More and more of the desperate gladiators agreed, until 200 men were in on the secret.

It was the height of summer in the rich city of Capua in southern Italy, the center for gladiator training. For weeks, Spartacus had eyed the gladiators around him, sizing up these men from far-off countries — Thracians like himself, as well as Gauls, Germans, and Syrians. Some were slaves, some condemned criminals, others prisoners of war. But many of them were free-born, and still carried the memory of freedom. It had been easy to convince them to act.

Their scheme was bold and simple: to gather in the training yard, slowly, without raising suspicion. There they would grab the training weapons at hand and rush the guards. With luck they'd overpower them by their sheer numbers. Beyond that they had no plan, and no idea what would be waiting outside for them. For now, getting out was all that mattered.

But on the humid summer evening before the escape, terrible news reached Spartacus: someone had talked. Their master and *lanista,* Lentulus Batiatus, knew of the plan and who the ringleaders were. A local militia was on its way to make an example of the would-be escapers. The gladiators looked at one another helplessly. What could they do?

"We go now," Spartacus replied firmly, "before the guards lock us in for the night." He knew they still had a chance if they acted swiftly.

Over half the plotters slunk away to their cells, fearing it would be crazy to plunge ahead now that the plan had been discovered. Those left behind quickly weighed their options. Their weapons were locked in the armory, leaving them defenseless.

"Think!" hissed a Gaul named Crixus, keenly aware that armed officials could be on the grounds at any moment. "Is there nothing to defend ourselves with?"

"The kitchen — we can still get in there!" Spartacus cried suddenly. Storming through the barracks, the gladiators burst into the school's kitchen. They grabbed knives, forks, cooking spits — anything sharp that could serve as a weapon.

Armed now, they streamed out of the kitchen into the moonlit training yard. Barely slowing down, Spartacus stooped to pick up a handful of stones, and hurled them at the startled guards. With cries and shouts the other gladiators followed his example, and the guards raised their arms to shield themselves. In that instant the gladiators rushed upon them with their knives and spits.

In minutes they had broken out of the school and flooded onto the streets of Capua, their hearts pounding.

"Look!" Crixus cried, breathless.

The gladiators stopped in their tracks, openmouthed. Spartacus couldn't believe their luck. Before them were two wagons loaded with gladiatorial weapons, destined for a contest in another city! Seeing the gladiators, the drivers quickly jumped off the carts and ran. The escaped men eagerly snatched up swords and shields and armed themselves.

About 70 gladiators had made it out. Now they'd need a plan if they were to have a chance of staying free. They chose their leaders on the spot. Two Gauls, Crixus and another man named Oenomaus, were quickly voted captains. But the overwhelming choice for commander was Spartacus. It was obvious to all that the Thracian had the brains and the courage to help them survive. What was more, Spartacus had a special insight into the enemy, having fought in their ranks. That could prove to be a valuable weapon.

But first, the new leaders agreed, they must get out of Capua.

Suddenly, distant shouts and the sound of running feet made Spartacus look up. From all directions, armed citizens were running down the city streets. In moments the escapers would be cornered.

Their backs to the wall, the gladiators clenched their swords and braced themselves for the attack. But in the fierce struggle that followed, the locals were no match for men trained to fight and desperate to stay free. The gladiators quickly overpowered and disarmed them.

Spartacus picked up a Roman weapon and balanced its weight in his hand. With his other hand he threw down the gladiator's sword he'd been holding, as did the others. Barbaric object, he thought. Tainted with dishonor. He'd never touch one again.

★ ★ ★

In Rome, the senators listened impatiently to the messenger's story of gladiators breaking out of a school in Capua. Let the local forces take care of it, they sniffed. Then word came that the rebels had left the city. A slave named Spartacus had led his followers up the treacherous mountain path to the very top of Mount Vesuvius. The gladiators had set up a camp in the volcano's crater. Worse, other runaway slaves were joining them daily, and their growing numbers posed a risk to the region.

Very well, the Roman authorities sighed. They would send a Roman commander. Not a consul — it would be beneath his

dignity— but a praetor, a lesser official. They'd draft a force of 3,000 men to put under his command. That kind of muscle would surely put a quick end to the revolt, the senate reasoned. There was no need to use Rome's highly trained regular army. They were dealing with *slaves,* after all.

In a confident and boastful mood, the newly drafted troops marched swiftly south to the foot of Vesuvius. There they prepared to surround and lay siege to the rebel slaves.

High above, Spartacus and his scouts peered over the tangle

of wild vines that covered the mountaintop, and watched grimly as the Roman army gathered in numbers far below. Roman guards were taking up their posts along the narrow road up the mountain — the only route down. All the other sides of the mountain were as steep and smooth as cliffs.

"They're trapping us," the scouts muttered. "We'll starve up here."

Spartacus was silent for a moment. "If it comes to that," he said at last, "I'd rather die by steel than perish by hunger."

Without another word he crept back from the edge and turned toward the camp in the crater. He wasn't going to give in so easily. Glancing up, he noticed the sun was already high in the sky. There was much to do before dark.

Spartacus put the gladiators to work until nightfall, ripping out the vines that grew all around them. Carefully they twisted the stems into chains, until they were long enough to snake down the face of the mountain. When darkness came they were ready.

Fastening their ropes to the cliff top, the slaves silently scaled down one of the steep, unguarded mountainsides. Above them, one gladiator stayed behind with the weapons until the last of his companions had reached the foot of the mountain. Then he rapidly tossed down the weapons one by one. When the last weapon hit the ground below, he slithered down the vines himself.

The slaves crept silently around the base of the mountain, circling the sleeping Roman camp from behind. Spartacus and his captains paused, listening in the dark for any sounds of enemy movement. But they heard nothing, only their own breathing. Then, at a signal from Spartacus, the slaves rushed forward in a fierce surprise attack. Overwhelmed and bewildered in the darkness, many of the Roman soldiers fled. Spartacus and his followers seized the camp and plundered it for weapons and supplies.

It was a stunning victory, beyond their hopes. And to the slaves of the surrounding countryside, it was the moment they'd dreamed of. Herdsmen and shepherds from the region ran to join the gladiators, who welcomed them. Spartacus knew how valuable such men could be. Their work made them strong and fast, and they could handle weapons — defending their flocks against wild animals and thieves had taught them that. Then came slaves fleeing from surrounding farms. Many weren't trained to fight, but they put their skill at weaving baskets from branches to good use, making shields for the rebels.

Spartacus quickly organized the newcomers according to their skills. Some were given heavy weapons, some turned into light-armed troops, others were made scouts. This was no longer a band of runaways. They were an army now. And a threat that Rome could no longer ignore.

Burning with shame, the Roman Republic sent another praetor to lead soldiers against Spartacus — with orders to swiftly undo the dishonor of the first one's failure.

The Roman defeats that followed were humiliating. The slave army harried the Romans with sudden attacks, surprising one commander while he was bathing, stealing another commander's horse out from under him! Frightened, Roman soldiers began to desert the army. A few tried to join Spartacus, but he turned them away. All the while Spartacus's army grew, from hundreds to thousands. Now, slaves boldly ran from their masters' homes to join them as they passed. The sight of the gladiator army made two things clear. Escape from slavery was possible, and even the Roman army couldn't force them back!

Rome no longer worried about the indignity of fighting slaves. This was no sordid rebellion. The slave army had swelled to tens of thousands of men and women and was moving freely through southern Italy. The whole Roman way of life — balanced so carefully upon slavery — was at risk of falling to pieces. Now fear spurred the Roman senate to put both of the Republic's consuls in command of two legions of infantry and cavalry, over 10,000 men. This time they would fight as they would against a powerful enemy.

But Spartacus knew better than to take on the full force of the Roman army. Some of his men, thrilled by their victories, clamored to march on Rome itself. Spartacus proposed another goal — they would march north to the Alps, and out of Italy to freedom.

"We'll cross the mountains, and then every one to his own homeland. To Gaul, to Germany... and to Thrace."

★ ★ ★

As the mid-winter of 71 B.C. approached, Spartacus stood on the southernmost tip of Italy and gazed out over the choppy waves. He and his army were camped on the bank of the Strait of Messina. Across the water lay the island of Sicily. He was about as far from the Alps as he could be.

It had been a stormy two years. The march north to the mountains had been slowed by arguments among Spartacus's followers, who had become unruly and hard to control. Many were over-confident, fired up by their freedom and victories, and thought only of sweeping through the cities of Italy for plunder.

"It's not gold and silver we need," Spartacus had warned them, "but iron and copper." Basic material for weapons and survival would keep them alive, not stolen ornaments and jewelry.

Other commanders in the slave army had taken revenge on their Roman prisoners of war, holding gladiatorial games and forcing the Roman prisoners to fight each other. Crixus had even split from Spartacus, taking with him a huge number of German slaves. On their own, Crixus's men had been savagely defeated by the consuls' forces.

Yet the two Roman legions had been powerless to stop the bulk of Spartacus's army, and the slaves kept pushing north. Then, just as freedom had seemed within their reach, a Roman governor of Gaul had moved thousands of his soldiers to block the slaves' escape route through the Alps. Spartacus had been forced to turn back. He led his army south, sticking to remote areas far from the cities.

The defeated Roman consuls had been recalled to Rome in disgrace, and it was revealed that their armies had been stripped of much of their weaponry by the slaves. At last the Roman senate grasped the danger they faced. They quickly named Crassus, a well-born and respected commander, as the general in charge of the war, and placed under his command eight legions of the best trained troops. And if Crassus did not crush the slaves fast enough, the famous commander Pompey would be summoned from Spain to finish the job.

That was the last thing Crassus wanted. Pompey was his rival for power, and he knew that whoever arrived last would take credit for winning the war. Crassus was determined to destroy the slave army before Pompey returned. His first action was to make sure his troops were more afraid of him than of Spartacus, and he harshly punished deserters and any soldiers accused of cowardice. Then he prepared for a massive onslaught against the slaves.

Now, almost two years after the breakout at Capua, Spartacus knew that despite all the victories, his army could not hold out any longer. On reaching the southern shores of Italy, Spartacus had bargained with Cilician pirates to take his men in their ships across the strait to Sicily. He knew that a slave revolt had been crushed on that island only a few years before, and he guessed that the memory of it would still be vivid there. Perhaps he and his followers could rekindle the sparks of rebellion.

The pirates took gifts from Spartacus and promised to return with more ships. But Spartacus waited in vain for them on the seacoast. In the meantime, Crassus had followed him south, and set up camp behind the slave army. There, he began to build a fortified wall lined with sharpened stakes and fronted with a deep ditch.

At first Spartacus laughed at the wall. But not for long. The barrier soon stretched from shore to shore straight across the neck of land that led to the southern tip of Italy. Crassus had trapped Spartacus between his wall and the sea.

But Spartacus had not yet run out of tricks. On a snowy winter night, he ordered his men to begin filling a part of the trench with earth and branches. Before Crassus was aware of what was happening, a third of the slave army had crossed the trench and clambered over the wall, and the rest soon forced their way across. Spartacus hoped that if they moved swiftly east to the port of Brundisium, they might sail from Italy across the Adriatic Sea.

He knew it was their last chance for escape, but by now many of his troops thought too highly of themselves to listen to their commander. Spartacus's strategy of sudden attacks followed by retreat — so successful in the past — now seemed beneath them. They were tired of staying on the defensive, forever on the move.

The slender thread of control Spartacus still held over his army snapped at last. Crassus's legions had been close on their heels for days, as the Roman general hoped to force a battle before Pompey's return. Spotting Crassus's nearby camp, a number of hotheaded slaves rushed to attack the soldiers nearest them. In no time, men from either side were leaping into the fray.

Spartacus watched grimly, and he knew that the decision to attack had been snatched out of his hands. On his reluctant command, the rest of his army wheeled around into battle formation, and Spartacus prepared to face Crassus head-on. Leading his men, he rushed straight for the Roman commander. In the brutal struggle that followed, Spartacus was last seen surrounded and outnumbered, defending himself with his raised shield and sword.

★ ★ ★

In the end, it had taken eight Roman legions — about 44,000 men — and two years to defeat Spartacus and his rebels. Pompey did arrive from Spain and stole the glory for the victory from Crassus by catching the last stragglers of the slave army fleeing the battle. The Romans took a terrible revenge on the slaves who had dared to defy them: 6,000 were executed as a warning to other slaves.

Yet even the Roman and Greek historians of the era, who would have liked to describe Spartacus as a low-life barbarian, were forced to admire his ingenuity and courage. To their shock, 3,000 Roman prisoners of war were found unharmed in Spartacus's camp after the slaves' defeat. And Spartacus had died as they believed a man should, boldly leading his troops in battle. It seemed scarcely believable, but this Thracian slave had behaved almost like — dared they say it — a Roman.

Over the Wall

Pössneck, East Germany, 1978

SOMETHING STRANGE WAS DEFINITELY GOING ON. That's the only conclusion 14-year-old Frank Strelzyk could come to. His parents had been going out a lot at night. And they *never* went out. His dad hated how you had to be careful what you said in public. You couldn't complain about your job or criticize the government without worrying that the person next to you would call the police. At least in my own living room I can speak my mind, his dad would say. So his parents usually stayed at home with Frank, watching West German TV. Until recently, that is.

And it wasn't just the nights out that were odd. His dad was spending hours in the garage with their neighbor, Günter Wetzel. Maybe that wasn't so strange — his dad, an electrician, often repaired things at home for extra money. But he usually loved to show Frank how to fix stuff. Now his workshop was off-limits. What were they doing in there?

One day Frank had snuck into the garage and seen the two men standing in front of something weird — it looked like a big airplane propeller. When they saw Frank they nearly jumped out of their skins. A couple of weeks later he passed the open door and had another peek. Inside, a giant roll of fabric leaned against the wall. His dad and Günter exchanged glances. "It's a tent," his dad said as he closed the door, blocking Frank's view.

Frank had wandered into the kitchen, where his mom was staring out the window, a faraway look in her eyes. She didn't even notice Frank at first.

What's happening? he thought. If something's wrong, why don't they tell me? He could understand if they didn't want to worry his younger brother, Andreas.

But why don't they tell *me?* he wondered helplessly. I'm not a little kid anymore.

★ ★ ★

Peter Strelzyk didn't like hiding things from his son, but he couldn't afford to take chances. Not now, not when they were so close.

It had started over a year ago, but back then it was just a game. A game that helped him forget the long hours he worked with nothing to show for it. A game that made him feel better when he could no longer read the newspapers without throwing them down in disgust. They were full of official lies about how good life was in Communist Germany. No one dared say anything different — the secret police's spies were everywhere. Troublemakers might be arrested in the middle of the night, and their neighbors would never find out what happened to them.

Sometimes Peter gazed across town toward the West. Not many miles away was another world he couldn't go see — because of the long stretch of barbed wire that snaked along the border between Communist East Germany and the democratic West. He'd never felt so trapped as when he visited Berlin and saw the looming concrete wall, first built in 1961, that sliced the city in half. The Communist government said it would safeguard the socialist way of life, but everyone soon discovered its real purpose — to keep people in, not enemies out.

And so he'd started playing a game in his head. If I wanted to get out, how would I do it? He asked his friend Günter what he thought.

"There's just no way out by land," Günter said in his usual slow, thoughtful tone. "The fences along the border are crawling with armed guards — in watchtowers and on the ground. They see everything. And even if you were able to get over the barbed wire, there's the death strip."

Peter nodded. Günter didn't have to explain what he meant: the barren strip of land between the barbed wire fence and the final wall bordering West Germany. It was covered with hidden mines that would explode under the lightest footstep, and trip wires that set off hails of automatic bullets.

"And there's no route by boat," Günter went on. "So that leaves only one way. Air."

"But where would we — I mean, someone — get an airplane, or a helicopter?"

Günter shrugged. They both knew it was impossible, unless you were very rich.

Peter couldn't remember who thought of it first. But one day at lunch, one of the friends nudged the other.

"I've got it — a balloon!"

"What?"

"Why don't we build ourselves a balloon?"

Both men grinned. So it wasn't just a game anymore! They were hooked on the idea from the start. Peter was known for solving problems on the assembly line at work. And there wasn't a car engine or machine that Günter couldn't fix. This would be the challenge of their lives!

But how *would* they build it? Neither of them had any first-hand knowledge of balloons.

"Hot air rises," Peter reasoned. "So we heat the cold air inside a big balloon with some kind of flame. But the flame has to be strong. We need enough heat to push the balloon, the basket, and all of us into the air."

That was about all they knew.

The next morning they stopped off at the People's Library to look for a book that could help them. In the sparse collection they found only two helpful items. And one was an entry in an encyclopedia about the first balloon flight in history — 200 years ago!

Peter wasn't discouraged. "If they could do it then," he whispered to Günter, "we should be able to do it today!"

★ ★ ★

Peter sat at the kitchen table, scrawling calculations on a pad. The balloon would need to carry four adults — Peter and his wife, Doris; Günter and his wife, Petra. Plus four kids — Frank, Andreas, and the Wetzels' two children. Then there was the weight of the basket, the heating system and the balloon itself. All in all, about 1,700 pounds!

Peter's pencil scratched until he arrived at the size of balloon they would need to lift it all. He stared at his results. Their balloon would have to hold as much air as a house — a big one! They'd need a huge amount of fabric.

Where would they buy all it all? Not in Pössneck, that was for sure. Stores were so badly stocked, Doris sometimes lined up for hours for groceries, only to find they were sold out when her turn came.

Peter and Günter drove from city to city. At last they found a roll of brown cotton in a department store.

"How much do you need?" asked the salesperson.

Peter glanced around to see if anyone was listening. He paused, then blurted out, "Eight hundred and eighty yards."

The salesperson's jaw dropped. "We run a camping club," he added hastily. "We need to line our tents."

Peter quickly paid cash with his savings and the two men lugged the rolls of fabric back to the car, shoving them into the trunk and back seat. After dark they drove to Günter's house and carried them up to the Wetzels' bedroom in the attic. They couldn't be too careful — a nosy neighbor might report any odd behavior to the police.

Over the next two days they cut the material into huge triangles and long, narrow rectangles. Günter hunched over Petra's forty-year-old sewing machine, pumping the foot pedal to sew the strips together, while Peter fed him the long pieces of fabric.

Outside the bedroom, Petra blocked the door with a ladder. "We're renovating," she told visitors. Günter put a second doorbell in the attic to warn them if someone came to call. After two weeks of labor, Günter's eyes were bleary and his ankles swollen, but they had their balloon — 50 feet wide and 66 feet long.

Next the men drew the curtains in Günter's workshop on the second floor and set to work on the basket and burner. Peter's welding torch sparked for hours as he pieced together the passenger basket from steel posts and wooden boards. He strung a clothesline between the posts for a guardrail.

The gas burner was trickier. It would have to be powerful. Peter rigged two propane bottles to a stovepipe, and prayed they would work.

The two men worked fiendishly, and within a few weeks it was time for a test. Peter and Günter drove around, looking for a place to try out the balloon in secret. Outside town they found a clearing in a wood of tall pine trees. Perfect!

Just before midnight, Peter and Günter stuffed the rolled-up balloon and equipment into the trunk and back seat of the car. Peter could hardly contain his excitement as they drove to the test site and quickly set up.

The burner shot out a flame, but the balloon stayed flat as a pancake. The fabric wasn't airtight! Peter groaned — they'd have to start over.

But they didn't dare buy so much material all at once again — it was too risky. The two men and their wives spread out to hunt for bits and pieces of fabric, driving to different towns and stores to buy airtight taffeta scrap by scrap.

★ ★ ★

On a cool May evening, little more than a month after the first test, the two couples spread their multicolored balloon across the clearing, and Peter started up the blower. The roar was deafening, even with the muffler Peter had added. Günter cringed at the noise.

"Don't worry," Peter shouted in Günter's ear. "People will think it's a motorcycle."

Günter, Doris, and Petra held up the neck of the balloon. Watching Peter, they braced themselves for the impact. Günter nodded, and Peter turned on the blowtorch and burner. The flame streaked out — higher than they expected. Doris and Petra jumped out of the way. Peter's hair was singed as he held the powerful burner steady.

The fabric on the ground began to stir, rippling as the air streamed through it. Peter stared at it as he gripped the burner. Come on, he thought. This time it *has* to work.

Ever so slowly, the colored stripes began to rise off the ground, snapping in the air. The balloon swelled as it lifted high above their heads.

All four stood with their heads tilted back, mouths open in amazement. It was beautiful! Like a dream, the balloon towered over the trees and swayed against the starry sky. Flushed with their first success, Peter shouted for joy.

It was time to tell Frank, he decided. He had worried that the kids would have a hard time keeping a giant balloon a secret. One little hint to their friends, and the whole plan was finished. Worse, they could be arrested. But now Frank was getting suspicious — it might be more dangerous to leave him guessing any longer.

Back at home, Peter led Frank to the garage, and this time he didn't hide anything from his son. As Frank stared at the deflated balloon, basket, and burner, Peter told him the story of their escape plan. Frank blinked with disbelief, then a slow smile spread across his face. It seemed too good to be true!

"We're almost ready to go," his father added.

★ ★ ★

Peter watched Günter as he wandered restlessly around the garage. He had been quiet tonight, even for Günter. Something was wrong.

Finally Günter spoke up. "Petra's been having bad dreams," he said slowly. "She's more afraid now — that we'll get arrested. That we'll crash."

"That's natural..." Peter began to say.

Günter cut him off. "It's not just Petra who's having doubts. Look, we've filled the balloon, but we still don't have enough lifting power." He looked down, avoiding Peter's eyes. "I'm just not sure that we can do it anymore."

Peter nodded. He turned his face to hide his disappointment. How could he blame them? Günter and Petra would have to risk so much.

"It might be better if we didn't see each other," he said at last. "I don't want the police arresting you and Petra as our accomplices."

There was nothing else to say. The two friends shook hands and Günter walked out into the night.

★ ★ ★

Peter stood in his backyard in the crisp spring air and stared at the propane tanks at his feet. It had been a year since that wonderful night when their balloon had filled the sky. Peter was still struggling alone to solve the puzzle of lifting power.

Peter sighed as he upended another used propane bottle. He turned the tap to empty the last bit of gas. Instantly propane streamed out through the opened tap. The pressure was incredible!

That's it! Peter thought. Turning the bottles upside down increases the pressure! That night he confirmed his theory at the test site — the burner's flame was at least 40 feet long.

Nothing was holding them back now. The Strelzyks waited nervously for the right flying weather — a clear night with a westward wind that would blow them over the border. Frank spent days at school staring out the window at a nearby weathervane. Doris and Peter made a point of taking on long-term projects at work, so no one would suspect they had a sudden departure on their minds.

Then one afternoon at school, Frank didn't hear a word his teacher said. The weathervane outside had been pointing steadily in the right direction for hours. The sky was blue — not a cloud in sight. Tonight would be the night!

Back at home, Doris grabbed the family's identification papers and made sure everyone had warm clothes — they would be soaring thousands of feet up in the cold night air. But they took little else with them. Extra weight would be disastrous.

The hours passed slowly as they waited for dark, then for their neighbors' lights to turn off. Slipping through the garage into the car, Peter told the boys to lie down in the back seat, so no one would see them out late.

The motion of the car soon put Andreas to sleep. But Frank was wide awake, his heart racing. He'd never felt so excited — or nervous.

At the clearing they set up quickly, and Peter made a final equipment check: flashlights, matches, altimeter. He started the blower and the balloon began to fill with cold air. Glancing up at the sky, he frowned. A few clouds drifted across the sky. They hadn't been there when they left. But he wasn't turning back now.

It was time to heat the air. He ignited the blowtorch and held the flame to the neck of the balloon. Frank quickly put the burner together. He watched for his dad's signal, then lit it.

The balloon rose so swiftly they were startled. The lines holding the basket to the fabric stretched to the breaking point.

"Come on," Peter shouted as he turned off the blowtorch and threw it down. The four of them scrambled inside and crouched down on the steel floor. Peter and Frank leaned over the sides and cut the cables holding them to the ground.

Slowly, gently, the basket swayed upward. Peter had not expected it would feel like this — he could hardly tell they were moving at all. Doris and the kids watched the trees below get smaller.

Peter kept his eyes on the gas flame. He mustn't let it touch the fabric, no matter what. He gripped the stovepipe to steady the flame in the center. It was as cold as ice! With a groan Peter remembered that he had left his work gloves lying on the ground. And beside them he had dropped the fire extinguisher!

The balloon kept rising in the darkness. Within minutes they had passed 3,000 feet, then 4,000, and still they soared higher. Peter guessed it would take them half an hour to reach West Germany. How much time had it been so far — 10, 20 minutes? Not long now, he told himself.

Suddenly Peter felt like he'd been drenched in a wet fog. They were in the clouds!

Don't panic, he thought. But he knew the balloon would soak up the water in the clouds like a sponge. It would make them heavier. And slower.

The basket started spinning, buffeted by strong winds. They'd hit turbulence! Peter quickly turned down the gas, and they sank under the clouds.

No one noticed at first that they kept sinking. Peter was blinded by the burner's hot flame. Why didn't I bring goggles? he thought uselessly. But when the others looked over the side, they saw the lights below getting bigger.

Shouts filled the balloon as everyone realized at once — they were going down.

"We're dropping!"

"Look out!"

There was no time to turn up the gas to lift them back up. Before Peter could react, he heard fabric tearing as the balloon sailed through the treetops. Pine branches gripped the balloon as it passed, slowing it down. Before they knew what was happening, they hit the ground.

"Everyone out!" Peter ordered. He didn't know what might

happen — the propane might explode, or the balloon might fall, trapping them.

One by one they hopped over the guardrail and ran into the woods. From a hiding spot they looked around, panting.

Where were they?

Peter's mind raced. They'd been in the air for more than half an hour. Chances were, they'd made it.

"Stay here while I look around," he said.

Peter walked alone out of the woods and spotted a fence up ahead. No, he thought. Two fences, high ones, with a strip between them. He tried to stay calm. Was it the border?

And which side were they on?

Peter returned to the woods. "Follow me," he whispered to his family. "Slowly."

They crept through the dark with the flashlight off, afraid its light would give them away. Peter stumbled on something. He lit the flashlight, shielding the beam with his hand and moved forward.

The light fell across something odd — wires spiraling across their path, about waist high.

Holding the others back, Peter swung his leg carefully over the wires. There were more ahead. He followed the length of one of the wires with the flashlight, and saw where it connected to a box.

Trip wires! Fear gripped Peter's mind. Do the West Germans use trip wires on their side? He didn't know. But they couldn't go any further in the dark, not with these deadly traps threading all around them. The slightest brush against them would set off an alarm — or automatic bullets. They'd have to wait until dawn.

Frank stooped down and picked something up. It was a torn package. Peter aimed his flashlight at it, and as they read the print, their hearts sank: "People's Owned Bakery, Wernigerode."

They were still in East Germany, just short of the border fences. Without speaking, Peter clicked off the flashlight. The four of them huddled together, and waited for first light.

★ ★ ★

If only. Those words haunted Peter when they got back home. If only they hadn't hit the clouds. If only he'd noticed sooner that they were sinking. He could have turned up the flame for the burst of speed they needed to carry them over the border. They were so close! The thought tortured him.

As the days passed, his hands stopped shaking, and he told himself that they had been lucky. A little further and they would have landed in the minefield.

Now something worse weighed on his mind — there was no going back to their old life. They'd left a balloon lying in the border zone. The police would search for the failed escapers. The newspaper had already carried a picture of the things they'd left in the abandoned balloon, asking people to come forward with information about the "crime."

It was only a matter of time before some clue — the fabric they'd bought, a witness who'd seen them driving to the clearing — led the secret police to their door.

There was only one thing to do: build another balloon. Fast. But this time Peter knew they couldn't do it alone.

★ ★ ★

Günter had pricked up his ears when he heard rumors of a torn balloon found near the border. Was it Peter's? He hadn't spoken to his friend since they'd agreed to go their separate ways.

When Peter knocked on his door, he had been surprised. He had listened eagerly to the details of the flight, the old excitement coming back. Peter described what had gone wrong.

"But you should have seen it, Günter! The takeoff and the flight were so smooth." Günter's eyes had grown brighter as he listened.

"If you had been there to navigate, Günter, we would have made it," Peter added. "I know it."

"I'll have to think about it, Peter."

But Günter had already known what his answer would be. Since they had backed out, he and Petra had regretted their decision more and more each day.

Now, standing beside Peter in the forest clearing, he couldn't help a feeling of pride as the balloon — their third one — rose before his eyes.

The filled balloon strained against the lines that held it to the ground. The ropes wouldn't hold for long.

"Hurry!" Günter called.

The two families scrambled inside. Frank and Günter reached down to slice the lines. But only two ropes were cut right through. Under the strain, the third peg flew out of the ground.

The basket tipped over, held by one line. Everyone tumbled to the side. Peter struggled to control the burner — at this angle it was grazing the balloon. To his horror, flames ran up the fabric. Günter aimed the fire extinguisher and with a steady burst put them out.

Then he dropped the extinguisher and frantically hacked at the last line with his knife. The basket tipped back and began to rise. They sailed up into the darkness. Peter held the burner, while Günter kept an eye on the altimeter. Doris and Petra made sure the kids were safe.

They were moving fast in a cloudless sky filled with stars.
Suddenly Günter's shout broke the silence. "Below! Spotlights!"

Beams of light from the border watchtowers swung across
the sky, crisscrossing in midair. Peter frantically tried to remember — do they have anti-aircraft guns at the border? He didn't
think so. He told himself that their machine guns couldn't fire
this high.

He opened the burner valve. The flame streaked higher into
the balloon, and they shot up above the lights.

Then, his heart sinking, Peter saw the flame sputter. Quickly he cranked open the valve as far as it could go. But he couldn't get a steady flame.

"How high are we?" he asked Günter.

"About 6,500 feet, but we're going down!"

The flame got smaller as Peter struggled with the burner. Then it dawned on him. We're out of fuel! How could that be? We've been flying for 23 minutes, he thought. We should have enough for 35 minutes. But there was no denying it. His calculations must have been wrong.

The flame flickered and went out. He could feel the balloon sinking. Below, they could see traffic lights. No, not yet, Peter thought wildly.

Günter grabbed the matches and tore out a handful. Striking them all at once, he held them to the burner. For a few seconds, a final flame streamed out.

The balloon soared upward briefly before the flame died. But was it enough?

Suddenly they were spinning, dropping, unable to steer. Peter strained to see through the darkness. Murky shapes were rushing toward them, getting larger as they fell earthward. Hills and trees, then farms.

They grabbed the posts and braced themselves for the crash. Branches brushed the basket's sides as they hurtled forward. Helpless, Peter clung to his post. Then he felt the earth beneath them.

The basket skimmed the grass, slowed, and came to a stop. Before they had caught their breath, it started to tip. Peter looked up — the balloon had caught in a tree and was dragging the basket over. He rushed to steady the propane bottles, while Günter cut the lines, freeing them of the balloon.

Everyone shook as they climbed out. They had flown for 28

minutes, thought Peter. Not long enough!

"Peter and I will look around," said Günter. "If it's safe, I'll light a flare. But if you don't see it, stay put!" Doris, Petra, and the kids hid in the trees as the two men walked away.

Across a field they spotted a large barn, its door hanging open. Peter and Günter ventured inside and swung the flashlight around.

The sound of a car pulling to a stop outside made them jump. Peter and Günter ducked behind the wall and peeked out. The car's headlights were aimed at the field. Peter could see two men in the front seats. Border police?

They must have tracked the balloon with the spotlights, then radar, thought Peter. They followed us straight to the crash site!

The two figures in the car got out and looked around.

Peter glanced desperately around for another way out of the barn. They're going to spot us any second, he thought.

Günter stared at the car — it was an Audi. Not what the cops usually drive, he thought. On its side, the single word "POLICE" shone in the dark. He'd never seen a police car like that before. Then suddenly it occurred to him.

That was no East German police car.

★ ★ ★

The police officers jumped when they saw two men running toward them from the barn. Wild-eyed, one of them was calling breathlessly, "Are we in West Germany?"

The policemen were so startled they just nodded. Shouts and hoots of joy pierced their ears. Before they had time to ask the strangers any questions, they were nearly knocked over as the two men hugged them.

"We made it!" the men shouted, jumping up and down. Then

one of them pulled a flare out of his pocket and lit it. The policemen looked at each other, mouths open. What was going on?

Now women and kids were running toward them across the field. Everyone was talking at once, but they managed to hear one thing clearly. These people claimed to have just landed in a hot-air balloon!

"Come on," the policemen chided. "Where did you people really come from?"

Petra led one of the officers to the site of the crash. But once there, she appeared to remember something. She reached inside the basket and drew out a carefully bundled package. Taking it back to the others, she unwrapped it while they watched.

"Champagne!" she cried, and they all laughed as she showed them the bottle. Petra had heard that every balloon flight needed a bottle of champagne for good luck.

★ ★ ★

It wasn't until four a.m. that the refugees popped the cork — in the town police station. Together they drank a toast to their amazing flight, and to the new life that lay ahead.

Reporters wanted to know why they had risked so much to escape to the West. Peter answered with the words he had carefully chosen to explain his actions. They wanted to live as free people, who could say what they thought and go where they wanted. And they wanted a good future for their children. The press called them heroes, but Peter disagreed.

"There's nothing heroic about wanting to be free," he said. "In any case, our desire for freedom far outweighed our fear."

Slaves of the Sahara

North Atlantic Coast of Africa, Off Cape Bajador, 1815

"TEN O'CLOCK!" CRIED THE MAN AT THE HELM. Through the fog, Captain Riley eyed the mainsail boom. It stretched far out to starboard, the ship running ahead of a strong breeze. The helmsman turned to port, and as the boom swung across the deck, Riley heard a roaring.

A squall? Startled, Riley glanced down the ship's lee side. Through a hole in the mist, he glimpsed rough water foaming below. Breakers!

"All hands on deck!" he shouted.

Working fast, the men dropped anchor and hauled in the sails. The ocean roared around them as they struggled to slow the ship before it hit the rocks. Waves swept across the deck, knocking the sailors off their feet.

For days, fog had made it hard to fix their position, but until now Riley had no idea how off-course they were. The *Commerce,* an American brig loaded with cargo, was headed from Gibraltar to the Canary Islands. Now its young captain knew the worst — they had been blown up against the North African coast, where deadly breakers pounded the rocky shoreline.

Riley's practical mind raced. The ship was beyond hope — pinned to the rocks and hammered by wave after wave. There was only one thing to do — save the crew before the vessel broke up and sank. The men worked quickly, knowing their lives depended on it. They grabbed all the water and provisions they could find, and threw overboard anything that would float. With luck some of it would wash ashore.

Riley fastened a sturdy rope to the ship's side. He signaled to his first mate, Porter, and the two men climbed down into the ship's small lifeboat, bringing the line with them. Waves broke over their bodies as they rowed desperately for the beach. A huge swell lifted their boat above the water, throwing them onto the sand. Riley scrambled for the line before it disappeared into the surf and tied it to a rock.

One by one the crew grasped the rope and lowered themselves out of the wreck, moving hand over hand along the line to shore. When the last exhausted sailor touched sand, they made a hasty camp on the beach. The ship's longboat washed ashore, its side smashed. Then came trunks of coins from their cargo. The men quickly buried the money in the sand.

Stopping to catch his breath, Riley scanned the sand dunes for other human beings. He wasn't in a hurry to see any. He knew that sailors shipwrecked on these shores were often captured and sold into slavery. Their best chance was to repair the leaky longboat and try their luck out at sea. The men set to work, until darkness forced them to quit for the night.

At first light, Riley's fears were realized. Heads appeared over the dunes. Down the sandy hills sprinted a nimble gray-haired man, holding a spear. Younger men followed, armed with scimitars. Further off, Riley spotted more figures on camels approaching across the dunes. Soon they'd be surrounded!

Panicking, the sailors scrambled into the half-repaired longboat and rowed frantically back to the *Commerce*. From the wreck,

Riley watched helplessly as the strangers plundered their camp. He gasped as one of them drove an axe into their casks, spilling the precious water onto the sand. Others dismounted from their camels and gathered the sea instruments and charts scattered across the beach. To Riley's horror, they burned them in a pile. Around him the crew clung to the wreck, tightening their grips with each sweeping wave that threatened to wash them off.

Then, to Riley's amazement, the men on the beach ran down to the water and put down their weapons at their feet. One of them held up a goatskin of water. Were they signaling peace?

The old man pointed to himself and then to the wreck. He wanted to come on board! He pointed to Riley and then to the beach. Riley understood: he was offering a trade — the captain for himself — to guarantee his safe return from the ship.

Riley quickly weighed their chances of getting out to sea through the pounding surf — slim indeed. They needed these people's help to survive. On a sudden impulse, he grabbed the line and worked his way back to the beach. The old man took Riley's place on the line and hauled himself toward the wreck. Once on board he looked around — for guns or money, Riley guessed.

Riley cupped his hands around his mouth and shouted to Porter: "Don't let him come back until they let me go!"

Porter put his hand to his ear and shook his head — he couldn't hear the captain over the roaring surf! Riley kept shouting, but his cries were lost in the din.

Finding nothing, the old man started back.

"Stop him!" Riley cried. He shot forward to the line. Strong hands grabbed his arms, as two men pulled him out of the water. Riley looked down at the scimitars they pointed at his chest, the metal blades glinting in the sun. He was their prisoner.

By now the old man had reached the sand, and the men started dragging Riley by the arms toward the dunes.

Riley thought fast. With frantic gestures, he signaled that a stash of coins was buried on the beach. The men stopped. One group headed for the spot he'd pointed out and began scraping at the sand. Two others sat Riley down with his face to the sea and pointed their scimitars at him — one to his chest, one to his head.

When they find the money, they'll probably shout, Riley thought. And my guards might look away for an instant. He'd have only one chance. Slowly, he drew his legs under him.

An excited shout was heard from behind. Riley's guards jerked their heads around. In a flash Riley sprung out from under their weapons and dove for the beach.

Riley knew he was running for his life. Sprinting to the water's edge, he felt his pursuers close on his heels. He plunged head-first into the waves and pushed his way underwater with desperate strokes. He didn't dare come up for a breath! Finally, his lungs bursting, Riley broke through the surface and gasped for air.

He stole a quick look around. The old man was close behind, up to his chin in the rough water. His arm was raised, his spear aimed at Riley. As he pulled back to let it fly, a huge surf rolled over both of them, hurtling the old man onto the beach.

Riley turned and swam furiously toward the wreck. Wave after wave broke over him. Each time he surfaced he glimpsed the crew on board, shouting and urging him on. At last he threw his arm up along the side, but a heavy surf pushed him down. Then he felt the grip of his mates' hands hauling him up.

Riley collapsed on the deck, exhausted. Over him stood Savage, the second mate, watching the beach. "What's happening?" Riley panted.

"Nothing — they're just staring out over the water. They can't believe you made it! Wait, now they're dragging our cargo toward the dunes." After a few moments, Savage shook his head. "I can't see them anymore... they're gone."

But they'll be back, thought Riley, pulling himself up. And there will be more of them. He gazed grimly at the rough sea. They wouldn't survive for long out there in the shattered longboat. But what else could they do? The wreck would soon smash to pieces. And the beach meant either slavery or death.

The longboat was their last chance. The crew threw in what little provisions were still on the wreck — a small keg of water, some salt pork, and a few figs. The eleven men took their places in the leaky hull, and two started bailing out water.

Riley put it to a vote. They could take their chances out at sea, or they could stick close to the rocky coast — and risk another wreck or attack. The men all agreed. They'd take the sea.

★ ★ ★

Riley's eyes were bleary from searching the horizon for a vessel. Six days at sea, and still nothing. Only the odd flash of lightning broke the gloomy haze. Under his feet the hastily patched boat creaked, and water seeped in constantly. He looked at the sunburned bodies of his crew, at the exhausted men who had to be prodded to keep bailing. His mouth was so parched that his orders came out in a hoarse whisper. How much longer would the water and pork hold out? As it was, their rations were barely giving them strength to row.

When the sun rose on the seventh day, Riley knew they couldn't go on. Then a shout broke through his grim thoughts.

"Land!"

Hope swept through the boat as the men turned in the direction of their mate's outstretched hand. Riley craned his neck — there it was! Far off, a perfectly smooth coast. No hill broke its straight line.

A desert, he realized, his heart sinking.

The men rowed for the coast. On shore Riley staggered from the boat and looked around. Jagged rocks loomed overhead, stretching as far as he could see in either direction. The men unloaded what was left of their water and salt pork and began to walk eastward along the coast — maybe they'd find a place to dig for water or get inland past the cliffs.

A fierce sun beat down on them. Hunger gnawed at Riley. He trudged onward, his eyes on the stony, red ground beneath him, baked hard by the sun. Spotting a few locusts, he grabbed them to stuff in his mouth, but they crumbled to dust at his touch.

I brought these men here, he thought. He stole a glance at young Horace, who was bravely keeping up with the bigger men. Riley had promised the cabin boy's mother that he would take care of him like a son.

After sunset, a crewman named Clark suddenly pointed ahead. "I see a light!" he cried.

A campfire! Hope thrilled through Riley. He saw the same feeling on the faces of his crew, but he raised an arm to hold them back. "Let's make camp for the night," he said. The men began to protest, but he shook his head. "Whoever they are, we don't want to alarm them by surprising them in the dark. Better to go in the morning."

The men wet their mouths with their last drops of water and settled down to sleep on the sand, which was still hot from the sun's rays. Riley lay awake, haunted by fears. They were unarmed, defenseless. Tomorrow they would probably be captured as slaves.

We must do what we can to stay alive, he told himself. Stay alive long enough to find a way, somehow, to get home.

★ ★ ★

Clambering over the dunes, Savage and Riley peered down into the valley nestled between sandy hills. Men and women milled around a well, fetching water for their camels — hundreds of them! Glancing up, a few men spotted the sailors and began to run toward them. At their sides, Riley could see the glint of steel in the sun — scimitars and muskets! Pulling Savage with him, he stepped forward.

The strangers wasted no time on words, and began to strip off the sailors' clothing. More people came running, and the air filled with shouts and excitement. Fights broke out over the windfall of new slaves.

The sailors were dragged away by their new masters, and women drove them toward the well with sticks. His shoes gone, Riley found it hard to walk barefoot over the hot sand, but each sharp whack from the stick sent him forward. Riley turned to the woman behind him and opened his parched mouth, pointing to it. She drew water from the well and began filling bowls.

The sailors fell upon the bowls of water. Slow down! Riley told himself. It was dangerous to drink so much at once when you have been dying of thirst. But he couldn't help himself. At last Riley raised his head from the bowl and, wiping his mouth, looked around.

The crowd was breaking up as each family moved off, its goatskins filled with water. We're going to be split up, Riley thought with horror. Porter and five other mates were already being led away on camels, their eyes wide and terrified. Riley had time only to grasp their hands as they passed. An instant later they slipped through a crevice in the cliff wall, and disappeared out of sight.

★ ★ ★

Riley clutched at the camel's hair, hanging on. His legs stretched painfully across the animal's broad back. Its backbone is as sharp as the edge of an oar's blade, thought Riley. Worst of all, the camel's sides, bloated with water, were perfectly smooth. Riley kept sliding down toward the camel's tail, then pulling himself back by its hair.

Frightened by the stranger on its back, the camel ran about, bellowing. Riley searched for a bridle or halter to guide it with — but found nothing. All he could do was hang on. Nearby, struggling in much the same way, were four of his shipmates — Savage, Clark, Horace, and Dick, the cook.

Up ahead their masters sat cross-legged on wooden saddles, their camels trotting across the flat landscape of sand and gravel. Women and children rode in huge baskets strapped to camels' backs.

The sun beat fiercely on Riley's bare skin and reflected off the sand, blinding him. Riley closed his eyes. His swaying camel felt like a small boat in a stormy sea.

Night came, and still there was no sign that the band of desert nomads would stop. The wind turned cold and cut through Riley's skin.

I can't take any more! he thought wildly. He looked down at the ground racing beneath him. If I fall off I could break my neck, he thought. But staying on was too painful. He let go and quickly slipped off the camel, tumbling to the ground. The group did not even pause. Riley scrambled on foot to keep up, the sharp stones cutting his unprotected feet.

At last the caravan stopped. The nomads milked the camels and gave the slaves a little to drink. Women quickly assembled tents for shelter from the cold night wind. Riley staggered toward a tent, but was beaten back with a stick. He and his crew were sent to lie down next to the camels. They collapsed onto the stony ground, where the desert wind swept over them unchecked.

Weeks passed in a blur of burning sun, swaying camels, and night winds. But Riley forced himself to stay sharp and listen to his masters' talk. It reminded him of Spanish — ancient Arabic, he guessed. He even learned a few words, and by watching their faces and hands, could catch the drift of their conversations.

That was how he discovered they were turning back to the well where he and his men had been captured. They couldn't survive any longer without water for the camels, whose milk was keeping them all alive.

Looking at the starved faces of his crew, Riley's heart sank. We're not going to make it there, he thought.

★ ★ ★

Riley panted in the shade of the tent — gratefully out of the midday sun. At his side lay Clark, barely conscious. Their masters had left early in the morning on their camels. The women had allowed the five slaves to rest near the tents in the meantime.

A month had passed since their capture, yet to Riley it seemed like years. He scanned the flat landscape that stretched in every direction. It's like the sea, he thought, like a smooth sea, when there's no wind. But the idea gave him no comfort.

His eyes grew heavy, but a movement on the horizon made him blink and open them wider. Two strangers on camels were approaching across the sand. As they came closer, Riley could see that their camels were loaded with goods and muskets that shone like silver in the sun. The riders stopped before the tent of Riley's master and, making their camels lie down, dismounted. Then they sat on the ground without a word, looking the other way.

The women of the family leapt up and began to rig an awning for the strangers. To Riley's surprise, his master's wife turned and approached him. Slowly, she spoke to him for the first time. Riley followed her words and gestures closely, piecing together her meaning.

"Sidi Hamet," she said, pointing to one of the strangers, "and his brother are cloth merchants from the Sultan's lands." She paused, then added in a low voice, "Perhaps he could buy you and take you there, where you might find your friends and kiss your wife and children." Then she walked away.

Riley's heart beat faster. He scanned the horizon again — no sign yet of his master. He snatched up a wooden bowl and ventured to the strangers' tent. Crouching down under their awning, Riley held up the bowl and showed his parched mouth to them. The man called Sidi Hamet asked him a question, and Riley recognized the word for "captain."

Riley nodded eagerly, "Yes, I am the captain."

Gathering heaps of sand in his hands, Riley made a coast on the ground. Then he drew the shape of a boat, adding a stick for a mast. With words and signs he prayed would capture the merchant's sympathy, Riley told the story of their shipwreck.

"I have a wife and five children back home... besides Horace, my son," he added, remembering his promise to the boy's mother. Hamet stared at him as he spoke, then turned his face away suddenly. Was he moved? How much had he understood? Riley wasn't sure.

Hamet motioned to his brother to give Riley some water, but the brother sullenly shook his head. Hamet signaled to Riley to hold up his bowl, and he poured it himself.

Clear, perfectly clear water streamed into the bowl. It was the first fresh water Riley had seen since they left the boat, and for a moment he was afraid he would faint. He drank half and then, gesturing toward Clark, asked to take the rest to him. Hamet nodded.

As Riley propped Clark up to drink, his shipmate's sunken eyes began to shine. Clark was mere skin and bones now, and Riley knew he would have to work fast.

The noise of approaching camels made Riley look up. Their masters were back. So soon! Riley felt sick with disappointment. His chance had slipped away — he did not dare approach the merchants again now. He'd have to watch for a chance to speak to them alone. In the meantime, his mind began to form a plan.

★ ★ ★

For days Riley shadowed the merchants as closely as he dared, terrified to take his eyes off them. They could be up and away at any moment.

Hamet feels sorry for us, he thought. I need to show him that helping us is worth his while! If he thinks there's money in it — a lot of money — he might buy us and carry us off the Sahara. If only I could get him alone! But Riley's master and his sons were never far away, and they glared ferociously at him whenever he lingered near the visitors.

Standing near the camels, Riley watched as his masters retreated from the afternoon heat into their tent. The two merchants moved back toward their own awning, Hamet trailing a little behind his brother.

This was his chance! Riley stumbled across the hot sand and fell to his knees before the merchant. With gestures and the few Arabic words he had practiced, he got his message across: "Carry me to the Sultan of Morocco, and my friend there will redeem me."

Riley's face fell as Hamet shook his head. The merchant stepped away, then paused.

"But," he said, turning back, "how much will you give me if I take you to Mogadore?" Riley had never heard of the place. With hand signs Hamet described it as a walled town and a seaport.

A seaport! Riley's heart raced. He made a pile of fifty stones. "That many dollars for myself and each of my men," he said, pointing.

Again, Hamet shook his head, waving his arm in the direction of the crew. "Not the others," he said. He jabbed a finger at the stones, then at Riley. "But how much more than that will you give me, if I buy *you?*"

Riley frantically counted out fifty more stones and added them to the first pile. "My friend will pay you as soon as you bring me to Mogadore," he said. His heart pounded as he watched Hamet's stony expression.

A moment passed in silence. At last Hamet nodded, pointing to Riley. "I will buy *you* then," he said. "But remember, if you deceive me..." He made a cutting motion across his throat.

Riley swallowed and nodded.

"Say nothing to your master," Hamet added as he turned to leave, "nor to my brother."

In the days that followed, Riley shadowed Hamet, begging him to buy just one more of the men — perhaps his son, Horace? "The ransom for all of us together would be even more," he promised.

But Hamet shook his head. "Impossible to get you all across the desert — robbers will attack us for our slaves, and my brother and I cannot fight them off."

Then Hamet pointed at Clark's wasted body. "He will not live more than three days. If I buy him, I'll lose my money!"

"I swear I will pay for him," said Riley, lowering his voice, "whether he lives or dies."

★ ★ ★

The merchants inspected the sailors from head to toe — parting their hair with sticks, frowning at their burned skin and blisters. They prodded their bones to see if they were in place.

Hamet's brother stood back and shook his head in disgust. "You will make a big mistake, my brother, to buy any more of them."

But one evening Hamet told Riley they would all leave at dawn. "I have used up all my goods buying the whole crew. My brother tried to talk me out of it," Hamet said. "He doesn't believe you have any rich friend who will pay for you." Riley looked down.

"You had better not deceive me," Hamet added, his tone menacing.

At first light they set off across the blowing sand. Savage muttered at Riley's side, voicing all the doubts Riley had ignored until now. "How do we know they're taking us where they say? And how on earth do you expect to pay them? There might not be an English consul — or any consul at all — at this seaport."

Riley stared ahead.

"And if there is," Savage went on, "you've promised too much! Who's going to lend you that much money? We're poor sailors, not rich men. Who pays a ransom for a poor man?" Riley was silent. Everything Savage said was true. He was taking a desperate gamble. And he remembered the penalty if he couldn't pay — his life.

The five sailors stumbled forward under the fierce sun. Like sleepwalkers they followed the merchants' swaying camels across endless stretches of sand. Riley had no idea how his wasted legs were able to keep moving, unless it was the new hope — a very slim one — that lay on the other side of the Sahara.

★ ★ ★

It took a moment for Riley's groggy mind to recognize the signs. Beneath his stumbling feet he saw something green. Something ragged and parched, but growing. Plants — they were near the edge of the desert! Then came the sound of distant voices, and small huts on the horizon.

As they made camp that night, Hamet took Riley aside. "I will set out in the morning for Mogadore," he said, "where I hope to arrive in three days. If your friend will pay the money for you and your men, you shall be free."

He stared hard at Riley. "If not, you must die for having deceived me, and your men shall be sold for what they will bring. I have suffered hunger and thirst to restore you to your family, for I believe God is with you. I have paid away all my money on your word alone."

"Take me with you," Riley begged. Hamet shook his head.

"My brother will guard you while I'm gone," he said firmly.

Riley looked down, but his new master beckoned to him. "Come, Riley. Write a letter." He held out a scrap of paper, smaller than Riley's hand. Riley took it, and Hamet gave him a little bit of black liquid and a reed.

Riley dipped the reed in the ink and held it for a moment over the shred of paper. All at once he saw how truly hopeless his scheme was. He had no "friend" in Mogadore, no idea if there was any consul there. Who would read his note? And if anyone did, why would they hand over so much money because of a scrap of paper from a stranger — a slave?

He glanced up and saw Sidi Hamet watching him. Taking a deep breath, he carefully began to write.

Sir,

> *The brig Commerce was wrecked on the 28 of August last. Myself and four of my crew are here nearly naked in slavery. I conjure you by all the ties that bind man to man… and by as much as liberty is dearer than life, to advance the money required for our redemption, which is nine hundred and twenty dollars. I can draw for any amount the moment I am at liberty…*
>
> *Should you not relieve me, my life must instantly pay the forfeit.*
> *Worn down to the bones — naked and a slave, I implore your pity…*
>
> *James Riley, late Master of the brig Commerce*

Riley folded the paper and paused. Who would he send it to? He dipped the reed in the little liquid that remained and scratched desperately,

> *To the English, French, Spanish or American consul, or any merchant in Mogadore*

He silently handed the paper to Sidi Hamet and watched his master turn and walk away. He had done all he could. Now his life was in someone else's hands.

★ ★ ★

Riley sat with his shipmates, watching the sun disappear behind the small huts that dotted the horizon. That makes it eight days since Hamet left for Mogadore, Riley thought grimly. Still they had heard nothing. He lay awake at nights, his mind swinging feverishly between hope and fear. He pictured Hamet searching in vain for someone who would read his letter — never mind pay the money! He must be angry by now, thought Riley. He must think I tricked him.

The sound of anyone coming — an opening gate, the trample of hooves — made Riley jump. He couldn't wait for his master to return, and at the same time he dreaded it. It would be the moment that either set him free, or ended his life.

A voice from nowhere made Riley and his men leap to their feet. "How de-do Cap-e-tan."

English! Riley couldn't remember the last time anyone but his crew had spoken to him in his own language. A man was walking toward them. Speaking in a mixture of English and Spanish, he explained that an Englishman had sent him from Mogadore. He handed Riley a letter.

Riley's heart was in his mouth as he took it. His shipmates stared at the letter with wide eyes, knowing it spelled out their fate. With shaking hands, Riley unfolded the paper and began to read.

My dear and afflicted sir,
    I have this moment received your note...

Riley's eyes scanned down the page to the only words that mattered.

    I have agreed to pay the sum of nine hundred and twenty dollars to Sidi Hamet on your safe arrival in this town with your fellow sufferers. He remains here as a kind of hostage for your safe appearance...
    ... with the hope of a happy end to all your sufferings, I subscribe myself, my dear Sir,
                Your friend,
                William Willshire

Riley stared for a moment at the name he'd never heard before. The name of a stranger. A stranger who had saved him. Joy and wonder began to swell inside him. He raised a hand to his gaunt face, and felt that his cheeks were wet with tears.

★ ★ ★

When Captain Riley returned home to the United States he wrote a book about his adventures. Riley's *Narrative* was read by over a million people, including a young boy named Abraham Lincoln. Some historians suggest that two events helped set the future American president's mind against slavery. One was his visit to a slave market in New Orleans when he was 19. And the other, earlier experience may have been reading Captain Riley's tale of slavery and escape.

Tickets to Freedom

Macon, Georgia, 1848

THERE WERE ONLY A FEW DAYS LEFT before Christmas, as a young black slave named William Craft hurried home through the dusk to the cottage he shared with his wife, Ellen. In the pocket of his coat he felt the pair of dark eyeglasses he'd bought moments before. Slaves weren't supposed to buy such things without their master's permission, but some storekeepers were ready to take a slave's money and not ask too many questions.

For weeks now, William had been buying pieces of clothing one at a time — a shirt here, a hat there, all at different stores so as not to attract too much attention. The green glasses were the finishing touch on a plan, a bold and dangerous scheme William and Ellen had worked out together: their bid for freedom.

★ ★ ★

William and Ellen had always known they were luckier than many slaves. Ellen worked in her mistress' house as a lady's maid. William's master had paid to train him as a carpenter and then hired him out, taking most of William's pay but letting him keep a little for himself. Life was better for them than for the slaves on a cotton plantation — theirs was hard, back-breaking work, never far from an overseer's watchful eye and sharp whip.

Still, they had longed for freedom. William was tired of working hard only to hand over his wages to someone else. And Ellen could never shake the fear that all they had could be snatched away. If either of their masters needed money, she or William could be sold and they would never see each other again. Worst of all, any children they might have could be taken from them. William had watched helplessly while his parents were sold at an auction to the highest bidder — and he felt the same anger and sadness whenever he remembered. Ellen had been taken from her mother when she was 11, and now she couldn't bear the thought of raising a child to be someone's slave. At first they had put off getting married, hoping to escape and marry once they were free.

Other slaves had done it. They'd followed the Underground Railroad — which wasn't a railroad at all, but a long line of hiding places and secret helpers that ran from the southern slave states through the free north, all the way to Canada. Some slaves had even made a desperate run for it, following the North Star at night, hiding in woods and swamps during the day. With luck, they stumbled upon a friendly person who could tell them the way to the next safe house, or "station" along the railroad.

But Ellen and William wanted to come up with a plan before they made their move. Whenever they were alone they whispered together about all kinds of schemes, yet every one had its problems.

"A train or boat would get us out of Georgia the quickest. We could save for the fare," Ellen ventured.

William shook his head. "Not without permission from our masters. We can't even walk the roads without that. Any white person could stop us and ask for our passes, to show we had a right to be there. And then what?" He paused and added, "They'd send slave catchers after us, that's what."

Ellen was silent. They both knew about professional slave hunters. The way they tracked down runaways — on horseback with guns and dogs — reminded William of a fox hunt. He shuddered as he imagined himself and Ellen being dragged back to slavery. And not to their old jobs, either. They'd be punished as a lesson to other slaves — separated and sold "down the river" to a much harder life on a plantation.

The more they talked, the more impossible it seemed to make it across the slave states to freedom — a journey of nearly a thousand miles. Ellen and William asked for their masters' permission to marry, and they tried to make the best of it. But they never forgot their dream, and kept their eyes open for the smallest hope of escape.

★ ★ ★

Mending a drawer in his workshop one December afternoon, William puzzled over the problems that stood in their way. Slaves couldn't get on a train or boat without permission. As he sanded, he pictured Ellen. She was so fair-skinned; she had a white father, after all. A bold plan began to form in William's mind. What if Ellen pretended to be white, while William traveled as her slave?

But no, he knew a southern lady would never travel alone with a male servant. Then a sudden idea made his hand pause on the wood. Ellen could disguise herself as a white *man*. They could escape in daylight, under the noses of the slaveholders themselves! They'd travel first-class to Philadelphia — in the free state of Pennsylvania — and from there through the northern states to Canada.

It was risky, he thought, but so unexpected that it might have a chance. He knew that some slaveholders gave their favorite slaves a few days' holiday around Christmas. If he and Ellen could get time off, it would give them a head start before they were missed.

That night William described his plan to Ellen. She was too shocked to speak at first. How could she keep up a disguise like that for hundreds of miles across the slave states? No, thought Ellen, it was too crazy. Then she pictured the life that lay before her if she did nothing — years of work without anything to call their own, not even their own bodies. And always the fear of losing her husband, her future children to the auction block. She looked at William and nodded — she would take the risk.

William began to buy as many pieces of her disguise as he could, a little at a time. Ellen was extra careful to please her mistress before she asked for a pass to be away for a few days, and the cabinetmaker gave William a pass without too much fuss. They hurried home to show each other their passes, but neither could read them — it was illegal to teach slaves to read. They'd have to trust that the passes said what they hoped.

So far all the pieces were falling into place. But as the day of escape drew closer, Ellen began to notice flaws in their plan. "William, any traveling gentleman would sign his name to register at a hotel — and I can't write!"

William slumped in his chair — he hadn't thought of that. Ellen paced the cottage floor anxiously. Then her face lit up. "I think I have it — I'll bind up my right hand in a sling, and ask the innkeeper to sign for me."

Then, glimpsing herself in a mirror, she frowned — her face was too smooth to convince anyone that she was a man! She pulled some cloth out of her sewing box and wound it into a bundle. Wrapping it around her chin with a handkerchief, she tied the ends over her head.

"As if I had a bad toothache," she explained, turning to show

William. He agreed it could work. And it would give her an excuse to avoid chatting with other travelers — the less she had to talk, the better.

Four more nights passed as they stayed up late, talking over their plan in the darkness. The sling and handkerchief gave William more ideas. If Ellen acted sick and lost in her thoughts, people wouldn't bother her. Like many slave owners, she'd count on her slave to fetch and carry for her — and answer questions from any nosy fellow travelers. And in only a few days, they could be free!

★ ★ ★

The moment they had so eagerly awaited was almost at hand. Ellen's costume was nearly finished. Whatever William hadn't been able to buy, Ellen had sewn herself in her moments alone. The evening before their escape, William brought home the pair of glasses that would complete the picture. The dark lenses would hide any fear in Ellen's eyes. They both knew she would have to sit surrounded by white men — and slave owners — wherever they traveled.

Just before dawn, William cut off Ellen's long hair. With trembling hands she slipped on her dark suit, cloak, and hat, then the high-heeled boots that would make her look taller. As she stood leaning on a cane, with one arm in a sling and bandages on her face, William took a long look at her. He smiled and shook his head in disbelief — she looked so much like a sickly white gentleman he was almost convinced himself!

It was time to go. They blew out the candles, and a sudden noise made them jump — was someone outside? Holding hands, they peeked out the cottage door. Everything was still. Silently they tiptoed outside and stood breathless, looking at each other.

From now on they would be traveling apart most of the time—blacks did not sit next to whites on trains and in boats. Without speaking they clasped hands, and then left in different directions for the rail station. William headed for the railcar reserved for blacks, and Ellen, leaning on her cane, limped to the first-class carriage. In her new identity as a young planter called Mr. Johnson, she bought a ticket for herself and one slave for Savannah — their first stop. There was no going back now.

Inside the carriage, Ellen took a window seat and stared outside. Sit still, she told herself. Don't attract attention. As the train slowly chugged away from the station, she glanced around the carriage — and froze. Mr. Cray, an old friend of her master who had known her since she was a child, had sat next to her while she was looking the other way. Ellen fought the urge to bolt, and turned slowly back toward the window. Why had he said nothing? Maybe he hadn't recognized her yet. If he strikes up a conversation, thought Ellen, he'll be sure to know my voice. Desperate, she decided to pretend to be deaf.

Mr. Cray soon turned to her and said politely, "It is a very fine morning, sir."

Ellen kept staring out the window. Mr. Cray repeated his greeting, but Ellen did not move. A passenger nearby laughed. Annoyed, Mr. Cray said, "I will make him hear," then, very loudly, "IT IS A VERY FINE MORNING, SIR."

Ellen turned her head as if she had only just heard him, bowed politely and said, "Yes." Then she turned back to the window.

"It is a great hardship to be deaf," another passenger remarked.

Mr. Cray nodded. "I will not trouble the gentleman anymore."

Ellen began to breathe more easily — he hadn't recognized her! Her disguise had passed a difficult test, but she realized more than ever how wary she must be.

The train pulled into Savannah early in the evening. William was waiting for Ellen outside her carriage, and they headed next for a steamboat bound for Charleston. Once on board, Ellen slipped into her room and shut the door. What a relief to be alone! But some of the passengers grumbled to William that this was strange. Why wasn't his young master staying up and being friendly?

William hurried to Ellen's room and told her about the reaction. They couldn't afford to do anything suspicious. But she couldn't very well play cards and smoke cigars without giving herself away! Ellen thought quickly: William could go heat up the bundle of medicine for her face on the stove in the gentlemen's saloon, to make it look as if his master was ill and going to bed early. The men in the saloon complained loudly about the smell the hot herbs made and sent William away. But they seemed convinced that his master must be pretty sick!

Once Ellen had turned in, William went on deck and asked the steward where he could sleep. The steward shook his head — no beds for black passengers, slave or free. William's heart sank, but he said nothing. As expected, his journey was turning out to be very different from Ellen's! Weary, he paced the deck for a while, then found some cotton bags in a warm spot near the smokestack and sat there until morning.

At breakfast, the ship's captain invited Ellen to sit at his table, and he asked politely about her health. William stood nearby to cut Ellen's food, since her arm was in a sling. When he stepped out for a moment, the captain gave Ellen some friendly advice: "You have a very attentive boy, sir; but you had better watch him like a hawk when you get on to the North."

A slave dealer sitting nearby agreed that William would probably make a run for it, and offered to buy him then and there. "No," Ellen answered carefully. "I cannot get on well without him."

Later up on deck a young southern officer warned Ellen that she would spoil her slave by saying "thank you" to him. "The only way to keep him in his place," he declared, "is to storm at him like thunder, and keep him trembling like a leaf."

I feel sorry for his slaves, thought Ellen. But from then on she remembered not to be so nice to William in front of people.

By now the boat had reached the wharf at Charleston, but when Ellen saw the crowd waiting for the steamer she shrank back. All those people — someone might recognize William. Or what if their owners already knew they had escaped and had sent someone to arrest them? She led William back to her cabin, where they waited nervously until every other passenger had left. At the last minute they stepped onto the empty wharf, and William ordered a carriage to take them to the best hotel.

When the innkeeper saw Ellen in her fine clothes and sling he pushed William aside and showed Ellen to one of the best rooms. Ellen would have loved to rest, but she knew the curious servants were expecting her downstairs for dinner. While she was led to the elegant dining room, William was handed a plate of food and sent to the kitchen to eat. Looking down, he saw that the plate was broken and that his knife and fork were rusty. William sighed but wasn't much surprised. He ate quickly and returned to wait on his "master," not wanting to leave Ellen alone for too long. As he entered the dining room he tried not to smile — three servants were already fussing over Ellen, each hoping for a tip from such a fine gentleman.

★ ★ ★

Ellen and William had planned to take a steamboat from Charleston to Philadelphia — and freedom! But at the inn Ellen learned that the steamer didn't run during winter. Their only choice now was the Overland Mail Route. They could take a steamer to Wilmington, North Carolina, and catch the mail train there. Ellen tried to hide her disappointment. This was a longer route — and the longer their journey, the more chances of being caught.

There was no choice but to press on. The next day, William and Ellen headed for the crowded ticket office, where Ellen asked for two tickets to Philadelphia. The mean-looking man behind the counter looked up and stared at William suspiciously. Then he asked Ellen to register her name and the name of her slave in his book.

Ellen ignored his glare. She pointed to the sling on her arm. "Would you kindly sign for me, please?" The man shook his head and stubbornly stuck his hands in his pockets. William glanced around and saw that people had stopped to stare at them. The last thing they wanted was more attention.

Stay calm, Ellen told herself, and she was thankful for the dark glasses that hid her eyes.

She was about to speak again when she heard a voice call "Mr. Johnson!" Ellen spun around. The young officer she had met on the last steamer — the one who had told her not to be so polite to her slave — was pushing through the crowd. He patted her on the back and cheerfully told the ticket seller, "I know his kin like a book."

At this the captain of the Wilmington steamboat, who had been watching silently nearby, spoke up. "I'll register the gentleman's name," he declared, no doubt realizing that he was about to lose a passenger, "and take the responsibility upon myself."

Once the steamer was on its way, the captain took Ellen aside to explain. They were always very strict at Charleston — you never knew when a sympathetic white person might try to help a slave run away by pretending to be his master.

"I suppose so," Ellen said casually.

The next day they switched to a train for Baltimore. Once again, William rode in a separate car while Ellen sat in a first-class carriage, this time with a gentleman from Virginia and his two daughters.

"What seems to be the matter with you, sir?" the man asked her in a kindly tone.

"Rheumatism," Ellen replied. He nodded and insisted that Ellen lie down.

Good idea, thought Ellen, the less chatting the better. The daughters made a pillow for her with their shawls and covered her with a cloak. While Ellen pretended to sleep, she heard one of them sigh and whisper, "Papa, he seems to be a very nice young gentleman." Her sister added, "I never felt so much for a gentleman in my life!" When Ellen told William about it he laughed. They had certainly fallen in love with the wrong man!

Before leaving the train, the girls' father handed Ellen a recipe — his "sure cure" for rheumatism. Ellen didn't dare pretend to read it. What if she held it the wrong way? So she thanked him and tucked it in her pocket.

★ ★ ★

It was Christmas Eve as the train slowed to its stop at Baltimore, where they would switch to a train for Philadelphia. This was the last "slave port" on their journey, and Ellen felt more nervous than ever. We're so close now, she told herself. Only one more night to get through. She and William knew that people kept a keen eye out for runaways in Baltimore, to stop them from escaping into the free state of Pennsylvania. They could lose everything just in sight of their goal.

As usual, William helped Ellen into the first-class carriage when they switched trains. He was about to board his own car when he felt a tap on his shoulder. He turned to face an officer, who asked sharply, "Where are you going, boy?"

"To Philadelphia, sir," William answered humbly, "with my master — he's in the next carriage."

"Well, you had better get him, and be quick about it, because the train will soon be starting. It is against the rules to let any man take a slave past here, unless he can prove that he has a right to take him along." He then brushed past William and moved down the platform.

William stood frozen for a moment, not knowing what to

do. Then he stepped into the first-class carriage and saw Ellen sitting alone. She looked up at him and smiled. He knew what she was thinking: they would be free by dawn the next morning. William struggled to keep his voice steady as he told her the bad news. Ellen's face fell. To be caught this close to freedom! She looked searchingly at William, but he was speechless. What choice did they have? Run for it now? They would be caught before they were outside the station. There was only one way — they would have to brave it out to the end.

Ellen led William to the station office and asked for the person in charge. A uniformed man stepped forward. Ellen felt his sharp eyes upon her.

"Do you wish to see me, sir?" she asked. The officer told her no one could take a slave to Philadelphia unless he could prove he was the rightful owner.

"Why is that?" Ellen demanded. The firmness in her voice surprised William. The officer explained that if someone posing as a slave owner passed through with a runaway, the real master could demand to be paid for his property.

This exchange began to attract the attention of other passengers. A few shook their heads and someone said that this was no way to treat an invalid gentleman. The officer, seeing that Ellen had the crowd's sympathy, offered a compromise.

"Is there any gentleman in Baltimore who could be brought here to vouch for you?"

"No," said Ellen. "I bought tickets in Charleston to pass us through to Philadelphia, and therefore you have no right to detain us here."

"Well, sir, right or no right, we shan't let you go," was the cold reply.

A few moments of silence followed. Ellen and William looked

at each other but were afraid to speak, in case they made a mistake that would show who they really were. They knew the officers could throw them in jail, and then it would only be a matter of time before their real identities were discovered and they were driven back to slavery. A wrong word now would be fatal.

Just then the conductor of the train they had left stepped in. He commented that they had indeed come on his train, and he left the room. The bell rang to signal their train's departure, and the sudden noise made everyone jump — all eyes fixed more keenly on them. Soon it would be too late.

The officer ran his fingers through his hair, and finally said, "I really don't know what to do; I calculate it is all right." He let them pass, grumbling, "As he is not well, it is a pity to stop him here."

Ellen thanked him and hobbled as quickly as she could with her cane toward her carriage. William leapt into his own railcar just as the train was leaving the platform.

Before long the train pulled to a halt alongside a river, where a ferry boat would carry the passengers to a train on the other side. When a porter asked Ellen to leave her seat and head for the ferry, she stood up and looked around for William. He always appeared as soon as the train stopped to "assist" her. Now he was nowhere in sight. On the platform she asked the conductor if he had seen her slave.

"No, sir," he said. "I haven't seen anything of him for some time." He added slyly, "I have no doubt he has run away, and is in Philadelphia, free, long before now."

Her panic rising, Ellen asked if he would look for William. "I am not a slave hunter," he huffed, and left her.

It was cold, dark, and raining as Ellen stood alone. Her mind started racing with possibilities — had William been left behind in Baltimore... or been kidnapped by slave catchers? Then with horror she remembered — she had no money. They had left it all with William because pickpockets wouldn't bother stealing from a slave. She looked down at the tickets in her hand, their tickets to freedom. They seemed worthless now that she had lost William.

Her time was up — everyone else had boarded the ferry. There's no going back, she thought. All she could do was press on to Philadelphia, and hope that someday she would find him.

★ ★ ★

William was closer than Ellen thought. They had been traveling day and night and sleeping very little. Fear and excitement had kept them awake until now. But finally, within hours of Philadelphia, William had nodded off. Sound asleep, he was tumbled out with the luggage onto a baggage boat.

A guard later found William and shook him awake. "Your master is scared half to death about you," he said.

William sat up, frightened — had something happened to Ellen? "Why?" he gasped.

"He thinks you have run away from him," the guard replied.

Relieved, William hurried to Ellen to let her know what had happened. The conductor and the guard laughed as if it were all a great joke. Then the guard took William aside and told him he really should run away once they got to Philadelphia.

"No, sir," William replied. "I shall never run away from such a good master." The guard was stunned, but William wasn't going to let anyone in on their secret — not yet.

Back in his own railcar, another passenger quietly told William of a boarding house in Philadelphia where he would be safe if he ran away. A station on the Underground Railroad! William thanked him, but did not say any more.

Just before dawn, William stuck his head out the train window. He could see flickering lights ahead in the distance. Then he heard a passenger say to his friend, "Wake up... we are at Philadelphia!" William felt as if a heavy burden had slipped off his back. He stared at the glittering city as the train sped on, and the sight made him lightheaded.

It was Christmas Day. Before the train had fully stopped, William was already running to Ellen's carriage. They hurried into a cab and William gave the driver the address of the boarding house he had heard about.

"Thank God, William, we are safe!" Ellen exclaimed, and broke into sobs. After pretending for so long, she felt drained. She leaned heavily on William as they stepped out of the cab and climbed the stairs to their room.

Ellen rested a while, then took off her disguise and changed into the women's clothing she had packed. She and William walked into the sitting room and asked to see the landlord. The man was confused. What happened to the young cotton planter he had seen arrive?

"But where is your master?" he asked William. William pointed to Ellen. "I'm not joking," the landlord replied, becoming annoyed.

It took some time to convince him of who they were! In the end, the innkeeper sent for some antislavery friends who could help them decide what to do next. William and Ellen had planned to go to Canada, following the Underground Railroad further north. But their new friends warned them that December in Canada would be much colder than they were used to in Georgia. They would face a hard first winter in an unfamiliar place.

But staying in Philadelphia wouldn't be safe either — slave catchers sometimes kidnapped runaways there, even though it was in a free state. Boston might be a better choice. Most people there were so against slavery that slave hunters didn't dare try. And so it was decided. Ellen and William stayed with a Quaker family until they were ready to leave for Boston, and a new life.

★ ★ ★

Even in Boston, the Crafts did not feel safe for long, however. Two years later, the Fugitive Slave Bill was passed. Slave catchers could now legally follow runaways into the free states and bring them back. With the help of Underground Railroad workers, Ellen and William escaped a warrant for their arrest and fled to Halifax, where they boarded a ship for England.

Sources

Abbott, G. *Great Escapes from the Tower of London*. London: Heinemann, 1982.

The Acts of Stephen, Roger of Wendover's Flowers of History. Excerpted in *Escape: An Anthology*. Edited by Michael Mason. London: Chatto & Windus, 1996.

The Anglo-Saxon Chronicle and *The Peterborough Chronicle*. The Online Medieval and Classical Library, University of California, Berkeley (sunsite.berkeley.edu/OMACL/Anglo).

Appleby, John T. *The Troubled Reign of King Stephen*. New York: Barnes & Noble Inc., 1970.

Bader, Douglas *Fight for the Sky: The Story of the Spitfire and the Hurricane*. London: Sidgwick and Jackson, 1973.

Bradley, Keith R. *Slavery and Rebellion in the Roman World: 140 B.C. – 70 B.C.* Bloomington, Indiana: Indiana University Press, 1989.

Brickhill, Paul. *Reach for the Sky: The Story of Douglas Bader*. London: Collins, 1954, 1967.

Chamberlin, Russell. *The Tower of London: An Illustrated History*. London: Webb & Bower Ltd., 1989.

Chancellor, Henry. *Colditz: The Definitive History*. London: Hodder and Stoughton, 2001.

Craft, William. "Running a Thousand Miles to Freedom." In *Great Slave Narratives: Selected and Introduced by Arna Bontemps*. Boston: Beacon Press, 1969.

Eggers, Reinhold. *Colditz: The German Story*. Translated and edited by Howard Gee. London: Robert Hale Ltd., 1961 (Charnwood Edition 1999).

Foot, M. R. D. and J. M. Langley. *MI9: Escape and Evasion 1939–1945*. London: Bodley Head, 1979.

Hilton, Christopher. *The Wall: The People's Story*. Phoenix Mill, Great Britain: Sutton Publishing Ltd., 2001.

Jackson, Robert. *Douglas Bader: A Biography*. London: Arthur Barker Ltd., 1983.

Kiger, Patrick. "The Escape Psyche." From the Learning Channel/Discovery website (www. tlc.discovery.com/convergence/escape/articles/psyche.html)

Larive, E.H. *The Man Who Came in from Colditz*. London: Robert Hale Ltd., 1975.

"A Letter from the Countess of Nithsdale, 1827 (describing events of 1716)." In *Escape: An Anthology,* edited by Michael Mason. London: Chatto & Windus, 1996.

Lucas, Laddie. *Flying Colours: The Epic Story of Douglas Bader.* London: Hutchinson & Co., 1982.

McFadden, Robert D., Joseph B. Treaster and Maurice Carroll. *No Hiding Place: The New York Times Inside Report on the Hostage Crisis.* New York: Times Books, 1981.

Mears, Kenneth J. *The Tower of London: 900 Years of English History.* Oxford: Phaidon Press, 1988.

"Memoirs of Henry Masers de Latude, during a Confinement of Thirty-five Years in the State Prisons of France." English translation, 1787. Excerpted in *Escape: An Anthology.* Edited by Michael Mason. London: Chatto & Windus, 1996.

Memoirs of the Bastille by Latude and Linguet. (Including "Despotism Unmasked," a memoir by Jean Henri Masers de Latude) Translated by J. and S.F. Mills Whitman. London: George Routledge & Sons Ltd., 1927.

Ortzen, Len. *Stories of Famous Shipwrecks.* London: Arthur Barker Ltd., 1974.

Pelletier, Jean and Claude Adams. *The Canadian Caper.* Toronto: Macmillan, 1981.

Petschull, Jürgen. *With the Wind to the West: The Great Balloon Escape.* Translated by Courtney Searls. London: Hodder and Stoughton, 1981.

Prestwich, Michael. *Armies and Warfare in the Middle Ages.* New Haven: Yale University Press, 1996.

Quétel, Claude. *Escape from the Bastille: The Life and Legend of Latude.* Translated by Christopher Sharp. Cambridge: Polity Press, 1990.

Reid, P.R. *Colditz: The Full Story.* London: Macmillan, 1984.

Riley, James. *Sufferings in Africa: Captain Riley's Narrative.* (First published 1817) New York: Clarkson Potter, 2000.

Shaw, Brent D., ed. and trans. *Spartacus and the Slave Wars: A Brief History with Documents.* New York: Bedford/St. Martin's, 2001.

Still, William (Secretary of Pennsylvania Anti-slavery Society's General Vigilance Committee). *The Underground Railroad: A Record.* Chicago: Johnson Publishing Company Inc., 1970 (first published 1871).

Warner, Philip. *The Medieval Castle: Life in a Fortress in Peace and War.* London: Arthur Barker Ltd., 1972.

William of Malmesbury's *Historia Novella,* in *Contemporary Chronicles of the Middle Ages* translated by Joseph Stephenson (1850, repr. 1988). Excerpted on California State University Northridge website (www.csun.edu).

About the Author

GROWING UP, Laura Scandiffio loved to read and write stories, draw pictures, put on plays with friends, and explore the woods and water near her home and cottage.

She has always been fascinated by stories of escape and survival, whether from real-life or in fiction. She enjoys traveling and the adventure of encountering different places, languages, and people.

Besides writing, Laura has worked as an editor of books for both children and adults. She is the author of *The Martial Arts Book,* also published by Annick Press. Laura lives in Toronto with her husband and two children.